Bilingual and ESL Classrooms

THIRD EDITION

Bilingual and ESL Classrooms

Teaching in Multicultural Contexts

CARLOS J. OVANDO
Arizona State University

VIRGINIA P. COLLIER
George Mason University

MARY CAROL COMBS
University of Arizona

FORWARD BY JIM CUMMINS
University of Toronto

AFTERWORD BY EUGENE E. GARCÍA
Arizona State University

Boston   Burr Ridge, IL   Dubuque, IA   Madison, WI   New York   San Francisco   St. Louis
Bangkok   Bogotá   Caracas   Lisbon   London   Madrid
Mexico City   Milan   New Delhi   Seoul   Singapore   Sydney   Taipei   Toronto

McGraw-Hill Higher Education

A Division of The **McGraw-Hill** Companies

BILINGUAL AND ESL CLASSROOMS: TEACHING IN MULTICULTURAL CONTEXTS

 This book is printed on acid-free paper.

4 5 6 7 8 9 0 FGR/FGR 0 9 8 7 6 5 4 3

ISBN 0–07–240737–9

Publisher: *Jane Karpacz*
Developmental editor II: *Cara Harvey*
Marketing manager: *Pamela Cooper*
Project manager: *Jean R. Starr*
Lead production supervisor: *Lori Koetters*
Coordinator of freelance design: *Mary E. Kazak*
Photo research coordinator: *Alexandra Ambrose*
Cover and interior design: *Asylum Studios*
Cover image: *© Vicky Kasala/Getty Images*
Typeface: *10/12 Sabon*
Compositor: *Precision Graphics Services, Inc.*
Printer: *Quebecor World Fairfield, Inc.*

Library of Congress Cataloging-in-Publication Data
Ovando, Carlos Julio.
    Bilingual and ESL classrooms : teaching in multicultural contexts /
Carlos J. Ovando, Virginia P. Collier, Mary Carol Combs.—3rd ed.
        p. cm.
    Includes bibliographical references and index.
    ISBN 0-07-240737-9 (softcover : alk. paper)
    1. Education, Bilingual—United States. 2. Multicultural education—
United States. 3. English language—Study and teaching—Foreign
speakers. 4. Community and school—United States.
    I. Title: Bilingual and English-as-a-second-language classrooms.
    II. Collier, Virginia P. III. Combs, Mary Carol. IV. Title.
LC3731 .O96 2003
370.117'5'0973—dc21   2002069571

To the memory of my ancestors,
who passed on to me
their cultural and linguistic heritage and
adventurous spirit.

—Carlos J. Ovando

To my mother and father,
who envision the world as one.

—Virginia P. Collier

To my bilingual and bicultural daughters,
Claudia and Sarah María

—Mary Carol Combs

About the Authors

Well known internationally for the first and second editions of this book, which has often been labeled a classic in the field of bilingual/multicultural/ESL education, Carlos Ovando and Virginia Collier and now joined by Mary Carol Combs, have again applied their deep expertise and experience to author this third edition.

DR. CARLOS J. OVANDO is Associate Dean for Teacher Education, Division Director for Curriculum & Instruction, and Professor of Education at Arizona State University—Tempe. He has taught at Indiana University—Bloomington, Oregon State University, the University of Alaska, and the University of Southern California. While at Indiana University, he served as chair of the Department of Curriculum and Instruction, as well as the director of the Bilingual-Bicultural Education Program. He has also served as a high school Spanish teacher. His research and writing focus on factors that contribute to the academic achievement of language-minority students and ethnically diverse groups. He has served as guest editor of two special issues of the *Educational Research Quarterly* and contributed to the *Bilingual Research Journal, Handbook of Research on Multicultural Education, Phi Delta Kappan, Educational Leadership, Educational Researcher, WCCI Forum, Kappa Delta Pi Record, National Forum, World Yearbook of Education,* and the *Harvard Educational Review.* With Colleen Larson, he authored *The Color of Bureaucracy: The Politics of Equity in Multicultural School Communities* (Wadsworth, 2001). He also edited (with Peter McLaren) *The Politics of Multiculturalism and Bilingual Education: Students and Teachers Caught in the Cross Fire* (McGraw-Hill, 2000). Professor Ovando has made presentations in Canada, Costa Rica, Cuba, Egypt, England, Guam, Mexico, Nicaragua, the Netherlands, the Philippines, Spain, and the United States. Born in Nicaragua, Dr. Ovando emigrated to the United States at the age of 15, and has therefore experienced first-hand many of the academic, sociocultural, and emotional issues that confront language-minority students in the United States. He is the recipient of two Teaching Excellence Recognition Awards from the School of Education at Indiana University.

DR. VIRGINIA P. COLLIER is professor of Bilingual/Multicultural/ESL Education at George Mason University in Fairfax, Virginia. Her award-winning national research studies on school effectiveness in language-minority education, conducted with Dr. Wayne Thomas, have had a substantial impact on school policies in the United States and abroad. A popular speaker, Dr. Collier has given over 110 keynote speeches at national, state, and international conferences and has conducted educational leadership training for superintendents, principals, and education policymakers in 27 states of the United States and 18 countries. She has over 40 publications in the field of bilingual/multicultural/ESL education. In 1989, she received the Distinguished Faculty Award from George Mason

University for excellence in teaching, scholarship, and service. Proficient in Spanish and English, having lived in Central America during her childhood, she has served the field of bilingual/multicultural/ESL education for three decades as parent, teacher, researcher, teacher educator, and doctoral mentor.

DR. MARY CAROL COMBS   is a research scientist at the Bureau of Applied Research in Anthropology, University of Arizona, where she directs research on bilingual education and language policy in Arizona and the Southwest. She also is an adjunct assistant professor in the Department of Language, Reading and Culture and teaches undergraduate and graduate courses in bilingual and multi-cultural education, English as a second language, and American Indian education. Dr. Combs is the recipient of academic fellowships from the National Endowment for the Humanities, the U.S. Department of Education, and the Marshall Foundation, and has received an outstanding teaching award from the University of Arizona.

Brief Contents

Contents

 *Foreword*

The term *globalization* is never far from the front pages of newspapers these days. It evokes strong positive or negative feelings depending upon whether it is being praised by the business community for opening up world markets to more extensive trade, or condemned by those who associate the term with the dramatically widening gap between rich and poor nations and people.

One aspect of globalization that has important implications for educators is the increasing movement of people from one country to another. Population mobility is caused by many factors: desire for better economic conditions, the need for labor in many countries that are experiencing low birthrates, a constant flow of refugees resulting from conflicts between groups, oppression of one group by another, or ecological disasters. One obvious consequence of population mobility is increased linguistic, cultural, racial, and religious diversity within schools.

In the "settler" countries of North and South America, Australia, and New Zealand, diversity of many kinds has obviously been a reality since their "discovery" by Europeans several centuries ago. However, continued high levels of immigration during the past 20 years, combined with the global reach of telecommunications and media, have opened up diversity of all kinds to much greater public awareness and scrutiny. Diversity is out in the open, visible, audible, and impossible to ignore.

Debates about social and educational policy increasingly are forced to address what dominant groups tend to characterize as the "problem" of diversity. Voices ranging from angry and xenophobic, to concerned and insecure, call on governments to put diversity back into the bottle and return the nation to the idealized homogeneity of previous eras. Other voices highlight diversity as a resource, an opportunity for enrichment and enlightenment among nations operating in the international arena. These voices frequently also point to the importance for nations that preach human rights in the international arena, of implementing human rights at home.

Clearly, issues of national identity are intertwined with debates about the social threats or merits of diversity. In societies around the world, dominant groups have frequently inculcated in their children the belief that national identity is essentially homogeneous. Furthermore, the central physical, cultural, and ideological components of national identity just happen to match those of the dominant group. Those who obviously don't fit into this fabricated mold are assumed either to be in the process of "melting" into it or to be of such little significance for the society that their marginalization is irrelevant to issues of identity. In the United States, Native American, Hawaiian, African-American, and Latino/Latina populations have, for centuries, occupied this excluded and occluded space outside the discourse of national identity. In Japan, indigenous groups such as the Ainu and more recent arrivals such as Koreans similarly have failed to disturb the mirror of homogeneity into which Japanese society has projected, and found reflected, its own identity. Similar examples could be found in most other countries.

Thus, the construction of national identity is largely a function of which societal groups have the power to define and which are subject to external definition. It is within this context of societal power relations that we can understand the significance of the debate on bilingual education in the United States and the contributions of the present volume to this debate.

The constitutional guarantee of equality for all, which for two centuries was largely ignored in the educational arena as well as in most other spheres, was given new impetus by Supreme Court decisions in the 1950s and by legislation in the 1960s that provided powerful tools whereby minority groups could challenge the patently inferior education provided to their children. Court decisions, particularly the *Lau* v. *Nichols* decision in 1974, forced school systems to take steps to address the learning needs of bilingual students. The promotion of transitional bilingual education as the most favored option by the Office for Civil Rights in the mid-1970s caused school systems to scramble to recruit bilingual teachers and classroom assistants. It also institutionalized linguistic diversity as a legitimate phenomenon within the nation's schools.

This recognition and partial institutionalization of linguistic diversity, together with continuing high rates of immigration, had evoked by the late 1980s a strong antagonistic response from those who saw the infiltration of diversity as undermining the fabric of nationhood. Diversity itself and what were seen as the "demands" of minority groups were viewed as the problem rather than the racism that for centuries had consigned these groups to the margins of society.

This problematization of diversity rather than culturally and racially homogenous conceptions of national identity is evident in the 1991 book written by Arthur Schlesinger, Jr., *The Disuniting of America* (New York: W.W. Norton), in which he announced his belief that "bilingualism shuts doors" and "monolingual education opens doors to the wider world." Schlesinger's opinion would probably be puzzling to the countless millions of children in schools around the world who are in the process of becoming bilingual and multilingual in order to benefit from the expanded personal and economic opportunities afforded by knowledge of languages in an increasingly interdependent world. Despite being absurd from any empirical or logical perspective, Schlesinger's views on bilingualism reflect the genuine fear of many commentators that legitimating bilingual and multicultural education will change the face of nationhood and destroy the identity that has been cultivated through two centuries of nation building. In recent years, these fears have found legal expression in Propositions 227 in California and 203 in Arizona that place severe restrictions on the use of bilingual children's mother tongues as languages of instruction in schools.

Carlos Ovando and his colleagues put these concerns to rest convincingly in their extremely clear and balanced overview of research on teaching in multilingual and multicultural contexts. Bilingual education is presented not as a plot by "Hispanic activists" (as some have argued) but as a series of approaches that are being implemented in countries around the world to provide effective learning opportunities for both language-minority and language-majority students. Growing up in Ireland in the 1950s, I experienced bilingual education (Gaelic-English) firsthand, as have countless students in countries as varied as Wales, Brunei, Canada, Australia, and Singapore. In fact, there is hardly a country in the world that does not implement some form of bilingual education for at least some of its student population. Bilingualism shuts doors? The reality is that any student who graduates from grade 12 with access to only one language is seriously disadvantaged in the global economic market in comparison to those who have multilingual skills. Especially significant in this regard is the information on "two-way" or "dual language" bilingual programs reviewed in this volume. These programs are intended for students from both majority language and minority language backgrounds and an increasing volume of research demonstrates that both groups of students develop fluent bilingual conversational and academic skills at no cost to their proficiency in English.

The relevance of cultural knowledge for students is emphasized strongly in this volume. There has been much talk in recent years about the importance of developing students' "cultural literacy"—their knowledge of the "basic facts"—historical, cultural, geographic, and so on-of their country. The perspective outlined in this volume is that cultural literacy must be expanded to include intercultural literacy, namely, knowledge about and sensitivity to cultural perspectives other than those into which we have been initially socialized. The logic here derives from the reality of cultural diversity in the international and domestic spheres: cross-cultural contact is at an all-time high in human history and will continue to increase as a result of population mobility throughout the world. Students who graduate with monocultural perspectives on their social realities are ill-prepared to contribute to their societies, domestic or international. They are simply not educated for the world into which they will graduate. This applies equally to students from both majority/dominant and minority/subordinated backgrounds.

What the authors of this book communicate strongly is their vision of a society that draws strength from its multifaceted cultural, racial, and linguistic identity, and their hopes for an educational system that will cultivate the richness of the identities that individual students bring to school. For prospective teachers who will prepare students to thrive in social and employment contexts that inevitably will be characterized by diversity, the authors offer no formulaic recipes. Instead, they chart promising directions and make us aware of the choices we will exercise every time we enter a classroom. We sense in these pages how the choices we make as we interact with students from culturally and linguistically diverse backgrounds not only define our own identities as educators but also sketch an image of our society as we would wish it to be and the contributions that our students can potentially make to the creation of this society.

This book provides us with the information to make powerful choices for both ourselves and our students. It also challenges us to use this information to create classrooms where learning is stimulated by caring and collaborative relationships across cultural and linguistic boundaries. The mirror held up to students in these relationships reflects not only who they are but who they can become.

Jim Cummins
Toronto, April 2002

 *Preface*

This third edition of *Bilingual and ESL Classrooms* is a very different text from the first and second editions published in 1985 and 1998 respectively. Since the release of the first two editions, the field has matured dramatically, and the research knowledge upon which it is based has expanded enormously. We think this is good news! In writing this third edition, we have worked hard to continue providing an accurate, carefully written, and detailed overview of our field and the research on which it is based.

The major goal of this book is to take a comprehensive look at research, policy, and effective practices in U.S. schools for students who are from culturally and linguistically diverse backgrounds. The demographic predictions are that students with close connections to their bilingual/bicultural heritages (now labeled "language-minority students" by the federal government) will be very large in number in the near future, becoming the majority in many states over the next two decades. Thus, we educators urgently need to provide appropriate, meaningful, and effective schooling for these students, who too often have been underserved by U.S. schools. This book speaks to all educators, with the goal of providing rich examples of effective practices and their underlying research knowledge base.

Audience

We feel that it is the responsibility of all educators, not just specialists, to prepare themselves to work with language-minority students. Therefore, *Bilingual and ESL Classrooms* is written for both preservice and experienced educators serving grades K through 12—mainstream, bilingual, ESL, and special education teachers, as well as administrators, school counselors, and educational policymakers.

We have written this book to serve a variety of purposes. It may be used as a core textbook for teacher education and education leadership courses that focus on linguistically and culturally diverse students. For example, the book can be used for introductory courses in bilingual/multicultural/ESL education such as foundations of bilingual education, methods of teaching ESL, methods of teaching in bilingual education, multicultural education courses designed to introduce teachers to issues in cultural diversity, and education leadership courses that prepare principals to serve in schools with culturally and linguistically diverse students. This book also may be used for ongoing staff development, to update teachers and administrators on the extensive research base and its implications for practice in the field of bilingual/multicultural/ESL education. Likewise, graduate and undergraduate students alike can use the book as a comprehensive reference on research, policy, and practice in our field. The book also can be used by bilingual/ESL faculty as a professional reference for mainstream teacher education faculty, providing an overview of our field.

Balance of Theory and Practice

In the chapters of this book we weave theories of bilingualism, second language acquisition, cultural transmission, content integration, assessment of language-minority students, bilingual-special education, policy and practice, and community relations. To examine and to bring to life the necessary interplay between theory and classroom application, we include engaging vignettes of students and teachers, and instructional guidelines features. Throughout this book we have emphasized that language and culture are integral components of the instructional process in all classes, for all students, and that instruction should be provided in a warm, supportive sociocultural environment that stimulates students' continuous linguistic, cognitive, and academic development.

We believe that bilingualism and the accompanying intercultural awareness is a source of great human richness. All the students we serve are learning formally and informally how to deal with the multiple worlds they live in at home and at school. Educators, through the quality of education that they provide, represent an important bridge to students' success in benefiting fully from the multiple languages and cultures they are experiencing. As with the first and second editions, this third edition emphasizes the integration of ESL and bilingual education. Bilingual and ESL staff serve the same student populations, coordinate programs and resources jointly, and often receive comparable professional training. Likewise, we envision schools where all staff work together, collaborating for the benefit of all students, rather than schools that operate separate, isolated programs. Everything in this book can be applied to all students and all educators, to enrich the schooling experience for staff and students together.

Terms

Recognizing that the first two editions of this book have been used over the past seventeen years as a foundations book for many teacher education programs for certifying bilingual and ESL teachers, in this third edition we have worked very hard again to utilize the most widely used but politically sensitive terminology in our field wherever possible. Over the years, many terms have been used in U.S. schools that have been offensive, derogatory, demeaning, or inaccurate in describing a given student population or education program. Throughout the book, with endnotes, we explain our chosen use of terms when there is variation in usage. We ask that educators continue to listen to the voices of the varying culturally and linguistically diverse communities that our schools serve and to be sensitive to lessened use of terms that offend or misrepresent the richness of all peoples' heritages.

New to the Third Edition

Pedagogical Structure

This new edition presents updated research on the education of English-language learners in the United States. The book also contains new features to make the text more accessible to readers, including opening vignettes, highlighted terms and concepts, figures and tables, blocked text, and photographs. These new features are designed to engage students and other readers more directly with the most current issues in pedagogy and practice.

The third edition also contains two new chapters: Chapter Eight, on authentic assessment, by Lorraine Valdez Pierce, and Chapter Nine, on bilingual special education, by Theresa Ochoa. Valdez Pierce, a leading authority on assessment for language-minority students, provides the latest research and information for bilingual and ESL teachers, as well as teachers of language-minority students in mainstream settings. Ochoa brings her expertise in the education of culturally and linguistically diverse students to a discussion of the unique needs of bilingual and ESL students with sustained academic difficulties.

Classroom Focus

Because of our desire to engage graduate and undergraduate students with the complex pedagogical issues we cover, we have attempted to present more applied content in the form of classroom sketches throughout the text. These sketches profile students and teachers in real-life classroom settings, and include teacher reflections about schooling and pedagogy. These sketches are frequently accompanied by yet another new feature in this edition—"Guidelines for Teaching"— or "how to" sections of recommended instructional strategies for use by teachers of English language learners. The new edition also contains highlighted and defined key terms and concepts, and provides reflection questions at the end of each chapter for continuing discussion and dialogue.

Updated Scholarship

Finally, the third edition provides readers with updated research on new and continuing controversies and findings in demographics, issues of assimilation and pluralism, federal and state legislation, antibilingual initiatives, school reform, achievement and assessment, second-language acquisition, content area instruction, bilingual special education, linguistic and ethnic identity, and community participation.

Chapter Overview

The text is organized into ten chapters:

Chapter One: Students   This introductory chapter defines the focus of the book: linguistically and culturally diverse students attending U.S. schools. Through poignant and personal examples, the authors guide educators to discover the complexity and richness of these students' life experiences. Among the topics explored in this chapter are the soaring demographics driving changes in schools; the sociocultural home and school contexts surrounding language-minority students; and the emotional, linguistic, and academic experiences these students face in school.

Chapter Two: Policy and Programs   Crucial reading for school administrators, written in the context of the current school reform movement, this chapter provides a policy overview of the development of the field of bilingual/ESL education in the United States. James Crawford, internationally known writer and independent journalist, begins this chapter with a section on the politics of the English Only movement and discusses state-level antibilingual ballot initiatives. The authors then analyze federal and state policies of the past four decades in language-minority education, including legislation and court decisions, with a look to the future. At the local educational level, the types of programs designed to serve language-minority students largely influence school policy. Thus this chapter ends with key distinctions among varying program models and their policy implications.

Chapter Three: Teaching   This chapter is designed for teachers, as well as administrators who supervise teachers and staff development personnel. The authors define the active, inquiry-based, interdisciplinary teaching style that is promoted throughout this book as a means to high student achievement, based on research on school effectiveness with culturally and linguistically diverse learners. Among the teaching strategies explored in this chapter are cooperative learning, critical pedagogy, and interdisciplinary, multisensory lessons, using as examples art, technology, and music incorporated into instruction that connects to students' lives inside and outside school.

Chapter Four: Language   The language and culture chapters (Four and Five) provide the deep research foundation for the unique resources that language-minority students bring to the classroom from their close connections to their bilingual/bicultural heritages. The authors present a comprehensive review of current research on first- and second-language acquisition for school, including linguistic, sociocultural, and cognitive processes that influence language acquisition. The second half of the chapter addresses current approaches to teaching English as a second language, teaching language arts in a bilingual classroom, and infusing the teaching of language and multicultural literature across the full curriculum.

Chapter Five: Culture   This second foundational chapter provides the crucial research base on culture and the integral role it plays in schooling students of diverse linguistic and cultural heritages. Rejecting superficial views of culture, the authors present an in-depth review of anthropological views of culture contrasted with popular perspectives, cultural transmission, biculturalism, acculturation, assimilation, cultural pluralism, and multicultural education. The chapter also covers issues of marked and unmarked languages and cultures, stereotypes, ethnocentrism, cultural relativity, cultural difference theories, socioeconomic and political factors, cultural compatibility studies, sociocultural theory, and knowledge construction studies.

Chapter Six: Mathematics and Science   This chapter explores the current school reform movement in the teaching of mathematics and science and its application to language-minority students and their diverse needs. Using the rich resources that can emerge in student contexts with linguistic and cultural diversity, the authors demonstrate through many examples the integration of cognitively rich mathematics and science content with the development and enrichment of students' knowledge base in first and second languages and cultures. Included are examples for using school and community resources and a review of resources for the teaching of multicultural science and math programs. Because the fields of mathematics and science represent "cultural capital" for our students in the school curriculum, the chapter argues that all students be provided with opportunities to access content in these areas.

Chapter Seven: Social Studies   This chapter provides teachers with practical strategies for the teaching of social studies integrated with language and culture. In the school reform context, the authors illustrate the power of social studies for cognitively challenging, linguistically rich, and culturally meaningful lessons. The authors provide rich practical examples for tapping community knowledge and resources for multicultural and global perspectives in social studies.

Chapter Eight: Assessment   Written for school administrators, bilingual and ESL teachers, as well as teachers working in mainstream settings, this new chapter by Lorraine Valdez Pierce provides an overview of assessment decisions in bilingual/ESL education, including federal and state policies. Topics include identification of culturally and linguistically diverse students, assessment practices upon entry into a school system, placement decisions, ongoing authentic classroom assessment, assessment for exit or reclassification when needed, accountability for individual student progress, and program evaluation.

Chapter Nine: Bilingual Special Education   This new chapter in the third edition, written by Theresa Ochoa, begins with a vignette of Andrés and then offers a definition of bilingual special education. It also includes a concise analysis of court cases directly related to the assessment and placement of English-language learners into special education programs. Special education researcher Theresa Ochoa acknowledges the legitimate concern of historical overrepresentation of language-minority students in special education programs, but unabashedly asserts that special education *is* appropriate for some English-language learners. Ochoa articulates the formidable challenges faced by general educators who work with English-language learners experiencing sustained academic difficulties. She asks special education educators and policymakers alike to consider whether those difficulties are related to second language acquisition or to cognitive deficiencies.

Chapter Ten: School and Community   Written for all educators—administrators, teachers, and counselors—this final chapter captures the celebration of school and community collaboration when schools begin to recognize the potential for deeper learning in partnership with their local communities of diverse linguistic and cultural heritages. This chapter provides varied examples of rich school and community partnerships that have transformed schools for the benefit of all—students, parents, educators, policymakers, and the community.

Acknowledgments

Many reviewers of this manuscript have provided thoughtful reactions and insightful suggestions to improve the quality of this book. We are grateful to the following individuals for their careful reading and valuable suggestions:

Harold S. Chi, *George Mason University*
Kathleen Chinn, *New Mexico State University*
Carlos Cruz, *Texas A&M University, Kingsville*
Ellen A. de Kander, *University of St. Thomas*
Rosa Castro Feinberg, *Florida International University*
Michele Hewlett-Gomez, *San Houston State University*
Ryuko Kubota, *University of North Carolina, Chapel Hill*
Annette Lopez, *Kean University*
B.E. Martin, *East Texas Baptist University*
Barbara Medina, *Adams State College*
Maria E. Medrano, *National University*
Eduardo Mendez-Bernal, *SUNY Fredonia*
Deborah L. Norland, *Luther College*
Yolanda Padron, *University of Houston*
Nancy E. Pappamihiel, *Florida State University*
Marc H. Rosa, *Wayne State University*

Julie Ruelas, *Los Angeles Mission College*
Milagros Seda, *University of Texas-El Paso*
Laura E. Sujo de Montes, *Northern Arizona University*
Cynthia K. Valenciano, *Chicago State University*
Luis Valerio, *University of Sothern Colorado*
Miroslava Vargas, *Texas A&M International University*
Gladys von Hoff, *Saginaw Valley State University*
Laurie Weaver, *University of Houston, Clear Lake*

We also wish to thank all the staff of McGraw-Hill Higher Education for their valuable support, patience, and encouragement in seeing this third edition to completion. Cara Harvey, our developmental editor, has been a gentle, supportive, patient, and efficient partner throughout the entire production phase. Gracias, Cara. Jane Karpacz, Publisher, shepherded the book through its initial stages of approval for the third edition. Jean R. Starr supervised the editorial production of the book.

We are especially grateful and indebted to Cristian R. Aquino-Sterling, Carlos Ovando's graduate assistant at Arizona State University, for his unselfish and exemplary dedication to this project. Un millón de gracias, Cristian. Last but not least, we also wish to thank Christy D. Hofsess and Daniel C. Rosen for their timely assistance with the project.

Students

CARLOS' STORY: I Couldn't Answer When You Called My Name
The oldest of nine children, I immigrated to Corpus Christi, Texas, from Nicaragua with my family in 1955, after a three-year residency in Guatemala and about a year in Saltillo, Mexico. There, my paternal grandmother, a younger brother and sister, and I waited for my

father, who had left us behind while he and another part of his family preceded us to the United States. As for many other immigrants from Latin America, Mexico for us was a stepping-stone to the richer and freer United States. According to my father, the primary reason for our move was freedom of religion and better economic and social conditions for the family. In other words, necessity and opportunity were the push-and-pull forces that propelled us to the United States.

*As a member of this family, I not only shared the primary cultural and linguistic patterns from Nicaragua, but also had values from both the Catholic and Protestant faiths. Nicaraguan language, food, and other cultural patterns continued for many years to dominate the socialization practices in my home. I did not, however, experience a deliberate push from my parents to achieve academically in my new country. For example, I do not recall my parents ever asking to see my report cards or expressing interest in visiting my school to talk to my teachers about which classes I should take or to find out how I was doing in my classes. As is the case with many other newly arrived immigrants, it may be that while tacitly interested in my academic well-being, my parents did not know how or were apprehensive to enter the unfamiliar American school. It could also be that because they were so involved in their own economic, linguistic, emotional, and economic survival, they entrusted their children's academic and peer socialization to school personnel—*los maestros son los padres de los estudiantes afuera del hogar/*teachers serve as in* loco parentis *(Larson & Ovando, 2001).*

In those years, schooling practices in south Texas for language minority students like myself were of the sink-or-swim variety. Although already about 14 years old, I was placed in the sixth grade upon arrival in Texas. Unable to make sense of what was going on in the classroom that year, I was retained. I also received my first paddling from the school principal, Mr. Hamshire, for speaking Spanish to an Anglo female student sitting next to me. While I was beginning to pick up English for social purposes after a few months of being exposed to it, my expressive skills were virtually nonexistent. Moreover, I was having a great deal of difficulty mastering the more abstract academic English that is necessary to do well in school—a process that some second language acquisition researchers claim may take up to seven years in optimally supportive sociolinguistic and schooling contexts (Cummins, 2000).

Such troublesome initial contact with the U.S. cultural experience in the schools made me question who I was and why we had left the cultural and linguistic safety of Nicaragua and Latin America for a strange and at times cold and hostile society. Why was I punished for speaking Spanish on school grounds? Why did many of my Mexican American schoolmates seem ashamed of speaking Spanish or reluctant to do so? Why did many such students only speak English? Why did Mexican Americans, African Americans, and European Americans (commonly referred to as Anglos in south Texas) live in segregated neighborhoods and attend segregated schools? Why were there separate drinking fountains for "Coloreds" and "Whites," and which fountain should I use? Was I stupid for not appropriating the English language quickly enough to keep up with my classmates? Why was I in classes with students who were much younger and more immature than I was? Oh, how I longed to show my teachers and classmates what I knew in Spanish in those days! I wish I could have been able to answer my teacher's questions in class to let my classmates know that I was intelligent and liked class discussions and ideas. Feeling alone in a strange world, having flunked sixth grade, I withdrew into a shell and began to entertain self-doubt about my intellectual abilities and my Latin American heritage.

Slowly, however, I rediscovered within myself the primary cultural, linguistic, cognitive, and athletic gifts that I had brought with me to the United States. I remember reassuring myself that I had once been an able student who had many friends and was good in sports. As I came to grips with who I was in this new sociocultural and linguistic reality, a big change occurred when my family moved from south Texas to Defiance, Ohio, about two years after entering the United States. In the new setting, suddenly the Spanish sounds and Latin American cultural patterns so ubiquitous in south Texas took a backseat to English and European American norms in northern Ohio. Now I had no choice but to choose my friends from the English-speaking world, and I felt simultaneously afraid and excited. Increasingly I saw myself becoming integrated socially, academically, and linguistically into another world that I did not fully understand but which pulled me to its epicenter. I made the varsity baseball team as a high school freshman, and it felt good to be recognized for doing something well. As it turned out, organized sports became a great peer equalizer and a source of ego strength for me. Academically, however, most teachers appeared color-blind and insensitive to my newcomer status to the United States. I often felt invisible in the school environment (see Olsen, 1997).

My academic career took a different path when somebody in the church congregation saw me coming out of a pool hall and told my father. Soon after that, in the hope of saving me from a life of sin, my father sent me to a private Mennonite high school in northern Indiana. There, I worked for my room and board, improved my conversational skills in English, and learned important lessons from the Mennonite community about the work ethic and about caring. One very culturally and linguistically sensitive teacher at the Mennonite school encouraged me to maintain and improve my Spanish, and this encouragement eventually led to my receiving an award for excellence in a statewide competition in Spanish. I subsequently received several scholarship offers from colleges and universities, and suddenly I envisioned myself in the world of ideas. I later majored in Spanish in college, taught it at the high school level, and then went on to receive a Ph.D. in Curriculum and Instruction, Latin American Studies, and International Comparative Education from a major research university in the Midwest.

Unlike many of my language minority peers who did not survive the Darwinian sink-or-swim schooling practices of the late 1950s, with the support of a very special teacher and a small network of caring friends and a somewhat resilient personality I was lucky to land on my feet. For a subsequent generation of language minority students—immigrants, children of undocumented workers, refugees, and U.S.–born indigenous minorities—a national experiment was waiting *in the wings that was to alter dramatically the way they would be treated and perceived in our schools. In 1968 the passage of the federal **Bilingual Education Act**[1] brought an exciting yet controversial approach to educating language minority students to the attention of educators throughout the United States. Educators and linguists in the area of English as a second language (ESL) had developed a substantial knowledge base in their field over the years, and educators had experimented with various forms of bilingual education in the United States since at least the early 1800s (Ovando, 1999).*

Thirty-two years after the passage of the federal Bilingual Education Act of 1968, the field of bilingual and ESL education has matured as a field theoretically, conceptually, and curricularly (Cummins, 2000). Yet there is still passionate controversy over the best ways to educate language minority students and induct them into mainstream society (see Crawford, 2000; Cummins, 2000; Ovando & Pérez, 2000). As we enter the new millennium, our society and our schools will continue to be challenged to serve the growing numbers of language minority students from Latin America and Asia (see related section on immigration in this chapter). Hence, it is crucial that educators, researchers, and policymakers listen attentively to the inner voices of language minority students, who may be prisoners of silence in English-dominant classrooms. It is axiomatic in educational circles that all students learn best when they experience curricular content and processes that mirror their lived cultures, languages, and socioeconomic realities (Gumperz, 1996; Minami & Ovando, 1995).

What Do We Mean by Bilingual Education and ESL?

Bilingual and ESL programs take on many, many different forms throughout the United States, depending on state regulations and guidelines, school district policies, the community context, and the composition of each local school population. In Chapter Two we will discuss the various types of bilingual and ESL programs, but let us begin here with a few basic definitions.

Bilingual Education

Any discussion about bilingual education should begin with the understanding that bilingual education is neither a single uniform program nor a consistent "methodology" for teaching language minority students. Rather, it is an approach that encompasses a variety of program models, each of which may promote a variety of distinct goals. For example, while some bilingual education program models promote the development of two languages for bilingualism and biliteracy, other programs may incorporate students' first language merely to facilitate a quick transition into English. There are bilingual education programs that aim to preserve an **indigenous or heritage language** as an ethnic, cultural or community resource.[2] There also are bilingual education programs with an explicit goal to assimilate or

Guidelines for Teaching

BASIC CHARACTERISTICS OF A BILINGUAL EDUCATION PROGRAM

In its most basic form a bilingual education program is one that includes these characteristics:

1. The continued development of the student's primary language (L_1).

2. Acquisition of the second language (L_2), which for many language minority students is English.

3. Instruction in the content areas utilizing both L_1 and L_2 (California Department of Education, 1981, p. 215).

---

socialize students into the mainstream of society (Baker, 1996). Consequently, bilingual education is "a simple label for a complex phenomenon," as Cazden & Snow (1990) have suggested, because not all programs necessarily "concern the balanced use of two languages in the classroom" (Baker, 1996).

(Throughout this book, the terms L_1 and L_2 will be used as they are described in the above quote, with L_1 referring to the child's first language and L_2 referring to the second language that the child is learning.)

Because of the inseparable connection between language and culture, bilingual programs also tend to include historical and cultural components associated with the languages being used.[3] The rationale for the inclusion of the cultural component in bilingual education programs is reflected in this quote from Ulibarrí (1972):

> In the beginning was the Word. And the Word was made flesh. It was so in the beginning and it is so today. The language, the Word, carries within it the history, the culture, the traditions, the very life of a people, the flesh. Language is people. We cannot conceive of a people without a language, or a language without a people. The two are one and the same. To know one is to know the other (p. 295) .

English as a Second Language

English as a second language (ESL) is a system of instruction that enables students who are not proficient in English (**English language learners**) to acquire academic proficiency in spoken and written English. ESL is an essential component of all bilingual education programs in the United States for students who are English language learners. In addition, ESL classes taught through academic content are crucial for English language learners when first-language academic instruction is not feasible, as is the case in contexts where low-incidence language groups (too few speakers of one language for bilingual education to be

Guidelines for Teaching

RECOMMENDATIONS ON THE ROLE OF BILINGUAL EDUCATION AND ESL

The professional organization **Teachers of English to Speakers of Other Languages (TESOL)** has taken the position that bilingual instruction is the best approach to the education of language minority students (TESOL, 1976, 1992b). In other words, according to the TESOL organization, ESL should be *part* of a larger bilingual program that also involves instruction in the student's L$_1$. This important position is shared by the authors of this book. The "TESOL Statement on the Education of K–12 Language Minority Students in the United States" (1992) recommends a four-prong bilingual configuration to meet the needs of language minority students:

- Comprehensive English as a second language instruction for linguistically diverse students that prepares them to handle content area material in English.

- Instruction in the content areas that is not only academically challenging, but also tailored to the linguistic proficiency, educational background, and academic needs of students.

- Opportunities for students to further develop and/or use their first language to promote academic and social development.

- Professional development for both ESOL (English to Speakers of Other Languages) and other classroom teachers that prepares them to facilitate the language and academic growth of

linguistically and culturally different children. (p. 12)

In addition, TESOL has recognized that the acquisition of English by English language learners is an extended and complex process. The organization issued a more recent policy statement (1999) on the acquisition of academic proficiency in English, in which it recommended that programs for ELLs incorporate the following elements:

- No time limits for services that support and move toward standards-based education.

- Sustained professional development for ESL and grade/content level teachers.

- Ongoing student assessment that uses fair, reliable, and valid qualitative and quantitative measures.

- Accountability for stakeholders (e.g., students, teachers) at different levels of implementation (e.g., school, district, state).

- Native language support to help students achieve academic progress.

- Cultural and linguistic diversity in school curriculum and programs.

- Emphasis on academic and content-based English language instruction.

- Active parental involvement in a student's education.

---

provided) are present. **ESL content (or sheltered) classes** may be self-contained, or students may attend ESL content classes for part of the school day and participate in monolingual English instruction in grade-level classes (in the "mainstream") the remainder of the day.

As mentioned before, however, it is not always feasible to implement such a bilingual program. When the number of English learners is insufficient, TESOL recommends monolingual instruction with an ESL component; the organization does not consider monolingual instruction *without* an ESL component adequate to provide language minority students with the specialized instruction they need to successfully acquire English language skills (TESOL, 1976, 1992b).

These brief definitions and position statements just begin to hint at the many issues involved in the implementation of bilingual and ESL programs, issues we will be considering throughout this book. In this first chapter, however, our most important task is to examine the reason for our professional existence: the academic and sociocultural well-being of our students. Who are the learners in bilingual and ESL classrooms? What particular and diverse needs do they have, and how can teachers be sensitive to all of their variations in personality, educational background, social class, culture, ethnicity, national origin, language competence, religion, learning styles, and special skills and talents? For the remainder of this chapter we will examine the range of students in bilingual and ESL classrooms, the backgrounds the students bring with them, what happens when such backgrounds are mixed into the culture of the schools, and how teachers can use this information to know their students better.

Demographics

Since the middle of the twentieth century—particularly during the last three decades—U.S. society has become increasingly multicultural and multilingual. Prior to 1965, when Congress abolished the national-origins quota system, Europe was the major source of immigrants to the United States. By the 1980s, however, 85 percent of immigrants to this country were coming from Third World countries (Crawford, 1992a, p. 3). As shown in Table 1.1, since 1970 the foreign-born population of the United States has increased rapidly due to large-scale immigration, primarily from Latin America and Asia. The total foreign-born population rose from 9.6 million in 1970 to 14.1 million in 1980, and from 19.8 million in 1990 (Gibson & Lennon, 1999) to 28.4 million in 2000.

According to 1990 census data, the total U.S. population grew by 9.8 percent between 1980 and 1990. The number of whites increased by 6.0 percent during this 10-year span, African Americans by 13.2 percent, American Indians (including Eskimos and Aleuts) by 37.9 percent, Asian and Pacific Islanders by 107.8 percent, Hispanic Americans by 53.0 percent, and "Others" by 45.1 percent. Of a U.S. population estimated at 248.7 million in the 1990 census, 30 million were African Americans (12 percent), 22.4 million were Hispanic Americans (9 percent), 9.8 million were "Others" (3.9 percent), 9.7 million were Asian Americans (3 percent), and 2.0 million were American Indians (0.8 percent) (Barringer, 1991, p.1).

In addition to these demographic variations, immigrants have continued to flow rapidly into the United States. By 2000, the Census Bureau estimated the country's total foreign-born population at 30 million, or roughly 11 percent of the nation's 281 million residents (Armas, 2001). That count included 35.5 million Hispanics nationwide—approximately 2.5 million more than had originally been estimated. The continuing influx of Asian immigrants, reported at 25.5 percent of the total foreign-born population for 2000 (Lollock, 2001), led the Census Bureau to project that San Francisco will soon become the second major U.S. city (Honolulu was the first) with a higher Asian than white population (McCormick, 2000).

TABLE 1.1 European, Hispanic, and Asian Immigrants within U.S. Total and Foreign-Born Population: 1970–2000. [In thousands, except as indicated (272,241 represents 272,241,000)].

| Year | U.S. Total | U.S. Foreign-Born[†] | U.S. Foreign-Born Populations* | | |
			Hispanics	Asians	Europeans
2000	281,421	28,379 (10.1%)	14,477 (51.0%)	7,246 (25.5%)	4,255 (15.3%)
1990	248,791	19,767 (7.9%)	8,407 (42.5%)	4,979 (25.1%)	4,350 (22.0%)
1980	226,546	14,079 (6.2%)	4,372 (31.0%)	2,539 (18.0%)	5,149 (36.6%)
1970	203,210	9,619 (4.7%)	1,803 (18.7%)	24,887[‡] (0.26%)	5,740 (59.6%)

*Percentages of the U.S. total foreign-born population.
[†]Percentages of the U.S. total population.
[‡]In hundreds.

Sources: Campbell J. Gibson, and Emily Lennon, Historical Census Statistics on the Foreign-born Population of the United States., February, 1999; U.S. Census Bureau, *Current Population Survey,* March 2000, Ethnic and Hispanic Statistics Branch, Population Division; U.S. Census Bureau, *Statistical Abstract of the United States, 2000.*

These population changes—sometimes referred to as the "demographic imperative"—have resulted in large numbers of school entrants whose first language is not English. Most educational discourse and learning environments to date, however, have continued to reflect the discourse practices of mainstream society, with often unfortunate results for nonmainstream students, including language minority students (Cazden, 1988; Gee, 1990; Michaels, 1981). According to John Gumperz (1996), linguistic minorities will soon outnumber monolingual English speakers in many places in the United States, and U.S. educators are not well prepared to work effectively in such diverse contexts. Banks (1991a) has succinctly summarized the changing demographics landscape and its impact on classrooms in the 21st century:

> The percentage of people of color in the nation will continue to rise throughout the early decades of the next century. Indeed, the 1990 census revealed that one out of every four people who live in the United States is a person of color and that one out of every three people will be a person of color by the turn of the century. Likewise, the ethnic and racial makeup of the nation's classrooms is changing significantly. Students of color constitute a majority in twenty-five of the nation's largest school districts and in California, our most populous state with a population of thirty million people. Students of color will make up nearly half (46 percent) of the nation's school-age youth by 2020, and about 27 percent of those students will be victims of poverty (p. 1).

Reflecting a general lack of preparedness for the increased "browning" of the United States student population is the nationwide critical shortage of well-prepared teachers who can work effectively with the large and growing number of students whose first language is other than English. This shortage will become even more severe in the next two decades, when, for example, the ratio of language minority teachers to language minority students will drop to an all-time low unless strong actions are taken to reverse current trends. For example, although Spanish-speaking students constitute the largest number of language minority students in U.S. schools, there is a dramatic shortage of teachers who come from Hispanic backgrounds (Crawford, 1999; Delpit, 1995). Applebome (1996) notes that the first challenge in the preparation of teachers for the 21st century will be to address the "growing mismatch between the background of teachers and the students they will be teaching" (p. 22).

Types of Language Minority Students

As used in this book, the term *language minority student* (in the United States) refers to a student who comes from a home where a language other than English is spoken. According to a 1992 **National Association for Bilingual Education (NABE)** publication, more than 7.5 million school-age children in the United States were from homes in which a non-English language was spoken. The predictions are that this language minority student population will surge to about 35 percent of all schoolchildren by the year 2000 (NABE, 1992, p. 3). Language minority children are now the fastest growing group in schools in the United States (McKeon, 1992).

This large language minority category includes a broad range of patterns of language proficiency. Language minority students may or may not have enough proficiency in English to do well academically in all-English instructional settings. They may be essentially monolingual in English, or they may be monolingual in a non-English language, or they may possess varying degrees and types of bilingualism. And, of course, their language proficiency status changes as they mature and as they progress through school. The parents or grandparents of monolingual English-speaking language minority students may still have varying degrees of proficiency in the ancestral language, but the children may be essentially only proficient in English, understanding just a few, if any, household words or phrases from the family's language of origin. At the other extreme are the children of recent immigrants, who are usually monolingual in the family's first language. (We say "usually" because these children may sometimes be bilingual in several non-English languages, or they may have some English proficiency from having studied English in their home country.) In between the two monolingual extremes are a complex array of mixes of bilingual proficiency. Although it is an oversimplification of the picture, such language minority students may be more proficient in English than in the ancestral language (English dominant), fairly balanced in proficiency in both languages, or more proficient in the second language than in English (e.g., Farsi dominant, Korean dominant, Spanish dominant, Vietnamese dominant, and so on.) This issue of various kinds of bilingualism will be explored further in Chapter Four.

Students who are either monolingual in the home language, or have some English proficiency but are still more fluent in their home language, until recently have been referred to as limited–English-proficient (LEP) students. Data from state education agencies receiving Title VII funding suggest that in 1989–90 there were about 2.2 million limited–English-proficient students in the United States (Meyer & Feinberg, 1992, p. 109). More recently, the Stanford Working Group (1993) estimated the number of LEP students to be much greater, perhaps as many as 3.3 million children between the ages of 5 and 17.

Although the term *LEP* has been used extensively in literature and demographic information about this group, the term has recently been criticized for its negative connotations. It has been argued that the use of the word *limited* in the term **limited–English–proficient** reflects a focus on what the child cannot do rather than on what he or she can do and that it implies a bias against non-English speakers as being less able than English speakers. Thus many educators have begun to use the more neutral term *English language learner* (ELL). This term conveys that the student is in the process of learning English, without having the connotation that the student is in some way defective until full English proficiency is attained. However, like LEP, the ELL designation is still somewhat problematic in that it focuses on the need to learn English without acknowledging the value of the child's proficiency in L_1 (Crawford, 1999, p. 17). Despite this drawback, we will generally use ELL throughout this book because we agree that it is a more positive and less stigmatizing term than LEP. However, LEP will appear occasionally when it was the original term used in a source we are citing.

Figures such as 7.5 million language minority children, or 3.3 million ELLs, although very important, do not reveal the rich mix of language minority students found in classrooms today, nor do they tell us who is eligible for bilingual services and how long they are to be served. Such students range from indigenous minorities whose ancestors have been here for tens of thousands of years to very recent immigrants from virtually every region of the world. As such, our language minority children represent both the oldest and newest members of American society. Throughout the nation's history, assimilative and acculturative factors have had powerful impacts on the lives of such students, producing many different configurations of language and culture. Language minority students in bilingual classrooms, for example, may include English dominant students with a language minority background, bilingual students who are proficient in both English and their home language, and English language learners.

A closer look at these groupings in bilingual classrooms, for example, reveals that English dominant language minority students may be involved in a bilingual program to improve academic achievement and perhaps additionally to develop their home language skills. An English dominant language minority student, for example, may be a Hispanic-American or American Indian child who speaks English predominantly or exclusively and yet is exposed to the family's other language through parents or grandparents. English dominant language minority students often come from stigmatized ethnolinguistic groups that, because of societal pressures, historical circumstances, or geographical location, have not fully maintained their ancestral languages. Although considerably acculturated into the English-speaking milieu, they may be socioeconomically or socioculturally marginal, and they may speak a variety of English that puts them at a linguistic disadvantage in the mainstream English classroom. (The issue of standard English as a second dialect will be discussed in Chapter Four.) Some of these English dominant language minority communities are undergoing linguistic and cultural revitalization today, and bilingual education has become an important avenue for the realization of their hopes for their children (Ovando & Gourd, 1996).

Besides these students whose parents want them to be reexposed to their ancestral languages through bilingual instruction, many bilingual students are enrolled in bilingual classes because of their desire to continue learning in two languages and living in two cultures. For such students who are already considerably fluent in two languages, bilingual instruction constitutes enrichment of their academic experience, an affirmation of the family's ethnolinguistic identity, and a highly valuable contribution to the nation's supply of well-educated, biliterate, bilingual citizens.

The language minority students most often associated in the public eye with bilingual and ESL instruction are, of course, the ELLs who upon school entry lack the necessary English skills for immediate success in an all-English curriculum. Bilingual instruction for such students is a way of providing educational equity and quality. Through bilingual instruction, including instruction in ESL, English language learners can begin to develop the linguistic and academic skills appropriate to their level of cognitive development. As these ELLs gradually become English proficient, they also enrich the nation's linguistic resources if they are able to maintain their home language through strong bilingual programs.

Student and Family Background

When I came from the Dominican Republic at the age of 11 and entered the New York City public schools, I felt as if all of a sudden my previous knowledge and lived experiences were disregarded and thrown out the window. It seemed as if most teachers focused their energies only on teaching me English. My sister and I cried many times, for we didn't know what was going on. (—Cristian Aquino-Sterling, Graduate student in College of Education at Arizona State University, 2001)

Very few, if any, educators would argue against the value of being familiar with students' cultural background, socioeconomic background, and previous schooling experience. While such information about any student is valuable, it becomes even more important when the student population includes children of language minority groups. Because of cultural and linguistic differences, insufficient knowledge in such situations can clearly lead to a greater risk of failure in school adjustment and cognitive growth. In this section, then, we will consider the cultural, social, and academic contexts that surround language minority students.

The Role of Culture

Because language and culture are so thoroughly intertwined, language minority students are almost by definition also cultural minority students. Given that the role of culture is so important in bilingual and ESL situations, an entire chapter of this book is dedicated to this issue (Chapter Five). Cultural traits are commonly associated with such salient features as language and racial background, name, clothing, and food. While such obvious cues are just the tip of the cultural iceberg, many of the negative attitudes found in society toward minority ethnic groups are rooted in fairly simplistic interpretations of items in those categories. However, beyond these obvious markers of being "different," many more subtle but important aspects of ethnicity contribute to a student's identity. For example, the roles assigned to individuals within and outside the family may vary significantly according to cultural backgrounds. Lines of authority and socialization expectations as manifested in birth order, sex roles, and division of labor are powerful agents in molding children's social relationships.

Values and religion, as expressions of belief systems, serve as windows to the interior of cultural structures. The things that we believe in, whatever they may be—independence, individual choice, freedom, conformity, nonconformity, economic success, community, optimism, idealism, materialism, technology, nature, morality, future time orientation, achievement orientation, the work ethic, democracy, socialism, capitalism, extended family, cooperation, competition, education, magic, horoscopes, Buddhism, pantheism, secular humanism, agnosticism, Judaism, Catholicism, Protestantism and on and on—provide a powerful synthesis of how we as humans attempt to make at least partial sense of the world surrounding us. The new linguistic and cultural environment that a language minority student encounters at school may intentionally or unintentionally affirm or negate the values of the child and his or her family. A young person who has been taught to be quiet and unquestioning when dealing with adults, for example, may find that his or her idea of the "good student" is not rewarded in an open, student-centered classroom.

Styles of nonverbal communication are also an important aspect of cultural identity. In communicating with each other, humans draw from many paralinguistic actions as well as from the verbal message. Cultural groups attach different meanings to types of body movements, spatial distance, eye contact, and emotional tone (Birdwhistell, 1970; Cazden, John & Hymes, 1972; Hall, 1959; Goodwin, 1990; Philips, 1983). The significance of a laugh, a pat on the shoulder, or a hug can be quite different depending on the cultural background of the person interpreting it. What message, for example, does a Chamorro student convey with the up-and-down motion of the eyebrows? (Among the Chamorros of Guam, raising the eyebrows and tilting the head back slightly indicate recognition of a person's presence. It is a silent hello.) Or what message does a Puerto Rican student convey by twitching the nose to a friend? (It is a way to signal a subtle message to the friend.) Knowledge of such nonverbal codes affects the outcome of intercultural communication between the culture of the home and the culture of the school.

Students who are new to the United States have usually had some type of exposure to the popular version of "American" culture before immigration. For some immigrants, impressions of the United States may be based on what Hollywood projects through the movies.[4] Others may have a more accurate vision of particular characteristics of life in the United States. Many, for example, have more realistic impressions of the country filtered through the interpretations of friends or relatives who have preceded them to the United States.

Once in the United States, many immigrant families continue to maintain strong ties with their ancestral lands. These ties are very enriching culturally and linguistically. However, they also sometimes contribute to an experience of bicultural ambivalence—the feeling of being treated as Americanized while visiting their country of origin, and yet not being accepted as "real" Americans by mainstream society in the United States. It is not uncommon for such students to report that when they visit their relatives in their home country they often feel uneasy and somewhat out of place culturally and linguistically—these students often have become highly acculturated to U.S. mainstream cultural patterns and they may not speak their ancestral language fluently, if at all. For example, after the election defeat of the Sandinista government in Nicaragua in 1990, the conservative government of Violeta Chamorro invited Nicaraguan expatriates to return from the United States. With this influx came a group of young people from the United States called the "Miami boys." Nicaraguans gave them the name because many of their cars had Florida license plates and their style of dress and taste in music reflected contemporary U.S. cultural and linguistic norms since many of these young people had become adolescents while in the United States. When their parents took them back to their country of origin, many of them experienced cross-cultural difficulties in Nicaragua.

Although born in the United States, indigenous language minority children also encounter mainstream cultural patterns that are alien to types of behavior and communication fostered at home. The children are exposed to these new patterns through migration to urban centers or simply through entry into the school system. How students and their families react to the differences they find in these new settings depends both on the impressions and attitudes toward the mainstream culture that they bring with them and on the way their cultural background is accepted in the school context.

The Social Context

Socioeconomic Status

⊠ *The single largest variable that predicts SAT scores is family income. If you want higher SAT scores, you need to get your kids born into wealthier families. You know, it's great to tell kids to pull themselves up by their own bootstraps, but you better put boots on them first. (—Paul Houston, American Association of School Administrators, Washington, DC, 1996)*

Many students in bilingual and ESL classrooms come from sociocultural groups that have been and continue to be the recipients of varying degrees of socioeconomic marginality and racial or ethnic discrimination. However, students served through bilingual instruction are not uniformly from lower socioeconomic backgrounds. Language minority students often have recently undergone changes in their socioeconomic status. Sometimes such students come from relatively well-educated middle-class families who face a different economic and social situation until they get themselves on their feet in the United States. Many language minority students, depending on the economic conditions, undergo social adjustments because of the change in the way they fit into society. This can be the case whether the family has moved from a higher socioeconomic status in the country of origin to a lower status in the United States or whether it is experiencing upward mobility.

Tied in with the social class of language minority students is the fact that much of what they represent is strongly linked to their geographical region of origin. Very often immigrants from rural areas have considerably different values and customs from their urban counterparts from the same country. Urban residents, for example, may have been exposed more frequently to the popular cultural version of the United States portrayed through the mass media, which serve as a powerful assimilator worldwide.

Prejudice and Discrimination   When considering the social context of language minority students, one has to explore the ways in which negative perceptions of their sociocultural and political status can affect their lives. How mainstream citizens perceive that language minority groups fit into the social texture of the nation can have a strong impact on both immigrants and indigenous minority populations. Some research indicates that the positive or negative perceptions of the mainstream population toward the minority population can affect the academic performance of language minority students as they internalize these perceptions (Jacob & Jordan, 1993; Ogbu, 1978, 1992; Skutnabb-Kangas & Cummins, 1988).

History, economic conditions, and political conflicts all play important roles in how various language minority groups are perceived. As an example of the changing political terrain, during the September 11, 2001, terrorist attack on the World Trade Center and the Persian Gulf War of 1991, many Americans felt hostility toward certain segments of the Arab population, especially those from Afghanistan, Saudi Arabia, and Iraq. Following the terrorist attack on the World Trade Center, for example, many Arab university and college students were ostracized by their U.S. peers and in some cases this caused them to withdraw from classes and return to their home countries. During the Persian Gulf War of 1991, an Anglo-American parent who had a brother fighting in the Persian Gulf War asked a teacher in Oregon to have her elementary students write letters of support to the U.S. soldiers stationed in the Persian Gulf. The teacher decided to refuse the parent's suggestion because some of her students were Arab, and she did not want to bring politics into the classroom. This, however, frustrated and angered some of the mainstream parents, who felt that the presence of the Arab children in the classroom should not preclude the option of letters supporting U.S. foreign policy.

As mentioned in our discussion of demographics, in recent years our classrooms have experienced an influx of students from such diverse regions of the world as Central America, Africa, Eastern Europe, the former Soviet republics, the Middle East, Southeast Asia, and the Caribbean. Many of these immigrants and refugees are fleeing from political strife, violence, and poverty. To these newcomers, the United States may seem to have a Jekyll and Hyde personality. On the one hand, the Statue of Liberty is a symbol that U.S. society welcomes the oppressed of the world. Yet, on the other hand, the United States also has a fairly consistent track record of xenophobia, especially when the economy is sputtering. Given this reality, immigrant and refugee families must be prepared psychologically to handle hostile treatment from members of U.S. society who may feel threatened by the presence of newcomers. Yet, immigrant and refugee children may also be the recipients of care and advocacy from many, including their bilingual and ESL teachers.

Today, worldwide trade issues also have the increasing potential to raise negative feelings toward individuals who represent countries where economic growth may threaten the U.S. economy. In the 1990s there was increasing talk about economic and regional nationalism. Thus, for example, the North American Free Trade Agreement (NAFTA), which includes Canada, the United States and Mexico, has generated heated discussions about winners and losers. This type of discussion can easily develop into hostile attitudes toward people whose countries of origin are perceived as harming our way of life. In the case of Mexico, for example, opponents of NAFTA fear "that Mexico intends to use its relatively cheap labor to steal American manufacturing jobs" (Golden, 1993, p. C1). Closer to home, tucked amidst the corn fields of the Midwest are Japanese car factories that, while providing jobs for the local population, also generate a fair amount of hostility toward the Japanese presence in the area.

Often, high numbers of newcomers to a community produce a powerful backlash as well. This has been the case, for example, in Dade County, Florida, where Cuban linguistic, cultural, and business practices compete with non-Cuban practices. Bretzer's (1992) excerpts from interviews she conducted in the Miami area illustrate the tensions experienced between Cubans and non-Cubans:

I couldn't believe it. I mean, it was like a foreign country . . . a Spanish-speaking country. You won't see a sign that's in English. . . . It was Spanish, every word on every building—it was Spanish. (p. 213)

The [Cuban] culture . . . has taken over—there is no integration. . . . If you are working someplace . . . the language is mainly Spanish; if you don't know it, you don't belong here. . . . They consider this Cuba across the water . . . They all carry guns as part of their culture. . . . Probably

98 percent of the drug arrests are from the element.... They brought a lot of things we really don't need, but it is a part of their culture.... Now it is up to us, with our tax money, to open schools that don't speak English. (p. 215)

Fearful of the potential economic, cultural, and linguistic impact that new immigrants could have on their communities, established residents in other parts of the country have expressed similar hostility towards their new neighbors. This has been the case, for instance, with the Hmong in Fresno, California, and Mexican migrant workers who have opted to establish permanent communities in rural areas of the nation. There are, however, instances where such initial hostilities are overcome by open-mindedness and goodwill. Such is the case in Monterey Park, California, a town of about 62,000 residents that was predominantly Anglo in the 1960s. Monterey Park experienced a 70.6 percent increase in Chinese immigrants from Taiwan, Hong Kong, and Southeast Asia between 1980 and 1986. Such a demographic shift brought about a strong backlash from established residents who thought their way of life was threatened. Horton and Calderón (1992) captured the evolution of the struggle over language politics and economic concerns between the Chinese community and the established residents of Monterey Park and its eventual resolution as follows:

> We trace the language struggle from an abortive attempt to declare Official English in 1986 to electoral support for Proposition 63, the state's Official English amendment later in the same year, to compromises on city codes regulating the use of Chinese business signs in 1989.[5] It is a story of initial polarization and conflict, followed by a lessening of language struggles and accommodation to the realities of a multiethnic community. (p. 187)

It would probably be safe to say that virtually all bilingual and ESL teachers are familiar with such community conflicts and that they can recall instances of prejudice or discrimination toward language minority students and their families. Pretending that such issues do not exist will not make them go away, and we will return to this theme again in this chapter when we look at the emotional issues for language minority students.

Previous Schooling Experience

In exploring language minority students' home backgrounds we have thus far considered the role of culture and the social context of the student's life. Another important aspect of getting to know our students that is related to the student's sociocultural background is the family's attitude toward formal schooling and the student's previous academic experiences. We will look at previous schooling and attitudes first from the point of view of the immigrant student, and then from the point of view of the indigenous student.

⊠ *The nature of an immigrant student or family's previous school experience depends on socioeconomic status, country of origin, and the circumstances of the geographical move. Some students have been provided with a sound base of knowledge that can be transferred to the English curriculum, whereas others have had almost no schooling. The cases of Beto and Mee, two language minority high schoolers, represent the extremes:*

- *Beto, a teenager who spent his childhood in the Dominican Republic, never had a chance there to attend school regularly and to learn how to read. Because his academic background knowledge is so extremely limited, he needs intensive instruction in the language he knows best, Spanish. Now, through lessons in Spanish, he has made three grades' progress in reading and math in one year, and he is beginning to learn enough English to transfer his reading and math skills to English.*
- *Mee, a Korean-born student, is already literate in her native language due to her previous education. Her literacy and broad knowledge base in Korean is helping her to understand materials in English, and she is excelling in mathematics because of previous exposure to the concepts.*

Even for children who come to the United States as preschoolers or who are born in the United States of recent immigrants, the parents' schooling experiences in the country of origin affect the way the child's schooling is perceived. Information about parents' and students' previous schooling is valuable not only for making curricular adjustments but also for taking an affirmative posture toward the learner. Some immigrant parents, for instance, arrive from countries that stress an authoritarian style within the school: The adult commands and the children play a strictly subordinate role. Placing a child from such a setting into one with a degree of academic and physical freedom often confuses the learner. In some countries children are exposed to a fairly standardized curriculum nationwide, and there is a high degree of uniformity in pedagogic methods. To families from such backgrounds, the variety of options available in most American school systems today may seem quite puzzling. A predominant approach to instruction in some countries emphasizes memorizing information rather than problem-posing, inquiry-driven, or open-ended learning activities. Students or parents accustomed to such pedagogy may feel uncomfortable initially with the critical thinking and discussion format that they may encounter in the new school environment. The student may have been rewarded previously for taking a passive learning role, or the family may have expected her or him to assume that role. A teacher who is aware of the different traditions that enabled the student or the student's parents to survive in the previous academic environment can help these students adjust to a more active role. Whether students have experienced small or large group instruction, whether time schedules and attendance requirements have been strict or lax, whether oral or written work has been emphasized, and whether there has been a cultural bias toward cooperation or competition and independence all have an effect. Finally, immigrant parents from any social class background may be unprepared for the design and value systems of schools in the United States. Standardized tests, authentic assessment, varied grading systems, learner-centered instruction, cooperative learning structures, and interactive, experiential learning are among many practices that may be unfamiliar to immigrant parents.

On the other hand, parents of indigenous minority students may be familiar with the operation of local school systems, but they may have experienced chronic failure in those systems. Their failure in turn influences what they want for their children as they are educated in the same systems. For example, Hispanic Americans have tended in the past to have less formal schooling than the mainstream population, with a relatively high rate of students dropping out before completing high school (Vargas, 1988, p. 9). Given the resultant lower incomes as well as generally weak academic skills, many such parents are not in a position to help their own children financially and academically. Against overwhelming odds, some of these Hispanic-American children will prosper academically. Unfortunately, however, many of them will ultimately replicate their parents' earlier paths of poverty and school failure by also dropping out of high school, at a rate as high as 45 percent in some school districts (Trueba, Spindler, & Spindler, 1989, p. 28).

What Happens at School

As we have seen, language minority students bring a very broad range of different sociocultural backgrounds and previous schooling experiences to school. Consequently, many researchers argue that much of the difficulty language minority children experience in school can be attributed to the apparent mismatch between the world of the home and the world of the classroom (Jacob & Jordan, 1993; Jordan, 1984; Mehan, 1991; Tharp & Gallimore, 1988; Ogbu, 1992; Trueba, Guthrie, & Au, 1981). The potential consequences of the home-school mismatch and the corresponding curricular and instructional challenge to create more culturally compatible classroom practices will be discussed in Chapter Five. To set the stage, though, we will look here at some of the emotional issues, the linguistic issues, and the academic issues facing language minority students when they arrive at school.

The Emotional Issues

A basic part of analyzing the level of integration of language minority students into the life of the school is a consideration of their emotional needs and experiences. Combining the variation in cultural patterns with the individual personality of each student results in many different ways that language minority children may react to a particular classroom situation. The following sketches illustrate just a few behaviors from the wide range these students exhibit:

- *Reserved, silent, seated in a corner, Lan prefers the isolation and comfort of written exercises. She prefers not to respond orally to the teacher or to Vietnamese peers. Who knows her innermost thoughts with her family gone and her familiar world taken away?*

- *Pedro is a highly energetic 13 year old who acts out his aggression in class. An Ecuadorian Indian, short compared to his classmates, he alternately is eager for lessons and teases classmates. He drives his teacher crazy.*
- *A handsome and bright new student, José, arrives from Venezuela. He is immediately popular and highly social, adjusts well to the new school context, and picks up social English extremely fast. He attends school faithfully and follows all the rules. Then the bilingual counselor discovers that he is a drug peddler in the back corner of the school yard.*
- *Yuki, an elementary Japanese student, has always spoken only in a whisper. Today she is playing an ESL game in which she acts out sentences such as "I am jumping." She becomes so involved in the game that she forgets her self-consciousness and speaks in an easily heard tone of voice for the first time.*

Teachers working with such students must be prepared to accept the likelihood that some of them may have some difficulty learning because of unhealed emotional scars from political and social upheavals. Their lives may represent on-and-off schooling experiences under very stressful conditions in their ancestral countries. They may have had dehumanizing refugee camp experiences in host countries. Some may be living with total strangers in the United States because their families sent them out of their war-torn countries in search of safety. Garbarino (1992), a child psychologist who specializes in the lives of children from the world's war zones, notes that "lethal violence in a young life often leads to nervousness, rage, fear, nightmares and constant vigilance" (p. 6). While it is unrealistic to expect bilingual and ESL teachers to be psychologists, social workers, immigration experts, and surrogate parents, it is important for us to be aware of these possible problems and to know where to find professional help for these students if they appear to need it.

Sensitizing oneself to the emotional needs of language minority students sometimes requires careful observation on the part of the teacher. In the business of the classroom day, we may not take time to notice and appreciate the messages we are being sent. A desire to express one's cultural or personal identity may come in very subtle ways. Consider the following story of an ESL teacher working with one of his students:

⊗ *Using Cuisenaire rods, the ESL teacher modeled an activity which reinforced color, direction, and prepositions. He sat with his back to a student, who gave him directions as to how to place the rods. If the student communicated her directions clearly in English, the teacher would end up with the same configuration of rods that she had formed. Kyun Sun did a great job, and her teacher ended up with the targeted design. The girl, very proud of her work, then explained to the teacher that he had formed the symbol for her name in Korean.*

Unfortunately, whether actual or perceived, subtle or blatant, some form of racial and ethnic discrimination is a reality of life in most culturally plural environments. The school may be one of the first places where language minority children discover that they are perceived by the mainstream culture as being different. An American-born language minority student from a rural background recalls, "When we came to this city I first experienced prejudice in school and that really cut me down. I wanted to go back where we came from, but my parents wanted me to stay here with them." As they mature, students, like their adult models, assess the sociocultural texture of society and notice what is valued and what is devalued. One impact that discrimination or prejudice can have on a person is a feeling of not being in control of the environment, which in turn can lead to low self-esteem (Cummins, 1986a; Ogbu, 1992). Although school, unfortunately, is certainly one of the places where language minority students may experience prejudice, school is also an important place where they can learn to confront it. Bilingual and ESL teachers, therefore, have an important role in encouraging their language minority students to believe in themselves and to affirm their ethnolinguistic heritage.

Another way language minority students may begin to feel alienated and defeated is to be placed in a grade that does not correspond to the student's age. In the past, new ELLs were often placed in a grade lower than they would normally be placed according to their age, the theory being that the work would be easier for them and that they would have more time to catch up as they learn English. Even if language minority students were initially placed in an age-appropriate grade, age-grade mismatch often occurred when the students were retained because they had not yet learned enough English to go on to the next grade. However, when the age-grade mismatch happens, it all too often results in the student just waiting to quit school. Regardless of language policy, research clearly shows that repeated grade retention ultimately leads to an extremely high probability of dropping out (Trueba, Spindler, & Spindler, 1989). A variety of alternative methods can be used in the elementary grades to provide age-appropriate, meaningful schooling to ELLs through such means as multilevel, nongraded classes and cooperative learning. Older than average high school ELLs need alternative secondary programs that can address their age-grade mismatch within a supportive environment, combining features such as individualized instruction, counseling, work experience opportunities, intensive language training, and academic preparation for postsecondary education.

The establishment of trust is another affective issue that may take on special features in the case of the language minority student. For example, students' and families' own academic expectations may differ from their view of the school's academic expectations for them. Where such differences exist, they can be a barometer of the level of trust between the school and the students and their parents. Regardless of whether they are justified, feelings on the part of some language minority students that less is expected of them are real and have to be faced. Take, for example, the thoughts of two language minority students with a high degree of resentment. One explains:

> *I want to be a doctor and I want to go to some third-world country because they need a lot of doctors there. What motivates me is when the white man tells me that I can't do it. It's up to me to prove that I can. It really makes me angry.*

The other student, a college-bound senior who entered the school system as an English language learner, reflects on the expectations she thought teachers had of her:

> *When I first came here to grade school the teachers thought I would have a lot of problems and they ended up putting me in a reading class a couple of grades below what I could read. I think it was a Dick and Jane book. In high school now, some of the teachers talk real slow, like I don't understand or something, but then others . . . Well, it seems like it's always either below my knees or above my head! I don't relate to my school counselor very well. I've done all the financial aid stuff for college pretty much myself.*

As students establish their ethnic identity, they also confront many emotion-laden issues. Many factors contribute to a child's formation of ethnic identity, and schools are an important arena in which these identities are shaped. For example, the nature of the ethnic identity children establish for themselves may depend partially on the ethnic composition of the school they attend. Although many other factors are involved in a student's self-concept, a school with a large proportion of language minority students sometimes may provide a supportive environment for more positive self-identification (Ovando, 1978a). Conversely, schools in which only a small number of students receive bilingual or ESL instruction may create the possibility of feelings of stigmatization. It is not unusual for children to feel uncomfortable about receiving any "special" academic assistance, but the fact that language minority youth are filtering their experiences through a different culture and language background may tend to make them particularly vulnerable. An ESL tutor, for example, wonders about the psychological impact of a pullout program on an ELL:

> *I am concerned about María Angela's feelings as to why I was asked to work with her. I don't want her to think, "I am an especially poor student, so they've assigned me a special tutor."*

The Linguistic Issues

For language minority students the process of acquiring English itself can be a highly emotional experience. Research syntheses by Brown (1994); Dulay, Burt, and Krashen (1982); Genesee (1987); and Schumann (1980) suggest that affective factors play a powerful role in the acquisition of a second language. As Mettler (1983) puts it, in learning a second language the "chances for success seem to be lodged as firmly in the viscera as in the intellect." (p. 1)

Language is usually the most salient issue as language minority students establish their role within the classroom. It is the dominant theme in the instructional process and the driving force behind the organization of bilingual and ESL classrooms. In addition to coming to the classroom with a different oral language base, language minority students also come with different literacy traditions: different writing systems, different concepts of sound-symbol relations, different modes of discourse, and different story patterns.

Finding the appropriate balance in instruction between the first and second language is another challenge. For example, a language minority student may appear to have very strong English oral communication skills in informal situations, but be very weak in reading and writing in English. It is often difficult for teachers, who have mastered the English language, to maintain a realistic perspective on the amount of time it takes a student to become academically proficient in a second language. After students have mastered the basics of informal, conversational English, it is easy for teachers to assume incorrectly that they comprehend the many forms of expression, vocabulary items, and sentence structures encountered in content-area class work in English. The amount of language information students must absorb becomes particularly striking past the primary grades, which rely on a simpler language base, more visual aids, and many more hands-on experiences. Two university students' journal entries on classroom observations of ESL students suggest the difficulties such students can face in the upper grades:

- *Several idiomatic expressions were really unfamiliar to Ounalom, such as "John Doe" and a "Dear John letter." "John Doe" was surprisingly difficult to explain. It makes you realize what is involved in English content mastery for an English language learner.*
- *Patricia has not yet decided what her report topic will be. Time lines are a possibility. She expresses considerable anxiety over this oral presentation. She is better able to communicate with pen and paper than verbally, and she admits to being embarrassed to speak in front of others.*

Another linguistic issue that has to be addressed is language variation. There are many Englishes throughout the world, and in the United States alone we have Black English, "Walter Cronkite" English, Brooklynese, Bostonese, Appalachian English, bush English in Alaska, Hawaiian Pidgin, Chicano English, and on and on. Language minority students acquire communicative competence in English from peers, other family members, sports activities, and the media, in addition to the formal classroom. Consequently, the type of language students learn varies with the context. English teachers sometimes become frustrated when language minority students use so-called incorrect English despite efforts to instill in them a standard version of the language. Students, however, learn to speak English not only to get good grades and please their teachers but also to survive socially and fit in with the sociolinguistic structure of their communities and peer subcultures. Keeping in mind the important sociocultural role that language patterns play in the lives of all students can help teachers value language variation in the lives of students across speech communities.

As in any linguistic community, language minority students also are likely to represent a wide range of language variation in their home language.

Hispanic-American students, for example, may be exposed to a standard form of Spanish in the bilingual classroom that differs markedly from the Spanish they are familiar with at home. Therefore, in getting to know the student's background, the bilingual or ESL teacher is not just dealing with standard English and the standard form of the home language; variation in language may be represented in English as well as in the other languages used by students.

Another facet of the language variation found among bilingual and ESL students is the existence of varying levels of proficiency in the first as well as the second language. It is easy to think of students in terms of two simple categories: English language learners and English proficient students. But another layer must be added to the construction of language categories: There are also students who, relative to their age, lack full communicative competence in both the home language and English. This may be the result of schooling experiences with "subtractive bilingualism" in which the first language is being lost as the second language is learned (California Department of Education, 1981, pp. 217–18).

Ancestral language loss also may occur because non-English–speaking parents, in an effort to help their children acquire English quickly, talk to them in their second language, English. Sometimes, unfortunately, this practice is catalyzed by teacher pressure. Moved by the desire to have non-English speaking students acquire English as quickly as possible, well-meaning but ill-advised teachers sometimes recommend that language minority parents use English with their children at home. When this happens, the nature of the communication between parents and children tends to become impoverished.

 Guidelines for Teaching

RECOMMENDATIONS TO SCHOOL PERSONNEL ABOUT THE USE OF L_1 AT HOME

Affirming the importance of authentically rich two-way communication processes at home through the first language, Coelho (1994), makes the following recommendation to school personnel:

- Inform parents of the value of continuing to use the first language rather than a poor model of English at home. Cummins (1981b) describes several studies that indicate the importance of the first language as a tool for the development of concepts that can be transferred into the second.

- If parents read or tell stories to their children in the first language, the children will continue to acquire a variety of rhetorical forms and genres of the written language as well as in the language of day-to-day interaction. The richer their experience with the first language, the more easily they will acquire the second. Children who already read and write the first language should continue to do so, as this will facilitate their reading and writing in English. (p. 324)

Parents, for example, may find it difficult, if not impossible, to share with their children their most subtle, rich, and intimate feelings and thoughts in a language that is alien to them.

While some language minority students may be struggling to hang on to their first language because English is used at home, fortunately there are also language minority students who speak only English but whose ancestral language is being revitalized. Although grandparents, adapting to the melting pot expectations of the past, might have suppressed their ancestral languages, some parents today want to restore traditional languages and cultures for their children (Ovando & Gourd, 1996). In areas such as Alaska and Guam, for example, which have strong oral traditions but little written literature, language revitalization has prompted the development of curricular materials in native languages (Ovando, 1984, 1997). An Inupiak Eskimo college student compares her elementary school language development, which included only English, with that of a younger niece today:

[X] *When I go back home from college I'm trying to tell my dad everything that has happened to me at school in our language [Inupiak], and he'll be really <u>exhausted</u> because he corrects me and tries to understand what I'm saying, so finally he says, "Why don't you tell your mother instead!" I started learning how to read and write my native language in college, but I have a niece in third grade who first learned how to read and write in Inupiak. We used to write letters to each other in Inupiak, and it was funny because we were both learning to write the language, I in college and she in first grade.*

Finally, in surveying the linguistic issues of students in bilingual classrooms, it is important not to forget the English proficient students who are not from language minority homes. Because it is illegal to intentionally school students in segregated contexts, bilingual classrooms should have a proportion of such language majority English-speaking students. These children may be in a bilingual classroom simply as a result of residence in a neighborhood where the school has a bilingual program, or they may have been intentionally enrolled in the bilingual program by language majority parents who value learning a second language and exposing their children to the multicultural reality of our society. For example, some bilingual programs are part of a magnet school that attracts students from several different neighborhoods. The native English-speaking students in bilingual classrooms may be from a variety of backgrounds. In some inner-city schools, for example, many bilingual classrooms are composed predominantly of language minority students and English-language-background African-American students, with perhaps a few English-language-background white students.

The ethnic and linguistic mix in bilingual classrooms helps to keep them from becoming isolated linguistic and cultural enclaves, and it makes it possible for many English-speaking children to have the academically and personally enriching experience of being exposed to different languages and cultures. TESOL's (1993) position illustrates the growing importance of seeing bilingual education as truly a national resource for *all* students, including monolingual English-speaking students:

> For students who come from homes where only English is used, bilingual education means the opportunity to add another language to their repertoire so that they, too, will have alternate means of learning and communicating beyond their families and immediate communities. The mix of language minority and language majority students in bilingual classrooms enables children in such contexts to play a mutually important role with each other as linguistic and sociocultural models. (p. 1)

A two-way bilingual classroom, one that provides second-language learning for *all* children, enriches the academic and the sociocultural experience of both language minority and language majority students. (See Chapter Two for more information about such two-way programs.) How the participation of language majority children in bilingual education can be beneficial to the individual and to the nation is colorfully illustrated in the following essay by a fourth grader of Japanese ancestry:

American people should study two languages. When you travel to another country you can make friends easier by speaking their language. When you grow up if you work for the government and the government wants to have a meeting with another country, if you can speak their language you can talk to them and you will know what they are saying. If you grow up and become a teacher and a new student is Japanese and you can speak Japanese, if the student doesn't know a word you can talk to them in Japanese and tell what the meaning is. When you go shopping in another country and there's a hamburger shop, if you want to buy two hamburgers you can. If you can't speak another language you don't get any hamburgers. In Japan most people study English and Japanese. In Canada most people speak French and English. In America most people do not speak two languages. It would be a good idea for Americans to learn two languages.

The Academic Issues

One of the principal reasons for bilingual education is to keep children from falling behind academically, and both the emotional and linguistic issues we have discussed thus far build directly into the key goal of helping each child reach his or her full educational potential. The principle of the educational use of language minorities' L_1, particularly in the early stages of learning, is not a new one. One of the primary justifications for the passage of the 1968 Bilingual Education Act was actually a 1953 UNESCO document entitled *The Use of Vernacular Languages in Education*. This publication was the result of a 1951 meeting of international experts who had concluded that "It is axiomatic that the best medium for teaching a child is his mother tongue" (United Nations Educational, Scientific and Cultural Organization, 1953, p. 11).

Because language minority students in the United States do not start on an equal playing field with their language majority peers, both the content of learning—math, science, social studies, language arts, music, art and so on—and the process of learning—cooperative learning, holistic assessment, culturally compatible classroom practices, and so on—must be made appropriate for them. Through bilingual education, children can be keeping up in the subject areas with instruction in their primary language while at the same time they are playing catch-up with the English necessary to function socially and academically in English dominant classroom settings. While the catch-up challenge can be great at all grade levels, it becomes even more critical in middle school and high school, which have more structured curricula with less emphasis on learning by doing and increased emphasis on abstract language. The key objective at all grade levels, however, is to provide academic experiences in a language that the child can understand, so that students become well educated at the same time that they are learning English. Throughout this book, of course, we will be addressing factors that either inhibit or promote academic success among language minority students in bilingual and ESL classrooms. In particular, the chapters on language, teaching, content areas, and assessment deal with academic issues.

Several years ago, while supervising elementary student teachers in Anchorage, Alaska, one of the authors had the following experience. It illustrates several points related to not only the implicit and explicit assumptions and expectations that teachers often have about language minority students' academic potential, but also how such notions may translate to either positive or negative outcomes:

⊠ *Following my customary routine, I stopped in the teachers' lounge to mingle with the cooperating teachers and student teachers before classes started. On this particular day I noticed an unusual joy on the part of my student teacher's third-grade cooperating teacher. She told me that she was eagerly anticipating today's arrival in her classroom of twin brothers who had just recently come from Japan. I asked her whether she was worried about possible linguistic, cultural, or academic difficulties. "Oh, no!" she replied. "On the contrary, I know that they will do very well in all those areas and our students will enjoy having them around. Furthermore," she continued, "I can always count on the ESL teacher to help out if I need any assistance." True to the cooperating teacher's prediction, the twin Japanese third graders adjusted well socially, did well academically, and very early in the semester learned the word "cuts," which they quickly began to use effectively to move ahead in the lunch line. Embedded in the teacher's sense of positive anticipation for her Japanese students was a set of notions related to the Japanese students' prior knowledge, schooling experiences, ability to acquire a second language, motivation, and family support that somehow corresponded to an ideal that would produce success.*

What is significant about this particular case is that the teacher ascribed all sorts of positive attributes to these students before she even knew them. Yet, while such attitudes existed for these boys, prior expectations about children of Alaskan native ancestry were often the opposite in this school. This attitude contributed, unfortunately, to negative academic consequences for many Alaskan native students in the school. This example illustrates the power of a teacher's expectations in either promoting or limiting academic success for language minority students. An antidote to the damage that preconceived notions can do is the ability to set aside certain expectations and be prepared to discover each child as an individual as you interact with him or her, with his or her family, and with the community. We turn now to just this theme—discovering the student.

Discovering the Student

⊗ *Sometimes I would try to look like I knew what was going on; sometimes I would just try to think about a happy time when I didn't feel stupid. My teacher never called on me or talked to me. I think they either forgot I was there or else wished I wasn't. (Indiana Daily Student, 1993, p. 13)*

Reflecting on her experience in grade school, a bilingual college student accentuates in the preceding quotation the importance of teachers having more than an illusion of knowledge about their students. Knowing as much as possible about the language minority student enables the teacher to relate with empathy and to foster a learning environment that is meaningful.

One of the most pervasive characteristics of human behavior is that we rarely ignore each other. As teachers, for instance, we are constantly monitoring the quality and quantity of our students' intellectual and social development. We may like to think that the intellectual observations we make are based on objective achievement criteria, but this is often not the case. The social or cultural profiles we develop of our students often are also based on stereotypic or assumed collective data about their worlds. Quite often when we meet a new language minority student, we tend to assign to that student our collective stereotypic view of his or her world. As teachers we are often unconsciously trapped by that perception, and we need to remind ourselves to move beyond it to see each student not only as a member of his or her culture, but also as an individual with idiosyncratic patterns. To do so, however, means taking time to develop trust and openness—with immigrants, refugees, and native-born language minority students. While it is only natural for us to continue to develop positive, neutral, or negative perceptions of persons based on subjective, impressionistic data, teachers of language minority students can benefit from a somewhat more systematic and rational approach to gathering information about our students. Notwithstanding all of the other rigorous demands of the classroom, it is useful to examine as much as possible the cultural details students bring because these details do have an important impact on the learning process.

Discovering the student is certainly not a process that has to wait until the teacher has a classroom of his or her own. It is extremely important for teachers in training to begin to develop the habit of sociocultural observation early in their careers. Although preservice teachers may not have the advantage of getting to know particular students over a long period of time, they may have the advantage of being able to take a little more time to explore different ways to discover students' backgrounds. Therefore, when we talk in this section about what teachers can do to get to know their students, we are addressing both preservice and in-service teachers. Preservice teachers, in addition to using their coursework on multiculturalism and community context, can use case studies, early observation experiences, internships, tutorial experiences, and student teaching experiences to develop their skills in sociocultural observation and reflection.

One approach to discovering the student is to read the available educational literature on various language minority groups. Unfortunately, because of the necessity to present conclusions, some of the information on language minority students found in the education literature tends to overgeneralize. Thus the teacher may acquire reductionist information about a cultural group that provides him or her with a sense of security but that also perpetuates stereotypes. Writers on education, like any other people, are bearers of their own cultural and social blinders and may therefore develop points of view about language minorities that are colored by their own background. Because teachers want to discover who their students are, they may receive information packets or take part in in-service training programs that provide lists of characteristics, language overviews, historical outlines, and sketches about holidays, customs, and foods. While there are certainly varying degrees of congruence between this kind of information and the actual lives of students, teachers are not always sufficiently exposed to the ever-changing and internally heterogeneous characteristics of cultural groups. Therefore, as we take time to focus on individual student variables that may affect teaching strategies, it is important not only to seek out the available information bases, but also to be open to variations and surprises. This is particularly true when working with information about "traditions," which may in some ways project an image that time has stood still. Overemphasis on descriptions of the traditional culture may lead to somewhat static or romanticized views that overlook the changes—some subtle, some glaring—that students are undergoing as members of contemporary cultural groups (Schafer, 1982, pp. 96–97). For example, a teacher learning about Japanese culture may be interested in kimonos and the tea ceremony, but his or her Japanese students may be more interested in sharing their comic books and robot toys.

Within the first days of school, teachers are immediately absorbed in time-consuming tasks that keep them from paying careful attention to who each student is. These tasks include completing regular paperwork, establishing classroom management and discipline procedures, organizing materials, supervising standardized testing, adjusting curriculum plans, and attending meetings. Many such duties interfere with the philosophical ideal of positive, caring student-teacher relationships. Yet we all want very much to show care and concern for the success of all our students. When everything seems to be going right—students are on task, classroom activities are varied and stimulating, behavior problems are minimal—then a teacher can feel fulfilled. But we rarely feel that we have accomplished that ideal. There are always students who seem hard to reach, who continually demand our attention but rarely settle down to accomplish a task, who would progress much better with one-to-one help that is not available, or who are obviously underchallenged by the tasks the class as a whole needs to master. Therefore, getting away from preconceived notions about language minority students and making a deliberate effort to take a fresh look is not always easy. Teachers, like anyone, are subject to the limitations associated with their own interpretations of and inferences about the world. One way to start is by examining our image of our own role vis-à-vis these students. For example, we might ask, "Do I see myself as a facilitator of student learning, a cultural and academic agent with the power to help children succeed, or do I see myself as an exploited cog in the bureaucratic machine of the school district?" The way we see ourselves will affect the way we see our students.

In looking at ourselves, our own ethnic or language background can serve as another point of departure. Members of our own families—if not our own generation, then perhaps our parents, grandparents, or great-grandparents—may have had experiences parallel to those of some of our language minority students today. How did our parents and members of our local communities interact with people of other cultural backgrounds when we were growing up? As adults, what positive and negative experiences have we had dealing with persons from cultural or language backgrounds different from our own? Also, what positive and negative experiences have we had in learning a second language ourselves? Many preservice and in-service teachers will attest to the tremendous value of writing an autobiography as a way of beginning to understand oneself as a cultural being. Through a written autobiography we can reflect in depth on events that have shaped our views of ourselves and of those who are unlike us.

Throughout this chapter we have discussed a wide variety of themes to be considered in exploring the identity of students in bilingual and ESL classrooms. Almost anyone, however, reading this chapter would question the practicality of expecting teachers to keep carefully prepared written ethnolinguistic profiles on each student. It is not unreasonable, however, for teachers to keep a running file of mental notes. We say "running" because it cannot be assumed that the child will remain static or that our perceptions at a given moment are completely accurate. Therefore, a valid student profile will reflect changing perceptions and changing behavior as the year goes on. Getting reliable information about a student will depend on the use of a variety of assessment and ethnographic sources. Outside of the classroom, for example, sources can include conversations with parents, the local ethnic media, community events, multicultural conferences and in-services, and literature on various cultural groups. Within the school context, understanding can be gained through such sources and activities as portfolios, student compositions, journals, discussions, role-playing, and informal classroom and playground observation.

Cutting across all of the above school contexts and community contexts is teaching style, which has an absolutely crucial role to play in the extent of opportunities to develop rich student profiles. Pedagogy that activates the student voice and embraces the local community provides a much richer environment for student understanding than pedagogy that treats students as if they were empty vessels into which knowledge is to be poured. In learning environments where students engage in extended discourse (rather than providing brief answers to teacher-initiated questions), and where students' community life and background experience provide a platform for the scaffolding of new knowledge, teachers are much more likely to be able to discover who their students are emotionally, socioculturally, and linguistically.

Guidelines for Teaching

DISCOVERING STUDENTS' LIVES

There are, of course, so many questions to ask and so little time to ask them. As long as we know what kinds of questions we need to be asking, and as long as we are alert for answers as they emerge, we will be well on our way to discovering the students in bilingual and ESL classrooms. Beyond the assessment of language minority students' L_1 and L_2 proficiency and the development of a basic cultural profile, the following topics can be used as an ongoing guide in the process of getting to know our students.

1. Background topics relevant to all language minority students
   a. Immigrant or native-born status
   b. Socioeconomic profile, including educational level of parents
   c. Rural versus urban backgrounds
   d. Parents' aspirations for themselves and their children, including expectations for schools
   e. Types of racial or ethnic prejudice that students may have experienced
   f. Attitudes toward maintenance or revitalization of home language and culture
2. Background topics generally more relevant to immigrant or refugee students
   a. Country of origin
   b. Length of residence in the United States
   c. Extent of ties with home country
   d. Political and economic situation in region from which they emigrated
   e. Reasons for emigration
   f. Other countries lived in prior to arriving in the United States
   g. Amount and quality of schooling in L_1 prior to arriving in the United States,

   including the extent of math and science training as well as literacy
   h. Languages other than English and their home language to which the students have been exposed
3. School observations
   a. Activities students enjoy or dislike, as a reflection either of cultural values or of their own personalities
   b. Students' nonverbal communication
   c. Students' comments on life in the United States, if immigrants, or comments about majority culture, if indigenous minorities
   d. Signs of positive and negative adjustment in peer relationships
   e. Comments that indicate a desire to share something of their home background
   f. Comments that reflect students' developing concept of their ethnic identity
   g. Students' own notions of the purpose of bilingual or ESL instruction as it relates to their own education.
4. Use of literature, media, classes, and in-service opportunities and participation in the life of ethnic communities
   a. Gathering information from a wide variety of resources
   b. Being alert to possible biases or distortions in materials or presentations
   c. Distinguishing between descriptions of traditional cultural patterns and contemporary patterns
   d. Cross-checking and relating what has been learned with the experiences of your own students and their families

Sylvia Ashton-Warner (1963), a creative, caring, and pioneering multicultural educator who worked among Maori children in New Zealand, captured quite cogently the importance of discovering and linking the life of the student with that of the school:

> The method of teaching any subject in a Maori infant room may be seen as a plank in a bridge from one culture to another, and to the extent that this bridge is strengthened may a Maori in later life succeed. (p. 28)

Education, as a bridge, should enhance communication, understanding, and human potential for language minority and language majority students alike. Although this is not an easy task, teachers have no choice but to continue exploring and growing as cross-cultural mediators for their language minority students. For, as the Mexican novelist, Carlos Fuentes (1992), puts it, "Cultures only flourish in contact with others; they perish in isolation" (p. 346).

Summary

This chapter focuses on the importance of getting to know the lived experiences of our language minority students as a sine-qua-non for creating exciting and academically promising teaching and learning classroom environments. Because the essence of life is often captured through personal narratives, the chapter opened with Carlos' story as a way to invite the reader to partake vicariously in the complex set of geographic, social, economic, religious, linguistic, academic, and emotional experiences surrounding his life.

Attempting to unpack the bilingual and English-as-a-second language (ESL) knapsack, the chapter then explains the symbiotic relationship between the different types of dual language instruction and ESL programs vis-à-vis state regulations and guidelines, school district policies, community support, and the composition of each local school population. Buttressed by policy statements from TESOL, the chapter recommends a set of instructional practices affirming the positive role of primary language in the cognitive, social, and emotional development of the students. TESOL also affirms research findings suggesting that the acquisition of English as a second language is an extended and complex process that is situated in sociocultural, political, pedagogical, ideological, and demographic contexts.

Since the mid-20th century, U.S. society has become increasingly multicultural and multilingual. Before 1965, when Congress terminated the national-origins quota system, Europe was the major source of immigrants to the United States. By the 1980s, however, 85 percent of immigrants to this country were coming from Third World countries (Crawford, 1992b, p. 3). These population changes—or "demographic imperative"—have produced large numbers of students whose first language is not English. Yet most teachers unfortunately tend not to be well prepared to work effectively with these students. Hence, a challenge in the preparation of teachers for this millennium will be to address the "growing mismatch between the background of teachers and the students they will be teaching" (Applebome, 1966, p. 22).

Language minority students represent a huge variety of sociocultural, economic, political, linguistic, and academic experiences. Thus educators need to become familiar with the push and pull forces that have produced these migration patterns to the United States. Equally important, however, language minority educators need to understand the historical facts and events that have shaped the attitudes and behaviors of indigenous populations toward assimilation and schooling practices in the United States. Too often stigmatized indigenous languages and cultures are seen as problems in school and society rather than as resources or as rights in our democratic and pluralistic society.

This chapter has suggested ways to affirm the lived experiences of our language minority students—their cultures, their social contexts, and prior schooling experience. Anchored in these past contexts, schools can then provide teaching and learning environments that maximize and take advantage of the plurality of experiences to create exciting teaching and learning challenges and opportunities for all of our students, not only those who speak Standard English and come from middle and upper class backgrounds.

Key Terms

Bilingual Education Act p. 5	ESL content (or sheltered) classes) p. 7
Indigenous or heritage language p. 5	Teachers of English to Speakers of Other Languages (TESOL) p. 7
English as a second language (ESL) p. 6	National Association for Bilingual Education (NABE) p. 10
English language learner (ELL) p. 6	Limited-English-proficient (LEP) p. 11

Reflection Questions

1. According to the authors, there is an important relationship between social class and academic achievement. Explain how the interplay between these two variables might impact the academic performance of foreign-born language minority students.
2. How might the previous schooling experiences of immigrant children (or, indeed, of their parents) influence these children's performance in an American classroom?

For example, if students have been exposed in their home countries to instruction that emphasizes rote memorization or passive learning, how might they react to the student-centered, problem-solving, or inquiry-driven approaches that characterize many American classrooms? More importantly, how would you—as their teacher—help ease their transition into the American educational system?

3. Consider the cases of Beto and Mee described on page 18. Why would content-area instruction in Spanish be more appropriate for Beto than an ESL-based curriculum? Similarly, why would Mee likely excel in ESL, with little or no support in Korean? What are the *pedagogical* and *policy* implications of these two cases for language minority education? Finally, although Mee might benefit from ESL instruction, while Beto would not, why is it critical for teachers to guard against a "model minority" stereotype of Asian or Pacific Islander students that portrays them as smart and hardworking?

4. Why do the authors argue that the loss of an ancestral or heritage language has cultural, emotional, or academic consequences for language minority students? How might students' schooling experiences with "subtractive bilingualism" lead to the loss of their first languages?

Resources

Immigration and Demographics

Dinnerstein, L., & Reimers, D. M. *Ethnic Americans: A history of immigration* (4th ed.) New York: Columbia University Press, 1999.

- *Ethnic Americans* is a compelling survey of immigration to the United States from 1789 until the 1920s. The authors give an engaging account of the ethnic conflicts and restrictions experienced by immigrants. The book also examines issues of ethnic mobility in contemporary society, including assimilation and recent immigration debates.

Portes, A., & Rumbaut, R. *Immigrant America* (2nd ed.) Berkeley: University of California Press, 1996.

- *Immigrant America* is a synthesis of "where we stand theoretically and empirically with respect to questions of immigration and ethnicity in the United States." The authors give a compelling analysis of the distinctive features of the new immigration dynamics.

San Juan Cafferty, P., & Engstrom, D. W. (Eds.). *Hispanics in the United States: An agenda for the twenty-first century.* New Brunswick: Transaction Publishers, 2000.

- *Hispanics in the United States* provides a much-needed foundation in research and policy agendas required for Hispanics in the new millennium. The authors establish historical, demographic, religious, and cultural contexts of the new immigrants. The book also describes major issues for Hispanics becoming integrated into the American social structure, especially those of health care, the labor market and education.

Suárez-Orozco, C., & Suárez, M. M. *Children of immigration.* Cambridge, MA: Harvard University Press, 2001.

- *Children of Immigration* addresses how immigrant children fare in America. Departing from the premise that one fifth of all school-age children in America are children of immigrants (in New York city the rate is 48 percent, and they speak over 100 languages), the authors discuss the socioeducational implications resulting from such a reality and answer questions such as "What thought has American society given to the special needs of these students?" "Have we done anything to accommodate them?" "What have they experienced?"

Takaki, R. *A different mirror: A history of multicultural America.* Boston, MA: Little, Brown and Company, 1994.

- *A Different Mirror* is a powerful narrative of the many peoples who comprise the United States of America—a new retelling of its history. Takaki turns the traditionally Anglo-centric vision inside out and offers us a lively account filled with the stories and voices of people previously left out of the historical canon.

Takaki, R. *Iron cages: Race and cultural in 19th Century America.* New York: Oxford University Press, 2000.

- *Iron Cages* provides a unique comparative analysis of white American attitudes toward Asians, blacks, Mexicans, and Native Americans in the 19th century. This work offers a cohesive study of the foundations of race and culture in America. In a new epilogue, Takaki argues that the social health of the United States rests largely on the ability of Americans of all races and cultures to build on an established and positive legacy of cross-cultural cooperation and understanding in the coming 21st century. Observing that by 2050 all Americans will be minorities, Takaki urges us to ask ourselves: Will America fulfill the promise of equality or will America retreat into its "iron cages" and resist diversity, allowing racial conflicts to divide and possibly even destroy America as a nation? *Iron Cages* is an essential resource for students of ethnic history and important reading for anyone interested in the history of race relations in America.

Social Class, Parental Education, and Academic Achievement

Lareau, A. *Home advantage: Social class and parental intervention in elementary education* (2nd ed.). Lanham, MD: Rowman & Littlefield, 2000.

- *Home Advantage* examines issues of social class and parent involvement in schooling, as well as issues of interconnectedness/separation between family and school settings. Laureau provides a thoughtful account of how social class influences parent involvement in schools.

MacLeod, J. *Ain't no makin' it: Leveled aspirations in a low-income neighborhood.*
Boulder, CO: Westview Press, 1995.
  • *Ain't No Makin' It* is a vivid account of friendships, families, school, and work.
    The ethnography resonates with feeling and vivid dialogue. MacLeod addresses
    one of the most important issues in modern social theory and policy: how social
    inequality is reproduced from one generation to the next.

Oakes, J. *Multiplying inequalities: The effects of race, social class, and tracking on opportunities to learn mathematics and science.* Santa Monica, CA: Rand Corporation, 1990.
  • *Multiplying Inequalities* is a provocative study that examines the distribution of
    science and mathematics learning opportunities for minority students in U.S. ele-
    mentary and secondary schools.

Oakes, J., & Lipton, M. *Making the best of schools: A handbook for parents, teachers, and policymakers.* New Haven: Yale University Press, 1991.
  • *Making the Best of Schools* examines schooling from a broad and theoretical per-
    spective. Oakes and Lipton assert that a single standard for school excellence will
    best insure all children's future. The book presents a few chapters on home sup-
    port for learning. Its main focus, however, is on how to determine the culture of
    a particular school and evaluate a classroom environment. The authors discuss
    and criticize learning theories, show how basic subjects could be taught in more
    meaningful ways, and evaluate testing, grading, tracking, and magnet schools.

Multicultural Case Studies

Carger, C. L. *Of borders and dreams: A Mexican-American experience of urban education.* New York: Teacher College Press, 1996.
  • *Of Borders and Dreams* is the story of Alejandro Suárez, Jr., a Mexican-
    American youth, his family, and their experiences in a bureaucratic and frustrat-
    ing public school system. It is an intelligent, probing portrayal of the problems
    that face bilingual and bicultural children in the United States.

Nieto, S. *The light in their eyes: Creating multicultural school communities.* New
York: Teachers College Press, 1999.
  • *The Light in Their Eyes* provides a spirited and provocative defense of multicul-
    tural education. Nieto defines multicultural education "as embedded in a
    sociopolitical context and as an antiracist and basic education for all students
    that permeates all areas of schooling, and that is characterized by a commitment
    to social justice and critical approaches to learning." The author proposes that a
    critical and comprehensive approach to multicultural education can provide an
    important framework for rethinking school reform.

Olsen, L. *Made in America: Immigrant students in our public schools.* New York:
The New York Press, 1998.
  • *Made in America* is an engaging study of marginalization and racial separa-
    tion in a school setting. Olsen spent two years observing life at Madison High

School—a prototypical American high school with 20 percent of its student body born abroad. Her interviews with students, administrators, and parents describe the challenges they face and create a disturbing portrait of racial separation. The author concludes that Americanization of immigrants marginalizes immigrant students, requiring them to give up their national identities and mother tongues in order to be accepted in a world that then denies them full participation.

Reyes, P., Scribner, J. D., & Paredes Scribner, A. eds. *Lessons from high-performing Hispanic schools: Creating learning communities.* New York: Teachers College Press, 1999.

- *Lessons from High-Performing Hispanic Schools* is an instructional volume that provides school administrators and teachers with tools they need to transform ordinary Hispanic schools into high-performing schools. The work provides a framework for creating successful learning communities and shows teachers specific classroom practices that academically motivate minority children.

Díaz Soto, L. *Language, culture, and power: Bilingual families and the struggle for quality education.* Albany: State University of New York Press, 1997.

- *Language, Culture, and Power* examines the political dimensions of bilingualism, bilingual schooling, and empowering education. The work is a disturbing examination of the racism underlying the opposition to bilingual education and its effect on a Puerto Rican community in Pennsylvania. The author shares her experiences in "Steel Town" after she is invited to a board meeting to explain the premises of bilingual education. Her transcripts, interviews with community members, and supporting research demonstrate that educating children can be the least priority in a setting where the unspoken but obvious agenda is creating ethnic superiority. The book invites us to support and collaborate with oppressed communities, for the purpose of successfully educating children.

Trueba, H., Jacobs, L., & Kirton, E. *Cultural conflict and adaptation: The case of Hmong children in American society.* London: The Falmer Press, 1990.

- During the last century, groups of Hmong have moved from southern China into Indochina, and about 90,000 of them have come to America in the last 13 years. *Cultural Conflict and Adaptation* is study of the history and plight of the Hmong and examines the alienation and cultural conflicts faced by the children of a small group of Hmong who have settle in La Playa, California.

Valdés, G. *Learning and not learning English: Latino students in American schools.* New York: Teachers College Press, 2001.

- *Learning and Not Learning English* is a brilliant ethnography about four Mexican students who struggle to learn English in American middle schools. It discusses various policy and instructional dilemmas surrounding English language education for immigrant children.

Endnotes

1. The federal Bilingual Education Act of 1968, long known as Title VII of the Elementary and Secondary Education Act, was changed to Title III in its most recent reauthorization.
2. We use the term "heritage language" to refer to an immigrant, ethnic community, or ancestral language.
3. While the literature sometimes refers to *bilingual-bicultural education,* in this book we use the term *bilingual education* generically, to include culture as well.
4. For a fascinating Japanese interpretation of U.S. stereotypic cultural patterns, derived largely through U.S. films shown in Japan, see Kolker and Alvarez (1991), *The Japanese Version* (videotape).
5. In 1988, Barry Hatch, the city councilman of Monterey Park presented a controversial ordinance to "require two-thirds English on all business signs" (Horton & Calderón, 1992, p. 190).

Policy and Programs

There is no equality of treatment merely by providing students with the same facilities, textbooks, teachers, and curriculum; for students who do not understand English are effectively foreclosed from any meaningful education.

Basic English skills are at the very core of what these public schools teach. Imposition of a requirement that, before a child can effectively participate in the education program, he must already have acquired those basic skills is to make a mockery of public education. We know that those who do not understand English are certain to find their classroom experiences wholly incomprehensible and in no way meaningful.

Supreme Court Justice William O. Douglas,
writing for the majority in Lau *v.* Nichols, *1974*

Schools in the United States are currently undergoing a gradual process of transformation. Administrative structures, instructional methods, curricular materials, and assessment practices are being analyzed, modified, and in some cases radically changed. A major impetus for the transformation is the reality of rapidly changing demographics. Increasingly heterogeneous classes are the norm in urban and rural areas of all regions of the country. If current population trends continue, as mentioned in Chapter One, it is projected that somewhere between the years 2030 and 2050, school-age children now labeled "minorities" by the federal government will be the majority in U.S. schools in all regions of the country (Berliner & Biddle, 1995).

The transformation of schools, now increasing in momentum, is a response to educational practices of the past several decades that have not been effective in promoting the academic achievement of all students. Students with close connections to their bilingual/bicultural heritages have been especially underserved by U.S. schools. Policy issues regarding how these students are served have evolved around power relations between groups in the broader society. Thus when educators view particular groups of students as having "problems" in need of "remediation," the deficit perspective tends to reinforce social status relations between groups that exist in the wider society. When educators genuinely strive for the academic success of all students, they are working towards assisting groups to move out of poverty and away from other risk factors, and thus they actually transform, in the long term, existing social status relationships between groups.

In general, U.S. school policies for serving culturally and linguistically diverse students that developed during the 1970s and 1980s focused on separate school programs to "fix" what was viewed as a "problem," the deficit perspective noted above. For example, bilingual and ESL educators were specialists to whom students with little proficiency in English were sent for extra help and special services. After receiving such assistance for some limited period of time, students were "exited" from those support services or "mainstreamed," similar to the approach taken in special education in the past.

But today, practices of tracking and ability grouping are being seriously questioned. Elementary and middle schools are restructuring to meet the needs of heterogeneous classes and to eliminate practices that tend to segregate students into what can become permanent tracks (Gamoran, 1990; Oakes, 1985, 1992; Oakes, Wells, Yonezawa, & Ray, 1997; Wheelock, 1992). Curricular reforms stress the interdisciplinary nature of learning and the importance of developing authentic, real-life language through meaningful academic content across the curriculum through active inquiry, discovery, and collaborative learning (Brophy, 1992; Leinhardt, 1992). The movement towards school-based management has encouraged shared decision making among the principals, teachers, and parents at each local school (Leithwood, 1992; McKeon & Malarz, 1991). Experimentation with performance and portfolio assessment has led to use of a wider range of assessment measures for instructional and program evaluation purposes (Herman, Aschbacher, & Winters, 1992; O'Malley & Valdez Pierce, 1996). These reforms may or may not assist linguistically and culturally diverse students. While they have the potential to transform schools, bilingual and ESL educators must collaborate actively in the transformation to create the deeper change needed to create equitable, safe, and meaningful environments for learning for all students.

This chapter examines school policies and programs for culturally and linguistically diverse students as they have developed in the United States over the past several decades. As we revisit some of the main events that have shaped educational services designed to meet language minority students' needs—the politics of the field, the history of federal and state legislation and court decisions, and the types of school programs that have developed in bilingual/ESL education—it is important to keep in mind the way in which power relations between groups play a role in decisions that are made. This framework sheds light on the ups and downs of the politics of the field, and it helps us clarify the vision of our long-term goal: the academic success of linguistically and culturally diverse students, which helps to ensure the academic success of all students. We will begin our exploration of policy issues with a discussion section on the politics of bilingual education.

The Politics of Bilingual Education

Bilingual education arouses strong emotions, both pro and con. It evokes conflicting views of American identity, ethnic pluralism, immigration policy, civil rights, and government spending for social programs. Popular attitudes about the field rarely stem from scientific understanding of second-language acquisition or pedagogy; yet they have exerted a major influence on policy-makers. Indeed, "politicization" is a commonly heard criticism of bilingual education. Ravitch (1985) alleges that "advocates press its adoption regardless of its educational effectiveness. . . . The aim is to use the public schools to promote the maintenance of distinct ethnic communities, each with its own cultural heritage and language."

Not surprisingly, bilingual education has attracted political support among the groups it serves—for example, from the Congressional Hispanic Caucus—although for stated reasons that have to do with academic excellence and equity, not ethnic separatism. It is also important to note that, where bilingual education is concerned, "politicization" is a two-way street. Many of the program's detractors themselves press an agenda that goes well beyond the classroom. Explaining his bill to terminate federal funding for bilingual education, Representative Toby Roth (R–WI) says: "I want all Americans to be the same. That is my mission" (Cohen, 1993).

Analyzing public opinion research conducted in 1983, Huddy and Sears (1990) conclude that "symbolic politics"—resentment of special treatment for minority groups, anti-Hispanic bias, and hostility toward immigrants—"play a large role in promoting opposition to bilingual education." More than a decade later, such feelings appear to have hardened, following the passage of numerous English Only laws and a groundswell of anti-immigrant agitation. In a Phi Delta Kappa/Gallup Poll, 71 percent of respondents said schools should "require [immigrant] students to learn English . . . before they receive instruction in any other subjects." (Of these, more than one-third believed that English should be taught "at their parents' expense before they are enrolled in public schools.") Only 27 percent favored bilingual instruction (Elam, Rose, & Gallup, 1993). Yet responses often vary, depending upon how questions are posed. In another poll, conducted by the National Opinion Research Center in 1994, 26 percent were strongly in favor and 38 percent somewhat in favor of bilingual education; whereas 15 percent were strongly opposed and 16 percent somewhat opposed to bilingual education (Donegan, 1996).

The Bilingual Education Act of 1968 (P.L. 90–247) became law in a very different political context. Passing Congress without dissent, it became **Title VII** of **the Elementary and Secondary Education Act,** a centerpiece of the War on Poverty. At the time the new law embodied a consensus that the prevalent "sink-or-swim" approach to teaching English was both an educational failure and a denial of equal opportunity for language minority students. Exactly how bilingual instruction would work remained unclear, but with Hispanic dropout rates approaching 75 percent in some areas, there was an eagerness to experiment with what the legislation called "new and imaginative elementary and secondary school programs." Senator Ralph Yarborough (D–TX), chief sponsor of the 1968 act, remained somewhat vague about its goals: whether the intent was solely to promote a transition to English proficiency or also to maintain and develop students' native language skills. If educators and researchers perceived any conflict between these objectives, they did not express it at the time (Crawford, 1992a, 1999); nor did federal officials who awarded discretionary grants to local school districts.

By the mid-1970s, however, mediocre results in early Title VII programs (Danoff, Coles, McLaughlin, & Reynolds, 1977–78) and symbolic objections to the use of public funds to perpetuate "ethnic languages" (Epstein, 1977) generated the first political backlash against bilingual education. Albert Shanker (1974), president of the American Federation of Teachers, criticized the goal of native-language maintenance as a diversion from schools' "melting pot" role of teaching English as rapidly as possible. Others warned that if bilingual education promoted minority languages and cultures, it might foster Quebec-style separatism in the United States. Reacting to such concerns, in 1978 Congress voted to limit Title VII support to transitional bilingual programs: The native language could be used only "to the extent necessary to allow a child to achieve competence in the English language" (P.L. 95–561; quoted in Leibowitz, 1980).

The English Only Movement

Senator S. I. Hayakawa (R–CA) linked the growing discontent with bilingual education to a wider critique of U.S. language policy. He argued that the nation sends "confusing signals" to immigrants by requiring them to learn English as a condition of naturalization while simultaneously inviting them to vote and attend school in their native tongues. Though "well-intentioned," such programs "have often inhibited their command of English and retarded their full citizenship" (Hayakawa, 1982). To "clarify" this situation, in 1981 Senator Hayakawa proposed a constitutional amendment declaring English the official language of the United States. But the measure went beyond mere symbolism. If ratified, it would have forbidden government agencies—federal, state, or local—from adopting or enforcing "laws, ordinances, regulations, orders, programs, [or] policies . . . which require . . . the use of any language other than English" (S. J. Res. 72, 1981). Two years later, on retiring from the Senate, Hayakawa helped to found an advocacy group, U.S. English, to lobby for Official English and against bilingualism in public life.

Thus began the English Only movement. It grew rapidly through media attention, direct-mail fundraising, and grassroots campaigns. Within five years of its founding, U.S. English claimed 400,000 dues-paying members and an annual budget of $6 million (Crawford, 1992b). By 2000, 24 states had adopted Official English legislation, including constitutional amendments passed by voter initiative (over the opposition of large language minority communities) in California, Florida, Arizona, and Colorado. In 1996, the U.S. House of Representatives passed the "English Language Empowerment Act," a statute that would have severely limited the federal government's ability to communicate in any other language. The bill died in the Senate, however, before becoming law. House Speaker Newt Gingrich and other Republican leaders in Congress, who had initially championed the legislation, soon abandoned the cause when they found that it alienated more voters (especially Latinos) than it attracted to their party (Crawford, 2000). Since that time, English Only bills have been bottled up in committee.

Most Americans are surprised to learn that the U.S. Constitution specifies no official language; in one survey, 64 percent of respondents assumed that English already enjoyed that status (Associated Press, 1987). On learning otherwise, many have viewed Senator Hayakawa's proposal as an innocent gesture, merely a recognition of the primacy of English in the United States. Proponents have strengthened this impression by couching their argument in positive terms. In a nation of immigrants, they say, English has served as our strongest "common bond," allowing Americans to overcome differences of race, religion, and national origin. By acting now to halt government's "mindless drift toward bilingualism" (Bikales, 1987), the United States can avoid future conflicts like those that beset Canada and other nations divided along language lines. Moreover, for immigrants, English is "the language of full participation . . . the door to opportunity" (U.S. English, 1990). In short, according to a U.S. English promotional brochure, "A common language benefits our nation and all its people."

Language minority advocates perceive a more sinister agenda. Behind the rhetoric of national unity, they say, lurks a mean-spirited, even racist desire to lash out against ethnic minorities by terminating bilingual services designed to ease their adjustment to American society. Language restrictionism distracts attention from their actual plans for immigration restrictionism, according to this view. Critics point out that U.S. English was founded by leaders of the Federation for American Immigration Reform, a lobby that has called for a moratorium on the admission of newcomers until the nation can assimilate those already here. Rather than producing social harmony, English Only campaigns have crystallized "anti-Asian and anti-Latino animosities" (Pérez-Bustillo, 1992), polarizing communities from Lowell, Massachusetts, to Monterey Park, California.

Why did the framers of the U.S. Constitution fail to designate an official language? Today many assume that bilingualism was simply "not an issue" at that time. Yet the United States has never been a linguistically homogeneous society. In the census of 1790, German Americans made up 8.7 percent of the population, a proportion comparable to that of Hispanic Americans, 9 percent, in the census of 1990 (Crawford, 1992a). Language legislation was considered at the nation's founding, notably a proposal by John Adams (1780) to establish an official academy "for refining, improving, and ascertaining" American English. But a majority of early leaders worried that such schemes might jeopardize civil liberties, opting instead for a "policy not to have a policy" on language (Heath, 1976). This is not to say that tolerance has always reigned supreme. Throughout U.S. history, there have been numerous instances of language-based discrimination and coercive assimilation, especially during periods of territorial conquest and large-scale immigration (Leibowitz, 1969). Yet rarely have language conflicts assumed national proportions.

Perhaps the more relevant question is why English Only fervor developed in the United States in the 1980s. Clearly, with the arrival of an estimated 8.7 million immigrants (U.S. Census Bureau, 1992), this was a decade of increasing linguistic and cultural diversity, as well as increasing anxiety about demographic change. Nativist lobbies, pointing to the social and economic costs of immigration, began agitating for tight quotas on legal entrants and aggressive "border control" to keep out the undocumented. Yet for many Americans, themselves the descendants of immigrants, such appeals are tainted with unfairness, recalling the days when Congress excluded or limited the admission of certain nationalities as racial undesirables. By contrast, the call to "defend our common language" carries no unsavory baggage, while still conveying (for some, if not all) a coded message: English First = America First.

Never mind that the "threat" to English is largely imaginary. For example, while the Spanish-speaking population is growing in the United States, thanks to immigration and higher-than-average birthrates, so too is that population's rate of "anglicization," or shift to English as the dominant language (Veltman, 1988). Among all U.S. residents over the age of four, all but 3 percent report speaking English "well" or "very well" (U.S. Census Bureau, 1992). So whence the concern about bilingualism? Fishman (1992) suggests that the English Only movement "may largely represent the displacement of middle-class fears and anxieties from the more difficult, if not intractable *real* causes . . . to mythical and simplistic and stereotyped scapegoats. If those with these fears are successful in passing Official English amendments, this would represent another 'liberation of Grenada,' rather than any mature grappling with the really monumental economic, social, and political causes of conflict" (p. 169).

Impact of Official English

Contrary to warnings by opponents, so far English Only legislation has had little direct impact on the rights of minority language speakers. To secure easy passage, proponents have often drafted simple declarations—for example, "The English language shall be the official language of Arkansas" (Arkansas Code, § 1–4–117)[1]—leaving courts and legislators to sort out the details. Such laws have generally been interpreted as symbolic statements about the role of English rather than as binding prohibitions on government's use of other languages.

At the state level, Arizona's Proposition 106 posed a serious legal threat to bilingual services, with its explicit mandate: "This State and all political subdivisions of this State shall act in English and no other language" (Ariz. Const. Art. XXVIII). The restriction applied not only to state and local agencies, but also to public schools and to government employees in the performance of their duties. Exceptions were permitted for purposes of public safety, criminal justice, foreign-language teaching, and native-language instruction "to provide as rapid as possible a transition to English." But these loopholes were so narrow that legal experts predicted the amendment would prohibit, among other things, instruction in Native American languages at state institutions, state-funded translations into Braille and American Sign Language, and parent-teacher communications in any language other than English. Proposition 106 never took effect, however, because a federal court ruled that it violated the freedom-of-speech guarantees in the U.S. Constitution (*Yñiguez* v. *Mofford*, 730 F. Supp. 309 [D. Ariz. 1990]). That decision was later "vacated" on technical grounds by the U.S. Supreme Court. But in 1998, the Arizona Supreme Court unanimously agreed that the English Only measure violated the First Amendment rights of state employees and of Arizona residents whose English is limited (*Ruíz v. Hull,* 191 Ariz. 441. [1998]). Later that year Alaska voters adopted a similar law and it, too, was blocked pending a court challenge.

Notwithstanding their limited legal effects, English Only campaigns have had damaging political effects on bilingual education. U.S. English worked hard to place Proposition 63 on the California ballot in November 1986, conscious that the legislature would shortly be deciding whether to extend the state's bilingual education law (Crawford, 1999). After the Official English measure passed with 73 percent of the vote, Governor George Deukmejian vetoed two attempts to extend the legal mandate for native-language instruction, once regarded as the nation's strongest; Governor Pete Wilson later vetoed another. This left a state with 40 percent of the nation's LEP[2] students with no law governing bilingual education, making the program vulnerable to political attacks a decade later.

Meanwhile, the landslide for Proposition 63 did not escape notice in Washington, where in early 1987 Congress began work to reauthorize the federal Bilingual Education Act. The California vote strengthened the hand of Secretary of Education William J. Bennett (1985), who had recently launched an attack on Title VII as "a failed path," "a bankrupt course," and a waste of $1.7 billion up to that time. He accused bilingual educators of attempting to promote "a sense of cultural pride" at the expense of "proficiency in English, our common language." As long as research remained "inconclusive" about its value, he asked, why should most schools receiving Title VII grants be required to use native-language instruction? Secretary Bennett proposed to expand federal support for "special alternative instructional programs" such as "structured immersion" in English, even though such approaches had rarely been evaluated for effectiveness in teaching language minority children.

Powerful members of Congress were initially cool to Bennett's arguments. At the request of the House Education and Labor Committee, an expert panel was assembled to evaluate his claim that there was "no evidence" for the benefits of native-language instruction. The panel concluded that, to the contrary, "the research showed positive effects for transitional bilingual education on students' achievement" in English and other subjects (U.S. General Accounting Office, 1987). A majority of the experts recommended that Title VII's preference for native-language instruction be retained.

Nevertheless, political winds in the spring of 1987 favored the critics of bilingual education. In the wake of Proposition 63, 37 state legislatures were considering English Only bills of their own. Public opinion polls showed overwhelming support for such legislation. Members of Congress who had supported bilingual education in the past suddenly became squeamish about defending a "mandate" for native-language instruction. After much backroom maneuvering, a compromise was reached that allowed up to 25 percent of Title VII grants to be diverted to nonbilingual programs (P.L. 100–297).

Meanwhile, English Only proponents expanded their lobbying activities, seeking to exert a direct influence on education policy. They also channeled substantial resources into organizations that specialize in opposing bilingual education, such as Learning English Advocates Drive (LEAD), a California-based teachers group, and the Institute for Research in English Acquisition and Development (READ), which funds and disseminates studies by researchers who favor alternative programs.

In response to the English Only movement, advocates for language-minority students rallied around a policy alternative known as English Plus. They argued that "the national interest can best be served when all members of our society have full access to effective opportunities to acquire strong English language proficiency *plus* mastery of a second or multiple languages" (English Plus Information Clearinghouse, 1992). While linguistic diversity entails certain costs, such as the need to provide bilingual services, it also brings benefits. As the world becomes more interdependent through mechanisms such as the North American Free Trade Agreement, government should actively cultivate skills in languages other than English through programs like developmental bilingual education. At the same time, it should enable linguistic minorities to acquire English, for example, by remedying the shortage of ESL classes for adults (a crisis that English Only proponents have strangely ignored). In sum, English Plus conceives bilingualism not merely as a problem but more importantly as a resource that "contributes to our nation's productivity, worldwide competitiveness, successful international diplomacy, and national security" (English Plus Information Clearinghouse, 1992, p. 152). Although this philosophy made limited inroads against the English Only movement, by the 1990s it began to exert an influence on policymakers concerned with bilingual education.

Changing Terms of Debate

While the critics of bilingual education inflicted only modest blows against the program in the 1980s, they did succeed in defining the terms of the policy debate. Public discussion focused heavily, sometimes exclusively, on the question of how to teach LEP children English as rapidly as possible: through bilingual or English Only approaches. Language of instruction, the key political issue, became for many the key pedagogical issue as well. Secretary Bennett (1985) described bilingual education and English as a second language as "alternative instructional methods," ignoring other details of program design. Beginning in 1984, Congress established Title VII grant categories along similar lines: special alternative instructional programs (no native language used), transitional bilingual education (native language used until students are proficient in English), and developmental bilingual education programs (native language continued after students are proficient in English). The U.S. Department of Education funded an eight-year, multimillion-dollar study to compare the effectiveness of structured immersion, "early-exit" bilingual, and "late-exit" bilingual program models, differentiated largely by quantity of native-language instruction (Ramírez, Yuen, Ramey, & Pasta 1991).

Educators and researchers, recognizing that numerous variables determine academic success or failure, have grown impatient with the obsessive and simplistic focus on language of instruction. While LEP students have unique needs (as well as unique abilities), they also have much in common with other students. Yet the politicization of the policy debate has tended to isolate these children—defining them solely by what they lack: English—and to perpetuate low expectations for their achievement. In recommendations to Congress and the Clinton administration, Hakuta and others of the Stanford Working Group (1993) argue that policymakers should respond to this problem in two ways: (1) "Language-minority students must be provided with an equal opportunity to learn the same challenging content and high-level skills that school reform movements advocate for all students," while receiving instruction and assessment that are linguistically and culturally appropriate; and (2) "Proficiency in two or more languages should be promoted for all American students," including language minority students, whose bilingualism should be valued and encouraged. These ideas were largely embraced and incorporated into the 1994 reauthorization of the Bilingual Education Act. For the first time, funding priority was given to programs that "provide for the development of bilingual proficiency both in English and another language for all participating students" (P.L. 103–382). In 2001, however, Congress reversed policy directions again, eliminating not only the goal of bilingual proficiency but even the word *bilingual* from the text of the law.

The Unz Era

This radical change at the federal level reflected still more radical moves by the states. In 1998, California voters approved an initiative mandating English-only instruction for LEP students—the first such law since the World War I era. Arizonans followed suit in 2000, and similar measures were scheduled for the 2002 ballot in Colorado and Massachusetts. These initiatives were financed and organized by a Silicon Valley millionaire and aspiring politician named Ron Unz. Unlike earlier English Only proponents, Unz dissociated himself from anti-immigrant lobbies; indeed, he posed as an immigrant advocate against schools that allegedly failed to teach English. He dubbed his campaign "English for the Children," a slogan with wide appeal, and portrayed the California initiative, Proposition 227, primarily as a way to improve second-language instruction for immigrant students. The measure's restrictive provisions were largely overlooked in media coverage. Editorials, whether pro or con, treated Unz as a school reformer whose ideas should be seriously considered. From the outset, public opinion polls reported overwhelming approval for the initiative—not only among native English speakers, but among Hispanic and Asian Americans as well (Crawford, 2000). Support slipped somewhat as voters learned about the darker side of Proposition 227 and its counterpart, Proposition 203 in Arizona. For bilingual education supporters, however, the problem was that most voters never heard those arguments. What they did hear was a simple and convincing case against bilingual education.

The sponsor of Proposition 227 built this case on a foundation of myths and misconceptions that were already widespread among the public. For example:

- The notion that young children should be able to learn a second language within a few months to a year at most; judged by that standard, 95 percent of California schools were failing each year, Unz claimed (English for the Children, 1997).

- The slander that bilingual programs do not teach English; thus they were to blame for high dropout and underachievement rates among Latinos, Unz argued.

- The belief that most immigrant parents oppose bilingual education; so schools' insistence on using native-language instruction denied parental rights to choose, Unz charged.

There was no need to produce evidence on behalf of such claims—not that any was available—because they reinforced the conventional wisdom about bilingual education. Again, in contrast to previous English Only arguments, which tended to be symbolic and emotional, these were practical and credible.

Neither researchers nor practitioners in the field had done much to address such fallacies over the years. To challenge them effectively in a short election campaign was probably impossible. Opponents of Proposition 227, however, did not even try. Rather than explaining what was right with bilingual education, they focused on what was wrong with the initiative, stressing its extreme provisions. These included:

- Mandating a one-size-fits-all approach for English language learners known as "structured English immersion," a program "not normally intended to exceed one year" (English Language in Public Schools, 1998; §305), despite the lack of scientific evidence for its effectiveness.

- Restricting the rights of language minority parents to choose the kind of program they want for their children; to be eligible for bilingual programs, students under age 10 must have "special needs" (§311).

- Threatening teachers and administrators with severe penalties for "willfully" violating the English Only rule, including lawsuits for personal financial damages (§320).

- Blocking future legislation to amend or repeal the initiative without a two-thirds "supermajority" vote in the California legislature or another ballot initiative (§335).

However valid these arguments, the initiative's opponents were not very successful in communicating them. They never found a clear message to counter the rhetoric of Ron Unz. Californians ultimately regarded Proposition 227 as a referendum on whether to stress English to the exclusion of native-language instruction. Their vote was a resounding Yes, 61 percent to 39 percent, although—contrary to the pollsters and pundits—Latinos ended up voting No by nearly 2 to 1.

Historical Background

Having visited some of the politics that prevail at this point in time, let us now travel back in time to review the history of the development of the field of bilingual/ESL education in the United States.

U.S. Schooling in Languages Other Than English

The 1800s   Contrary to commonly held current beliefs in the United States, during the 18th and 19th centuries, multiple languages other than English were used as the languages of instruction in U.S. schools. As different groups of varied languages and countries of origin established homesteads in U.S. territory, a general sense of geographical and psychological openness existed. Some communities were self-sufficient and agrarian based; others were ethnic pockets in urban areas (Ovando, 1978b). Historical records show that during the 19th century, many public and private schools used languages other than English as mediums of instruction. In 1900, for example, records show that at least 600,000 children in the United States were receiving part or all of their schooling in German in public and parochial schools (Crawford, 1999; Kloss, 1977; Tyack, 1974). During the 19th century, following annexation of the Territory of New Mexico, either Spanish or English or both could be the language of a school's curriculum (Leibowitz, 1971), and more than a dozen other states passed laws providing for schooling in languages other than English (Crawford, 1992a, 1999). During the second half of the 19th century, bilingual or non-English–language instruction was provided in some form in some public schools as follows: German in Pennsylvania, Maryland, Ohio, Indiana, Illinois, Missouri, Nebraska, Colorado, and Oregon; Swedish,

Norwegian, and Danish in Wisconsin, Illinois, Minnesota, Iowa, North and South Dakota, Nebraska, and Washington; Dutch in Michigan; Polish and Italian in Wisconsin; Czech in Texas; French in Louisiana; and Spanish in the Southwest (Crawford, 1999; Kloss, 1977).

The 1900s   Toward the end of the 1800s, however, there were increasing demands for all immigrants to be assimilated into one cultural and linguistic mold. Between 1900 and 1910, a surge of new immigrants—over 8 million— were admitted to the United States, with the largest numbers coming from southern, eastern, and central Europe (Stewart, 1993). Those northern and western European immigrants already established in the United States clamored for power to control institutions, and one solution to the power struggle focused on schools. Thus schools were charged with the task of "Americanizing" all immigrants, and by 1919, 15 state laws had been passed calling for English Only instruction (Higham, 1992). This push for English-dominant cultural and linguistic homogeneity became established as a pattern within schools during the first half of the 20th century. It was spurred by many factors, such as the standardization and bureaucratization of urban schools (Tyack, 1974), the need for national unity during the two world wars, and the desire to centralize and solidify national gains around unified goals for the country (González, 1975). During the half-century from World War I to the 1960s,

> language-minority students were subjected to severe punishment whenever they resorted to a language other than English on the playground or in the classroom. The legacy of that period continues today, as demonstrated by language minority parents whose ambivalence toward bilingual education often reflects fears that their children will be punished for using a non-English language (Arias & Casanova, 1993, p. 9).

In the early 1920s, the U.S. Congress passed extremely restrictive immigration laws creating a national-origins quota system that discriminated against eastern and southern Europeans and excluded Asians. With fewer numbers of new immigrants, second-generation immigrants stopped using their heritage languages, and bilingual instruction disappeared from U.S. public school instruction for nearly half a century (Crawford, 1992a).

The experience of indigenous groups, whose land was eventually incorporated into what is now U.S. territory, was even more repressive. From the 1850s to the 1950s, indigenous Spanish speakers in Texas and California endured mandated English Only instruction, and Mexican Americans in Texas were placed in segregated schools until segregation was ruled illegal. While the U.S. government initially recognized the language rights of the Cherokees under an 1828 treaty, the record for most other American Indian[3] groups reflected repression of native languages and cultural traditions, a policy also applied to the Cherokees in time. In 1879, federal officials began sending American Indian children to boarding schools, away from their families, where they were punished for speaking their native language, a policy that continued into the 1950s, leading to enormous language loss among many indigenous groups (Crawford, 1999). Of over 300 original languages of North America, 210 of these languages remain, 175 in the United States. But only about 18 of these languages are still being passed on to the children: in Hawaii, Hawaiian; in Alaska, Siberian Yupi'k and Central Yupi'k; in Arizona and New Mexico, Cocopah, Havasupai, Hualapai, Yaqui, Hopi, Navajo, Tohono O'odham, Western Apache, Mescalero, Jemez, Zuni, Tiwa, and Keresan; in Oklahoma, Cherokee; in Mississippi, Choctaw (Krauss, 1996). After such a long history of language loss, Reyhner (1996) passionately portrays the reasons for stabilizing and restoring indigenous languages:

> Many of the keys to the psychological, social, and physical survival of humankind may well be held by the smaller speech communities of the world. These keys will be lost as languages and cultures die. Our languages are joint creative productions that each generation adds to. Languages contain generations of wisdom, going back into antiquity. Our languages contain a significant part of the world's knowledge and wisdom. When a language is lost, much of the knowledge that language represents is also gone. (p. 4)

As one result of this historical pattern of repression of many immigrant and indigenous languages among the U.S. populace, the lack of foreign-language skills became evident during World War II, with the sudden need for military and civilian personnel who were proficient in many world languages. U.S. personnel returning from overseas duty helped to change the prewar disregard for the importance of multiple language resources (Peña, 1976a). Eventually, as the cold war mentality and the Soviets' launching of Sputnik, the first earth-orbiting satellite, increased the need for the United States to compete for international status and power, the **National Defense Education Act of 1958** provided federal money for the expansion of foreign-language teaching.

Although this step represented an improvement in foreign-language policy, it did not resolve the two conflicting philosophies prevalent in U.S. policy that remain to this day. On the one hand, the federal government has recognized the need to develop and support foreign-language instruction for improved international relations, economic development, and national security purposes. On the other hand, a natural resource that new immigrants bring to this country is lost as U.S. schools continue to encourage the loss of native languages of linguistic minorities through insistence on exclusively English instruction. The majority of newcomers entering U.S. schools do not have access to classes taught through their native language. In schools where bilingual education is available, the most widely implemented form is transitional bilingual education, which is designed as remedial instruction to be offered for only two to three years, after which students are expected to function exclusively in English.

English as a Second Language

At the beginning of the 20th century, when English classes were taught for immigrants, largely for purposes of "Americanization" (Perlmann, 1990), there was not yet a conscious effort to professionalize the field of **English as a second language (ESL)**. The first U.S. steps towards formalizing this field of teaching focused on the teaching of English as a foreign language (EFL) in other countries. In 1941, the U.S. Department of State and the Rockefeller Foundation supported the founding of the English Language Institute at the University of Michigan, which began formal training of U.S. teachers for teaching EFL abroad and taught intensive EFL courses to 2,100 international students in its first 10 years of existence. Also during the 1940s, the first EFL textbooks and teacher references were published (Alatis, 1993).

The profession of teaching English as a second language within the United States began to expand in the 1960s in response to increasing numbers of immigrant and refugee children entering the country, as well as to the growing numbers of international students attending U.S. universities. The 1965 immigration law dramatically increased the number of immigrants allowed to enter the United States and eliminated the national origins quota system, thus providing for more diversity among immigrants from all regions of the world. The professional organization Teachers of English to Speakers of Other Languages (TESOL) was established in 1966, development of ESL textbooks expanded, and courses in linguistics and ESL methodology were increasingly demanded (Paulston, 1976).

With specialized classes in which students received instruction at their level of English proficiency, ESL instruction represented a significant change in school policy. In the early 20th century, the approach to schooling had been to immerse immigrants with native-English-speaking students in all content-area classes taught in English with no form of special support. Cohen (1976) coined this sink-or-swim approach, "**submersion.**" A few immigrants survived the submersion process, but most suffered low educational attainment. ESL instruction improved the process of teaching English to speakers of other languages, but in the first decades of ESL expansion, little thought was given to helping students keep up with academic work in math, science, social studies, and other curricular areas. Even as late as 1975, the *TESOL Guidelines for the Preparation of ESOL Teachers* (formally approved by the professional organization that year) made no mention of the need for ESL teachers to teach the English language through academic content, other than to "help students gain knowledge of American social customs, traditions, folklore, history and literature" (Norris, 1977, p. 31). The ESL curriculum of the 1950s and 1960s placed little emphasis on the importance of using a student's home language and culture as a knowledge base on which to build academic success through two languages of instruction. Even with the expansion of ESL teaching during this period, it is important to remember that few students had access to ESL support (Crawford, 1999).

Bilingual Instruction of the 1960s

The Cubans' arrival in Miami following the revolution of 1959 reintroduced bilingual instruction into U.S. schools. During this period, bilingual instruction was a response to very specific local conditions—the need to provide education for the Cuban refugees as they poured into Miami. Cubans quickly established private schools with classes taught in Spanish, with the hope that they would eventually return to their island; but as they recognized that the political situation would not be easily changed, they began to persuade the public schools to establish some bilingual classes. The nation's first new bilingual program in this century began at Coral Way Elementary School in Miami in 1963, and its success soon led to the establishment of other bilingual schools in Dade County, Florida, as well as in other states in the United States. González (1975) suggests that many special factors influenced the Cubans' success in establishing bilingual schools, such as their middle- and upper-middle-class status; the presence of trained Cuban teachers among those who resettled; the aid of the Cuban Refugee Act in providing special training and jobs for the refugees; special sympathy for the refugees, who were seen as victims of their political situation; and a lesser degree of racism expressed towards them because of the predominance of Hispanics of light-skinned European stock among the first groups to arrive.

In 1964, following Florida's example, Texas began to experiment with some bilingual instruction in two school districts. By 1968 bilingual education was being provided in at least 56 locally initiated programs in 13 states. The large majority were Spanish-English programs, but six other languages were represented (Andersson & Boyer, 1970). These bilingual programs were locally developed and funded, and they were supported by the local community of each school. By 1971, the first International Bilingual/Bicultural Education Conference was held in the United States (Mackey & Andersson, 1977), and the National Association for Bilingual Education was officially incorporated as a professional organization in 1975 (Peña, 1976b).

Historical Overview of Title VII Legislation, 1968–2001

Federal influences on bilingual/ESL schooling are one part of the policy picture. But it must be kept in mind that the U.S. Constitution does not mention education as a duty of the federal government; thus the responsibility for education policy decision making resides at the state and local levels by provision of the 10th Amendment. At the same time, over the past half century, the federal government has gradually redefined its role in education as the responsibility for assessing the condition and progress of educational achievement in the United States (Beebe & Evans, 1981).

> The government has a responsibility to improve education through initiatives in research, development and evaluation. The government must also preserve individuals' rights to equitable participation in the educational system. When

this is nonexistent, it must intervene to address critical educational problems which affect the entire country. . . .

The education of limited-English-proficient (LEP) students enrolled in the nation's public schools constitutes an unmet educational need that has national impact. Several factors catapult this need to national attention: (1) the number of LEP students is significant and growing; (2) LEP students have educational rights that are protected by federal laws and statutes; and (3) this group has traditionally not been well served by the educational system. (Sosa, 1996, p. 34)

We will first explore the federal perspective, while keeping in mind that federal funding represents approximately 6 to 9 percent of the total amount spent on education in the United States, which limits the amount of federal influence. However, the federal government can have an impact on school policy decisions indirectly, through denial of federal funds that provide support for students in the categories of federal funding. In the sections that follow, we will review the two major categories of federal influence on bilingual/ESL education: federal legislation and court decisions. Secada (1990) presents the federal role in this way:

Federal policy in bilingual education since 1960 has been driven by efforts to mandate and efforts to entice. Both are efforts to ensure equal educational opportunity for minority-language children of limited English proficiency. Mandated programs are coercive. They grew out of court decisions enforcing civil rights legislation such as **Title VI of the Civil Rights Act of 1964** and the **Equal Educational Opportunities Act of 1974.** Enticement programs, on the other hand, are voluntary. They grew out of the Great Society's War on Poverty, which funded local district efforts to improve educational opportunity for the disadvantaged, as in the Elementary and Secondary Education Act of 1965. The distinction between mandate and enticement is like that between a carrot and a stick: Funding is the carrot and legal mandates are the stick. (p. 83)

Title VII of the Elementary and Secondary Education Act

The first federal legislation for bilingual education (the first "enticement") was passed by Congress in 1968 under Title VII of the Elementary and Secondary Education Act. The new law created a small but significant change in federal policy for linguistic minorities. The civil rights movement and the climate of social change of the 1960s had spurred the passage of legislation focusing on the special needs of minorities. The Bilingual Education Act of 1968 represented the first national acknowledgment of some of the special educational needs of children of limited English proficiency.

This was a popular piece of legislation with bipartisan support; 37 bilingual education bills were introduced in the 1967–68 Congress. The final version focused on the needs of children of poverty who had little or no proficiency in English, with mostly a remedial, compensatory focus (Crawford, 1999; Lyons, 1990). The original sponsors of the bill had hoped to emphasize the advantages to the nation of developing students' bilingualism/biculturalism, resulting in increased academic achievement and bilingual resources for the United States. Modest funding was provided at $7.5 million for fiscal year (FY) 1969 (a federal fiscal year referring to the period from October 1, 1968, to September 30, 1969), with 76 projects funded to support educational programs, train teachers and aides, develop and disseminate instructional materials, and encourage parental involvement (Crawford, 1999).

Provisions of the Original 1968 and 1974, 1978, 1984, 1988 Title VII Reauthorizations

Funding Appropriations   The Bilingual Education Act was **reauthorized** in 1974 and 1978, with appropriations increased each year until FY 1980, when $166.9 million was spent and 564 projects were funded. The lower appropriations that followed during the Reagan years from 1980–1988 represented a 47 percent reduction from the spending level in 1980 for Title VII programs, at a time when support for all other education programs declined by 8 percent (Lyons, 1990). During this period, media reports gave the impression that support for bilingual education had ended in most public school programs, a misrepresentation of what was actually happening at the local level. In FY 1996, $128 million was appropriated for Title VII programs, and in FY 1997, $156.7 million, indicating continuing minimal support at the federal level in comparison to other federally funded education programs, at a time when the number of students with little or no proficiency in English was increasing at a rapid rate (Zapata, 1996). Figure 2.1, expanded from Crawford (1997, p. 30), provides an overview of Title VII funding from 1980 to 2001, adjusted for inflation.

Students Eligible for Federal Services   The 1968 Bilingual Education Act specified that services were to be provided to "children who come from environments where the dominant language is other than English" and from families with incomes below $3,000 per year. The 1974 amendments changed the law to include eligibility for all children of "limited-English-speaking ability" (LES—defined as limited in listening and speaking skills in English), ending the low-income requirement, and the 1978 law expanded the definition to include eligibility for children of limited-English proficiency (LEP—listening, speaking, reading, and writing). The last change allowed students to remain in a program until they reached deeper proficiency in both oral and written English, rather than requiring that they be tested and exited solely on the basis of oral skills (Leibowitz, 1980). It was an important step for the federal definition of who is eligible for Title VII funds to include students who do not yet know how to read and write the English language. Unfortunately, the overall impact of both definitions, LES and LEP, was that many programs funded with Title VII funds from 1968 to 1994 maintained a remedial, compensatory perspective, keeping students in a separate program until they

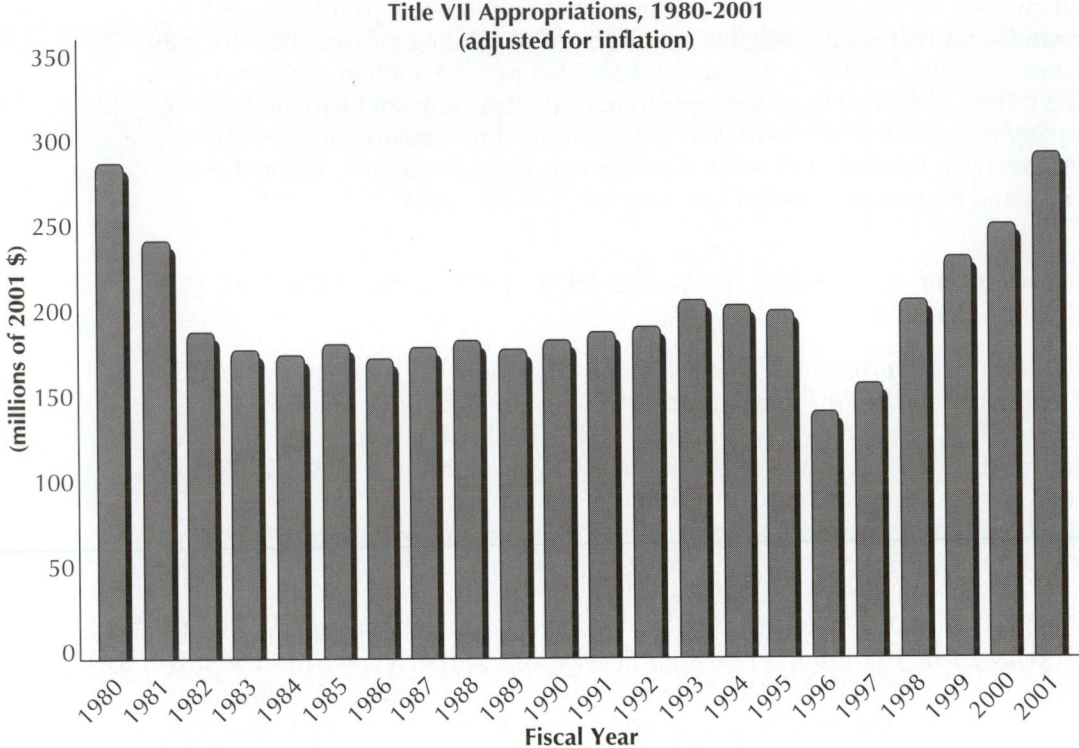

Figure 2.1   *Title VII Appropriations (Adjusted for inflation)*
Source: Crawford, 2001

reached a certain level of performance, after which they were exited from the special services. The 1994 federal funding, which will be discussed in a section below, attempted to change this perspective. Many bilingual/ESL educators and students dislike the acronym *LEP*, introduced with good intentions in the 1978 law and still used in most states, because of the pejorative connotations of the term, which implies that these students have a problem, rather than recognizing that their knowledge of another language and bicultural or multicultural experiences bring rich resources to the classroom.

Purposes of the Federal Funding   The three purposes of the 1968 Bilingual Education Act were to "(1) increase English-language skills, (2) maintain and perhaps increase mother-tongue skills, and (3) support the cultural heritage of the student" (Leibowitz, 1980, p. 24). The reauthorizations in 1974 and 1978 placed increasing emphasis on the importance of mastery of English-language skills as the main purpose of the bill. The 1978 bill also allowed participation of English-speaking children in bilingual programs funded by Title VII, as long as the number did not exceed 40 percent. The inclusion of English speakers was a small beginning toward addressing the conflict in federal language policy. By providing funding for integrated bilingual classes, foreign-language education for language-majority students was enhanced, and at the same time, a few policymakers viewed native-language maintenance for language-minority students as a national priority for the first time. The main intent of the 1978 change, however, was to prevent the segregation of students on the basis of national origin, to comply with legal requirements. The law cautioned that "the objective of the program shall be to assist children of limited English proficiency to improve their English language skills, and the participation of other children in the program must be for the principal purpose of contributing to the achievement of that objective" (Lyons, 1990, p. 70).

The 1984 Bilingual Education Act introduced several new grant programs. Previously, most of the funding had been used for transitional bilingual education, a short-term (two- to three-year) bilingual program. The new categories of funding included family English literacy (to include parents and out-of-school youths in services provided), special populations (to provide services for preschool, gifted, and special education students), academic excellence (to replicate exemplary models), developmental bilingual education (to support native-language maintenance), and special alternative instructional programs (to provide program alternatives for low-incidence language groups). The academic goals of Title VII of the 1984 act were stated more precisely as "allowing a child to meet grade-promotion and graduation standards" (Crawford, 1999, p. 55).

The introduction of **developmental bilingual education** (DBE) as a category of funding in the 1984 reauthorization represented another breakthrough in moving away from compensatory, remedial perspectives to viewing bilingual education as an additive, enrichment school program. Developmental bilingual programs extended provisions in the 1978 law that "where possible," DBE programs should enroll approximately equal numbers of native English-speaking children and children 'whose native language is the second language of instruction in the program' (Lyons, 1990, p. 76). However, subsequent appropriations bills provided little funding for this category relative to the larger amounts provided for the long-standing Title VII transitional bilingual programs. English only proponents supported more funding for "special alternative instructional programs," and the 1988 law authorized up to 25 percent of the funding to be spent in this category, but through FY 1997, Title VII funding remained largely for programs that provided instructional support both in the home language and in English. The 1988 law placed a three-year limit on funding for any applicant, requiring that most students be "mainstreamed" in three years. Thus it continued to emphasize short-term transitional bilingual education as the main model supported by federal funds. However, the 1994 law radically changed this perspective by deemphasizing program models and encouraging schools to develop responses to the reform movement that encompassed the whole school and the whole school system.

Training and Resources   The 1968 Bilingual Education Act provided for training of bilingual personnel through grants, contracts, and fellowships to local educational agencies (LEAs), state educational agencies (SEAs), and institutions of higher education (IHEs) that were expanded in 1974 and 1978. In addition, beginning in 1974, the federal Office of Bilingual Education began to fund a network of institutions designed to provide resources and services to state and local school districts. In 1994, the specialized resource centers funded under Title VII were combined and streamlined within new comprehensive regional assistance centers funded by general funds across all federal programs in education.

In 1977, the National Clearinghouse for Bilingual Education (NCBE) was established to collect, analyze, synthesize, and disseminate information related to linguistically and culturally diverse students in the United States. This is the central information center for the field of bilingual/ESL education in the country. As of the 1990s, NCBE operates a site on the Internet that includes an online library with bibliographic databases, technical assistance network information, and numerous NCBE publications that provide research syntheses on current issues in the field.

Title VII of the Improving America's Schools Act of 1994 and School Reform

Among the many changes occurring at federal, state, and local levels, the reauthorization in 1994 of the federal legislation for education, Improving America's Schools Act (IASA—formerly ESEA) and its companion legislation, Goals 2000: Educate America Act (which provided a framework for state reform), had some impact on shaping education for language minority students. In order to bring language minority students' issues to the discussion table in the reform movement, in 1992–93 a group of researchers and language minority advocates called the Stanford Working Group convened a series of national meetings that resulted in a report proposing changes to the federal legislation:

> For too long, LEP children have been kept on the margins of American education and education reform. . . . The goal of the Working Group . . . is to ensure that LEP students' unique needs and bilingual potential are addressed within the context of raising education achievement for all. . . . A survey of the current condition of education for LEP students reveals areas of dire need, as well as unfulfilled potential. (Stanford Working Group, 1993, pp. 1–2)

The report of this group, as well as proposals from the Congressional Hispanic Caucus and many other advocacy organizations, resulted in substantial changes to federal funding for language minority education. Funding for language minority students became available through both Title VII and Title I funds, whereas before, LEP students had generally been excluded from Chapter I (now Title I) services.

Moving away from the remedial, compensatory, deficiency model of bilingual education to enrichment and innovation, the new Title VII funding

Guidelines for Teaching

"NO CHILD LEFT BEHIND"—PL 107–110

School reform presented a rare opportunity for bipartisanship following the disputed presidential election of 2000. Immediately after taking office, President George W. Bush offered his proposal for reauthorizing the Elementary and Secondary Education Act—"No Child Left Behind"—and made it the centerpiece of his domestic agenda. Lawmakers responded by putting aside ideological divisions and seeking ways to compromise. For Democrats the top priority was increased funding for school programs; for Republicans, more local "flexibility" and less federal control over how the money would be spent. Both parties stressed greater "accountability for results" in the form of higher academic standards, required annual testing in grades three through eight, and increasingly severe sanctions for "failing schools." The final bill ran nearly 1,200 pages, incorporating these and other policy changes, the most sweeping since 1965. When it came to bilingual education, Congress moved to demolish the structure it had created seven years earlier. It is fair to say that the Bilingual Education Act, as conceived in 1968, died a quiet death in 2001; most of its functions were inherited by the states.

Under the new law, Title VII, the Bilingual Education Act, has been renamed Title III, the English Language Acquisition, Language Enhancement, and Academic Achievement Act. It replaces the system of federally administered, competitive grants for school programs with "for-

mula grants" administered by state education agencies. Bilingual education programs will remain eligible for funding, without restrictions (e.g., a three-year limit on student enrollment) that Republicans had proposed. At the same time, however, the 75 percent set aside for native-language programs was repealed. States are merely required to distribute funding to local school districts on the basis of their LEP student and immigrant student populations—unless the annual appropriation dips below $650 million. In that (unlikely) event, the old federally administered grant program would be reinstated. National grants for professional development have been retained, but their funding will be capped at 6.5 percent of annual spending—considerably less than before. As the law's title implies, the pedagogical emphasis will be on English acquisition and academic achievement in English—not the cultivation of bilingualism, as stressed in the Improving America's Schools Act of 1994. Failure to meet "benchmarks" for second-language acquisition will make states and districts vulnerable to financial penalties. Finally, the National Clearinghouse for Bilingual Education survives, albeit under a name that suggests a new mission: the National Clearinghouse for English Language Acquisition and Language Instruction Educational Programs. While the impact of these changes is difficult to predict, there is no doubt about their magnitude.

was designed with the following principles, which came directly from the Stanford Working Group:

1. All children can learn to high standards.
2. Limited-English-proficient children and youth must be provided with an equal opportunity to learn the challenging content and high-level skills that school reform efforts advocate for all students.
3. Proficiency in two or more languages should be promoted for all students. Bilingualism enhances cognitive and social growth and develops the nation's human resources potential in ways that improve our competitiveness in the global market (U.S. Department of Education, 1995, p. 16).

To lead school districts to reform efforts, the old program models were deemphasized, and replaced by four major categories of funding that focused on the function that the funding served: *program development and implementation grants, program enhancement projects, comprehensive school grants,* and *systemwide improvement grants.* By moving away from funding that focused on programs differentiated by the language(s) used for instruction to a more comprehensive and flexible approach to program, school, and school system reform, the funding encouraged creativity, innovation, and revitalization.

School districts were encouraged to create comprehensive school reform plans that integrated bilingual/ESL education into the core of the school system, and were financed by local, state, and federal funding sources. Systemwide, integrated bilingual/ESL education programs included effective, research-based teaching and assessment practices, year-round professional development, innovative curricula supported by interactive education technology, and close partnerships for learning with the linguistically and culturally diverse school community (G. N. García, 1994). The implementation of two-way developmental bilingual education programs, where possible, was strongly encouraged as part of the plan for reform efforts because of their proven effectiveness. "The additive bilingual environment of developmental bilingual education programs is designed to help students achieve fluency and literacy in both languages, meet grade-promotion and graduation requirements by providing instruction in content areas, and develop positive cultural relationships" (U.S. Department of Education, 1995, p. 18).

Court Decisions And The Office For Civil Rights

While the debates in Congress have continued on language policy issues, with limited funds provided under Title VII for school districts that wish to apply for extra funding to meet their continually changing demographic needs, another level of federal policymaking ruled by the federal courts and the executive branch of government has had considerable influence on the developments in U.S. language-minority education—and these decisions are mandates. Federal court decisions of the 1970s and 1980s, as well as enforcement guidelines monitored by the Office for Civil Rights, a function of the executive branch of government, have forced school systems in many regions of the United States to reexamine their practices in schooling language-minority students.

Basic Rights of Language Minority Students

Over the past several decades, federal policy for the protection of the educational rights of language-minority students has gradually evolved through court decisions and federal legislation that have extended the interpretation of basic rights provided in the U.S. Constitution. Three important federal laws that establish these basic rights are the Fourteenth Amendment of the U.S. Constitution (passed in 1868), which guarantees all persons equal pro-

Guidelines for Teaching

THE *LAU* V. *NICHOLS* SUPREME COURT DECISION, 1974

Of all the court decisions based on one or more of the above federal laws, the landmark U.S. Supreme Court decision *Lau* v. *Nichols* (1974) has had by far the most significant impact in defining legal responsibilities of schools serving limited English proficient students. In the early 1900s, the few court decisions that issued rulings related to language policy were mainly concerned with preserving and promoting English as one of the key elements in the formation of U.S. national identity (Teitelbaum & Hiller, 1977b). *Lau* v. *Nichols* did not deny the importance of learning English, but the Supreme Court justices ruled unanimously, on the grounds of the Civil Rights Act of 1964, that some 3,000 Chinese students in San Francisco were not being provided an equal educational opportunity compared with their English-speaking peers.

The Supreme Court decision did not specify the remedy for schools to provide a more "meaningful education" for students of limited English proficiency, although it described bilingual education and ESL as possible remedies. In the consent decree that followed, the San Francisco school district agreed to provide bilingual/bicultural education for students of limited English proficiency. The *Lau* v. *Nichols* decision had a direct and immediate impact on the growth of bilingual education programs.

Although it did not expressly endorse bilingual education, the *Lau* decision legitimized and gave impetus to the movement for equal educational opportunity for students who do not speak English. *Lau* raised the nation's consciousness of the need for bilingual education, encouraged additional federal legislation, energized federal enforcement efforts, led to federal funding of nine regional "general assistance *Lau* centers," aided the passage of state laws mandating bilingual education, and spawned more lawsuits. (Teitelbaum & Hiller, 1977a, p. 139)

tection under the laws of the United States; Title VI of the Civil Rights Act of 1964, which bans discrimination on the basis of "race, color, or national origin" in any federally assisted program; and the Equal Educational Opportunities Act of 1974, which states that:

> No state shall deny equal educational opportunity to an individual on account of his or her race, color, sex, or national origin, by . . . the failure of an educational agency to take appropriate action to overcome language barriers that impede equal participation by its students in its instructional programs. [20 U.S.C. §1703(f)] (cited in Lyons, 1992, p. 10)

U.S. Office for Civil Rights

In August 1974, Congress passed the Equal Educational Opportunities Act, which gave legislative backing to the *Lau* decision and extended its scope to apply to all public school districts, not just those receiving federal financial assistance. Additional pressure on school districts to implement some kind of meaningful instruction for students of limited English proficiency came from the **U.S. Office for Civil Rights (OCR)**, which issued the 1975 *Lau* **Remedies.**

Guidelines for Teaching

THE 1970 OCR MEMORANDUM

An important precedent to the *Lau* Remedies was the OCR Memorandum of May 25, 1970, sent by the then Department of Health, Education, and Welfare to the Chief State School Officer of every state and to the superintendents of school districts with large numbers of language-minority students. The 1970 memorandum was upheld in the *Lau* v. *Nichols* decision and was incorporated into the OCR manual of compliance procedures for Title VI of the Civil Rights Act (Castro Feinberg, 1990). It stated:

1. Where inability to speak and understand the English language excludes national origin–minority group children from effective participation in the educational program offered by a school district, the district must take affirmative steps to rectify the language deficiency in order to open its instructional program to these students.

2. School districts must not assign national origin–minority group students to classes for the mentally retarded on the basis of criteria that essentially measure or evaluate English language skills; nor may school districts deny national origin–minority group children access to college preparatory courses on a basis directly related to the failure of the school system to inculcate English language skills.

3. Any ability grouping or tracking system employed by the school system to deal with the special language skill needs of national origin–minority group children must be designed to meet such language skill needs as soon as possible and must not operate as an educational dead-end or permanent track.

4. School districts have the responsibility to adequately notify national origin–minority group parents of school activities that are called to the attention of other parents. Such notice in order to be adequate may have to be provided in a language other than English. (Pottinger, 1970)

The 1975 Lau Remedies   The 1970 OCR Memorandum and the *Lau* v. *Nichols* Supreme Court decision led to expansion of Title VI enforcement under the Ford and Carter administrations, resulting in the 1975 *Lau* Remedies, developed to provide OCR guidelines for compliance. The guidelines specified procedures for identifying language-minority students and assessing their English language proficiency (to be presented in Chapter Eight), determining appropriate instructional treatments, deciding when students were ready for mainstream[4] (grade-level) classes, and determining the professional standards expected of teachers of language minority students (Lyons, 1990). The *Lau* Remedies strongly encouraged school districts to implement bilingual education wherever feasible, for example, in each school district that had at least 20 students of limited English proficiency who spoke the same primary language. Schools were generally required to provide these students with ESL support combined with academic content taught through the student's strongest language, until students reached sufficient proficiency in English to experience academic success in monolingual English classes.

Furthermore, these guidelines redefined bilingual education to include bilingual/bicultural program models that go beyond transitional to provide ongoing bilingual/bicultural instruction after students are proficient in English, resulting in students who can function equally well in both languages and cultures (González, 1994).

The *Lau* Remedies represented a new level of federal requirements where none had existed previously. School districts were now required to demonstrate that they had some kind of effective educational program for students of limited English proficiency. If a school district were found to be out of compliance, it could be threatened with loss of federal funds (Teitelbaum & Hiller, 1977a). Lyons (1990) describes the results:

> The *Lau* Remedies quickly evolved into de facto compliance standards as DHEW moved aggressively to enforce Title VI during the Ford and Carter administrations. Between 1975 and 1980, OCR carried out nearly 600 national-origin compliance reviews, leading to the negotiation of 359 school district *Lau* **plans** by July 1980. (p. 72)

The Proposed 1980** Lau **Regulations   The 1975 *Lau* Remedies were never published in the *Federal Register,* and after a court decision questioned their enforceability, in August 1980, a new set of *Lau* **regulations** was proposed. Written in substantial detail, these regulations specified identification and assessment procedures and proposed alternative methods of instruction for limited-English-proficient students, such as transitional, maintenance, or two-way models of bilingual education, and ESL for low-incidence language groups. The proposed regulations drew intense criticism for being too specific (whereas the 1975 remedies were considered too ambiguous), and coming three months before the presidential election, the regulations became a campaign issue. As a result, the regulations were withdrawn. New *Lau* compliance standards were developed in 1985, based chiefly on *Castañeda* v. *Pickard* (to be discussed below), but these guidelines were not published as official regulations. Many fewer OCR compliance reviews were conducted during the Reagan and Bush years (González, 1994; Lyons, 1990).

In 1988, "Congress acted to restore its intent to deny *all* Federal assistance to school districts that violate the educational rights of students because of race or color or national origin in any of its programs" (Lyons, 1990, p. 31); however, the Bush administration did not greatly increase enforcement of OCR compliance reviews. When Clinton became president in 1993, the newly appointed assistant secretary for civil rights, Norma Cantú, began an intensive effort to initiate numerous compliance reviews, focusing on whole school systems. Priorities in OCR investigations have focused on access for limited-English-proficient students, overinclusion of minorities in special education, testing and admissions bias, and underrepresentation of women and minorities in mathematics and sciences (Pitsch, 1994; Schnaiberg, 1994b). For school districts cited as out of compliance, OCR reviews have focused on

Guidelines for Teaching

FEDERAL COURT DECISIONS AFTER *LAU* V. *NICHOLS*

Since the *Lau* v. *Nichols* Supreme Court decision in 1974, a number of important federal court decisions have continued to refine the interpretation of the educational rights of language-minority students that are guaranteed in the Equal Educational Opportunities Act of 1974. "Parents frustrated by OCR's inaction retain the option of taking their complaints directly to federal court" (Crawford, 1999, p. 58), and that is precisely what parents have done in state after state. Even before *Lau,* the judicial trend of mandating some form of bilingual instruction had begun with cases such as *United States* v. *Texas* (San Felipe del Río School District, 1971) and *Arvizu* v. *Waco* (Texas, 1973). Soon after *Lau,* a lawsuit filed by Mexican-American parents in *Serna* v. *Portales* (New Mexico, 1974) resulted in a federal court mandate to implement a bilingual/bicultural curriculum, revise assessment procedures to monitor Hispanic students' academic achievement, and recruit bilingual personnel.

   Aspira v. *Board of Education of the City of New York* (1974) was a decision with far-reaching implications for bilingual education. On behalf of 150,000 Hispanic students, the consent decree, which remains in effect today, mandates a system of identification of Hispanic students in need of special instruction, describes necessary teacher qualifications, and sets standards for instruction in English and Spanish (Crawford, 1999). Bilingual instruction was also required as part of the overall desegregation plan in the three desegregation cases of *Morgan* v. *Kerrigan* (Boston, 1974), *Bradley* v. *Milliken* (Detroit, 1975), and *Evans* v. *Buchanan* (Wilmington, Delaware, 1976) (Teitelbaum & Hiller, 1978).

   In *Cintrón* v. *Brentwood* (1978), the court ordered this New York school district to keep recently hired bilingual teachers who were being dismissed because of declining enrollment in the district. Two plans submitted by the school district were rejected by the court as violating desegregation guidelines and the *Lau* Remedies. The school district was ordered to develop a new plan for bilingual/bicultural education that included identification, long-term assessment of LM students'

academic performance, development of appropriate and high-quality desegregated programs for all students, and professional development for bilingual teachers (Lyons, 1992). In *Ríos* v. *Read* (1977), a district court ruled that the school district of Patchogue-Medford, New York, was obligated under *Lau* to provide a *quality* program for students of limited English proficiency. The court rejected the school district's practice of providing mostly ESL instruction with 40 to 50 minutes of content instruction in Spanish for kindergarten and first grade only. Again, the school district was ordered to identify language-minority students, validly assess their abilities, and provide ESL and bilingual instruction by competent bilingual personnel.

Castañeda v. *Pickard,* 1981
"Perhaps the most significant court decision affecting language minority education after Lau" (Lyons, 1992, p. 19) is *Castañeda* v. *Pickard* (1981). The school district in Raymondville, Texas, was charged with violation of language minority students' basic rights under the **Equal Educational Opportunities Act of 1974.** In this case, the Fifth Circuit Court of Appeals formulated three criteria for evaluating programs serving LEP students: (1) the school program must be based on "sound educational theory;" (2) the program must be implemented effectively, with adequate resources and personnel; and (3) the program must be evaluated and determined to be effective, not only in the teaching of language, but also in access to the full curriculum—math, science, social studies, and language arts (Crawford, 1999). Since this court decision, the "*Castañeda* test" has been applied by the courts in other cases and has been used as a standard in OCR guidelines for compliance with the *Lau* v. *Nichols* Supreme Court decision.

   In another well-publicized case, *U.S.* v. *the State of Texas* (1981), U.S. District Judge William Wayne Justice ordered bilingual instruction for grades K through 12 for all Mexican-American students in Texas with limited English proficiency,

continued

Guidelines for Teaching, continued

stating that "the state of Texas had not only segregated students in inferior 'Mexican schools,' but had 'vilified the language, culture, and heritage of these children with grievous results'" (Crawford, 1999, p. 44). At the time, Texas had state-mandated bilingual education in grades K through 3 only. A year later, though, a federal appellate court reversed the ruling.

Court decisions of the 1980s built on the *Castañeda* criteria included *Keyes* v. *School District #1* (1983), in which a U.S. District Court ruled that the second and third criteria for the transitional bilingual program had not been met. The program was judged as being not adequately implemented. The court declared that more bilingual teachers needed to be hired; standards for measuring teachers' bilingual proficiency needed to be established; adequate professional development for bilingual/ESL teachers must be provided; and appropriate assessment instruments must be used to measure the program's effectiveness. In 1987, in *Gómez* v. *Illinois State Board of Education*, under the Equal Educational Opportunities Act, it was ruled that state education agencies are also responsible for ensuring that language minority students' educational needs are met, including identification and assessment of language minority students and placement of students in appropriate programs.

Special Education for LM/LEP Students

Several court decisions have focused on the legal responsibilities of schools for serving language minority students with special needs (see Chapter Nine for a more extensive discussion of the special education for culturally and linguistically diverse students). Overrepresentation and underrepresentation of LM students in special education classes are continuing concerns. Federal legislation such as the 1975 Education of the Handicapped Act (P.L. 94–142) and Section 504 of the Rehabilitation Act of 1973 provides important protection under the law (Lyons, 1992). Under P.L. 94–142, students of limited English proficiency must be assessed in their primary language to determine appropriate educational program placement. The court case *Diana* v. *California* (1970) first brought legal attention to the overrepresentation of language minority children in classes for the mentally retarded. As a result of this settlement and the federal legislation, IQ has ceased to be the predominant construct for special education assessment, replaced by measurement of adaptive behavior and linguistic and cognitive tasks in the student's primary language (Figueroa, 1980). School districts continue to be held accountable through court decisions such as *Y. S.* v. *School District of Philadelphia* of 1988, brought on behalf of 6,800 Asian-American students in Philadelphia's schools. One of the students named in this suit, a Cambodian refugee, had been placed in classes for the mentally retarded based on tests developed for English-speaking students (Lyons, 1992).

Plyler v. *Doe*, 1982

Another landmark case taken all the way to the U.S. Supreme Court was *Plyler* v. *Doe* (1982). The resultant ruling of the highest court in the United States guarantees the rights of undocumented immigrants to free public education. Based upon the equal protection provisions of the 14th Amendment to the U.S. Constitution, public schools are *prohibited* from (1) denying undocumented students admission to school, (2) requiring students or parents to disclose or document their immigration status, or (3) requiring social security numbers of all students (Carrera, 1989).

School districts may not arbitrarily require students to present social security numbers, maintain lists of students with alien registration numbers, report or refer students to the US Immigration and Naturalization Services (except in the case of an I–20 visa matter with parental authorization), nor classify undocumented or other immigrant students on the basis of their federal immigration status as nonresidents under state school attendance laws. However, districts may collect information for the purpose of documenting eligibility for funding by the Emergency Immigration Act or the Transition Program for Refugee

continued

Guidelines for Teaching, continued

Children by asking whether a student has arrived in the United States within the last three years and is in his or her first district of school attendance, and whether the student has status as a refugee under federal immigration law. (Castro Feinberg, 1990, p. 146)

The *Plyler* v. *Doe* Supreme Court decision figured prominently in a federal judge's ruling striking down many of the provisions of Proposition 187, a ballot measure passed by California voters in 1994 in an attempt to slow down illegal immigration. The new law required public school personnel to report to law enforcement agencies and the Immigration and Naturalization Service of the U.S. Department of Justice all persons—children and parents—who were not able to prove their legal immigration or nationality status in the United States (Macías, 1994). "Judge Pfaelzer's ruling

responded to arguments by civil rights and education groups that immigration is a federal responsibility and that the U.S. Constitution does not permit a state to establish its own system. The judge agreed that requiring schools and other public agencies to verify and report immigration status violates the Constitution" (Schnaiberg, 1995, p. 13). The judge's ruling rejected as unconstitutional all of Proposition 187's provisions involving elementary and secondary schools. However, this and other issues are being contested in lawsuits, and lengthy court battles are predicted. In 1996, Congress attempted to pass legislation, known as the Gallegly amendment to the immigration-reform bill, HR 2202, allowing states to deny a free, public K through 12 education to undocumented immigrants. Bipartisan support for immigrants' rights resulted in its defeat (Schnaiberg, 1996).

the following issues for language minority students who are limited in English proficiency (LM/LEP students): identification and assessment of LM/LEP students, education programs for these students based on sound theory and research, program participation data, program staffing and training, designation of exit criteria if the program is separate from the mainstream, program evaluation and modification, notices to parents in home language, segregation and facilities, access to special opportunity programs (e.g., gifted, magnet schools, advanced placement programs), and appropriate placement and services in special education when needed.

State Policies

State Legislation

Since the U.S. Constitution delegates most education decision making to the states, school policies for language-minority students are strongly influenced by legislation and funding sources at the state level. This book cannot provide the rich detail of developments in state policies due to limited space; it is important that educators gather information from individual state education agencies on the requirements and resources for their jurisdictions because they vary greatly from state to state.

During the first half of the 20th century, several states had statutory prohibitions against the use of languages other than English for instruction. But along with the federal passage of the 1968 Bilingual Education Act, many states passed legislation to assist local school districts with implementation of bilingual and ESL services, repealing or ignoring the earlier laws (González, 1994; Gray, Convery, & Fox, 1981). By 1971, 30 states permitted or required some form of bilingual instruction, while 20 states prohibited such instruction (National Advisory Council for Bilingual Education, 1978–79). By 1983, bilingual education was explicitly permitted by law in 43 states. And as of 1996, bilingual education was mandated, with specific guidelines for the requirements, in nine states: Alaska, Connecticut, Illinois, Massachusetts, Michigan, New Jersey, Rhode Island, Texas, and Wisconsin. Although laws in seven states—Alabama, Arkansas, Delaware, Nebraska, North Carolina, Oklahoma, and West Virginia—still prohibit instruction in languages other than English, these bans are no longer enforced. Of the states that permit or mandate bilingual education, 21 provide some form of special funding for school districts to use for LM/LEP students (Crawford, 1999; Gray, Convery, & Fox, 1981).

In 1969, New Mexico was the first state in this century to pass legislation authorizing instruction in languages other than English (Crawford, 1999). But the first state legislation to *mandate* bilingual education was enacted by Massachusetts in 1971. The Massachusetts state law contributed to the institutionalization of transitional bilingual education as a program model that, in the early 1970s, was also adopted in many other states' laws regarding the education of LM/LEP students (González, 1994). (We will define this and other historical program models in the next section.) All states require the inclusion of ESL as an essential component of all bilingual programs. Ten states explicitly permit the inclusion of monolingual English speakers in two-way bilingual classes for desegregation purposes, and other state laws prohibit the segregation of LEP students. A few states have provisions for bilingual maintenance programs.

California is an interesting example of strong state laws that come and go with the politics of bilingual/ESL education. In 1986, California had a comprehensive bilingual education law, with specific policies for implementation. As the state with the largest number of limited-English-proficient students, with 40 percent of the national LEP enrollment in 1994–95 (Silcox, 1997), California has immense needs. The California Department of Education found in 1994 that 27 percent of California LEP students (over 300,000 children) received no special language services at all, and only 28 percent of the state's LEP students received bilingual instruction that included both primary language content instruction and English language development (Affeldt, 1996). Yet in a political climate in which California voters declared English the state's official language in 1986, when the bilingual education statute came up for reauthorization in the same year, even though it was endorsed by "virtually every school board and educators' organization in California . . . and it breezed through the legislature," the governor vetoed the measure. The California state bilingual education legislation had been

> a virtual bill of rights for language-minority children, providing guarantees unmatched in other states (p. 195) . . . popular with many parents and

educators because it clarified the schools' obligations: how to evaluate and reclassify LEP children, when to establish bilingual classrooms and what to do about a shortage of qualified bilingual teachers. These strict requirements also bred opposition, especially among teachers who had to learn a second language or risk losing their jobs. (Crawford, 1999, pp. 63, 195).

However, in spite of the demise of the law, many of the requirements have remained in effect, through use of other state statutes and continuing state monitoring visits. Prior to the passage of Proposition 227, no California school districts had chosen to dismantle their bilingual programs, and numerous school districts continued to expand and improve the quality of bilingual services. Bilingual schools that were cited by the state or federal government as exemplary have continued to excel, and innovative bilingual curricula and models have spread to other schools (Crawford, 1999).

The state of California has also pioneered in cooperative work between OCR and the state education agency to assist school districts with plans for accountability when they have been cited as out of compliance with federal or state guidelines. One example was the comprehensive bilingual education plan negotiated with the Oakland Unified School District, following a class action suit filed by nine families of LEP students in 1985. With the development of a five-year plan that met the concerns of all parties, bilingual education state funds were reinstated (Affeldt, 1996; Schnaiberg, 1994a).

State Certification of Bilingual/ESL Teachers

Another level of state policymaking that influences implementation of school programs is formal teacher certification or licensure. According to a 1999 survey of state education agencies, 41 states and the District of Columbia offered either ESL *or* bilingual/dual language teacher certification or endorsements. Of these, 22 states offered *both* ESL and bilingual certification or endorsements; 23 states had legislative requirements that teachers placed in ESL classrooms must be certified in ESL. Similarly, 17 states had legislative requirements that teachers placed in bilingual/dual language classrooms must have bilingual/dual language certification. Ten states did not provide either a bilingual or ESL endorsement: Alaska, Idaho, Louisiana, Mississippi, Oklahoma, Pennsylvania, Rhode Island, South Carolina, South Dakota, and Vermont. States that offered ESL but not bilingual teacher certification were Arkansas, Florida, Georgia, Hawaii, Iowa, Kentucky, Maryland, Missouri, Montana, Nebraska, North Carolina, Oregon, Tennessee, Virginia, and West Virginia. Three states—Michigan, North Dakota, and Wyoming—offered bilingual but not ESL teacher certification (McKnight & Antinuez, 1999).

One of the major problems with the development of these licensing standards for teachers is that many of the states' standards for ESL teachers were developed in the 1970s or early 1980s, when ESL teachers were expected to teach only the English language. Thus the typical state-required coursework for ESL teachers focuses mostly on theoretical and applied English linguistics courses that analyze the structure of the English language (Collier, 1985). But

Guidelines for Teaching

ESL OR BILINGUAL TEACHER CERTIFICATION

State	ESL Certification or Endorsement	Bilingual-Dual Language Certification or Endorsement	State	ESL Certification or Endorsement	Bilingual-Dual Language Certification or Endorsement
Alabama	Yes	Yes	Montana	Yes*	No
Alaska	No	No	Nebraska	Yes*	No
Arizona	Yes	Yes	Nevada	Yes*	Yes*
Arkansas	Yes	No	New Hamphire	Yes	No
California	Yes*	Yes*	New Jersey	Yes*	Yes*
Colorado	Yes*	Yes*	New Mexico	Yes	Yes
Connecticut	Yes*	Yes*	New York	Yes*	Yes*
Delaware	Yes	Yes	North Carolina	Yes*	No
Dist. of Columbia	Yes	Yes	North Dakota	No	Yes
Florida	Yes	No	Ohio	Yes*	Yes*
Georgia	Yes	No	Oklahoma	No	No
Hawaii	Yes	No	Oregon	Yes	No
Idaho	No	No	Pennsylvania	No	No
Illinois	Yes*	Yes*	Rhode Island	No	No
Indiana	Yes*	Yes*	South Carolina	No	No
Iowa	Yes	No	South Dakota	No	No
Kansas	Yes*	Yes*	Tennessee	Yes	No
Kentucky	Yes*	No	Texas	Yes*	Yes*
Louisiana	No	No	Utah	Yes*	Yes*
Maine	Yes	Yes	Vermont	No	No
Maryland	Yes	Yes	Virginia	Yes*	No
Massachusetts	Yes*	No	Washington	Yes*	Yes*
Michigan	No	Yes*	West Virginia	Yes	No
Minnesota	Yes*	Yes*	Wisconsin	Yes*	Yes*
Mississippi	No	No	Wyoming	No	Yes
Missouri	Yes*	No			

*In addition to *offering* certification, this state has legislative *requirements* for certification.

Source: A. McKnight & B. Antinuez (1999). Sate survey of legislative requirements for educating limited English proficient students. National Clearinghouse for Bilingual Education (NCBE).

in the 1980s, the movement toward content-based ESL, recognizing that LEP students must receive access to the full curriculum (math, science, social studies, and language arts), resulted in the need for ESL teachers to be licensed to teach across the curriculum. Some states actually require dual licensure, adding ESL as an endorsement on top of standard teacher certification, but other states require only the coursework in English linguistics. This leads to the serious problem that often ESL teachers are not prepared to teach the subject areas that they are assigned to teach, and in some states they are not given the coursework in child and adolescent development and teaching methods that prepare them for their work. In some states, the bilingual teaching credential has some of the same problems, but most states require bilingual teachers to be fully licensed across the curriculum, using the same standards as those for all grade-level (mainstream) teachers, plus coursework in bilingualism and second language acquisition, foundations of bilingual education, and incorporation of a cross-cultural or multicultural perspective into the curriculum.

Program Models

While federal and state policies have a strong impact on school programs, at the local school level many policy decisions are made that focus on the specifics of program implementation. The program models for bilingual/ESL education that have evolved in the United States over the past three decades represent a mixture of federal, state, and local policy influences. In addition, research on program effectiveness in bilingual/ESL education has had some influence on the policy decisions regarding implementation of these program models at the local level.

Historically, many different names have been given to program variations in bilingual/ESL education. Not infrequently, educators define these differently from school to school. Likewise, researchers, politicians, and journalists have sometimes used program labels in bilingual/ESL education inappropriately and have caused confusion for the field. Included here are concise clarifications of the most common terms used to define differences in programs among bilingual/ESL educators in the United States.

Use of the Primary Language of Language Minority Students

The most prominent characteristic that defines differences among programs in bilingual/ESL education is how much the primary language (L_1) of the students is used for instruction. Historically, programs have defined this for language minority students by the number of years of exposure to English. Under this approach, students receive bilingual instruction until they are proficient enough in English to achieve academically in their L_2 (English) at the same level as native English speakers. Currently, programs are changing from this remedial perspective for bilingual instruction to an enrichment perspective, recognizing that the research clearly demonstrates the benefits of additive bilingualism. As a result, the strongest models with an enrichment perspective, the 90–10 bilingual immersion model (also referred to as two-way bilingual or dual-language education), ultimately designed for grades K through 12, are increasing in number across the country.

Enrichment or Remediation?

The remaining differences between program models boil down to the social perception of the program, as viewed by school staff, students, and community, and the social consequences of the program design. When the underlying goal of the program is to "fix" students who are perceived as having a problem, the program generally separates the students from the mainstream and works on "remediation." The consequence is usually that students receive less access to the standard curriculum, and the social status quo is maintained, with underachieving groups continuing to underachieve in the next generation. When the focus of the program is on academic enrichment for all students, with intellectually challenging, interdisciplinary, discovery learning that respects and values students' linguistic and cultural life experiences as an important resource for the classroom, the program becomes one that is perceived positively by the community, and students are academically successful and deeply engaged in the learning process (Chiang, 1994; Clair, 1994; McKay & Wong, 1988). We shall examine some of the historical program models from this point of view.

ESL or ESOL

English as a second language (ESL), also known as ESOL (English to speakers of other languages), is an integral and crucial component of all bilingual programs. During the English portion of the instructional time, ESL-trained teachers provide students with access to the standard academic curriculum, taught from a second-language perspective. The ESL teacher is also responsible for teaching age-appropriate English language arts objectives from a second-language perspective. In team-teaching situations, the ESL and bilingual teachers closely coordinate the curriculum together, providing for content reinforcement without repetition in each language. In addition, in schools with low-incidence language groups, where there are too few speakers of one language in one or two adjacent grades to provide bilingual support, ESL teachers serve the essential role of providing English language learners with access to English and academic content, taught from a second-language perspective.

ESL Pullout

ESL pullout is the most expensive of all program models in bilingual/ESL education because it requires hiring extra resource teachers who are trained in second language acquisition (Chambers & Parrish, 1992; Crawford, 1997). In the United States, ESL pullout is the most implemented and the least effective model (Thomas & Collier, 1997).[5] Problems with this model are lost time in students' access to the full curriculum, lack of curriculum articulation with grade-level (mainstream) classroom teachers, and no access to primary language schooling to keep up with grade-level academic work while learning English. The social assumption is that the language the child speaks is a problem to be remediated, and students often feel that they are stigmatized by attending what is perceived as a remedial class.

ESL pullout teachers have to struggle with many issues. If the teacher is lucky enough to have a resource room, ESL students may come and go during the day, some staying a short time and others a long time. Students of many ages may be together in one given time period—some may be missing science while others are missing social studies or math. The ESL teacher has little time to plan individual content lessons for each student, so students miss important academic work. Many ESL teachers are itinerant teachers who have to travel to several schools in one week.

Alternatives to ESL pullout currently under experimentation include various models of inclusion. The least effective inclusion models are those that place the ESL teacher or aide in the back of the classroom to tutor students individually using worksheets. The most promising models are team teaching with the grade-level teacher, where the two teachers share equal teaching responsibilities for the whole class, have joint planning time, and collaborate well together. The big advantage of team teaching is that students do not have to be exited from a separate program, and they are part of the mainstream in a more socially supportive environment.

ESL Content, or Sheltered Instruction   In the 1980s, the field of ESL began to move away from models that taught only the English language, recognizing that students inevitably get behind in their schooling while they are learning English so language and academic content should be taught together. Content ESL teaching is a very effective method for teaching the English language when delivered by a trained specialist in second-language acquisition, who clearly has both language and content objectives in each lesson. Research has found that in ESL content teaching the school curriculum can be a natural, motivating, hands-on way to acquire language through experimenting in science, solving problems in math, analyzing the community from a social studies perspective, exploring authentic children's literature, and reading and writing across the curriculum.

ESL content classes are often self-contained at the elementary school level for one to two years, with a gradual shift towards placing students in their age-appropriate grade-level classes. At the secondary school level, students attend classes in subjects that they need to graduate from high school, taught by dual-certified ESL teachers or by subject-matter specialists who have been trained in second-language acquisition. Throughout the eastern half of the United States, the term *ESL content* or *content ESL* is most often used for this type of program, whereas the West Coast, especially California, uses the term *sheltered instruction,* or more recently, *Specially Designed Academic Instruction in English (SDAIE).* Sheltered instruction refers to a content subject (science, math, or social studies) taught to ESL students by a teacher who has certification in the content area being taught as well as specialized training in instructional strategies designed to meet the linguistic and cultural needs of English language learners. That teacher might also have certification in ESL or might team with an ESL teacher. Sheltered English instruction provides students with continuing English language development, access to the core curriculum, and opportunities for classroom interaction. It is based on the premise that language is best learned when it is taught as "comprehensible input," (Krashen, 1985) or instruction that is understandable. For instruction to be comprehensible, it must be specially designed to "make sense" to the students and to provide them with opportunities to participate in learning activities. Sheltered instruction also promotes the idea that instruction is best taught through context-embedded experience. In other words, students acquire second language skills when these skills are taught in meaningful context and are not isolated from subject matter (Crawford, 1997, 1999; Glendale Unified School District, 1990; Northcutt Gonzales, 1994; Peregoy & Boyle, 1997; Valdez Pierce, 1988).

In sheltered English instruction, "meaning is conveyed not through language alone but with the help of gestures, body language, visual aids, demonstrations and hands-on experience" (Glendale Unified School District, 1990, p. 2). Other sheltered strategies include slow but natural levels of speech, clear enunciation, short, simple sentences, repetition and paraphrasing, controlled vocabulary and idioms, visual reinforcement, and frequent comprehension checks (Lessow-Hurley, 1996, p. 78).

ESL content teaching or sheltered instruction is much more effective than ESL pullout because students have access to more of the curriculum while they are learning English. Sheltered instruction typically is a component of bilingual education programs, and serves as a bridge from an ESL class to an all-English academic content class. It is important to note, however, that it is the consensus of the research and practitioner literature on sheltered English instruction that this method is best used with students who have acquired an intermediate or advanced level of proficiency in English, particularly for classrooms in which English learners and mainstream students are present.

As with ESL pullout, sometimes mainstream staff and students may perceive ESL or sheltered content classes as remedial in nature, making it hard to undo the social stigma attached to the program. However, enrichment bilingual programs and other such innovations have successfully transformed the school community's perception of ESL content classes into "gifted" or "accelerated" curricula. The more teachers plan together to develop age-appropriate, cognitively complex, thematic ESL content lessons (to be discussed in the next chapter), the more students and the school community can come to view ESL as enrichment. On the issue of cost-effectiveness, if ESL content teachers are incorporated into the mainstream staff providing ESL students access to the core curriculum, this model can be much more cost-effective than ESL pullout.

Newcomer Programs

Over the last several years, newcomer programs have been developed for newly arriving immigrant students in some school districts. These programs combine teaching ESL with content instruction, as well as some L_1 academic support when feasible, and they provide social service information to assist families with adaptation to this country. For desegregation purposes, students are not generally kept in a separate newcomer program for more than one to two years.

"Structured Immersion"   **Structured immersion** is a misnamed program model that was promoted by English-only proponents with a political agenda in the early 1980s. The name was taken from Canadian immersion programs with the plan to implement immersion in the United States. But immersion programs in Canada are very strong bilingual programs with academic instruction through two languages for grades K through 12. The U.S. planners failed to implement the Canadian model, leaving out the crucial L_1 component, and providing instruction only in English. Thus, this is just another form of ESL content teaching in a self-contained class. The term *structured* was used to refer to highly structured materials that introduce students step-by-step to the English language, and the first materials used in the program, "Distar Reading, Language, and Arithmetic," were designed for students with learning disabilities. In the first evaluations of this model, as ESL students moved through the grades, their scores plummeted as they reached cognitively more complex work in fifth and sixth grades. As originally designed, "structured immersion" did not prove to be an effective program model because the materials did not match the natural second-language acquisition process, which is not sequential and is very complex (as will be seen in Chapter Four). ESL content classes using discovery learning across the curriculum have been much more effective than structured approaches to teaching language. It is unfortunate that anti-bilingual education ballot initiatives in California and Arizona have targeted young English language learners—the very group for whom a structured immersion model and sheltered English instruction is most problematic. School districts that dismantle their bilingual programs in favor of structured English immersion face both the legal and curricular challenge of providing English language learners with *full* access to the academic core content areas. Anything short of this may result in "watering down" the curriculum, thus denying students the equal education they are legally entitled to (Becijos, 1997; Crawford, 2000; Valdés, 2001).

Bilingual Education

Transitional or Early-Exit Bilingual Education   In **transitional bilingual** classes, students who are not yet proficient in English receive instruction in their native language in all subject areas as well as instruction in English as a second language, but only for a limited number of years (typically two to three), with a gradual transition to all-English instruction. Native-language academic work is provided to keep students on grade level while they are learning English. Such a short-term program offers fewer opportunities to include English speakers, so this is generally a segregated model. The highest priority of most transitional bilingual programs is teaching English, with the goal of mainstreaming students into grade-level classes as soon as possible. In transitional bilingual programs, students have made greater gains than in ESL pullout programs, but students have been much more academically successful in enrichment bilingual programs such as immersion, **two-way,** and developmental or late-exit (Ramírez, Yuen, Ramey, & Pasta, 1991; Thomas & Collier, 1997).

The transitional model has many problems. As with ESL pullout, transitional bilingual classes are generally perceived as a remedial program, a lower track for slow students. Teachers complain that they feel so much pressure to implement all-English instruction that they have to water down the academic content in students' L_1 to have enough time to teach English, which lessens the cognitive complexity of the work in which students engage in either language. Transitional bilingual education is often perceived by staff and students as another form of segregated, compensatory education, which in general has had limited success in raising students' achievement scores. Some researchers and vocal minority groups criticize transitional bilingual instruction as another means of perpetuating the status quo of the society, keeping language-minority students in separate groups that are perceived as having low ability, thus maintaining their lower-class status (Hernández-Chávez, 1977; Kjolseth, 1972; Spener, 1988, Valdés, 2001).

Another major problem with the transitional model is the common misconception that two years is sufficient time to learn a second language for schooling purposes. All research findings in studies following students' long-term success show that the longer students remain in a quality bilingual program, the more they are able to reach academic parity with native English speakers and sustain the gains throughout the remainder of their schooling (Collier, 1992c; Thomas & Collier, 1997). The native English speaker is constantly gaining 10 months of academic growth in one school year. Thus students not yet proficient in English, who initially score very low on the tests in English (typically three or more years below grade level, because they cannot yet demonstrate in L_2 all that they actually know) have to outgain the native speaker by making 15 months' progress on the academic tests in L_2 (one and one-half years' academic growth) with each school year over a six-year period, in order to reach the typical performance level of the constantly advancing native English speaker. When students are allowed to keep up to grade level in academic work in their primary language for more than two to three years, they are able to demonstrate with each succeeding year that they are making more gains than the native English speaker and thus closing the "gap" in achievement as measured by tests in English. After five to six years of quality bilingual schooling, students are able to demonstrate their deep knowledge on the school tests in English as well as in their native language, achieving on or above grade level (Thomas & Collier, 1997).

Transitional bilingual education has generally been the main model for bilingual schooling implemented in the United States during the 1970s and 1980s. This model has been most widely supported by federal and state funding. Spener (1988) points out that this may be purposeful:

> If U.S. society needs to recruit and prepare new candidates for a growing number of low-status, poorly compensated slots in the opportunity structure, transitional bilingual education programs for non-English-speaking

immigrants may be construed by the majority as part of a "reasonable" set of educational policies for the nation. . . . Educational policy can serve to reinforce caste distinctions in the society by providing, more or less intentionally, non-White people with an inferior education. In doing so, the educational system plays a role in creating a pool of adults who are "qualified" to be economically exploited, unemployed, or underemployed. (p. 148)

Many researchers, including Spener, have found that enrichment models of bilingual schooling are much more effective for students' long-term academic success. The remaining models of bilingual schooling to be discussed below are all considered to be enrichment, additive models.

Maintenance or Late-Exit or Developmental Bilingual Education   The maintenance model, now generally referred to as developmental bilingual education, places less emphasis on exiting students from the bilingual program as soon as possible. Students in bilingual classes receive content-area instruction in both languages throughout their schooling, or for as many grades as the school system can provide. The large majority of maintenance bilingual programs implemented throughout the United States in the 1970s and 1980s were for grades K through 5 or K through 6, with no continuation at the middle school or high school level. For this reason, David Ramírez coined the term *late-exit* to refer to programs that were first developed as a transitional bilingual model but were able to continue L_1 support through the end of the elementary school years. In a longitudinal study comparing structured immersion, early-exit bilingual education, and late-exit bilingual education, Ramírez found that students in the late-exit bilingual classes were the only ones reaching parity with native speakers on standardized tests in English (Ramírez, Yuen, Ramey, & Pasta, 1991). Other studies of maintenance or late-exit or developmental bilingual education have shown that high academic achievement can be demonstrated on tests in the second language after four to six years of bilingual schooling (Collier, 1992c; Cummins, 1996b; Thomas & Collier, 1997).

Ideally, maintenance or developmental bilingual education would include classes taught through both languages in a curriculum infused with a multicultural perspective for grades K through 12, with continuing dual language offerings at the university level. Realistically, the only way such programs might develop in the United States would be through the demands of English-speaking parents whose children attend two-way bilingual classes. Politically, the term *maintenance* prompted a flurry of political controversy back in the 1970s over how federal money should be spent, with some concern raised that native-language maintenance was not the task of the federal government (Epstein, 1977). However, maintenance bilingual education supported at the local level has become an issue of great political and economic significance for local communities that wish to maintain their cultural and linguistic heritage, and it has created new pride and dramatic improvement in achievement in some bilingual Navajo schools in the Southwest (Cantoni, 1996; Reyhner, 1986). To avoid the politics associated with the term, most programs have shifted from the term *maintenance* to *developmental*. Another form of developmental bilingual education is dual-language or bilingual immersion, to be described next.

Bilingual Immersion, Two-Way Bilingual, or Dual-Language Education

The **immersion model** was originally developed in Canada in the 1960s for majority language students to receive their schooling through both French and English from K through 12. The term *early total immersion* is used to refer to the initial immersion experience, in which 90 percent of the school day is in the *minority* language (the language less supported by the broader society), for kindergarten and first grade. Following the introduction of literacy and math through the minority language in grades K through 1, the majority language is introduced into the curriculum in grade 2 or 3, and time spent using the majority language gradually increases until the curriculum is taught equally through both languages by grade 4 or 5. This model, called the 90–10 model in the United States, is becoming increasingly popular for two-way programs, especially in California and now in Texas. For the English speakers it is a **bilingual immersion program,** emphasizing the minority language first, and for the language minority students it is a bilingual maintenance model, emphasizing their primary language first for literacy and academic development. Both groups stay together in this model throughout the school day and serve as peer tutors for each other. In research studies on this model, in both Canada and the United States, academic achievement is very high for all groups of students participating in the program, when compared to comparable groups receiving schooling only through English (Cummins & Swain, 1986; Dolson & Lindholm, 1995; Genesee, 1987; Lindholm, 1990; Lindholm & Aclan, 1991; Lindholm & Molina, 1998, 2000). The Case Studies schools in California followed this model with great success. (For a detailed description of the Case Studies schools, see Crawford, 1999).

Another form of dual-language programs that works well is the 50–50 model, in which half of the instructional time is in English and half of the instructional time is in the minority language for grades K through 12. In both the 90–10 and the 50–50 models, maintaining separation of languages is an important principle, and the appropriate percentage of instruction in each language is carefully planned. Lessons are never repeated or translated in the second language, but concepts taught in one language are reinforced across the two languages in a spiraling curriculum. Teachers might alternate the language of instruction by theme or subject area, by time of day, by day of the week, or by the week. If two teachers are teaming, each teacher represents one language. Two teachers would share and exchange two classes. This is a mainstream bilingual model and can be the most cost-effective of all models, if the same pupil-teacher ratio is followed as the desired pupil-teacher ratio for the whole school system.

The term *developmental bilingual education* was first introduced in the United States in the 1984 Title VII federal legislation as another way to describe this type of enrichment program, which is designed for both language minority students and native English speakers. This term emphasizes the linguistic, cognitive, and academic developmental processes in both L_1 and L_2 that are ongoing throughout the school years in a developmental, or dual-language, or two-way bilingual immersion program. All of these names are used for the same enrichment model. These enrichment bilingual programs are immensely successful in promoting all students' long-term academic achievement (Thomas & Collier, 1997).

As stated earlier, Stern (1963) coined the term *two-way* to differentiate between one language group being schooled bilingually ("one-way" bilingual education) and two language groups being schooled bilingually through each other's languages ("two-way" bilingual education). Two-way bilingual programs integrate language minority and language majority students in a school setting that promotes full bilingual proficiency and high academic achievement for both groups of students. "By uniting these two groups of students, two-way bilingual programs help to expand our nation's overall language competence by conserving and enhancing the language resources that minority students bring to school with them and promoting the learning of other languages by English speakers" (Christian, 1994, p. 3). Criteria for success in two-way bilingual education include a minimum of four to six years of bilingual instruction, focus on the core academic curriculum, quality language arts instruction in both languages, separation of the two languages for instruction, use of the non-English language for at least 50 percent of the instructional time (to a maximum of 90 percent in the early grades), an additive bilingual environment that has full support of school administrators, a balanced ratio of students who speak each language (e.g., 50 to 50 or 60 to 40, preferably not to go below 70 to 30), promotion of positive interdependence among peers and between teachers and students, high-quality instructional personnel, and active parent-school partnerships (Lindholm, 1990). Two-way programs are growing in number and in the diversity of languages taught (Christian & Whitcher, 1995). This is a promising enrichment model for bilingual schooling, and an effective way of promoting school reform (Cloud, Genesee, & Hamayan, 2000; Dolson & Lindholm, 1995; Lindholm & Aclan, 1991; Lindholm & Molina, 1998, 2000; Lindholm-Leary, 2001; Thomas & Collier, 1997).

Leading School Reform at the Local Level

With the current school climate focused on restructuring, realigning curricula, school improvement, and systemic reform as described at the beginning of this chapter, educators are continually redefining the changes that need to be made in schools. The challenge is to stimulate policy changes at all levels: innovating in school leadership, recruiting qualified bilingual/ESL teachers, continuing professional development, developing challenging bilingual/bicultural materials across the curriculum, and developing authentic assessment measures for the classroom and program evaluation measures that provide students access to future educational opportunities. We bilingual/ESL educators are part of this educational transformation. We have pointed out the inequities in student achievement and the need for major changes in U.S. schools. Now it is crucial that we lead our schools, joining in collaboration with all educators to create a more equitable, safe, and meaningful learning environment for all students. The chapters of this book that follow provide a thorough, comprehensive, research-based guide to effective educational practices that will lead culturally and linguistically diverse students, as well as all students, to high academic achievement.

Summary

The history of language minority education over the last two centuries has been contradictory. While the 18th and 19th Centuries were marked by a general tolerance toward the use of immigrant languages for instruction in both private and public schooling, growing anti-immigrant sentiments and subsequent restrictive immigration legislation in the 20th Century resulted in widespread "Americanization" efforts and English only instruction as a national policy. American Indian students endured a repressive education in boarding schools located far from their families and homes. The result of this historical pattern was a severe loss of cultural and linguistic resources among immigrant and indigenous groups alike.

Although the federal government increasingly acknowledged the growing need for linguistically competent military and civilian personal, especially during World War II and the Cold War, it has never fully accepted the linguistic resources that new immigrants bring to our country. Most immigrant students still receive their education in English only, with some instruction in English as a second language. If bilingual education is available, it typically is transitional, designed as remedial instruction for only two or three years, after which students are expected to continue their education in English only. Unfortunately, reauthorizations of the federal Bilingual Education Act since 1968 have not addressed this contradiction. While early Title VII legislation was characterized by its promotion of compensatory, deficit models of bilingual education, the 1994 reauthorization encouraged the development of bilingualism and biliteracy. The most recent authorization of the BEA, renamed Title III, Language Instruction for Limited English Proficient and Immigrant Students, returns to a pedagogical emphasis on English acquisition and achievement in English, not the development of bilingualism and biliteracy.

Key Terms

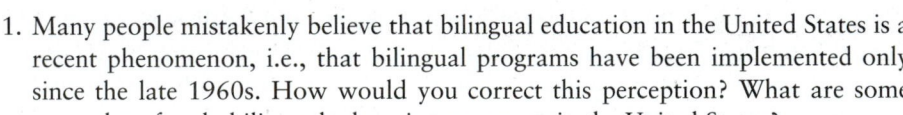

Bilingual Education Act of 1968 p. 43

Title VII of the Elementary and Secondary Education Act p. 43

National Defense Education of 1958 p. 53

English as a second language (ESL) p. 54

Submersion p. 54

Title VI of the Civil Rights Act of 1964 p. 56

Reauthorization p. 57

Development or maintenance bilingual education p. 59

U. S. Office for Civil Rights (OCR) p. 63

Lau Remedies p. 63

Lau plans p. 65

Lau regulations p. 65

Equal Educational Opportunities Act of 1974 p. 66

English as a second language (ESL) p. 73

Structured English immersion p. 76

Transitional bilingual education (early-exit bilingual education) p. 76

Immersion model p. 79

Two-way, dual-language, or bilingual immersion education p. 79

Reflection Questions

1. Many people mistakenly believe that bilingual education in the United States is a recent phenomenon, i.e., that bilingual programs have been implemented only since the late 1960s. How would you correct this perception? What are some examples of early bilingual education programs in the United States?
2. The U.S. Supreme Court's decision in *Lau* v. *Nichols* (1974) is considered to be among the strongest federal endorsements of the right of English language learners to a "meaningful" and equal education. Why did the Court rule that Chinese students in San Francisco were receiving an "unequal" education? In other words, why might an education provided on "equal terms" (the standard in *Brown* v. *the Board of Education*), in fact, not be equal? Did the Supreme Court's decision in *Lau* make bilingual education mandatory across the nation?
3. Currently, the federal government uses the three-part "*Castañeda* Test" to determine school district compliance with federal civil rights laws. What might trigger this test? How does the test work?

4. Trace the development of the Bilingual Education Act since 1968. How has the legislation changed over each subsequent reauthorization? What were some of the political forces that influenced these reauthorizations?

Resources

Bilingual Education Policy and Practice

Crawford, J. *Bilingual education: History, politics, theory, and practice.* 4th Edition. Los, Angeles, CA: Bilingual Education Resources, Inc., 1999.
- An excellent introduction to bilingual education for both graduate and undergraduate students. The book covers the early and present history of bilingual education in the United States, including an extensive discussion of federal bilingual education policy and the reauthorization of the Bilingual Education Act.

Crawford, J. *At war with diversity: U.S. language policy in an age of anxiety.* Clevedon, England: Multilingual Matters, 2000.
- This book features a collection of essays written by one of the country's leading experts in language policy, and bilingual education. These essays analyze the prominence of English only activism in U.S. politics, sources of the current antibilingual education efforts, as well as the impact of those efforts on education policy. The book also explores efforts to resist the English only trend, including projects to revitalize American Indian languages.

Freeman, R. D. *Bilingual education and social change.* Clevedon, England: Multilingual Matters, 1998.
- This book provides a general introduction to bilingualism, bilingual education, and minority education in the United States. It also contains an ethnographic/discourse analytic study of how one "successful" dual-language program challenges mainstream U.S. educational programs that discriminate against minority students and the languages they speak. Implications for research practice and practice in other school and community contexts are emphasized.

García, O., & Baker, C., eds. *Policy and practice in bilingual education: Extending the foundations.* Clevedon, England: Multilingual Matters, 1995.
- An excellent collection of articles on policy and practice in bilingual education around the world, focusing on the United States. The articles are organized under four broad categories: policy and legislation on bilingualism in schools and bilingual education; implementation of bilingual policy in schools: structuring schools; using bilingualism in instruction: structuring classrooms; using the bilingualism of the school community: teachers and parents.

Kloss, H. *The American bilingual tradition.* 2nd edition. McHenry, IL: Delta Systems, 1998.

- This second edition of *The American Bilingual Tradition* contributes to the current debate over bilingualism and language diversity in the United States. Written by an eminent European language historian, it challenges widespread myths about alleged differences between recent immigrants to the United States and those of past generations. The authors provide a thorough analysis of the evolution of federal, state, and territorial language policies and of the general historical climate toward language minorities in the United States.

Piatt, B. *¿Only English?: Law and language policy in the United States.* Albuquerque: University of New Mexico Press, 1990.

- The book provides a theoretical and legal discussion about the notion of "language rights" in different domains: the classroom, the workplace, the courtroom, social service agencies, and broadcasting. The author concludes with a legal and moral plea for the need to recognize both individual and group rights to language.

Ricento, T., & Burnaby, B. *Language and politics in the United States and Canada.* Mahwah, NJ: Lawrence Erlbaum Associates, 1998.

- This volume critically analyzes and explains the goals, processes, and effects of language policies in the United States and Canada from historical and contemporary perspectives. It explores parallel and divergent developments in language policy and language rights in the two countries, especially in the past four decades as a basis for reflection on what can be learned from one country's experience by the other.

Endnotes

1. After signing the measure into law in 1987, then-governor Bill Clinton insisted that the legislature add a proviso: "This section shall not prohibit the public schools from performing their duty to provide equal educational opportunities to all children." Nevertheless, bilingual education remains illegal in Arkansas under another state law (§6–16–104), which authorizes a fine of up to $25 a day for teachers who use a language other than English for instruction.
2. While we have chosen throughout this book to avoid use of the phrase *limited-English-proficient students* wherever possible because of the pejorative connotation associated with the word *limited* and its acronym *LEP,* throughout most of this chapter we shall use *limited-English-proficient students* and *LEP* because we are referring to the official term used in government documents, court cases, and federal and state legislation. In general, the acronyms LEP and LM/LEP (language minority/limited-English-proficient students) are still the most common terms used in most U.S. federal and state policy documents.
3. In this book, we use the term *American Indian* to refer to all indigenous groups descended from the original inhabitants, prior to the Europeans'

arrival, of the land defined by current U.S. political boundaries. While the U.S. government uses the term *Native American,* (to avoid the misnomer originally created by Christopher Columbus who thought he had discovered the water route to India), the term *American Indian* is still preferred by most indigenous groups of American Indian heritage. Our use of the term *American Indian* is not to be confused with the descendants of those who have emigrated to the United States from the country of India in South Asia.

4. Throughout this book, wherever possible, we have substituted the term *grade-level* for *mainstream,* to use terminology introduced by Enright and McCloskey (1988) that has fewer negative associations in our field. However, we continue to use the term *mainstream* in this chapter when policy documents use this term, or when we wish to emphasize the contrast between the curricular mainstream and separate bilingual and ESL classes that are not taught on grade level during the portion of the day that is taught through the second language.

5. In the state of Arizona, for example, ESL pullout is even illegal. The consent decree in a recent federal court decision, *Flores v. Arizona,* requires that English language development be combined with content area instruction for all English language learners in the state.

Teaching

Then said a teacher, Speak to us of Teaching.

And he said:

No man can reveal to you aught but that which already lies half asleep in the dawning of your knowledge.

The teacher who walks in the shadow of the temple, among his followers, gives not of his wisdom but rather of his faith and his lovingness.

If he is indeed wise he does not bid you enter the house of his wisdom, but rather leads you to the threshold of your own mind.

—*Kahlil Gibran*, The Prophet.

Do you tend to see your students as empty vessels to be filled by you? Do you tap into the student's lived experiences to anchor your classroom activities? Do you tend to see other people's children as your own and see yourself in their futures? Do you tend to see your students as being "at risk"? Do you identify with Kahlil Gibran's words? What motivates you to be in the classroom? When do special moments happen? Which experiences excite you? Teaching, we all agree, is about making a difference in our students' lives. And we know we do make a difference in many different ways, but teaching decisions are often hard, and in the spontaneous energy of a classroom full of humans, we have to respond to the moment and hope our decisions are good ones. As new teachers, we sometimes feel overwhelmed with the responsibilities we are given. Experience helps, but as we build up a repertoire of teaching strategies, we can also become stale, bored, perhaps out of touch. Those of us who are experienced teachers often need to renew the energy from our imaginative preteaching days by discovering new instructional strategies that work, as well as exploring new knowledge with our students. We teachers today must reflect on our teaching for professional growth, renewal, and insights into the teaching process. This chapter presents current research on variations in instructional teaching styles that are especially important to consider when working with language minority students.

Portrait of a Traditional Classroom

Desks in rows facing the front, students quietly take notes as the teacher lectures, using the blackboard at the front of the room. Students are instructed to open their textbooks to read a section and answer the questions connected to what the teacher has just presented. Perhaps the teacher passes out worksheets to expand the points made. Students practice rote learning through memorization and recall of facts. The teacher makes every classroom decision. Students raise their hands to be called on, and the teacher chooses who gets to speak, one at a time. Students do not leave their desks unless given special permission by the teacher.

Worldwide, most classrooms still function in this way, especially in high schools and universities. Teachers who were schooled under this system of teaching prefer the convenience of sequenced textbook lessons that require little effort in lesson planning on the teacher's part, and strict teacher control of the class. Knowledge transmission is the goal of these classes, based on an assembly line, factory model from the industrial age of the 19th and early 20th centuries. Why, then, if it is so easy to teach this way, are current teacher educators pushing for major changes in teaching styles? What is motivating us to try to change the way that schools facilitate learning?

The Workplace of the 21st Century

Among the many changes taking place in the transformation from an industrial age to an information-driven, technological age is the demand for a well-educated workforce. But "well educated" is defined differently in the professional world of today than it was a century ago. In the past, the number of years of schooling a student completed implied that student's mastery of a given body of knowledge. But today the knowledge explosion is overwhelming in all fields of study. Students stay in school longer and longer, as the expected credentials for many jobs are being expanded. Yet when a degree is completed, graduates know that they still have much to learn. Since it is no longer possible for students to master everything there is to know in their given field during their formal studies, and since new knowledge will continue to transform the basic knowledge base, it is essential that students learn how to get access to all sources of knowledge.

This means that we can no longer rely on the traditional classroom to provide the learning context needed for student inquiry. The knowledge explosion occurring in all fields requires access to greatly varied technology and print sources, as well as developing a different way to approach the learning process, through active, inquiry-based learning. The workplace of today, from low- to high-income professions, requires extensive collaboration with other employees and workers' willingness to expand their own professional development through implementing new uses of technology, developing new roles in the workplace, and tackling new problems to be solved.

Students need extensive experience with collaborative knowledge gathering and problem solving for reasons beyond preparation for the workplace, however. Research and theory from cognitive psychology have led us to a new view of the learning process itself. Today we view learning as "a highly interactive process of constructing personal meaning from the information available in a learning situation and then integrating that information with what we already know to create new knowledge" (Marzano, 1992, p. 5). We shall explore this new perspective on learning after a glimpse at some less helpful practices in bilingual and ESL classes.

Passive Learning

In 1991, a large congressionally mandated longitudinal study was completed to assess the relative effectiveness of three types of programs for language-minority students (Ramírez, Yuen, Ramey, & Pasta, 1991). One of the many findings of the study focused on the type of teaching style found in ESL and bilingual classrooms. Classroom observational data, collected from 1984 to

1989 among 51 elementary schools and 554 classrooms in nine school districts and five states (California, Florida, New Jersey, New York, and Texas), revealed a preponderance of bilingual and ESL classrooms that were teacher dominated, where students were treated as passive learners and were assigned only cognitively simple tasks.

Without exception, across grade levels, . . . teachers do most of the talking. . . . Students produce language only when they are working directly with a teacher, and then only in response to teacher initiations. In over half of the interactions that teachers have with students, students do not produce any language (i.e., using nonverbal responses such as listening, gesturing, etc.). When students do respond, typically they are providing simple information recall. Rather than being provided with the opportunity to generate original statements, students are asked to provide simple discrete close-ended or patterned responses. Not only does this pattern of teacher/student interaction limit a student's opportunity to create and manipulate language freely, but it also limits the student's ability to engage in more complex learning. . . . In summary, teachers do not teach language or higher order cognitive skills effectively. Teachers in all three programs offer a **passive learning** environment, limiting student opportunities to produce language and to develop more complex language and conceptual skills. (Ramírez, Yuen, Ramey, & Pasta, 1991, pp. 421–22)

But this pattern is not unique to bilingual and ESL classrooms. Other large-scale studies of U.S. education have found the same phenomenon prevalent across many classrooms of all grade levels (Goodlad, 1984; National Coalition of Advocates for Students, 1991; Oakes, 1985; Porter, 1989; Sirotnik, 1983). If passive classrooms are still common practice, how do education researchers and school reformers characterize active learning, our goal in U.S. education reform?

Active, Inquiry-Based Learning

Students actively engaged in solving a problem, discovering new ways of perceiving their world, intensely applying learning strategies to the next task, developing family-like community among classmates, sharing the excitement of a special discovery—these glimpses of invigorating, deep learning occur naturally in a classroom that promotes active learning.

An **active learning** environment requires students and teacher to commit to a dynamic partnership in which both share a vision of and responsibility for instruction. In such an environment, students learn content, develop conceptual knowledge, and acquire language through a discovery-oriented approach to learning in which the learner is not only engaged in the activity but also with the goal of the activity. Essential to this approach is the view of the learner as responsible for discovering, constructing, and creating something new, and the view of the teacher as a resource and facilitator. . . . Active learning implies the development of a community of learners . . . and supports opportunities for authentic communication rather than rote language drills. Additionally, integration of the student's home, community, and culture are key elements of the active learning approach. (Fern, Anstrom, & Silcox, 1995, pp. 1–2)

Almost a century ago, John Dewey (1916) spoke passionately of the benefits of discovery learning for all students. Today teacher educators have extended Dewey's vision of active learning as crucial to education in a democratic society, and educational research has demonstrated the power of this instructional approach for the academic success of diverse students of many different backgrounds (Apple & Beane, 1995; Brooks & Brooks, 1993; Harmin, 1994). But while an active learning classroom environment benefits all students, it is even more critical to language-minority students' success.

When examining the length of time that it takes for students who are not yet proficient in English to achieve academically in English at the typical performance level of native English speakers in all content subjects (4 to 12 years or more), it becomes exceedingly clear that we are holding language-minority students back, and therefore increasing the gap between native and non-native English speakers, in passive classrooms emphasizing basic skills approaches to teaching. Research examining language-minority student performance in bilingual, ESL, and grade-level classes taught through collaborative discovery learning using meaningful, cognitively complex, interdisciplinary content has found that active learning accelerates language-minority students' academic growth, leading to eventual high academic performance comparable to or exceeding that of native English speakers (Thomas & Collier, 1997). In this research, based on over 700,000 language minority student records from 1982 to 1996 in five school districts in several regions of the United States, Thomas and Collier found that the major factors that accelerate language-minority students' academic achievement in the second language are cognitively complex on-grade-level academic instruction across the curriculum through students' first and second languages; the use of current approaches to teaching in an interactive, discovery learning environment at school; and a transformed sociocultural context for language minority students' schooling.

Other research on the effectiveness of language minority education suggests the importance of creating a classroom environment that promotes active learning. Such an environment includes cognitive complex lessons, an integrated and thematic curriculum, collaborative learning, and building upon the language-culture-knowledge base that the student brings to the classroom (Au, 1993; Chamot, Dale, O'Malley, & Spanos, 1992; Cummins, 1996b; Dalton & Sison, 1995; García, 1991, 2001; 1994; Goldenberg, 1991; Henderson & Landesman, 1992; Lockwood and Secada, 1999; Moll, 1988a; Ovando, 1994; Ovando & McLaren, 2000; Panfil, 1995; Rivera & Zehler, 1990; Romo, 1999; Rosebery, Warren, & Conant, 1992; Tashakkori & Ochoa, 1999; Tharp & Gallimore, 1988; Thomas, 1994; Valdés, 2001; Valdez Pierce, 1991; Warren & Rosebery, 1995).

Summarizing effective classroom practices for language-minority students, García (2001) suggests that an interactive, student-centered learning context, anchored on the language and culture of the home, plays a major role in the academic and social success of language-minority students (see next page).

Guidelines for Teaching

PRINCIPLES OF EFFECTIVE CLASSROOMS FOR LINGUISTICALLY AND CULTURALLY DIVERSE STUDENTS

- Any curriculum, including one for diverse children, must address all categories of learning goals (cognitive and academic, advanced as well as basic).

- The more linguistically and culturally diverse the children, the more closely teachers must relate academic content to a child's own environment and experience.

- The more diverse the children, the more integrated the curriculum should be. That is, multiple content areas (e.g., math, science, social studies) and language learning activities should be centered around a single theme. Children should have opportunities to study a topic in depth and to apply a variety of skills acquired in home, community, and school contexts.

- The more diverse the children, the greater the need for active rather than passive endeavors, particularly informal social activities such as group projects in which students are allowed flexibility in their participation with the teacher and other students.

- The more diverse the children, the more important it is to offer them opportunities to apply what they are learning in a meaningful context. Curriculum can be made meaningful in a number of creative ways. Science and math skills can be effectively applied, for example, through hands-on, interactive activities that allow students to explore issues of significance in their lives. (García, 1994, p. 275).

Moreover, in identifying ways to address cultural and linguistic diversity in responsive learning communities, García (2001) proposes the following conceptual dimensions for teacher practices:

Guidelines for Teaching

CONCEPTUAL DIMENSIONS OF A RESPONSIVE PEDAGOGY

- Bilingual/bicultural skills and awareness

- High expectations of diverse students

- Treatment of diversity as an asset to the classroom

- Ongoing professional development on issues of cultural and linguistic diversity and practices that are most effective

- Basis of curriculum development to address cultural and linguistic diversity:
  - Attention to and integration of home culture/practices
  - Focus on maximizing student interactions across categories of [native language], Spanish and English proficiency, and academic performance
  - Focus on language development through meaningful interactions and communications

As García notes, in committing to a dynamic partnership with the students, it is crucial that teachers select and apply instructional strategies that acknowledge, respect, and build on the language and culture of the home. Teachers play the most critical role in students' academic success, and students become important partners with teachers in the teaching and learning enterprise (García 2001, p. 153).

Activating Students' Prior Knowledge

An underlying, basic concept of the active, inquiry classroom is that authentic, personally meaningful learning must connect to students' prior knowledge. This crucial principle means that learning in a diverse class incorporates the rich linguistic and cultural life experiences that each student brings to the classroom. Students' diverse experiences growing up are gifts, resources, and a rich knowledge base. Cognitive psychologists' theories are grounded in this basic concept: that we learn by connecting new knowledge to our existing schemata. In second-language learning, we get the "aha" through lots of rich clues to meaning, among the most important clues being those that connect to what we already know.

To activate students' prior knowledge, the teacher must become an active partner in the learning process so that students and teachers are both learners and meaning-makers (Cummins, 1996b; Goodman & Wilde, 1992). Thus students actively participate in choosing the curricular themes that are developed, exploring community knowledge, and creating writings (text) that are generated from exploration of the theme. Visuals, manipulatives, posters, time lines, science experiments, journal writing, rich storybooks, puppets, and many other concrete experiences can activate students' prior knowledge and life experiences. In the sections on art, technology, and music in this chapter, we will explore glimpses of classes that activate students' prior knowledge. **Critical pedagogy** and **accelerated learning**, also to be examined briefly in this chapter, are based on connecting closely to the linguistic and cultural learning context outside of school, bringing community and school into a collaborative, meaningful partnership for authentic inquiry.

Cooperative Learning

Now that we have examined the general definition of active learning and the research base that has found active, discovery learning to be a key ingredient in language-minority students' success in school in the United States, we shall explore the specifics of implementation. **Cooperative learning,** also referred to as collaborative learning in secondary and higher education contexts, is one element in an active learning classroom that is crucial to management of an interactive class. Cooperative learning, as implemented in the United States, generally refers to many varied ways to structure a class in small, heterogeneous student groups (usually of two to six members, with four an ideal size) to accomplish individual or group goals for learning that require cooperation and positive interdependence.

Throughout human history, group learning has been an ancient and honored tradition for passing on the knowledge of the elders from one generation to the next. Over the centuries, humans have used small-group collaboration for most forms of learning, until the 20th century when the numbers of students being formally schooled increased so dramatically that class size led teachers towards knowledge transmission through lecture. Cooperative learning structures have helped teachers return to the most time-honored approach to learning, in a small-group context, even when class size is large.

Research on Cooperative Learning

Today many forms of cooperative learning are practiced in countries around the world (Nunan, 1992; Slavin, 1989). In the United States since the 1970s, cooperative learning has been used to improve cognitive, academic, social, and affective outcomes in classrooms as an alternative to individualistic, competitive structures. The research base for cooperative learning is strong, with hundreds of studies documenting the effectiveness of this instructional approach for teaching diverse student populations (Calderón, 1994; Holt, 1993; Jacob, 1999; Jacob, Rottenberg, Patrick, & Wheeler, 1996; Johnson, Johnson, & Holubec, 1986; Johnson, Johnson, & Smith, 1991; Kagan, 1986, 1992; Kessler, 1992; Slavin, 1988a, 1989, 1990; Slavin, Sharan, Kagan, Hertz-Lazarowitz, Webb, & Schmuck, 1985). Research has found cooperative learning for bilingual students:

> (1) to support interaction and thus the development and use of the first language in ways that support cognitive development and increased second language skills; (2) to increase the frequency and variety of second language practice through different types of interaction; (3) to provide opportunities to integrate language with content instruction; (4) to provide inclusion of a greater variety of curricular materials to stimulate language use as well as concept learning; and (5) to provide opportunities for students to act as resources for each other and thereby assume a more active role in learning (Calderón, Tinajero & Hertz-Lazarowitz, 1992; McGroarty, 1989). (Tinajero, Calderón & Hertz-Lazarowitz, 1993, p. 242)

Students participating in a two-way bilingual program derive even greater benefits from the use of cooperative learning. Because native speakers of each language are present in each cooperative group, these peer teachers stimulate higher levels of linguistic and content accuracy, including interaction at challenging cognitive levels. In addition, "the students' first language acquires high status, and their self-esteem flourishes as they become experts for other students," transforming the bilingual program into an enrichment program. "The bilingual/bicultural cycle enables inclusion of a greater variety of curricular materials, real-life experiences, and authentic literature from diverse cultures," in which "newcomers find that their expertise in language and cultural capital is valued and nurtured" (Calderón, 1994, pp. 96–97).

Principles of Cooperative Learning

When first introduced to cooperative learning, sometimes teachers express skepticism as they try out one or two suggested structures presented in a staff development session. But it is very important to think of cooperative learning as diverse in its definitions, characteristics, and potential uses. The concept is adaptable, flexible, and meant to be used creatively by teachers. As teachers experiment with cooperative learning structures, each class responds differently, and new ideas emerge for implementation (Holt, 1993). Hertz-Lazarowitz and Calderón (1994) present a comprehensive professional development model to train, coach, and provide follow-up support systems for teachers implementing cooperative learning.

Keeping in mind the adaptability of varied approaches to cooperative learning, we present a few guidelines from some of the key thinkers in the field. David and Roger Johnson, teacher educators who helped to initiate the current movement towards use of cooperative learning in the United States:

Guidelines for Teaching

FIVE ELEMENTS OF COOPERATIVE LEARNING

1. Positive interdependence, a sense of working together for a common goal and caring about each other's learning.

2. Individual accountability, whereby every team member feels in charge of their own and their teammates' learning and makes an active contribution to the group. Thus there is no "hitchhiking" or "freeloading" for anyone on a team—everyone pulls their weight.

3. Abundant verbal, face-to-face interaction, where learners explain, argue, elaborate, and link current material with what they have learned previously.

4. Sufficient social skills, involving explicit teaching of appropriate leadership, communication, trust, and conflict resolution skills so that the team can function effectively.

5. Team reflection, whereby the teams periodically assess what they have learned, how well they are working together and how they might do better as a learning team. (Kohonen, 1992, p. 35)

Working from these principles, Kagan (1992) has collected a wide variety of teaching strategies that help teachers experiment with cooperative learning, including structures that focus on building team and class social skills, structures that assist with academic information sharing and content mastery, and structures that build communication and thinking skills. Most of Kagan's key concepts focus on practical advice to teachers for implementation strategies that are crucial to classroom management. Kessler (1992) provides another excellent teacher reference for bilingual/ESL teachers on the use of cooperative learning in teaching L_1 and L_2 through mathematics, science, and social studies, as well as language and cognitive development. The following sections review a few teaching decisions to consider when first implementing cooperative learning.

Forming Teams

Heterogeneous student teams are very important for students' academic and social development; this idea is a fundamental concept for many cooperative learning specialists. The rationale for diversity within one team is that heterogeneity maximizes the possibilities for peer tutoring and improves intercultural communication across groups. Generally in cooperative learning, teachers assign students to teams by mixing students by gender, ethnicity, language proficiency, and academic achievement. If students select their own teammates, status hierarchies persist. If random selection is used, teachers run the risk of creating "loser" teams. Yet there is no prescriptive rule to follow for assigning students to teams. Sometimes students' self-selection of team members can serve a purpose in one lesson; random selection is occasionally meaningful; and homogeneous groupings can serve an important purpose for language-minority students. Thus the overall guide for teachers is to use great variety, to change team members so that the same group of students does not work together for weeks, and to change team formation patterns (Kagan & McGroarty, 1993; Kohonen, 1992).

A special issue when working with language-minority students is to balance homogeneity with heterogeneity in team formation. This is a complex issue that must be carefully planned, depending upon the goals and instructional objectives for each group of students. During the academic portion of the day when subjects are taught in students' primary languages, students may be grouped homogeneously by language. Likewise, beginning ESL students need times when specialized ESL through content lessons are tailored to their proficiency level. Thus homogeneous groupings may be very important for language-minority students at times during the instructional day (Kagan & McGroarty, 1993). Yet without access to native English-speaking peers for some portion of the school day, language-minority students can get stuck in low-status tracks that do not lead to academic success. In two-way bilingual programs, homogeneous student groupings are not often needed, since peer tutoring is a crucial component of this model for academic work in two languages. Again, flexibility and variety in cooperative learning teams, classroom structures, and program designs are an important part of teacher decisions in lesson planning.

Structuring Team Activities

Many details of a cooperative learning activity need to be carefully planned ahead of time, more than can be included in this short review. Among the decisions that a teacher needs to make (some of which should be decided democratically with students) are the physical arrangements, role assignments for team members, group procedures that will promote interaction, rules for group work, and systems for managing movement and noise in the classroom (Goor & Schwenn, 1993). Possible role assignments (to be rotated among team members) might include quiet captains, timekeepers, materials monitors, praisers and cheerleaders, equalizers and encouragers (to encourage less involved students to contribute and to motivate the team when it gets bogged down), recorders (to write down each significant group decision), presenters (to share group findings with the class), coaches (to facilitate peer assistance), task masters (to help the group start and stay on task), reflectors (to reflect back to the group how well they worked together), and question commanders (to help answer or redirect team questions before calling on the teacher for help) (Goor & Schwenn, 1993; Kagan, 1992, Chapter 14, pp. 10–12). Other suggested role assignments that are especially helpful for English language learners are checkers (to check for preparation, completeness, agreement, or understanding among teammates), and bilingual facilitators (negotiating meaning and understanding through both L_1 and L_2 as needed) (Kagan & McGroarty, 1993). For other details of classroom management, it is very helpful to refer to references on cooperative learning, such as Holt (1993), Kagan (1992), and Kessler (1992).

Team and Class Building

Kagan emphasizes the importance of activities that "help students get to know each other, build a positive sense of team identity, accept individual differences, provide mutual support, and develop a sense of synergy" (Kagan & McGroarty, 1993, p. 59). These are especially important for students who have had little previous experience with group work, including recent arrivals from other countries. Many of the team and class building activities proposed in Kagan (1992) and Kessler (1992) assist with language and content acquisition and involve negotiation of meaningful topics. These activities help to develop a supportive, safe, trusting classroom environment that builds students' self-esteem and willingness to participate.

An important caution must be mentioned here. Newcomers recently arrived from other countries may initially experience negative feelings towards cooperative learning. Negative reactions may include counterproductive behavior by students and parental feelings that teachers are not doing their job when students are asked to teach one another and to pursue discovery learning (Saville-Troike & Kleifgen, 1986). Students who have been taught from a knowledge-transmission perspective may initially perceive cooperative groups as play rather than learning and feel that the teacher does not have control of the class. With patience and the assistance of students (peer teachers) in the class who understand and value cooperative learning, along with bilingual staff and parents who can provide support to new parents, new arrivals can gradually come to perceive and value the class process as one in which deep learning is taking place.

Structures for Learning

To provide one example of the difference between competitive and cooperative classroom structures in teacher training sessions, Kagan demonstrates a common competitive structure "Whole-Class Question-Answer" and contrasts it with the simple cooperative structure "Numbered Heads Together." In the competitive structure, the teacher asks a question, and students who wish to respond raise their hands. The teacher calls on one student, who attempts to state the correct answer.

In this arrangement, students vie for the teacher's attention and praise, creating negative interdependence among them. In other words, when the teacher calls on one student, the others lose their chance to answer; a failure by one student to give a correct response increases the chances for other students to receive attention and praise. Thus, students are set against each other, creating poor social relations and establishing peer norms against achievement. (Kagan, 1993, p. 10)

In contrast, Numbered Heads Together uses the following strategy to call on students. At the beginning of the lesson, students number off within each group of four, remembering their assigned numbers. When the teacher asks a question, students put their heads together in their groups and discuss the answer, making sure every team member understands the answer. The teacher then calls a number (1, 2, 3, or 4) and students with that number raise their hands to respond.

Positive interdependence is built into the structure; if any student knows the answer, the ability of each student is increased. Individual accountability is also built in; all the helping is confined to the heads-together step. Students know that once a number is called, each student is on his or her own. The high achievers share answers because they know their number might not be called, and they want their team to do well. The lower achievers listen carefully because they know their number might be called. Numbered Heads Together is quite a contrast to Whole-Class Question-Answer in which only the high achievers need participate and the low achievers can (and often do) tune out. (Kagan, 1993, pp. 10–11)

A teacher can use this simple example of a cooperative learning structure to check for comprehension and emphasize key concepts. But overuse of Numbered Heads Together and other structures of the same type could lead to student learning that emphasizes low-level knowledge recall with little higher-order cognitive development. Thus it is important for teachers to use a wide range of cooperative learning structures that lead to deep academic, cognitive, and linguistic development. Other types of structures Kagan (1992) presents in great detail include structures for communication building, mastery of content, and concept development.

Jigsaw, originally developed by Elliot Aronson and his colleagues (Aronson, Blaney, Stephan, Sikes, & Snapp, 1978), is a good example of a strategy for peer exploration of readings, with many variations and uses for heterogeneous classes. Using Jigsaw for second-language classes taught through content is demonstrated in Coelho (1992). Other structures focus on peer learning of a given body of knowledge, including structures developed by Robert Slavin and his colleagues, such as Student Teams Achievement Division and Teams-Games Tournaments, Team-Assisted Individualization, and Cooperative Integrated Reading and Composition (Slavin, 1989). Many structures work on developing students' thinking skills, such as Think-Pair-Share and the use of Venn diagrams (Kagan, 1992). Cooperative project designs include such strategies as Group Investigation, developed by Shlomo Sharan (Sharan & Sharan, 1976), and Co-op Co-op, developed by Spencer Kagan to eliminate between-team competition and emphasize expressive, probing, problem solving (1992).

Evaluating Student Outcomes

Decisions need to be made regarding assessment that include evaluation of group processes, individual student accountability, and team accountability. Students' monitoring of their own learning process as well as their group's achievements, can be structured into the activities (Goor & Schwenn, 1993). Classes should set team goals that encourage cooperation across teams, rather than competition between teams. Individual student testing is an important part of assessment within a cooperative learning classroom, but tests should be authentic and meaningful, connected to the goals of class work within teams. Many cooperative learning structures include ways to assess individual student and team achievement.

Coaching Teacher Colleagues

Cooperative learning is not easily implemented after only one staff development session. Once teachers make a commitment to try cooperative learning strategies, they need extensive collegial support. School administrators need to build in ongoing staff development training, attend the sessions with teachers to serve as mentors and facilitators, provide plenty of opportunities for collegial coaching and teaming across classrooms, allow time for teacher growth and experimentation, avoid fast and simple solutions, and have a focused vision and mission for the school (Hertz-Lazarowitz & Calderón, 1994). The same principles of cooperative learning for students apply to collaborative teaching. Holt's summary on cooperative learning is a fitting statement to close this section:

> Cooperative learning has become popular for many reasons. It adds variety to the teacher's repertoire. It helps teachers manage large classes of students with diverse needs. It improves academic achievement and social development. It prepares students for increasingly interactive workplaces. However,

one of its most powerful, long-lasting effects may be in making school a more humane place to be by giving students stable, supportive environments for learning. (Holt, 1993, p. 8)

Accelerated Learning

Now we are ready to explore another aspect of active learning. Cooperative learning provides a system for dynamic partnership in the learning process. But if the curricular content presented to students is frequently low in cognitive demand, an interactive class can still be deadly. How can we assure language-minority learners' engagement in discovery learning, enabling our students to make the leaps needed to achieve academic success with each succeeding year of schooling?

We are adopting the term *accelerated learning* as symbolic of cognitively complex, discovery learning. In the next section we will combine this concept with a crucial additional dimension from language-minority educators who understand the importance of critical pedagogy and empowerment. Henry Levin (1987, 1988; Levin & Hopfenberg, 1991; Hopfenberg, Levin & Associates, 1993) has developed a model for accelerated schools and applied it to a substantial number of schools with culturally and linguistically diverse student populations. The model helps schools with high concentrations of "at-risk" students to change their governance structure and to implement an inquiry curriculum that incorporates community funds of knowledge, so that parents, teachers, students, administrators, and the community take responsibility for turning the school into a high-achieving school. Remedial classes and pullout programs have been found to slow down learning. Accelerated schools focus on enrichment rather than remediation, building on the strengths that all children bring to the classroom as well as the community knowledge and resources that are often untapped (Rothman, 1991).

Levin describes his work in the 1980s examining school practices with so-called at-risk students, in which he conducted research syntheses, visited schools around the country, and interviewed members of school communities at local, state, and federal levels:

> ⊠ *I came to a startling conclusion: The inevitable consequences of existing educational practices used with students in at-risk situations actually undermined the future success of these students. Even though these students started school behind other students in academic skills, they were placed in instructional situations that slowed down their progress. They were stigmatized as remedial students or slow learners and assigned boring and repetitive exercises on worksheets. . . . School districts, with the support of the publishers, had saddled schools with "teacher-proof" approaches that consisted of low-level textbooks in combination with student workbooks full of dull and tedious exercises. Rarely did I see opportunities for problem solving, enrichment, or applications of knowledge that drew upon student experiences and interests.*
>
> *To me the solution seemed obvious: Instead of slowing down these students . . . we needed to accelerate their progress. . . . Finally, I found the appropriate learning approach in the*

enrichment strategies used for gifted and talented students—the design of creative approaches
that build on strengths . . . . Accelerated school staff and parents use a pedagogy constructed on
the strengths and cultures of the children (and indeed all members of the school community),
with a heavy reliance on relevant applications, problem solving, and active, "hands-on" learning
approaches as well as an emphasis on thematic learning that integrates a variety of subjects
into a common set of themes. Finally, parental involvement both at home and school is central to
the success of an accelerated school. (Hopfenberg, Levin & Associates, 1993, pp. xii–xiv)

The perspective, still dominant in many U.S. classrooms, that we need to teach basic skills before students can move into more cognitively complex work is no longer supported by most current research. Educators have experimented with honors classes, enrichment programs, magnet bilingual schools, and other forms of accelerated learning for minority students, in which the *social perception* of schooling is changed—not the students. Our students have the potential giftedness that sensitive teachers can tap, if we can provide the learning context that allows all students to flourish. Examples from accelerated bilingual schools in California and Texas are provided in Hopfenberg, Levin & Associates (1993) and Calderón and Carreón (1994).

Critical Pedagogy

To probe deeper into how and why cognitively complex lessons work best for the beginning ESL student and the young bilingual learner as well as students of all social classes, ages, and special needs, analyses from **critical pedagogy** provide important insights. Paulo Freire (1970, 1973) warned educators over two decades ago that we need to get away from stultifying, boring, debilitating curricula that have no meaning in students' lives. Cummins (1989a) portrays how little we have changed in the two decades since Freire's original work:

> Unfortunately, the reality is that schools continue to promote rote memorization rather than **critical thinking** and encourage consumption of predetermined knowledge rather than generation of original ideas; the curriculum has been sanitized such that students rarely have the opportunity to discuss critically or write about issues that directly affect the society they will form. Issues such as racism, environmental pollution, U.S. policy in Central America, genetic engineering, global nuclear destruction, arms control, and so on, are regarded as too "sensitive" for fragile and impressionable young minds. Instead, students are fed a neutralized diet of social studies, science, and language arts that is largely irrelevant to the enormous global problems that our generation is creating for our children's generation to resolve. (pp. 5–6)

When we do introduce thematic units that tackle tough issues connected to students' life experiences, students quickly become deeply engaged in the learning process. An imaginative teacher can explore burning questions with no clear answers with students. Together they can choose a unit that has meaning in students' lives, and pursue a deeper knowledge base, all with class members collecting many different sources of information, developing research skills, analyzing, evaluating, actively collaborating, and working on solving problems while tolerating the ambiguity that is a part of all deep knowledge gathering.

Critical pedagogy involves problem posing, reflective thinking, knowledge gathering, and collaborative decision making. It helps students and teachers find and express their voice, in oral and written form (Torres-Guzmán, 1993). Three teachers explain it this way: "Students recognizing that they are the protagonists in the story of their own lives, and feeling adequately empowered to act upon this knowledge, has become paramount to our vision of education" (Adkins, Fleming, & Saxena, 1995, p. 202). Critical pedagogy also involves teacher risk taking by exploring new knowledge and being open to new ways of perceiving the world, including thinking about ways to transform power relations that exist within and outside schools. A bilingual high school teacher speaks out passionately for change in school curriculum and school structures:

 Critical pedagogy has become a way of learning and living for my students and me. . . . Unfortunately, most of my oppressed students' social injuries are very deep; the oppressive educational practices they have experienced have left them seriously scarred. They do not trust teachers, administrators, police, or any person holding a position of high authority at school or in the community. It takes much time, understanding, and patience to peel off the layers of distrust, fear, and hate created by teachers and a curriculum that seldom has validated their language, their culture, their daily experiences—in sum, their authentic selves and history. (Terrazas, 1995, pp. 280, 284)

Guidelines for Teaching

CHACTERISTICS OF A PEDAGOGY FOR EMPOWERMENT

Cummins (1986a, 1989a, 1989c, 1992, 1993, 1995, 1996b) has written extensively on the coercive relations of power between subordinate and dominant groups, with school serving as one of society's institutions that perpetuates existing power relations. In order for language-minority students to experience success in school, Cummins encourages a pedagogy for empowerment with the following characteristics:

- Minority students' language and culture are incorporated into the school program.

- Minority community participation is encouraged as an integral component of children's education.

- The pedagogy promotes intrinsic motivation on the part of students to use language actively in order to generate their own knowledge.

- Professionals involved in assessment become advocates for minority students by focusing primarily on the ways in which students' academic difficulty is a function of interactions within the school context rather than legitimizing the location of the "problem" within students. (Cummins, 1989a, p. 58)

Critical pedagogy applied to the young student includes transforming the process of literacy development in school to creative bilingual/bicultural methods of reading (Ada, 1980, 1988, 1991; Pérez & Torres-Guzmán, 1996) and the use of numerous forms of meaningful print and genres of writing to help children construct meaning; enjoy reading and writing; and use the written word to learn about, interpret, reflect, explain, analyze, argue, and act upon the world (Faltis & Hudelson 1998; Hudelson, 1989, 1991, 1994). Walsh (1991a, 1991b, 1995, 1996), expresses the transformation needed in literacy practices in schools in an impassioned voice:

> Traditional skills-based approaches to literacy assume that knowledge is neutral, universal, and verifiable information that must be formally acquired and taught. Instruction breaks this knowledge down into manageable, discrete pieces that are systematically fed to students in a controlled way. . . . These approaches tend to exacerbate racial/ethnic, language, class, and gender stratifications, deny what it is children do know, and track students into levels that they forever carry with them. . . .
>
> Whole language challenges the traditional approach by presenting a view of knowledge that is connected to the student, her/his social context, and personal/social needs. The acquisition of knowledge (i.e., learning), is considered to be a part of a natural meaning-making process in which the student actively draws from prior knowledge and lived experience to construct meaning; the teacher helps facilitate and encourage such exploration and interaction. . . . But from a critical perspective, the problem with whole language is that it tends to treat all experience as neutrally lived and equally accepted. . . .
>
> Critical [pedagogy] approaches recognize knowledge as always partial and problematic, as bound in complex ways to the social, political, cultural, linguistic, and economic conditions of the society and to the meanings, experiences, and lived lives of students. In practice, critical approaches challenge teachers and students to work together . . . to construct new and sometimes different ways of interpreting, understanding, reading, writing and acting in the classroom, with one another and the world. (Walsh, 1995, pp. 93–94).

For readers wishing to explore more writings on critical pedagogy, Paulo Freire (1970, 1973, 1978, 1985; Freire & Macedo, 1987; Shor & Freire, 1987), a Brazilian educator who played a significant role in transforming educational contexts in Africa, Latin America, and Europe, provides a worldwide perspective. Henry Giroux (1988, 1992, 1993; Giroux & Simon, 1989) writes from a theoretical sociology of education perspective, applying the theory to U.S. institutional contexts. Ovando & McLaren (2000) examine contested political and pedagogical issues surrounding multiculturalism and bilingual education in U.S society.

Within the field of language minority education, the previously cited work of Jim Cummins and Catherine Walsh is seminal. A book produced by the California Association for Bilingual Education (Frederickson, 1995) provides the first volume written by both "experts" and teachers that examines ways teachers have collaborated as they wrestle with critical pedagogical perspectives to transform schooling for language-minority students. A very readable source written by Sonia Nieto (2000) presents creative strategies meaningful to teachers and case study data with students' voices as illustrations of theory, research findings, and teacher implementation.

Weaving It All Together

How, then, can teachers prepare cognitively complex lessons that are multidimensional? We do it through celebrating life in all its complexity in the classroom, through multisensory experiences that weave together math, science, social studies, language, literature, technology, music, art, dance, movement, games, and folklore, while connecting to students' and community knowledge across many cultural dimensions. In Chapters Four through Seven, you will examine many ways to explore and to integrate the standard academic content areas in your teaching. In the remainder of this chapter, we will explore further dimensions of life experiences that stimulate the learning process for language-minority students.

Why do we recommend multidimensional learning? Psychologists' theories of intelligence have helped educators understand that in formal schooling we tend to develop and reward only certain narrow aspects of the human brain's capabilities. For example, Robert Sternberg's research has led him to identify three major intellectual abilities—analytical, creative, and practical. Creative intelligence allows us to cope with novelty, and practical intelligence enables us to apply what we know to everyday situations. Sternberg's research has found that intelligence is not an inborn trait; instead it is mediated by the environment and can be taught and enhanced (Viadero, 1994). Howard Gardner's theory of multiple intelligences (1983, 1993) identifies seven different forms—linguistic, logical-mathematical, spatial, bodily kinesthetic, musical, interpersonal, and intrapersonal intelligence. Gardner posits that each person possesses all seven intelligences (and perhaps more yet to be identified), with some developed more than others, and they work together in complex ways. Both Sternberg and Gardner agree that IQ tests measure only one form of intelligence that is rewarded in school which may not be the key to success outside of school (Viadero, 1994).

Applying Gardner's theory to the classroom, Armstrong (1994) proposes multimodal teaching—"reaching beyond the text and the blackboard to awaken students' minds" (pp. 49–50)—through thematic experiences that cross the whole spectrum of human experience. We shall explore several examples of the potential of these modalities, with the hope that teachers will collaborate to create other multidimensional lessons stimulated by these ideas. Many other modalities not presented here for lack of space, such as drama, folklore, games, puppetry, storytelling, and all forms of written narrative, should be explored in active, discovery classrooms. The order of the following sections is not presented hierarchically in order of importance. Instead, the use of art, technology, music, and other dimensions of life are to be viewed as a whole, to be blended into lessons in meaningful, multisensory ways.

Art

Etched deeply in our psyche is a powerful desire to affirm, to recognize, or to create beauty. For some of us our spiritual and mental selves have found a bond through the reflection of a full moon on the surface of a glasslike, tranquil, and secluded lake, or a stunning and prolonged sunset over an ocean bay. For others, beauty has manifested itself in the form of the delicate and smooth texture of an infant's skin, an extraordinarily handsome face, a mother duck surrounded by her ducklings. As humans, we universally decorate our artifacts or ourselves—notice for example, the current popularity of tattoos across varying age groups. People from all cultures create designs, textures, smells, colors, and forms that express intimate feelings, bonds, identity, and knowledge. Art, as a universal form of human expression, is an essential ingredient of learning to be woven into thematic lessons.

Artistic expression in the form of drawing, painting, weaving, pottery, crafts, puppetry, photography, computer graphics, print making, sculpture, collage, origami, calligraphy, beadwork, masks, gardening, cooking, and woodworking evokes in us strong emotional and cognitive responses. Art allows us to create a socioculturally rich environment, stimulating linguistic, cultural, cognitive, affective, and psychomotor development. By engaging the senses of touch, taste, smell, sight, and sound, teacher and students are pushed and pulled toward each other's perspectives and encouraged to exchange and expand their views of the world. As an example of the natural integration of art into science lessons with a diverse class, one teacher, Karen Gallas (1994), provides a glimpse of her vibrant classroom:

🔀 *One afternoon in early June, six children and I crowd around a butterfly box watching a painted lady chrysalis twitch and turn as the butterfly inside struggles to break free. Juan, who is seated on a chair next to the box, holds a clipboard on his lap and is carefully sketching the scene. This is his third sketch of the day chronicling the final stage in the life cycle of the butterfly. It will complete a collection he began in early May, when mealworms arrived in our first-grade classroom. As he draws, the children agonize over the butterfly's plight. They have been watching since early that morning, and they all wonder if the butterfly will ever get out. Sophia smiles to herself and then begins to hum a tune.*

"I'll sing it out," she says.

"Yeah, let's sing it out!" agrees Matthew, and all the children begin to improvise a song. Juan looks up, smiles, and continues to sketch.

Events such as these have become almost commonplace in my classroom. Over the course of the school year, this particular class of children questioned, researched, wondered, and discussed their way through a wide variety of subject matters and concepts. What distinguished their learning process from that of many other children, however, was the presence of the arts as an integral part of their curriculum: as a methodology for acquiring knowledge, as subject matter, and as an array of expressive opportunities. Drawing and painting, music, movement, dramatic enactment, poetry, and storytelling: Each domain, separately and together, became part of their total repertoire as learners. . . .

Juan arrived in September from Venezuela, speaking no English but filled with joy at being in school. As I struggled during our first few weeks together to find out what he could and could not do . . . he would suggest cheerfully, "Paint?" Paint, for Juan, meant drawing, painting, modeling, or constructing, and it was his passion. . . . His visual representations became a catalogue of science information and science questions, and that information began to provide material for his involvement in reading and writing and learning a new language. (pp. 130–132)

This kind of spontaneous magic occurs when teachers plan and gather numerous resources for exploring a theme in multidimensional ways. When integrating art into a thematic unit, it is important to approach the process from an art education perspective that is nontraditional. After a theme has been chosen and collaborating teachers and students gather many resources for studying the theme in depth, art experiences will naturally emerge from the data gathering that include students' participation in artistic creation as well as responding to other artists' works. By giving learners an opportunity to engage in truly personal expressive choices, teachers can avoid the homogenizing tendencies often exhibited in arts and crafts activities in traditional approaches to art in education. Perhaps too often, children are given a subject—for example, a duck—followed by instructions, after which the students faithfully produce ducks that all look remarkably similar. But words of advice from an experienced art teacher warn teachers not to succumb to "assembly-line" art production:

⊠ *Too much concern with how a product is made inhibits expression. Educators too often teach technique, directing the use of materials in lock-step procedures that guarantee a particular outcome. . . . I ask students to start their artwork "in the middle." They understand that to mean, literally, the center of what they are looking at, such as the nose or surface of the face of an animal in a photograph or the red of the apple in a still life. They know to let their work grow from that place, although they may choose the particular place to start. . . .*

When observing an artifact, students may do several exercises with different media. Second graders are given the four colors they need to analyze the patterns in Kente cloth from Ghana. The paper they work on is cut to the size they need to show one segment of the cloth, and the whole of the paper is colored. Then they actually weave their own interpretation of the pattern, doing as many as two or three weavings that measure four by ten inches. They are given the time to experiment, to see if they can show diagonals, or to decide how many strings they need to use to make a consistent pattern. (Grallert, 1991, pp. 264, 267)

As our students connect to their heritages, exploring art from a global perspective, folk art can be examined at the local museum, collected at secondhand shops, and discovered through human resources of the community (Schuman, 1992). "Folk art is the visual manifestation of the cultural environment of a people. . . . The folk art objects brought to the classroom need not be exotic or one-of-a-kind, because it is sometimes the simple common items that provide more insight into the lives of their creators and their users" (Carrillo Hocker, 1993, p. 156). Suggestions for using folk art and artifacts include examining how each piece was made, how it was used, the environment within which it existed, where it fits in chronological time, influences on its design, and its function in deeply rooted value systems as well as comparing it to similar artifacts from other cultures (Carrillo Hocker, 1993).

Cross-cultural experiences through art with young adolescents can delve into deeper connections to historical, sociopolitical, and ethnolinguistic roots. Powerful connections to heritage are present in every form of aesthetic expression:

Myths, folk tales, drawings, carvings, and paintings objectify a cultural group's concept of reality. Forces that are not explainable appear concrete and often are thought of as the force itself. Ceremonies, rituals, and artifacts explain weather, hunting and gathering successes, and crops growing or failing. (McFee & Degge, 1977, p. 291)

Students may want to explore traditional and modern art forms of cultural groups represented in the classroom. To what extent are the murals of East Los Angeles the personal artistic expressions of the individual Chicanos who painted them, and to what extent are they extensions of the ethnic experience as expressions of social protest? What symbolism and myth are present in an Inuit sculpture of smooth black stone? What emotions and philosophical perspectives are conveyed in producing different kinds of Japanese watercolor brush strokes? In summary, art is powerful for connecting to the imagination, developing language, examining the natural world in science, exploring cultural roots, and deepening sociopolitical awareness in social studies.

Technology

A phenomenon very different from art but powerful in its potential to enhance student learning is the pervasiveness of technology. In schools, teachers have increasing access to audio and video equipment, compact disc players, cameras, computers, interactive videodisc players, and other technological devices to deepen instructional possibilities. Furthermore, technology is here to stay, assuming no major global catastrophe. In fact, technology seems to be defining the future of our whole world in many ways.

As we incorporate the use of technology into education, however, we are reminded that any innovation has a downside along with the benefits and excitement that it generates. Technological devices may get purchased but lie unused when teachers are intimidated by the hardware, or the available software may not meet curricular objectives, or often the school budget shortsightedly ignores the maintenance and repair costs of the technological equipment. Language-minority students have much less access to computers in schools than native-English-speaking students (Becker, 1990; Neuman, 1994; Roberts, 1988). And even when they do have access, computers are too often used for individualized drill and practice activities with low-level cognitive demand, or as rewards for completing assignments, rather than as an integral part of meaningful, complex thematic instruction. At home, children may sit passively in front of the television for hours. As Brown (1993) explains,

> Bilingual teachers are interested in using technology but want to do so in a way that is consistent with their goals of encouraging students to actively and critically examine and question the world around them, all the while interacting with and learning from one another and the community in which they live. . . . The unfulfilled promises associated with technology use have left bilingual teachers with mixed feelings. . . . How to justify the greater use of machines that have traditionally placed the student in a passive role?
>   . . . The wisest and most powerful uses of technology are likely to come from sound pedagogical principles and from a knowledge of the language-minority students in our classroom and their communities. The most important factors in exploring what those uses might be are not related to technical expertise but rather to trusting our instincts as humane teachers. (pp. 178–179)

Thus, using technology does not ensure excellent teaching. Teachers should first focus on creating an active learning environment and then use technology as one of many important components of effective teaching. In this section, we examine a few examples of technology use in an interactive, discovery classroom for language-minority students. We will focus on technologies that are accessible, inexpensive, and that have been shown to work well in culturally and linguistically diverse classes.

Telecommunications

For general information on the use of telecommunications in education, a comprehensive reference is Roberts, Blakeslee, Brown, and Lenk (1990). Among the most exciting uses of technology with language-minority students, the Orillas network is a well-cited example of creative school partnerships across distances using relatively inexpensive telecommunications technology (Brown, 1993; Brown & Cuellar, 1995; Cummins & Sayers, 1990, 1995; DeVillar & Faltis, 1991; Faltis & DeVillar, 1990, 1993; González-Edfelt, 1993; Johnson & Roen, 1989; Sayers, 1993a, 1993b, 1996). This project, formally titled De Orilla a Orilla (From Shore to Shore), links bilingual, ESL, and second/foreign language classes in many schools across the United States, including Puerto Rico, with schools in Argentina, Canada, Mexico, Costa Rica, France, and Japan. Promoting bilingual literacy acquisition and maintenance through interactive discovery learning with native-speaking peers and long-distance school partnerships through telecommunications (using a computer, modem, and local phone line) has led to student-produced bilingual books, newspapers, and journals; collecting and analyzing oral histories and folklore from extended families and community; intercultural analyses of community life through social science methods of research; and cross-linguistic analyses (Brown, 1993; Sayers, 1993a, 1993b). The education technology column in *NABE News* provides electronic mail addresses for bilingual/ESL educators' networks (see Sayers, 1996).

Electronic mail (e-mail) is only one of many uses of the computer for purposes of communication with others nearby and in far distant places. Through the phone lines, which are used to link computer systems around the world, the Internet has emerged as a rich source of information and interconnections of people throughout the world. The World Wide Web interface was developed to provide users easy access to the Internet through graphics, sound, animation, and video, using hypertext that provides clearly visible links to other documents (Randall, 1996). Possibilities abound for uses of this massive and relatively inexpensive teaching resource. With one microcomputer in your class linked up to a local phone line of an Internet service provider, you have a world library at your fingertips. Bilingual and ESL teachers must demand access to these resources and let their students become experts on the Web. Once students recognize the power of this resource, literacy in L_1 and L_2 becomes desirable and meaningful, and students become collaborators in the learning process. As Snell (1996) notes, however,

> After human teachers, the Internet would represent the most important educational resource in the world if every student had a computer. That not being the case, the Internet as it stands is an exercise in the expansion of inequality. By and large, the students who now have access to the Internet already have access to well-supported schools, well-paid teachers, and well-stocked libraries. . . . However, by familiarizing themselves with the educational resources the Internet offers, teachers, administrators, and parents may acquire the ammunition they need to sell their schools on the necessity of classroom computing. . . . Newsgroups, IRC [Internet Relay Chat—in many world languages] channels, Gopher menus, and Web pages can offer access to a world of information about, and exchange with, other cultures and communities and experts in every field. It's the best all-around encyclopedia, textbook, and teaching video money can buy. (pp. 93–94)

Video

Another example of an accessible technology that is both relatively low in cost and easy to use is the videocassette player. Endless uses of video abound for educational purposes, including language learning, but teachers are cautioned to use it meaningfully, for authentic, cognitively complex learning, not as a filler for passive viewing. The field of ESL enthusiastically embraced video in the 1980s, with several publications providing lots of advice on teaching techniques (e.g., Allan, 1985; Duncan, 1987; Hutchings, 1984; Lonergan, 1984; Maxwell, 1983; and Stempleski & Tomalin, 1990), including such tips as selecting short clips of one to five minutes, planning previewing activities to prepare students for what they will see, experimenting with prediction and other critical analyses through silent viewing or sound only, and planning meaningful postviewing follow-up. Some of these sources approach language lessons as brief, entertaining experiences that stand by themselves rather than as interconnected acquisition of thematic academic content, as practiced in more current approaches. But when teachers use video segments for meaningful development of a thematic unit, the potential for deep learning is strong (Pally, 1994). Closed captioning in the form of television subtitles, developed for the hearing-impaired TV viewer and available for many current educational TV programs, has been found to improve beginning, intermediate, and advanced ESL students' oral and written comprehension and vocabulary acquisition dramatically, making authentic material more accessible to nonnative speakers (Neuman & Koskinen, 1990; Spanos & Smith, 1990; Vanderplank, 1993).

The video camera has still more power to transform lessons. Just as students feel proud of their own pictures that teachers snap of them working and display in the classroom, the video camera captures special moments. Brown (1993) describes a remarkable experience in a family literacy program for Spanish-speaking families in the Pájaro Valley Literacy Project in California, when videotapes made for the evaluators turned into an effective teaching tool. Project facilitators decided to videotape the presentations by group leaders, the discussion circles where parents (who were also developing emergent literacy along with their children) related the themes in the books to their own lives, and the open dialogue that followed, reflecting on the books their children had written that they had read together during the past week. Some parents requested that they be allowed to check out the videotapes. At home, families repeatedly watched themselves on videotape and invited other family members to watch with them, and parents and children gained more confidence with each succeeding week.

As the school year progressed, . . . these parents . . . had become leaders and policymakers in their community. The videos, originally intended only for use by the teachers for documentation purposes, became a highly significant part of the whole project. . . . In contrast to education videos, whose purpose is to introduce new facts and concepts and to bring into the classroom scenes from the outside world, here the video is used to capture images of the participants themselves in the process of learning and engaging in dialogue to create knowledge together. Encouraging the participants to reflect more critically on their own learning provides them greater insight into their own experiences as learners, while giving them greater confidence to act upon these insights. (Brown, 1993, p. 182)

Microcomputers

Extensive sources are available on use of the microcomputer in language minority education. This glimpse can only hint at the possibilities. We have already seen the power of electronic mail in the Orillas project, connecting classrooms across countries for discovery learning. Other examples of ESL/EFL students' participation in interactive writing using e-mail are illustrated in Gaer and

Ferenz (1993), Goodwin, Hamrick, and Stewart (1993), Krauss (1994), Sullivan (1993), and Sutherland and Black (1993). For all ages of students, process writing is fun to do on the microcomputer. When students see their own writing in published form, it gives them strong incentives to take responsibility for their own editing process with multiple drafts, especially since word processing makes it easy to correct errors (Monroe, 1993). Less research has been conducted on language-minority students' response to the writing process with word processing, but initial studies find the technology a very promising and important tool (e.g., Neu & Scarcella, 1991; Peyton & Mackinson-Smyth, 1989; Phinney, 1991; Salavert, 1991; and Susser, 1993). An excellent, practical teacher reference for the use of microcomputers in teaching the reading and writing process from a constructivist, inquiry perspective is one by Willis, Stephens, and Matthew (1996). This book provides many tips on useful software, electronic mail, and the World Wide Web.

Microcomputer software for bilingual/ESL classes is another story. Since most of the instructional software that has been developed for bilingual and ESL classes by commercial publishers is very low-level in cognitive demand and tends to encourage passive learning environments, teachers need to develop a very critical, analytical perspective when reviewing software for use. In a search for innovative computer-based programs exhibited at the 1993 TESOL Convention, Hunt (1993) concluded:

> Most of the software focused on typical vocabulary or grammar drill and practice. . . . The very nature of drill and practice software runs counter to the natural acquisition approach for L$_2$ instruction because it tends to present isolated, noncontextualized exercises that focus on accuracy rather than fluency. (p. 8)

Hunt (1993) found only "a small number of exemplary multimedia products designed for the ESL learner" (p. 8). As a technology specialist, she advises ESL and bilingual teachers to look for instructional products that have flexibility, for use with a range of grades and levels of proficiency; thematic presentation of materials within a rich contextual framework; appropriate, relevant, current content; opportunities for students to listen, speak, read, and write; open-ended questions and writing prompts that allow creative student responses; plenty of opportunities for natural interaction with peers; mixed media in the package (e.g., laserdisc, microcomputer, and/or CD-ROM resources, audiotapes, and print materials); extensive system guides; and in-service training provided by the publishers (Hunt, 1993, pp. 8–9). Microcomputer software developed for teaching L$_2$ has generally included activities focused on tutorial help, drill, and practice, problem solving, instructional games, text manipulation, text generation, and simulations (presented here from low to potentially higher cognitive demand) (González-Edfelt, 1993).

Another issue of importance to language teachers when using microcomputers has been their silence, limiting the development of students' listening and speaking skills. Technology has continued to make great strides in development of peripheral audio devices as well as digitized and synthesized speech and speech processing systems, but these are expensive to use. The latest developments in interactive videodisc technology and interactive hypermedia are the most promising for active learning environments, with the development of inexpensive large storage capability through CD-ROM (Compact Disc–Read Only Memory) making it possible to create exciting multimedia for schooling (González-Edfelt, 1993; Soska, 1994).

Principles for Technology Use

These examples of the potential of technology use provide only a glimmer of things to come. Technology specialists in our field describe the technology revolution that is taking place worldwide in this way:

> The development of educational technology in the past five years has been so rapid as to leave us gasping. Our ability to realize the fantastic implications for us and our students, to capitalize on the potential of each new discovery for enhancing our efforts, and to implement the latest capability always lags far behind the dramatic announcement [of each new development] . . . (Garett in Dunkel, 1991, p. xiii)

It seems fitting to close this section with principles for technology use that were developed by Kristin Brown (1993), based on the writings of Paulo Freire, Celestin Freinet, Mario Lodi, and Alma Flor Ada, as well as current research on language acquisition, the writing process, and collaborative learning. This small portion of her advice to teachers demonstrates the wealth of ideas for technology use in active, collaborative bilingual/ESL classes.

Language-minority students must have access to technology (Mielke & Flores, 1994), the force driving us into a new era, referred to increasingly as the information age. Schools are changing, and "technology . . . can contribute substantially to the active, experiential learning that Dewey advocated decades ago" (O'Neil, 1993, p. 1). We language-minority educators can lead the way, by creating meaningful social contexts for learning that use technology to transform "deficit, remedial" perspectives into "languages-and-cultures-as-resource" perspectives for collaborative learning.

Music

Music is such an integral part of young people's lives these days that it would be foolish to ignore the power of this sensory experience for storing knowledge permanently in memory. Music stimulates our emotions, relaxes or intensifies the senses, and increases stimuli for retention of an experience. The more multilayered a learning experience is, the more mechanisms we have for retrieving knowledge imprinted on long-term memory (Stevick, 1976). Taste, touch, smell, sight, and sound stimulate extrasensory mechanisms for memory retrieval. Thus music integrated into a thematic unit is a natural means to explore students' multiple intelligences (Gardner, 1993).

Guidelines for Teaching

GUIDING PRINCIPLES FOR CHOOSING TECHNOLOGY

- *Look for technologies over which you can get control, especially communications technologies.* Find ways to use technologies as tools for creating knowledge in social contexts. Tool applications might involve producing and filming original plays with a videotape recorder, using audiocassette recorders for intergenerational interviews, writing with a word processor, doing research with databases, or mounting joint projects with distant classes through telecommunications. In particular, look for . . . technologies that will allow your students to capture, record, and share their own words and worlds.

  In searching for tools that will be useful in your classroom do not overlook the potential uses of old or "out-of-date" machines such as overhead projectors, thermofax machines, or slide projectors that may be gathering dust on the shelves at your school. Consider using technologies that are not usually found in classrooms, such as fax machines, to exchange student artwork and illustrated poems with other classes or to consult with local business or community organizations. Finally, getting control over technology may mean not using the machines with the materials or software that come with them. A ditto machine does not have to be used for worksheets; a roomful of expensive drill and practice software may be less useful than a single public domain word processing program with Spanish fonts.

- *Look for technologies that will allow students to publish their writing.*

- *Look for technologies that will allow you to record oral language.*

- *Encourage students to work collaboratively to create group texts.*

- *Encourage students to use technology in responding creatively and critically to the books they read.*

- *Use technology to promote critical reflection.*

- *Use technology to engage your students in dialogue with another class: long-distance team-teaching partnerships.* (Brown, 1993, pp. 193–197)

Today, with technology as a resource, many natural experiences with music can be woven into thematic lessons. Children naturally try out rhythms, foot stomping, skipping, jumping, hand clapping, finger snapping, and moving to the sounds, adding another stimulus for storage of a learning experience in long-term memory. Young adolescents prefer to be cautious in their response to music or any other stimulus because of all the changes occurring to them emotionally and physically. Thus for middle and high school students, a democratic process, through which students and teacher together choose the musical experiences to be integrated into the curriculum, helps to create the socio-affective environment for maximum learning.

The possibilities are endless. Suppose that your class, composed of several students from Central America, after watching portions of the movie *El Norte*, chooses to develop a thematic unit on the Maya and their descendants in southern Mexico and Guatemala. Your local museum, library, and community residents help you and your students gather resources. You have contacted the Orillas coordinator, who finds a partner e-mail class in Oaxaca, Mexico, to exchange materials and serve as a data collection site for the research questions the sister classes develop. Ancient and contemporary art, music, and folklore from the peoples inhabiting the Yucatan peninsula, gathered through this process, could lead the class to many research questions to be explored in history, geography, sociology, anthropology, science, and mathematics. Music your class discovers might include contemporary music with heavy influences from the United States, ethnomusicologists' collections of folk traditions passed on through the centuries (e.g., Bensusan & Carlisle, 1978; Macías, 1991), marimba bands playing both ancient and contemporary music, guitarists and harpists exploring ancient melodies or creating current protest music, traditional musicians playing flute and drum in ceremonies in the highlands of Guatemala, orchestras playing music of Europe, and so on. Your class might get curious about what musical instruments are used, what they are made of, and how they are handcrafted. Where do the materials come from to make the instruments? What produces the sound? How are they used? For the musical instruments that the Maya descendants use, what kind of history time lines demonstrate new influences from what other cultures? Who enjoys what kinds of music across social classes, ethnic groups, ages, gender, geographic regions? What factors produce changes in music, and how is music passed on from generation to generation? How does immigration to the United States affect musical traditions and preferences for first-, second-, third-generation families?

Developing a unit such as "the Maya and their descendants" can feel quite daunting to a first-year teacher, imagining collecting all these materials alone. In all thematic lesson building, teaming across classrooms, perhaps the whole school, makes it possible to collect and share the resources needed to explore learning at a deep level. Once the project takes off and students accept their responsibility for data collection, community resources or "funds of knowledge" (Moll, Amanti, Neff, & González, 1992) will emerge from parents and the community.

Other ways to explore music include playing or singing composed music (the most common strategy of teachers), as well as creating music (mainly done by the music educator or the budding young musician). Singing a song is often perceived by a class as side entertainment, and is only meaningful when students see the song's direct connection to the unit they are working on. The key to the use of every curricular area, including music, is to work on lessons that provide students with *variety* in every aspect of its use. Humans have created music varying greatly by type, purposes for use, geographic region, environmental conditions, cultural patterns, language(s) used, musical instruments used, and all social patterns of human life. When students experience that variety in human expression, it expands their perceptions of the world and each other (Dobbs, 1992). Music deepens their knowledge base and energizes the learning process.

You can help students listen to all types of music from all peoples of the world by using music when students enter and leave class, during breaks, and at meaningful points in lessons connected to thematic content. Together you can sing, dance, and play music. You can analyze the words in music, musical instruments, social uses of music and politics of music. You can experience the intense emotions stirred up by music, explore the imagination, feel the connections between music and every other aspect of human life. Students can affirm and celebrate their bilingual/bicultural heritages and understand the deep function that sounds, sights, touch, smells, and tastes have in defining what is important and meaningful in people's lives.

Summary

The content and process of teaching and learning do not occur in a vacuum. The lived experiences of students and teachers should provide a rich context to engage the learning community in a critical, meaningful, and life-affirming educational experience. Anchored in the linguistic, cultural, and cognitive background of students, teachers face the challenge of uncovering and implementing effective ways for teaching and learning in a pluralistic society.

Research findings suggest that culturally and linguistically compatible classroom practices that are active, inquiry based, and cooperative in nature tend to function well for language-minority students. Hence, this chapter proposed that the traditional "banking" model of schooling, be replaced with promising curricular and instructional approaches that lead students to 'the threshold of [their] own minds.'

Key Terms

Passive Learning p. 89

Active Learning p. 89

Critical Pedagogy p. 92

Accelerated Learning p. 92

Cooperative Learning p. 92

Reflection Questions

1. What do you believe to be the role/responsibility of teachers in providing a meaningful and effective education to students of linguistically and culturally diverse backgrounds?
2. According to the authors, teachers can no longer rely on the traditional classroom to provide the learning context needed for student inquiry. Based on your

own understanding of the nature and demands of contemporary society, elaborate on reasons that would support their claim.

3. What are the effects of "passive learning" approaches to education? What other approaches do you find to be more effective, especially when faced with the challenge of teaching in linguistically and culturally diverse contexts? Explain why.

4. Explain the role of critical pedagogy in the bilingual and ESL classroom. Identify ways in which you could begin to implement this practice in your own teaching and learning. Are there risks associated with taking a pro–social justice agenda in classroom activities?

5. What do the authors mean by the concept of "multidimensional" teaching and learning? Design a lesson that incorporates its aspects.

6. How can art and technology serve as mediums to enhance teaching practices in the bilingual and ESL classroom? What artistic and technological activities have you found to be of specific value when teaching in linguistically and culturally diverse contexts? Explain why.

Resources

Educating Minority Language Students: Active, Inquiry-Based Learning, and Critical Pedagogy

August, D., & Hakuta, K., eds. *Educating language-minority children*. Washington, DC: National Academy Press, 1998.

- In *Educating Language-Minority Children* August and Hakuta summarize for teachers and education policymakers what has been learned over the past three decades about educating minority-language students. The book discusses a broad range of educational issues: how students learn a second language; how reading and writing skills develop in the first and second languages; how information on specific subjects is stored and learned and the implications for second-language learners; how social and motivational factors affect learning for English-language learners; how the English proficiency and subject matter knowledge of English-language learners are assessed; and what is known about the attributes of effective schools and classrooms that serve English-language learners.

Beykont, Z. F., ed. *Lifting every voice: Pedagogy and politics of bilingualism.* Cambridge, MA: Harvard Education Publishing Group, 2000.

- *Lifting Every Voice: Pedagogy and Politics of Bilingualism* considers the political and cultural significance of bilingual education, and discusses the importance of bilingualism for democracy, the practices of bilingual education, and education reforms. The book assesses the current contribution of bilingual education. Contributors include public school teachers, teacher educators, linguists, and scholars in language studies.

Christian, D., & Genesse, F., eds. *Bilingual education.* Teachers of English to Speakers of Other Languages, Inc. (TESOL), 2001.

- Bilingual education is a series of case studies that covers the diversity of environments in which languages can be learned bilingually. It provides a wealth of information on how to teach bilingually, and attests to the value of community and individuals that can result from bilingual forms of education. The eleven programs described demonstrate the linguistic, cultural, and academic contributions that bilingual approaches to education can make around the world.

Darling-Hammond, L., & Sykes, G., eds. *Teaching as the learning profession: Handbook of policy and practice.* San Francisco: Jossey-Bass Publishers, 1999.

- *Teaching as the Learning Profession* is an in-depth overview of the issues and challenges facing the teaching profession today. It includes case studies of innovative approaches to school improvement, principles for better staff development, proposals for the reform of unions, and offers conceptual as well as practical advice on recruitment, licensing, redefining the teaching career, enhancing diversity, developing leadership, and expanding such innovations as networks and other sustained forms of teacher-to-teacher learning. The book discusses issues such as preparing teachers for diversity; strengthening the connections between teacher and student learning; teacher recruitment, selection, and induction; and staff development and instructional improvement.

Delpit, L. *Other people's children: Cultural conflicts in the classroom.* New York: The New Press, 1995.

- In *Other People's Children,* Delpit uses analyses of cultural clashes in classrooms from Alaska to Papua New Guinea to get at the highly charged issue of race in our schools, discussing what must happen if we are to educate teachers to accommodate ethnic and cultural diversity. She argues that many minority students are erroneously labeled "underachievers" due to failures of communication between teachers and students. The author introduces the idea of teachers as "cultural translators" for students struggling to understand the sometimes "foreign" ways of American public schools.

Faltis, C. J., & Hudelson, S. J. *Bilingual education in elementary and secondary school communities: Towards understanding and caring.* Needham Heights, MA: Allyn and Bacon, 1998.

- *Bilingual Education in Elementary and Secondary School Communities* is an introduction to bilingual education for education majors interested in becoming bilingual teachers. The book presents a set of principles that form the foundation of how children and adolescents acquire literacy, and illustrates what actually happens in certain bilingual classrooms and schools through detailed vignettes of social interaction involving students and teachers.

————— *Joinfostering: Teaching and learning in multilingual classrooms* (3rd ed.). Upper Saddle River, NJ: Merrill/Prentice-Hall, 2001.

- *Joinfostering* makes a claim for the need to reform teacher preparation if we are to succeed in American schools. The book speaks to the present and future generations of American teachers and emphasizes the need to understand the role of teachers facing multiple home languages and students' difficulty in acquiring English literacy. Faltis has written a volume that offers teachers an excellent perspective on the most significant and neglected aspect of teaching and learning, "joinfostering," which is a process of cooperative, personalized, and effective teaching for all students.

Gay, G. *Culturally responsive teaching: Theory, research, and practice.* New York: Teachers College Press, 2000.

- This volume in the *Multicultural Education Series,* edited by James A. Banks, is designed to provide teachers and preservice educators with texts that analyze the theory, research, and practice related to the education of ethnic, racial, cultural, and language groups in the United States. Gay identifies four critical aspects of culturally responsive teaching—caring, communication, curriculum, and instruction—and offers useful explanations and examples for working with culturally diverse groups. Particular care is taken to address the factors of gender, age, and social class as well.

González, J., & Darling-Hammond, L. *New concepts for new challenges: Professional development for teachers of immigrant youth.* Washington, DC: Center for Applied Linguistics, 1997.

- In *New Concepts for New Challenges* the authors develop a framework for considering what teachers need to understand about their students, what kinds of professional experiences are likely to facilitate those understandings, and what kinds of teacher education programs and school settings are able to support their ongoing learning. González & Darling-Hammond describe promising new structures and practices for professional development, particularly those that promote community, collegiality, and collaboration.

Hollins, E. R., King, J. E., & Hayman, W. C., eds. *Teaching diverse populations: Formulating a knowledge base.* Albany, NY: SUNY Press, 1994.

- *Teaching Diverse Populations* attempts to formulate a knowledge base for teaching diverse students. The book describes the need for cultural congruence in instruction and the purpose of schools for students from diverse racial and ethnic backgrounds. Rather than focusing on specific content or curriculum areas, the overall text emphasizes the purpose and process of schooling. The work has direct implications for teacher preparation and staff development programs for veteran teachers.

hooks, bell. *Teaching to transgress: Education as the practice of freedom.* New York: Routeledge, 1994.

- *Teaching to Transgress* is an informally written, autobiographical polemic on teaching and alternative strategies to traditional forms of educational pedagogies. The author borrows heavily from the works of Paulo Freire and other critical/feminist scholars to suggest that traditional forms of teaching suppress liberatory movements, oppress people from different cultures and traditions, and continue a "white supremacist capitalist patriarchy." hooks begins her meditations on class, gender and race in the classroom with the confession that she never wanted to teach. hooks declares that education today is failing students by refusing to acknowledge their particular histories. The book is full of hope and excitement for the possibility of education to liberate and include.

Howard, G. R. *We can't teach what we don't know: White teachers, multiracial schools*. New York: Teachers College Press, 1999.

- This volume in the *Multicultural Education Series,* edited by James A. Banks, is designed to provide teachers and pre-service educators with texts that analyze the theory, research, and practice related to the education of ethnic, racial, cultural, and language groups in the United States. Howard offers an insightful discussion of the responsibilities that white teachers have in challenging racism and creating learning environments that can accept, affirm, and build on the identities of all students.

Ladson-Billings, G. *Crossing over to Canaan: The journey of new teachers in diverse classrooms*. San Francisco: Jossey-Bass, 2001.

- *Crossing Over to Canaan* tells the story of eight novice teachers working in urban, elementary school settings. It details their struggles and triumphs as they confront challenges in the classroom and respond with innovative strategies that turn cultural strengths into academic assets. Ladson-Billings offers a model of teaching that focuses on academic achievement, cultural competence, and socio-political consciousness. Drawing from her own experiences as a young African-American teacher working in Philadelphia, she successfully weaves together narrative, observation, and scholarship to create an inspirational and practical book that will help teachers everywhere as they work to transcend labels and categories to support excellence among all students.

The dreamkeepers: Successful teachers of African American children. San Francisco: Jossey-Bass Publishers, 1994.

- *The Dreamkeepers* discusses important aspects of culturally relevant teaching. The author discusses culturally relevant teaching as a pedagogy that uses cultural referents to impart knowledge, skills, and attitudes; culturally relevant teaching practices derived from her own three-year ethnographic study of eight teachers; and how teachers' perceptions of themselves and others affect the way in which they structure social relationships. Ladson-Billings shows through classroom vignettes how this teaching helps students construct knowledge, and challenges the contradictions in the curriculum as they relate to students' real life experiences. The conclusion examines ways in which culturally relevant teaching may become a part of teacher preparation programs.

Ovando, C. J., & McLaren, P. *The politics of multiculturalism and bilingual education: Students and teachers caught in the crossfire*. Boston: McGraw-Hill, 2000.

- *The Politics of Multiculturalism and Bilingual Education* is an empowering, provocative book that examines current contested political and pedagogical issues surrounding multiculturalism and bilingual education in the United States. The engaging voices and styles are woven together to create a unified, student-accessible text which analyzes the role of culture in the construction of privilege and prejudice, and provides a realistic account of the issues of multicultural and bilingual education facing teachers today.

Shor, I. *Empowering education: Critical teaching for social change.* Chicago: The University of Chicago Press, 1992.

- In *Empowering Education,* Shor describes the "kind of learning process that can empower students to perform at their best." Holding that education is socialization, and is never neutral, the book is a discussion of the educational values and processes that can develop citizens who think critically and act democratically. Some of those values are participation, affect, problem posing, dialogic, desocializing, researching, and activism, with participation obviously the more encompassing and initiating value. Shor's pedagogy is student-centered, but it is not permissive or self-centered.

Tashakkori, A., & Ochoa, S. H. *Education of Hispanics in the United States: Politics, policies, and outcomes.* New York: AMS Press, 1999.

- *Education of Hispanics in the United States* addresses the historical nature and evolution of the educational access and outcomes for Hispanics in the United States; the status of educating Hispanics in the midst of recent controversies regarding minority issues; the educational outcomes for the next decade, given current demographic trends; and policy and curriculum changes necessary to improve future outcomes for Hispanic students. The editors recognize that "Hispanics are a very heterogeneous group, consisting of different races, ethnicities, and national backgrounds. . . ." The essays address concerns that include the political and legal status of Hispanic education in the United States; issues of access and outcomes in the elementary and secondary education of Hispanic children; and higher education and Hispanic students.

Art

Goldberg, M. *Arts and learning: An integrated approach to teaching and learning in multicultural and multilingual settings.* New York: Longman, 1997.

- *Arts and Learning* explores the relationship between arts and learning. The book is an introduction to the practice of integrating the arts and education, particularly for teachers who want to make the arts—music, visual arts, and poetry, for example—part of the learning experience in their classrooms.

Technology

Gorski, P. *Multicultural education and the Internet: Intersections and integrations.* Boston: McGraw-Hill, 2001.

- *Multicultural Education and the Internet* focuses on the Internet's ability to help facilitate multicultural ideals of inclusive, interactive, and collaborative teaching and learning. The first section covers practical strategies for using the Internet to supplement multicultural teaching practices and will list existing Internet resources with annotations. The second section provides detailed chapter-length lists of Internet resources such as ESL and bilingual sites, subject-specific multicultural sites, lesson plan sites, online journals, and more. Screen shots, site explanations from site creators, and short case essays by teachers who have used the Internet successfully in multicultural teaching practice expand each chapter. www.mhhe.com/multicultural

Language

Language is very much like a living organism. It cannot be put together from parts like a machine, and it is constantly changing. . . . Language does not contain meaning; rather, meaning lies in the social relationships within which language occurs. Individuals in communities make sense of language within their social relationships, their personal histories, and their collective memory. . . . Our own language practices come from our cultural experience with language, but our individual language practices along with those of others collectively make the culture. Indeed the different ways people use language to make sense of the world and of their lives are the major distinguishing features of different cultural groups.

At the same time, language is always changing as we use it. Words acquire different meanings, and new language structures and uses appear as people stretch and pull the language to make new meanings. Consequently, the meaning that individuals make from language varies across time, social situation, personal perspective, and cultural group. . . . School actually plays a modest role in language acquisition, the bulk of which occurs outside the school. In schools we must learn to teach language in a way that preserves and respects students' individuality at the same time that we empower them to learn how to be responsible and responsive members of learning communities.

(International Reading Association and National Council of Teachers of English, 1994, pp. 7–9)

School personnel serving language-minority students often wonder what works best. What factors strongly influence students' development of their first and second languages? How long does it take to learn a second language? What are the most effective instructional practices that foster students' academic success? This chapter provides answers to these questions based on the most recent research, as well as an overview of current instructional practices for teaching language in schools. The knowledge base presented in this chapter can be applied to the teaching of English as a second language (ESL) and to English language arts (English as a first or dominant language), as well as to any other language (Spanish, Vietnamese, Arabic, and so on) taught as a first or second language.

The teaching of language is intimately connected to the major education reform movement described in Chapters Two and Three. Language teachers can no longer teach language in isolation from the rest of the curriculum. At elementary and middle schools, teachers are collaboratively planning thematic units that cross curricular areas, so that students discover the interdisciplinary connections and uses of knowledge outside of school. While high schools are still organized by isolated subject areas, the reforms at elementary and middle school levels are beginning to have an impact on high schools through some experimentation with structural reforms.

In the United States, the teaching of English language arts has undergone radical transformation over the last two decades. The focus of the older curricular approaches taught discrete skills in grammar, spelling, punctuation, and vocabulary memorization, with critical thinking applied mainly to literary analysis. The old discrete-skills curriculum isolated language structures from context, established artificial sequences of language skills to be mastered, simplified texts to control sentence structures and vocabulary, and emphasized measurement of student progress through discrete-skills tests.

The current movement toward a constructivist, whole-language philosophy of learning places emphasis on the integration of language and content, fostering personally and academically meaningful language development. The four language modes (formerly referred to as "skills") of listening, speaking, reading, and writing are taught as an integrated whole, with written and oral language developed simultaneously. Lessons are learner centered and meaningful to students' lives inside and outside school. Language lessons engage students in social interaction and collaborative learning. The focus is on the social construction of meaning and understanding the process of reading and writing (Freeman & Freeman, 1992, 1994; Goodman, 1986). Students first acquire literacy through their own writings and share children's literature as well as experiences across the curriculum through, for example, science experiments, recipes, games, instructions for making things, math problem solving, interactive computer communications, and map reading. Most of all, language is developed for meaningful purposes within and outside of school. The current curricular standards for the teaching of language arts reflect the perspective articulated by the International Reading Association and the National Council of Teachers of English (1994) in the opening quote of this chapter.

A large body of research on language acquisition has provided the theoretical base for this shift to a constructivist, whole-language philosophy for teaching language. Recent media coverage has inaccurately presented whole-language advocates as embroiled in controversy with those who support phonics instruction. In contrast to the oversimplified stories in the press, the general philosophy of whole language incorporates phonics and other analytic skills into the natural language acquisition process. Phonics advocates push for phonics to be taught first in literacy development; whereas whole-language approaches start the initial stages of literacy with focus on meaningful, authentic, natural uses of language, with explicit instruction in phonics and other skills, as needed, when learners are developmentally ready. We shall discuss this in more detail in the section of this chapter on whole-language approaches.

Research in first-language acquisition, second-language acquisition, and the simultaneous acquisition of two languages can provide teachers with insights into the language acquisition process with implications for the classroom. This chapter will explore (1) important research findings on language acquisition; (2) instructional approaches to teaching a second language; (3) teaching language arts in a bilingual classroom; and (4) teaching language and multicultural literature across the curriculum for bilingual, ESL, and grade-level classrooms.[1]

Language Acquisition

Teachers and parents have many misconceptions about language learning. Contrary to popular belief, second-language learning is difficult and complex for all ages, including young children. Acquiring a first or second language takes a long time, and the process of second-language acquisition varies greatly with each individual learner. The notion that first language "interferes" with a second language has been resoundingly rejected by extensive research findings on the positive role the first language plays in second-language acquisition. Cognitive and academic development of a student's first language provides especially crucial support for second-language acquisition. This section of the language chapter provides an overview of current research findings in language acquisition that have strong implications for the classroom teacher.

The Prism Model: Language Acquisition for School

The following conceptual model was developed by Thomas and Collier (1997) to illustrate the interrelationships among the four components that influence first- and second-language acquisition in a school context. The developmental process that all students experience throughout the school years is subconscious and ongoing. Figure 4.1 illustrates this developmental process by showing the interdependence of all four components—sociocultural, linguistic, academic, and cognitive processes—which occur simultaneously. While this figure looks

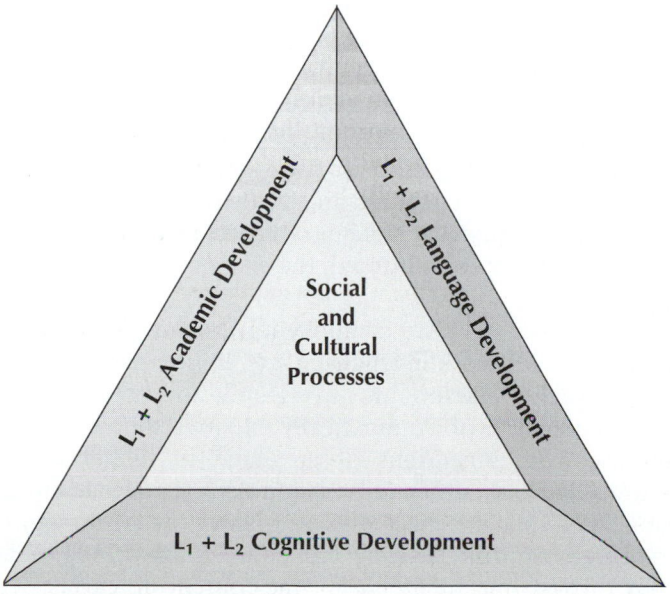

Figure 4.1   *Language Acquisition for School: The Prism Model*
Source: W.P. Thomas & V.P. Collier, 1997

simple on paper, it is important to imagine that this is a multifaceted prism with many dimensions.

Sociocultural Processes   At the heart of the figure is the individual student going through the process of acquiring a second language in school. Central to that student's acquisition of language are all of the surrounding social and cultural processes occurring through everyday life within the student's past, present, and future, in all contexts—home, school, community, and the broader society. Sociocultural processes at work in second-language acquisition may include individual student variables such as self-esteem, anxiety, or other affective factors. At school the instructional environment in a classroom or administrative program structures may create social and psychological distance between groups. Community or regional social patterns such as prejudice and discrimination expressed towards groups or individuals in personal and professional contexts can influence students' achievement in school, as well as societal patterns such as the subordinate status of a minority group or acculturation versus assimilation forces at work. These factors can strongly influence the student's response to the new language, affecting the process positively only when the student is in a socioculturally supportive environment.[2]

Language Development   Linguistic processes, a second component of the model, consist of the subconscious aspects of language development (an innate ability all humans possess for acquisition of oral language), as well as the metalinguistic, conscious, formal teaching of language in school *and* acquisition of the written system of language. This includes the acquisition of the oral and written systems of the student's *first and second languages* across all language domains, such as phonology (the pronunciation system), vocabulary, morphology and syntax (the grammar system), semantics (meaning), pragmatics (how language is used in a given context), paralinguistics (nonverbal and other extralinguistic features), and discourse (stretches of language beyond a single sentence). To assure cognitive and academic success in a *second* language, a student's *first* language system, oral *and* written, must be developed to a high cognitive level at least through the elementary school years.

Academic Development   A third component of the model, academic development, includes all school work in language arts, mathematics, the sciences, and social studies for each grade level, K through 12, and beyond. With each succeeding grade, academic work dramatically expands the vocabulary, sociolinguistic, and discourse dimensions of language to higher cognitive levels. Academic knowledge and conceptual development transfer from first language to second language. Thus it is most efficient to develop academic work through students' first language, while teaching second language during other periods of the school day through meaningful academic content. In earlier decades in the United States, we emphasized teaching second language as the first step, and postponed the teaching of academics. Research has shown us that postponing or interrupting academic development is likely to promote academic failure. In an information-driven society that demands more knowledge processing with each succeeding year, students cannot afford the lost time.

Cognitive Development   The fourth component of this model, the cognitive dimension, is a natural, subconscious process that occurs developmentally from birth to the end of schooling and beyond. An infant initially builds thought processes through interacting with loved ones in the language of the home. This is a knowledge base, an important stepping-stone to build on as cognitive development continues. It is extremely important that cognitive development continue through a child's first language at least through the elementary school years. Extensive research has demonstrated that children who reach full cognitive development in two languages (generally reaching the threshold in L_1 by around age 11 to 12) enjoy cognitive advantages over monolinguals. Cognitive development was mostly neglected by second-language educators in the United States until the past decade. In language teaching, we simplified, structured, and sequenced language curricula during the 1970s, and when we added academic content into our language lessons in the 1980s, we watered academics down into cognitively simple tasks. We also too often neglected the crucial role of cognitive development in the first language. Now we know from our growing research base that we must address linguistic, cognitive, and academic development equally, through both first and second languages, if we are to assure students' academic success in the second language.

Interdependence of the Four Components   All of these four components—sociocultural, academic, cognitive, and linguistic—are interdependent. If one is developed to the neglect of another, this may be detrimental to a student's overall growth and future success. The academic, cognitive, and linguistic components must be viewed as developmental, and for the child, adolescent, and young adult still going through the process of formal schooling, development of any one of these three components depends critically on simultaneous development of the other two, through both first and second languages. Sociocultural processes strongly influence, in both positive and negative ways, students' access to cognitive, academic, and language development. It is crucial that educators provide a socioculturally supportive school environment that allows natural language, academic, and cognitive development to flourish in both L_1 and L_2 (Collier, 1995a, 1995c).

Linguistic Processes

The synthesis of research on language acquisition that follows presents three of the four major dimensions of the Prism Model: *linguistic, sociocultural,* and *cognitive.* The *academic* dimension of the Prism, focused on the specifics of language acquisition *in a school context,* will be discussed in more detail in the second half of this chapter, as well as in the Mathematics and Science and Social Studies chapters. Most major theories of second language acquisition developed in the last decade have incorporated these three overall dimensions of language development—linguistic, sociocultural, and cognitive processes (Ellis, 1985, 1994; Larsen-Freeman, 1985; Larsen-Freeman & Long, 1991; McLaughlin, 1987; Wong Fillmore, 1985, 1991a). We shall begin with the linguistic dimension.

First-Language Acquisition   A common misconception of parents and teachers is to assume that it takes a short time to acquire a language. Research on first-language (L_1) acquisition can help us to understand the complexity of language development, a lifelong process (Berko Gleason, 1993). Development of oral language is universal; all children of the world have the same capability, given no physical disabilities and access to a source of human language input. From birth through age five, children subconsciously acquire oral language (listening and speaking), advancing to the level of a five-year-old in L_1 phonology, vocabulary, grammar, semantics (meaning), and pragmatics (how language is used in a given context). While we think of this as a fantastic accomplishment, L_1 is not yet halfway completed at this age. From ages 6 to 12, children subconsciously continue oral development of complex grammar rules, subtle phonological distinctions, vocabulary expansion, semantics, discourse (stretches of language beyond a single sentence), and more complex aspects of pragmatics (Berko Gleason, 1993; de Villiers & de Villiers, 1978; Goodluck, 1991; McLaughlin, 1984, 1985). This oral L_1 development is not formally taught; it is subconsciously acquired through *using* the language.

Formal instruction in school introduces L_1 written language—the modes of reading and writing—to be mastered across all the language domains mentioned above. Each grade level adds to the cognitive complexity of language development needed for each subject (mathematics, sciences, social studies, language arts). By adolescence, L_1 proficiency, developed both in and out of school, has reached a very complex level. Even so, there are aspects of first-language acquisition that continue across one's lifetime, including vocabulary development, writing skills, and many pragmatic aspects of language (Berko Gleason, 1993; Collier, 1992a; Harley, Allen, Cummins, & Swain, 1990; McLaughlin, 1985).

Simultaneous Bilingual Acquisition   Acquisition of a second language (L_2) is equally complex. A young child who is raised from birth as a simultaneous bilingual goes through the same subconscious acquisition process with both languages. Most children being raised bilingually experience a developmental stage of appearing to combine at least some aspects of the two languages into one system, followed by several stages that lead to separating the two languages into distinct language systems sometime between three to five years of age. Given regular exposure to, and cognitive development in, both languages over time, the same level of proficiency develops in two languages as a child acquiring one language reaches (Goodz, 1994; Hakuta, 1986; Harding & Riley, 1986; Hatch, 1978; McLaughlin, 1984). Children who are fortunate enough to develop strong academic proficiency in both languages are likely to experience cognitive advantages over monolinguals (Baker, 1993; Bialystok, 1991; Díaz & Klingler, 1991; Genesee, 1987; Hakuta, 1986).

Second-Language Acquisition: Social Language   While some children are raised bilingually from birth, many more are successive bilinguals who begin exposure to their L$_2$ at a later age. The purposes of acquiring the L$_2$ and opportunity for exposure to that language have significant influence on the amount of proficiency developed. Crucial components to the language learning process are

> (1) *Learners* who realize that they need to learn the target language and are motivated to do so; (2) *Speakers of the target language* who know it well enough to provide the learners with access to the language and the help they need for learning it; and (3) A *social setting* that brings learners and target language speakers into frequent enough contact to make language learning possible.

All three components are necessary. If any of them is dysfunctional, language learning will be difficult, or even impossible. When all three are ideal, language learning is assured. Each of them can vary in a great many ways, however, and some of this variation can critically affect the processes by which language is learned (Wong Fillmore, 1991a, pp. 52–53).

For example, when a child is using the L$_2$ for communication with friends in play, conversation may begin to flow within a few months. Given the three essential components outlined above, for communicative purposes the vocabulary, grammar, phonology, semantics, and pragmatics of L$_2$ will develop over a two- to three-year period, although "differences of up to five years can be found in the time children take to get a working command of a new language" (Wong Fillmore, 1991a, p. 61).

In this book, we use the term **social language** to refer to the dimension of language proficiency first referred to by Cummins as "basic interpersonal communicative skills" (BICS) or "context-embedded" or "conversational" or "contextualized" language (Cummins, 1979a, 1981b, 1986b, 1991, 1996b). In social language, meaning is negotiated through a wide range of contextual cues, such as nonverbal messages in face-to-face interaction or written feedback in a letter from a friend or an e-mail message. Social language is more than the acquisition of listening and speaking; it includes the development of literacy for use in situations such as shopping, use of transportation, or access to health services. Children, adolescents, and adults generally develop substantial proficiency in L$_2$ social language within two to three years, given access to L$_2$ speakers and a social setting that encourages natural interaction. For those just beginning L$_2$ acquisition as adolescents or adults, retention of an accent is so universal that non-native pronunciation is not considered to be an issue in proficiency development, unless the accent impedes the flow of communication.

Age of Initial Exposure to the Second Language   A myth also exists that young children are the fastest learners of a second language. Adults are fooled by the nativelike pronunciation that young children acquire quickly, but this is one of the few advantages that young children have over older learners. In fact, substantial research evidence has shown that young children may not reach full proficiency in their second language if cognitive development is discontinued in their primary language (Bialystok, 1991; Collier, 1988, 1989c, 1992c). Given the necessary prerequisites for L_2 acquisition to happen as defined above by Wong Fillmore, older learners from approximately ages 9 to 25 who have built cognitive and academic proficiency in their first language are potentially the most efficient acquirers of most aspects of academic L_2, except for pronunciation. An accent-free pronunciation is more possible if a second language is introduced before puberty. Adult learners past their 20s just beginning a second language may have more difficulty than the adolescent or young adult (Harley, 1986; Long, 1990; Scovel, 1988; Singleton & Lengyel, 1995). However, adults usually experience less difficulty with third- and fourth-language acquisition if they are already very proficient in the oral and written systems of their first two languages.

A research synthesis on the optimal age question written two decades ago (Krashen, Scarcella, & Long, 1982) concluded that "older is faster but younger is better." Now we know that this generalization applies mainly to conversational or oral language development. When reading and writing are added to the picture, a very different conclusion emerges. To state that one age is better than another to begin second-language acquisition would be greatly oversimplifying the complex interrelationships between development of language and cognition as well as social, emotional, and cultural factors (Collier, 1987, 1988, 1989c, 1992a). As proficiency in academic language develops at school, age interacts with many other variables that influence the language acquisition process, to be discussed below.

Second-Language Acquisition: Academic Language   When the purpose of L_2 acquisition is for use in educational settings, then the complexity of language proficiency development expands greatly. We use the term **academic language** to refer to "a complex network of language and cognitive skills and knowledge required across all content areas for eventual successful academic performance at secondary and university levels of instruction" (Collier & Thomas, 1989, p. 27). Cummins (1979a, 1981b, 1986b, 1991) first popularized this dimension of language, referring to it as "cognitive academic language proficiency" (CALP) as well as "context-reduced" or "decontextualized" language. This dimension of language proficiency is an extension of social language development. In other words, social and academic language development represent a continuum; they are not separate, unrelated aspects of proficiency. However, academic language extends into more and more cognitively demanding uses of language, with fewer contextual clues to meaning provided other than the language itself, as students move into more academically demanding work with each succeeding grade level.

A good teacher incorporates social and academic language development into every lesson. Activating students' background knowledge and prior experience might begin with social language, including many contextual supports through, for example, visuals, maps, charts, manipulatives, music, and pantomiming. As the lesson continues, new knowledge is developed and applied through increasingly cognitively complex tasks that extend students' cognitive and academic development through meaningful application in cooperative groups. Development of academic language is using language "to explain, to classify, to generalize, . . . to manipulate ideas, to gain knowledge, and to apply that knowledge" across all academic subjects (Swain, 1981, p. 5). Academic language development crosses all levels of Bloom's (1956) taxonomy of educational objectives in the cognitive domain—knowledge, comprehension, application, analysis, synthesis, and evaluation—for all grade levels and all content areas. Developing L_2 academic language is not watering down the curriculum; instead, students actively participate in lessons through meaningful, contextualized language that stimulates their cognitive and academic growth.

Academic Language: How Long?   When one realizes that academic language development is a continuous process throughout a student's schooling, the length of time required for this complex process can be better understood. For example, in the United States, native-English-speaking students are constantly acquiring a deeper level of proficiency in academic language in English. A newcomer who has had no previous exposure to English must build proficiency in social and academic language in English *and* catch up to the native speaker, who is not standing still waiting for others to catch up, but is continuing to develop higher levels of academic proficiency (Thomas, 1992). Cultural knowledge embedded in the native speaker's past experience adds to the complicated task the second-language student must face. Research has shown that when immigrants in the United States and Canada are schooled only in L_2, it takes a minimum of 5 to 10 years to attain grade-level norms in academic L_2, and it takes even longer when students do not have a literacy base in L_1 (Collier, 1987, 1989c, 1992c; Collier & Thomas, 1989; Cummins, 1981b, 1991, 1992; Cummins & Swain, 1986; Dolson & Mayer, 1992; Genesee, 1987; Ramírez, 1992). However, when students are schooled in L_1 and L_2 at least through grade 5 or 6, they are able to maintain grade-level norms in L_1 and reach grade-level norms in academic L_2 in four to seven years (Collier, 1992c; Genesee, 1987; Ramírez, 1992). Furthermore, after reaching grade-level norms, students schooled bilingually stay on or above grade level; whereas those schooled only through L_2 tend to do less well in school in the upper grades (Thomas & Collier, 1997).

Interdependence of First and Second Languages

Many studies have shown that cognitive and academic development in L_1 has a strong, positive effect on L_2 development for academic purposes (Collier, 1989c, 1992c; Cummins, 1991; Díaz & Klinger, 1991; Freeman & Freeman, 1992, 1994; García, 1993; Genesee, 1987, 1994; Hakuta, 1986; Lessow-Hurley,

1990; Lindholm, 1991; McLaughlin, 1992; Snow, 1990; Tinajero & Ada, 1993; Wong Fillmore & Valadez, 1986). Academic skills, literacy development, concept formation, subject knowledge, and learning strategies all transfer from L_1 to L_2 as the vocabulary and communicative patterns are developed in L_2 to express that academic knowledge. Cummins (1976, 1979a, 1981b, 1986b, 1991) refers to this phenomenon as **"common underlying proficiency"** or the **"interdependence" of languages.** Cummins' view is supported by research in linguistic universals, which has found many properties common across all languages at deep, underlying structural levels (Ellis, 1985, 1994). Only in surface structures do languages appear to be radically different. But still deeper than language itself is the underlying knowledge base and life experience that students have developed in L_1, all of which is available to them once they have the ability to express that knowledge in L_2. L_1 literacy is considered a crucial base for L_2 literacy development. Many research studies have found that a wide variety of skills and learning strategies that are developed in L_1 reading and writing can have positive transfer to L_2 reading and writing (Au, 1993; Bialystok, 1991; Cummins, 1989c, 1991, 1996b; Cummins & Swain, 1986; Freeman & Freeman, 1992; Genesee, 1987, 1994; Hudelson, 1994; Johnson & Roen, 1989; Lessow-Hurley, 1990; Lindholm, 1991; Snow, 1990; Tinajero & Ada, 1993; Wong Fillmore & Valadez, 1986). Some studies indicate that if a certain academic and literacy **threshold** (Cummins, 1976) is not reached in L_1 (at least four to five years of L_1 schooling), students may experience cognitive and academic difficulties in L_2 (Collier, 1987; Collier & Thomas, 1989; Cummins, 1976, 1981b, 1991; Dulay & Burt, 1980; Duncan & De Avila, 1979; Skutnabb-Kangas, 1981). Not only are L_1 literacy skills important to L_2 literacy in languages with obvious transfer possibilities, but also literacy skills from non-Roman-alphabet languages (such as Arabic, Hindi, Korean, and Mandarin Chinese) assist significantly with acquisition of L_2 literacy in a Roman-alphabet language such as English (Chu, 1981; Cummins, 1991; Thonis, 1981). Swain, Lapkin, Rowen, and Hart (1990) found that L_1 literacy has a strong positive impact on academic achievement even in L_3 for language-minority students attending Canadian bilingual immersion programs.

A number of researchers have criticized Cummins's threshold hypothesis as well as his distinction between social and academic language, suggesting that both are rooted in the deficit theory of **semilingualism,** or the belief that some language-minority children do not know any language at all, or speak their native and target languages with only limited ability (Edelsky, et al, 1983; Edelsky, 1996; MacSwan, 2000; MacSwan & Rolstad, in press; Martin-Jones & Romaine, 1986; Wiley, 1996). This belief has little theoretical or empirical validity, they argue, because all normal children acquire the language of their speech community, and thus are unlikely to arrive at school without the ability to understand or speak it. Moreover, the term "semilingualism" fits all too well into popular stereotypes about children who do not know English and do not know their mother tongue either, and therefore do poorly in school settings (MacSwan, 2000).

Cummins initially used the term in the context of the threshold hypothesis to characterize the low levels of academic proficiency that some bilingual students appeared to manifest in their two languages. He argued that failure to attain strong academic proficiency in either language "might mediate the consequences of their bilingualism for cognitive and academic development" (cited in Cummins, 2000, p. 100). Cummins made clear that such a condition was the result of discriminatory schooling and the systemic denial to language-minority students the opportunity to access literacy and academic language in either L_1 or L_2. Over the years, Cummins has repudiated his earlier use of the term (1979a, 2000), stating that it "has no theoretical value in describing or explaining the poor school performance of some bilingual students" (2000, p. 99). Nonetheless, he argues forcefully that the attainment—or not—of academic language proficiency is the principal variable in school success:

> . . . The denial of the theoretical utility of the construct of 'semilingualism' does not imply that the academic language proficiency (CALP) that bilingual students develop in their two languages is irrelevant to their academic progress. In fact, there is overwhelming evidence that for both monolingual and bilingual students, the degree of academic language proficiency they develop in school is a crucial intervening variable in mediating their academic progress. The vast majority of those who have argued that 'semilingualism does not exist' have failed to realize that theoretical constructs are not characterized by existence or nonexistence but by characteristics such as validity and usefulness, or their opposites. Most have also declined to engage with the question of how language proficiency is related to academic achievement and how individual differences in academic language proficiency should be characterized (2000, p. 99).

MacSwan (2000) and MacSwan and Rolstad (in press) extend the discussion about semilingualism and academic language proficiency in recent works. In a review of research studies of language variation, linguistic structure, school performances, and language loss, they argue that all of the research findings are either spurious or irrelevant. The authors maintain that semilingualism, as the basis of the threshold hypothesis, is essentially indistinguishable from classical prescriptivism, because it ascribes special status to the language of school, and hence to the language of the educated classes. Thus, the threshold hypothesis itself, like semilingualism and the BICs/CALP distinction, assumes that the "academic" language of the school is richer or inherently superior to the "social" language spoken by minority children at home. While first language literacy "and knowledge of academic discourse and vocabulary are certainly relevant to *academic* achievement, they are not relevant to *linguistic* achievement. All normal children achieve linguistically" (MacSwan, 2000, p. 35, emphasis in original). Wiley (1996), in his own critique of Cummins' distinction between "context-embedded/cognitively undemanding" social language and "context-reduced, cognitively demanding" academic language, similarly argues against the perspective that "literate academic language is *intrinsically* more cognitively demanding than oral language" (p. 171).

The deficit implications of the threshold hypothesis for policy and pedagogy have not been fully explored. On the one hand, the theory hypothe-
sizes that helping children achieve academic or cognitive thresholds in L_1
first—which then theoretically contribute to academic success in L_2—is
only possible at school (in a bilingual education program, for example) and
not in a language-minority home where there are perceived linguistic and
literacy deficiencies. On the other hand, the threshold hypothesis has been
widely embraced by teachers and researchers alike and has been used as
the justification for bilingual education program models that emphasize
academic instruction in L_1, accompanied by a gradual increase in English
language development. Indeed, as we discussed earlier, many studies have
indicated that cognitive and academic development in students' first language contributes positively to both the acquisition of English and academic
success in school.

The old notion that L_1 "interferes" with L_2 has not been supported by
research evidence (Larsen-Freeman & Long, 1991; McLaughlin, 1984, 1985,
1992). It is clear that L_1 serves a function in early L_2 acquisition, but it is a
supportive role rather than a negative one. In the beginning stages of L_2
acquisition, acquirers lean on their L_1 knowledge to analyze patterns in L_2,
and they subconsciously apply some structures from L_1 to L_2 in the early
stages of interlanguage development. Most linguists look upon this process as
a positive use of L_1 knowledge. Less reliance on L_1 structures occurs naturally
as the acquirer progresses to intermediate and advanced stages of L_2 acquisition. Overall, research has found less L_1 influence on L_2 vocabulary and
grammar development once students move beyond the beginning levels of
acquisition. Students beginning L_2 exposure as adolescents and adults experience some L_1 influence on L_2 pronunciation throughout their lives. Also,
research in L_2 academic writing has found considerable influence from L_1 on
L_2 rhetorical thought patterns (Connor & Kaplan, 1987).

Input and Interaction   Essential to the language acquisition process is a
source of input. This is best provided by speakers of the target language in
a social setting in which the target language speaker selects and modifies
the L_2 input in the context of social interaction with the L_2 learner so that
real communication takes place (Wong Fillmore, 1991a). Krashen (1981,
1982, 1985) posits that the key to L_2 acquisition is a source of L_2 input
that is understood, natural, interesting, useful for meaningful communication, and approximately one step beyond the learner's present level of
competence in L_2. In L_1 acquisition for children, adults and older children
provide natural input through caregiver speech, a modification of vocabulary and structures to enable meaningful communication with the child.
Some common characteristics of caregiver speech are focusing on the here
and now, shortening sentences, repeating through rephrasing, inserting
pauses, modeling what the child seems to want to say, correcting errors
indirectly, and focusing on communication rather than language form

(Berko Gleason, 1993; de Villiers & de Villiers, 1978; Snow & Ferguson, 1977; Wells, 1985). A natural stage of beginning L_1 acquisition can also be observed in beginning child L_2 acquisition, a "**silent period**" of several months when children mostly listen to the new language, without being forced to produce the new language. Young ESL beginners who rarely speak in the new L_2 have been found to make just as much, and frequently more, progress in L_2 acquisition as their more talkative classmates by the end of the first year of exposure to L_2 (Dulay, Burt, & Krashen, 1982; Saville-Troike, 1984; Wong Fillmore & Valadez, 1986).

While respecting an initial need for a silent period, as research has continued to discover the complexities of L_2 acquisition, most linguists today would agree that language acquisition does not generally occur purely through a source of input, but through *interaction* with that source of input (Allwright & Bailey, 1991; Chaudron, 1988; Ellis, 1985, 1990, 1994; Gass & Madden, 1985; Hatch, 1983; Swain, 1985; Wong Fillmore, 1989, 1991a). Researchers focusing on teacher talk as a source of L_2 input have found modifications in speech similar to those in caregiver speech, such as nonverbal pauses, gestures, and facial expressions; changes in volume and manner of delivery; simplification of syntax; repetitions, paraphrases, and expansions; use of visual aids and realia; and comprehension checks. Interactional features of teacher talk have added to the above strategies clarification and confirmation checks, explicit error correction and modeling appropriate form, as well as introducing playfulness with language (Smallwood, 1992).

While spoken input in L_2 comes from conversations, written input comes from reading in L_2. The most useful texts for L_2 learners have characteristics similar to spoken language. Meaningful readings are written in readable, natural language that is interesting, useful, and approximately one step beyond the student's present proficiency level in L_2 (Krashen, 1985). For a text to be meaningful, readings that are cognitively appropriate for a student's maturity level are crucial, but they are hard to find for older preliterate students. Also important is that readings activate the students' background knowledge and life experiences, which is best done through readings that present a bicultural or multicultural perspective (Au, 1993; Smallwood, 1991; Tharp & Gallimore, 1988; Tinajero & Ada, 1993).

Output is just as essential as input (Swain, 1985). Output comes from the L_2 learner in the form of speaking and writing. Interactional features mentioned above in spoken language are also available to students in written language through feedback from teachers and peers. Writing experienced through the writing process, with stimulation from peer and teacher interaction in response to each stage of the writing, leads to new language acquisition (Enright & McCloskey, 1988; Freeman & Freeman, 1992; Goodman & Wilde, 1992; Hudelson, 1994; Johnson & Roen, 1989). In summary, the negotiation of meaning through oral and written language between L_2 learners and native speakers is considered central to the acquisition process.

Second-Language Acquisition as a Natural, Developmental Process

Research evidence has found that many aspects of L_2 acquisition appear to be driven by an internal capability of the brain to facilitate this natural process. This innate ability is available to children, adolescents, and adults, in both untutored and classroom-assisted L_2 acquisition (Chomsky, 1957, 1965). Research on interlanguage (L_2 acquirers' language produced at various stages of L_2 acquisition) and language universals (properties common to many or all languages) continues to identify aspects of the process that most L_2 acquirers experience. While each student varies in the order and the rate at which specific language features are acquired, there are general, predictable stages that most learners pass through (Brown, 1994a; Ellis, 1985, 1994; Hakuta, 1987; Krashen, 1981; Larsen-Freeman & Long, 1991).

For example, there is a developmental sequence to the acquisition of negation, interrogation, and relative clauses in ESL acquisition. In the first stage, most acquirers commonly produce a word order that does not necessarily reflect the standard word order of English, and some sentence constituents are omitted. In the second stage, the acquirer begins to use English word order and most required sentence constituents are there, but grammatical accuracy is not. Grammatical morphemes begin to be used more systematically and meaningfully in the third stage. In the fourth stage, the acquirer moves to acquisition of more complex sentence structures (Ellis, 1985, pp. 58–64). Studies of ESL morpheme acquisition also provide evidence for a natural developmental sequence, regardless of the learner's background or L_1. For example, as a general pattern, the morpheme *-ing,* the plural, and the helping verb *to be* are acquired much earlier than the regular past tense, third-person singular present tense, and the possessive (Ellis, 1994; Krashen, 1977, 1981; Larsen-Freeman & Long, 1991).

Teachers can facilitate the natural process by recognizing that acquisition of any given feature in the language cannot be mastered quickly. A morpheme, for example, will be acquired in stages, with gradual awareness and refining of rules surrounding that morpheme, as the detail of complexity of its use becomes more evident to the acquirer. Formal instruction cannot speed up the natural developmental process, but it can facilitate it. Errors need not be viewed as lack of mastery but as positive steps in the L_2 acquisition process. While recognizing that the natural L_1 acquisition process is an innate capability also available to L_2 acquirers, much greater individual variation occurs in L_2 acquisition than in L_1 acquisition (Bialystok & Hakuta, 1994; Hakuta, 1986, 1987; Wong Fillmore, 1991a). This variation is due to the interaction of many other factors in second-language acquisition, including those discussed in the preceding section on linguistic processes, as well as sociocultural and cognitive variables to be discussed in the following sections.

Social and Cultural Processes

Social and cultural factors in the second-language acquisition process represent a wide range of mostly external forces that strongly affect the instructional context, such as students' socioeconomic status and past schooling, the functions of L_1 and L_2 use within a community, attitudes toward L_1 and L_2, social and psychological distance between L_1 and L_2 speakers, subordinate status of a minority group, cross-cultural conflict, and many more potential factors. While many social and cultural factors may not be easily modified by teacher or student, educators can adapt existing instructional practices and educational structures to provide as supportive an educational environment as possible for students' acquisition of L_2 and their successful academic achievement.

Extensive research from anthropology, sociology, sociolinguistics, psycholinguistics, social psychology, and education has identified many very powerful sociocultural influences on L_2 acquisition for schooling. To ignore these factors is equivalent to setting up a system for the academic failure of many L_2 students. The sociocultural context is different in each school setting, and it is therefore difficult to generalize findings from one community or school to another. However, research in each school setting can provide new insights into sociocultural patterns to illustrate the complexity of their interaction with the L_2 acquisition process. This brief review does not begin to cover the wide range of social and cultural processes that can interact with linguistic and cognitive variables. Only a few examples will be presented here, with expansion of this discussion in Chapters Five and Ten.

Language Use at School   An issue as seemingly simple as language use is fraught with sociocultural complications. Within school, what is allowed is often a reflection of language status within a given community. When the majority group wishes to keep a minority group in subordinate status, often school rules are subconsciously used to maintain the hierarchical relationship between groups. Use of a minority language is sometimes perceived as a threat by monolingual majority language speakers. Educational historians' analyses of U.S. school patterns in the 20th century are replete with examples of repression of minority language use at school—including physical punishment (Crawford, 1992a; Tyack, 1974). Why do we feel so threatened?

While in most other countries of the world bilingualism is the norm and is present in everyday life for all classes of society and all age groups (Grosjean, 1982), in the United States the pattern during the 20th century has been to encourage the eradication of bilingualism as quickly as possible. Yet in spite of this pattern, bilingualism persists. L_1 is used at home or in the language-minority community because a person's L_1 is intimately connected to his or her self-identity. It is the first means of expression of soul, kinship, emotions, tastes, sounds, and smells. L_1 is associated with the most important and intimate aspects of existence. To take L_1 away is to rob a person of his or her most basic identity and meaning in life.

Estimates from the 1990 U.S. Census have found that 55.9 million persons, or 22.5 percent of the total U.S. population, speak a non-English language at home (Waggoner, 1991). While the fear is expressed that immigrants are not learning English, this is far from the reality. Research clearly shows that language shift to English as the primary language occurs among language minorities faster in the United States than anywhere else in the world (by the second or third generation). Our high rate of immigration, with new arrivals daily, masks the language shift to English as the primary language that is actually occurring at a very rapid rate (Crawford, 1992a; Grosjean, 1982; Veltman, 1988).

Bilingual school personnel and educated language-minority parents, who work on building students' cognitive development in L_1, describe what an uphill battle it is to fight U.S. societal pressure for children to switch to English and lose L_1 as quickly as possible. Lambert (1975, 1984) refers to the lack of societal support for a minority language, with gradual loss of L_1, as subtractive bilingualism, a consequence of social pressure sometimes present in majority-minority relations. If L_1 loss occurs too early in life, though, it is associated with negative cognitive effects. Subtractive bilinguals (who lose L_1) perform less well on many cognitive and academic measures than additive bilinguals (who acquire L_2 *and* maintain L_1).

Societal and community patterns are reflected in school in relationships among various ethnolinguistic student groups and among students and staff. Conscious analysis of these forces can lead to constructive, democratic decisions for change for a classroom as well as for the whole school. Bilingual programs that provide strong instructional support for both L_1 and L_2, with more equal status given to the two languages, are the most successful programs for language-minority students, for both L_2 academic development and building students' self-confidence and self-esteem (Collier, 1989c, 1992c; Thomas & Collier, 1997). Among indigenous groups, L_1 revitalization in schools is crucial for cognitive development, to connect to the deep knowledge passed on within each ethnolinguistic community from generation to generation (Ovando, 1994; Ovando & Gourd, 1996), such as intimate knowledge of the ecology of a region and human responses to that environment. L_1 loss can lead to "a destruction of intimacy, the dismemberment of family and community, the loss of a rooted identity" (Slate, 1993, p. 30). In schools with no instructional support for L_1 for language-minority students, decisions can be made regarding social language use that reflect respect for the functions of L_1 for identity and cognitive development, as well as social and emotional support. Creating a school context for additive bilingualism demands respect and valuing of all minority languages, dialects, and cultures (Cummins, 1996b; Trueba, 1991).

Language use decisions apply not only to majority/minority languages in use in the school community, but also to regional varieties of language (such as the use of nonstandard dialects of a language). Linguists look upon all varieties of language as equally complex, grammatical, and purposeful (or they would not exist). Acknowledging that a language variety serves an important function in a given community and then assisting students with an analysis of the uses and contrasting features of that variety and the standard variety affirm students' identity and help with the process of bidialectal acquisition (Ovando, 1993).

Sociolinguists and anthropologists have amassed a significant body of knowledge examining the functions of language use in many culturally varied ethnolinguistic communities for a comparison with typical genres taught in U.S. schools. These studies have generally found a wealth of functions of language use that support and broaden the academic uses of language in school, much richer than narrow stereotypical perceptions that school staff members have of language development at home and in the community (Díaz, Moll, & Mehan, 1986; Heath, 1986; Minami & Ovando, in press; Trueba, Guthrie, & Au, 1981). When closer school-community relations are developed, what is frequently revealed is a richer, more complex range of language use in the home, community, and professional life, and a very narrow, restricted focus of uses of language at school. In several regions of the United States where a large ethnolinguistic community exists that has experienced discrimination and resultant low academic achievement in school, researchers and school staff have worked together to forge linkages between the community and school, resulting in contagious excitement among students and staff as an expanded school curriculum is developed that recognizes the social and cultural nature of learning and language development. Exciting, ongoing school-community linkages have radically transformed school practices and L_2 academic achievement among, for example, African Americans (Heath, 1983), Ethiopian Americans, Haitian Americans, Portuguese Americans (Warren, Rosebery, & Conant, 1990), Hawaiian Americans (Au & Jordan, 1981; Tharp & Gallimore, 1988; Vogt, Jordan, & Tharp, 1993), Mexican Americans (Ada, 1988; Delgado-Gaitán, 1987, 1990; Moll & Díaz, 1993; Moll, Vélez-Ibáñez, Greenberg, & Rivera, 1990), and Navajo students (Rosier & Holm, 1980; Tharp & Gallimore, 1988; Vogt, Jordan & Tharp, 1993).

Students' Socioeconomic Status   Any group of educators gathered together can very quickly identify many student background factors that they believe affect their students' success or lack of success in the classroom. How much these factors affect the L_2 acquisition process has not yet been analyzed extensively because it is difficult to control these variables in research, and their influence on L_2 development varies greatly from one student to another. For example, socioeconomic status (SES) was identified in educational research of the 1960s and 1970s as one of the most powerful variables influencing student achievement. A common approach to language teaching of the 1970s and early 1980s was to assume that students of low SES background were best taught through a carefully structured, sequenced, basic skills approach to language arts. Today, substantial research has found that this practice actually widens the gap in achievement between middle- and low-SES students as the students move into the upper grades; whole language approaches to language teaching hold more promise for addressing the language needs of students of all income backgrounds (National Coalition of Advocates for Students, 1988; Oakes, 1985; Rothman, 1991; Valdez Pierce, 1991).

For language minorities, severe poverty is not necessarily closely correlated with L_2 academic failure. The circumstances for each ethnolinguistic family in the United States may vary greatly, and many other factors may interact with SES to make it a less powerful variable in academic language development. Most new immigrants go through a shift in SES from home country to host country, some from higher SES to lower status in the United States, and others experiencing upward mobility upon emigration. Recent research on effective schools for language-minority students has found that low SES is a less powerful variable for students in schools that provide a strong bilingual/bicultural, academically rich context for instruction (Collier, 1992c; Cummins, 1996b; Krashen & Biber, 1988; Lucas, Henze, & Donato, 1990; Rothman, 1991; Thomas & Collier, 1997; Valdez Pierce, 1991).

Students' Past Schooling and Escape from War   Past educational experience is another factor in students' background that is much more powerful than SES for acquisition of academic L_2. Immigrants from an economically depressed region of the world may have experienced fewer school hours per day because of overcrowding of schools, or they may have come from a rural area with limited accessibility to formal schooling. Over the past decade, large numbers of new students have arrived in the United States from war-torn areas of the world, where they experienced long periods of interrupted schooling or crowded refugee camp conditions with little opportunity for instructional support. Very little research has been conducted on recent arrivals with little or no formal L_1 schooling. These students appear to need lots of academic support in the language in which they are cognitively more mature, L_1, to develop literacy, mathematics, science, and social studies knowledge as quickly as possible to make up years of missed instruction. In special programs developed for students from war-torn areas, teachers say that some students may also need lots of emotional support and counseling to deal with the scars of violence they have witnessed, lost family members, and continuing trauma of establishing stable family relations and meeting their basic survival needs.

In an analysis of Hmong adaptation to the U.S. school culture, Trueba, Jacobs, and Kirton (1990) concluded that the Indochinese children they studied who had escaped war and emigrated from refugee camps needed bicultural learning environments "to break the vicious cycle of stress, poor performance, humiliation, depression and failure" (p. 109). The researchers recommended school curricula for the Indochinese students that provide a meaningful way to integrate language, culture, and community knowledge, making each academic activity functionally meaningful and connecting it to students' prior knowledge, based on the model developed by Tharp and Gallimore (1988). This model has been successfully applied to language-minority students in Hawaii, Arizona, and California, significantly increasing academic L_2 achievement.

Caplan, Choy, and Whitmore (1992) examined 6,750 Southeast Asian boat people who emigrated to the United States following devastating hardships suffered in war and relocation camps. The researchers collected extensive information on these Indochinese parents and their children, using survey data, interviews conducted in L_1, and students' academic records at school, including grade point averages and standardized test scores. Contrary to the researchers' expectations, they found that the strongest predictors of L_2 academic success for these Indochinese children were parents' maintenance of L_1 at home, reading books in L_1 to their children, and strong retention of their own cultural traditions and values, including providing a supportive home environment that placed a high value on love of learning. These were families who, for the most part, had not had extensive opportunities for formal schooling in the past; education had been a restricted privilege for the well-to-do. In spite of parents' lack of formal education and lack of English proficiency, they were able to provide the family support needed to help their children excel in L_2 academic achievement through continuing development of their first language and cultural heritage at home.

Length of Residence in the Country of Immigration   For immigrants, length of residence in the country of immigration is a key variable in L_2 acquisition for the first five years of exposure to the natural L_2 environment (Cummins, 1991). Teachers can expect immigrants who have received at least four to five years of schooling in L_1 to make substantial progress in academic L_2 with each succeeding year of exposure to L_2. For example, after five years of exposure to English in the United States, many immigrants with strong educational backgrounds from their home country begin to reach the stage of L_2 proficiency where they can successfully compete with native speakers on standardized measures of academic achievement. Five years is the shortest amount of time found in any study of immigrants being schooled completely in L_2 after arrival (Collier, 1989c, 1992c; Thomas & Collier, 1997). But it is important to understand that it takes at least five years because school measures of academic success are school tests that change with every year of school in contrast to a language proficiency test, which is a more static measure. Non-native speakers are being compared to native speakers who are also growing linguistically, academically, and cognitively with each year of schooling, and the tests for each grade level change to reflect this growth.

Thus it is unreasonable to expect students to make faster progress. Language acquisition cannot be accelerated; it is a developmental process that occurs over many years, given the basic conditions for acquisition: access to speakers of the target language and a social setting that encourages natural interaction with target language speakers. Exiting students from special support in ESL classes after two to three years should be done only with the clear understanding among grade-level teachers that L_2 development is at the most half completed and that these students will still be continuing to acquire L_2 skills with each succeeding year within the mainstream. Length of residence in the country of immigration is one of several very strong variables influencing L_2 development, but only through the first five to seven years in the new country.

Interestingly, quantity of L_2 input applies to number of years of exposure to L_2, but not to number of hours per day. Those who prefer "sink-or-swim" all-English instruction, although providing no special support of any kind for limited-English-proficient students is not in compliance with U.S. federal standards,[3] argue that the more instruction provided in English, the faster immigrants will learn English. While this argument sounds logical, the research on this topic has clearly shown that half a day of instruction in L_2 is just as effective as a full day, when the other half of the day consists of continuing academic instruction in L_1. Students being schooled bilingually, who receive only a half day of L_2 exposure, have generally taken four to seven years to reach L_2 academic proficiency comparable to that of a native speaker. Academic skills being developed in L_1 transfer to L_2, and this can be a crucial base for L_2 academic development (Collier, 1992c, 1999; Wong Fillmore, & Valadez, 1986).

The Classroom Environment and Affective Factors   The social context within the classroom can affect students' L_2 acquisition in many varied ways. Wong Fillmore (1991a) describes some of the basic social processes needed for natural L_2 acquisition to occur:

> Learners have to make the speakers aware of their special linguistic needs, and get them to make whatever accommodations and adjustments are necessary for successful communication—a difficult task. Communication with learners is never easy because it takes special thought and effort to make oneself understood, and to figure out what the learner is trying to say. . . . When target language speakers and learners interact, both sides have to cooperate in order for communication to take place. The learners make use of their social knowledge to figure out what people might be saying, given the social situation. The learners assume that the speech used by the speakers is relevant to the immediate situation; if the target language speakers are being cooperative, this will indeed be true. This is possible when the social settings in which learning takes place provide meaningful contacts between learners and speakers of the language. (pp. 53–54)

To create an acquisition-rich classroom environment, teachers need to plan lessons that begin by activating students' background knowledge and lead to discovery of new knowledge through problem-solving, interactive tasks. Cooperative learning (explored in Chapter Three) can serve as a classroom management structure for grouping students in varied ways to allow for peer interaction and discovery learning.

Establishing a cooperative learning environment among students is not an easy task, but it is essential to language acquisition. Research in L_2 acquisition has shown that a student's lowered anxiety level, self-confidence, and self-esteem are important affective factors that enhance the language acquisition process (Brown, 1994a; Krashen, 1982; Richard-Amato, 1996). Students need a supportive classroom environment in which affective or emotional development is valued as much as the cognitive side of learning. While most current L_2 acquisition theories emphasize a balance of linguistic, social, and cognitive factors, there is no doubt that the *interaction* of social, affective, and cultural factors with linguistic and cognitive factors can strongly influence the language acquisition process.

Societal Factors   One more example of the wide range of potential sociocultural influences on acquisition of L_2 for schooling can be classified as societal factors. These are powerful influences that are sometimes very difficult for a school staff to overcome. However, they can be modified by creating a school culture different from the society around it, when the staff and students decide that they really want the sociocultural context for schooling to change.

Societal factors basically revolve around relations between groups, such as social and psychological distance between L_1 and L_2 speakers, perceptions of each group in interethnic comparisons, cultural stereotyping, intergroup hostility, subordinate status of a minority group, patterns of assimilation (losing first culture when acquiring second culture) or acculturation (acquiring and affirming both first and second cultures) (Brown, 1994a; McLaughlin, 1985; Schumann, 1978). These factors can immensely complicate the L_2 acquisition process, but research is imprecise in determining the extent and range of their influence. Majority-minority and interethnic relations are at the heart of these factors influencing L_2 acquisition. The term *empowerment* has come to symbolize the struggles embodied in each group's access to education and general success in life.

Some analyses of societal structures can be very depressing, such as Ogbu's (1974, 1978, 1987, 1992, 1993) conclusion that the United States is essentially a caste society that excludes true participation of subordinate and indigenous minorities (incorporated into this country against their will through slavery, conquest, or colonization) in access to education or career opportunities for advancement. Oakes (1985; Oakes, Wells, Yonezawa, & Ray, 1997) has found extensive evidence of institutionalized racial bias in the U.S. educational system, with minority students still being counseled into nonacademic tracks and generally denied many educational opportunities. She encourages major U.S. educational reform to eliminate tracking and to use cooperative learning for interactive, interdisciplinary, multicultural, and problem-solving classes.

Other analyses of language-minority education have examined, for example, inequality and discrimination in U.S. schools (Suárez-Orozco, 1987, 1993), language-minority parents' perceptions of school and the need for closer school-community linkages (Delgado-Gaitán, 1987, 1990), and the role of transitional bilingual education in maintaining the status quo in majority–minority relations because their short-term support for both L₁ and L₂ development is too limited to be of help (Hernández-Chávez, 1977, 1984; Spener, 1988). Cummins (1995) presents a major analysis of U.S. societal patterns from a language-minority perspective and proposes "empowerment pedagogy" (pp. 70–86) as the best way to challenge societal structures reflected in education. Instead of a knowledge transmission approach in which "the teacher's role is to drill skills into reluctant skulls" (p. 71), empowerment pedagogy creates an interactive, experiential classroom in which critical thinking skills are developed; cooperative learning is used for interactive, small-group problem solving; and process writing is developed. Social and cultural factors influencing language acquisition will be discussed in much more detail in Chapters Five and Nine.

Cognitive Processes

Cognitive processes refer to the aspects of language development that occur inside a student's head. In contrast to the natural, subconscious linguistic processes described earlier, some cognitive processes can be mediated by the learner and influenced by the teacher and the instructional setting. How central these conscious cognitive processes are to second language acquisition is the subject of an ongoing debate. Krashen (1981, 1982) popularized a distinction between subconscious acquisition and formal, conscious learning, basing his ideas on Chomsky's and other linguists' work. Chomsky (1957, 1965) posits that an innate language acquisition device is the central mechanism in first-language acquisition. Krashen believes that this innate mechanism is also central to the acquisition of a second language, thus taking the position that formal learning in the classroom serves a very limited role in the language acquisition process. However, others such as Ellis (1985, 1990), Wong Fillmore (1991a), McLaughlin (1987), and O'Malley and Chamot (1990) give conscious cognitive processes a more central role in second-language acquisition. Wong Fillmore (1991a) describes some of the cognitive processes that she considers central to second-language acquisition:

> What learners must do with linguistic data is discover the system of rules the speakers of the language are following, synthesize this knowledge into a grammar, and then make it their own by internalizing it. . . . Learners apply a host of cognitive strategies and skills to deal with the task at hand: They have to make use of associative skills, memory, social knowledge, and inferential skills in trying to figure out what people are talking about. They use whatever analytical skills they have to figure out relationships between forms, functions, and meanings. They have to make use of memory, pattern recognition, induction, categorization, generalization, inference, and the like to figure out the structural principles by which the forms of the language can be combined, and meanings modified by changes and deletions. (pp. 56–57)

Many linguists have analyzed a great variety of ways in which cognition plays a role in second-language acquisition, more than can be reviewed in this brief discussion (see, for example, the journal *Language and Cognitive Processes*). The studies on language transfer have found that L_2 acquirers rely on their knowledge of L_1 for learning the L_2, noticing features in the input in L_2 and comparing those features with their internal language systems. Interlanguage theory analyzes the stages that learners go through in hypothesis testing regarding the rules of the new language system, although this occurs mainly at the subconscious level. Ellis (1994) presents a detailed analysis of cognitive accounts of second-language acquisition.

Studies on linguistic universals provide further evidence for the role of cognition in second-language acquisition. In the theories that explore the role of innate knowledge, some linguists have analyzed linguistic universals by attempting to identify typological universals through the study of many world languages. Other researchers have followed the generative school started by Chomsky, studying each individual language in great depth, in order to identify the principles of grammar underlying and governing specific rules, referred to as Universal Grammar (Ellis, 1994). This research provides further evidence for what Cummins refers to as the interdependence of languages, or common underlying proficiency (1976, 1979a, 1981b, 1986b, 1991, 1996b), an important concept for bilingual and ESL educators to understand (discussed earlier in this chapter).

Learning Strategies   As cognitive psychologists and linguists have continued to explore the relationship between language and cognition in first-language acquisition, Chamot and O'Malley (1986, 1987, 1994; O'Malley & Chamot, 1990) have extended this research to second-language acquisition. They have found that second-language learners' use of learning strategies makes a significant difference in their academic success in the second language. Learning strategies are the techniques that students use to understand and retain information and to solve problems.

Oxford's (1990) classification of strategies used in language learning includes three general categories of indirect strategies—metacognitive, affective,

Guidelines for Teaching

LEARNING STRATEGIES

Metacognitive strategies—planning for learning, monitoring one's own comprehension and production, and evaluating how well one has achieved a learning objective.

Cognitive strategies—manipulating the material to be learned mentally (as in making images or elaborating) or physically (as in grouping items to be learned or taking notes).

Social/affective strategies—either interacting with another person in order to assist learning, as in cooperative learning, and asking questions for clarification, or using affective control to assist learning tasks. (Chamot & O'Malley, 1994, pp. 60–61)

and social strategies—and adds three categories of direct strategies—memory, cognitive, and compensation strategies. Oxford (1990) defines learning strategies as "operations employed by the learner to aid the acquisition, storage, retrieval, and use of information . . . to make learning easier, faster, more enjoyable, more self-directed, more effective, and more transferable to new situations" (p. 8). Research has found that second-language learners who receive instruction with explicit teaching of learning strategies become more efficient and effective learners (Oxford, 1990; Thomas, 1994; Wenden & Rubin, 1987).

L_1 Cognition and L_2 Academic Language Development   Cummins' (1991) research synthesis on attribute-based aspects of L_2 proficiency (internal to the learner) has shown that cognitive processes are much more responsible for *academic* language development and less closely correlated with *social* language development. In contrast, L_2 social language development is strongly related to both the personality of the learner and the quality and quantity of L_2 input received by the learner (Cummins, 1984b, 1991). Furthermore, strong research evidence demonstrates consistent crosslingual relationships between L_1 and L_2 cognitive and academic language development. Acquisition of academic L_2 is closely connected to cognitive development in L_1. The research evidence overwhelmingly shows that when a student's cognitive and academic growth in L_1 is more fully developed, the student's proficiency and academic development in L_2 will deepen (Collier, 1992c; Cummins, 1991; Thomas & Collier, 1997).

This has implications for the language spoken at home. Many well-meaning U.S. teachers advise language-minority parents to speak only English at home. Yet this is the worst advice that can be given. When parents and children speak the language they know best, they are working at their highest level of cognitive maturity and are continuing cognitive development. Parents do not have to be formally schooled to provide this crucial support. For example, solving problems together, building or fixing something, cooking meals, talking about a television program, or going somewhere together are cooperative family activities that can stimulate the continuation of children's cognitive processes. Once language-minority parents understand the importance of L_1 cognitive development and the role they can play in reinforcing their children's cognitive growth, they are usually overjoyed to assist schools with L_1 cognitive development at home (Arnberg, 1987; Caplan, Choy, & Whitmore, 1992; Delgado-Gaitán, 1990; Dolson, 1985; Genesee, 1994; Moll, Vélez-Ibáñez, Greenberg, & Rivera, 1990; Saunders, 1988; Skutnabb-Kangas & Cummins, 1988; Wong Fillmore, 1991b).

Another important implication of the research on crosslingual transfer of cognitive development is that we can no longer afford the time wasted in teaching language in isolation from the rest of the curriculum. For the deepest level of proficiency in a second language, both first and second languages should be developed through continuing cognitive and academic growth in L_1

and L_2 through cognitively demanding mathematics, language arts, science, and social studies interdisciplinary problem solving.

Individual Variation   Probably the strongest generalization that could be made regarding second language acquisition is that there is great individual variation among students acquiring L_2. This is due to the large number of interacting variables across the four dimensions of language acquisition just described in this chapter: linguistic, sociocultural, cognitive, and academic. Personal attributes such as personality, age, aptitude, and cognitive styles, as well as the sociocultural circumstances of learning and many other factors interact with each other in extremely complex ways. The interwoven relationship between linguistic, sociocultural, academic, and cognitive processes is an everyday reality that teachers must face by creating a classroom context where the magic can happen. The next section on instructional approaches to teaching a second language addresses that reality.

Instructional Approaches to Teaching a Second Language

Second-language teaching approaches (such as teaching ESL, or teaching Spanish or Vietnamese or Arabic as a second language in a two-way bilingual class) have gone through a radical transformation over the past decade, keeping in stride with curricular reform occurring in mathematics, science, social studies, and language arts for native speakers. Some of this change has occurred more easily in the elementary grades because school structures are smaller and more flexible and curricular subjects are not as tightly defined by time periods and by specialists for each subject as they are in high schools. This change has not by any means occurred everywhere, and many teachers who have more recently completed their teacher education training and have embraced the new ideas bemoan the slowness of school systems to change. Nevertheless, the curricular reforms are spreading rapidly across the United States. The difference from previous "fads" in education is that the suggested changes are backed by considerable research evidence that these changes will make a substantial difference in all students' academic achievement.

Reflecting the reality of a decade ago, the language chapter of the first edition of this book focused on the teaching of language mostly as a subject by itself. Now ESL and bilingual teachers increasingly are being asked to team teach with other subject area teachers, or to coordinate curricula more closely with grade-level teachers, or to serve as a second-language specialist across the curriculum within the grade-level classroom, or to continue to teach in a separate classroom but to teach language and content areas simultaneously. Language is no longer taught as an isolated subject area.

In this chapter, while we take time to focus on particular aspects of language teaching, all of these aspects of language development take place not in isolation, but in a context in which the teaching of language is integrated with academic content and uses all language modes (listening, speaking, reading, and writing). Throughout this book, we also make a strong case for providing wherever possible for the social integration of minority and majority students, for the instructional integration of all staff, and the integration of home and school contexts. All current research findings imply that the most promising classroom practices for heterogeneous classes are (1) having language taught through meaningful content, usually organized by themes; (2) chosen through teacher-student collaborative inquiry and discovery learning; (3) in a cooperative learning setting, with use of a wide variety of classroom structures that involve extensive interaction among students; (4) leading to tasks that involve creative problem solving and stimulate the development of higher-order thinking skills; (5) and making use of the latest technological advances available to students to prepare students for the workplace of the 21st century where workers will need to problem solve cooperatively, be comfortable with technology, and know how to get access to information resources. It is in this context that the following comparative analysis of the range of instructional approaches to teaching second language is presented.

Traditional Approaches to ESL Instruction

Throughout this section, we will refer to the teaching of ESL as an example of second-language instruction, so as not to exhaust the reader with repetition of all the other possible languages to which this discussion can be applied. Thus when we refer to ESL, we also imply SSL (Spanish as a second language), KSL (Korean as a second language) or any other language taught to English speakers in a bilingual classroom. The second language to be taught does not change the basic instructional approach. In contrast, foreign language teaching (language taught as a subject in a setting in which students receive little exposure to the language either from peers or outside the classroom) is very different from second-language teaching and may change greatly depending on the context and the language to be taught. Second-language teaching involves students' natural acquisition of the language through meaningful academic tasks and through informal contact with peers who speak the second language.

Traditional approaches to teaching ESL in general have been (1) teacher-centered and teacher-controlled, (2) very carefully structured, (3) sequenced mostly by grammar structures to be taught, (4) with discrete units of language taught separately (part to whole), (5) focused mostly on producing correct form, (6) with the learner treated as a passive recipient of knowledge *about* the language, (7) with little focus on language *use* for communicative or other meaningful purposes, and (8) with ESL taught as a subject by itself. Some examples follow.

Grammar-Translation   In English as a Foreign Language (EFL) teaching around the world, grammar-translation is still used by many teachers who are not native speakers of English and who feel less comfortable with their level of proficiency in English. The students' L$_1$ is used a great deal in a grammar-translation course to explain the grammatical structures of English, to define vocabulary, and to translate readings in English. Emphasis is on the development of reading, writing, and grammar, with less concern for oral English language development because of the lack of access to native speakers of English. This method usually involves memorizing long vocabulary lists out of context, deductive instruction of grammar in which rules are taught explicitly, practice of extensive verb conjugations that are committed to memory, and reading literature passages through translation, with the teacher serving as an authority figure and providing immediate error correction. Grammar-translation was developed in the mid-19th century and remained popular in the United States as a method for teaching foreign languages until the mid-20th century. It is still used in the United States to teach classical languages such as Greek or Latin. (For more description, see Chastain, 1988; Larsen-Freeman, 1986; Richards & Rodgers, 1986.)

Audiolingual Method   This method was developed in reaction to grammar-translation's lack of emphasis on oral skills. Experimentation with the audiolingual method was accelerated during World War II, when U.S. military personnel were in need of crash courses in communicative skills in foreign languages, and it peaked in popularity in the United States during the 1960s. Even with heavy criticism from cognitive linguists during the 1970s, many current ESL textbooks are heavily based on audiolingual methodology, although they may claim to be more up-to-date. This method is also used extensively for EFL teaching around the world.

The audiolingual method is based on theories from structural linguistics and behavioral psychology. ESL is taught through mimicry and memorization and through repetitive, manipulative drills. Grammar structures are carefully sequenced and taught inductively, with immediate error correction. All four language skills (now referred to as "modes") are considered important, but the sequence of teaching listening and speaking first, followed later by reading and writing, led many language teachers to assume that an oral base was an essential prerequisite to the written word. Reading research today, on the other hand, shows that with school-age learners, listening and reading can be acquired simultaneously and are reinforced by speaking and writing. Tapes, language labs, and visual aids are considered crucial for authentic implementation of the audiolingual method. Minimal use of students' L_1 used to be the rule, but practice in EFL settings frequently includes substantial use of L_1 for explanations.

The audiolingual method has been heavily criticized for producing students who could model perfect sentences in English with nativelike pronunciation but could not use the language in a real communicative situation with native speakers. Student graduates of the method criticize it for its military-like drills; its boring repetitions, which do not encourage students to focus on meaning; and the long dialogues to be memorized, which have little transfer to real language use. Cognitive linguists criticize the method for the structural linguistic principles on which it is based, such as language learning as habit formation, and the emphasis on many discrete points of language to be mastered before reaching the stage of meaningful communication (part to whole). (For further reading, see Bowen, Madsen, & Hilferty, 1985; Celce-Murcía, 1991; Chastain, 1988; Larsen-Freeman, 1986; Richards & Rodgers, 1986.)

Direct Method Another reaction to grammar-translation is the direct method, which has been in existence for a century or more as a natural way to learn language through acquisition. Sometimes the term *immersion* is used in referring to direct method, but this use of the word should not be confused with immersion bilingual programs, in which there is always substantial native-language support in school. The direct method focuses on total immersion in L_2 throughout each language lesson, with no use of L_1 allowed in the L_2 classrooms. New material is frequently presented through films, tapes, and readings that are situational or organized around topics. However, the direct method may be structured with a plan for sequencing the vocabulary, verb forms, and grammar points to be mastered. As in the audiolingual method, grammar structures are intended to be picked up inductively rather than consciously taught. The direct method does not focus on manipulative drills as does the audiolingual method. Instead, it involves an open-ended response to the materials the teacher brings into the classroom, which leads the class towards a more natural acquisition process, focused on authentic activities. We classify this method as one of the traditional methods because in practice in classes such as those using the Berlitz method (which is one of the few curricula left today in which the direct method is claimed to be used), ESL tends to be taught in a very structured, sequenced curriculum that is very teacher controlled. (For further reading, see Bowen, Madsen, & Hilferty, 1985; Diller, 1978; Larsen-Freeman, 1986; Richards & Rodgers, 1986.)

ESL Methods in Transition

Language teaching innovations of the 1960s, 1970s, and 1980s, which some teachers faithfully tried, have brought important changes to our ways of thinking about ESL teaching, but none of these methods has been adopted for general practice by the large majority of ESL teachers, with the exception of the Natural Approach (discussed later). These innovations appear to have served as a transition towards current approaches, which embody an eclectic mix of techniques from historical and more recently developed ESL methods, combined with some major changes in the philosophical conception of the teacher-student relationship to one of collaborative inquiry with highly interactive classes, focused on the teaching of language through meaningful content rather than language as an isolated subject. The methods or approaches described in this section have some characteristics that are more typical of traditional approaches, while introducing some aspects of instructional practice that have led to the most current approaches.

Silent Way Caleb Gattegno developed the Silent Way, an approach that forces the teacher to be silent at least 90 percent of the time and to let students generate language on their own. There is no use of students' L_1 allowed during formal presentation of the lesson. Students begin with childlike experimentation with sounds. In an initial lesson, the teacher points to color-coded graphemes on charts that cover all visual representations of the phonemes in English. As students discover the sounds of the new language, precision with phonemes, stress, and intonation is reinforced through repetition and teacher signals, but with little teacher talk, with the teacher modeling a sound or expression only once. As the lesson progresses, Cuisenaire rods (color-coded by size and traditionally used for teaching math) are used to teach simple grammar points inductively. Word charts, wall pictures, and worksheets are used as the course develops to increase vocabulary and provide topics for conversation and composition. Students initiate and generate language that is teacher-guided and teacher-sequenced. Error correction is initiated by student peers with no judgment expressed by the teacher. The key is that students help other students, with teacher guidance but not teacher control.

While the Silent Way attempts to develop learner independence, the approach cannot be classified as learner centered because the teacher controls the curriculum, and the material is carefully structured and sequenced, still emphasizing mastery of small parts of language before moving to more meaningful language use. In most ways, this experiment remains closer to the traditional approaches to teaching ESL, using the structured, sequenced, part-to-whole, grammar-driven curriculum. Its contributions to language teaching are the use of Cuisenaire rods as abstract symbols for teaching some features of a language, the color-coded phonemic charts (which are more useful for languages with a closer sound-symbol correspondence than that afforded by English), and the philosophy that the learner can take more responsibility for his or her own learning process, with less dependence on the teacher. (For a more detailed description, see Gattegno, 1976; Larsen-Freeman, 1986; Richards & Rodgers, 1986; Stevick, 1980.)

Suggestopedia   Developed in Bulgaria by Georgi Lozanov, this method also emphasizes childlike experimentation with ESL. The Suggestopedic teacher takes a strong role as guide and authority figure in deciding what takes place in class; however, students also initiate and generate language, with the guidance of the teacher. The physical setting for lessons must be relaxing and aesthetically pleasing. Music, art, drama, yoga, and physical exercise are used to encourage relaxation, stimulation of the subconscious, and informal, natural communication. On entering class, students accept a surrogate identity for role playing. Long dialogues are presented in phases and include long spaces of silence with classical baroque music played in the background. Later, students engage in interaction activities based on the dialogue. The teacher is expected to be lively and to uphold the overall goal of reducing the anxieties of students. Error correction is minimal. Students' L_1 may be used for explanations and discussion. A major goal is to tap students' natural subconscious processes that will allow more retention in long-term memory.

Suggestopedia's emphasis on learning in a relaxed setting, teaching language through the arts and physical exercise, and focusing on language use rather than language form, have provided contributions to current approaches. However, Suggestopedia still remains traditional in its teacher-directed curriculum, with focus on long dialogues as the main form of new material presented to students. (For further reading, see Bancroft, 1978; Larsen-Freeman, 1986; Lozanov, 1978; Lozanov & Gateva, 1988; Richards & Rodgers, 1986; Stevick, 1980.)

Community Language Learning   Developed by Charles Curran, Community Language Learning is based on principles from humanistic psychology. The most important goal is creation of a cooperative learning community, in which students are responsible for each other (similar to that of Silent Way). On the first day, learners are seated in a closed circle (a maximum of six students is ideal), with the resource person (the teacher, called the "knower") outside the circle. The learners initiate conversation in L_1 and the knower provides translation in L_2, close to the student's ear, in a clear, gentle, supportive voice. The sentences generated are taped. After 8 to 10 sentences, the students and knower work with this material, guided by the knower through occasional short silent periods followed by questions (e.g., "Do you remember anything we said?"). Students may ask anything they desire, and discussion may flow freely in L_1 and L_2. The knower serves as facilitator rather than dominant authority figure and engages in minimal error correction. Group problem solving, with lessons generated by students, is somewhat like a therapy group, and often becomes personal and very realistic. Anxieties are lowered; natural L_2 acquisition is encouraged; and a learning community is created in which the students actively support, counsel, and motivate each other. The use of L_1 is very gradually phased out as L_2 acquisition expands.

This approach to teaching EFL/ESL has received attention in publications but has been implemented in few classrooms due to the small preferred class size and the full bilingual proficiency that the teacher must have to be accurate with the translations from students' L_1 to L_2. The translation required in this method is not practical for an ESL class with students of many language backgrounds. Nevertheless, Community Language Learning brought language teaching methods still closer to the goals of current approaches used today. The curriculum includes language taught through meaningful content generated by students, discovery learning that is learner centered, and a focus on language for communicative use as opposed to focus mostly on form. However, it was designed mainly to teach language alone, rather than language taught through academic content. (For further reading, see Curran, 1976; Larsen-Freeman, 1986; Richards & Rodgers, 1986; Stevick, 1980.)

Total Physical Response   This technique, developed by James Asher, is very useful for the early stages of second-language acquisition as one strategy to be incorporated into teachers' repertoire of activities within current ESL approaches. The teacher gives a command and models the physical movement to carry out the command. In the first stages, students focus only on listening comprehension by responding to the commands with the appropriate physical movement. Speaking, reading, and writing the commands come soon after. Adding touch and movement to the stimulants of sight and sound increases the potential for storage into long-term memory. Many natural activities make use of mostly commands and can be successfully incorporated into lessons; for example, cooking, operating a machine, physical exercise, doing artwork, giving directions, putting together a do-it-yourself project, driving a car, doing mathematics operations, conducting a science experiment, learning how to use the library, and so on. While Asher describes this technique as a method, most teachers would agree that this technique cannot stand alone but can be used as one of many strategies for varied lessons. (For more reading, see Asher, 1982; Larsen-Freeman, 1986; Oller, 1993; Richards & Rodgers, 1986.)

Natural Approach   In the late 1970s, Tracy Terrell and Stephen Krashen proposed a method of teaching second language that emphasizes the centrality of the acquisition process. Techniques in this approach focus on providing a context in the classroom for natural language acquisition to occur, with acquirers receiving maximum "comprehensible input" (Krashen, 1985), and establishing the best conditions possible for reducing the affective factors that may inhibit students' L_2 acquisition (Krashen, 1982). This is done through a teacher's simplification of his or her speech, similar to modifications in caretaker speech, and through the creation of low-anxiety situations. Other factors include (1) a focus on each student's needs and desires, (2) little overt error correction, (3) avoidance of forcing production until acquirers are ready, and (4) a positive acceptance of the children's native language, while modeling the second language. Traditional drills that are focused on a specific grammar point fail as a source for acquisition and thus are not used. In the early stages, the Natural Approach uses Total Physical Response techniques, allowing the acquirer as long a silent period as needed. As the acquisition process expands, pictures, manipulatives, games, problem solving, and humanistic activities focus students' attention on the content of language rather than on form. As social language is developed, academic language is increasingly taught.

When Krashen and Terrell (1983) published their first detailed description of this approach to teaching a second language, basing it on Krashen's second-language acquisition theory, they presented the Natural Approach as "designed primarily to enable a beginning student to reach acceptable levels of oral communicative ability in the language classroom" (p. 131). However, the approach has evolved over time into an expanded version of the authors' original conception, as it has been widely adopted in ESL classrooms on the West coast of the United States (Solís, 1989). The teaching of reading and writing through the language experience approach and other whole-language approaches has been incorporated by most teachers into beginning ESL lessons using the Natural Approach. In addition, ESL Natural Approach classes are now generally taught through meaningful thematic academic content. The

Natural Approach as it has actually been implemented by teachers has come the closest to the goals of current eclectic approaches to language teaching (Solís, 1989). The focus is on communicative language use (oral and written), with all four language modes integrated into each lesson, and error correction is indirect. Language is taught through meaningful content (whole to part), focused on discovery learning in a cooperative learning setting, leading to creative problem solving, with the teacher serving as facilitator rather than authority figure. (For additional reading, see Blair, 1982; Krashen & Terrell, 1983; Richard-Amato, 1988; Richards & Rodgers, 1986; Solís, 1989; Terrell, 1981.)

Current Approaches to ESL and Bilingual Instruction

In the 1990s, U.S. educators called for major reforms in all areas (instructional methods, curricular materials, assessment practices, and administrative structures) to respond to dramatic demographic changes (increased immigration to the United States and mobility within the United States) and major shifts in the economy and the workplace as we move into the 21st century. Current approaches to language teaching are a response to these global changes, as well as a reflection of new insights from research in language acquisition, reviewed in the first section of this chapter.

In the United States, heterogeneous classes are a reality that is here to stay. As teachers have responded to this reality, we have recognized that no single method of language teaching is effective with all students (Hamayan, 1993). Recent second-language acquisition research has also discovered many complex interacting factors that influence the process of language development, with great variability from one learner to another. Therefore, current instructional approaches represent a blend of past and present techniques that have evolved over time, in response to students' needs, changing assumptions about the language-learning process, and implications from research on second-language acquisition. No convenient label can be used to identify one specific approach or instructional method that is currently fashionable. In the following paragraphs, we will try to summarize some of the most salient features of current approaches to second-language teaching.

Integration of Language and Content   The overriding drive in current changes occurring in second-language teaching is the need to teach language through something essential and meaningful to the student. When the goal of an ESL class is to prepare students for academic success in classes taught in English, as is the case in teaching ESL in grades K through 12, then ESL is best taught through lessons that teach meaningful mathematics, science, social studies, and language arts concepts simultaneously with second-language objectives. Thus we have shifted from an ESL approach that focused mainly on *grammatical knowledge* of English, which was in vogue for the first half of the 20th century, to the goal of *language use* common to the varied communicative approaches introduced in the 1960s and 1970s, to current approaches that teach *language use in a meaningful context* begun in the late 1980s and 1990s. Teaching meaningful academic language requires establishing close coordination with teachers who teach students of the same age. The ESL teacher needs to know the curricular objectives for each grade level and each subject area of the students assigned to his or her classes. Depending on the circumstances of students' past educational experiences, an ESL teacher needs to know not only the age-appropriate objectives but also all prior grade-level objectives to help students catch up and keep up with the academic work required of their age group. Schools with bilingual instruction provide crucial support with this process.

Teaching language lessons through academic content does not mean taking all the fun out of ESL. In fact, these can be exciting, magical classes. How about a primary school ESL math/science project to plan and build a terrarium or any other type of enclosure for some plants and animals for your classroom, with careful research on an ecologically sound environment for these living creatures that will join your class? At the secondary level, you might plan a math/science/social studies unit with your Central American students on the destruction of tropical rainforests and the ecological consequences for the Americas, through examination of statistical graphs and charts gathered from environmental agencies, exploration of political and economic patterns in U.S.–Central American relations, analysis of birds' migratory patterns across the Americas as well as species threatened with extinction in the rainforests, geographical analyses of land use and topographical features, and future planning for the ecological health of the Americas. The chapters on culture, social studies, mathematics, and science that follow this language chapter will provide many more examples of ways to develop meaningful language through content lessons. (For readings on ESL taught through content, see Adamson, 1993; Brinton, Snow, & Wesche, 1989; Cantoni-Harvey, 1987; Chamot & O'Malley, 1994; Cocking & Mestre, 1988; Crandall, 1987, 1993; Crandall, Dale, Rhodes, & Spanos, 1989; Faltis, 1997; Fathman & Quinn, 1989; Fathman, Quinn, & Kessler, 1992; Mohan, 1986; Padilla, Fairchild, & Valadez, 1990; Richard-Amato & Snow, 1992; Rosebery, Warren, & Conant, 1992; Short, 1991, 1993; Smallwood, 1991; Snow, Met, & Genesee, 1989.)

Content ESL and Sheltered Content Teaching   Chapter Two of this book defined content ESL and sheltered content instruction, and discussed the benefits and policy limitations of both approaches. While content ESL and sheltered content instruction represent significant improvements on ESL pullout or more traditional approaches to ESL, English language learners themselves may view sheltered classes as remedial or socially stigmatized, especially if students are segregated from age and grade peers in mainstream classes (Valdés, 2001). Additionally, English Only ballot initiatives in California and Arizona impose sheltered instruction on young learners of English as a second language, the very group for whom this approach may be inappropriate.

Guidelines for Teaching

WHAT IS SHELTERED CONTENT INSTRUCTION? WHO BENEFITS FROM IT?

Linda Northcutt Gonzales (1994, p. 5), in a useful book designed for teacher inservices on sheltered content instruction, defines sheltered teaching as a *"synthesis of several components of quality teaching and second-language acquisition research. It has been called the missing link for those students who need to learn academic English and engage skills mastered in the first language. Sheltered instruction offers a solution to those schools that have a number of language groups to serve with limited staff."* Northcutt Gonzales also offers the following formal guidelines for determining which English language learners would benefit from sheltered teaching. Typically, these are English language learners...

1. Who come from strong academic backgrounds in the first language.

2. With intermediate fluency in the second language who have acquired English and basic skills in the American school system.

3. Who were born in the United States, but who were not given the opportunity of primary language learning and English as a second-language program.

4. Who speak languages in which bilingual staff are not available.

Nevertheless, sheltered content instruction for English language learners with intermediate fluency in English can be highly effective, since it provides students with access to academic subject matter through comprehensible language and context (Echevarria & Graves, 1998). Skilled sheltered content teachers use a variety of strategies and materials to convey meaning to English language learners, including the use of props, graphic organizers and other visuals, multimedia, demonstrations, modeling, and expressive body language (Northcutt Gonzales, 1994).

Whole Language   Current ESL and bilingual approaches advocate a whole language philosophy, originally developed for English speakers in English language arts classes, as central to the second-language teaching process. The whole language philosophy of teaching is based upon results of language research conducted over the last 20 years analyzing the developmental process that occurs naturally as children acquire their first language (oral and written). The same natural processes are at work in second-language acquisition, and increasing research evidence shows that the same strategies can be extremely effective in second-language teaching (Enright & McCloskey, 1988; Freeman & Freeman, 1992; Hamayan, 1993).

Whole language approaches focus on use of authentic language that is meaningful to students, proceeding from whole to part, integrating development of multiple language modes and domains. Whole language focuses on *using* language, focusing on meaning first, getting students to write early and

Guidelines for Teaching

SHELTERED CONTENT INSTRUCTION STRATEGIES

Echevarria and Graves (1998), in a highly readable book about the theoretical foundations and practical applications of sheltered instruction, provide excellent suggestions for how teachers can incorporate these strategies into their teaching:

- *Modeling.* The teacher models what is expected of the students. Before students begin solving word problems in math, the teacher takes the students through a word problem step-by-step, modeling useful strategies for solving such problems. Students with diverse levels of ability benefit from concrete, step-by-step procedures presented in a clear explicit manner.

- *Hands-on manipulatives.* This approach can include learning aids from Cuisenaire rods in math, to microscopes in science, to globes in social studies.

- *Realia.* For a unit on banking skills, students might practice filling out actual bank deposit slips and check registers. When learning about geology, students might be given samples of rocks and minerals. For consumerism, students might read actual labels on products.

- *Commercially made pictures.* There are a variety of photographs and drawings on the market that depict nearly any object, process, or topic covered in the school curriculum.

- *Teacher-made pictures.* As an alternative to buying pictures to enhance lessons, the teacher can draw pictures or cut them out of magazines.

- *Overhead projector.* As material and information are introduced, the overhead projector can be used to give constant clues to students. Teachers jot down words or sketch out what they are presenting. The written representation of words gives students learning English a chance to copy the words correctly, since certain sounds may be difficult to understand when presented orally. Students with learning problems often have difficulty processing an inordinate amount of auditory information and are helped with the visual clues offered through an overhead projector.

- *Demonstration.* In a middle-school class studying archeology, a student asked how artifacts get buried deep underground. Rather than relying on a verbal explanation, which would have been meaningless to many of the students learning English, the teacher demonstrated the process. First, he placed a quarter in a pie pan and proceeded to blow dirt on the quarter, covering it slightly. He then put dried leaves on top, followed by a sprinkling of "rain." Finally, he put some sand on top, and the quarter was then underneath an inch or so of natural products. Although the process was described in the text, most students did not have the reading skills or English proficiency to understand it. The demonstration made a much greater impression on the students and was referred to later when discussing the earth's layers and other related topics.

- *Multimedia.* Technology offers a multitude of options in this area, from something as simple as listening to a tape recording of Truman's announcement of the dropping of the atomic bomb to an interactive laser computer display. Videos, filmstrips, CD-ROM programs, and tape recordings are examples of multimedia that can enhance comprehension for English-language learners.

- *Time lines.* These are particularly useful in the social sciences. As one lesson progressed through Western Civilization, a time line was mounted along the length of a wall that visually represented each historical event as it related to other events and periods in history. As an event was studied, the teacher made some visual representation on the time line and continued adding to it throughout the course of the year.

- *Graphs.* Information represented visually often makes greater impact and is easier to remember. Graphing the students' weekly consumption of junk food, fruits and vegetables, and milk products is more interesting and meaningful than simply reading about the various food groups

continued

Guidelines for Teaching, continued

and recommended servings. The text becomes more understandable when the graphing activity is completed before reading the text. Many of the terms and concepts will then already be familiar to the students.

- *Bulletin boards.* Visual representation of lesson information can be put on bulletin boards for reference, whether it is an example of a business letter, some friendly letter formats, or a three-dimensional paper model of stalactites and stalagmites with labels.

- *Maps.* This can be one of the most effective means of easily creating context, since many subjects relate to geography. When talking about the rain forest in science, its location can be shown on a map. History class lessons about wars can become more meaningful if the territories are shown on a map.

- *Real-life activities.* These might include surveys, letter writing, simulations, or constructing models. Students should get lots of opportunities for listening, speaking, reading and writing.

- *Previewing new vocabulary or terms.* New words should be introduced, highlighted, and written for students to see. Vocabulary knowledge in English is one of the most important aspects of oral English proficiency for academic achievement. To be more effective, vocabulary development needs to be closely related to subject matter.

- *Creating a word bank,* on butcher paper and posted around the room. Word banks can then become reference points for students to remember definitions and relationships between terms and to model correct spelling.

- *Reducing the linguistic load of teachers' speech* through the following techniques:
  - Slower speech.
  - Clearly enunciated speech.
  - Use more pauses between phrases.
  - Use consistent vocabulary.
  - Use appropriate repetition or natural redundancy.

  - Songs, chants, raps, patterned stories.
  - Reinforce vocabulary, language structures and intonation.
  - Communicate the same idea repeatedly using different words.
  - Clarify terms and vocabulary.
  - Use gestures and body language.
  - Use an abundance of positive reinforcement.

- *Interaction between students.* It is especially important for students learning English to practice using the new language in meaningful ways. Grouping, or cooperative learning is critical when working with students with a variety of language and learning abilities. Heterogeneous grouping is encouraged, both with respect to language proficiency and academic skill level. Group activities offer students with diverse abilities an advantage by utilizing one student's strengths to compensate for a classmate's weakness. Grouping gives students the opportunity to clarify key concepts in their primary language as needed, by consulting an aide, peer, or primary language text. One of the benefits of sheltered instruction is that students are exposed to good models of English language as well as the opportunity to practice using English in academic settings.

- *Linking concepts to students' background.* This process is twofold: It taps the students' previous knowledge on the topic being studied and ties it to the lesson, and it validates students' cultural background and experience by providing opportunities for students to talk about their lives and relating them to the topic.

- *Relating content material to previous lessons.* English-language learners need relationships between new learning and past lessons explicitly stated to clarify the connection between lessons.

- *Vary your instructional strategies.* Effective sheltered instruction offers a variety of learning opportunities for students, including explanation, modeling, demonstration, and

continued

Guidelines for Teaching, continued

visual representation. When students are acquiring a new language, varying delivery modes assists in comprehension and helps keep students engaged in learning throughout the lesson.

- *Frequent checks for understanding.* These can be done individually or by asking group questions.

- *Vary your reading options.* These might include teacher read-alouds, buddy reading, and silent reading. Listening to reading on tape is also effective. Varying the reading format allows students to have reading experiences that are assisted or scaffolded by others. *Scaffolding* is the process of providing support

as needed, with less support required as students move toward independent functioning.

- *Design lessons to provide students with a wide variety of learning opportunities.* These will include opportunities to use higher-level skills, including problem solving, hypothesizing, organizing, synthesizing, categorizing, evaluating, and self-monitoring.

Source: Echevarria, J., & A. Graves. *Sheltered content instruction: Teaching English-language learners with diverse abilities.* Boston, MA: Allyn and Bacon, 1998, pp. 65–75.

often, accepting invented spelling for beginners but expecting conventional spelling as students advance in the writing process, exposing students to high-quality literature and authentic texts from diverse writing genres, allowing students to make choices in reading, and encouraging all to be voracious readers (Willis, 1995).

Part-to-whole approaches to language teaching dominated first- and second-language teaching in the United States until the 1970s. Isolated units of language—sounds, letters, grammar rules, and words—were emphasized as a first step in learning language. Whole language emphasizes a focus on meaning first and the parts come naturally later, as students are ready to focus on the details of language, through reading authentic text and the students' own writing. Whole language teachers avoid the practices of teaching skills in isolation or in a strict sequence, using readers with controlled vocabulary, or using worksheets and drill. In contrast, a whole language lesson might start with reading a story together, collecting litter in the schoolyard and classifying it by attributes, hand-making tortillas and eating them, or creating an origami figure.

Whole language principles are very humanistic, respecting the strengths each student brings to the classroom and encouraging discovery learning through extensive social interaction, with students and teachers as partners in the learning process. Curriculum is constantly negotiated to meet the students' interests and needs. Building on students' prior knowledge and experiences, in a culturally and linguistically diverse class, the rich linguistic and cultural resources shared by students and teacher create a dynamic, empowering context for learning. Whole language allows self-correction to emerge by addressing accuracy through engagement in functional contexts that emphasize fluency over accuracy. While some policymakers portray whole language as responsible for low student achievement and propose a return to basic skills approaches, research has found that U.S. students are achieving at higher and higher levels with each succeeding year and therefore the standards are raised each year, in what David Berliner calls "the manufactured crisis" (Berliner & Biddle, 1995). While the newspaper headlines present the dialogue as though teachers must choose between whole language and phonics (e.g., Sánchez, 1996), most teachers have adopted a whole-language perspective that incorporates the teaching of phonics concepts when students reach the "teachable moments" in the natural language development process. (For more reading, see Au, 1993; Cazden, 1992; Carrasquillo & Hedley, 1993; Edelsky, 1996; Edelsky, Altwerger, & Flores, 1991; Enright & McCloskey, 1988; Freeman & Freeman, 1992, 1994; Genesee, 1994; Goodman, 1986; Goodman, Bird, & Goodman, 1991; Goodman & Wilde, 1992; Harste, Burke, & Woodward, 1981; Heald-Taylor, 1989; Hudelson, 1989; Noden & Vacca, 1994; Spangenberg-Urbschat & Pritchard, 1994; Strickland & Morrow, 1989.)

Cognitive Development   Language, academic, and cognitive development all go hand in hand. As our students increase their knowledge of a second language across all subject areas, they need to have continuing development of thinking skills. As we have seen in the language acquisition section, continuing L_1 cognitive development is crucial while L_2 is being developed. Faster acquisition of cognitive skill development occurs in L_1 because the student is functioning cognitively at his or her age or maturity level in L_1. But along with continuing L_1 cognitive development in school and out of school (wherever possible with parents, weekend schools, bilingual classes, and peer and sibling tutoring), thinking skills can consciously be developed in ESL classes, from beginning through advanced levels, as well as in grade-level classes. Once students discover that they can regulate their own learning, they can take control of the learning process.

O'Malley and Chamot (1990) have conducted extensive research on the learning strategy acquisition of ESL students. They define learning strategies as "the special thoughts or behaviors that individuals use to help them comprehend, learn, or retain new information" (p. 1). The learning strategies that students develop are one important aspect of cognitive development that can make a significant difference in students' academic achievement. Teachers can consciously assist students with learning strategy acquisition by finding out what strategies students are already using through interviews and think-aloud tasks, selecting new strategies to be taught, and assisting students with transfer of strategy use to new academic tasks. Earlier in this chapter, metacognitive, cognitive, and social/affective learning strategies were defined. Details for teaching specific learning strategies can be found in Chamot and O'Malley (1994). Another practical reference for teaching learning strategies is Oxford (1990).

Chamot and O'Malley (1994) have developed their own L_2 teaching approach that incorporates many of the characteristics of current approaches described throughout this section. But their Cognitive Academic Language Learning Approach (CALLA) is unique in one particular way: CALLA trains teachers how to focus on students' explicit acquisition of learning strategies at the same time that language is being taught through content. CALLA is designed to meet the academic needs of limited-English-proficient students in upper elementary and secondary schools at intermediate and advanced levels of ESL; students need to have at least a basic level of proficiency in the language of instruction to benefit from the conscious focus on learning strategies. ESL student achievement in CALLA math classes looks very promising in an examination of student progress over a three-year period (Chamot, Dale, O'Malley, & Spanos, 1992; Thomas, 1994).

CALLA does not simplify the curriculum, but it presents cognitively demanding activities at ESL students' developmental level:

> A common reaction to the less-than-fluent English of a student is to teach content from a lower grade level and to expect from LEP students only lower-level cognitive skills such as simple recall. CALLA demands the opposite. LEP students need to learn content appropriate to their developmental level and previous educational experience; higher-level thinking skills are as much to be expected from them as from any other student. Instead of watering down content for LEP students, CALLA teachers make challenging content comprehensible by providing additional contextual support in the form of demonstrations, visuals, and hands-on experiences, and by teaching students how to apply learning strategies to understand and remember the content presented. When asking LEP students higher-order questions, CALLA teachers evaluate responses on the basis of the ideas expressed rather than on the correctness of the language used. (O'Malley & Chamot, 1990, p. 194)

Chamot and O'Malley recommend beginning CALLA lessons with ESL science, which provides many natural opportunities for hands-on discovery learning. ESL mathematics should be next, because in the upper grades math is highly abstract and has a more restricted language register than science. Social studies is third, and English language arts the fourth subject introduced because of the complex level of reading and writing required as well as underlying cultural assumptions (Chamot & O'Malley, 1994; O'Malley & Chamot, 1990).

In general, cognitive development includes every aspect of the development of complex thinking skills, across all aspects of life—academic, professional, and personal. For students, cognitive development takes place both at home and in the classroom. But many times school staff unconsciously hold ESL students back by presenting material far below students' cognitive abilities. ESL lessons can be cognitively complex even when students' English language proficiency is quite limited. Including students' first language and culture in their school experience can be another powerful way of continuing cognitive development at age-appropriate levels.

Valuing Students' First Languages   Current approaches to bilingual and ESL instruction provide strong affirmation of students' first languages. All school staff and parents who are not familiar with language acquisition findings of the last 20 years must be reeducated regarding the incorrect assumptions of foreign language educators that first language "interferes" with second language. The research evidence is very clear that first-language development provides crucial support for second-language development. The more that students are given positive opportunities for L_1 development, the better they will succeed academically in L_2. This confuses some ESL teachers who interpret L_1 support to mean that they should let their students speak L_1 in the ESL classroom as much as they want to. This is not needed as long as students have other opportunities to develop cognitively and academically in L_1. Once you have established clear objectives for each aspect of the instructional process, you can mediate with your students the times when L_1 is allowed and other times when all communication is expected to be exclusively in L_2. Most of an ESL class should be conducted in L_2. But during the first year of beginning ESL, it can be very important for students to be able to use L_1. For example, the Natural Approach allows students to use L_1 while they are in

Guidelines for Teaching

SUPPORTING STUDENTS' FIRST LANGUAGES

Teachers can support students' first languages by:

- Teaching academic content courses in L_1. Hiring bilingual school staff (counselor, librarian, janitor, everyone).

- Using L_1 volunteer tutors (including parents, cross-age and peer tutors).

- Providing books and other resources in L_1 in the library and all classrooms.

- Preparing units in lessons that incorporate other languages in a meaningful way (e.g. bilingual storytellers, L_1 pen pals across classes or schools through e-mail, journal writing in L_1, environmental print in L_1 for young readers, show and tell in L_1, learning centers in L_1).

- Building partnerships with parents to continue L_1 cognitive/academic development at home.

- Using the school building for after-school or weekend school taught in L_1. Encouraging students to contribute articles in L_1 to student publications.

- Inviting ethnic community members as resource persons.

- Allowing social use of L_1 outside of classes.

- Encouraging extracurricular activities and school celebrations in L_1. Providing signs throughout the school in the different languages of the community.

- Sending newsletters and school information to parents in L_1. Providing family math and literacy programs evenings or weekends.

Sources: See Cummins, 1996b; Freeman & Freeman, 1992; Scarcella, 1990; Tinajero & Ada, 1993.

the preproduction and early speech production stages. The structured immersion program model also allows students to respond to the teacher in their native language during the first year of academic work in second language.

Translation of sentences or thoughts is no longer considered to be a very useful skill for purposes of language acquisition. Instead, students are encouraged to think in their L_2. However, translation of words can be a very efficient way of acquiring vocabulary, especially for abstract words that are not easily pantomimed or illustrated. Bilingual dictionaries can be a handy resource in the ESL classroom, not a crutch. Another use of L_1 can be appropriately planned times for peer tutoring. If your school is unable to provide a bilingual teacher or teacher aide for your students, allowing peers time in the lesson to analyze a problem to be solved in their native language can be a very effective reinforcement for content instruction. Other means of support for students' L_1 are shown in the Guidelines box.

Incorporating Multicultural/Global Perspectives   Education research findings have clearly established that students learn best when lessons connect to their past experiences (Au, 1993; Genesee, 1994; Tharp & Gallimore, 1988). Activation of students' prior knowledge is considered the first step in any meaningful instructional activity (Chamot & O'Malley, 1994; Freeman & Freeman, 1992). What better way to do this than through lessons that approach each theme or topic from a multicultural or global perspective, using the natural resources that language-minority students bring to the classroom from their past experiences?

However, most teachers immediately interpret multicultural perspectives to mean emphasizing a few points about other nations, or celebrating holidays and heroes of other cultures, activities that usually degenerate into superficial glimpses of culture and lead to stereotyping and woefully inaccurate misinformation. The type of multicultural/global perspective that we encourage is presented in depth in the next chapter on culture. It involves examination of how we humans lead our lives every day, or the complexity of the human spirit and mind in response to our environment. It also includes being open to a more global perspective as we address each theme of our class.

For example, homelessness and hunger are phenomena affecting the world in strikingly global ways. ESL and bilingual social studies lessons that examine the environmental reasons for the existence of these conditions and the effect that they have on people who experience them can include many ways of presenting and sharing multicultural, global perspectives. Immigrants to the United States are often shocked to find out that here, too, many people experience homelessness and hunger, and they feel angry and want to understand why and how such conditions could exist in one of the wealthiest nations of the world. When students go through a process of gathering information on an urgent topic, a multicultural/global perspective unfolds with time and in-depth research together.

Close home-school collaboration brings a natural bicultural or multicultural perspective into the classroom. Many collaborative research projects that link community and schools are described in Saravia-Shore and Arvizu (1992) as well as other sources mentioned in this chapter under sociocultural processes of language acquisition, and in Chapters Five, Seven, and Nine.

Students and Teachers as Partners in Learning   Another feature of current approaches to second-language teaching that contrasts sharply with methods of most of this century involves a major shift in the teacher-student relationship. In many ways, we are returning to John Dewey's philosophy of the early 20th century that emphasized student-centered, discovery learning. While the ESL or bilingual teacher serves as a guide or facilitator, teacher and students together are exploring new knowledge and new ways of perceiving the world. Together, teacher and students might study the natural world, solve practical mathematics problems, or examine social and historical patterns in human behavior. Or following Freire's approach, problems are posed and acted upon (Freire, 1985; Freire & Macedo, 1987; Shor & Freire, 1987). In this process, the teacher is no longer the "expert," but is discovering new ways of exploring knowledge along with the students. This might mean that sometimes students lead the class in new curricular directions, depending upon how a unit develops. The teacher might initiate a theme, but as it unfolds, students contribute considerably to gathering the knowledge base that the class develops.

An integral component of the teacher-student partnership is the affective dimension. As students and teachers gradually become friends, the classroom can become a place for sharing at the level of family or close community. Igoa (1995) presents an eloquent, inspiring story of a teacher's reflections on her students' "inner world." Through the voices of the immigrant children in her classroom and through her own reflections on her teaching, this book provides examples of creative ways to integrate art, music, language arts, and content learning with the emotional side of learning, in a familylike, supportive, loving partnership.

Thus, the role of the learner has changed from that of a passive recipient of knowledge about the language he or she is learning, and from an automatic applier of rigid language rules, to an active decision maker in the language learning process and a creative generator of newly acquired language. This notion applies to very young learners as well as to older students. (Hamayan, 1993, p. 17)

A major rationale for the shift to learner-centered, experiential approaches is based on the current knowledge explosion. As we move into the 21st century, it is becoming more impossible with each passing year for any professional to know everything he or she needs to know in one field. Knowledge transmission methods of instruction appeared to be effective when the knowledge base remained the same. But now we must prepare students to know how to gain access to new knowledge and to critically apply, evaluate, and solve problems based on changing knowledge (Cummins, 1986a, 1989c, 1996b).

Interactive Classrooms   Since the teacher is no longer the authority figure around whom all activity is centered in a second-language classroom, teachers need to provide an appropriate environment for students to work with each other on academic tasks. The rationale for creating a highly interactive class is based on the centrality of peer interaction for stimulating the second-language acquisition process (Brown, 1994b; Faltis, 1997; Wong Fillmore, 1989, 1991b). Other reasons for creating a classroom climate in which students spend considerable time working in small groups or pairs are that cooperative learning structures result in dramatic academic gains, especially for students at risk (Calderón, 1994; Johnson, Johnson, & Holubec, 1986; Kagan, 1986; Slavin, 1988c); that cooperative learning helps develop prosocial skills; and that students need to be prepared for an increasingly interdependent workplace (Kagan, 1992). (See Chapter Three, for an overview on cooperative learning with language-minority students.)

Thematic, Interdisciplinary Instruction   Current approaches to teaching ESL and bilingual classes also take an interdisciplinary approach. Earlier in this section we introduced the integration of language and content. Thematic approaches to teaching provide a meaningful framework for development of units that teach language through exploration of multidisciplinary material. Themes can be broad or narrow in focus, but they should capture students' imagination enough to stimulate them to gather information, and they should naturally lead to application across multiple content areas.

We have already mentioned two problem-posing themes that can be approached from a global perspective: hunger and homelessness, and the ecological interconnectedness of the rainforests of the world. Young children might explore themes that develop self-awareness and discovery of their community and its resources. Other themes might develop feelings, such as remembering someone special and recreating that person's geographical and historical setting; or leaving home—the trauma or joy surrounding that event, the circumstances that can cause people to migrate to new homes, and the changes the move brings to their lives. Some themes could focus on improving the quality of life where the students live, investigating how something works, understanding an everyday event such as the detailed weather report on the local news and the importance of that information for several professions, analyzing one current event in international news in great depth, or exploring the knowledge base of an ancient non-Western culture, such as the Maya in southern Mexico and Central America or the Han Dynasty in China, by examining their uses of mathematics, the sciences, art, music, literature, sports, religion, and the geographical and historical circumstances of their existence.

Themes generally focus on something that is a universal experience, where through gathering knowledge students can identify with some of the information and can apply, analyze, synthesize, and evaluate the material, creating new knowledge that leads to additional curiosity and new problems to be solved. Sometimes specific curricular objectives required in each subject area for each grade level can at first discourage teachers from developing rich thematic units. But collaborative planning with other teachers usually leads to many creative ideas for reaching the specific curricular objectives through authentic and meaningful themes that explore the universal human experience. In the chapters that follow, we will present other examples of themes that can be explored through integrated language, mathematics, science, and social studies.

Use of Technology   Given the explosion of the uses of technology in the workplace, home, and school over the past decade, it is essential that current approaches to teaching ESL and bilingual classrooms incorporate into the thematic material for lessons many meaningful experiences with electronic devices and greatly varied uses of instructional multimedia. The use of audio-cassette players, video equipment, cellular phones, compact disc players, cameras, computers, interactive videodisc players, CD-ROMs, modems and other networking equipment, voice recognition and voice synthesis systems, and other electronic devices soon to be available can enliven student interaction, enrich knowledge gathering, and deepen language-minority students' experiences in preparation for the workplace of the 21st century. Using computers in instruction can expand students' language and academic skills through use of word processing software, spreadsheets, database software, communications programs, graphics packages, hypermedia, and access to telecommunications such as electronic mail and the Internet. (Approaches to uses of technology in bilingual and ESL classrooms were explored in Chapter Three.)

Teaching Language Arts in a Bilingual Classroom

Empowering bilingual students by providing them with the academic strategies and cognitive strengths they need to be effective learners is the overall goal of bilingual classes. The instructional approaches outlined in the previous section—incorporating whole language approaches taught through thematic, interdisciplinary academic content with a multicultural perspective, in an interactive classroom using the latest technology, with students and teachers as partners in discovery learning—are crucial to bilingual students' academic success. In other words, what works well in ESL and grade-level classes also is very effective in bilingual classes.

The most conclusive research findings to date on the role of native language instruction point to the critical importance of literacy and cognitive development in the students' primary language as crucial to academic success in the second language (Au, 1993; Bialystok, 1991; Cummins, 1989c, 1991, 1996b; Cummins & Swain, 1986; Freeman & Freeman, 1992; Genesee, 1987, 1994; Hudelson, 1994; Johnson & Roen, 1989; Lessow-Hurley, 1990; Lindholm, 1991; Snow, 1990; Tinajero & Ada, 1993; Wong Fillmore & Valadez, 1986). When students receive high-quality instruction in their first language, then academic skills, literacy development, concept formation, subject knowledge, and learning strategies will all transfer from L_1 to L_2 as the vocabulary and communicative patterns are developed in L_2 to express that academic knowledge. Thus, in a bilingual language arts class taught in students' primary language, the teacher is developing language skills that will enhance students' cognitive and academic growth. What, then, is the goal that a bilingual teacher should strive to reach in a language arts class?

Defining Bilingual Proficiency

Goals of a bilingual program differ, depending on the amount of proficiency in the two languages desired by the school community. We believe strongly that basic L_1 literacy developed in transitional (or early-exit) bilingual programs is not sufficient to reach the threshold level that Cummins (1976) posits is crucial to second-language success. Students need to receive at least four to five years of high-quality L_1 schooling to avoid the risk of cognitive difficulties in L_2 (Collier, 1987; Collier & Thomas, 1989; Cummins, 1976, 1981b, 1991; Thomas & Collier, 1997).

The reason for these widely differing definitions of bilingualism centers around the context in which the two languages will be used. Fishman (1966a) and other sociolinguists posit that the purposes of using two languages vary greatly from one region to another and from person to person, according to

Guidelines for Teaching

THE CONTINUUM OF BILINGUALISM

Linguists have a wide range of definitions of bilingualism, forming a continuum from a very strong version proposed by Bloomfield (1933) to weak versions proposing minimal competence in L_2. For example, a bilingual is one who

1. Has nativelike proficiency in two languages (Bloomfield, 1933).

2. Can use two languages alternately (Weinreich, 1953).

3. Can produce meaningful sentences in L_2 (Haugen, 1969).

4. Can use two languages alternately, although the point at which a person actually becomes bilingual is arbitrary or impossible to determine (Mackey, 1962).

5. Can engage in communication in more than one language (Fishman, 1966a).

6. Possesses at least one language skill (listening, speaking, reading, or writing) in L_2 to a minimal degree (Macnamara, 1967).

7. Can use a passive knowledge of L_2 and a little lexical competence to transact business in L_2 (Diebold, 1961).

8. Speaks only one language but uses different language varieties, registers, and styles of that language (Halliday & Strevens, 1964).

the topic, listener, and context. Linguists would consider it unrealistic to require that bilingualism always be defined as the complete mastery of two languages in all contexts.

Nevertheless, we encourage the strong definition of bilingual proficiency proposed by Bloomfield (1933) within a school context for the following reasons. First, all public school programs in the United States have as one of their goals the development of full proficiency in English. In order to reach a deep level of academic proficiency in English as a second language, it is necessary to build a sufficient level of proficiency in the first language. Without that academic and literacy base in L_1, students are likely to suffer cognitive difficulties in L_2. The most conclusive research to date on comparisons of different types of L_1 support for language-minority students comes from the state of California, where the programs with the most minority language instruction are the ones in which language-minority students are excelling in academic achievement (California Department of Education, 1991; Crawford, 1995; Krashen & Biber, 1988; Wong Fillmore, 1991a).

The goal of strong bilingual proficiency includes the development of listening, speaking, reading, and writing modes in both languages and the ability to use both languages for all academic work across the curriculum at each grade level. In the United States, schools rarely provide bilingual instruction beyond the elementary grades; yet bilingual immersion educators in Canada believe that a bilingual program should provide academic instruction in both languages throughout grades K through 12. U.S. educators need to provide much more L_1 support for bilingual students in secondary education. Overall, high school language-minority students are not doing at all well in school at the present time (Collier & Thomas, 1989; Dentzer & Wheelock, 1990; Minicucci & Olsen, 1992, 1993; Thomas & Collier, 1997).

Dialect Diversity

In a whole-language approach to teaching language arts in a bilingual classroom, a good bilingual teacher uses authentic language that is meaningful to students, developing oral and written language in each lesson through shared multicultural children's literature, students' own writing, and problem solving across the curriculum. As students write and write, communicating ideas and using inventive spelling at beginning stages, the multiple drafts in the writing process help them gradually understand the process of transforming speech to print, with editing for form emphasized in the later stages of development of a good piece of writing.

When implementing quality language arts instruction, all teachers must face instructional decisions regarding their attitudes towards the great variety of language usage that students bring to the classroom from the communities in which they have lived. This can be a thorny issue in bilingual language arts classes, because some bilingual teachers have been trained to teach the language as a foreign language and have become accustomed to correcting errors from the point of view that one standard form represents the only "accept-able" form of the language. Sometimes teachers may see the particular oral language varieties represented in class as in need of remediation, to be eradicated in favor of a standard variety. It takes special sensitivity to understand the full complexity of all the language varieties represented in a class and the appropriate varieties to teach (Merino, Trueba, & Samaniego, 1993; Valdés, 1981). The following vignette illustrates the dilemma bilingual teachers face:

⊠ *In a first-grade bilingual classroom, composed primarily of children of very recent immigrants from rural Mexico, the assignment is to write about something that happened in the story "Jack and the Beanstalk." Marta's sentence reads as follows: "Jack jue ne ca la giganta." "Ne" is a spelling error for "en," but the rest of the sentence is written correctly according to the Spanish that the child speaks. In standard Spanish, the sentence would read: "Jack fue a la casa de la giganta."*

Now that inventive spelling is encouraged in the early grades, teachers of young students have become more accustomed to accepting the varied ways that students write down what they hear as cute and creative. But teachers of grades 3 through 12 struggle with the appropriate time for error correction and the form error correction should take. This type of instructional decision is usually made still more complicated by the wide range of spoken dialects that the students bring to the classroom.

First, it is helpful to recognize that spoken languages are constantly in a process of change. For example, while strict English grammar teachers complain, spoken English continues to split infinitives, place prepositions at the ends of sentences, and accept incomplete sentences as legitimate, complete thoughts. Changes occur to spoken languages when a language is moved to a geographical location separate from its origin, or when its speakers are socially isolated. Geographical or social isolation in the new setting ensures the development of a new language variety. Languages also change when they come in contact with other languages. As members of one language community interact with members of another and, as a result of the contact, some members begin to use aspects of both languages for different tasks, each language influences the other (Ferguson & Heath, 1981; Fishman & Keller, 1982; Grosjean, 1982; Heath, 1983; Hernández-Chávez, Cohen, & Beltramo, 1975; Ovando, 1993; Valdés, 1981, 2001; Wolfram & Christian, 1989).

Most bilingual teachers must deal with some form of language contact, raising the issue of which variety to teach. Standard? If so, from which country or region? Local dialect? What should they do with a mixed variety when two languages are in close contact? After the first step of recognizing why these spoken varieties exist, the next step is to respect and affirm each spoken variety that each student brings to the classroom. The same affirmation of the benefits of bilingualism applies to multidialectalism. These varieties do not harm children. Linguists view each variety as a creative and rich example of human language development. Researchers have found that, contrary to the common assumption that a first language "interferes" with the second language, the relationship between L_1 and L_2 is a very positive one. Likewise, dialect researchers have discovered that analysis of the differences between spoken varieties of a language and the written standard variety can lead teacher and students to new insights that bring cognitive benefits similar to those associated with proficient bilingualism (Heath, 1983, 1986; Wolfram & Christian, 1989).

Bilingual teachers need not worry about learning a new version of the standard variety of language that they speak. Using Spanish as an example, teachers from Spain, Argentina, Cuba, Mexico, Puerto Rico, California, Colorado, or Texas usually represent greatly varied regional varieties of *standard* Spanish, with vocabulary and pronunciation patterns unique to each region. Students will likely bring still more regional varieties to the bilingual classroom. The bilingual teacher models her own variety, making it clear to the students where she is from and helping them to become aware of language differences between countries, regions, cities, and even city blocks (Zentella, 1981). She can affirm the varieties represented by students in class, and as students become older and more cognitively aware, they can benefit from understanding the differences and affirming spoken varieties as creative uses of language. The teacher can model the standard written variety and talk about it as acquisition of a new language, radically different from spoken language.

Dialects become more of a challenge to affirm and incorporate into instruction when they are stigmatized by the dominant language group in a given region. Educators in the past have tended to blame a stigmatized language variety, home environment, or both for the student's lack of success. The solution proposed in the past was eradication of the stigmatized variety:

> Eradication, . . . which may be said to be the traditional view of the English-teaching profession as a whole, looks upon dialects other than the standard as deficient in themselves, as deserving of the stigma they have attracted, and as the causes of severe problems in the total learning process including the acquisition of reading and writing skills. Educators who hold this view look upon the educational process as a means by which one is made to distinguish "right" from "wrong." They see themselves as the tools by which a particular student can rid himself of stigmatized dialect features and become a speaker of the "right" type of English—well known to be a passport to achievement, success, and acceptance. They insist that as educators they have a solemn duty to their students, that includes the total eradication of nonstandard dialects (Valdés, 1981, pp. 14–15) .

Eradication, applied for most of this century, has not significantly altered the school achievement of minority students.

Another strategy used in a few inner-city schools has been to teach a spoken and written version of the variety of African-American English used in a particular city, assuming that students will be able to function more effectively in that community and attempting through the schools to give more affirmation to acceptance of that variety. This position of appreciation of dialect differences is a very positive way to affirm local varieties, but it does not deal effectively with the reality of the workplace, in which minorities are held back from jobs on the basis of the language variety they speak and write. In the 1960s, when curricular materials developed especially for African-American English speakers were first proposed, many African-American educators and community leaders opposed the idea on the basis that even though the materials were linguistically justifiable, the use of such materials would likely result in the resegregation of African-American children (Stewart, 1987).

The most popular current view among linguists and bilingual educators is the acceptance of bidialectalism. This position affirms the importance of home dialect and its appropriate use within the community in which it is spoken, while at the same time teaching the standard written and spoken varieties of language. Affirming home language means that students may speak in native dialect in the classroom without being told that they are wrong. Instead, teacher and students together analyze the differences between their dialects and the standard variety. Students are thus empowered, through affirmation of their linguistic roots and through the cognitive stimulus of multidialectal development, which eventually brings additional resources to their professional life:

> Cognitive psychologists . . . tell us that we build our cognitive repertoire on prior knowledge, experiences, attitudes, and skills. It is a layering process. Educators, therefore, dare not destroy what was there before. The goal should be to build on and add to what is already present in the lives of students. Creative bridges using the early socialization patterns of the home language and culture can be useful in motivating students to learn. This means that such students will come to see their teachers as professionals who understand the value of their nonstandard languages and use their structure and function to build another layer of linguistic skill that will enable these students to negotiate the prestige varieties of [their two languages] in the larger society and thus to have more options in their lives (Ovando, 1993, pp. 223–24).

Language Distribution in the Bilingual Language Arts Classroom

Another instructional decision that is extremely important in a bilingual classroom is the distribution of the two languages across the curriculum. The percentage of use of each language for language arts, mathematics, science, and social studies sends a clear message to students regarding the esteem and importance of each of the two languages, as valued by the school community. When a school program has chosen to emphasize both languages equally in the curriculum, students are more likely to take seriously their academic work in both languages, as well as to build a deep level of oral and written proficiency in both languages.

In Chapter Two, we reviewed the major variations in the distribution of the two languages within a bilingual program, alternating the language of instruction by teacher, by content areas, by time of day, or by day(s) of the week. In the first years of experimentation with U.S. bilingual education of the late 1960s and early 1970s, it was quite common to see language arts classes in which switching from one language to the other occurred often in the bilingual classroom, especially in the geographic regions of the United States in which English and Spanish are in close contact and many bilinguals use the two languages interchangeably, including the use of code-switching. As researchers have analyzed the advantages and disadvantages of the concurrent use of the two languages, increasing research evidence points to the importance of separation of the two languages, especially for language arts instruction (Christian, 1994; Crawford, 1999; Cummins & Swain, 1986; Legarreta, 1979, 1981; Lindholm, 1990, Lindholm-Leary, 2001; Milk, 1986; Ulanoff & Pucci, 1993; Wong Fillmore, 1989). Today, more and more bilingual language arts classrooms are clearly defining the language of instruction by blocks of time devoted to one language at a time. If any concurrent bilingual teaching is done, it might take place in some content teaching, but the languages are kept separate within each language arts block. The California Department of Education, after many years of research analyzing student progress within many different types of programs, has concluded that separation of the two languages through clear curricular decisions is the best strategy for language-minority students' long-term academic achievement (California Department of Education, 1991; Crawford, 1999).

Language and Multicultural Literature Across the Curriculum

This chapter would not be complete without a final section addressing the teaching of the four language modes—listening, speaking, reading, and writing—as well as the second major component of language arts classes—literature. However, traditions of only a decade ago regarding the teaching of these skills in second-language classes are radically different from approaches to instruction in English language arts, ESL, and bilingual classes as practiced today.

The shift to whole-language approaches has radically changed the focus of teaching from an emphasis on discrete language subskills in isolation (such as phonics, spelling, punctuation, grammar points, and vocabulary words to be memorized) to the integration of all four language modes (listening, speaking, reading, and writing) combined with other content areas, and the use of authentic literature rather than simplified basal texts. "The ideas that undergird whole language are here to stay. . . . Textbooks have already changed radically in response to the whole language movement. . . . Use of whole language is pretty widespread. . . ." (Willis, 1993, p. 8).

The discrete-skills curriculum isolated language skills from meaningful contexts, established artificial sequences of language skills to be taught from simple to complex (as defined by the textbook writer), simplified texts to control sentence structures and vocabulary, and emphasized measurement of student progress through discrete-skills tests. In contrast, whole language puts strong emphasis on meaning first. Listening, speaking, reading, and writing are taught as an integrated whole, with each lesson developing oral and written language. The focus is on the social construction of meaning and understanding the process of the acquisition of reading and writing. Whole-language lessons are learner centered and meaningful to students' lives inside and outside school (Cazden, 1992; Edelsky, Altwerger, & Flores, 1990; Enright & McCloskey, 1988; Freeman & Freeman, 1992; Goodman, 1986; Goodman & Wilde, 1992; Hamayan, 1993; Heald-Taylor, 1989; Hudelson, 1994; Peregoy & Boyle, 1993; Pérez & Torres-Guzmán, 1996; Scarcella & Oxford, 1992; Tinajero & Ada, 1993).

Does this mean that teachers no longer need to teach or assess language subskills? Of course not. Whole language includes development and careful monitoring of each detail of language acquisition for each learner, but the *context* of discrete skill development has changed to emphasize listening to and reading authentic, meaningful texts, as well as expanding the speaking and writing genres developed in school, and understanding the writing process. The learner takes increasing responsibility for developing a repertoire of learning strategies in listening and reading and for communicating effectively, as well as correcting his or her own errors in speaking and writing (Freeman & Freeman, 1992; Willis, 1993).

Stepping back in time to revisit older approaches to teaching second or foreign languages, the rationale for isolating and emphasizing each of the four language skills was to encourage teachers to provide a balanced approach to each. For example, the grammar-translation approach was rightfully criticized for its emphasis on the teaching of reading and writing while neglecting oral language development. The audiolingual method in its early years overemphasized listening and speaking by holding students back from reading and writing in the second language for the first six to eight weeks of a course. Most revised audiolingual texts modified the approach to provide a balance of the four skills from the beginning, but these texts still inappropriately emphasized a sequence of skill acquisition as first listening, then speaking, then reading, and finally writing. Current research does not support this sequence. The experimental methods of the 1970s and early 1980s such as Silent Way, Community Language Learning, Total Physical Response, and Natural Approach also tended to emphasize oral language development first, followed by very simplified written work in later lessons (Celce-Murcía, 1991; Larsen-Freeman, 1986; Richards & Rodgers, 1986).

Today, reading and writing research has proven that these artificial sequences do not foster natural language acquisition. Instead, the learning process occurs in an integrated fashion, through the stimulation of a meaningful context in which language is developed. Isolating subskills and analyzing their use is a natural part of a process in whole-language classes, but the focus is on a meaningful context through which students understand why they need to learn these details of language use. The misconception that oral language must be mastered by young children before written language is taught has been replaced by the early emphasis on reading and writing from the beginning stages of exposure to the second language for students of all ages in grades K through 12 (Enright & McCloskey, 1988; Freeman & Freeman, 1992; Goodman, 1986; Hudelson, 1994).

Another way to understand the relationship between the four language modes (formerly called skills) is to focus on the contrast between receptive and productive language. Listening and reading are the receptive modes, which always exceed the productive modes of speaking and writing. Our receptive vocabulary is often 10 times that of our productive vocabulary. In other words, students can comprehend much more through listening and reading than they demonstrate in speaking and writing tasks in school. To be held back from the reading process by well-meaning teachers who think that students must have a speaking knowledge of ESL before they can start reading is a faulty assumption not supported by the reading research (Edelsky, Altwerger, & Flores, 1991; Enright & McCloskey, 1988; Goodman, Goodman, & Flores, 1979; Goodman & Wilde, 1992; Hudelson, 1994; Peregoy & Boyle, 1993; Tinajero & Ada, 1993).

Teaching Listening and Speaking

With the understanding that all four language modes are integrated into each lesson in bilingual, ESL, and grade-level language arts classes, we will mention a few points regarding the differences between spoken and written language. For example, spoken English is much more informal in grammatical expectations: There is no differentiation between who and whom; prepositions occur at ends of sentences; verb contractions are assumed; infinitives are split. Natural variations in sound patterns occur when native speakers speak at normal speed, leading to contractions and omissions of words and sounds (e.g. "whuchagunnadoo?" for "What are you going to do?").

Spoken language has variations in nonverbal aspects of language, as well as intonation, emotional overtones, redundancy, corrections, pauses, hesitations, fillers, false starts, colloquialisms, and register (the social context in which language is spoken and resultant modifications needed in style of speech). Spoken language can produce grammatical sentences without subjects, verbs, auxiliaries, or other parts of speech, and can drop grammar markers not essential to meaning. Spoken conversations are interactive, with meaning negotiated between two or more people; special situations have to be constructed for immediate feedback in writing, such as peer feedback in a writing workshop (Long & Richards, 1987; Omaggio Hadley, 1993; Scarcella & Oxford, 1992).

The best way to teach spoken language is to use live language, spoken by native speakers, from a variety of natural and rehearsed sources, using technology to capture conversations and formal spoken language through radio, television, newspapers, magazines, telephone recordings, museums, performances, and events. For example, some Total Physical Response materials tend to emphasize artificial sequences of commands to develop listening comprehension, but the idea of responding physically to commands can be applied to natural uses of language, such as learning to use a piece of equipment in the classroom, following instructions for origami, cooking, conducting a science experiment, or doing physical exercises. Other authentic listening comprehension activities can be dialing recorded messages such as the time or the weather; listening to classroom directions or lectures; attending a large public gathering such as a concert, religious service, movie, or performance by a famous speaker; and taking a guided tour of a farm, zoo, museum, business, government facility, or historic site.

Interactive academic tasks, with lots of opportunities for talking to occur through peer interaction in partnerships, small groups, and total-class work, are essential. Each lesson directly connects students' reading and writing tasks to the oral work. The teacher serves as a model and as the facilitator to achieve the multiple aims of each lesson. Shared literature or nonfiction can activate students' background knowledge and provide the stimulus for activities to reinforce the content and language objectives. Video and audiocassette players and computers can incorporate art, music, and photography into lessons, taking the place of the language laboratory and allowing students to develop, expand, and choose new learning experiences.

Problem solving, interviews, storytelling, drama, role-playing, simulations, and cooperative games can expand student uses of spoken and written language. Guests from the multiethnic communities of the school neighborhood, field trips, and use of multicultural community resources are rich stimuli for meaningful lessons. For older students, survival skills and consumer knowledge provide endless sources for expansion of authentic lessons using live language, such as use of the telephone, the media, the library, bank, social services, housing, shopping for food and clothing, transportation, and medical assistance.

Literacy in First and Second Languages

Reading and writing are the most crucial language modes for school success. Yet an amazing number of transitional bilingual and ESL programs for primary school children consider competence in oral English as the main exit criterion for placing students in grade-level classes. Some students who miss developmental stages in reading and writing are able to acquire those skills on their own, but many more do not fill in the gaps and stay behind in academic preparation. The teaching of reading and writing in both first and second languages provides the backbone for any school program and for full development of proficiency in academic language. This does not mean that students need three or four hours per day of language arts classes in first and second languages. Reading and writing are effectively taught through science, math, and social studies lessons, as well as through language arts.

An early bilingual program decision to be made when addressing the teaching of beginning reading to students of multiple language backgrounds involves the language chosen for students to learn to read first. Can literacy skills be developed simultaneously in a student's two languages? Does it make any difference whether students begin to learn to read in their primary language or in their second language?

For language-minority students, the research indicates that the most successful long-term academic achievement occurs where the students' primary language is the initial language of literacy (California Department of Education, 1984, 1991; Collier & Thomas, 1989; Crawford, 1999; Cummins, 1979a, 1981b, 1986b, 1991; Hakuta, Butler, & Witt, 2000; Krashen & Biber, 1988; Ramírez, Yuen, Ramey, & Pasta, 1991;Thomas & Collier, 1997; Wong Fillmore & Valadez, 1986). In contrast, language *majority* students who are taught to read initially in their second language show no negative consequences (Genesee, 1987; Thomas & Collier, 1997). Researchers have found that speakers of the dominant language learning to read first in L_2 often pick up reading in L_1 before formal instruction of literacy in L_1 is introduced in bilingual classes. Thus, students in a 90–10 two-way bilingual program in which majority and minority students are working together can follow a sequence similar to early total immersion used in Canada. This program model introduces the minority language as the language of instruction for 90 percent of the school day for the first two years (grades K through 1), gradually adds English literacy in second or third grade, and by fourth or fifth grade presents half of the instruction in each language. The state of California has concluded that the 90–10 two-way bilingual immersion program is their most successful model of bilingual instruction. Early total immersion has also been the most successful program model among bilingual immersion programs in Canada. Researchers cited in Cummins (1996b), Tucker (1980), Skutnabb-Kangas and Cummins (1988), and the California Department of Education (1984) explain that in contexts in which the language-minority group feels ambivalence or hostility toward the majority group, the insecurity and confusion results in low academic performance. Use of the minority language at the beginning stages of instruction builds language-minority students' identity and feelings of self-worth and reduces feelings of ambivalence toward the majority language and culture. Thonis (1981) concludes

> The case for native-language reading instruction for language-minority students is strong. The rationale can be defended on logical grounds and empirical evidence. . . . Once language-minority students have learned to read well and have understood the strategies for obtaining meaning from print, these abilities provide a solid foundation for literacy skills in the second language. (p. 178)

A second choice for literacy development is to develop reading skills in the two languages simultaneously. This appears to cause some initial confusion, which is generally short-lived and does not affect long-term academic achievement. Researchers of bilingual immersion programs in Canada have found that students studying in two languages who receive sequential literacy acquisition reach nativelike levels of proficiency in L_2 one year sooner than those acquiring literacy simultaneously (California Department of Education, 1984; Cummins & Swain, 1986). However, in the United States, several two-way bilingual schools that implement half a day of instruction in each language for all elementary school grades (K through 5 or K through 6) have chosen to teach literacy in the two languages simultaneously with no negative academic consequences for students. Instead, both language-minority and English-speaking students achieve above the 50th percentile on all academic measures in second language by fifth or sixth grade and remain high achievers throughout their schooling (Thomas & Collier, 1997).

The clearest, unambiguous finding of hundreds of research studies on bilingual literacy is that first-language literacy is a crucial variable influencing second-language literacy in a very positive way. As reviewed earlier in the section of this chapter on language acquisition, many studies show that numerous skills in reading transfer from one language to another (Au, 1993; Bialystok, 1991; Cummins, 1989c, 1991, 1996b; Cummins & Swain, 1986; Freeman & Freeman, 1992; Genesee, 1987, 1994; Hudelson, 1994; Johnson & Roen, 1989; Lessow-Hurley, 1990; Lindholm, 1991; Pérez & Torres-Guzmán, 1996; Snow, 1990; Tinajero & Ada, 1993; Wong Fillmore & Valadez, 1986). Even when the two languages do not use the same writing system, researchers have found that general strategies, habits and attitudes, knowledge of text structure, rhetorical devices, sensorimotor skills, visual-perceptual training, cognitive functions, and many reading readiness skills transfer from L_1 to L_2 reading (Chu, 1981; Cummins, 1991; Mace-Matluck, 1982; Swain, Lapkin, Rowen & Hart, 1990; Thonis, 1981). Students who are literate in L_1 generally progress much faster in L_2 reading than those who are not literate in their primary language.

In long-term research on academic achievement, Collier and Thomas (1989) found that by grade four, language-minority students who were not literate in their first language because they were schooled exclusively in English in the United States were three years behind their peers who had received at least three years of schooling in their first language before emigrating to the United States. This means that parents should be encouraged to continue the use of L_1 at home with children for development of full proficiency, including reading and writing if possible, especially if the school does not have the resources to provide bilingual personnel for all language groups. Any use of L_1 at home, both oral and written, will benefit students' cognitive development, all of which will transfer to cognitive and academic development in L_2 when the students acquire L_2 vocabulary and communicative patterns to express that knowledge.

Over the past decade, greatly increasing numbers of immigrants or refugees, arriving from war-torn countries or regions that have suffered catastrophic natural disasters, have experienced interrupted schooling or may never have had the opportunity to attend school. Older preliterate students present a special challenge to bilingual and ESL teachers, because of the general policy in U.S. schools to place students according to their age, regardless of the grade level they have reached in past schooling. Some schools have arranged for special one-to-one literacy instruction for these students in L_1 and L_2 through the use of teacher aides, student teachers, and volunteers. Other schools provide special needs classes taught by an ESL teacher. The most meaningful instruction for these students is intensive L_1 cognitive and academic development and L_1 counseling to deal with emotional issues that they often need to resolve from recent and past experiences, coupled with initial oral work in ESL, followed by reading and writing in ESL as soon as a solid literacy base is established in L_1. The greatest challenge these students present is to find ways to integrate them socially with students of their own age, while at the same time to present meaningful lessons at both their level of maturity and their level of cognitive development.

Teaching Reading and Writing

Many wonderful sources are available that provide detailed strategies for the teaching of reading and writing in bilingual, ESL, and heterogeneous grade-level classes. Our limited space here cannot do justice to this very important knowledge base for teaching. We will provide the reader with a few glimpses of the richness of current approaches to teaching reading and writing and refer to a few of the many resources available for teachers today.

Our overall goal in teaching reading and writing is to enable students to use and enjoy reading and writing "to learn about and interpret the world and reflect upon themselves in relation to people and events around them . . . and to explain, analyze, argue about, and act upon the world" (Hudelson, 1994, p. 130). Au (1993) emphasizes the importance of constructing meaning through written language by making students' background experiences central to the literacy process, using culturally responsive instruction.

In a literate society, children become aware very early of the importance of written language in their world through books, the media, signs, printed containers, logos, instructions, letters in the mail, and endless forms of environmental print. Reading and writing are natural processes that most students can readily acquire when they are given a classroom environment for learning to read and write that makes full use of the natural reading activities surrounding them (Goodman, 1986; Hudelson, 1994). Children might first learn to read stories that they dictate to the teacher (the language experience approach), directions for class responsibilities that students create (e.g., "feeding our rainforest tree frogs"), e-mail letters with a brother/sister bilingual school in another country or state, dialogue journals or peer journals, personal filmstrip stories that share inner feelings (Igoa, 1995), games, recipes, instructions to make things, a class newspaper, math puzzles, results of science experiments, maps of the school neighborhood, and published stories and poems created by classmates using word processing.

Dialogue journals have been used extensively in bilingual, ESL, and grade-level classrooms to develop writing skills as well as to enhance personal communication and mutual understanding between teacher and student.

Using this technique, each student keeps a notebook in which a private written conversation is carried on between teacher and student or between two peers in class. The writing style is informal, conversational language, and each student is free to write about anything of interest to the writer. The teacher makes no error correction other than modeling correct form through the response given. A teacher's comments should be warm, supportive, and responsive to the student's attempt to communicate. While the main focus of dialogue journal writing is on functional, personal, interactive use of the language, teachers report that students also improve in grammar, spelling, form, and content as the year goes on, without direct error correction, and students are extremely proud of their progress when they compare early entries with their writing at the end of the year (Johnson & Roen, 1989; Hudelson, 1989; Peyton, 1990; Peyton & Reed, 1990).

Formal writing is now taught as a process that involves several stages, including multiple drafts and revision through peer feedback. Students from kindergarten through grade 12 and beyond are writing and writing, first using invented spelling (in kindergarten) and later refining their revision skills as the nature of text development evolves with their developing language competence. As students write, they gain greater confidence and take on responsibility for the writing process.

In the prewriting stage, students need many opportunities to develop the ideas and information that will become the text of their writing. Extensive time should be allowed for prewriting, which is a significant proportion of the writing process (up to 40 percent of the total time involved). In this stage, teachers can provide a context that facilitates the prewriting process, including such strategies as brainstorming ideas, fantasizing, storytelling, word mapping or webbing, conversations with peers, strategic questioning, information gathering through interviews and reading, free writing or quick writing (in the form of stream of consciousness, with any style acceptable), creating an illustration, or sharing an experience (Adamson, 1993; Enright & McCloskey, 1988; Hudelson, 1994; Scarcella & Oxford, 1992). Goodman and Wilde (1992) describe the importance of creating a writing environment that empowers writers:

> The opportunity to move around the classroom and the availability and accessibility of appropriate writing materials and resources invite writers to "live off the land," a metaphor Donald Graves uses to describe how writers make use of a rich classroom environment. Such an environment provides opportunities and resources for children to think about, read about, talk about, and extend their composing. The freedom to use reference books and dictionaries and to stare out the window or at the ceiling, as well as to interact with teachers, peers, paraprofessionals, and others who participate in the community life of the classroom, dynamically influences children's writing. (p. 8)

The second stage of writing involves getting the first ideas down on paper, focusing on communicating thoughts to a known audience. Fluency is more important than accuracy at this stage. The third stage includes sharing and responding to this first draft, usually in small groups or pairs of classroom peers. When a new class begins this process, the total class can be the context for the teacher to model strategies to be used in a peer writer's workshop. Peer feedback does not happen naturally; teachers have to facilitate the process through guidance and careful modeling of positive feedback to each writer (Samway, 1992). Teacher-student conferences can be another form of writing feedback.

The fourth stage of writing includes revision in response to feedback, additional peer feedback, and more revision. Revision should first focus on communicating ideas, organizing the writing, making sense to the desired audience, use of beginnings and endings, transitions, and choice of words. The fifth stage involves editing for the mechanics of usage and spelling, and can be done with peer editors, dictionaries, spell checks on the computer, and all resources needed to "get it right." Publishing is the final stage in the writing process, and can be done through displays of student work, either hand-written or written using word processing on the computer (Enright & McCloskey, 1988; Johnson & Roen, 1989; Scarcella & Oxford, 1992). These stages described above provide a starting point for teachers and students becoming familiar with the writing process. With a stimulating classroom environment and experienced teachers, many other creative ways to approach the writing process emerge.

Many different genres of writing should be developed in the classroom, ranging from personal eventcasts, narratives, formal academic writing, letters, list making, form filling, literary writing, and journalistic writing, to all types of writing required for each subject area at each grade level (Heath, 1986; Kaplan, 1988). Writing is the most difficult language skill to be mastered in both first and second languages. For older students acquiring second language, written discourse (formal thought patterns) in first language is likely to have considerable influence on second-language writing (Connor & Kaplan, 1987; Purves, 1988).

Writing stimulates reading. Reading stimulates writing. And talking about one's own writing and other authors' writings, as well as connected life experiences, leads to continuing cognitive and academic growth through language acquisition: a full circle. Emergent literacy is stimulated through a print-rich classroom environment; sharing oral and written personal narratives, journal writing, and conversational writing with student partners; fluent readers (including the teacher) reading aloud daily, using predictable and familiar books; read-alongs and sing-alongs; story mapping; and sharing oral narratives from home, such as storytelling, commenting, questioning, jointly constructing a story, teasing, jokes, and riddles (Au, 1993; Hudelson, 1994; Pérez & Torres-Guzmán, 1996; Tinajero & Huerta-Macías, 1993). Phonics and other subskills of the reading process are taught within a meaningful context, through a combination of student discovery and teacher guidance.

Guidelines for Teaching

THE ACQUISITION OF THE WRITING PROCESS

Following two years of research on the acquisition of the writing process among Tohono O'odham children in Arizona, Goodman and Wilde (1992, p. 224) described a set of principles that emerged from observing these Tohono O'odham classrooms and are fundamental to any sound curriculum in writing:

- Children learn to write by writing.

- Children learn to write in a social environment that encourages and supports writing.

- Children learn to write as they know their audiences and use writing for a variety of purposes of communication.

- Children learn to write as they express themselves through many varieties, modes, and genres of writing.

- Children learn to write as they read a wide range of different kinds and genres of reading materials.

- Children learn to write as they make personal choices and decisions about what to write and what to read.

- Children learn to write as they experiment, take risks, and invent new forms of writing while they try to express their meanings through writing.

- Children learn to write as they talk about and critique their own compositions with others and as they discuss and critique the compositions of others with them.

- Children learn to write when they share with others through writing what they've learned about specific content in social studies, science, math, or other areas of the curriculum that they care about and are interested in.

- Children learn to write when they have important ideas or concerns to share with others.

- Children learn to write as they make miscues (errors) and inventions and self-monitor and self-correct their own writing.

- Children learn to write with teachers who understand the factors that influence writing and can organize rich literacy environments that support children's learning.

Most important of all is the recognition that literacy acquisition is "a profoundly social phenomenon" (Hudelson, 1994, p. 137). All reading and writing researchers in language-minority education emphasize the importance of collaborative activities with peers, cross-age tutors, and adults in many varied interactive settings as essential to reading and writing acquisition (Adamson, 1993; Au, 1993; Cantoni-Harvey, 1987, 1992; Carson & Leki, 1993; Cook & Urzua, 1993; Delgado-Gaitán, 1990; Enright & McCloskey, 1988; Freeman & Freeman, 1992; Goodman & Wilde, 1992; Heath & Mangiola, 1991; Hudelson, 1994; Johnson & Roen, 1989; Pérez & Torres-Guzmán, 1996; Peyton, 1990; Peyton & Reed, 1990; Rigg & Enright, 1986; Samway, 1992; Scarcella & Oxford, 1992; Tharp & Gallimore, 1988; Tinajero & Ada, 1993; Williams & Snipper, 1990).

Research in language-minority schools, homes, and communities has uncovered the rich "funds of knowledge" or "cultural resources" within each community (Moll & Díaz, 1993) that schools often overlook. Through collaborative research on reading and writing acquisition, teachers and researchers have discovered exciting ways to connect home and school literacy development in Native-American communities (Au, 1993; Goodman & Wilde, 1992; Vogt, Jordan, & Tharp, 1993), Hawaiian-American communities (Au, 1993; Tharp & Gallimore, 1988; Vogt, Jordan, & Tharp, 1993), Mexican-American communities (Ada, 1988; Campos & Keatinge, 1988; Delgado-Gaitán, 1987, 1990; Edelsky, 1986; Heath, 1986; Heath & Mangiola, 1991; Moll & Díaz, 1993; Moll, Vélez-Ibáñez, Greenberg, & Rivera, 1990), and other Hispanic-American communities (García, 1991; Hudelson, 1989, 1994; Pérez & Torres-Guzmán, 1996; Saravia-Shore & Arvizu, 1992; Tinajero & Ada, 1993).

Multicultural Literature

Finally, a language arts class incorporates books, poems, and stories written by authors who are skilled using the magic of words to create humor, excitement, suspense, beauty, joy, struggles—mirroring life in all its social and cultural complexity. A wealth of rich and original literature can excite and overwhelm the teacher trying to choose appropriate materials for students. Yet whole-language approaches are based on the principle that original literature (sometimes referred to as "trade books") is much more motivating and meaningful than the simplified texts that were typical of basal readers and ESL readers of the 1970s and 1980s.

Annotated teacher references are widely available in libraries for classical and contemporary literature used in U.S. classrooms, but they are focused mostly on U.S., British, and Canadian authors. To address teaching in the

Guidelines for Teaching

STRATEGIES FOR INCORPORATING LITERATURE FOR LANGUAGE-MINORITY ADOLESCENTS AND YOUNG ADULTS

Strategies for incorporating literature into lessons for language-minority adolescents and young adults may include the use of award-winning adolescent novels that deal with culturally complex issues (Sasser, 1992); the use of poetry, folktales, myths, and authentic world literature (Bosma, 1992; Lott, Hawkins & McMillan, 1993; Sasser, 1992); and reading aloud sensitively chosen children's literature with universal themes, using the following selection criteria:

- Interest-provoking titles.

- Simple structure with a strong, meaningful theme.

- Fresh and challenging vocabulary.

- Creative and vivid illustrations.

- Irreverent, rebellious stories with a twist. (Khodabakhshi & Lagos, 1993, p. 52) multicultural classroom, Smallwood (1991) created one of the first comprehensive, annotated guides for multicultural/multiethnic literature available in English for grades K through eight that can be used in ESL, bilingual, and grade-level classes. Bosma (1992) provides annotations of folk literature from around the world. Other references with lists of multiethnic books but no annotations include Tiedt and Tiedt (1990) and Harris (1993). Analyses of multicultural children's literature with annotations of selected books are provided in Harris (1992), which includes chapters analyzing the Puerto Rican (Nieto, 1992) and Mexican-American (Barreras, 1992) experiences as represented in children's literature. A number of publishers that exhibit at the annual conference of the National Association for Bilingual Education have produced some beautiful children's literature in Spanish and other languages.

Using multicultural literature in the classroom, students and teachers can experience the power and magic of language through oral and written words passed on through the generations from myths, folktales, novels, short stories, and poetry. We can reflect on our own life experiences in crossing cultures through the eyes of contemporary artists. We can study the multitude of ways people have interpreted reality, varying cultural values, the depth of cultural traditions, environmental reasons for varying behavior, and the changes occurring in the world now as a result of technology. Students can experience global perspectives and can recreate in their own writing or through dramatizations the stories that have power for them personally.

Language is enchanting, powerful, magical, useful, and personal. Language is our means of discovery of the world and our response to the world. As teachers we serve as catalysts for our students to make the best use of their two or more languages. Our languages are the most powerful tools we have.

Summary

This chapter has considered the complex processes involved in second-language acquisition. As we have seen, the process of acquiring a second language is neither simple nor short term, but involves the interaction of social, linguistic, academic, and cognitive variables. Although often counterintuitive to people outside of the field of bilingual or ESL education, research has provided consistent evidence for the interdependence of first and second languages. In other words, first-language academic development is strongly correlated with second-language acquisition and academic success in school.

For language-minority students, L_2 acquisition typically occurs in a school context, where students also are expected to learn academic content knowledge.

Consequently, instructional approaches designed for English language learners must effectively address their language needs as well as their academic development. While traditional approaches to ESL instruction emphasized the grammatical knowledge of English, more contemporary strategies have focused on the teaching of language *use* for meaningful communicative or academic purposes. Increasingly, ESL and content area instruction is being integrated to develop students' second language and to help them acquire the academic knowledge necessary for school success.

Key Terms

Social language p. 127

Academic language p. 128

Common underlying proficiency/
interdependence of languages p. 130

Threshold hypothesis p. 130

Semilingualism p. 130

Silent period p. 133

Reflection Questions

1. Although research studies suggest otherwise, many people persist in believing the myth that young children are faster and more efficient learners of a second language than are adults. Why do you think people continue to believe such a myth? What does the research, in fact, suggest about young second-language learners?
2. Why do the authors argue that the low socioeconomic status of many language-minority students is not an accurate predictor of their academic success or failure in school?
3. Why are some researchers critical of the "threshold hypothesis" and argue that it is related to the theory of semilingualism? What are the implications of the threshold hypothesis for policy and practice in bilingual education?
4. Consider some of the traditional approaches to ESL teaching. How do they compare to more contemporary ESL methods?
5. Why do researchers and practitioners argue that in K–12 classrooms it is more beneficial to integrate language and content instruction, rather than teach them as isolated subjects?

Resources

Bialystok, E., & Hakuta, K. *In other words: The science and psychology of second language acquisition.* New York: Basic Books, 1994.

- This is an engaging and comprehensive review about the process of first and second language acquisition. It considers second-language learning from a variety of perspectives.

Collier, V. *Promoting academic success for ESL students.* Elizabeth, NJ: New Jersey Teachers of English to Speakers of Other Languages-Bilingual Educators, 1995.

- A well-written introduction to the complex topic of academic second language acquisition for language-minority students in the United States. The book discusses the linguistic, social and cultural processes involved in second-language acquisition, as well as the cognitive and academic benefits for these students of first-language development.

Cummins, J. *Language, power and pedagogy: Bilingual children in the crossfire.* Clevedon, England: Multilingual Matters, 2000.

- A review of research and theory relating to the instruction and assessment of bilingual students. It focuses on issues of language learning and teaching, as well as the ways in which power relations in the wider society affect patterns of teacher-student interactions in classrooms. In this volume, Cummins also responds to critiques of several of more influential theories, including semilingualism, the threshold hypothesis, and the social versus academic language distinctions.

Echevarria, J., & Graves, A. *Sheltered content instruction: Teaching English-language learners with diverse abilities.* Boston, MA: Allyn & Bacon, 1998.

- This useful book provides both the theoretical basis for sheltered content instruction, or Specially Designed Academic Instruction in English (SDAIE), and strategies for its successful implementation in the classroom. The authors provide specific examples of sheltered content instruction and scenarios of classroom interaction during such instruction.

Ellis, R. *The study of second language acquisition.* Oxford, England: Oxford University Press, 1994.

- At 824 pages, this book is a veritable encyclopedia of second-language acquisition theory. It begins with a general framework for the study of second-language acquisition, then provides descriptions of the language of second-language learners, external and internals factors of SLA, and individual differences in language learning. The book also reviews expanding research on classroom second language acquisition.

Hakuta, K. *Mirror of language: The debate on bilingualism*. New York: Basic Books, 1986.

- An early and influential comprehensive account of the psychological, linguistic, educational, and social aspects of bilingualism.

MacSwan, J. The threshold hypothesis, semilingualism, and other contributions to a deficit view of linguistic minorities. *Hispanic Journal of Behavioral Sciences,* 22(1), 2000, 3–45.

- The author argues that the construct of semilingualism contributes to a deficit view of English language learners, and that Cummins's threshold hypothesis, which incorporates the semilingualism thesis, is similarly rooted in deficit theory and should be abandoned on empirical, theoretical and moral grounds.

Wiley, T. *Literacy and language diversity in the United States*. Washington, DC: Center for Applied Linguistics and Delta Systems, 1996.

- A well-written and interesting introduction to issues pertaining to literacy and language diversity in the United States. The book critiques policies and practices that view language and other forms of human diversity as problems that must be remedied through education and points to recent positive developments in adult literacy that accommodate language diversity and use it as a resource.

Endnotes

1. We have adopted the term *grade-level* classroom from Enright and McCloskey (1988) to replace the term *mainstream* or *regular* classroom, in the spirit of many professionals' concerns to use terms with fewer negative associations in our field. *Mainstream* is used by the field of special education to distinguish between classes that all students attend and special education classes in which students might be placed for a short or long period of time when students have special needs that cannot be met in the mainstream classroom. This term has been adopted by our field, but in many contexts it is not appropriate. When students are placed in ESL classes, they are generally a part of the mainstream for most of their school day, and ESL provides additional mainstream support to their schooling, an additive process. Likewise, transitional bilingual classes provide extra support for students' cognitive and academic development, as a part of the mainstream process, an added benefit. Two-way bilingual classes are grade-level, mainstream classes for all students who wish to receive the positive benefits of schooling in two languages. Therefore, *grade level* in our book refers to classes in which students are performing age-appropriate academic tasks at the level of cognitive maturity for their age and grade level. Many bilingual and ESL classes are also grade-level classes.

2. The theoretical concept of sociocultural processes is very similar to Jim Cummins' work on "negotiating identities" (Cummins, 1996). Emphasizing that human relationships are at the heart of schooling, Cummins shows that when powerful, affirming, respectful, and trusting relationships are established between teachers and students, students experience academic success that transcends poverty, societal subordination of groups, or past experience with war or other trauma. "Within this framework, *empowerment* can be defined as *the collaborative creation of power*. Students whose schooling experiences reflect collaborative relations of power develop the ability, confidence, and motivation to succeed academically. They participate competently in instruction as a result of having developed a secure sense of identity and the knowledge that their voices will be heard and respected within the classroom. They feel a sense of ownership for the learning that goes on in the classroom and a sense that they belong in the classroom learning community. In other words, empowerment derives from the process of negotiating identities in the classroom." (Cummins, 1996, p. 15)

3. The U.S. Supreme Court decision in *Lau* v. *Nichols* (1974) stated that merely providing limited-English-proficient students with the same facilities, textbooks, teachers, and curriculum that native-English speakers receive is equivalent to denying limited-English-proficient students a meaningful education. The Supreme Court justices ruled that U.S. public schools must provide some kind of special support to limited-English-proficient students. Most subsequent court decisions have ruled in favor of some combination of academic instruction in students' native language plus support from ESL specialists. "Sink-or-swim" practices can result in an OCR investigation. Also note that although we have chosen throughout this book to avoid use of the phrase *limited-English-proficient students,* because of the pejorative connotation associated with the word *limited* and its acronym *LEP,* we use the federal government term here to be consistent with federal terminology still used in federal legislation and court decisions.

Culture

Ethnographic Approaches to Cultural Understanding
Cultural Compatibility Studies
Sociocultural Theory and Knowledge Construction Studies

Culture . . . is not so much a matter of an inert system in which people operate, but rather a historical construction by people that is always changing. This change is not necessarily for better, not necessarily for worse, but always changing because the essence is not order, the essence is volition. The essence is how people work to create culture, not what culture is.

—Henry Glassie, folklorist, 1992

In the lives of language-minority students in our schools and communities we can see many different cultural processes at work. Such processes, however, can often defy easy understanding on the part of educators, because they can be interpreted (or misinterpreted) in conflicting ways. On the one hand, cultural processes are the complex, fluid, mysterious, and subtle ways in which we both transmit and create culture. But on the other hand, in interpreting them, we can end up with fixed labels that reduce cultural patterns to simplistic and dangerous stereotypes. Thus, at times, we may agree with Glassie's sense of the disorderliness of culture, while at other times we may be eagerly looking for pegs on which to hang cultural labels—labels that will confirm our desire for cultural stability and predictability.

Numerous factors contribute to cultural identity and have the potential either to bring us together or to separate us from each other. Some of the factors that contribute in varying degrees to cultural identity are ethnicity, geographical region, national origin, social class, level of education, types of contact with other cultural groups, religion, gender, and age. Yet, for all of the good pedagogical intentions associated with the process of identifying such factors and attaching cultural labels, there is always the danger of doing a disservice to the complex nature of cultural processes and thus to the individual student. As Maxine Greene states (1993):

> No one can be considered identical with any other, no matter what the degree of gender, class, ethnic or cultural identity ostensibly shared. Neither fixed in place nor voiceless, no one can be conceived as an endlessly reproducible repetition of the same model, to be counted for in accord with general laws of behavior. Nor can any human be predefined. The self is not something ready-made, John Dewey wrote; "but something in continuous formation through choice of action." Within that flux, the person is forever embarking on new beginnings, reaching beyond what is to what might be.

Embracing the dynamic and volitional nature of cultural processes suggested by Greene, we interpret culture in this chapter as a deep, multilayered, somewhat cohesive interplay of language, values, beliefs, and behaviors that pervades every aspect of every person's life, and that is continually undergoing modifications. When we study culture, it becomes an abstraction—albeit a useful one—for giving meaning to human activity. What it is *not* is an isolated aspect of life that can be used mechanistically to explain phenomena in a multicultural classroom or that can be learned as a series of facts. When we discard the dynamic and multidimensional views of culture for a series-of-facts view of culture, our efforts to implement **multiculturalism** become unrealistic when compared to the complex day-to-day events in the cultural life of the classroom. With respect to culture there *should* be an uneasy and creative tension between theory and practice, because this reflects the elusive and impermanent nature of cultural knowledge and processes (Ovando & Gourd, 1996).

To establish a broader basis for what we mean and do not mean by the word *culture,* in the first section of this chapter we consider various perspectives on the concept of culture—first the anthropological view and then popular views. In the second section we look at processes involved in the development of children's cultural identities: cultural transmission, biculturalism, acculturation, and assimilation. For the remainder of the chapter we delve into multicultural education as it relates to language-minority students. To do this, in the third section of the chapter we introduce the principles of cultural pluralism and multicultural education. In the fourth section we examine cultural concepts relevant to prejudice and discrimination, and in the fifth section we explore the role of culture in the school success of language-minority students. In the final section, we continue to examine the role of culture in achievement more closely through a survey of relevant ethnographic studies.

Throughout the entire chapter, we ask the reader to remember the importance of personal reflection on the topics that we address. Making educational decisions regarding cultural differences can be much more slippery or abstract than making decisions about how to set up a bilingual cooperative learning group, how to introduce reading in a second language, or how to make use of L_1 during content area instruction, for example. Whether you are a preservice or an in-service teacher, we ask that you pause throughout this chapter to reflect on how the topics relate to your own experiences—experiences that you have had with your family, in your own schooling, with your peers and friends, with your co-workers, in your travels, in community activities, or with your students. Unless we personally confront cultural issues such as acculturation, assimilation, ethnocentrism, stereotyping, discrimination, and deficit theories— just to name a few—we cannot assume that we have adequately "covered" culture (M. Calderón, personal communication, December 16, 1996).

Perspectives on the Concept of Culture

The Anthropological View of Culture

The concept of culture has been something of an enigma for social scientists. There is, to begin with, disagreement as to how culture should be defined (Wax, 1993). A common point of departure for discussion, however, is the definition formulated in 1871 by one of the earliest anthropologists, E.B. Tylor: "Culture . . . is that complex whole which includes knowledge, belief, art, law, morals, custom, and any other capabilities and habits acquired by man as member of society" (Kroeber & Kluckhohn, 1963, p. 81). Such broad, listlike definitions of culture have served as natural seedbeds for cultural analysis and intellectual enrichment for many years. However, if one views culture as an innumerable and complex set of nongenetic characteristics, as suggested by Tylor's definition, anthropological analysis runs the risk of limiting itself to what Geertz (1973) refers to as

> turning culture into folklore and collecting it, turning it into traits and counting it, turning it into institutions and classifying it, turning it into structures and toying with it. (p. 29)

For this reason, contemporary anthropologists have suggested a less segmented and more conceptually intricate perspective (Geertz, 1973; Jacob & Jordan, 1993). As a proponent of a deeper view of culture, Geertz (1973) offers the following interpretation:

> Believing, with Max Weber, that man is an animal suspended in webs of significance he himself has spun, I take culture to be those webs, and the analysis of it to be therefore not an experimental science in search of law but an interpretive one in search of meaning.
>
> Cultural analysis is intrinsically incomplete. And, worse than that, the more deeply it goes the less complete it is. It is a strange science whose most telling assertions are its most tremulously based, in which to get somewhere with the matter at hand is to intensify suspicion, both your own and that of others, that you are not quite getting it right. . . . Anthropology, or at least interpretive anthropology, is a science whose progress is marked less by a perfection of consensus than by a refinement of debate. What gets better is the precision with which we vex each other. (pp 5–29)

Culture Is Learned   In other words, culture is not carried in the genes. Consider a child who accidentally touches a hot object. The immediate

Guidelines for Teaching

AN ANTHROPOLOGICAL DEFINITION OF CULTURE

Despite conceptual disagreement over a specific definition of culture (Wax, 1993), anthropologists do tend to agree on three of its most basic characteristics (Hall, 1976, p. 13):

1. Culture is not innate, but learned.

2. Culture is shared and it has an important role in defining the social boundaries of different groups.

3. The various facets of culture are interrelated.

withdrawal of the hand is a physical reflex that does not have to be taught. However, whether the unpleasant surprise elicits from the child a scream of "Ay!" or "Ow!" becomes a cultural artifact, something transmitted through social interaction. Because a newborn child comes equipped with virtually no cultural baggage, an essential characteristic of being human is the manner, consciously and unconsciously, in which we transmit cultural patterns to succeeding generations. The premise that culture is learned, not inherited, is so basic to all considerations of the concept that it has often been used as a definition of culture by itself. Long before children enter the formal classroom, a rich mixture of culturally coded behavioral patterns have been learned through enculturation, a term described by Margaret Mead (1963) "as the actual process of learning as it takes place in a specific culture" (p. 185).

Because cultural patterns are learned, they are highly variable. Administration of justice among children, for example, does not follow one pattern that is innate to all humans. A pattern observed among some native Hawaiian families is that when children are involved in argumentative behavior with siblings or friends, parents tend to discipline all involved rather than attempting to identify the guilty parties. Consequently, these children may learn that it pays to take care of their concerns within their peer groups rather than sharing them with the adults (Gallimore, Boggs, & Jordan, 1974; Tharp & Gallimore, 1988). But the same children may also learn that in their classrooms, which generally operate out of a different cultural system, the teacher may often want to know who is responsible for the unacceptable behavior. Such an approach may teach children different ways of interacting with each other and with adults.

Culture Is Shared   Culture exists only in relation to a specific social grouping. Humans acquire and create culture only as members of society. Therefore, as groups constantly maintain some aspects of their identity while periodically modifying other aspects, individuals serve the dual function of being culture bearers as well as culture makers. This continual flux reflects what Berger (1967) refers to as "the cultural imperative of stability and the natural state of culture as unstable" (p. 6). To put it another way, human beings are constantly in the process of becoming "*a part of*" and "*apart from*" a given cultural context (Adler, 1972). For example, a child becomes a part of her home cultural environment as she learns ways to give or get information and to give or get attention appropriate to her ethnic group (Goodwin, 1990; Hymes, 1979). In school, however, she may grow apart from these patterns to some extent as she learns alternative forms of communication that characterize the classroom setting (Heath & Mangiola, 1991). Through such social contact with members of her own and other cultural groups her cultural identity develops.

While culture plays a role in defining ethnic boundaries, these boundaries are usually quite porous. To use a saying that folk singer Pete Seeger attributes to his father, "plagiarism is basic to all culture." Throughout history, societies have borrowed a great deal from each other (Wax, 1993). This borrowing has been a principal source of the instability of culture and of the constant development of cultural patterns "apart from" the original ones. This perpetual state of becoming—of new beginnings crafted on old ones—gives culture its dynamic and fascinating character.

Cultural Components Are Interrelated   The cultural traits of a particular group of people are largely integrated with each other into an interrelated whole. In other words, cultural traits are not a random hodge-podge of discrete customs with no relation to each other. To some extent this integrated consistency derives from adaptation to the environment. For example, in preindustrial societies, the traits of low population density, a nomadic lifestyle, and limited material possessions relate to a hunting and gathering society. Higher population density, permanent communities, and more acquisition of material possessions emerged with the development of agriculture-based societies. Cultural patterns tend toward a psychological integration of values and beliefs as well. For example, child-rearing practices and family living arrangements within a particular cultural group tend to reflect the same values and beliefs that the groups' folktales portray (Ember & Ember, 1988, p. 26). Of course, no two individuals within any cultural group are completely alike, and change is constantly occurring. Therefore, cultural components are not always in complete harmony with each other, but there is certainly an adaptive tendency toward reasonable consistency.

Because cultural patterns are integrated, a change in one aspect of the culture can, and probably will, affect many other facets of the culture. Looking just at examples involving education, consider the introduction of compulsory formal schooling into remote Alaskan native villages. Athapaskan Indians of the Yukon traditionally followed a seminomadic way of life, moving from fishing camps to hunting camps as the seasons changed. In the 1930s, however, "compulsory education forced parents to keep their children in school and thus abandon their traditional seasonal rounds" (Simeone, 1982, p. 100). Thus, with changes in the form of education also came changes in residential patterns, along with concomitant changes in subsistence patterns, the local economy, patterns of social interaction, and the loss or weakening of indigenous languages (Ovando, 1994). The Micronesian island of Pohnpei underwent a comparable process when the introduction of Western schooling patterns brought about many other changes in cultural patterns (Falgout, 1992).

The above generalizations—that culture is learned, shared, and integrated—provide some important grips on the concept of culture, but they do not give one a comprehensive hold. Culture is learned, but most of the teaching of culture is unreflected on, and the content is somewhat modified as it is transmitted. Culture is shared and defines boundaries, but the exact same culture is not shared by all members of a social group, and the boundaries are highly permeable. Components of a culture seem to be interrelated as in a system, but this system does not always seem to behave according to clear, systematic rules.

Finally, to make the understanding of culture even more evasive, there is the problem of inevitable bias. Because we are all culture bearers, when we study or simply observe the behavior of members of a cultural group, we cannot dissociate our own cultural background completely from the topic of inquiry. Because we all view the world through our cultural lenses, objectivity is a goal we can only hope to approach but will probably never reach. If we implement a critical pedagogy that activates students' prior experiences, incorporates community knowledge, and addresses sociocultural issues of concern to students, we will certainly have a wealth of important cultural information to use in the teaching and learning process. But as we make instructional decisions based on our observations of students' cultural background, it is extremely important to remember that our interpretations will always be colored by our own cultural and individual values. This issue of subjectivity will be discussed further in the third section of this chapter, when we take a look at cultural concepts relevant to prejudice and discrimination.

Popular Views of Culture

The High Civilization View   Educators have often tended to use the word *culture* as meaning the accumulation of the so-called "best" knowledge, ideas, works of art, and technological accomplishments of a particular group of people. This "high civilization" or "highbrow" view of culture (Levine, 1988), in the case of Western civilization, conjures up the image of the sophisticated cognoscente familiar with the likes of Shakespeare, Dante, Cervantes, Socrates, Mozart, Michelangelo, and so on. Such a sophisticated person may scoff at the unfortunate slob who "doesn't have any culture." Curricula in the United States have implicitly and explicitly stressed the importance of Western ideals as the hallmark of culture. This view of culture (minus the snobbery) can be justifiably taught as an appreciation of a historical heritage, and it can be an important component of the liberal arts curriculum (Banks, 1993; García, 1993). However, a monocultural view of the accomplishments of the Western or English-speaking world, at the expense of the social, cultural, and linguistic realities that surround minority learners, may have significant negative effects. Lack of acknowledgment of multiple cultural traditions can be related to high dropout rates, alienation, and low academic achievement (Banks, 1993; Ogbu, 1978, 1992; Stanford Working Group, 1993; Tharp & Gallimore, 1988; Trueba, 1987).

The Set-of-Traits View   Another common approach to culture—one that we refer to as the "set-of-traits" point of view—is the tendency to view culture as a series of significant historical events and heroes, typical traditions, and culturally coded concepts or terms. Erickson has referred to such superficial treatment as "cultural tourism"—a focus on the more colorful and salient aspects of a group of people (Erickson, 1997, p. 46). Tongue in cheek, the set-of-traits point of view has also been called the "laundry list" approach and the "facts, fun, and fiestas" approach. Using the laundry list approach to Mexican-American culture, for example, an educator could conclude that students should know about such items as Benito Juárez, César Chávez, Dolores Huerta, *la Virgen de Guadalupe*, *Cinco de Mayo*, *La Raza*, *cholos*, *Aztlán*, and *la quinceañera*. The argument for this approach is that the better informed students are about a culture, the less prejudiced they will be. And there is some empirical evidence to support the argument (Banks, 1991b; Glock, Wutnow, Piliavin, & Spencer, 1975; Lambert & Klineberg, 1967).

The set-of-traits view, however, is extremely limited and easily promotes the view that culture is highly static rather than being a complex, interrelated, and varying construct. The approach obscures the reality of individuals as culture bearers and culture makers, who not only carry their culture but also may help to reconstruct their world if they so desire. It does not lend itself to the consideration of people's **acculturation** or **assimilation**, nor does it portray **culture** as an integrated configuration adapted to a particular context. There is also the danger that this type of approach may lead to stereotyping, especially of already stigmatized minorities. One is inclined to assume falsely that everything on the cultural "list" is meaningful in the same way to every member of the cultural group. This view of culture may also encourage one to feel a sense of distance from the everyday immediacy of cultural phenomena. The "bits" of culture become discrete abstractions, items that can be reduced to "right" or "wrong" on a multiple-choice test. Instead, it is important to observe the actual behaviors of students and parents in and outside of the classroom and to ask many questions. For example, instead of assuming that a given holiday or celebration is meaningful for *all* members of a particular ethnic group, the teacher may wish to ask the students and parents themselves, "What holidays or celebrations are most important to you? Why?" (Saville-Troike, 1978, p. 37). The responses to such inquiries may confirm what was already known, but they may also reveal new dimensions to a student's ethnic identity.

Both the high-civilization view of culture and the set-of-traits view have some pedagogical validity, but they are not in and of themselves sufficient to achieve an understanding of culture in the multiethnic classroom. Both views deprive us of an awareness of culture as an integral aspect of our own lives—as the web we all weave, together and separately, day after day. Both views bypass a premise particularly essential to multicultural education: that no child or teacher is without culture. This premise is the critical source for the role of culture in the classroom. An awareness of culture is not only the discovery of "others," but also the discovery of ourselves, and of our own webs. To illustrate this point, consider the reaction of a group of adult students, learning to read for the first time, to a picture of their village—the first they had ever seen. (This incident occurred in São Tomé, an island off the west coast of Africa.)

⊠ *The class first looked at the picture in silence, then four of them got up as if by arrangement and walked over to the wall where the picture code of the village was hung. They looked attentively at the picture, then they went over to the window and looked at the world outside. They exchanged glances, their eyes wide as if in surprise, and, again looking at the picture, they said, "It's Monte Mario. That's what Monte Mario is like, and we didn't know it." (Freire, 1981, p. 30)*

Processes in the Development of Cultural Identities

As teachers, we are working with young people who are not only developing physically, emotionally, socially, academically, and cognitively; we are also working with children who are developing culturally. As stated in the first section of this chapter, children are not born with a culture; they learn it. In the case of language-minority children, the process is a particularly interesting one as they build their cultural identity within the multiple contexts of their home environment, the school environment, and the larger dominant sociocultural environment. To better understand this process of cultural development, we will consider Mead's model of cultural transmission, and then we will look at the interrelated issues of biculturalism, acculturation, and assimilation.

Cultural Transmission

We have already introduced Mead's concept of enculturation when we described the child's process of learning cultural patterns. However, the process is not a simple, straightforward one in which children always learn "all there is to know" from older family members. A lifelong student of cultural transmission in Western and non-Western societies, Margaret Mead (1978) concluded that the process by which new members learn the scope and detail of their own culture is not, and never has been, a smooth and painless one. She identified three kinds of cultural transmission processes: postfigurative, cofigurative, and prefigurative.

Postfigurative Transmission   In postfigurative transmission, adult community members pass on values, beliefs, and behaviors to the upcoming generation with little alteration. Usually in such contexts the children question the cultural patterns they receive from their elders very little. In the United States, for example, the Amish and Hutterite subcultures closely represent postfigurative processes. Immigrants from traditional or rural societies may also have a background of strong postfigurative cultural transmission.

Cofigurative Transmission   In cofigurative transmission communities there are multiple cultural role models—old ones and contemporary ones. Emergent cultural traits may be attributed to the sharing between parents and children at a time when the traditional cultural patterns have lost some power over the young. Cofigurative communities may be represented, for example, by immigrant groups that are partially disengaging from the past and are beginning to relate in different ways with their children growing up in the United States. "But Mom, that's not the way you do it here," may be a beginning signal that cofigurative culture change is occurring within the ethnic community.

Prefigurative Transmission   In this type of cultural transmission the children to a large extent create culture change. For example, immigrant parents in prefigurative situations vicariously experience much of American society and culture through their children. The reality that such children present to their parents has been secured from the formal school system and from many informal channels—peers, street culture, television, radio, magazines, newspapers, clubs, and organizations. These children are frequently the source of many answers for their parents' concerns. They serve as translators at the doctor's office, for example, or they write the school absence excuse for their younger siblings. Virtually everything new is filtered through the children, who may put aside some of their old values as being obsolete. Frustration and stress may sometimes begin to characterize many of the interactions between parents and children. There may also be a sense of power or superiority on the part of the prefigurative youth. As Handlin (1951) put it years ago, referring to the acculturation process across immigrant generations, "the young wore their [U.S.] nativity like a badge that marked their superiority over their immigrant elders" (pp. 253–54).

While Mead analyzed the development of cultural identity across generations, another important way to look at the process is from the standpoint of interaction between various cultural groups. From this point of view we will look at biculturalism, acculturation, and assimilation.

Biculturalism

A person is bicultural when he or she has the capacity to negotiate effectively within two different cultural systems. Being bicultural, however, does not necessarily mean giving equal time to both cultures in terms of behavior. There may be many traits from one culture or both that the person understands but doesn't necessarily act out, such as religious rituals or family traditions (Kim, 1988; Paulston, 1992; Saville-Troike, 1978). The following statement by a Greek-American scholar provides a window into the dynamics of **biculturalism** in the United States:

Living in two worlds, the one American, the other of the immigrant Greek, was not an emotional strain. It was a natural thing to do and made it possible to achieve early in my life a sense of identity, something which we are trying now to achieve with the cultural minority groups in our schools. . . .

Phenomenologically, my work world and my social world are a seamless fabric of a continuing experience. This bicultural experience provides me with an active comparative and contrastive set of insights into American and immigrant cultures as continuing lived experiences. . . . I feel that the opportunity to experience cultural conflict and the cultural integrity earned through the resolution of that conflict are vital affective education. (Cited in Havighurst, 1978, pp. 15–16)

Although one would think that an understanding of biculturalism would be an important aspect of public policy on bilingual education, surprisingly little theorizing has been given to the concept (Harris, 1994). Anthropology, for example, which has so much to say about culture, has very little to say about biculturalism. The term receives only a small paragraph, as a subheading under the term *acculturation,* in the *International Encyclopedia of Social Sciences* (Sills, 1968, p. 24). The *Dictionary of Anthropology* does not even include a listing for the term *bicultural* (Seymour-Smith, 1986). And while perhaps a majority of bilingual programs are described as "bilingual/bicultural" programs, the extent to which learning a second language actually implies becoming bicultural is something that has not been significantly analyzed. Paulston (1992) substantiates the lack of work on this topic. In her search of the literature she found only five entries under *biculturalism.*

The tendency in the United States has been to perceive biculturalism as an abnormality (Social Science Research Council, 1954, p. 982). This tendency to view biculturalism negatively is related to much linguistic and psychological work done during the first half of this century that suggested that bilingualism was an undesirable trait. Such research alleged, for example, that bilinguals "had lower IQ scores than monolinguals, were socially maladjusted, and trailed monolinguals in academic performance" (Reynolds, 1991, p. 145). Similarly, Diebold (1968) pointed out that in the past a common perception in the United States was that bilingualism was detrimental to personality development because the knowledge of two languages was thought to imply two separate, culture-bound personality structures operating within the same individual.[1]

A more positive view of biculturalism emphasizes the maintenance of identity by means of changes in cultural patterns. For example, studies by Clark, Kaufman, and Pierce (1976); Delgado-Gaitán (1994); Merino, Trueba, and Samaniego (1993); Suárez-Orozco (1989); Suárez-Orozco and Suárez-Orozco (1995); and Spindler and Spindler (1990) suggest that culture contact in the United States generates "situational ethnicity"—individuals have a range of types of bicultural behavior that vary in their emphasis on minority cultural patterns and majority cultural patterns. For example, in an investigation of the ethnic identity of Mesquakie Indians, Polgar (1960) found that the teenagers he studied regularly went through a process of biculturation. Through their reservation life and contact with the outside community (especially through the schools) they had been simultaneously enculturated into traditional Mesquakie life and media-influenced dominant culture lifestyles.

Based on research among Eskimo students in rural Alaska, Kleinfeld (1979) has also concluded that institutions such as schools play a highly significant role in the establishment of young people's cultural identities. She has noted two characteristics that can foster the "bicultural fusion" of the minority child:

1. Significant reference groups in the majority culture (such as teachers, majority-group classmates, media) hold the minority culture in esteem and significant reference groups in the local minority culture (such as parents, peers, older youth who are trendsetters) hold the majority culture in esteem.

2. Central socialization settings (home, school, religious groups, ethnic organizations) fuse elements from both cultures rather than separate them. (Kleinfeld, 1979, p. 137)

Kleinfeld's findings suggest that school personnel and community members who have mutual respect for each other's values and who also are open and adaptable in their interaction with one another enhance children's ability to function biculturally as both members of an ethnic group and participants in American society at large.

Acculturation

Although the term *biculturalism* has not been researched extensively in the field of anthropology or education, the related terms *acculturation* and *assimilation* have been used exhaustively to analyze culture contact. Acculturation is a process by which one cultural group takes on and incorporates one or more cultural traits of another group, resulting in new or blended cultural patterns. The *Dictionary of Anthropology* describes acculturation as "processes of accommodation and change in culture contact" (Seymour-Smith, 1986, p. 1). For example, as rural Mexican immigrant youngsters start wearing baseball caps and listening to heavy metal music, they are acculturating to outward aspects of contemporary U.S. culture. However, although these children may quickly adopt some U.S. clothing styles and musical tastes, such things as their language usage patterns, gestures, facial expressions, value systems, and social interaction styles will most likely remain more Mexican for a much longer period of time. As Nieto (1996) puts it, students often maintain such "deep culture" while they acculturate to their new cultural environment in more superficial ways.

Cultural change through acculturation does not necessarily mean loss of the original cultural identity. For example, a Koyukon Athapaskan who uses a snowmobile instead of sled dogs is still an Athapaskan Indian. It is not a set of particular traits that counts in ethnic identity as much as it is the fact that the Athapaskan *considers* him or herself as a member of a distinct group (Erickson, 1997). Acculturation can frequently be seen as an additive process, one that can result in bicultural or even multicultural identities. Acculturated individuals are able to employ situational ethnicity because they have the knowledge and skills to function in two or more different cultural contexts.

As Erickson points out, in today's world most humans actually are multicultural, especially those who live in large, complex societies (Erickson, 1997).

Assimilation

Acculturation, instead of resulting in biculturalism and situational ethnicity, can alternatively result in assimilation. Assimilation is a process in which an individual or group completely takes on the traits of another culture, leaving behind the original cultural identity. The absorption of many European immigrant groups into majority U.S. cultural patterns and social structures has generally been described as a process of assimilation. For many years in the past one of the goals of many school programs in the United States has been to assimilate indigenous and immigrant minority children into the majority culture. For example, the policy of assimilating American Indian youth through education is clearly reflected in the 1887 statement by J.D.C. Atkins, Commissioner of Indian Affairs: "If we expect to infuse into the rising generation the leaven of American citizenship, we must remove the stumbling blocks of hereditary customs and manners, and of these language is one of the most important elements" (Adams, 1988, p. 8).

Because the concept of the assimilative **melting pot** has been such a strong theme in the history of the United States, there is a tendency to still assume today that many young people will want to entirely assume dominant cultural patterns. However, Nieto (1996, 1994) found in her own case studies of 12 high school students, as well as in other researchers' work, evidence that many contemporary minority students—despite some conflicts and mixed feelings—have pride in their background and express a desire to maintain their language and culture. As one of the students in her case study said, "You gotta know who you are" (1996, p. 284). She also notes research evidence that suggests that students who resist assimilation may also be more successful academically. For example, one study of Southeast Asian students found a positive correlation between higher grades and maintenance of pride in ethnicity.

Multicultural Education

Cultural Pluralism as a Basis for Multicultural Education

As language-minority students enter adulthood, they will have to confront the degree to which United States society is prepared to accept their multiple cultural identities through an ethos of cultural pluralism. Cultural pluralism characterizes a society in which members of diverse cultural, social, racial, or religious groups are free to maintain their own identity and yet simultaneously share equitably in a larger common political organization, economic system, and social structure. Cultural pluralism is an extremely sensitive political issue in many nations throughout the world. Biculturalism can conceivably be seen as a matter of individual choice, but a positive or negative stance on cultural pluralism as a national policy touches on the most basic definitions of nationhood. In the United States, for example, with its growing diversity, there is a renewed public debate regarding the best way to induct historically marginalized groups into the sociocultural fabric of society. Some argue that unless diversity is harnessed through an assimilative process into a common culture and language, the country will become divided into many ethnic enclaves with very particular agendas that could threaten the unity and future of the nation. For example, the works of Bennett (1984), Bloom (1987), D'Souza (1991), Epstein (1977), Finn, Ravitch, & Fancher (1984), Glazer (1985), Gray (1991), Hirsch (1991), Ravitch (1990), and Sowell (1993) reflect this general point of view. The American historian, Arthur Schlesinger, Jr., in his controversial book, *The Disuniting of America: Reflections of a Multicultural Society* (1992, p. 18), echoes the above concerns, asking, "Will the center hold? Or will the melting pot give way to the Tower of Babel?" Looking specifically at education, Lutz (1994) reports that some writers hold that cultural pluralism will lower academic standards through an emphasis on "feel good" learning, and further that it will teach wrong values and infringe on the right to freedom of speech through enforcement of political correctness.

Supporters of cultural pluralism, however, argue that it is not only possible but necessary to affirm ancestral cultural and linguistic roots while concurrently sharing a set of pluralistic democratic principles, especially through the school curriculum. Supporters of cultural pluralism hold that the inclusion of diversity in both the content and the process of schooling practices gives society its sociocultural coherence. Cultural pluralism in fact puts into practice *e pluribus unum* and thus enables us to live up to the founding democratic principles of our society (Banks, 1993; Graff, 1992).

The above interpretation of cultural pluralism is of course an ideal, which has, so far, come quite short of its mark in the United States. With respect to public school policy, the controversy cannot be resolved to suit everyone's ideological or pedagogical persuasion. Cultural pluralism elicits strong passions because it challenges us to rethink not only our conception of a just society but also of who we are as Americans and what makes us unique. Critics of cultural pluralism who fear a loss of national character would do well to consider whether or not that supposed character has ever been a constant. National character, if it can even be identified, is not a straitjacket—an all-encompassing yet vague force that causes particular types of behavior in particular groups. It has always been a developing and adjustable framework, very responsive to social and economic conditions. For example, it would be very difficult to find many cultural similarities between the "typical American citizen" of 1797 and the "typical American citizen" of 1997, even if we could find such a thing as a "typical" citizen. Maintenance of any ethnic identity within the United States is not a result of adherence to rigid cultural laws but occurs within the context of adjustments to social and economic conditions and cross-cultural contacts. Language-minority children in a school that values their ethnic heritage would be highly unlikely, as a consequence of such schooling, to lock themselves into all the behaviors and values traditionally held by members of their ethnic group. While remaining secure in their ethnic identity, they would more likely alter some of the characteristics of that identity as they experiment with new behaviors that are effective in new social contexts.

Dimensions of Multicultural Education

Multicultural education is built on the premise of the need to prepare all children, minority and majority, to participate equitably in a culturally pluralistic society. And like its conceptual partner, cultural pluralism, it too has been subject to severe criticism, as suggested above by Lutz. Cummins (1996a) argues that the debate is so heated because multicultural education

> entails a direct challenge to the societal power structure that has historically subordinated certain groups and rationalized the educational failure of children from these groups as being the result of their inherent deficiencies. Multicultural education . . . challenges all educators to make the schools a force for social justice in our society. (p. xvi)

Multicultural education is challenging and controversial not only because it has the potential to mobilize communities of learners as social change agents, but also because it makes us rethink our ideas of what constitutes effective teaching: Are teachers to be merely transmitters of consensus values and dominant culture knowledge, or are they to be coparticipants with students in knowledge construction and social action?

 Guidelines for Teaching

CHARACTERISTICS OF MULTICULTURAL EDUCATION

1. Multicultural education is antiracist. It does not gloss over the presence of racism in society but addresses it.

2. Multicultural education is basic. It is an integral component of education along with other core subjects.

3. Multicultural education is vital for both majority and minority students.

4. Multicultural education is pervasive in the entire schooling process. It is not a separate subject.

5. Multicultural education is education for social justice. It connects knowledge and understanding with social action.

6. Multicultural education is a process. It is ongoing and dynamic and involves relationships between people as much as it does content.

7. Multicultural education is critical pedagogy. Teachers and students in a multicultural learning environment do not view knowledge as being neutral or apolitical.

As suggested by these broad issues of social justice and knowledge construction, multicultural education today is defined by leaders in the field as a comprehensive approach to schooling that can touch on virtually every aspect of the educational process, from power and decision-making structures to curricular content to instructional practices to community relations (Banks & Banks, 1997; Bennett, 1995a; Grant & Sleeter, 1989; Ladson-Billings, 1994; Nieto, 1996). Nieto (1996, pp. 306–23), for example, anchors her broad approach to multicultural education within the sociopolitical context of contemporary society, and she identifies seven key characteristics of multicultural education, which we summarize and paraphrase in the Guidelines box on p. 200.

This multifaceted definition shows that multicultural education is a highly challenging concept that can be viewed as an organizing principle for systemic school reform. Nieto (1996) argues that without such a transformative sociopolitical approach, multicultural education is just a trip to "fairyland" (p. 9), another set-of-traits or cultural tourism approach to the issue. Erickson (1997, p. 53) provides us with a good illustration of the limits of a multicultural approach that does not address the larger sociocultural and political factors that affect school achievement. Distinguishing between what he calls the visible and the invisible aspects of culture, he describes a potential scenario in which a classroom has visible signs of a multicultural curriculum—for example, a poster of Frederick Douglass is displayed, the children learn vocabulary in Swahili or Yoruba, and they also study about West Africa from a positive point of view. However, in this same early childhood classroom, cultural variation in language use patterns—a less visible aspect of culture—is not recognized, resulting in lower expectations for some students. Erickson gives the example of the teacher's assessment of "reading readiness." The teacher holds up a sheet of red paper and asks a low-income

 Guidelines for Teaching

FIVE DIMENSIONS OF MULTICULTURAL EDUCATION

Given the extensive boundaries of multicultural education, how can bilingual and ESL educators play an active role in its implementation? To address this question, we will use the five dimensions of multicultural education that Banks and Banks (1995) have identified as useful guides to educators who are trying to implement multicultural school reform. The dimensions are:

1. Content integration.

2. The knowledge construction process.

3. Prejudice reduction.

4. An equity pedagogy.

5. An empowering school culture and social structure. (Banks & Banks, 1995, pp. 4–5)

African-American child, "What color is this?" Because the child comes from a cultural background in which adults tend not to use such known-answer questions in conversations with children, he or she is confused by the nature of the question and answers in Black English, "Aonh-oh". (I don't know.) The teacher makes a negative evaluation of the child's nonstandard English pronunciation coupled with an assumption of limited vocabulary development, and the child may well be on his or her way to a tracked program of low achievement, despite the presence of an outwardly multicultural curriculum.

In this book, reflecting the premise that multicultural education should be comprehensive, we address many different aspects of the multicultural approach throughout the entire text. We discuss Banks and Banks's first dimension, content integration, in a variety of contexts. In particular, Chapter Three (including art, music, and technology) and the chapters on language, social studies, math, and science address incorporating multicultural materials and perspectives. (Another useful resource for content integration is Grant and Gómez's book *Making Schooling Multicultural: Campus and Classroom* (1996), which includes separate chapters on multicultural content integration in math, science, social studies, art, music, physical education, health, theater, and television and film.) We describe how Banks and Banks's second dimension, knowledge construction, is related to the concepts of active learning and critical pedagogy in Chapter Three. We also consider knowledge construction later in this chapter and in Chapter Seven. The final three dimensions—prejudice reduction, equity pedagogy, and empowering schooling—also appear indirectly throughout the book as we consider the many different ways in which to provide an equitable education for language-minority students. However, we will focus most directly on these three dimensions in the remainder of this chapter. We will first look at prejudice reduction in light of the issues of marked and unmarked cultures, stereotyping, and ethnocentrism and cultural relativism. We will then look at equity pedagogy and empowering schooling environments as we examine the role of culture in the school success of language-minority students.

Prejudice and Discrimination

Through the civil rights movement, educators developed a greater awareness of prejudice and discrimination in schools. For example, one study done in the early 1970s for the U.S. Commission on Civil Rights, based on observations of 494 classrooms in the Southwest, revealed that teachers directed 21 percent more questions to European Americans than to Mexican Americans, praised or encouraged European Americans 35 percent more often, and accepted or used European Americans' ideas 40 percent more often (Jackson & Cosca, 1974). Despite the growth of such awareness in the 1960s and 1970s, the fact remains today that prejudice and discrimination are still frequent presences within schools across the nation. ESL and bilingual educators have both firsthand and secondhand knowledge of this discrimination as they work with children from a broad range of backgrounds. Nieto (1994) gives the example of the thoughts of one immigrant high school student from Cape Verde (an island nation west of Senegal) who came to the United States at the age of 11:

When American students see you, it's kinda hard [to] get along with them when you have a different culture, a different way of dressing and stuff like that. So kids really look at you and laugh, you know, at the beginning. (p. 47)

We will focus our examination of prejudice and discrimination on the implications of the following cultural concepts: marked and unmarked cultures, stereotypes, and ethnocentrism and cultural relativism. Teachers who bring an understanding of such concepts to the school environment will be better prepared to analyze and address the discrimination that occurs in bilingual and ESL settings.

Marked and Unmarked Languages and Cultures

The terms **marked** and **unmarked language**, and by extension, **marked and unmarked culture**, distinguish between the different degrees of status assigned to particular cultural groups. Fishman (1976), a linguist who analyzed the education of language-minority students from a broad, international perspective, introduced the terms. In the context of bilingual education, Fishman (1976) defined a marked language as one "which would most likely *not* be used *instructionally* were it not for bilingual education, that is to say, it is precisely bilingual education that has brought it into the classroom. Conversely, a language is *unmarked* in a bilingual education setting [if it] would most likely continue to be used instructionally, even in the absence of bilingual education" (pp. 99–100). In other words, marked languages are the ones associated with less social status and political power. In the United States the unmarked language is standard English.

Expanding the concepts of marked and unmarked languages to the groups they most closely represent, unmarked culture in the United States tends to be associated with white, middle class, nonethnic, English-speaking groups. It is unmarked in the sense that it reflects a somewhat mythical generalization of the way the typical "American" is "supposed" to be. Marked culture, on the other hand, is associated with the stigmatized and sometimes subordinate status of socioeconomically or culturally defined minority groups. Most curricula in public schools in the United States tend to emphasize unmarked cultural values, because the unmarked culture is the one that wields by far the most power in educational institutions.

Spolsky (1978, p. 28) suggested that one goal of bilingual education should be to enable language-minority students to experience unmarked civic life outside the boundaries of their marked culture without being stigmatized. For schools to allow this would imply their unprejudiced acceptance of the blending of characteristics of the unmarked and marked cultures. We are all too often unable to approach this ideal, of course, and the stigmatization of marked languages and cultures in the United States continues to be a problem as evidenced by the chronic difficulty in gaining full acceptance of bilingual programs that have a strong, long-term use of L_1 and a strong cultural component.

Nieto (1996) effectively describes the potential burden of carrying a marked cultural background in school:

> "*Who does the accommodating?*" This question gets to the very heart of how students from nondominant [marked] groups experience school every day. Dominant-group students, on the contrary, rarely have to consider learning a new language to communicate with their teachers. They already speak the acceptable school language. The same is true of culture. These students do not generally have to think about their parents' life-styles and values because their families are the norm. . . . Students from other groups, however, have to consider such issues *every single day*. Their school experiences are filled with the tension of accommodation that students from the dominant group could not even imagine. (p. 334)

The intuitive awareness of marked and unmarked languages and cultures appears to develop in children at a fairly young age. Consider the following dialogue that a colleague of one of the authors overheard, which reflects an awareness of marked and unmarked status among three elementary-age students:

⊠ *Three middle class teachers who work at a largely Hispanic-American, lower-income elementary school have come to school on a Saturday to catch up on work. These three teachers have all brought their daughters along, all of whom attend middle class elementary schools. The children are all native English speakers—two European-American girls and one Mexican-American girl who is very acculturated to the unmarked culture. They are working at a table cutting out decorations when a local, Mexican-American mother comes into the classroom and carries on an extended conversation in Spanish with one of the teachers. After the mother leaves, this conversation arises among the children:*

> *Linda (Mexican American): I know how to speak Spanish—my grandmother taught me. But I don't like to!*
>
> *Laurie (European American): I know. There's a girl in my class who all she does is speak Spanish and she's so dumb! All she does is copy my work.*
>
> *Jennifer (European American): People who speak Spanish aren't dumb. They just can't help it.*

Cummins (1989b) found the same phenomenon in a study of four first-generation Mexican-American fifth graders. Although these students were not fully proficient in English, they rarely used their native language, Spanish, explaining that this language was just for "dumb kids." The adverse pedagogical implications of this bias against the marked language are significant.

As Cummins points out, the students' avoidance of use of the marked language, coupled with the school's failure to capitalize on the student's experiences and language-rich home environment, resulted in serious limits on their opportunities to employ more abstract discourse and higher levels of cognitive functioning.

The case of immersion bilingual education programs provides another revealing example of the role of marked and unmarked cultures in educational outcomes. Edelsky (1996), reflecting on the studies she and Hudelson conducted in two Spanish-English two-way immersion programs in the late 1970s, noted that for children in such programs, "clues mount up quickly over which language must be learned" (p. 26). For example, in one of the programs, which was an alternate day program, the unmarked language, English, very frequently crept into use during Spanish days—much more so than Spanish crept into use during English days. On Spanish days, English speakers were often given comprehension checks in English, whereas on English days, Spanish speakers were less likely to be given such assistance through their L_1. Because English was the unmarked language, it was taken for granted by children and teachers alike that this was the language that all students would have to learn. Spanish speakers made great strides in English over the course of the year, while English speakers knew little more than colors, numbers, and social routines in Spanish after months of exposure to the marked language.

Edelsky suggested that, although the outside effects of the larger social structure cannot be totally neutralized, intensive efforts can be made within the school to lessen the degree of markedness of the marked language by making greater efforts to use the languages equitably. This stance is borne out by the findings in California, alluded to in Chapters Three and Four, that suggest that a 90 percent marked/10 percent unmarked pattern of language use in the early grades is the most effective form of immersion education for both language majority and language-minority students. The heavy emphasis on the marked language in the early grades helps the marked language speakers to develop their cognitive skills in a less prejudiced atmosphere, and it provides the unmarked language speakers with an environment in which—within the confines of the school—the marked language is actually the one that counts the most.

Stereotypes

The American Heritage Dictionary of the English Language defines a **stereotype** as "a conventional, formulaic, and oversimplified conception, opinion, or image." Although we have all been victims as well as users of stereotypes, they become particularly significant when talking about marked cultural groups. The following comments from a high school student of Lebanese origin reflect his mixed feelings over stereotypes and his desire to be judged as an individual rather than according to the generally negative view of Middle

Easterners portrayed in the media. Despite this student's statement that it doesn't matter, one gets the feeling from his overall comments that perhaps the stereotype does matter to him:

> *Some people call me, you know, 'cause I'm Lebanese, so people say, "Look out for the terror- ist! Don't mess with him or he'll blow up your house!" or some stuff like that... But they're just joking around, though... I don't think anybody's serious 'cause I wouldn't blow up anybody's house—and they know that... I don't care. It doesn't matter what people say.... I just want everybody to know that, you know, it's not true. (Nieto, 1994, p. 35)*

Hispanic Americans in the United States are often stereotypically lumped into one cultural group by non-Hispanic Americans. Judging from the media, one might assume all Hispanic Americans are in pursuit of a soccer ball, are Roman Catholics, have large extended families, and like to eat jalapeño pep- pers. Hispanic Americans, however, are not at all a homogenous group: They form a cultural, social, and historical mosaic. Mexicans eat tortillas, but Cubans do not. Most Hispanic Americans are associated with Catholicism, but a growing number are Protestant, and many have African-influenced reli- gious traditions. Some have become so acculturated that they speak little or no Spanish, whereas many have maintained a strong language loyalty. Many Hispanic Americans in the Southwest are second only to American Indians as our earliest residents, but many are newcomers who have immigrated recently. Some have strong rural ties, whereas others are firmly rooted within the urban context (Arias, 1986b). Even within a single Mexican-American barrio, one encounters many different Mexican Americans, not "the typical Mexican American." Here is a description of El Hoyo, a Chicano neighbor- hood in Tucson, Arizona, by the author Mario Suárez (1973):

> *Perhaps El Hoyo, its inhabitants, and its essence can best be explained by telling a bit about a dish called capirotada. Its origin is uncertain. But, according to the time and the circum- stance, it is made of old, new, or hard bread. It is softened with water and then cooked with peanuts, raisins, onions, cheese, and panocha. It is fired with sherry wine. Then it is served hot, cold, or just "on the weather" as they say in El Hoyo. The Sermeños like it one way, the Garcías like it another, and the Ortegas still another. While it might differ greatly from one home to another, nevertheless it is still capirotada. And so it is with El Hoyo's Chicanos. (p. 102)*

Region of origin is one example of a factor that may account for some of the deviation a child shows from stereotyped patterns of behavior for a given cultural group. Just as a great variety of regional cultural patterns can be found in the United States, there are also very striking regional differences within the countries of origin of most immigrant families (Delgado-Gaitán & Trueba, 1991; Stevenson, 1994). Some Cambodians established in the United States, for example, may be offspring of Hmong tribesmen, who are from rural, nontechnological mountain villages, whereas others may be the children of white-collar apartment dwellers from Phnom Penh. Although all of them are Cambodians, the behavior and adjustment patterns exhibited by the two groups will be considerably different. The significance of place of origin also explains why one first-grader in a school composed predominantly of recent immigrants from rural Mexico doesn't "seem" like the other children and occasionally points out to her teacher and peers that her family is from the Mexican city of Ensenada, rather than from a small farm or *rancho*. She has taken upon herself the responsibility of making sure that the teacher doesn't stereotype her.

While overgeneralization is one problem with stereotypes, another is that actual behavior patterns can change much faster than stereotypes do. Gender roles provide just one example of the many ways in which this may happen. All cultural groups have developed expectations, attitudes, and values associated with a person's gender, and institutions such as the family serve to maintain these expectations. Consequently, outsiders to a culture may expect masculine or feminine behavior of a group member to conform to stereotyped notions. For example, many Mexican families used to place little importance on formal education for girls, resulting in females' lower educational aspirations. However, gender roles are changing both in Mexico and Mexican-American society. Research evidence suggests that today Mexican-American girls may actually place a higher value on education than their male counterparts (Bennett, 1995b, p. 665; Carter & Wilson, 1994; Ovando, 1978a).

Because of the damage that negative stereotypes have inflicted on individuals and groups over time, educators are "supposed" to think of stereotyping as a bad thing. And yet, like ants, stereotypes do not seem to go away no matter how hard we try to eradicate them. Some educators argue that precisely because stereotyping is here to stay we should make the concept useful by subjecting it to critical interrogation. For example, one can make an effort to distinguish between personal traits and ethnic traits (Bem, 1970; Longstreet, 1978). For the teacher this distinction becomes a process of balancing an awareness of general cultural or subcultural traits with an affirmation of the absolute uniqueness of every child. It also becomes a process of contrasting the cultural variations represented by actual students with the existing stereotypes. As a step toward effective teaching in the bilingual or ESL classroom, it is therefore important to assess the within-culture diversity already existing in the school's cultural microcosm. In a multiethnic environment, the interplay between stereotyped behavior patterns and personal patterns is amazingly intricate for children as they adjust to their culturally varied settings—the home culture versus the world of television, school versus the street, first-generation adult values versus second-generation youth values, and so on. The sociocultural background of the child in the bilingual or ESL classroom, therefore, emerges not in clear-cut stereotyped patterns but in varied types of behavior. In understanding a student's behavior, it is helpful to strike a balance between a more culturally based stereotypic perspective and a totally individualized perspective. The misperceptions stemming from a stereotypical perspective are well known, but on the other hand a totally individualized perspective is skewed because it does not take into account the powerful molding forces of culture (Robert & Lichter, 1988).

Teachers, of course, are not the only people with stereotypic views. Students and parents bring their own stereotypic views to the bilingual or ESL classroom. Some Mexican-American children may arrive in the kindergarten classroom with unconsciously formed expectations about *gabacho* behavior based on parents' or older siblings' perceptions. (*Gabacho* is a term used by Mexican Americans to refer, often derogatorily, to European Americans.) A Korean immigrant parent may approach his first meeting with an American teacher with certain stereotypical assumptions about the teacher's high degree of permissiveness. In considering the presence of prejudice in school environments, therefore, teachers also need to be aware that students and parents may bring negative stereotypes to school interactions.

Ethnocentrism

Ethnocentrism, the belief in the superiority of one's own ethnic group, can emerge in many different configurations within the multiethnic classroom. Ethnocentric reactions may occur on the part of the teacher toward the student, on the part of the student toward the teacher, between students, on the part of the parent toward the teacher, and so on. The sense of group identity attained by prejudice against another group is demonstrated with the following story. After India gained its independence from Britain, there was a strong push to soften the rigid caste system. A group of idealistic students supposedly approached some members of the Harijan caste (the untouchables) and started to talk with them about the past injustices of the caste system. The students suggested to the Harijans that they should become politically involved and elect officials who would improve their lot. No sooner had the speaker finished his speech, when one of the outcast members said, "The only way the system can improve is to develop another group below us so that we can look down upon them."

In multicultural societies, such as the United States, the balance between cultural pride and negative ethnocentrism—with its resultant prejudice and discrimination—is delicate. Just how much ethnocentrism is innocuous cultural pride and how much is damaging to the social fabric? Consider the emotional high many Hispanic-American soccer fans may feel when an Argentine or Mexican player scores a goal for his national team in a critical World Cup match. Most would say that this is not ethnocentrism, just healthy cultural pride. Bidney, an anthropologist who studied ethics from a cross-cultural perspective, suggested that cultural pride itself need not be equated with ethnocentrism. He stated that it is not "the mere fact of preference for one's own cultural values that constitutes ethnocentrism but, rather the uncritical prejudice in favor of one's own culture and the distorted, biased criticism of alien cultures" (Bidney 1968, p. 546). It is this type of critical prejudice that can do so much damage to the development of the minority child. What happens, for example, to the self-concept of a language-minority child who absorbs so many negative evaluations of his cultural background that by the time he is 10 he prefers to hide his ethnicity as much as possible and even avoids being seen with his parents?

Cultural Relativism

Cultural relativism is an important concept for bilingual and ESL educators because it serves as an antidote to the damaging effects that conscious or unconscious ethnocentrism can have on the emotional and academic development of language-minority children. Cultural relativism, as described by Bidney, involves "tolerance based on skepticism of universal, objective standards of value as well as the idea of progress" (1968, p. 547). As a *philosophical* doctrine, cultural relativism can imply that there are no universal norms by which all cultural groups should be judged, and as such, the concept can raise many ethical problems. For example, is female circumcision or the use of corporal punishment that leaves bruises or other longer lasting effects to be considered objectively acceptable on the basis of adherence to cultural relativism? As a *method* for coming to understand a cultural system and for viewing cultural change, however, cultural relativism is basic to all cultural inquiry. It constitutes an attempt to interpret data from the viewpoint of the people being observed or studied, rather than applying the values of one's own cultural system to the subject (Bidney, 1968, p. 543). The novelist (and former anthropology student) Kurt Vonnegut (1974), in an introduction to a children's book, *Free to Be You and Me,* proposes cultural relativism as a way of looking at how people may interpret their multiple worlds:

> One thing I would really like to tell them [children] about is cultural relativity. I didn't learn until I was in college about all the other cultures, and I should have learned that in the first grade. A first grader should understand that his or her culture isn't a rational invention; that there are thousands of other cultures and they all work pretty well; that all cultures function on faith rather than on truth; that there are lots of alternatives to our own society. (p. 139)

Cultural relativity is, of course, easier to talk about than to practice in the classroom, especially when members of cultural groups subscribe to beliefs, values, or behaviors that run counter to those prescribed for traditional educational settings in the United States. For example, from a culturally relative point of view, standard and nonstandard versions of a language are of equal validity in terms of performing the function of communicating a message. Yet, within the classroom, teachers of language-minority students may find it difficult to accept the nonstandard dialect as a valid one and still believe that they are providing adequate standard language preparation for the students. To consider an example involving teachers' own language varieties, teacher-training institutions generally consider the ability to use standard English as part of the requirements for becoming certified. An aspiring Alaskan teacher who wished to return to teach in her home village, however, expressed doubts to one of the authors as to whether teacher certification was worth the price of alienating herself from her home community by giving up her bush English—a variety of English spoken by many Native Alaskan villagers.

All of us grow up with a basic core of set values; to have to reexamine them vis-à-vis other modes of behavior can be a disturbing task. However, cultural relativism is an important tool for educators as it enables us to move toward less prejudiced perceptions. For an American with a relativistic point of view, the British do not drive on the *wrong* side of the road. They simply drive on the *left* side of the road. To achieve the perspective of cultural relativism, understanding the *underlying premises* for the behavior is as important as understanding the behavior itself. Because culture is accumulated learning, it involves a long history of people responding as needed to environmental conditions and problems. Consider another example from the Alaskan bush. An imported teacher from the "lower 48" was trying very hard to have her Athapaskan youngsters develop cuddly feelings for a pet rabbit that she had brought to the classroom. When the children responded in unexpected ways she became very puzzled. After all, she had assumed that all children liked rabbits as pets. In order to accept the children's behavior, she had to understand that in their subsistence-oriented environment, a rabbit was more likely to be considered a source of food than something to be petted. From the children's point of view, it was the teacher's behavior that was puzzling.

Having an awareness of marked and unmarked cultures, the role of stereotyping and ethnocentrism, and the framework of cultural relativism will help us to better understand the ways in which prejudice and discrimination appear in schooling contexts. However, simply being aware of such issues will not reduce the incidence of various forms of bias. Considering ways to reduce prejudice brings us back to the pervasive nature of effective multicultural programs. For example, Nieto (1996, pp. 330–31) refers to a variety of research findings that suggest, in essence, that actions speak louder than words. Explicit "antiprejudice" lessons for students or "one-shot" treatments seem to be less effective than broad-based programs that are infused into the curriculum through such practices as cooperative learning and the inclusion of social justice issues within academic content. A "before" and "after" lesson plan from Grant and Sleeter (1989, p. 110–11) illustrates how prejudice reduction can be built in to academic learning without explicitly addressing it as a separate lesson topic. In Grant and Sleeter's monocultural example of a unit on American Indians, the listed objectives are to identify reservations in the students' state and name the tribes, to list geographical features in the state that have American Indian names, and to appreciate local American Indian art and literature. In a multicultural unit design on the same subject, the objectives change significantly: The students will identify areas of good and bad agriculture on a state map, analyze the distribution of land to whites and American Indians and the consequences of that distribution, make bar graphs from numerical data, differentiate between institutional racism and individual prejudice, and appreciate the potential of their own actions against institutional racism. This lesson plan demonstrates the important role of critical pedagogy (Giroux, 1992) in prejudice reduction, as students involved in the above lesson would be examining power issues within a historical context and also exploring avenues of social action.

Looking beyond individual lessons to overall school climate, we began this section by noting that it is the marked students who traditionally have had to do most if not all of the accommodating in school. Díaz, Moll, and Mehan (1986) suggest a schoolwide process of "mutual accommodation" in which both teachers and students make modifications which build toward more equitable school success at the same time that they allow for integrity of marked cultures. Such an atmosphere of mutual accommodation allows fewer opportunities for prejudice and discrimination to impinge on the quality of the school environment for language-minority students.

The Role of Culture in Language-Minority Achievement

We now look at Banks's last two multicultural dimensions, equity pedagogy and empowering school structures, by more closely examining the role of culture in the school success of language-minority students. Language-minority students reflect a very broad range of achievement levels: Some of the nation's finest young scholars are language-minority students, whereas other language-minority students fail to complete high school or exit with a very inadequate education. These students find themselves without the necessary literacy and learning skills to find adequate employment opportunities or to participate effectively as citizens in a democracy.

Explanations for school failure or success, of course, are heavily colored by the assumptions on which they are based. When searching for factors to help explain the tendency toward lower educational achievement of many language-minority students, educators and policymakers in the past all too often pointed fingers in the direction of the students' sociocultural backgrounds, suggesting that the students possessed deficiencies that impeded academic success. For example, educators often placed recently arrived language-minority students in the lowest curriculum track, thus virtually guaranteeing low achievement levels (Arias, 1986a). Hispanic Americans for a number of years were very frequently misplaced in classes for the educable mentally retarded, based largely on IQ tests that did not take into account language proficiency or cultural bias (Figueroa, 1980). The apparent assumption underlying such practices was that lack of English language skills equaled lack of academic potential (California State Department of Education, 1986).

Some progress has been made since the days when many ELLs were erroneously placed in highly inappropriate programs, assuming that it was up to the individual to sink or swim. There is recognition today that a complex variety of social, economic, cultural, and personal factors can all play roles in influencing the education outcomes of such students. As we look at the role of culture in school success, therefore, we must also take into consideration the relationship of cultural factors to other variables. As Banks and Banks (1997) point out, "It is necessary to conceptualize the school as a social system in order to implement multicultural education successfully" (p. 1). Exploration of education for language-minority students with a map drawn from social and cultural analysis is important because such a map can help us to discover the "hidden curriculum"—that is, the concealed norms, values, and beliefs of the school culture and social system that can hinder or promote children's cognitive, linguistic, and social development (Beyer & Apple, 1988).

To better understand the role of culture in the school success of language-minority children, first we will look at the legacy of deficit theories and its impact on school success. Then we turn to the development of cultural difference theories, and next we put these perspectives within the context of larger socioeconomic and political factors. (The reader may want to consult Cortés, 1993, Jacob and Jordan, 1993, and Nieto, 1996, for their more in-depth discussions of the complex array of theories that have been used to explain the tendency toward the academic underachievement of many minority students.)

As we proceed through this discussion of cultural factors in school achievement, it is useful to recall Thomas and Collier's prism, which was introduced in Chapter Four. At the center of the triangular prism are "sociocultural processes," which are interrelated with all three interconnected anchoring points of the prism: language development, cognitive development, and academic development. Through our discussion of the role of culture in school success, we will be examining a range of such sociocultural processes as they affect language-minority students' linguistic, cognitive, and academic development. By building a strong awareness of the role of these sociocultural processes within the prism, bilingual and ESL teachers are in a better position to take an effective role in the implementation of equity pedagogy and empowering sociocultural structures within the schools.

Deficit Theories

There are essentially two aspects to deficit theory: genetic deficit and cultural deficit. (Ginsburg, 1986, may be consulted for a detailed review of deficit theories.) The genetic deficit framework, which has existed in a variety of forms for many years as a justification for personal and institutional racism, resurfaced in new ways in the 1960s. At this time, some researchers suggested through statistical analyses that a group's overall capacity to learn is enhanced or constrained by their inherited genes. Researchers such as Jensen (1969) suggested that the academic underachievement of minorities had little to do with the environment, class, ethnicity, or the nature of assessment procedures and much to do with the kinds of genes inherited by the individual. It is important to note that despite the general lack of respect that social scientists have had for such genetic determinism theories, Herrnstein and Murray (1994) in the 1990s again renewed a national debate over the role of genetics with the publication of *The Bell Curve: Intelligence and Class Structure in American Life*. Their genetically deterministic argument rekindled the debate over Jensen's discredited genetic view. It seemed to have tapped racist and xenophobic sentiments in the country, as evidenced by the large amount of media coverage and the number of weeks that the book was on the best seller list of the *New York Times*. Despite all of the interest in the book, the genetic heritage explanation, with its racist base, is flawed and extremely harmful to the education of minority students. It compares such students, who have varied cognitive, linguistic, socioeconomic, political and cultural patterns, with language majority students, who serve as the criterion for intellectual and sociocultural "normalcy" (Delpit, 1995).

The second view, the cultural deficit view, which emerged in the 1960s and 1970s, is perhaps as pernicious as the genetic deficit explanation. This "culture of poverty" approach that implied academic underachievement among many groups of minority students was anchored in their socioculturally, economically, linguistically, and intellectually impoverished environments, tended to devalue the sociocultural and linguistic background of students as well as to blame the victim (Ovando & Gourd, 1996). Jacob and Jordan (1993) have summarized some of the key areas in which culture of poverty children were said to be deficient: "cognitive development," "attention span," "expectations of reward from knowledge and task completion," "ability to use adults as sources of information," "ability to delay gratification," and "linguistic and symbolic development" (p. 5). Looking more closely at linguistic development, language skills have been an important component of much cultural deficit research in the past (Jacob & Jordan, 1993; Guthrie & Hall, 1983), and there still is a lingering yet erroneous view among some educators today that lower-income ethnic minorities enter school with faulty oral language and literacy patterns that inhibit their intellectual development.

Like the genetic deficit viewpoint, the cultural deficit viewpoint is flawed in that it brings to the research a predetermined idea of what constitutes "normalcy." Researchers evaluate children's performance based on their discipline's culturally influenced ideas about "normal" affective, cognitive, and language development patterns. Then, when they identify other patterns within particular groups, the implication is that these patterns are defective, rather than simply being different.

As mentioned in Chapter Two, the effect of cultural deficit perspectives on bilingual and ESL instruction for ELLs has been evident in the preponderance of programs that have tended to view lack of English proficiency as a problem that had to be fixed through remedial programs, with the goal of exiting the children into mainstream classrooms as soon as they have become, so to speak, "normal." One bilingual teacher in the 1970s reflected on her feeling that public bilingual education would not be so threatening to its opponents if it were not associated with allegedly "culturally deprived" groups:

⊠ *If I were telling people that I taught in a French/English program at an elite private school, I think it would be easy to rave about the virtues of bilingual education and get agreement from virtually everyone. But that is not quite the context of my bilingual school, which is about 95 percent minority and in one of the lowest income neighborhoods of the city. My students are too often perceived as problems rather than as promises, as members of the "culture of poverty" whose cultural values need to be changed.*

Cultural Difference Theories

The basic premise of cultural difference theories is that the failure of schools to effectively address discrepancies between sociocultural and linguistic patterns in the home and in the school produces underachievement (Forman, Minick, & Stone, 1993; Jacob & Jordan, 1993; Lomawaima, 1995; Tharp & Gallimore, 1988). Rather than blaming minority students for their underachievement, which genetic and cultural deficit theories would do, cultural difference theories proceed from the anthropological notion that "minority students and their families and communities are no less well endowed, in basic intelligence, talents, language, culture, or life experience, than members of the majority population. Therefore, clashes with majority culture schools, when they occur, are matters not of deficit, but of difference" (Jacob & Jordan, 1993, p. 10).

Within this field of culturally based research into minority student achievement, a number of interrelated terms have been used. One of the early terms was *home-school mismatch.* Other terms that researchers and practitioners use for instruction derived from cultural difference theories are *culturally compatible, culturally congruent, culturally appropriate, culturally responsive,* and *culturally relevant* (Nieto, 1996, p. 146). Despite differences in focus and in the degree to which educators believe that school practices must mimic home practices, the general concept of this type of research remains that schools that make accommodations according to cultural backgrounds will enhance minority achievement. For example, Ladson-Billings, who developed her concept of "cultural relevance" through a case study of highly effective teachers within a predominantly African-American community, found that the teachers in her study were able, through culturally relevant teaching, to provide an environment in which students could "choose academic excellence yet still identify with African and African-American culture" (Ladson-Billings, 1994, p. 17).

Such home-school differences can manifest themselves in a very broad range of ways in the classroom. Three of the major ways that we will examine here are cognitive styles, language variation, and language use patterns.

Cognitive Styles   Teachers today are aware through their training and experience that children vary in their cognitive styles, and a body of research suggests that these styles may be influenced by cultural background (Bennett, 1995a). Banks (1988) in a review of studies on cognitive style, for example, found that ethnicity tended to have a greater influence on cognitive style than did social class, suggesting that there is a link between cultural background and approaches to learning. Childrearing practices, degree of stress on individual orientation versus group orientation, ecological adaptations to the environment, and the ways that language is used are just some of the factors that may result in patterns of cultural differences in cognitive styles (Bennett, 1995a).

While an awareness of potential differences in cognitive styles can be valuable, it can also be misleading. Notions about culturally influenced cognitive styles can be based on faulty research and can also lead to stereotyping. The difficulty in finding clear answers about the relationship between culture and cognitive styles is evident in many studies. Cole and Scribner (1974) did an international review of research on culture and cognition, covering the areas of language, perception, conceptual processes, memory, and problem solving, and two of the main things that they learned from the careful review was how *not* to ask questions and how *not* to design and carry out research in culture and cognition (p. 173). For example, apparent difficulty in performing certain cognitive tasks, as a researcher looking for cultural differences presents them, may not necessarily be related to a difference in cognitive styles but instead to different schemata, or networks of background knowledge. A Navajo from a remote rural area, for example, may be more likely to successfully complete sequencing tasks if initially they are based on the care of sheep rather than on small pictures of a trip to an urban supermarket (Bingham & Bingham, 1979; U.S. Commission on Civil Rights, 1975).

We can use the issue of so-called "field-dependent" or "field sensitive" learning to illustrate how cognitive style research can lead to negative stereotyping. In the 1970s research by Ramírez and Castañeda (1974) suggested that Mexican-American children had a field-dependent learning style. Other research studies emerged suggesting that African Americans and American Indians also shared this type of learning style. According to these researchers, field-dependent students did not prosper academically in U.S. schools because they tended to rely heavily on learning styles that were deductive, global, highly personalized, cooperative, and group normed rather than relying on field-independent styles that were inductive, linear, analytical, fomulaic, impersonal, independent, and individually oriented. (Ramírez & Castañeda, 1974, p. 142). Irvine and York (1995, p. 484), in a survey of the literature concluded, however, that findings on patterns of field dependence and field independence had been "premature and conjectural." Nevertheless, the concepts, for a period of time, influenced many educators and had a negative effect on the perceptions of minority students, because the field-dependent style had a less positive connotation than the field independent style from the point of view of dominant cultural patterns.

Another problem with theories on cultural differences in cognitive styles is that implementation in the classroom of culturally compatible learning strategies can be difficult. Nieto (1996, p. 139), for example, refers to at least 14 identified types of learning style differences and 13 learning style theories. As has been suggested many times now, culture is truly complex, deep, and changing. As we survey lists of observable behaviors that have been developed to supposedly identify learning styles, we need to remember that there are usually uncharted waters surrounding those behaviors and we may not be in a position (by virtue of knowledge, training, or experience) to penetrate them. Just as the essence of culture is not order but change, students' cognitive styles are not necessarily static. In a constructivist sense, students are developing multiple learning styles in response to their learning environments.

Despite the difficulties with cognitive style theories, the concept of cultural variability in such styles does have a role to play in understanding cultural factors in the achievement of language-minority students. Confirming the inconclusive but at the same time promising aspects of learning styles, Irvine and York (1995) state:

> The research on the learning styles of culturally diverse learners is neither a panacea nor a Pandora's box. The complexity of the construct, the psychometric problems related to its measurement, and the enigmatic relationship between culture and the teaching and learning process suggest that this body of research must be interpreted and applied carefully in classrooms of culturally diverse students.... However, learning-styles research has significant possibilities for enhancing the achievement of culturally diverse students. This body of research reminds teachers to be attentive not only to individual students' learning styles but to their own actions, instructional goals, methods, and materials in reference to their students' cultural experiences and preferred learning environments. (p. 484)

Language Variation   In Chapter One, we introduced the notion that a great deal of language variation can exist within the bilingual or ESL classroom, in both English and in the non-English languages. In a bilingual setting in Los Angeles, one teacher identified three varieties of English and three varieties of Spanish in her classroom. Each variety carried with it information about social status and the cultural background of the speaker: Instruction officially went on in the standard forms of English and Spanish, but students used two other varieties of English—Black English and Chicano English—and two other versions of Spanish—Chicano Spanish and a rural northern Mexican variety.

Related to the issue of standard and nonstandard language is the process of word borrowing, which occurs naturally in language contact situations. Consider the word *grocería*. A Nicaraguan living in the Midwest may use this word to refer to a grocery store, when in fact *grosería* (spelled differently, but pronounced the same way) means "cuss word" in standard Spanish. However, in the Midwestern Spanish-speaking community where the speaker lives, *grocería* is a natural and legitimate word for grocery store, especially because the usual places in which one buys food in Nicaragua are very unlike the physical set-up of large supermarkets in the Midwestern United States—words used in Nicaraguan Spanish for places to buy food don't really fit well in the new context. However, this natural process of language adaptation can be negatively misinterpreted as a reflection of weak language skills. For example, nonlinguists sometimes refer derogatorily to the blend of Spanish and English as "Spanglish."

Code-switching is another important aspect of language variation that affects language-minority students. Suppose that a bilingual Mexican American child says to another peer, "*Ándale, pues,* I don't know," or "Gimme the ball, *que le voy a decir a la maestra.*"[2] Such language behaviors, sometimes erroneously labeled as reflections of "semilingualism," are also natural adaptations to language contact situations. Research, for example, suggests that code-switching among bilingual people is both a predictable and a creative skill that follows patterns and performs special communicative functions (Ferguson & Heath, 1981; Jacobson & Faltis, 1990; Timm, 1993; Valdés, 1980).

To the purist, both word borrowing and code-switching may seem to be a threat to the integrity of the standard language, but such language mixture has always been a part of language change and as such is part of the larger and inevitable process of culture change (Dulay, Burt, & Krashen, 1982). However, students who navigate two overlapping linguistic worlds in a school environment that is not accepting of cultural differences may find barriers to school success. A bilingual education researcher describes his personal questioning of his language identity:

⊗ *With what language was I raised? What language do I speak in the Chicano community? Is it Spanish? Is it English? Is it even a language? Early in my elementary school days I learned that I was not speaking English; and later, in high school, when I was enrolled in what I thought would be an easy course, Spanish, I was told that I didn't speak Spanish! (Carrasco, 1981b, p. 191)*

Because of the use of nonstandard language patterns, many of the children who qualify for bilingual or ESL instruction represent linguistic backgrounds that all too often are still perceived as being "deficient" by speakers of standard English. Such judgments are unconsciously woven in with judgments of the quality of the child's cultural background, and can result in lower expectations of the child's ability, which will in turn lead to lower achievement by the child. When we introduced these language differences in Chapter Four, in the context of language arts instruction, we noted the importance of accepting nonstandard language varieties in the classroom at the same time that standard forms are added to the students' repertoire of language proficiencies. Erickson (1997, p. 32) provides an example of lost learning opportunities due to culturally insensitive approaches to language differences. Referring to Piestrup (1973), he describes a first-grade reading lesson in which the teacher wanted the children to read aloud and "remember your endings" (the final consonant sounds at the ends of words). The teacher had one student re-read "What did Little Duck see?" four times until he or she finally pronounced the final "t" in "what." Such an approach certainly does not encourage a child to perceive reading as a pleasurable experience. The time spent insisting on pronunciation of final consonants is at the expense of time that could be spent bringing some personal meaning and higher level thinking skills to the story of Little Duck. Erickson calls this an example of a "cultural border war" that results in lower achievement, and we will return to this concept later in the chapter.

Language Use Patterns   We have learned from ethnographic studies of human communication that there are cultural differences in the ways in which people communicate with each other. Using videotapes, audiotapes, and participant observation, researchers interested in differences in how cultural groups use language to communicate collect data on a variety of classroom and community interaction patterns: for example, types of listening behaviors, ways of showing attention, turn-taking structures, questioning patterns, the ways in which topics of conversation are organized, body movements, and the rhythm and cadence of conversations. Researchers who have studied these differences in classrooms and minority communities have in some cases found evidence to suggest that some modification of school patterns to more closely resemble home and community patterns may have a positive effect on school success for language-minority students. In the last section of this chapter, "Ethnographic Approaches to Cultural Understanding" we will return to look more closely at some examples of home-school differences in participant structures and other language use patterns.

Social, Economic, and Political Factors in Achievement

Cultural difference theories—addressing such issues as cognitive styles, language variation, and language use patterns—have contributed greatly to our understanding of schooling outcomes for language-minority students. However, the issue of cultural congruence cannot provide a complete explanation for the lower achievement levels of some groups of language-minority students. Ogbu (1986), for example, argues that cultural differences alone cannot explain differences in school success, pointing out a pattern in which culturally different recent immigrant students are more likely to succeed academically than culturally different castelike minority students who have been subject to generations of discrimination. Whether immigrant or castelike minority, there are also cases where minority children achieve success even though the instructional practices at their school are not culturally congruent, suggesting that "other factors not related to cultural conflict must be involved as well" (Nieto, 1996, p. 149).

Some theorists use a distinction between microforces and macroforces to analyze cultural versus sociopolitical factors in school success for minority students. The behaviors and human interactions that teachers, students, family members, and community members engage in every day both inside and outside the classroom constitute the microforces that may affect student success. Such microforces are associated with cultural difference theories about school achievement, because cultural difference research focuses in very closely on the minutia of human interaction. Macroforces, on the other hand, are those large socioeconomic and political patterns that are generally not accessible to intervention strategies on the part of educators. They have to do with who holds wealth and power in the society and how the distribution of such status is maintained or altered. We will look at these macroforces first by considering in a general sense the role of socioeconomic status (SES) in the school success of language-minority students and then by examining social reproduction theory as it applies to language-minority students.

Socioeconomic Status   The ability to perceive the interplay between SES and cultural variables is important in the context of bilingual and ESL instruction because people often associate the terms *ethnic group, language minority,* and *English language learner* with lower SES. However, it is important to remember, as we mentioned in Chapter One, that they do not necessarily go hand in hand. For example, using a typology that distinguishes between ethnic groups that have tended to be relatively successful socioeconomically and those that have not, Havighurst illustrated a variety of patterns that emerge through the interplay of ethnic identity, cultural models, and socioeconomic structures. Through this interplay, it emerges that some minority groups have in the past managed to position themselves successfully within the given educational and socioeconomic structure, while other groups have not been served fairly by existing educational and economic opportunities (Havighurst, 1978, pp. 14–18). However, despite the fact of socioeconomic diversity within the language-minority community, it is true that a disproportionate number of language-minority children do come from lower-income homes.

It is no great surprise that parents' SES can be a strong factor in school success for both majority and minority students. Using an approach called status attainment research, investigators such as Coleman et al. (1966) and Jencks et al. (1972) gathered extremely large sets of research data from across regions, ethnic groups, and social classes and performed a variety of statistical analyses to isolate the extent to which such variables as family background, innate ability, peer influences, and schooling practices explained students' variation in performance on standardized tests. Jacob and Jordan (1993) indicate that such status attainment researchers have generally concluded "that family background is highly related to student performance on standardized tests and that school variables, except for some characteristics of teachers, are not significantly related to student test performance" (p. 6). An important component of family background is SES—parents' education level, occupation, and income level.

From a cynical point of view, then, we could conclude that the best way for language-minority students to ensure their academic success is to "choose their parents well." However, macrolevel status attainment research, like microlevel cultural difference research, has been criticized for its inadequacy in explaining the variability in achievement among minority students. There are also methodological challenges to the types of measurements used. Critics also fault this type of approach for ignoring the microforces at school that must come into play for the macro input variables such as parents' SES to result in particular outcomes (Jacob & Jordan, 1993, pp. 6, 7). We can use an interesting example from the 1970s to illustrate one way in which microforces may intervene between macro input variables and achievement outcomes. The U.S. Civil Rights Commission found in a 1972 study that the degree of acceptance of the use of Spanish by Hispanic children was related to the income level of the students' families. The no-Spanish rule, which was present in many schools in the Southwest at this time, "was more likely to be enforced when the proportion of Chicanos in the school was high and the socioeconomic status of the population was low" (Peñalosa, 1980, p. 11). The macro-input variable of low SES resulted at the microlevel of daily school interactions in the discriminatory treatment of the students' L_1, which in turn could be argued to have contributed to the outcome of low achievement. Thus, one could argue that it was not the SES that caused the low achievement, but the ensuing prejudicial treatment that stemmed from the low status of the students.

Social Reproduction Theory   Social reproduction theory provides another type of sociopolitical macro explanation for schooling outcomes. Associated with such researchers as Bowles and Gintis (1976), proponents of social reproduction theory hold that, as instruments of the dominant classes, the schools' implicit and explicit curricular infrastructures serve as vehicles through which the larger society's socioeconomic and cultural inequalities are reproduced. This view of society suggests that macro-structural forces in society largely determine how well children will succeed in school. Thus, if language-minority students attend poor neighborhood schools with a working class student population, the chances are great that such students' outcomes will be influenced not only by what they experience in the courses they take, but also through many other aspects of the school environment. Such things as the physical layout of the school (prisonlike or campuslike, for example), the nature of the relationships between students and teachers, and the quality of the courses (watered-down "basic" courses versus challenging course content) all may be said to reflect the dominant versus the subordinate status of different schools (Nieto, 1996, p. 235).

Social reproduction theory has been challenged, among other things, for being excessively deterministic and overstating the connection between highly varied local school practices and the larger capitalistic structure of society. Theorists also challenge social reproduction theory, such as status attainment theory, for also failing to address at the microlevel the school practices that produce the unequal outcomes (Mehan, 1989). Some social reproduction theorists, however, have to some degree incorporated microfactors into their model by introducing the concept of "cultural capital." By defining cultural traits as a form of "capital" within the socioeconomic system, they argue that marginalization of minority students occurs because their cultural capital has little value in the social structure of the school. Consequently, they find themselves at a disadvantage compared to students who have large amounts of dominant society "cultural capital" to invest in school success (Bourdieu & Passeron, 1977; McLaren, 1989).

Another variation of social reproduction theory is Erickson's resistance theory. Erickson (1987) combines aspects of cultural mismatch theory with the socioeconomically deterministic premise of social reproduction theory to suggest a process in which early cultural differences in the schooling process initiate school failure. This failure then becomes entrenched within some groups as they actively begin to resist the school's culturally hegemonistic social reproduction patterns. For example, students may resist "selling out" to the dominant culture's expectations through attitudes and classroom behaviors that have negative effects on their learning. From this perspective, minority students are not just victims of the reproduction of social inequalities: They become actors who are involved in a struggle. As we mentioned previously in this chapter, Erickson (1997) has described such conflicts as cultural border wars. Our earlier reference to the teacher who battled with her students over the pronunciation of final consonant sounds was an example of such a cultural border war. We can also see evidence of resistance theory in the results of a year-long study comparing teachers who negatively sanctioned Black English with teachers who accepted the presence of Black English. At the end of the school year, the students in the sanctioned classroom actually used more Black English than they had at the beginning of the year. The students whose Black English had been accepted, however, used more standard language patterns by the end of the year (Erickson, 1997, referring to Piestrup, 1973). Erickson's resistance theory mitigates the deterministic implications of social reproduction theory by suggesting that schools that are willing to acknowledge and address sociocultural issues are less likely to set off cycles of resistance. As Erickson (1997) states, "in the short run, we cannot change the wider society. But we can make school learning environments less alienating. Multicultural education, especially critical or antiracist multicultural education, is a way to change the business as usual of schools" (p. 50).

While acknowledging the power of strong macroforces such as socioeconomic inequality, perpetuation of power structures, and the presence of racism, many researchers agree that there is evidence that schools that embody a multicultural approach to education can provide more equitable opportunities than schools that ignore multicultural issues. In other words, despite socioeconomic and political macroforces, treatment of cultural differences still has a role to play in school success. Nieto points out that while racism, inadequate health care, substandard housing, and all the other negative effects of poverty are serious causes for concern, there are schools that manage to be more successful than others in such contexts. Social and economic hardships "do not in and of themselves doom children to academic failure" (Nieto, 1994, p. 26). Faltis (1997), surveying the field of culturally appropriate learning environments, cites a variety of studies that indicate that teachers' changes in the context for learning that are based on an under-standing of cultural differences between the home and the school can lead to improved school success. Also, looking specifically at bilingual programs, in Chapter Four we referred to evidence suggesting that SES can be a less pow-erful variable in academic achievement for language-minority students in schools that have a strong, academically rich bilingual program. The Significant Bilingual Instructional Features Study (Tikunoff, 1985; Tikunoff et al., 1991) provides broad-based evidence for the key role that cultural rele-vance can play in the quality of programs for language-minority children. This large study involved observation and data collection in 58 classes with stu-dents from many different linguistic origins at six sites throughout the United States. Through analyses of all of the data, researchers identified several cul-turally relevant factors in effective bilingual instruction (Tikunoff, 1985, p. 3).

To summarize our exploration of the role of culture in school success for language-minority students thus far, we return again to Nieto (1996, p. 245), with whom we began this section by listing her defining factors of multicul-tural education. In her extensive review of factors in school success for minority students, she concluded that

> School achievement can be understood and explained only as a multiplicity of sometimes competing and always changing factors: the school's tendency to replicate society and its inequalities, cultural and language incompatibili-ties, the limiting and bureaucratic structures of schools, and the political rela-tionship of ethnic groups to society and the schools. Nevertheless, it is tricky business to seek causal explanations for school success and failure. . . . Structural inequality and cultural incompatibility may be major causes of school failure, but they work *differently* on different communities, families, and individuals. How these factors are mediated within the school and home settings and their complex interplay probably are ultimately responsible for either the success or failure of students in schools. (Nieto, 1996, p. 245)

As bilingual and ESL educators, we have an important role to play as to how these factors are mediated within the local schools. Díaz, Moll, and Mehan (1986) emphasize the role of "pedagogically optimistic teachers" in this process. Such teachers are able to change the classroom social organiza-tion patterns for full participation of students from a variety of backgrounds through a variety of culturally appropriate learning environments. Through such actions, teachers in bilingual and ESL classrooms can help to foster mul-ticultural programs that nurture equity and an empowering school climate.

Ethnographic Approaches to Cultural Understanding

In the previous section on the role of culture in school achievement we have just concluded that, despite the acknowledged power of socioeconomic and political macroforces, teachers can have an effect on learning outcomes through the devel-opment of multicultural learning environments. By surveying some examples of ethnographic studies that examine sociocultural processes in the classroom and the community, we can develop a more specific understanding of the evolving ways in which educators can effectively address cultural diversity. Such ethnographic studies have had and will continue to have an important role in helping educators to understand cultural processes in bilingual and ESL classrooms. **Ethnography** is a vital tool in the construction of culturally sensitive learning environments for language-minority students. Ethnographic approaches enable us to see the school as a sociocultural system; they explore the insiders' perspective on the schooling process; and they place education within the context of the community to see how communication and learning takes place both inside and outside of the classroom walls. Microethnography, a type of ethnography that focuses in on selected aspects of human interaction and language use, can, for example, provide insights into "how learning is mediated by adults in the classroom and how concrete activities of communication shape the way children cope cognitively with different learning tasks" (Moll, 1981, p. 442).

As we consider the following ethnographic studies in a progression from earlier work up to more recent work, we will see a general move away from the idea that home and school cultures must be closely matched, and we will also see a movement toward greater interest in culturally relevant knowledge construction processes in classrooms. As we move into the discussion of knowledge construction processes, we will also consider the important role of teachers in ethnographic research.

Cultural Compatibility Studies

We start by discussing one of the best-known and most comprehensive projects on cultural compatibility, the Kamehameha Early Education Program (KEEP). During the 1970s and 1980s KEEP researchers conducted a series of studies on home-school mismatch, looking at social interaction in the home, in the community, and in the classroom. Psychologists, cultural anthropologists, sociolinguists, and curriculum specialists collaborated in a broad spectrum of applied research studies on the academic achievement of children of native Hawaiian ancestry, who have tended to have some of the lowest achievement levels of any group in the nation. In searching for cultural explanations for the tendency of minority groups toward lower academic achievement, Kamehameha researchers operated under the following assumption:

> Minorities are members of coherent cultural systems and that their difficulties are not the consequence of personal and/or social deficits and pathologies. Second, the classroom is held to be an interface of cultures in which the learning process is disrupted because teachers and pupils have incongruent expectations, motives, social behaviors, and language and cognitive patterns. (Gallimore, Boggs, & Jordan, 1974, p. 261)

KEEP project members used a three-stage process for improvement of instruction for Hawaiian children. First, KEEP researchers developed a knowledge base regarding Hawaiian children within the context of their home culture and their school experience. They gathered information on such topics as home socialization, social motivation, language production, phonemics, sociolinguistics, cognitive strategies, and standard English acquisition. (For example, one area of cultural mismatch that they identified was the value placed on personal autonomy. The researchers observed that in their homes the children were socialized to value being contributors to the family's well being rather than to value independent living (Tharp, 1994). In the classroom, however, personal accomplishment was valued for its own sake rather than as a contribution to the needs of others.) In the second stage, researchers and teachers collaborated to apply this database to the development of an effective program in the project's laboratory school. Finally, through in-service training and collaboration between consultants and teachers, the instructional program was implemented in public schools that had a concentration of Hawaiian students (Tharp et al., 1981; Tharp, 1994; Vogt, Jordan, & Tharp, 1993). One of the project's videotapes, *Coming Home to School: Culturally Compatible Classroom Practices*, demonstrated how teachers, by getting a glimpse of native Hawaiian students' natural home cultural environment, saw these children demonstrating talents seldom revealed in the classroom. Teachers were then able to use the filmed information as a guide in selecting culturally and instructionally appropriate learning environments.

While KEEP researchers considered a culturally responsive curriculum to be a keystone for effective schooling, identifying what is and is not essential in the match between the home and school was also important. Some important home cultural patterns were positively applicable to the classroom. Language use patterns in the home, for example, were transferred to classroom reading instruction through emphasis on comprehension rather than phonics, and through an open, relaxed, "talk story" discussion approach in place of the "teacher-asks-a-question/one student-answers/teacher-evaluates" format. (The "talk story" is a particular type of discourse pattern that the researchers observed to occur regularly in Hawaiian homes.) The researchers concluded that other home cultural patterns, however, seemed to have a neutral effect on classroom performance. For instance, they found that the English of the classroom did not have to match the students' variety of English, Hawaiian Pidgin, for achievement to improve.[3]

A variety of ethnographic studies published in the 1980s focused on communication patterns and participant structures of language. For example, Mohatt and Erickson (1981) conducted a study on language use patterns in Native American classrooms by comparing an Indian and a non-Indian teacher. Mohatt and Erickson observed such behaviors as how teachers gave directions and how they monitored student activities. They also studied the rhythm of the teachers' pause times between questions and answers. They found that the Indian and non-Indian teachers used different participation structures in the classroom. For example, the non-Indian teacher used more direct commands and singling out of students for individual responses or contributions. However, it is also interesting to note that as the school year progressed the non-Indian teacher began to use more of the participation structures that were characteristic initially of the Native American instructor only. Mohatt and Erickson's study thus suggested two things for the teacher in the bilingual or ESL classroom. First, the ethnicity of the instructor can have an effect on the participation structure that evolves in the classroom and on the degree to which that structure complements the students' own communication styles. Second, if teachers' ethnicity differs from that of students, it may be possible for teachers to adapt their style as they gain experience with classroom participants.

In another investigation of language patterns, Morine-Dershimer (1983) studied the effect of teachers on the "communicative status" of students in multiethnic classrooms. Students with high communicative status were defined as those with a high frequency of classroom verbal participation and were viewed by classmates as people one could learn from. In her research, Morine-Dershimer found that teachers could "create" varied distributions of communicative status within their classrooms, depending on the types of instructional strategies they employed. The types of students who attained high communicative status via a textbook-based teaching approach, for example, differed from the types of students who attained high status via an experience-based approach. This research implied that a more equitable distribution of communicative status opportunities could be realized in multiethnic classrooms through the intentional use of varied types of instructional strategies.

Philips's study on the Warm Springs Indian Reservation in eastern Oregon was a sociolinguistically based investigation that compared interaction styles within the classroom and the community. In her research Philips studied the cultural differences in attention structure and regulation of talk between home and school. Among her principal findings were that Warm Springs Indian students "speak too softly, hesitate too long before speaking, and engage in too much visually received signaling *from the point of view of teacher expectations* [italics added]" (Philips, 1983, p. 129). Philips, however, pointed out that one's position in the social structure influenced how researchers and educators perceived such miscommunication. That is, because of the teacher's higher social status and authority, observers tended to conclude that it was the students who misunderstood, whereas logically it could just as well be said that it is the teacher who misunderstands. In other words, it would be just as reasonable to say that the teachers talked too loudly, didn't pause long enough before speaking, and didn't make use of sufficient visual signaling. Based on her research, Philips suggested that even if teachers had good intentions, they and their students could miscommunicate nonverbally. She argued that because nonverbal behavior is extremely difficult to monitor consciously, ethnic discrimination by teachers might continue to occur even if deliberate efforts were made to eliminate it.

Another influential study of language use patterns was Heath's research with children in a community in the Piedmont Carolinas, where many African-American residents spoke a nonstandard variety of English. Heath found that these children in her study tended to be very unresponsive to the teachers' questions in school, and consequently educators perceived the children to be deficient in language skills. Through her ethnographic work, Heath observed that the questioning patterns used in the home were different than those used at school. Consequently, when teachers changed their questioning style at school to one more similar to the home style, there was a significant change in the students from a passive to an active role in classroom discussions. This success then served as a bridge to traditional classroom questioning patterns (Heath, 1983).

As ethnographic studies of language-minority education continued into the 1990s, researchers began to question some of the conclusions regarding cultural patterns and learning styles previous researchers had made. To varying degrees some researchers set aside the notion that cultural patterns in the classroom necessarily had to emulate those found in the home. For example, McCarty et al., (1991), based on their research on the Rough Rock Indian reservation, concluded that the idea of the nonverbal Indian student was a myth. In reaching that conclusion, they raised questions about the very concept of culturally based learning styles. The researchers noted that in the past educators in an effort to establish culturally compatible classrooms, had tended to favor nonverbal and short-answer types of instruction for American Indian students. The result, according to McCarty et al., has been detrimental to the students' development of higher-order thinking processes and the use of inquiry methods. The researchers worked with Navajo staff members from the Native American Materials Development Center to design and implement a bilingual inquiry–based social studies program. Teachers using this program were to emphasize inquiry and information-seeking questions. Project members designed the program to use the students' prior knowledge of the local community as a bridge to their understanding of new problems and their solutions. Because they were working in an instructional environment that was based on their own experience and knowledge and that was designed to emphasize inquiry, the researchers observed that the students did indeed become more verbal. They concluded that it was classroom discourse patterns that had previously limited the nature of their verbal responses.

Sociocultural Theory and Knowledge Construction Studies

A growing number of studies based in sociocultural theory reflect the move away from a focus on culturally compatible classroom practices. From the point of view of sociocultural theory, "both student and teacher are engaged in the process of constructing their minds through social activity" (García, 1994, p. 146). The work of Vygotsky (1978) can be seen as a link between research in cognitive styles and the development of the sociocultural framework. Vygotsky postulated that children's cognitive structures are developed through the actions and speech of their caretakers and are transmitted through social interaction. It follows, therefore, that culturally coded styles of speech and social interaction result in culturally related patterns of cognitive structure. To come to an understanding of students' cognitive structures, it is therefore important to develop a data base on the sociocultural patterns surrounding the learner. Therefore, the use of ethnographic methods continues to be important in the context of sociocultural research.

Building on sociocultural theory, it follows that the extent to which the cultural and linguistic resources of the community are used in the knowledge construction process will positively or negatively affect the teaching and learning process. For over 10 years, Moll and his colleagues have been using a sociocultural approach in their field studies that links schools closely with their Hispanic-American communities in the Southwest. Guided by principles from anthropology, psychology, linguistics, and education, and building on the research of Vélez-Ibáñez (1993) and Vélez-Ibáñez and Greenberg (1992), Moll and his colleagues have examined resources Hispanic-American communities use to survive economically as well as to provide academic, linguistic, cultural, and emotional support for their children. This body of research suggests that the use of the Hispanic-American community as a resource can play a key role in the academic and sociocultural well-being of Hispanic-American students (Moll, 1992a; Moll, 1992b; Moll & Díaz, 1993). We have already alluded to this concept of the use of local funds of knowledge when we discussed literacy development in Chapter Four, pointing out that connections between home and school literacy development can enhance language-minority students' learning. We will return to the theme again in the final chapter of the book, "School and Community."

Sociocultural theory implies that certain instructional approaches will be more favorable than others for the establishment of an environment in which knowledge construction thrives. Some instructional approaches used in socioculturally based classrooms are dialogue, teacher co-learning, peer collaboration, questioning, use of students' prior knowledge, and joint knowledge construction (Wells & Chang-Wells, 1992). Moll and Díaz (1993), using the framework of knowledge construction, focus on the "immediate environment of learning" rather than on the possible mismatch between the home culture and the school culture. In a series of studies they collaborated with teachers to compare the reading instruction of elementary-age native Spanish speakers in Spanish and English. They also studied the English writing instruction of junior high school native Spanish speakers. In both cases they found evidence of a "watered-down curriculum" that did not use the students' cultural and linguistic resources in the knowledge construction process. In the case of the elementary students, they observed that students who could read very well in Spanish and who demonstrated sophisticated comprehension skills during Spanish reading instruction were being given only very simple decoding lessons during English reading instruction, with an emphasis on correct pronunciation. Once the English reading teacher was given an opportunity to observe the students' skills in Spanish reading, the researcher and teacher were able to work together to change the social organization of instruction and to use bilingual support through L_1 to remove the unnecessarily simplified constraints of the previous English reading program.

A similar pattern of reductionist instructional strategies was observed in writing instruction at the junior high school. The native Spanish speakers were doing very little extended writing in English, ostensibly because of their lack of English skills. The researchers began by studying uses of writing in the students' community and by talking to parents about local issues that were important to them. This generated possible topics for writing assignments from which students could choose. Then in a two-phase process, students collected information on their topics through homework assignments, usually consisting of interviews of community members. Then they wrote and revised their essays or reports. Although the products contained many grammar errors, the important point was that the students were now doing work that was comparable to what the native English speakers were doing in terms of development of expository skills. In both this case and the previous one, the principal question of the investigators and the teachers was "how to maximize the use of available resources to overcome reductionist instructional strategies" (Moll & Díaz, 1993, p. 74). Reflecting the shift away from emphasis on home-school cultural mismatch, the authors argued that "to succeed in school one does not need a special culture; we know now, thanks to ethnographic work, that success and failure is in the social organization of schooling, in the organization of the experience itself" (Moll & Díaz, 1993, p. 78).

We conclude this brief review of several ethnographic studies by noting the valuable role that teachers can and do play in such research.[4] Because one of the goals of ethnography is to gain some understanding of a cultural system from the insider's perspective, collaboration between researchers and teachers is valuable. In fact, the distinction between teacher and researcher can become blurred as they both take on the role of learners. Collaboration between researchers and teachers was an important component of Moll and Díaz's (1993) studies, which we just described. The teachers involved in these studies kept journals of their observations and innovations, and the research team used these to help guide their investigations. Using a similar approach, Calderón (1996) developed a project in which teachers were trained to work as microethnographers within their classrooms. In this study of two-way bilingual programs in a Texas-Mexico border town, pairs of teachers team taught. This made it possible for team partners to observe classroom sociocultural interaction on a regular basis. The purpose of the observations was to help the teachers to be able to step back and develop an understanding of such things as the different types of discourse that were valued in Spanish and English instruction and the different types of social relationships of power that were sanctioned or encouraged. The 24 teachers involved in the study formed a Teachers Learning Community, which met regularly to discuss their observations. With the data collected, the teachers developed new ways of looking at their daily routines. According to Calderón (1996),

> By creating a culture of inquiry through ethnography, professional learning was focused and accelerated. With the tools of "teacher ethnography" the teams of monolingual and bilingual teachers grew closer together. They learned about their teaching by observing children and their partner. Their partner provided a mirror for their teaching. Change became meaningful, relevant and necessary. Although far from perfect still, the teachers' continuous

Guidelines for Teaching

THE ROLE OF CULTURE IN EDUCATION

Trying to summarize all of this as succinctly as possible, we conclude that the 1978 resolution of the Council on Anthropology and Education on the role of culture in educational planning is still quite valid:

1. Culture is intimately related to language and the development of basic communication, computation, and social skills.

2. Culture is an important part of the dynamics of the teaching–learning process in all classrooms, both bilingual and monolingual.

3. Culture affects the organization of learning, pedagogical practices, evaluative procedures, and rules of schools, as well as instructional activities and curriculum.

4. Culture is more than the heritage of a people through dance, food, holidays, and history. Culture is more than a component of bilingual education programs. It is a dynamic, creative, and continuous process, which includes behaviors, values, and substances shared by people, that guides them in their struggle for survival and gives meaning to their lives. As a vital process it needs to be understood by more people in the United States, a multiple society which has many interacting cultural groups. (Saravia-Shore, 1979, p. 345)

learning is bringing about instructional program refinement and greater student gains as evidenced by preliminary academic and linguistic data for the experimental and control students in the study. (p. 8)

It is clear that ethnographic approaches can be used in many ways to enable educators to better understand the role of culture in bilingual and ESL classrooms. Ethnographic approaches help educators to analyze the dynamics of human interaction in the learning process, they provide us with broader perspectives on the assessment of student competencies, they develop our awareness of culturally influenced patterns of communication, they provide a window into the character of the local community, and they increase our sensitivity to the cultural influences on social, curricular, and organizational structures of school. Through all of the above, they provide insightful ways for teachers to observe and improve the multicultural learning process.

Summary

Given the all-encompassing nature of culture, our discussion in this chapter has ranged far and wide. We started by arguing for a complex view of culture as an elusive but powerful force in students', families', and teachers' lives. Then we explored children's development of cultural identities and found a multifaceted and dynamic process. Next, we turned to the broad dimensions of multicultural education as an organizing concept for how to capitalize on cultural diversity in bilingual and ESL settings. Within this context, we examined cultural concepts relevant to prejudice and discrimination, and we then turned to the role of culture in school success for language-minority students. Armed with the argument that culturally relevant instruction did have a role to play in school achievement, we finally looked at ethnographic studies as important tools in the development of locally sensitive educational environments that take advantage of the cultural and linguistic wealth of their communities.

In 1968 Jackson wrote in *Life in Classrooms* that schools have a hidden curriculum, and today we are still exploring all of the implications for language-minority children. These children adapt to, learn from, contribute to, or rebel against the largely concealed and yet powerful beliefs, values, behaviors, and language use patterns that schools embody. At the same time these children are maintaining, modifying, or discarding the largely unstated and yet powerful beliefs, values, behaviors, and language use patterns that they bring to school from their homes and communities. To the degree that we can make these changes mutual learning processes instead of battles, we can enhance the life opportunities for language-minority students.

We return to our initial theme in this chapter: the perplexing webs that we all weave as cultural beings. The thoughts of a Vietnamese-origin high school student powerfully illustrate the elusive nature of culture. Referring to his teachers, he said,

> They understand something, just not all Vietnamese culture. Like they just understand something *outside*. . . . But they cannot understand something inside our hearts. (Nieto, 1994, p. 53)

We cannot understand cultures completely, but we can know and accept that we do not understand everything; we can be prepared to learn from as well as with the students in our schools. For teachers in bilingual and ESL settings the significance of culture will always be so close and yet so difficult to capture. The patterns and perceptions are always changing, because "the essence is how people work to create culture, not what culture is" (Glassie, 1992). As culture bearers and culture makers we are all continuously transmitting and constructing new realities. As bilingual and ESL educators, we can play an enormously important role in working together with our students as culture-bearers and culture-makers to create culturally peaceful schooling realities that foster each child's full potential.

Key Terms

Multiculturalism p. 188	Assimilation p. 193
Acculturation p. 193	Culture p. 193

Reflection Questions

1. How would *you* define culture? In what terms do you think of yourself as a "cultured" person? Do you agree with the idea that culture is learned, not inherited? Explain.
2. Elaborate on the differences between the anthropological and the popular views of culture presented in this chapter.
3. How does Margaret Mead's model of "cultural transmission" presented in the chapter relate to individuals growing up in a multicultural society like the United States? What challenges does the model present when considering the adaptation process of immigrant families?
4. How are the concepts of *biculturalism*, *acculturation*, and *assimilation* related? Which concept(s) will best aid you in describing your own process of development of cultural identity? Do you view cultural diversity as a positive or negative phenomenon? Explain.
5. Elaborate on the importance of *cultural pluralism* as a basis for multicultural education. What are some political connotations underlying the concept when viewed from the perspective of nationalism? Are there concrete ways in which our society promotes and/or hinders *cultural pluralism*? Explain.
6. Bilingual and ESL educators play an active role in the implementation of multicultural education. Using the "five dimensions of multicultural education" identified by Banks and Banks (1995) as a point of departure, design an action plan for implementing the various dimensions within a multicultural school community or classroom.
7. How is ethnocentrism related to prejudice and discrimination? In what sense does cultural relativism provide an "antidote" to the damaging effects of conscious or unconscious ethnocentrism? Design a lesson plan geared to introduce your students to the concept of cultural relativism as a method for cultural inquiry and understanding.
8. What implications do the various "deficit theories" discussed by the authors have on the educational achievement of minority language students? Design an argument that would render both theories as flawed.
9. What is the role of ethnography or naturalistic inquiry in multicultural education?

Resources

Banks, J. A. *Cultural diversity and education: Foundations, curriculum, and teaching* (4th edition). Boston: Allyn and Bacon, 2001.

- *Cultural Diversity and Education* is designed to help educators clarify philosophical and definitional issues related to pluralistic education. The book serves as a guide for preservice and in-service educators in the implementation of effective teaching strategies that reflect ethnic and cultural diversity, and prepares sound guidelines for multicultural programs and practices. This book describes actions that educators can take to institutionalize educational programs and practices related to ethnic and cultural diversity.

Hutner, G., ed. *Immigrant voices: Twenty-four narratives on becoming an American.* New York: Penguin Putnam, 1999.

- *Immigrant Voices* is a collection of narratives that provide historical perspectives on the struggle and successes of immigrants in the United States.

LeBlanc Flores, J., ed. *Children of La Frontera: Binational efforts to serve Mexican migrant and immigrant students.* Charleston, WV: Clearinghouse on Rural Education and Small Schools, 1996.

- *Children of La Frontera* is a compilation of essays addressing the particular realities and needs of children along the U.S.–Mexican border. The authors address issues that elucidate on who are the children of La Frontera, and what do we need to know in order to help these youngsters become the next group of U.S. college students, technicians, professionals, artists, and participating citizens.

Levinson, B. *We are all equal: Student culture and identity at a Mexican secondary school, 1988–1998.* Durham and London: Duke University Press, 2001.

- *We Are All Equal* is the first full-length ethnography of a Mexican secondary school available in English. Levinson observes student life at a provincial Mexican junior high to study how the school's emphasis on equality, solidarity, and group unity dissuades the formation of polarized peer groups and affects students' eventual life trajectories.

Nieto, S., ed. *Puerto Rican students in U.S. schools.* Mahwah, NJ: Lawrence Erlbaum Associates, Publishers, 2000.

- *Puerto Rican Students in U.S. Schools* is a compilation of scholarly chapters and personal reflections that focus on the history and experiences of Puerto Rican students in the United States. The authors address issues of identity, culture, ethnicity, language, gender, social activism, community involvement, and policy implications.

Rosaldo, R. *Culture and truth: The remaking of social analysis.* Boston, MA: Beacon Press, 1989/1993.

- *Culture and Truth* is a classic in cultural anthropology. Describing the inadequacies of the traditional conception of culture as static and monolithic, and of detached, 'objective' observers, Rosaldo argues for a new approach for thinking and writing about culture—namely, one that acknowledges and celebrates diversity, narrative, emotion, and the unavoidability of subjectivity.

Weatherford, J. *Native roots: How the Indians enriched America.* New York: Crown Publishers, 1991.

- *Native Roots* is a study of the Indians of North America and their essential role in the making of the United States.

Endnotes

1. Current linguistic studies find no basis for the idea that bilingualism is detrimental to personality development or cognitive functioning. In fact, in many studies bilinguals have been found to have a more diversified pattern of abilities than their monolingual peers (Bialystok, 1991; Hakuta & Díaz, 1985, p. 322; Moran & Hakuta, 1995). For further discussion of the cognitive aspects of bilingualism, see Chapter Four.

2. Translations: "Gosh, well, I don't know." "Gimme the ball, or I'm gonna tell the teacher."

3. KEEP programs did result in improved test scores for many students, and the KEEP studies on cultural factors in school success have been very influential in guiding research and practice in language-minority settings. However, recently some Kanaka Maoli (Native Hawaiians) have placed the findings and practices of KEEP educators under new scrutiny. For example, Hewett (in press), a native Hawaiian educator, criticizes KEEP researchers, who were not generally Kanaka Maoli, for having represented the voice and curricular perspectives of the colonizer. Hewett questions the research approaches and the generalizations they made about Hawaiian children and how they learn. For example, she takes issue with KEEP's reification of "talking story," as it is referred to among the Kanaka Maoli, into "the talk story" and then using it in the classroom without fully understanding the meaning of this cultural practice. As Hewett sees it, "talking story" is an intricate part of the Hawaiian way of life—part of a web of social communication—not something to be turned into an instructional method. This and other points that Hewett raises demonstrate once again the complexity of cross-cultural studies: our cultural lenses and our place in the sociopolitical structure continually affect our perceptions and consequently our conclusions and actions.

4. There are other informative ethnographic studies that we do not refer to in this chapter. In the last chapter, "School and Community," we will discuss several of these ethnographies, which are important in the field of bilingual and ESL education.

Mathematics and Science

Humans have never lost interest in trying to find out how the universe is put together, how it works, and where they fit in the cosmic scheme of things. The development of our understanding of the architecture of the universe is not complete, but we have made great progress. Given a universe that is made up of distances too vast to reach and of particles too small to see and too numerous to count, it is a tribute to human intelligence that we have made as much progress as we have in accounting for how things fit together. All humans should participate in the pleasure of coming to know their universe better. The terms and circumstances of human existence can be expected to change radically during the next life span. Science, mathematics, and technology will be at the center of that change—causing it, shaping it, responding to it. Therefore, they will be essential to the education of today's children for tomorrow's world.

Rutherford & Ahlgren, 1990

Given the importance of science and mathematics, a bilingual or ESL program that is designed to ensure quality instruction in these areas will be doing a better job of preparing its children for tomorrow's world. Before we examine the issues and approaches involved in mathematics and science education for language-minority students, let us take a look at one English language learner's experience in kindergarten mathematics, told from the point of view of the child's ESL teacher.

Rui's Encounter with More and Less

⊠ *I am an ESL teacher, and one of my students is Rui, a kindergarten boy. Rui arrived from Japan very recently, and consequently his English expressive skills are at this time limited to one- or two-word responses. Rui is the only English learner in his classroom and I work with him individually for 45 minutes a day. Although I am bilingual, I do not happen to speak Japanese, and among the activities which I use with Rui are mathematical, manipulative-based ones.*

Rui's classroom teacher often puts in "special requests" for vocabulary or concepts to be taught during Rui's ESL time, and one day when I came to get Rui, she asked me to teach him the meanings of "more" and "less." I used a variety of paired sets of real objects, and I had one of my puppets ask me which set had more or less. For each of the puppet's questions I modeled the target response by pointing to one of the sets and responding with the appropriate word, "more" or "less." Rui understood immediately and began taking his turn responding to the puppet's questions, exclaiming intermittently in English, "Easy, easy!" (He had learned this word from his kindergarten peers.) After a little practice with real objects, I tried the exercise with paired workbook pictures of sets, and he always responded correctly. Then, at a more symbolic level, I showed him paired numerals, again asking, "Which one is more/less?" He continued to respond correctly, minus some typical kindergarten confusion with sixes and nines. It was clear that within the span of 10 minutes of instruction I had not taught him the concept of more and less; he showed that he already had that concept in his repertoire of cognitive skills. I had just taught him to associate the English words "more" and "less" with that concept.

Rui's teacher is concerned that he is not keeping up with the other students, and she often asks me for a quick progress report when I bring him back to the classroom. When I told her on this particular day that Rui could respond to more and less problems now, she threw up her arms in delight, went over to Rui, and exclaimed, "Boys and girls, boys and girls! Rui! Rui, tell all the boys and girls what more means!" Virtually every curious kindergarten eye was on Rui as he responded with frightened, uncomfortable silence. The teacher tried prompting. "More means . . ." but Rui was no more ready to explain with words in English what more meant than I was ready to explain long division in Japanese. The teacher looked over at me and smiled as she shook her head.

"He needs objects or numbers. He can show you," I explained.

"Oh, yes. Well. I see. Rui, that's all right, honey. I'm going to give you a big hug."

By this time Rui was almost in tears. Rui's teacher means well, and when I talked to her later in the day she realized without my saying very much that she had gone about probing his skills in a less than ideal manner. Still, for Rui's sake, and for the sake of the other students' perceptions of Rui, I wish the incident had not happened.

From Rui's point of view, the "more–less" day was probably not one of the better ones in his kindergarten career. The point we wish to emphasize is that Rui had already mastered, within a Japanese language context, the *concept* of more and less and what he was being taught on that day was to associate the English words with the concept. This is an important distinction that, when overlooked, can lead to the underestimation of the math and science knowledge base of children who are learning English. And there are many other experiences, in many other classrooms, for many other language-minority students, that are less than optimal for the acquisition or demonstration of mathematics and science skills.

What conditions can enhance the achievement of language-minority students in mathematics and science classrooms? To arrive at an answer to this question we will discuss six interrelated topics: (1) the mathematics and science achievement of language-minority students, (2) current **mathematical standards** and reform in math and science education, (3) opportunity to learn standards for language-minority students, (4) approaches for the effective use of L_1 and L_2 in mathematics and science instruction, (5) cultural issues in math and science instruction, and (6) theme-based math and science instruction.

Achievement of Language-Minority Students in Mathematics and Science

Educators often predict informally that language-minority students will have fewer problems with mathematics than language arts because "math is a universal language." Maybe they haven't talked to a teacher who has tried to help an ELL solve a word problem that is written in English. In reality, teachers and students employ a great deal of language in the math and science teaching and learning process. Research in the mathematics achievement of the student population as a whole suggests a connection between math and language in that there is a somewhat positive relation between mathematics achievement and verbal proficiency. Although the question of how these two areas influence each other is largely unanswered, Cocking and Chipman (1983) note that the so-called universal mathematical language is mediated in the classroom through the oral and written language of instruction, and thus proficiency in the language of instruction can reasonably be expected to have an effect on the acquisition of concepts and skills.

When we look at achievement data for minority students (which, of course, include many language-minority students and speakers of nonstandard varieties of English), we can find both promising patterns and inequitable patterns. The promising news is that between the 1980s and the 1990s, Scholastic Achievement Test (SAT) scores in math for most ethnic groups have been rising. For example, Puerto Ricans have gained 18 points; Mexican Americans, 20; Asian Americans, 14; and African Americans, 28. The exception to this positive trend in SAT scores among ethnic groups has been American Indian students, whose scores dropped six points on mathematics ("SAT scores seesaw," 1994, pp. 1, 2). However, despite the general pattern of gains, the average SAT math scores of most minority groups still tend to fall behind those of European-American students. Data from the 1994 National Assessment of Educational Progress (NAEP), which tracked performance from 1969 to 1992 in 4th-, 8th-, and 11th-grade science and mathematics, also indicated that despite modest gains, the gap in scores between white and African-American students and between white and Hispanic students remained wide.[1] For example, in a survey done in the early 1990s, white students scored 58 points higher than African-American students and 44 points higher than Hispanic students ("NAEP trends show turnaround," 1994, pp. 1–3, 5, 6). In the NAEP measurement of basic math and science competency, two-thirds or more of whites and Asian/Pacific Islanders achieved at or above the basic level of proficiency, while fewer than half of American Indians, African Americans or Hispanics demonstrated achievement at the basic level (Mullis, Dossey, Owen, & Phillips, 1993, pp. 2, 3). (*Basic* refers to partial mastery of knowledge and skills necessary for professional work.)

Achievement data reported in problematic census categories such as "white" and "Hispanic" reveal overall deficiencies in the quality of education offered to African Americans, Hispanic Americans, and American Indians, but they also hide the complexities of the issue. For the sake of generalization the categories compare racial groupings with ethnic and linguistic groupings. White, for example, is a racial categorization, while Hispanic is essentially a linguistic-origin categorization. Also lost is the extensive cultural, sociological, and socioeconomic heterogeneity within each group, as well as the effect of language proficiency and length of residence in the United States for ELLs.

Tsang (1982), for example, points out that the image of Asian Americans as the "model minority" is reflective of research done largely in the 1960s that focused principally on Chinese-American and Japanese-American samples. The present Asian-American population, however, is a much larger and more diverse one. While the overall pattern for the group is one of strong achievement in math and science, there are groups within the larger group for whom this is not necessarily the case. For example, Ovando (2000) argues that the so-called 'model minority' stereotype oversimplifies the lived experiences of many Asian students, masking the diversity within Asian-American communities due to social class, religion, language, ethnicity, migratory status, length of residence, and education (p. 4). On the other hand, the generalized census category data also hide the many exciting individual success stories among language-minority students. For example, out of the 40 highly competitive Westinghouse Science Awards given in 1995, four went to students from New York City's Stuyvesant High School, and all four of these students were language-minority students, the children of immigrants.

Nevertheless, despite the exceptions and despite the limitations of lumped statistical data, most bilingual and ESL teachers would probably agree that all too often language-minority students are not being given opportunities to achieve at the same level in math and science as English proficient majority students. The explanations for such gaps in achievement, not surprisingly, are many. The generally lower performance of minority students in math and science cannot be attributed to any one factor: There are complex and interrelated sociopolitical, socioeconomic, cultural, linguistic, and instructional factors. Regarding assessment, Cocking and Chipman (1983) note that the actual competence of minority students may be undermeasured because the style or format of the instrument fails to tap their actual concepts and skills. For example, a consumer testing group called FairTest argues that the SAT continues to be biased in its questions about topics and concepts more familiar to affluent students and males (Carmody, 1994, p. 16A). Even though there is evidence that the usual assessment tools may undermeasure actual achievement, it is still reasonable to suppose that actual proficiency is lower than it should be based on classroom performance.

Focusing in on American Indians, Schindler and Davison (1985) offer the following four reasons for their general pattern of lower math proficiency: (1) math anxiety related to low sense of self-efficacy; (2) difficulty with English language processing for ELLs; (3) a cultural orientation of the traditional school math curricula that is quite different from students' experiences, and (4) the lack of use of visual and manipulative modalities in the curriculum, which is dominated by abstract and symbolic modalities (pp. 148, 149). Using a contextually interactive model, Cocking and Mestre (1988, pp. 19, 20) suggest that in general, language-minority students' performance in mathematics is influenced by both linguistic and nonlinguistic factors such as (1) entry characteristics of the learner (cognitive ability patterns such as mathematical concepts, language skills, reading, and learning ability); (2) educational opportunities provided to the learners (such as time on task, quality of instruction, appropriate language, and parental or other assistance); and (3) motivation to learn (such as motivation to engage by including cultural/parental values, expectations for awards, and motivational nature and cultural appropriateness of instructional interaction).

In looking at one factor, socioeconomic status (SES), we see in the case of the SAT that lower scores in general do tend to correlate with lower family income levels and lower levels of parent education. However, in Chapter Five we discussed how school micro forces may either perpetuate the socioeconomic pattern through unequal educational opportunity or potentially mitigate to some degree the effects of low SES. One recent study of Asian Americans, which considered the relative weight of school experience factors versus racial-ethnic and family background factors, found that, particularly in the area of mathematics, school experiences were as important as family background in determining the amount of student learning. In other words, as the authors state, "students can excel if they are given or guided to proper school experiences" (Peng, Owings, & Fetters, 1984, p. 17).

Further suggesting that school factors can make a difference in math and science achievement, Ginsburg (1981) found that differences among young children in mastery of basic mathematics concepts were not related significantly to social class or racial background. In other words, preschool children from the varied backgrounds he studied had very similar levels of the understanding of basic number concepts. For school-age children of some language-minority groups, however, there was evidence that as they advanced through the grades their average scores start to lag farther and farther behind the averages for majority students. For example, the mathematics achievement gap for Hispanic Americans and American Indians increases at each age level, ages 9, 13, and 17 (Cocking & Chipman, 1983, p. 17). This certainly suggests that school opportunities may be a strong factor.

In a nationwide statistical study of the distribution of opportunities for math and science learning, Oakes (1990) also found strong evidence that lower-income minority students tended to be served inequitably. Such students were more likely to be placed in low-track classes, and they had less access to a full math and science curriculum. In addition, they were taught by less qualified teachers, had less access to math and science equipment and facilities, and were less likely to receive instruction that was active and inquiry based, thus having less opportunity to develop problem-solving skills.

Looking specifically at the minority-student subcategory of language minorities, Cocking and Chipman (1983) also noted that teachers of language-minority students were actually less likely to have adequate training and skills in mathematics pedagogy, and that the amount of instructional time allotted to mathematics might be insufficient because of the emphasis on language development for ELLs. Despite progress during the past decade in the integration of math and science instruction with language development, all too often language-minority students are not receiving the service that they need in order to reach their full potential in the areas of science and mathematics. For example, McKeon (1994) reports from a study of California schools that language minorities were much less likely than majority students to have access to computers. Looking specifically at English language learners, the researchers found that only 11 percent of those who would benefit from bilingual programs were enrolled in such programs. With so few students receiving instructional support in their first language, it is no wonder that far too many would fall behind in math and science proficiency. The same survey also found that more than half of the California high schools in one study did not offer adequate content area bilingual or ESL classes in such subjects as math and science—classes specifically designed to meet the needs of English language learners. The result of the lack of such course offerings is reflected in the following quote from an 11th-grade native Spanish speaker who immigrated from Mexico at the age of 14:

⊗ *"For me, they shouldn't have put me in Basic Math. I should have been in Algebra. But there is more English vocabulary in Algebra so they said I couldn't take it until I learned more English. I felt I was spending time with things I already knew, but then that's required of Latin immigrants. We waste our time because we don't know English yet." (Olsen, 1988, p. 50)*

Current Standards and Math and Science Reform

⊗ *Imagine a classroom, a school, or a school district where all students have access to high-quality, engaging mathematics instruction. There are ambitious expectations for all, with accommodation for those who need it. Knowledgeable teachers have adequate resources to support their work and are continually growing as professionals. The curriculum is mathematically rich, offering students opportunities to learn important mathematical concepts and procedures with understanding. Technology is an essential component of the environment. Students confidently engage in complex mathematical tasks chosen carefully by teachers. . . . Students are flexible and resourceful problem solvers. . . . Orally and in writing, students communicate their ideas and results effectively. They value mathematics and engage actively in learning it. (—Principles and Standards for School Mathematics (2000), p. 3)*

Buttressing NCTM's vision above for equity, quality, and relevance in mathematics education, the National Council of Teachers of Mathematics, the National Science Teachers Association, the American Association for the Advancement of Science, the National Science Resource Center, and the National Science Foundation, along with many other organizations, have called for reform in math and science education for *all* students. Catalyzed by general evidence of math and science illiteracy in the United States, such organizations have proposed the implementation of more rigorous mathematics and science curricula that are inquiry-based, holistic, hands-on, lifelike, interdisciplinary, and equitable. The current standards in these fields call

Guidelines for Teaching

SIX PRINCIPLES FOR SCHOOL MATHEMATICS

- *Equity.* The vision in mathematics education challenges a pervasive societal belief in North America that only some students are capable of learning mathematics. Excellence in mathematics education requires high expectations and strong support for all students. That is, all students should have access to an excellent and equitable mathematics program that provides solid support for their learning and is responsive to their prior knowledge, intellectual strength, and personal interests.

- *Curriculum.* A curriculum is more than a collection of activities: It must be coherent, focused on important mathematics, and well articulated across grades. A coherent curriculum effectively organizes and integrates important mathematical ideas, and gives guidance about when closure is expected for particular skills or concepts.

- *Teaching.* Effective mathematics teaching requires understanding what students know and need to learn and then challenging and supporting them to learn it well. It requires knowing and understanding mathematics, students as learners, and pedagogical strategies. Teaching mathematics well is a complex endeavor, and there are no easy recipes.

- *Learning.* Students must learn mathematics with understanding, actively building new knowledge from experience and prior knowledge. The requirements for the workplace and for civic participation in the contemporary world include flexibility in reasoning about and using quantitative information. Conceptual understanding is an important component of the knowledge needed to deal with novel problems and settings.

- *Assessment.* Assessment should support the learning of important mathematic skills and furnish useful information to both teachers and students. Whether the focus is on formative assessment aimed at guiding instruction or on summative assessment of students' progress, teachers' knowledge is paramount in collecting useful information and drawing valid inferences. Assembling evidence from a variety of sources is more likely to yield an accurate picture.

- *Technology.* Technology is essential in teaching and learning mathematics; it influences the mathematics that is taught and enhances student' learning. Electronic technologies—calculators and computers—are essential tools for teaching, learning, and doing mathematics. Technology, however, should not be used as a replacement for basic understanding and intuitions. The possibilities of engaging students with physical challenges in mathematics are dramatically increased with special technologies.

for curricular reform that will enable students from all backgrounds to understand and value math, science, and technology in their daily lives. The National Council of Teachers of Mathematics (NCTM) (1989, pp. 5, 6), for example, has established the following goals for students: to learn to reason mathematically, to learn to communicate mathematically, to become confident in their mathematical abilities, and to become mathematical problem solvers. These NCTM goals imply an emphasis on problem solving and conceptual understanding, with less emphasis on rote memorization.

Building on the foundations of the original *Standards* (1989, 1991, & 1995), the National Council of Teachers of Mathematics (2000) has also established six *Principles* emphasizing high quality mathematics education for *all* students. Concerned about equity issues, NCTM has likewise developed *Content* and *Process Standards* for all students. The document describes the understanding, the knowledge, and the skills all students should acquire in grades pre-K–12 (see guiding principles below). Guided by the above overarching principles, NCTM also provides a set of content and process standards to inform curricular goals and practices (see below).

Also interested in making the science curriculum accessible to all students, the National Science Teachers Association has proposed that the current "layer cake" approach to middle school and high school science be abandoned (Aldridge, 1995). (The layer cake approach refers to the practice of taking one full year of biology, then never going back to it; one full year of

Guidelines for Teaching

CONTENT AND PROCESS STANDARDS FOR SCHOOL MATHEMATICS PRE-K–12

Content Standards:

- *Number and operation.* Instructional programs K–12 should enable all students to understand numbers, the ways of representing numbers, relationships among numbers, and number systems; understand the meanings of operations and how they relate to one another; and compute fluently and make reasonable estimates.

- *Algebra.* Instructional programs K–12 should enable all students to understand patterns, relations, and functions; represent and analyze mathematical situations and structures using algebraic symbols; use mathematical models to represent and understand quantitative relationships; and analyze change in various contexts.

- *Geometry.* Instructional programs K–12 should enable all students to analyze characteristics and properties of two- and three-dimensional geometric shapes and develop mathematical arguments about geometric relationships; specify locations and describe spatial relationships using coordinate geometry and other representational systems; and apply transformations and use symmetry to analyze mathematical situations.

- *Measurement.* Instructional programs K–12 should enable all students to understand measurable attributes of objects and the units, systems, and processes of measurement and apply appropriate techniques, tools, and formulas to determine measurements.

- *Data analysis and probability.* Instructional programs K–12 should enable all students to formulate questions that can be address with data and collect, organize, and display relevant data to answer them; select and use appropriate statistical methods to analyze data; develop and evaluate inferences and predictions that are based on data; and understand and apply basic concepts of probability.

Process Standards:

- *Problem solving* or engaging in a task for which the solution method is not known.

- *Reasoning and proof* or a formal way of expressing particular kinds of reasoning and justification.

- *Communication* or a way of sharing ideas and clarifying understanding.

- *Connections* or emphasis on the interrelatedness of mathematical ideas.

- *Representation* or the ways in which mathematical ideas are presented and used by the students to model physical, social, and mathematical phenomena.

Guidelines for Teaching

WHO CAN LEARN MATH? ALL STUDENTS!

Along with these promising proposals for reform, the issue of equity has become very important in the design of standards for math and science instruction. The phrase *all students* is used often in the publications of the NCTM. Authors of the Professional Standards for Teaching Mathematics (NCTM, 1991) define *all students* to include:

- Those who have been denied access to opportunities as well as those who have not.

- African Americans, Hispanic Americans, American Indians and other minorities as well as majority.

- Female as well as male.

- Those who have not been successful as well as those who have.

chemistry, then never to going back to it, and so on.) Instead, the association recommends that all middle and high school students take science every year for six years, covering fewer topics in greater depth each year and spreading out each discipline over several years. In other words, the new high school science curriculum would include a biology component each year, a chemistry component each year, a physics component, and an earth/space science component each year. Throughout these strands the focus would be on *how* we know what we know and *why* we believe it to be true.

In our postmodern world, mathematics, science, and technology have become an important source of "cultural capital" for particular segments of the U.S. student population. Unfortunately, however, as Schoenfeld (2002) notes, ". . . disproportionate numbers of poor, African American, Latino, and Native-American students drop out of mathematics and perform below standard on tests of mathematical competency, and are thus denied both important skills and a particularly important pathway to economic and enfranchisement (p. 13)." It is thus particularly important that NCTM, the leading organization of mathematic educators, is concerned that all students in our society receive a high level of instruction in mathematics.

Opportunity to Learn Standards

Equity, of course, is much easier to talk about in principle than to carry out in action. For example, some educators initially feared that the excellence reform movement would backfire for language-minority students. They anticipated increases in the drop-out rate because of tougher math and science requirements for graduation. However, as requirements generally increased in the 1970s and 1980s, the increase in drop-out rates that some expected did not occur. For example, Mirel and Angus (1994) observed that from 1982 to 1990 the percentage of Hispanic Americans taking three years of math and science in high school increased from 6 percent to 33 percent. During this time, however, the drop-out rate for this group did not increase. Based on these findings, Mirel and Angus posited that in the long run the raising of academic standards *can* potentially result in more equal educational opportunities.

However, notwithstanding the good intentions and the potential of the current standards for all students, equitable math and science opportunities for many language-minority students remains an unfulfilled goal. As Apple (1992) noted on the possibilities and limitations of the NCTM standards (1989, 1991), the proposals have not been sufficiently grounded in or discussed in the context of the sociocultural, economic, and ideological realities found in today's schools. For example, the standards do not forcefully address the need for systemic, multicultural reform that is relevant to the needs of language-minority students in math and science classrooms. To use just one illustration, is it really fair to hold English-language learners to the same common standards as English proficient students? As McKeon (1994, pp. 45–49) observed, holding English-language learners to "common" standards may, in fact, be uncommonly high for LEP students, asking them to perform at a much higher cognitive and linguistic level than their monolingual English-speaking peers." As an illustration, if you speak limited Russian and have to write a report on photosynthesis in Russian, "you are actually performing a much more difficult task than your Russian speaking peers" (McKeon, 1994, p. 3). The task is even more difficult if you have never studied photosynthesis in English to begin with.

Applying these standards more specifically to math and science, language-minority students need access to a multicultural math and science environment that builds on the background and interests that they bring to the classroom, age-appropriate instruction in math and science instead of watered-down instruction, math and science classes that make appropriate

Guidelines for Teaching

"OPPORTUNITY TO LEARN" STANDARDS

In this situation, the key word in equal educational opportunity is *opportunity*. The authors of the "TESOL Statement on the Education of K–12 Language-Minority Students in the United States" argue, for example, that along with more demanding academic standards, there must be "opportunity to learn" standards for English-language learners. These "opportunity to learn" standards are:

- Access to positive learning environments.

- Access to appropriate curriculum.

- Access to full delivery of services.

- Access to equitable assessment. (TESOL, 1992, pp.12, 13)

use of L_1 and that use effective second-language methods of content instruction, and opportunities to show their math and science competence in a variety of ways.

Bilingual and ESL teachers obviously need strong conceptual understandings of first- and second-language development as well as principles of multicultural education in order to work toward the realization of such opportunities for math and science. In addition, teachers' attitudes, motivation, and competencies in mathematics and science are critical to the student's affective and academic development. Most bilingual and ESL teachers are not specialists in math or science, but they can make the best of the math and science skills that they do possess by collaborating with math and science specialists and by modeling for their students an appreciation for the fields. Language-minority students are more likely to find these areas engaging and meaningful, and thus to succeed in these subjects, when their teachers:

1. Understand the functions of mathematics and science historically as well as in contemporary society.
2. Make the mathematics and science curricula responsive to the local cultures and languages.
3. Are themselves enthusiastic and curious about the mystery, complexity, and simplicity of mathematical and scientific concepts, applications, and processes.[2]

With these "opportunity to learn" standards established, we turn now more specifically to the use of language and culture in math and science classrooms. As we discuss first language and then culture, we again find Thomas and Collier's prism (Chapter Four) useful. In science and math classrooms, academic development, cognitive development, and language development all form an interdependent triangle. As we look at the use of language, we will see that in active, integrated learning environments the development of language proficiencies, thinking skills, and math and science knowledge are all intertwined. When we look at culture and theme-based instruction in the final sections of the chapter, we are touching on the center of Thomas and Collier's prism, the sociocultural processes that interact with the outer points of language, cognition, and math and science knowledge.

Language in Mathematics and Science Classrooms

Teachers may have in their science or mathematics classes quite a mix of students: ELLs, bilingual students, English monolingual majority students, and English monolingual minority students. How can they meet the language development needs of these students while at the same time providing all of them with opportunities to fully develop their mathematics and science knowledge at grade-appropriate levels? There are no immediate, absolute, or universal answers. As with bilingual and ESL programs in general, math and science solutions have to be adapted to the local context. However, because of the primacy of language as a vehicle for cognitive and academic development, how it is used in the bilingual or ESL classroom can have a significant impact on the quality of math and science learning environments. In this section we will first discuss the use of L_1 in math and science contexts. Next we look at content ESL. We will finish with a look at several programs that exemplify the principles of language-rich environments for math and science at the same time that they exemplify principles of active, inquiry-driven math and science instruction in bilingual or ESL contexts.

Use of L_1 for Math and Science Instruction

As noted in Chapters Two and Four, the research by Cummins (1981), Thomas and Collier (1997), and Collier (1989), suggests that it can take anywhere from 5 to 10 years or more for English language learners to reach the necessary levels of academic language proficiency to compete on par with native English speakers in content areas such as math and science. Collier and Thomas also indicate that in order for English-language learners to do well academically through instruction in a second language, their first-language oral and literacy skills ideally must be developed at least to threshold levels commensurate to a sixth-grade education. Because scientific and mathematical skills and knowledge acquired through L_1 transfer across languages, instruction in such subjects in the first language is an efficient and culturally appropriate way of developing math and science literacy for language-minority students while they are learning English (Cummins, 1992, p. 91).

The following three studies provide evidence of the effectiveness of L_1 instruction for math achievement. Students in bilingual education programs in Fremont and San Diego, California, outperformed a control group of students of the same socioeconomic status who were not in bilingual programs in the math portion of the California Test of Basic Skills in grades three through six (Krashen & Biber, 1988, p. 60). Ramírez (1992, p. 91) likewise found in his research that primary language support through bilingual instruction enhanced mathematical achievement. In a study of alternative instructional programs such as newcomer centers, sheltered English programs, and content ESL programs, researchers also found that use of L_1 was one of the important factors for concept development in subject areas such as math and science (Tikunoff et al., 1991).

Assessment   For ELLs an adequate diagnosis of math and science knowledge requires that the teacher speak the child's first language or secure the assistance of a speaker of the learner's first language. Through this initial screening teachers can determine what the students know in their primary language. Because of the broad range of language-minority student backgrounds, the knowledge base can range from that of students who have had virtually no formal training in math and science in their country of origin to that of foreign-born students who are far ahead of most U.S. students of their age in math and science. For skills and knowledge students have already gained through their home language, the teacher may plan to focus instruction on the acquisition of English-language competencies that will enable them to transfer the abilities to the English-language instructional context. However, for skills and knowledge that English language learners have not yet developed in their home language, instruction in L_1 will more likely ensure successful learning. In other words, new math and science content instruction is generally most effective if done in the home language; it will take time for the skills to be demonstrated in the second language.

L_1 Delivery Approaches   An important instructional decision for math and science lessons in bilingual classes is the alternation of the two languages. As discussed in Chapter Four, today more and more bilingual classes are clearly defining the language of instruction by blocks of time devoted to one language at a time. Decisions regarding the amount of instructional time spent in each language are made by alternating languages by subject area or theme, by time of day, by day of the week, or by week. In this section, we will examine some of the historic patterns of language use in bilingual classes: alternate, preview–review, and concurrent approaches. However, as part of the reform movement, bilingual teacher educators have frequently chosen the alternate approach, keeping the languages of instruction clearly separated, as the preferred model. Research has clearly shown that separation of the two languages leads to higher academic achievement in the long run.

The alternate language approach clearly structures a separation between the two languages in a bilingual program. In subject area alternation, for example, one year of a program might include mathematics in Spanish, with science in English. The following year math would be in English, with science in Spanish. For a half-day alternate bilingual program, on one day all lessons conducted in the morning might be in English, and those in the afternoon in Spanish. On the following day, Spanish would be the language for morning lessons and English the language in the afternoon. Alternate approaches to bilingual content area avoid the repetition of lessons in each language within the class period, which can happen with poorly implemented concurrent approaches.

For students of very limited proficiency in one of the languages of instruction, the alternate model may not be appropriate, as such students may miss too much math or science content during the time that teaching is done in the second language. As they develop increasing proficiency in a second language, the students may be introduced to an increasing amount of science and mathematics instruction in their second language, at which point an alternate program might be more appropriate to their needs. It is within a bilingual maintenance program, in which students have fairly strong proficiencies in both languages, that the alternate language approach may be the most appropriate for math and science instruction.

In the older preview–review approach, the teacher introduces a mathematics or science lesson in one language and presents the body of the lesson in the second language. In the preview session, the teacher or bilingual assistant gives an overview of the concept and accompanying science and mathematics terminology to be presented in the lesson, so that they will be understood when they appear in the main body of the lesson in the second language. For example, part of the preview of an elementary science lesson to be presented in English on measurement of temperatures might include an explanation in Korean of the meaning of such English words as *increase* and *decrease*. After the main body of the lesson is completed, the lesson might be reviewed in one of several ways. For example, the students might be divided by language dominance, with reinforcement activities conducted in each group's dominant language, or the lesson may be reviewed and expanded with all the students together, using the concurrent approach to elicit what was learned from the presentation. This approach rests to some extent on well-informed decisions by the teacher on when to use which languages most effectively. Although two languages are used in the preview–review method, the main body of the lesson is presented in only one language. Therefore, this approach may lend itself best to lessons that have many visual or physical cues. For example, if an integrated mathematics and marine biology lesson involves the measurement on the playground of the average length of the blue whale, the activity itself will provide many cues even though the student does not understand the language in which the activity is being conducted. On the other hand, if a lesson is more abstract, such as in a written explanation of how photosynthesis works, a student who does not speak the language of the main presentation may become lost despite the introduction in his or her native language.

The concurrent approach, switching back and forth in one lesson between two languages, is in disrepute with most linguists and educators because it may not control for instructional balance of the two languages, and it may not motivate students to learn the second language because first-language explanations are so immediately available. However, the concurrent approach is still used in many math and science classrooms. For teachers who have a full command of two languages or who have a bilingual team partner or paraprofessional, the skilled use of both languages helps all students, both English-dominant and English learners, understand and participate actively in math and science thought processes. Concurrent teaching, however, is a skill. It requires giving equivalent rather than literal translations as well as avoiding unnecessary repetitions of material. It requires careful decisions about switches to the other language based on knowledge of students' proficiency levels in each language and the context of the moment. It also requires that the teachers and paraprofessionals have a sound knowledge of science and mathematics terminology in both languages. The rationale for the skilled use of the concurrent approach in mathematics and science is to make sure that the information contained in the lesson is comprehensible to all students and is accessible in an intellectually challenging way. ELLs, for example, might be able to follow simple, visually cued instructions for an experiment in

English, but they might not be able to generate hypotheses or analyze results without access to L_1. Teachers using the concurrent approach can encourage contributions in whichever language the child speaks best, and then have those ideas restated in the other language if necessary so that every child, regardless of language background, participates in the math or science discussion.

Content ESL

Unfortunately, full bilingual programs in mathematics or science are not available for many English language learners. However, content ESL programs in math and science will increase the opportunities for such language-minority students to master mathematical and scientific concepts despite little or no use of L_1. Ideally, however, content ESL programs should be coupled with strategies to provide some access to L_1 if at all possible. For example, a bilingual tutor or paraprofessional may be available, or students may be grouped so that bilingual children can assist ELL classmates through their L_1. Content ESL classes can be used in a variety of contexts. Content ESL approaches to math and science are important for students who have never had access to bilingual programs, but they are also important for students who have left early-exit bilingual programs. Such students are still developing their academic language skills in L_2 and will therefore benefit from the specialized support that content ESL provides for math and science. In addition, content ESL approaches can be found in bilingual programs because math and science may be used as a medium for developing the second language.

As a means of providing English language learners with instruction that simultaneously develops second language skills and content-area knowledge, content ESL has grown tremendously in recent years. Content ESL is based on two important linguistic concepts. The first one is Krashen's (1982) familiar concept that language acquisition occurs when students, in an interesting, low-anxiety context, are provided with comprehensible input that is slightly above the students' level of understanding. The second one is that second-language proficiency entails control not only of social, but also of academic language. As discussed in Chapter Four, academic language tends to be more abstract and complex, and thus more challenging for students. It takes more years to master than social language. This is the type of language that is present in math and science classrooms, and by integrating these subjects with linguistically appropriate support in L_2 development, the student has a better opportunity to develop academic language. According to Crandall (1987)

> Many content-based ESL programs have developed to provide students with an opportunity to learn CALP [academic language], as well as to provide a less abrupt transition from the ESL classroom to an all-English-medium academic program. Content-based ESL courses—whether taught by the ESL teacher, the content-area teacher, or some combination—provide direct instruction in the special language of the subject matter, while focusing attention as much or more on the subject matter itself. (p. 7)

Guidelines for Teaching

THE INTEGRATION OF SECOND-LANGUAGE ACQUISITION WITH SCIENCE CONTENT

Fathman, Quinn, and Kessler (1992) identify the following strategies for use in classes that integrate second-language acquisition with science content, and the same principles would apply for math:

- Promoting collaboration between teachers and among students.
- Modifying language.
- Increasing the relevancy of science lessons to students' everyday lives.
- Adapting science materials.
- Using language teaching techniques in presenting science concepts. (p. 4)

One can imagine a range of instructional emphases for content ESL. At one end of the continuum, we have ESL lessons that happen to use a math or science topic as a means for developing second-language skills. At the other end, we have lessons whose main objective is to develop math or science concepts but that use techniques of second-language acquisition to maximize students' understanding of the content. Lessons that focus more specifically on second-language development tend to be found within the confines of an ESL class composed of ELLs, whereas an emphasis on content instruction with the adjunct use of second language principles is somewhat more likely to be found in a classroom of mixed proficiencies. Situations arise in which each end of the continuum may be appropriate, and, as a continuum, there is not always a clear demarcation between the ESL focus and the content focus.

We will look more closely now at aspects of the second and last items on the above list, modifying language, and using language teaching techniques. Specifically, we will consider identification of language objectives, the role of error correction, use of **multiple modalities,** vocabulary development, modeling, learning strategies, and integration of reading and writing. As we look at these strategies, we will be giving examples of content ESL math and science approaches or programs that reflect specific strategies. However, as we proceed, notice that the various programs we describe reflect many different strategies, not just the one we are highlighting.

Identification of Language Objectives   As math and science activities proceed in the second language, students encounter a very large vocabulary and a considerable array of sentence structures. As they participate in the lesson, however, teachers can design the activities to focus on certain vocabulary sets or grammatical structures as they occur naturally in the context of the lesson. Following are some brief examples of second-language objectives that may be developed while children are engaged in mathematics or science activities.

Classification activities can provide students with a variety of simple language structures appropriate for beginning second-language learners. If beginning ELLs are building a vocabulary of plants and animals while they are using classifying skills in science, the following sentence patterns can emerge as the students give each other directions on how to sort picture cards:

The turtle is not a plant.
The pine tree is a plant.

Teachers may use attribute blocks to simultaneously develop beginning language skills and classification thought processes. Attribute blocks are sets of geometric figures possessing several specific attributes—size, thickness, color, and shape, for example. There is a large thick blue circle, a small thick blue circle, a large thin blue circle, a small thin blue circle, a large thick red circle, a small thick red circle, and so on. As Cantieni and Tremblay (1979) pointed out in their description of an immersion program, attribute blocks provide an "immediate concrete situation in which vocabulary can be learned and questions and answers formulated" (p. 249). While they classify attribute blocks according to varying traits, students can learn descriptions for color, shape, and size. They may also develop adjective placement as teachers and other students model statements such as "the red triangle" or "the big red triangle." If students are classifying the blocks into a six-compartment grid based on two attributes (e.g., color—red, yellow, or blue—and size—big or little), the following question and answer exchange could take place:

(Holding up a block) Where does it go?
(Taking the block and placing it in the grid) It goes here.
Or, at a slightly more advanced second language level:
Where does this big red block go?
It goes in the third box in the first row.
Where does this little blue block go?
It goes in the first box in the second row.

Cuisenaire rods are another device that allows learners to make the linguistic connection between manipulation of a mathematical concept and use of a second language. Opportunities to use comparisons, for example, can be combined with the exploration of mathematical equality and the commutative property:

One orange rod is as long as 10 white rods.
Ten white rods are as long as 1 orange rod.

As ELLs become literate in English, they may gain writing practice in the second language by composing mathematics word problems. Using supermarket advertisements, students can combine development of a food vocabulary with practice in the solution of real-life mathematical problems that their classmates or parents might face:

※ Masumi has $20. He wants to buy one box of cereal, three frozen pizzas, and two bottles of soda. The cereal costs $2.59; the pizzas cost $3.79 each; and the soda costs $1.89 a bottle. Does Masumi have enough money?

The Role of Error Correction   Even though the primary focus of a science or math activity may be language development, error correction generally should not become a part of this teaching process. Suppose that in a particular ESL lesson, the teacher is using the topic of the circulatory system. If a child says, "the heart pump blood" instead of "the heart pumps blood," he or she has adequately communicated the scientific fact despite the grammatical error. Some teachers may feel compelled to consistently correct such errors, but most errors are developmental and thus temporary anyway. Furthermore, error correction does not seem to cure the mistakes (Dulay, Burt, & Krashen, 1982), and teachers who focus on errors may impede the maintenance of a positive language-learning environment. Focus on the communicative function of English as opposed to its form is theoretically sound for young ELLs and it also lends itself more naturally to lessons in math and science content. When students are excitedly comparing relative sizes of fractions using slices of pizza, no one will want to stop for error correction.

Use of Multiple Modalities   Mathematics and science topics possess great motivating powers for engaging English language learners. Children are great admirers of natural and human-made mathematics and science phenomena. The snake in a cage in the book corner or the new row of computers in the media center fascinates them. Therefore, the teacher who is able to integrate second-language development activities with mathematics and science content will be providing highly motivating contexts for both language and content development. Students like to smell, touch, see, hear, taste, connect, disconnect, heat, cool, and quantify things. They like to know why certain things work the way they do and why others work differently. And because mathematics and science deal with quantifiable and material subjects, it is possible to frame much learning in such a way that students are able to develop cognitive skills in these subject areas as they receive instruction in L_2. Because much of the content of mathematics and science lends itself to physical representation, ESL teachers can use many manipulatives, demonstrations, and experiments to involve students not only in the discovery of new subject knowledge, but also in the practice of newly acquired L_2 proficiencies. This type of integrated content and language instruction in math and science fits well with the linguistic premise that learners acquire a second language more quickly when they are interested in what they are learning and when they are allowed a sufficient level of manipulation of the language through group work and the use of visuals, realia, and manipulatives.

The use of hands-on and visual math and science pedagogy can result in both the acquisition of content area and development of academic language use. For example, if teachers present algebra problems involving such terms as "twice as long as," "half as wide as," or "10 times as many as" in a visual and manipulative manner, the English-language learner will learn not only how to solve the problems but also English terms that can subsequently be applied in more academically demanding paper-and-pencil assignments.

Metaphors can often be of value in giving concrete context to a lesson that might otherwise be too abstract. Metaphors provide a bridge between the familiar and the unfamiliar or the available and the unavailable. Students cannot directly feel the pumping action of a human heart, but with a bicycle pump students can feel the bursts of air and transfer that first-hand experience to the concept of the heart's rhythmic bursts of blood. As the lesson is refined, students can explore areas of similarity and dissimilarity between the pump and the heart. It is also impossible to bring a live baleen whale into the classroom (along with a large supply of sea water), but the feeding function of the baleen can be demonstrated using a coffee filter/baleen metaphor.

An additional argument for multiple modalities has to do with children's cognitive development. Natural competencies in mathematics and science generally do not go beyond the Piagetian developmental stages predicted for their age groups. General research in elementary science education, however, indicates that teachers and books frequently present lessons in abstract formats that are beyond the logical thinking stage of the students. This often results in failure to master targeted concepts even when language proficiency is not an issue (De Luca, 1976). For young children at the preoperational and concrete stages, for example, manipulation of objects enhances the logical thinking process. Macbeth (1974) found that the extent to which pupils manipulated materials was positively associated with the acquisition of elementary science skills. The problem of developmentally inappropriate science lessons becomes increasingly serious for ELLs who may be processing the concepts in their L_2 in addition to dealing with the developmentally inappropriate instruction. Thus use of materials that students can touch, push, pull, smell, taste, cut up, heat, cool, weigh, measure, and so on takes on even greater importance in a classroom in which more than one language is represented. Such activities make the concepts cognitively accessible at the same time that they provide a linguistically appropriate environment. Children who are not fully proficient in English are going to be more likely to master a mathematics or science lesson presented in English if they are dealing only with a partial language barrier and not with a language barrier combined with a cognitive barrier.

Vocabulary Development Teachers who use content ESL in conjunction with math and science instruction develop a strong awareness of the need to identify and develop key vocabulary words. Much vocabulary development occurs naturally through the context of math and science activities, especially

Guidelines for Teaching

VOCABULARY DEVELOPMENT IN MATH AND SCIENCE

Vocabulary development in math and science should include words that convey *how* the thinking processes in math and science occur. For example the following note to students at the beginning of a content ESL workbook on Earth Science and Physical Science calls the students' attention to such vocabulary as *consult* and *hypotheses*.

With this book you will learn to follow the scientific thinking process. You will do the following things:

- *Consult with others:* Share ideas in cooperative groups

- *Make hypotheses:* Guess possible answers to questions or problems

- *Experiment:* Watch and take notes on what you see

- *Read:* Learn new information and remember it

- *Classify:* Put things or ideas into groups or categories

- *Compare and contrast:* Discover how something is different from another or the same as another thing. (Christison & Bassano, 1992, p. vii)

when the subjects are taught actively using visuals, realia, models, experiments, manipulatives, role playing, and so on. However, it is important for teachers to have in mind and to introduce in a relevant context the major terms that students will need in order to understand a particular activity or concept. The Pre-Algebra Lexicon (PAL), published by the Center for Applied Linguistics (Hayden & Cuevas, 1990), is an example of a resource teachers can use to guide them in identification and development of vocabulary. This publication lists over 300 terms and phrases that are most commonly found in prealgebra courses and texts, and it includes ideas for instructional strategies that will enhance the ELL's acquisition of the terms in meaningful classroom contexts. PAL also provides techniques for the assessment of math vocabulary development as a natural part of daily instruction.

Modification of Language and Modeling   Although some commercial math and science ESL materials are available, often the materials that teachers use for science and math activities, especially at the elementary level, are not ones that have been specifically designed for ELLs. Therefore, teachers will want to modify the language involved so that it is comprehensible to students. As sentence structures and vocabulary are simplified, however, it is important to keep the conceptual content of the lesson intact. For example, language for carrying out an experiment on air pressure can be simplified, but it must be done in a way that maintains the concept that air occupies space and has weight.

Extensive modeling of modified language during science and math instruction provides students with comprehensible input. Fathman, Quinn, & Kessler (1992) have developed a three-stage approach for ESL science instruction that demonstrates the importance of modeling. The three stages are (1) teacher demonstration, (2) group investigation, and (3) independent investigation. In the first phase the teacher directs and demonstrates a science activity as he or she models the language the students will be using. The teacher demonstration gives students the opportunity to listen and observe before having to produce the language involved in the activity. During the second phase the students have natural opportunities to use the modeled language for communication in the group activities. A mix of language proficiency levels within each group will enrich the language learning environment during this stage. In the final phase the students initiate independent activities in which they further develop the language. Teachers tailor the third phase to the individual proficiency level of each student. In all three phases the focus is on inquiry: Even the teacher demonstration is carried out in a way that fosters critical thinking and interaction. The following example illustrates how the three language stages can be used as students study electrical forces:

Concept: Electrical Energy Causes Motion

Teacher Demonstration.   *Use an inflated balloon to pick up small pieces of paper.*

Group Investigation.   *Use an inflated balloon to cause another balloon to move.*

Individual Investigation.   *Use an inflated balloon to test what objects it will pick up.*

In developing a lesson or unit using this approach, the teacher not only has to think about the particular science concept. He or she will also need to be thinking about the language functions needed to carry out the activity, designing the activities in such a way that they promote reading and writing skills in addition to listening and speaking. Here is what Arturo, an eighth-grade ESL student, wrote in his reflection on a three-prong lesson about how light waves are bent:

The science help us comprehend the phenomenons of the Nature. For this reason the experiment was very interesting because working in groups helped us practice english... Also I learned new vocabulary words for example: beam, divergent, coin, convergent, inclined surface, measure, path, refraction etc. I like the experiment because I learned the objective of the experiment "the refraction of the light" I would like to make more experiments. (Fathman, Quinn, & Kessler, 1992, p. 1)

Integration of Reading and Writing   We have already mentioned the integration of reading and writing activities in Fathman, Quinn, and Kessler's (1992) three-prong design for science lessons. Because one of the purposes of content ESL is to develop children's academic L_2 proficiency, reading and writing across the curriculum is an important component of complete math and science ESL programs. The next example, although not from a content ESL class, applies well to ESL contexts. It illustrates the integration of language arts into

Guidelines for Teaching

LEARNING STRATEGIES

Learning strategies are the activities that students engage in across subject areas as they "learn *how* to learn." For example, they may use a diagram to help them understand a relationship, or they may comprehend a new concept by connecting it to an experience they have had in their own life. The Cognitive Academic Language Learning Approach (CALLA) (Chamot & O'Malley, 1994) is a content ESL approach that makes extensive use of learning strategies as it addresses the academic and cognitive needs of English-language learners and prepares them for content area instruction in all-English classrooms. First introduced in Chapter Four, CALLA is an approach in which teachers explicitly teach learning strategies at the same time that they develop language and content knowledge. The learning strategies provide extra support for the negotiation of content-area instruction in the second language. By developing the habit of using learning strategies, the students have transferable skills that will stay with them as they progress to higher levels of academic instruction in math and science. Because of their accessibility through physical representations, math and science are the recommended gateway courses into CALLA (Chamot and O'Malley, 1994), with CALLA instruction in social studies and language arts coming next.

Chamot and O'Malley (1994) have identified three types of learning strategies:

1. *Metacognitive Strategies*
   Advance organization
   Organizational planning
   Selective attention
   Self-management
   Monitoring comprehension
   Monitoring production
   Self-evaluation

2. *Cognitive Strategies*
   Resourcing

Grouping
Note taking
Elaboration of prior knowledge
Summarizing
Deduction/induction
Imagery
Auditory representation
Making inferences

3. *Social/Affective Strategies*
   Questioning for clarification
   Cooperation
   Self-talk (pp. 60–64)

As part of the learning strategy approach, students and teachers in CALLA classrooms frequently talk about how they learn. Here is an example of how one student responded to the researcher's question about what strategies he was planning to use to solve a math problem: "Ask yourself what do you know. What do you need to find out? What is the progress (meant *process*)?" (Chamot, Dale, O'Malley, & Spanos, 1992, p. 23).

CALLA shows evidence of being valuable to ESL students in math classes. For example, researchers compared students in classes with high use of CALLA to students in classes with low use of CALLA. The results showed that, when given a story problem to solve, "Significantly more students in high-implementation classrooms were able to solve the problem correctly than were students in low-implementation classrooms" (Chamot, Dale, O'Malley, & Spanos, 1992, p. 1). The CALLA model has been incorporated into several commercially available content math and science ESL materials for middle and high school students, such as those by Chamot and O'Malley (1988), Christison and Bassano (1992), and Johnston and Johnston (1990).

the math curriculum in an American Indian context. To promote literacy at the same time as they taught math, resource teachers in a Crow American Indian community had students keep math journals recording what they had learned and their reactions to problems. Students also recorded math vocabulary definitions in their own words and brainstormed key words and phrases related to a target word. (For example, if the target word were *fraction,* the brainstormed key words and phrases might be "part of something, part of a whole, a piece, number, denominator.") Students also wrote their own story problems in groups and shared them. Students gained self-confidence in math, and throughout the year their math conversations became more focused and they used more math vocabulary. The students' writing also increased in amount and complexity (Davison & Pearce, 1992, pp. 150–152).

An example of a large-scale project that integrates reading and writing is "Cheche Konnen: An Investigation-Based Approach to Teaching Scientific Inquiry" (Warren, Rosebery, & Conant, 1990). The Cheche Konnen program integrates math and science with literacy development and computer skills, and an important component of the program is communicating to others the results of the students' science projects. *Cheche Konnen* means "search for knowledge" in Haitian and was originally targeted for Haitian immigrant students of high school age. The aim of the model is twofold: (1) "to help LEP students become mathematically and scientifically literate through collaborative learning activities," and (2) "the development of teacher resources to enable others to develop and implement an investigation-based approach in their classrooms" (Santos, 1992, pp. 251–52). The project has resulted in a set of activities, a handbook, a training plan, and videotape materials that can be used in a variety of language-minority contexts. Many of the participants in Cheche Konnen have been illiterate in their mother tongue and in English, have had little or no school experience with science or math, have been considered academically at risk, and thus fit the profile of students who all too often wind up in the basic memorize-the-facts science class. However, with Cheche Konnen, such students successfully designed and carried out their own scientific investigations and reported the findings. Guided by their own research questions, the students in the Cheche Konnen program acted as scientists, formulating hypotheses, collecting and analyzing data, and then writing and sharing final reports with an audience. They gained an understanding of the scientific process at the same time that they developed literacy, math, and computer skills. The teachers also learned to guide rather than to direct, and they developed greater expectations of the students' potential. As a very important additional benefit, research projects that Cheche Konnen students shared with the larger student body improved other students' perceptions of language-minority students and resulted in more frequent interaction between the groups (Rivera, 1990).

Linguistically and Cognitively Rich Environments

Now that we have looked at the use of L_1 and content ESL to teach math and science to language-minority students, we close this section on language use by looking at examples of linguistically and cognitively rich environments. Whether in a bilingual or an ESL context, effective language strategies have to go hand in hand with well-designed curricula that emphasize mathematical problem-solving abilities and scientific process skills in a rich context of social interaction.

It is extremely difficult through the written medium to effectively portray the dynamics of a math or science lesson that is alive with thinking skills and social interaction. Teachers may want to view a video such as *Communicative Math and Science Teaching* (Center for Applied Linguistics, 1990) in order to see and hear the nature of such instruction. *Communicative Math and Science Teaching* documents the characteristics of classroom interaction in exemplary math and science programs for language-minority students, and the program also includes interviews with teachers and students as they reflect on their experiences.

Keeping in mind the importance of first-hand or video experience with math and science classroom interaction, we will attempt to provide a flavor here for linguistically and cognitively rich environments by briefly describing four models. The four models that we examine are cooperative learning through *Finding Out/Descubrimiento,* realistic problem solving through the 3-D Project, the cognitive apprentice model, and cognitively guided math instruction.

Cooperative Learning: Finding Out/Descubrimiento   Specifically designed for diverse cultural, academic, and language backgrounds, the *Finding Out/Descubrimiento* (FO/D) (DeAvila, Duncan, & Navarrete, 1987) program offers over 100 math and science activities for grades two to five. Each activity has two phases. The first phase involves activities that introduce children to social aspects of fulfilling roles within small groups (i.e., asking for help or giving help). Phase two deals with the specific content activities. For example, fourth-grade students may work in groups to identify the ways in which magnetic forces work on a variety of actual objects. The role of the teacher is to ask questions, to foster student interaction, to suggest problem-solving strategies, to encourage cooperative behavior, to help students analyze problems without directly giving the solutions, and to make generalizations about concepts and principles. Communicating, observing, classifying, predicting, and interpreting are some of the key cognitive skills that children develop as they engage in FO/D activities. All instructions, activity cards, worksheets, and other materials are in Spanish and English, so that in Spanish/English bilingual settings children also develop their L_1 and L_2 through their interaction with each other in mixed language groups. A Stanford research group evaluated FO/D pilot bilingual schools in San José, California, and concluded that:

- FO/D students showed significant improvement in problem solving ability, reading, and English proficiency
- "Low achievers" gained as much in math and problem solving as high achievers
- FO/D students showed gains on the California Test of Basic Skills (CTBS). (De Avila, Duncan, & Navarrete, 1987, p. 19.)

Realistic Problem Solving: The 3-D Project   The 3-D Project focuses on "(1) deeper and higher-order understandings of elementary mathematics, (2) realistic problem solving situations, and (3) diverse types of mathematical abilities" (Lesh, Lamon, Behr, & Lester, 1992, p. 408). Teachers working with the 3-D math curriculum use a set of problem prototypes that can be adapted to fit the interests of local students. 3-D Project teachers identify students whose math talents have not been recognized through traditional instruction and assessment, and they work to help them develop their math literacy through the use of realistic problems that do not have quick-answer, one-rule solutions. These researchers have found that "when students work on model-eliciting problems selected to fit their interests and experiences, and when the tasks emphasize a broad range of abilities, a majority of students routinely invent (or extend, or refine) mathematical ideas that are far more sophisticated than their teachers would have guessed could be taught" (Lesh et al., p. 416). The following example illustrates the process of using a 3-D activity in mathematics to solve real-life problems:

Students are to design a carnival game that will actually be played at a school fundraiser. The game involves throwing discs onto a game board to win CDs. The students need to design their game so that some people win (for incentive to play), but they cannot have so many winners that the game will not make money. Using many different math skills, the game plan has to include information about the size of the game board and target, prices to charge for throws, chances of winning, and estimated profits.

The 3-D Project does not specifically target language-minority students, but its design is congruent with a conceptually sound language development approach for language minorities that emphasizes students' experiences and involves group projects to foster communication, concept development, and problem-solving skills.

The Cognitive Apprentice Model   Building on sociocultural theory (see Chapter Five), Moll (1986, 1989) sees the bilingual classroom as a cultural microcosm in which knowledge can be effectively developed through a cognitive apprenticeship model. Such an approach addresses social and cultural contexts of learning while developing higher levels of cognition (Collins, Brown, & Newman, 1989, p. 161). In order to do this in the bilingual context, both languages are used concurrently as needed to ensure that the instructional environment is meaningful to all students. In the cognitive apprentice model that was used in the bilingual classrooms Moll studied, the teacher's role was that of a craftsman who was sharing knowledge with the students—apprentices—as they carried out meaningful science and math activities together. To do this, teachers used modeling strategies and scaffolding strategies (building from what the students already know to new concepts). They also used evaluating strategies (such as talking about how a problem was solved, what worked, and what didn't), and peer collaborative strategies. Trained in ethnographic methodology, the teachers in Moll's study also conducted research in the effectiveness of the cognitive apprenticeship model for math and science. According to Thornburg and Karp (1992), bilingual teachers trained in the apprenticeship model "appear able to communicate both second language skills and higher order thinking within mathematics and science lessons" (p.175). Moreover, "the model appears to facilitate their (the teachers') responsiveness to students' efforts to comprehend, apply, and reason through concepts and procedures using the second language" (pp. 175–76).

Cognitively Guided Instruction   In cognitively guided math instruction, teachers and learners are always talking about why they are doing what they are doing, and they come to expect that doing mathematics should make sense. With a traditional math curriculum, the idea that math should make sense often gets lost as children do repeated paper-and-pencil problems. For example, Powell and Frankenstein (1997, p. 193), referring to Pulchalska and Semadeni (1987), tell the story of a school child who was given the following problem: "You have 10 red pencils in your left pocket and 10 blue pencils in your right pocket. How old are you?" The child answered that he was 20, just as many schoolchildren would. He knew that he was seven years old and he understood addition, but he *didn't* have an expectation that math should make sense. Rather, he was mechanically operating out of his classroom experience that told him that when you answer a math question in school, you use the numbers given to you in the story.

Tieing the math reform movement with the needs of language-minority children, Secada and Carey (1990) and Secada and De La Cruz (1996) provide excellent examples of the use of cognitively guided instruction in bilingual math classrooms. In Secada and De La Cruz (1996) we step into a fraction lesson in a second-grade bilingual classroom. The description demonstrates how a cognitively guided approach can show children that math should make sense to them. The students have plenty of opportunities to figure things out for themselves, with help as needed from the teacher. Through their work, they come to expect that giving a reason for what they did is a natural part of the learning process in mathematics. The following excerpt provides a glimpse of the interaction that one may find in cognitively guided math discussions.

Second-graders have been playing a manipulative math game in which they use fractions to add up to 1. There has been much discussion among the children as they figure out what combinations of fractions work to add up to 1. Now they are reporting their observations in a whole class discussion. Some children have argued that 1/3 + 1/2 + 1/4 equals 1.

[⊗] *Teacher: ¿Quiénes piensan que estos suman a uno? (Who thinks that these add up to one?) [A group of children raise their hands.] ¿Y quiénes dicen que no? (And who says no?) [Some other children raise their hands.] ¿Y quién no sabe? (And who doesn't know?) Bueno, discútanlo entre ustedes mismos. (Well, discuss it among yourselves.*

In a spirited conversation, some children bring out strips to show others how 1/3 + 1/4 + 1/2 is too big to equal 1. Other children write on paper. Listening to each group's reasoning, the teacher sends groups that achieve consensus to the other groups to help them resolve the problem. After a while, there is quiet.

> *Teacher: ¿Qué decidieron? (What did you decide?)*
>
> *María: Es más que uno. (It is more than one.)*
>
> *Teacher: ¿Cómo lo sabes? (How do you know that?)*

Paraphrasing from Secada and De La Cruz, María then went to the overhead and showed with strips of paper that the fractions added up to more than one. She re-explained with the strips of paper again for some children who said they didn't understand. Then the teacher went on to ask "Who did it a different way?" Another student came to the chalkboard, and showed, using a written approach, how she also concluded that 1/3 + 1/4 + 1/2 could not equal one, by comparing it to 1/4 + 1/4 + 1/2, which she already knew equaled 1 (Secada & De La Cruz, 1996, p. 291).

Cultural Issues in Mathematics and Science

We cannot leave the topic of math and science instruction in bilingual and ESL settings without a consideration of cultural issues. We will look at research on cross-cultural cognition and developmental universals as they relate to math and science. Then we will explore the fields of **ethnoscience** and **ethnomathematics.** From there we move into activating student and community resources for culturally relevant math and science instruction. In doing so we will be building on the principles of multicultural education that we discussed in Chapter Five.

Cross-Cultural Research and Developmental Universalities

How do learners under various cultural and environmental conditions come to grips with knowledge about their worlds? Knowing "how people perceive the environment, how they classify it, how they think about it" (Cole & Scribner, 1974, p. 5) is very relevant to bilingual and ESL math and science instruction. In the areas of math and science, to what extent do culturally diverse students approach learning in different ways, and to what extent do they approach it in the same ways? As the reader will recall from our discussion about cultural influences on cognitive styles in Chapter Five, while evidence exists that there may be differences, the specific nature, degree, and cause of the differences is elusive. In asking such a question, therefore, we do not intend to suggest a straitjacket cultural determinism position. We are not, for example, suggesting that "Adel is Egyptian. Therefore, Adel categorizes in the same way that all Egyptians categorize." However, cross-cultural research on math and science enables us to better understand the potential influences of culture in these areas.

Does the human brain, across cultures and languages, have one single "innate mathematical structure," comparable to the "universal grammar" proposed by Chomsky? According to Crump (1992, p. 27), "All the evidence suggests that there is but one universal grammar of number." Despite cultural differences in such things as counting systems and applications of math to everyday life, the above statement by Crump positively reaffirms from the mathematical point of view the principle that all humans share a common cognitive heritage. Children's mathematically based games from throughout the world reflect this reality. As Crump states, "Games foreshadow the acquisition of elementary mathematical skills in the intellectual development of the child," and "The intellectual basis of games is universal and logical, rather than particularistic and linguistic." One illustration is the Japanese game of "janken." (This game appears in different forms in many cultures—in English it is the "scissors, stone, paper" game.) Young children learn very easily to play "janken," but behind the game "the mathematical theory is both profound and difficult" (Crump, 1992, pp. 117–18). To use another example of universality of math thought patterns, Ginsburg found through his research in the Ivory Coast that all children, regardless of any formal preschool experience and regardless of tribal affiliations, have been given a "good mathematical "head start'" (Ginsburg, 1978, p. 43). He found, for instance, that all the children in his sample could solve the majority of "more" problems. His results also indicated that "in judgments of *more,* African children use the same methods of solution as do American children" (Ginsburg, 1978, p. 37). In essence, before even entering a classroom, children throughout the world appear to possess an intuitive notion of "more." Thus when a teacher concludes that a kindergarten child does not demonstrate understanding of more, this assessment may be mistaken. The child may not understand the language of instruction, the context, or the format used for assessment, but he or she probably understands the concept.

Piaget's focus on the development of logicomathematical structures in children makes it particularly relevant to a discussion of cultural similarities and differences in mathematics and science learning.[3] One of the early implications of Piaget's work was that his four stages of logicomathematical thought structure would be universal across varied cultural contexts, and Piagetian scholars produced a variety of cross-cultural research evidence that seems to confirm this (Dasen, 1977). However, while early cross-cultural research into Piagetian stages suggested universality, reviews of later studies suggested that perhaps the characteristics and timing of the stages were not as universal as earlier thought (Lancy, 1983).

However, it is difficult to ascertain the origins of differences that have been noted. For example, differences in the development of formal operations among adolescents might be seen not as a product of Western versus non-Western cultural patterns, but of the presence or lack of formal postelementary schooling, which places great emphasis on formal operations. The effect of culture and other social experiences such as formal schooling on Piaget's stages of intellectual development is therefore a complex and unresolved issue. Saxe and Posner (1983) suggest that Piagetian studies, because of the premises under which they operated, are inherently unable to "explicate the manner in which cultural factors contribute to the development process" (p. 300) in such areas as numerical thought.

The work of Vygotsky (1962) is useful in understanding possible cultural differences in approaches to math and science learning. Saxe and Posner (1983) have compared the Piagetian and Vygotskian approaches to the development of mathematical thinking from a cross-cultural perspective and point out that while the Piagetian approach focuses on logical operations, the Vygotskian approach focuses more on the cultural context of how problems are solved. Whereas from the Piagetian perspective children are seen to interact with the physical world directly, from the Vygotskian perspective cognition is a mediated activity in which children interact with representations of the world, including such culturally rooted systems as language and numeration. The basis of Vygotsky's approach is that there are two types of learning: (1) the learning of "spontaneous concepts," which the child engages in independently and which entails specific solutions to particular problems, and (2) the learning of "scientific concepts," which is carried out through interaction with formal and informal adult teachers. This learning entails generalized knowledge structures that can be applied in a variety of contexts and that comprise part of the group's cultural value system. The interaction between these two types of learning is the mechanism for the development of the intellect within a particular culture. The scientific concepts learned through interaction with mature members of the group gradually begin to direct children's approaches to their own spontaneous problem solving. Although they become more independent in their ability to solve problems, the style of cognitive functioning which they use is more or less a replica of that of their cultural group.

Researchers basing their work on Vygotsky hypothesize that culturally different groups will exhibit different approaches to the solution of mathematics problems. Looking at numeration systems in particular, Saxe and Posner (1983) point out that "in general, the research consistent with Vygotsky's approach has provided documentation concerning the way numerical skills are interwoven with particular numerational systems and culturally organized practices" (p. 306). For example, Hatano (1982), in a review of studies, found cultural influences in the mathematics achievement of Japanese students. Extensive abacus training provided calculation skills that transferred to pencil-and-paper computations. Also, number words are regular and reflect place value in the Japanese language. (For example, the Japanese equivalent for 11 is "10–1," 12 is "10–2," 21 is "2–10s–1," and so on.) Hatano argued that this cultural trait facilitated the comprehension of multiple-digit operations. In addition, the Japanese language also happens to provide a regular rhyming system for the memorization of multiplication facts.

Saxe and Posner (1983) concluded that because of the different emphases of the Piagetian and Vygotskian approaches, a combination of the two holds the greatest promise for an understanding of the development of mathematical thought from a cross-cultural perspective. In some ways the dichotomy between the two is akin to the issue of nature versus nurture. As Lancy asks, "At what point does genetic evolution stop and cultural evolution take over in managing the development of cognition?" (in Saxe & Posner, 1983, p. 196). Saxe and Posner (1983) propose that the "formation of mathematical concepts is a developmental process simultaneously rooted in the constructive activities of the individual and in social life" (p. 315).

Just as cultural variables may alter expression of mathematical or scientific thought processes, some researchers suggest that the development of dual language skills may work interdependently with the development of mathematical and scientific ways of thought. Saxe (1983) cited studies that indicated that bilingual children have a greater awareness of the "arbitrary property of number words" (p. 23). Kessler and Quinn (1980) cited many studies from a variety of sociocultural contexts that indicated that bilinguals may have an advantage over monolinguals in some measures of cognitive flexibility, creativity, and divergent thinking. In their own research, they compared the ability of monolingual and bilingual sixth-graders to formulate hypotheses for science problems. They found that the bilinguals scored significantly higher than the monolinguals in hypothesis quality. Basic to Piaget's theory of intellectual development is that the child's observation of discrepant events produces conflict within his or her existing thought system, which in turn results in intellectual development through assimilation and accommodation. (A discrepant event, for example, would be the observation that a crayon that sank in a tub of tap water floated in a tub of salt water.) Kessler and Quinn suggested that bilingual children, through their experience of learning two languages, have experienced more conceptual conflict than monolinguals, and that this conflict activates the equilibration processes of assimilation and accommodation for cognitive development. There is not, however, an extensive research database to support the existence of a positive relation between bilingualism and hypothesis-generating abilities, or between bilingualism and any other logicomathematical operations. The definite effects of bilingualism on Piagetian equilibration processes, as well as any resultant relation between such processes and mathematical and scientific development, are still largely unresolved.

Related to the issues of cognitive universals and the influence of bilingualism is the hypothesis that language determines an individual's worldview, long associated with Sapir and Whorf. With respect to science and mathematics we still have to at least consider Whorf's (1956) statement that "we dissect nature along lines laid down by our native languages" (p. 213). Is our interpretation of observed phenomena directly influenced by the lexicon and syntax of our mother tongue? It is true that the word or grammatical structure used in a language to describe a scientific or mathematical concept may not have an equivalent in another language. For example, there is no word for *line* in some American Indian languages (Lovett, 1980, p. 15). Does this mean that an American Indian child for whom English is a second language will have more trouble than an English-dominant American Indian child in learning to identify a line? Some research does in fact indicate that "people more readily discriminate between things they have different names for" (Berelson & Steiner, 1964, p. 190). However, despite variation in the way languages categorize or describe scientific and mathematical concepts, languages do not form impermeable walls closing off cross-cultural transmission of scientific or mathematical content. A loan word will give a label to a concept that can be mastered in any language. Algebra was developed in an Arabic cultural context, and the English word *algebra* is of Arabic origin. However, there is no evidence that non-Arabs consistently have more difficulty than Arabs in mastering algebra. In this case we have to go back to the empirical universality of certain basic cognitive processes. Crucial to this discussion is the expandability of all languages. Because languages have always borrowed extensively from each other for vocabulary to express new objects, ideas, or processes, language by itself is not a boundary preventing the acquisition of nonnative concepts.

Ethnoscience and Ethnomathematics

Most of us, regardless of our own cultural background, have been educated monoculturally in the fields of math and science. Textbooks and teachers generally presented the subjects as empirical, fact-based endeavors that were devoid of social or cultural content. However, there is a large and fascinating world that opens up to us and to our students when we develop a multicultural perspective on math and science. As reflections of logical processes and verified facts, mathematics and science have universal currency. But as instruments of cultural and social content they also carry with them all the richness, creativity, and variety associated with such systems. "Ethnomathematics" and "ethnoscience" enable us to see mathematical and scientific systems within their rich cultural contexts. Ethnoscience, as described by Kessler and Quinn (1987), refers to "theories and procedures for learning about the physical world that have evolved informally within cultures to explain and predict natural phenomena" (p. 61). Borba defines ethnomathematics as "mathematical knowledge expressed in the language code of a given sociocultural group." Ethnomathematics includes "the mathematical ideas of peoples, manifested in written or nonwritten, oral or nonoral forms, many of which have been either ignored or otherwise distorted by conventional histories of mathematics" (Powell & Frankenstein, 1997, p. 9). The infusion of ethnomathematical and ethnoscientific perspectives into math and science instruction is one of the ways in which we can affirm the diversity and develop the multicultural literacy of minority students, at the same time that we develop the multicultural literacy of majority students.

Such things as the historical origins of math terms used today, or the cultural significance of certain numbers or shapes, serve as reminders of the interrelationships between math, science, and culture. For example, the English measurement of "acre" is derived from an old calculation of the amount of land that could be plowed in one day (Crump, 1992, p. 75). The measurement of 60 seconds into 1 minute and 60 minutes into 1 hour is a survivor from ancient Babylonian sexagesimal numerals (Crump, 1992, p. 36). Consider also the functional and symbolic meanings surrounding the number "three" in the Western tradition. Besides its counting function, the number three shapes Western stories, which generally have a predictable three-part format: beginning, middle, and end. Even Christian theology, with its affirmation of the Holy Trinity, is an example of a numerical concept associated with a cultural meaning. The number three, however, may not have the same symbolic, magical, or organizational importance in other cultures. Athapaskans, for instance, tend to divide stories into four rather than three logically integrated subparts. To take a different example, the geometric figure of the mandala, used throughout Southeast Asia, has cultural meaning coded into its defining geometric shape. The shape underlies important historical, political, and architectural patterns. The core (manda) of the figure is unitary, while the outer part of the figure, called the container (-la) is always a multiple of two. The mandala is not only the model for the temples at Angkor Wat (in Cambodia) and Borobudur (in Indonesia), but it is also the model for the political structure of a king who is dominant over a circle of subordinate princes (Crump, 1992, pp. 70, 71).

Many examples of the ethnoscientific perspective involve the comparison of systems for classification. For example, plants and animals have been traditionally classified by the Cree and Ojibwa people based on their function and use. In the formal Western scientific system, however, they are classified according to their structure. Both systems are valid and both involve an underlying cognitive process of classification. Powell and Frankenstein (1997, p. 197) retell an interesting account of a cross-cultural classification study conducted by Western experimenters with non-Western individuals from a rural, agrarian society. The researchers had 20 objects that, from their Eurocentric perspective, they expected to be sorted into four "logical" categories: food, clothing, tools, and cooking utensils. However, the people in the study based their sorting on the practical connections between pairs of objects. For example, they paired the knife with the orange because the knife cuts the orange. As they sorted, they occasionally commented that such was the way that a wise person would group the objects. Puzzled by the approach, a researcher finally asked how a *fool* would group the objects. This time individuals in the study produced the four categories that the Western researcher had considered to be the "correct" solution!

There are many examples of how our understanding of the scope of science and math development has been biased by the traditional curricular focus on Western mathematicians and scientists who recorded and published their findings. When we open math and science to a broader definition of knowledge, we find fascinating perspectives on the development of knowledge throughout the world. For example, Mendel did controlled studies and recorded his work with plant genetics. In the larger context, however, humans had been doing genetic research for thousands of years. For example, the ancestor of today's corn plants was a stubby little grass that had evolved naturally. Through generations of selection of seeds with desired traits, North and South American Indians developed much larger and more useful domestic varieties for human consumption. In 1721, Cotton Mather learned from Onesimus, an African-American slave, of the Banyoro tribe's method of inoculating against smallpox. He reported this method to Boylston, who later received honors in the Western scientific community for the "discovery" of the smallpox vaccine. The traditional knowledge on which he had built his discovery was ignored. Westerners learned of the treatment for malaria, quinine, from American Indians in Peru. For generations, many Hispanic parents have known of the use of *manzanilla* tea for children's fever, aches, and pains. *Manzanilla* contains acetylsalicylic acid, which we more commonly know as aspirin (Barba, 1995, p. 57). Ethnoscientific and ethnomathematical knowledge helps children to see that humans throughout the world and throughout history have been observing and making conclusions about the natural world. Science and math are not just the domain of people in lab coats who conduct formal experiments and publish their results.

Ethnoscience and ethnomathematics also provide rich opportunities for an interdisciplinary approach to math and science. For example, while doing a scientific study of the various structures and functions of spider webs, children can also learn about ways in which American Indians have traditionally used spider webs as protection against bad medicine. Archeology is particularly representative of the integration of culture with mathematics and science. Students learn "how people, separate from themselves in time, technology, and worldview, shaped and were shaped by the environment" (Tirrell, 1981, p. 1). At the same time they may learn about such things as measurement, coordinates, statistics, radioactivity, and the effect of climate on plant communities. For example, study of the solar equinoxes and solstices can be clearly related to the astronomical observations of the Maya, Inca, and Anasazi. The fact that their astronomical achievements now serve as a basis for a newly created field called archeostronomy serves as evidence of the significance of their accomplishments. In such an integrated unit of study all students gain information that reinforces astronomical concepts. At the same time the content affirms the background of Hispanic-American or American Indian students who may be speculating about who their ancestors were and what they did. Teaching that applies mathematics and science concepts to cultural phenomena or that uses examples drawn from disparate cultural backgrounds to illustrate mathematics or science objectives is intellectually stimulating for both the teacher and the students.

Activation of Student and Community Resources

As valuable as ethnoscience and ethnomathematics are, they have to be implemented within the context of the local community. Cultural themes derived from the ethnoscientific or ethnomathematic perspective should be integrated in ways that are relevant and meaningful to all students, majority and minority. For example, when teachers integrate an aspect of a particular group's cultural heritage into a lesson, they cannot assume that all the children from that group will find it affirming. If a teacher presents a unit on the Mayan numerical system in such a way that it appears to be a curiosity "on behalf of" students of Mexican or Central American origin, the unit might actually engender negative attitudes. Instead, such a unit can be presented as an example of a numerical system that illustrates the concept of the use of various mathematical patterns to solve problems. Language-minority children continually assess, consciously and unconsciously, the pros and cons of affiliation with their home culture, and if they have a strong sense of the marked status of their cultural background, they might not initially want to look at Mayan gods or Hopi motifs on the margins of their mathematics worksheets. Despite the importance of corn in Mexican culture, a Mexican-American student living in Anchorage, Alaska, may have no more feeling for the development of a corn seed into a mature plant than a fourth-generation Swede living in Los Angeles has for the chemical processes involved in the preparation of *lutefisk*. (*Lutefisk* is a traditional Scandinavian dish of dried cod soaked in lye for several weeks before the final process of boiling.) With these warnings in mind, we conclude that if topics are presented in such a way that it is clear that they have a bearing on actual mathematics or science content, and if they are presented as lessons to be absorbed by all students regardless of linguistic background, they can have academically sound and culturally enlightening results. The infusion of multicultural content into the math or science curriculum, rather than being an added nuisance that "softens" the subject, can help students internalize new concepts.

We turn now to the more everyday aspects of culturally diverse children's lives that can be incorporated into math and science instruction. Because all children, regardless of cultural and environmental conditions, come to know aspects of the physical and mathematical world in their daily lives outside of the classroom, bilingual and ESL teachers who start by affirming and searching for these natural competencies are going to be better able to encourage the development of new math and science skills. Returning again to the concept of "more," a pretest that comes with a commercial math curriculum, with its culture-based format, may indicate that a child has not mastered the notion, when in fact he or she has. Basing instruction on the pretest results without delving any deeper would result in a waste of valuable instructional time and, worse, in the teacher's underestimation of the child's ability.

While young children's cognitive developmental stages may be fairly universal, the way in which they are manifested in math and science contexts may be somewhat specific to a given cultural matrix. Knowing this we are more apt to question the nature of the mathematics and science lesson formats as they relate to the experience of the child, rather than questioning exclusively the child's capability. A case in point is Secada's work with Hispanic-American bilingual first-graders. He found that these children, in both Spanish and English, actually were able to come up with correct solutions for word problems that, based on usual assessment procedures, teachers did not expect them to be able to solve. Freed to use their own invented solutions, the children showed that they had a good mathematical understanding of many of the problems they supposedly were not ready to solve (Secada, 1991).

Work on differences between street mathematics and school mathematics by Nunes, Schliemann, and Carraher (1993) confirms that people are more successful and creative in solving math problems when the problems are set in a familiar context. For example, the researchers found that unschooled street vendors in Brazil (many of them children) were able to solve math problems that were connected to everyday life experiences in the marketplace. For example, the street vendors were able to adjust the prices of goods according to how many the customer wanted to buy. However, the same vendors had difficulty solving similar problems when the problems were presented to them with school-like terminology and procedures.

Certain concepts may be almost self-evident to a child based on their application to home experiences, whereas others may require more reinforcement in school due to a lack of related exposure in the home or community. Ginsburg, in comparing two tribes in Africa, for example, found that one group promoted the development of the mathematical concepts of more and less through extensive commercial activities, whereas the other group, because of its lesser amount of commercial activity, was less likely to provide opportunities for children to practice the concept. In a formal school lesson on more and less, a child from the former ethnic group might appear to have more ability than a child from the second group, whereas in fact their innate ability levels could be the same but their experience unequal. In another study that reflects the role of cultural practices in the development of specific math abilities, the investigators found Kpelle tribesmen to be better than Yale undergraduates at estimating the number of objects in a pile (Gay & Cole, 1967). From the point of view of the Kpelle, the Yale student might be considered "culturally deprived" because of his poor estimation abilities; he would need "remedial" work in estimation if school math curricula were designed by the Kpelle.

Opportunities to apply home and community experiences to math and science instruction are innumerable. A student who has observed his or her parents slaughter goats or pigs has some important background information or questions to contribute to the classroom study of internal organs (as a part of a sixth-grade health curriculum, for example). A child who is familiar with herbal remedies has valuable information to share with the class when they are studying the properties of plants or the use of drugs in the treatment of illnesses. Beginning with the first chapter of this book, we have stressed the importance of developing an awareness of the community in which our students live and learn, and this knowledge can significantly enrich the math and science curricula and instructional processes. As such, the application of scientific or mathematical principles should not be limited to traditional cultural artifacts or to the students' culture as it existed in the country of origin. (Again, consider the culture change that a Mexican American in Anchorage, Alaska, experiences.) The study of energy can be related to the oil well just behind the student's backyard fence, or principles of physics can be applied to the antics of a low-rider car. A good example of the effective use of community knowledge in an integrated approach is that of the Innovative Approaches Research Project carried out in a Mexican-American working-class community in the Southwest. During a sixth-grade bilingual classroom's unit on construction, parents and relatives involved in local construction were invited to share their knowledge. Students learned about such things as measurement of height, perimeter, and area; the use of fractions for the mixture of mortar; the construction of arches; and calculation of time and money. Social topics naturally became integrated into the theme as they explored such things as cost versus quality and the history of local buildings (Moll, Vélez-Ibáñez, & Rivera,1990, pp. 33, 34).

A Theme-Based Approach: Science, Technology, and Society

In Chapter Three, we argued for the value of theme-based, interdisciplinary teaching approaches for language-minority children. Throughout this chapter, we have seen in a variety of examples that interdisciplinary instruction can bring science and math to life for students. In discussing content ESL we pointed out the need to integrate reading and writing development with instruction in science and mathematics. When discussing the role of culture in math and science instruction, we saw how ethnoscience, ethnomathematics, and use of local community resources can afford opportunities to reach into history, geography, folklore, careers, and many other areas.

It might be argued by some that mathematics and science should be culture free, that because they contain an enormous amount of challenging information to be mastered there is no time or use for the integration of other subjects into such objective disciplines. However, many bilingual and ESL teachers will testify to the value of integrated instruction to promote meaningful learning for language-minority students. Our minds are made to integrate separated concepts and knowledge into unified wholes. Although it is true that pinpointing and drawing out the connections among subjects may require creative approaches, the inherently interdependent infrastructure is always there. As the biologist Lewis Thomas (1975) put it, "the circuitry seems to be there, even if the current is not always on" (p. 15).

While we already have seen how different subject areas can be related to math and science, we have not yet directly considered thematic instruction, in which the focus of study is a single broad topic. In a theme-based approach, students learn math, science, language arts, and other subjects through the medium of a main topic. The example that we will use has to do with the incorporation of technology and social issues into the science curriculum. The following statement by the American Association for the Advancement of Science (1993) affirms the importance of technology as the application of science to human endeavors:

> Technology—like language, ritual, values, commerce, and the arts—is an intrinsic part of a cultural system and it both shapes and reflects the system's values. Anticipating the effects of technology is therefore as important as advancing its capabilities. (p. 55)

Science-technology-society education (STS) (Barba, 1995; Wraga & Hlebowitsh, 1991; Yager, 1990) is an approach that links science education with technological and social issues. This approach to science education naturally incorporates some of the key dimensions of multicultural education as we discussed them in Chapter Five. The dimensions that are most clearly reflected in STS are education for social justice and the use of critical pedagogy. Through STS education, children not only learn science; they learn how science, technology and society are interrelated.

The possibilities for STS themes seem endless: "acid rain, air quality, deforestation, drugs, erosion, euthanasia, food preservatives or additives, fossil fuels, genetic engineering, greenhouse effect, hazardous waste, hunger, land usage, mineral resources, nuclear power, nuclear warfare, overpopulation" and so on through the alphabet (Barba, 1995, p. 323). With these themes, students learn about scientific concepts alongside social issues. For example, in an illustration given by Barba (1995, p. 321) students do an STS unit on land usage. Using three different samples of soil from three different areas in their community, they use scientific processes to compare and contrast the qualities of the three soil samples. Based on their analysis of the samples from the three different locations, students then discuss which area of their community would probably be the best location for an imaginary new housing development. With such a theme-based approach, children develop the ability to deal knowledgeably with scientific, technological, and social issues. Through STS, they engage in reading, writing, sharing, critical thinking, and problem solving. They come to see the value and worth of science in the real world.

When combined with sound principles of first- and second-language acquisition, STS education can be of great value for language-minority children. As we think back on the topics that we have covered in this chapter—achievement status, current standards and reform, opportunity to learn standards, language use, and cultural issues—we can see that STS education is a promising avenue for critical pedagogy that provides language-minority students with more equitable opportunities to learn math and science.

The tension that often exists in all societies between tradition and technological innovation was brought home to one of the authors quite forcefully once through a play presented by a theater group of Greenlandic Eskimos. This theater group used the name *Tukak,* meaning harpoon in the Inuit language.

The *tukak,* or harpoon, was their symbol of their search for innovation at the same time that they maintained an attachment to the past. Reflecting on the harpoon metaphor, many Alaskan Eskimos today are interested in nurturing their ethnic identities through whatever benefits science and technology may bring to their circumpolar region of the world. Snowmobiles, air transportation, modern medicine, motorboats, heating systems, and use of computer technology, for example, can potentially be used to strengthen their communities rather than destroying them.

The harpoon can also serve as a metaphor for the "opportunity to learn" standards for language minorities that we discussed at the beginning of this chapter. Math and science instruction that is culturally relevant and non-Eurocentric will anchor them in their cultural identities at the same time that cognitively and linguistically sound instruction will provide them with the math and science knowledge and skills to move forward into the 21st century.

Summary

This chapter explores the current school reform movement in the teaching of mathematics and science and its application to English language learners and their diverse needs. Using the rich resources that can emerge in student contexts with linguistic and cultural diversity, the chapter demonstrates through many examples the integration of cognitively challenging mathematics and science content with the development of students' knowledge base in first and second languages and cultures. The chapter includes examples for using school and community resources (funds of knowledge), computers, calculators, and a review of current standards in mathematics and science education for the teaching of multicultural science and mathematics programs. The chapter hinges on the premise that the disciplines of mathematics and science represent "cultural capital" that should be available to *all* students, including English language learners who may be poor and from non Standard English language

Key Terms

Mathematics standards p. 236

Multiple modalities p. 250

Learning strategies p. 256

Ethnoscience p. 261

Ethnomathematics p. 261

Reflection Questions

1. The prediction that language-minority students will have fewer problems with mathematics than language arts because "math is a universal language" is not supported by either research or practice. Why is mathematics often a difficult content area for students who are acquiring English as well?
2. What is the role of the student's first language in the teaching and learning of mathematical and scientific skills? What are some of the instructional approaches that bilingual and ESL teachers can use to help English language learners acquire these skills? What are the advantages and disadvantages of some of these approaches?
3. Review the discussions about content ESL and sheltered English instruction in Chapters Two and Four. Select a topic or concept in math or science. How would you shelter your instruction to make the topic meaningful and comprehensible to English language learners?
4. Why do the authors advocate a "multiple modalities" approach in the teaching of mathematics and science to English language learners? What do they mean by the term? Why is this approach more effective than other, more traditional approaches to math and science instruction?
5. What do the authors mean by "ethnomathematics" and "ethnoscience"? How can educators infuse ethnomathematical and ethnoscientific perspectives in math and science instruction?

Resources

Math and Science Content ESL

Crandall, J. *ESL through Content Area Instruction: Mathematics, Science and Social Studies*. Englewood Cliffs, NJ: Prentice-Hall, 1987.
  • Provides a framework on the whys and hows of content ESL, and also contains a variety of examples of lessons in elementary science and mathematics.

Fathman, A. K., Quinn, M. E., & Kessler, C. *Teaching science to English learners, Grades 4–8*. Washington, DC: National Clearinghouse for Bilingual Education, 1992.
  • A good summary of techniques to use in the integration of science instruction with language development, including a model for designing science units for ELLs. To give the reader a better picture of the processes involved, the booklet includes sample lessons on heat, animals, and plants.

Hiebert, J., et al. *Making sense: Teaching and learning mathematics with understanding.* Portsmouth, NH: Heinemann, 1997.

- *Making Sense* is a guide that presents current research-based ideas on how to design classrooms that help students learn mathematics with understanding. It is based on the authors' work in four separate research programs, all of which investigated the effects of specific instructional approaches. Out of their ongoing discussion emerged a striking consensus about what features are essential and what features are optional, information they share in this book. By describing the essential classroom features that support students' mathematical understanding and by offering pictures of several classrooms that exhibit these features, the authors create a valuable framework with which elementary teachers can reflect on their own practice.

Kessler, C., Quinn, M. E., & Fathman, A. K. "Science and cooperative learning for LEP students." In C. Kessler, ed. *Cooperative language learning.* Englewood Cliffs, NJ: Prentice Hall Regents, 1992, pp. 65–83.

- *Cooperative Language Learning* fosters a rich communicative environment for the hand-in-hand development of science and language. This article contains information on how to use cooperative learning with ELLs in the science classroom.

Moses, R. P. *Radical equations: Math literacy and civil rights.* Boston: Beacon Press, 2001.

- *Radical Equations* is a thought provoking field manual based on Robert Moses's investigations and development of an approach to middle school mathematics that aims at preparing every child for high school and college mathematics. Moses argues that "the most urgent social issue affecting poor people and people of color is economic access . . . [and] economic access and full citizenship depend crucially on math and science literacy." In this sense, "The ongoing struggle for citizenship and equality for minority people is now linked to an issue of math and science literacy."

Scott, J., ed. *Science and language links: Classroom implications.* Portsmouth, NH: Heinemann, 1993.

- *Science and Language Links* explores how language supports science learning and conversely how science instruction can be used to develop language. The book provides theoretical background as well as classroom suggestions. It has one chapter devoted specifically to science instruction for second-language learners.

Short, D. J. *How to integrate language and content instruction: A training manual,* 2nd edition. Washington, DC: Center for Applied Linguistics, 1991.

- A succinct yet comprehensive treatment of the subject that goes into organizational issues as well as pedagogy. It presents an overview of basic classroom strategies and techniques for content-area instruction for ELLs, and also addresses important issues in the implementation of content-area ESL. For example, Short discusses collaboration between ESL and content specialists, scheduling of classes, administrative support, classroom organization, and student placement. She outlines several models for implementation and staff development and also lists resource centers. Some of the lesson samples are in math and science, and they all reflect the use of multiple media, the fostering of thinking skills, and student-centered organization of instruction.

Multicultural Math and Science Programs

The curricular possibilities for more equitable approaches to science and mathematics instruction through multicultural infusion are truly exciting. We refer here to several resources that provide an idea of the types of materials that teachers may want to work with as they incorporate cultural themes into math and science instruction. Bilingual and ESL teachers will also want to collaborate with math and science specialists in order to stay abreast of new materials or approaches as they develop. As valuable as teachers may find certain resources to be, they should keep in mind that effective multicultural education defies "cookbook" approaches. It has to be developed, as suggested above, within the context of the local community.

Alcoze, T. *Multiculturalism in mathematics, science and technology: Readings & activities.* Reading, MA: Addison-Wesley, 1993.

- An activity book that helps teachers infuse cultural diversity into the high school math or science curriculum. It has over 30 units, each one focusing on a scientific or mathematical principle as it is manifested within a particular cultural context. For example, there is a unit on Zuni engineering techniques that protect against soil erosion. Each unit begins with a reading, followed by critical thinking questions and one or two activities that help students better understand the scientific or mathematical principles involved.

Barba, R. H. *Science in the multicultural classroom: A guide to teaching and learning.* Boston: Allyn and Bacon, 1995.

- A comprehensive resource for teachers that addresses a very wide range of issues in achieving equity in science education. Each chapter addresses a particular aspect of multicultural science instruction and then concludes with a sample unit. An instructor's manual with transparencies and activities for actual classroom use is also available.

National Science Teachers Association. *Science for all cultures: A collection of articles from NSTA's journals.* Arlington, VA: NSTA, 1993.

- A collection of 14 informational articles for teachers from the NSTA's journals. The collection includes articles on such areas as the scientific achievements of Africans, American Indians, Arabs, and the Islamic world.

Zaslavsky, C. *The Multicultural Math Classroom.* Portsmouth, NH: Heinemann, 1996.

- Contains rich cross-cultural information on such mathematical topics as counting systems, numerals, calculating devices, games, and geometry and measurement in architecture. Each topical chapter includes ideas for discussion and activities that encourage critical thinking.

Endnotes

1. We have used the term *white* here instead of *European American* (our preferred term throughout this book), and *Hispanic* rather than *Hispanic American* because these were the terms used for the categories in the NAEP study.

2. *Sciences for All Americans* (Rutherford & Ahlgren, 1990) explores the many connections of science to our daily lives. Rutherford and Ahlgren describe what scientific literacy entails and establish why all people need to be scientifically literate. Bilingual and ESL teachers who read this book can gain a greater appreciation for the teaching of science and will be better equipped to find their own connections between science instruction and other curricular areas.

3. Piaget (1929, 1954) originated a theory of intellectual development that is based on a series of four distinct predictable stages of thought, or logicomathematical thought structures. Children progress through these stages—sensorimotor, preoperational, concrete operational, and formal operational—by a process of equilibrium, in which they reconcile discrepancies between their current forms of understanding and new physical experiences that contradict those forms of understanding.

Social Studies

From the Other Side

Oh my God. I wrote notes and to-do lists yesterday
Before we were struck.
Now nothing looks the same . . .

I've got to be still
And silent as the trees
To find the presence
To witness
The humanity
Implied in the halftone photograph
Of the man falling head first
From tower top to asphalt
Preferring this terrible dying
To the horror
Of allowing himself to be
Consumed in flames.

Merciless.

Someone's technology saved a visual record
Of one man's last living moment
And so I see
A life turned upside down
Someone frozen in free fall
Breathing the last of a gloriously beautiful day
Ripped Dear God by rage
So furiously hot
I must ask
What
Is behind this
What drove people to condemn and execute so many
So ruthlessly
Let me look into the faces of the perpetrators and let me
Listen, Dear God, let me learn
What those World Trade Towers
Mean, What the Pentagon means
From the other side.

When we stopped paying our dues at the U.N.
What did it look like from the other side?
When we refused to abide by the judgments of the World Court

What did it look like from the other side?
When we refused to be bound by the laws of the International Criminal Court
What did it look like from the other side?
When we refused to sign the Land Mine Treaty
What did it look like from the other side?
When we refused to sign the Kyoto Agreement
What did it look like from the other side?
When we walked out of the International Conference on Racism
What did it look like from the other side?
When we embargo and bomb Iraq daily—without a thought—
Without a moment's reflection on the flaming buildings,
The broken bodies, the human suffering that we're causing,
For the first time I can say I have a clue
What it feels like
From the other side.

> *—Lou Ann Merkle, Artist, Art Teacher, and SEED Seminar Leader in the Upper Dublin School District, 1994–1998 and the Crefeld School, 2001. Poem read at SEED Seminar Meeting on September 12, 2001, Plymouth, PA.*

When you hear the term *social studies,* what comes to mind? Teaching about countries and capitals, lakes and rivers? Exotic cultures and unfamiliar customs? Presidents and legislation, wars and more wars? Terrorism, conflict resolution, foreign policies, and global interdependence? How does the opening poem above speak to conflict resolution in the global village?

Boring? Incomprehensible? Maybe not to you, but it could be for your students. The field of **social studies** poses a variety of challenges for language minority children. Often the instruction they receive is incomprehensible and the assessment is inappropriate. Social studies classes tend to be heavily dependent on the extensive use of literacy skills, and both reading and writing assignments frequently involve genre and sentence structures that are unfamiliar to English language learners (ELLs). In addition, social studies involves a heavy load of new vocabulary, much of it fairly abstract. To compound these challenges, many traditional social studies classes offer limited use of realia and other nontextbook materials. Also, social studies curricula often assume a base of prior knowledge that language-minority students may not have because of their sociocultural background or varied educational history (Short, 1994a). Finally, social studies instruction may, to varying degrees, be culturally biased. Certainly many ingredients combine to make the subject potentially boring and incomprehensible.

Yet social studies certainly doesn't have to be boring. When taught in a manner appropriate to language-minority students, it provides a fascinating context for children to develop their own sociocultural identity, to reach out and learn about the world and their place in it, and to begin to exercise their role as citizens in a democracy and as citizens of the world. At the same time, social studies provides a rich linguistic environment in which

Guidelines for Teaching

SOCIAL STUDIES IN ACTION

Social studies doesn't have to be boring! Consider the following examples of social studies in action in a variety of multilingual schools, elementary through high school, across the United States:

"*¿Dónde agarraron los ladrillos?*" ("Where did they get the bricks?") an inquisitive sixth-grader asks a classmate during a social studies presentation in a bilingual classroom. The class has been working on a long-term simulation project in which they first develop a community from a group of people lost on an island, and then they write a history of the community's changes over time. The child who is asked about the bricks is a recent immigrant who is barely literate in his L_1 and has very little English. However, he is clearly an active member of this learning community as he explains the presence of bricks for home construction (Heras, 1993, p. 292).

At an elementary magnet school in New Jersey that has about 40 ELLs from 25 different countries, fourth-graders are studying about their state as part of the district's social studies curriculum. Included within their studies is an exploration of the numerous ways in which New Jersey is linked to other parts of the world. This is just part of the entire school's commitment to global education across subject areas (Gidich, 1990).

In an urban middle school, students in a Spanish-English bilingual social studies class work in cooperative groups on dioramas that depict different points of view of Columbus' encounter with the "new" world. Students use both Spanish and English to convey their ideas to each other, and they use English and Spanish texts as references. Thus they are actively employing all of their linguistic resources for problem solving and higher-order thinking as they make decisions about how to portray their perspectives (Hornberger & Micheau, 1993).

In a middle school sheltered social studies class, ELLs are involved in a global, theme-based unit on conflicts in cultures. The unit incorporates writing in a variety of genres, including poetry. Two students reflect their understanding of Inca social classes in the following diamante poems:

Priests
respected, faithfull
praying, sacrificing, advising
loyally, religiously; poorly, faithfully
tilling, growing, working stealing: common, poor
Farmers

by Mindy

Farmers
humble, poor
enjoying; growing; hardworking
faithfully: noisely: selfishly: powerfully
stealing: imposing: counting
royal: amazed
Emperor

by Sofia
(Short, 1997)

Southeast Asian high school students develop their L_1 proficiency, their English proficiency and their knowledge of history and culture as they produce a magazine to share with the larger community. They record interviews of immigrant community members in their L_1, transcribe the interviews in L_1, and then work with a peer tutor to translate the transcriptions into English. Articles in the magazine include "Across the Ocean: Pen Ouk's Sad Journey," "Hmong Marriage Rites," and "Farming in Laos" (Anderson, 1990).

Two Dade County, Florida, high schools with very diverse populations have implemented schoolwide global education programs. For example, at one of the schools, located in the heart of Miami's "Little Havana," global education cuts across the entire curriculum. The foreign language, social studies, and language arts departments draw on many topics and materials from the Caribbean and Central American countries represented by the student body. In economics classes students may learn about interdependence in trade and communication; in history classes they may compare 19th-century immigration with contemporary immigration patterns; and in home economics

continued

Guidelines for Teaching, continued

they may learn about cultural differences in courtship patterns or child-rearing practices. Students at the second high school also develop global literacy across all of the subject areas. Through their studies they become conscious of multiple ways of living; develop an awareness of the general state-of-the-planet; link current events with historical patterns; develop an awareness of cross-cultural commonalities and differences; understand the global interdependence of cultural, ecological, economic, political, and technological systems; and act locally through a variety of community service projects (Fuss Kirkwood, 1990a, 1990b).

High school students in a predominantly Puerto Rican–American community watch a student-made oral history video about a Puerto Rican who is recalling his experiences during the time of World War II. The students are amazed about the knowledge that this man with little formal education has about the war, sparking their interest in an event that otherwise might seem very distant to them (Olmedo, 1993).

students constantly develop the listening, speaking, reading, and writing skills that contribute to their academic language proficiency and that will provide a sound basis for lifelong learning and active participation in society.

The students in the vignettes above have had opportunities to become engaged in social studies in ways that will have a positive impact on their lives and on their abilities to function as knowledgeable citizens in a complex, interdependent world. Throughout the chapter, we will be referring back to each of these vignettes as they illustrate particular aspects of social studies instruction for language minority students. As the above vignettes reflect, we advocate a language-sensitive, active approach to social studies that is developed from a multicultural, global perspective. In presenting such an approach, we explore four areas: (1) a defining framework for social studies in multilingual contexts, (2) bilingual and ESL classroom settings for social studies, (3) instructional methods, and (4) models of theme-based social studies units for language minority students.

Multiple Perspectives: A Framework for Social Studies

To address social studies issues for language minority students, we first need to establish a framework for the subject area. The issues that social studies educators are debating at the general level have a direct impact on the quality of social studies instruction for language-minority children. To establish this framework, we will take a walk around social studies, so to speak, looking at the field from four different perspectives. We will consider first the National Council for the Social Studies' definition of social studies, accompanying ideals for powerful teaching, and the ten thematically based curriculum standards. Then we will look at social studies from the point of view of the major types of approaches that have actually been used to teach social studies during this century. Our last two perspectives will be from the point of view of multicultural education and global education.

A Social Studies Definition, Guidelines for Powerful Teaching, and Thematically Based Curriculum Standards

We are all very familiar with social studies classes from our own school experience as children and from our professional experience as educators. But because social studies is so much a part of our lives, we sometimes take it for granted. Exactly what is social studies? The answer depends on who you ask, but we have chosen to base our discussion on the 1993 definition of the National Council for the Social Studies (NCSS):

> Social studies is the integrated study of the social sciences and humanities to promote civic competence. Within the school program, social studies provides coordinated, systematic study drawing upon such disciplines as anthropology, archeology, economics, geography, history, law, philosophy, political science, psychology, religion, and sociology, as well as appropriate content from the humanities, mathematics, and the natural sciences. The primary purpose of the social studies is to help young people develop the ability to make informed and reasoned decisions for the public good as citizens of a culturally diverse, democratic society in an interdependent world. (National Council for the Social Studies, 1993, p. 213)

To bring life to this definition in the classroom, the National Council for the Social Studies (1993) focused its accompanying position statement around the theme of "powerful" social studies teaching and learning. The authors of the position statement define powerful social studies as being "meaningful, integrative, value-based, challenging and active" (p. 214). Paraphrasing from the position statement, we will look at each of these features, briefly pointing out the implications for social studies instruction for language minority students. (See Guidelines for Teaching, p. 284.)

Many readers will agree that these five features are highly desirable ones to attain, but the task force itself acknowledges that it is talking about an ideal situation. In reality, many current school structures do not allow enough classroom time, preparation time, appropriate material, and enough flexibility in schedules and curricula for full attainment of the ideal.

Moreover, NCSS has also developed a set of social studies curriculum standards for the K–12 curriculum to assist teachers and students in addressing pressing issues in our pluralistic and democratic society. Interdisciplinary in nature, the standards suggest a holistic framework for state and local social studies curriculum practices.

Notwithstanding the obstacles associated with the attainment of the ideals represented in the above standards (see earlier discussion in the chapter), we believe that bilingual and ESL educators do have the necessary skills and perspectives to implement the above ideals and curriculum standards in creative ways. The terms *meaningful, integrated, value-laden, challenging,*

Guidelines for Teaching

SOCIAL STUDIES INSTRUCTION

- *Meaningful.* Students learn to see networks of interconnecting themes, and they can use this understanding both inside and outside of the classroom, establishing relationships with their own experiences. Thus, meaningful instruction gives language-minority students the opportunity to bring their own culturally diverse resources to the social studies classroom. Through real-life activities, students begin to see the big ideas that are embedded in the specific topics they are exploring. For example, two of the big ideas underlying a study of the westward movement of European Americans in North America are human migration and conflict over territory. These are obviously themes that can be applied universally to the real-life experiences of language minority children.

  In meaningful instruction, the emphasis is on depth of development of important ideas rather than superficial coverage of many disparate bits of knowledge. This is another aspect of meaningful instruction that is important for language-minority students. Often, immigrants are playing "catch up" with majority students; they have to absorb previous years' knowledge that native students have already covered, plus new grade-level concepts. Instruction that focuses on the big ideas rather than numerous facts enables such students to quickly develop schema for broad social studies concepts.

- *Integrative.* Tied in with the focus on big ideas, powerful social studies integrates across the curriculum and includes effective use of new technology. It also integrates values and possibilities for social action with knowledge acquisition. For ELLs, one of the most important ways in which social studies benefits from integration is through the incorporation of language develop-

ment (listening, speaking, reading, and writing) into the social studies curriculum.

- *Value-based.* In a powerful social studies class, teachers and students consider controversial issues. There are opportunities to think critically and to learn to deal with ethical issues, social values, and policy implications. Students learn to respect multiple points of view, be sensitive to cultural diversity, and accept social responsibility. Such value-based social studies instruction provides language-minority students with a supportive forum in which their distinctive voices can be heard and in which they can develop their sociocultural identity. The extensive verbal classroom interaction in value-based settings also encourages language development for language-minority students.

- *Challenging.* Teachers have high expectations for students to be serious and thoughtful participants in individual and group efforts. Teachers model critical and creative thinking and establish an environment in which dialogue and debate can be conducted with civility. For language-minority students, a challenging environment assures them that regardless of their level of proficiency in English, they can receive an age-appropriate curriculum rather than a watered-down curriculum.

- *Active.* Classrooms focus on a broad range of authentic activities that reflect the ways social events happen in the real world. For example, students develop models or plans, act out historical events, perform mock trials, conduct interviews, collect data, or become involved in community service or social action. Active social studies learning provides ELLs with the types of hands-on and experiential activities that help to make instruction linguistically comprehensible and personally meaningful.

and *active* have a familiar ring in the ears of bilingual and ESL educators, as these terms parallel many of the principles of effective second-language instruction. We believe that bilingual and ESL teachers can have a valuable role to play in helping their schools to approach the ideals of the NCSS position statement on powerful social studies teaching and learning.

Transmission, Social Science, and Critical Thinking Approaches

Turning from the idealism of the NCSS's five features of powerful social studies instruction to the reality of social studies in the classroom, Barr, Barth, & Shermis (1977) identified three distinct social studies traditions that have been used in American classrooms during the 20th century: social studies taught as citizenship transmission, social studies taught as social science, and social studies taught as critical (or reflective) thinking. These three traditions can still be seen in use today (Thornton, 1994). They are all reflected in the NCSS definition of social studies, and in reality the three approaches overlap and are often mixed in the classroom. One of the approaches may be used at one moment, while a different approach may be underlying another activity. The three approaches are useful to keep in mind, however, as guideposts that will help us understand what we are accomplishing with social studies in our bilingual and ESL classrooms, and we will be seeing them again later in the chapter.

In the tradition of social studies as citizenship transmission, nurturing a good citizen tends to mean transmitting predetermined knowledge and values. Teachers transmit content through fairly structured procedures such as use of textbooks and lecturing, and there is a pattern of vertical pedagogical authority. In practice in the United States, the general theme of a transmission curriculum tends to be the rise of democracy, with a belief in "fairly continuous progress" and a focus on the most powerful political and economic systems. This approach has been criticized as being Eurocentric by educators who favor more diverse perspectives (Thornton, 1994, p. 238).

Proponents of the approach of teaching social studies as social science suggest that effective citizenship comes about through an understanding of the various fields of social science—history, geography, political science, economics, sociology, anthropology, and psychology, for example. In this approach, educators teach a simplified version of the concepts and processes that scholars use in academic social science disciplines. The social science approach is more commonly found in secondary schools, where specific social science courses are taught, but it can also be found at the elementary level in certain types of activities. In the social science approach, students may learn to observe and analyze events and issues in ways similar to those that practicing social scientists would use. For example, they may do historical research, engage in a simulated archaeology dig, or make ethnographic observations from photographs of unidentified cultural settings. However, when it is taught with traditional textbook and recitation methods, the social science approach often is similar in teaching style to the transmission approach (Thornton, 1994, p. 228).

Unlike social studies taught as citizenship transmission and social studies taught as social science, social studies taught as critical thinking bases citizenship preparation on the reasoning powers of the individual rather than on a particular set of values transmitted from the top down or a body of social science knowledge per se. This approach stresses reasoning skills as students

Guidelines for Teaching

NINE THEMATIC STRANDS IN SOCIAL STUDIES

- *Culture.* The study of culture is concerned with preparing the students to answer questions such as: What are the common characteristics of different cultures? How do belief systems, such as religion, or political ideals, influence other parts of the culture? How does the culture change to accommodate different ideas and beliefs? What does language tell us about culture? This theme typically appears in units and courses dealing with geography, history, sociology, and anthropology.

- *Time, continuity, and change.* Human beings seek to understand their historical roots and to locate themselves in time. This would allow us to develop a historical perspective and to answer questions such as: Who am I? What happened in the past? How am I connected to those in the past? How has the world changed and how might it change in the future? This theme typically appears in courses in history.

- *Peoples, places, and environments.* The study of people, places, and human-environment interactions assists students as they create their spatial views and geographic perspectives of the world beyond their personal location. Students need the knowledge, skills, and understanding to answer questions such as: Where are things located? Why are they located where they are? This theme typically appears in units and courses dealing with geography.

- *Individual development and identity.* Personal identity is shaped by one's own culture, by groups, and by institutional influences. Students would consider questions such as: How do people learn? Why do people behave as they do? What influences how people learn, perceive, and grow? How do people meet their basic needs in a variety of contexts? How do individuals develop from youth to adulthood? This theme typically appears in units and courses dealing with psychology and anthropology.

- *Power, authority, and governance.* Understanding the historical development of structures of power, authority, and governance and their evolving functions in contemporary U.S. society and other parts of the world is essential for developing civic competence. In exploring this theme, students confront questions such as: What is power? What forms does it take? Who holds it? How is it gained, used, and justified? What is legitimate authority? How are governments created, structured, maintained, and changed? How can individual's rights be protected within the context of majority rule? This theme typically appears in units and courses dealing with government, politics, political science, history, law, and other social sciences.

- *Production, distribution, and consumption.* Because people have wants that often exceed the resources available to them, a variety of ways have evolved to answer such questions as: What is to be produced? How is production to be organized? How are goods and services to be distributed? What is the most effective allocation of the factors of production (land, labor, capital and management)? This theme typically appears in units and courses dealing with economics concepts and issues.

- *Science, technology, and society.* Modern life as we know it would be impossible without technology and the science that supports it. Technology, however, brings with it many questions: Is new technology always better than old? What can we learn from the past about how new technologies result in broader social change, some of which is unanticipated? How can we cope with the ever-increasing pace of change? How can we manage technology so that the greatest number of people benefit from it? How can we preserve our fundamental values and beliefs in the midst of technological change? This theme draws upon the natural and physical sciences, social sciences, and the humanities, and appears in a variety of social studies courses, including history, geography, economics, civics, and government.

continued

Guidelines for Teaching, continued

- *Global connections*. The realities of global interdependence require understanding the increasingly important and diverse global connections among world societies and the frequent tension between national interests and global priorities. Students will need to be able to address international issues such as health care, the environment, human rights, economic competition and interdependence, age-old ethnic enmities, and political and military alliances. This theme typically appears in units or courses dealing with geography, culture, and economics, but may also draw on the natural sciences and the humanities.

- *Civic ideals and practices*. An understanding of civic ideals and practices of citizenship is critical to full participation in society and is a central purpose of the social studies. Students confront such questions as: What is civic participation and how can I be involved? How has the meaning of citizenship evolved? What is the balance between rights and responsibilities? What is the role of the citizen in the community and the nation, and as a member of the world community? How can I make a positive difference? This theme typically appears in units or courses dealing with history, political science, cultural anthropology, and fields such as global studies, law-related education, and the humanities. (Parker & Jarolimek, 1997)

interact with their teachers and with each other. Social studies educators have also called this approach a transformative approach, as opposed to the more passive transmission approach. This critical thinking/transformative approach resists using prepackaged materials. It can encompass many different kinds of classroom experiences and is therefore somewhat difficult to define. However, its general characteristics are "(a) connecting students' experiences and the curriculum; (b) providing at least some opportunity for students to construct meanings for themselves; (c) allowing for the possibility, even the likelihood, that different students will take away different understandings from a lesson; and (d) questioning students' taken-for-granted views of the world" (Thornton, 1994, p. 233). One of the common criticisms of this approach is that it may sacrifice good coverage of content, leaving children with harmful gaps in their knowledge. Hirsch (1987), for example, feels that children given a social studies diet rich in the critical thinking approach could be at a disadvantage in society because of not knowing "what every American needs to know."

Despite concerns about content coverage, we believe that bilingual and ESL teachers, as part of their commitment to powerful social studies teaching and learning, can take a leadership role in bringing more critical thinking approaches into the social studies classroom. Social studies as critical thinking fits the linguistic and cultural needs of language-minority students very well. Looking back at the four characteristics of the approach listed in the previous paragraph, we can see that these characteristics clearly imply the establishment of a language-rich environment and that they also capitalize on the diverse sociocultural experiences of language-minority students. In the process of living in a variety of geographical, social, cultural, educational, and linguistic environments, language-minority students already have had direct experience with multiple perspectives, and they have also had experience with making sense out of new environments. A social studies approach that makes clear connections with students' experiences enables them to share and to learn from others, and it allows them to use their own knowledge about how individuals and groups face and solve social problems.

Despite the fact that the critical thinking/transformative approach tends to be emphasized in teacher preparation programs, the textbook-and-recitation transmission model is still the most widely used approach today (Thornton, 1994, p. 229). Therefore, bilingual and ESL educators who choose to become advocates of a more transformative approach will need to work actively to provide optimal social studies learning environments for the language-minority students in their schools. They may also have a positive influence on the overall quality of social studies instruction in their school as they collaborate with other teachers in the establishment of social studies programs that meet the needs of language-minority students in a variety of classroom settings.

Multicultural Education

We now turn the corner and take a look at social studies from the perspective of **multicultural education.** Notwithstanding some observers' pessimism over the chances for reform in social studies, multicultural education is certainly one area in which some change has been achieved over the past several decades.

The damage that a monocultural perspective has had on generations of minority Americans is captured in the observation of the writer Adrienne Rich (1986): When you study about "our" society and you are not in the picture, it produces "a moment of psychic disequilibrium, as if you looked into a mirror and saw nothing" (p. 199). Not as psychologically damaging, but just as deceiving is for European-American children to look into the mirror of society and see only the reflection of themselves. The historian Ronald Takaki (1993, p.2) points out that based on current demographic trends, by 2056 the majority of Americans will trace their descent from some group other than white Europeans. In addition, the proportion of Americans who are of mixed racial heritage will be much larger than it is today. The overall effect will be a change in the idea of what it means to be American. Through multicultural education, ESL and bilingual educators have the opportunity to be leaders in the movement to prepare children of all language, ethnic, and racial backgrounds for this reality. They can do this, for example, by providing opportunities for language minority students to serve as cross-cultural informants for all the students in the school as they all learn to view issues from multiple perspectives. Also, as bilingual and ESL teachers collaborate with other teachers, they may bring their multicultural experience to bear on course content and instructional strategies.

Multicultural education influences subject areas, pedagogy, and school structure, but its home base is in the social studies. However, because multicultural education has often been promoted as something new and innovative, it is easy to overlook its natural home as part of social studies, a subject that teachers have been teaching for years. What multicultural education really amounts to is an alternative, less ethnocentric lens with which to focus on an old subject: people and how they interact with one another and with nature. Multicultural education is a crucial focal point for bilingual and ESL educators as we implement social studies instruction that makes extensive use of the critical thinking approach, and that is meaningful, integrated, value-laden, challenging, and active.

We cannot begin to adequately cover the many dimensions of multicultural education within the limits of this book, but Chapter Five provides a basis for understanding how a multicultural perspective affects the instructional process throughout the entire school day. Here we will focus only on how the multicultural perspective affects knowledge construction within the specific context of social studies instruction, and on how multicultural education is aligned with the critical thinking/transformative approach to social studies.

Banks and Banks (1997, pp. 21, 22) describe the processes through which teachers can help students see that cultural perspectives influence how knowledge is constructed, and therefore, how it is presented in books. For example, United States history textbooks have traditionally referred to the European "discovery of America" and "the New World." If we are aware of the cultural influences on knowledge construction, then we notice that the terms *discovery* and *New World* tell us that the story is being told from the point of view of the Europeans. The terms also say something about the general attitudes of the Europeans toward the people who had been living here for tens of thousands of years before they arrived. For the people who already lived here, America was neither discovered, nor was it a new world. Another example is the teaching of the westward movement of European–American settlers in the United States. How would this be described by the Lakota Sioux? Perhaps as the invasion from the east?

Through a multicultural approach to social studies, students learn how point of view affects how knowledge is constructed. Consequently, they develop the ability to see multiple perspectives. The middle school students in our introductory vignette who were making dioramas of different points of view of Columbus's arrival in the "new" world were learning to see social studies knowledge from multiple perspectives. *Thinking and Rethinking U.S. History* (Horne, 1988) is an example of a resource for both teachers and students who want to develop an awareness of multiple perspectives. The publication addresses six major social justice issues and their treatment in U.S. history textbooks up through Reconstruction: racism and people of color, colonialism, sexism, militarism, classism, and social change movements. One of the activities for both teachers and students is to take sample sentences from popular textbooks and write them from a different point of view. For example, "To live in the South was to live in daily fear of slave violence" (p. 343), when rewritten from an African-American perspective, might become "To live in the South was to live in daily hope of successful revolts of African-American people" (p. 344).

Banks and Banks (1997) note the need for continuing development of multiple perspectives in their statement that commercially available multicultural content today is "usually presented from mainstream perspective" (p. 232). For example, Sacajawea, who did not challenge European-American expansion, is likely to get more coverage in textbooks than Geronimo, who did challenge the invasion of his people's lands. Another example is the way in which material on non-European Americans is often fragmented and presented in special sections, rather than being integrated into the main text as a meaningful part of the real story. This add-on approach distorts reality, a reality in which the true story of American history is a story of "multiple acculturation." This **multiple acculturation** is a process through which "the common U.S. culture and society emerged from a complex synthesis and interaction of the diverse cultural elements that originated within the various cultural, racial, ethnic, and religious groups that make up U.S. society" (Banks & Banks, 1997, p. 239). The fact is that majority U.S. sociocultural patterns are not purely composed of Anglo-Saxon Protestant elements; they are imbued with numerous elements from other cultural groups. *A Different Mirror* (Takaki, 1993) is a useful reference for teachers who want to improve their own knowledge of the multiple acculturation of the United States. This book tells the story of U.S. history from the multiple perspectives of Native Americans and people coming from England, Africa, Ireland, Mexico, Asia, and Russia.

Another important aspect of multicultural education that relates very directly to social studies instruction is its alignment with the critical thinking/transformative approach. The critical thinking emphasis on multiple perspectives, connections with students' lives, and reasoned decision making provides a framework in which multicultural education can come to life and be much more than the passive transmission of information about minorities. Building from the transformative approach, Banks & Banks describe, for example, a framework for multicultural learning through social action. Using this framework, a social studies unit might start with a problem to be addressed through a decision-making process. Students would then conduct research to acquire relevant data. Then, through activities such as case studies or role-playing, students would explore the attitudes, beliefs, and feelings associated with the problem. Finally, students would make their own decisions about the issue and take a course of action after considering a variety of options and their consequences (Banks & Banks, 1997, p. 242). Looking at multicultural education from this perspective, it becomes an integral aspect of any social studies program that aspires to promote effective citizenship and bring the nation closer to its democratic ideals.

Global Education

We complete our walk around social studies with a view from the perspective of **global education.** We have already gotten a glimpse into the nature of global education in the introductory vignettes to this chapter. We described the fourth-graders who, as part of their study of their home state, were exploring the numerous ways in which New Jersey was connected to many other parts of the world. We also introduced the two southern Florida high schools where a global perspective pervaded the entire curriculum, as students learned about the interdependence of global systems and the relationship of local and global issues across a variety of subject areas.

As defined by the Center for Human Interdependence, global education involves learning about those problems and issues that cut across national boundaries, and about the interconnectedness of systems—ecological, cultural, economic, political, and technological. Global education involves perspective taking—seeing things through the eyes and minds of others—and it means the realization that while individuals and groups may view life differently, they also have common needs and wants. (Tye, 1990a, p. 163)

Global education is fertile ground for the use of the five NCSS features of powerful social studies. It can also constitute a broad platform for both the social sciences approach and the critical thinking approach to social studies. It is also, of course, a very close partner to multicultural education. However, it is also the most controversial of the topics in this discussion of a social studies framework for bilingual and ESL educators. As Tye (1990a) explains it, global education "is a value-oriented movement in that it is part of a larger societal change that involves a new view of how the United States (or any nation) relates to the rest of the world" (p. 162). Proponents of global education tend to be advocates of cooperation instead of competition, interdependence instead of domination, and a human-centric rather than a state-centric social studies curriculum.

Some educators and others have criticized global education for, among other things, challenging the assumption that the American system is always the best and that therefore Americans have a mission to bring their own values to the rest of the world. Global educators openly acknowledge the human-centric values that underlie their endeavors, but they stress the importance of substance over "value-laden mush" in the implementation of global education programs. *Substance* means that a global education program should help learners collect and use verifiable information about the state of the planet, use analytical and evaluative skills, and participate in open dialogues and debates. A global educator is aware of his or her own value orientation, but does not promote a "specific policy agenda nor unfairly discourage students from conducting critical analysis" (Lamy, 1990, pp. 52–55).

Teachers in a global education program use substantive knowledge about world geography, history, and current events to help students build their own awareness and develop their own conclusions. Consequently, a global educator needs to have the following traits: "open-mindedness, anticipation of complexity, resistance to stereotyping, inclination to empathize, and non-chauvinism." In addition, a global educator also needs a "consciousness of one's own perspective" (Wilson, 1994, p. 55). Looking at this list, we see that effective bilingual and ESL teachers will already have many of the characteristics needed, and we encourage interested teachers to take advantage of opportunities to learn more about global education and to advocate for schoolwide global perspectives. Global education is one more avenue through which bilingual and ESL teachers can also capitalize on the rich sociocultural resources that language-minority students and their communities bring to the school setting. *Global Education: From Thought to Action* (Tye, 1990a) and *Global Education: School-Based Strategies* (Tye, 1990b) are both good resources for beginning to learn more about the concept of global education. The books provide numerous examples of the implementation of global education in a variety of school settings.

Having completed our tour around the multiple frameworks of social studies, we note that teachers of language minority children will face several opposing forces as they address social studies from these varying perspectives. There is the responsibility to "give students the tools that enable them to function effectively in [U.S.] society" (King, Fagan, Bratt, & Baer, 1987, p. 95), yet at the same time there is the responsibility to capitalize on students' diverse backgrounds and give them the tools to function effectively on the global stage. By helping immigrant students develop key concepts of American history—for example, the "spirit of independence," the "sense of individualism," and the Bill of Rights—bilingual and ESL teachers are helping them acculturate to U.S. society and participate from a position of strength (King et al., 1987, pp. 95, 96). By teaching from a more global perspective, teachers are helping language-minority students define their unique sociocultural identity and become knowledgeable participants in an increasingly interdependent world order. In theory these two responsibilities are complementary, but in reality they can compete for time and administrative support.

The other opposing forces are the themes of unity and diversity. Although much progress has been made in multicultural education and, to a lesser extent, in global education, there are still strong voices against the value of diversity in the social studies curriculum. As we saw in Chapter Five, and we will see again in Chapter Ten, there is a long history of debate in the United States over the alleged danger that cultural diversity can lead to social and political disintegration. However, many others argue very convincingly that it is precisely through an honest understanding of our long history of diversity that our children will be better equipped to maintain the sociopolitical unity of the nation (Ovando & McClaren, 2000; Takaki, 1993).

There are no set paths as bilingual and ESL teachers negotiate between a U.S. focus and an international focus, between a focus on unity and a focus on diversity. However, bilingual and ESL teachers who have as a framework the NCSS features of a powerful social studies program, who are able to include a strong dose of critical thinking in their repertoire of social studies approaches, and who infuse their work with a multicultural and global perspective should be able to find a balance and to provide their students with sociocultural understanding and the knowledge, skills, and values needed for effective citizenship.

Classroom Settings for Bilingual and ESL Social Studies

We take quite a jump now, from the general development of a theoretical framework for social studies for language-minority students to the specifics of classroom settings. However, these classroom settings set the stage for the next section of the chapter, "Methods for Social Studies Instruction," where we will begin to see more clearly again the importance of a guiding framework.

Differences in bilingual/ESL program models, scheduling patterns, grade levels, language proficiency levels, and heterogeneity of students will all influence the structural setting for social studies for language-minority students. It is difficult to generalize about program structures. As we know from Chapter Two, there are probably about as many bilingual and ESL program designs as there are bilingual and ESL programs. It follows, then, that there are numerous configurations for incorporating social studies into the curriculum. Therefore, as we look first at elementary settings and then at middle school and high school settings, it is important to keep in mind that we will not be covering all of the possible designs for social studies instruction.

Elementary Social Studies Classroom Settings

In some elementary settings, students may be segregated by language proficiency for social studies, with the subject being taught in the students' L_1 or as part of a second-language development curriculum. However, whether in a bilingual or ESL setting, most elementary teachers more often than not find themselves teaching social studies as part of a self-contained classroom with children of mixed language backgrounds and mixed levels of language proficiency. Bilingual and ESL teachers have the dual responsibilities of developing both language and content during social studies instruction, and in doing so they are drawing on the important principle that language can very effectively be developed through content such as social studies. A great deal of first- and second-language acquisition can occur naturally through children's strongly motivated involvement in social studies activities that are not focused solely on language. Compared to the typical secondary structure, the elementary classroom usually lends itself well to the use of interdisciplinary theme-based instruction, which can include a wide variety of activities—physical movement, visual stimuli, things to touch and make, field trips to community sites and museums, and music and art.

Given the range of literacy levels and language proficiencies in multilingual elementary classrooms, teachers need to capitalize on this diversity by creating an environment in which children can learn social concepts and skills from each other as well as from the teacher and instructional assistants. This can be done by using a variety of whole class, small group, and individual activities, with the teacher and instructional assistants working frequently as facilitators while children do research, carry out projects, prepare presentations and discuss ideas.

The traditional curriculum that language-minority children may encounter at the elementary level is the expanding environments sequence, in which children in the early grades learn about themselves and their families. Then, by third grade they study their community, and in fourth grade they learn about their state. In the final elementary grades they focus more on the nation as whole, with an emphasis on geography and history. However, as part of the process of making new social studies standards, changes are occurring. For example, Florida and California have begun statewide efforts to introduce more history at a younger age. California's elementary social studies curriculum is anchored in the chronological study of history, with an emphasis on the use of such materials as narratives and biographies to tell the *story* of history. History told as stories enables children to see cause-and-effect relationships and to see the big ideas that unite disparate historical events (Thornton, 1994, pp. 231, 32). Short (1994a) notes that these changes may in some ways be of value for language minority learners, as the context of "stories" is one that children from a variety of backgrounds can relate to. However, the chronological approach can cause problems in that children who were not in the United States in the early grades will have missed out on earlier historical periods. Or even if they were here, they may have missed out on the content because the instruction they received was not adapted to their language needs.

The ideal situation to meet language needs in the context of social studies instruction is usually a bilingual classroom environment. However, situations often arise in which ELLs are not in a bilingual setting. For example, at a school with an early-exit bilingual program, a fourth-grader may no longer be in a bilingual classroom with L_1 instruction, but he or she may not have acquired enough academic proficiency in English yet to benefit fully from social studies instruction carried out entirely in English. In such cases a teacher trained in bilingual or ESL methods may need to collaborate with teachers in nonbilingual classrooms to design a social studies environment that is as comprehensible as possible for English-language learners. Sometimes a bilingual or ESL teacher or instructional assistant may be assisting children with social studies content on a pull-out or an inclusion basis. (These terms are explained in Chapter Two.) In some districts, recent immigrants at the elementary level may attend classes for all or part of the day in a separate program for newcomers. Social studies is often a major part of the curriculum in which children learn basic concepts and vocabulary related to such topics as the family and the community, or maps and globes. Regardless of the elementary setting, basic principles of language and cognitive development apply to social studies: When the resources are available, L_1 should be used as a platform for elementary social studies instruction.

Middle School and High School Social Studies Classroom Settings

While the setting for social studies instruction may be fairly straightforward and uncomplicated at the elementary level, a look at middle school and high

Guidelines for Teaching

LANGUAGE-MINORITY STUDENTS IN MIDDLE AND HIGH SCHOOLS

Some of the possible social studies backgrounds of students coming into middle schools from elementary programs in the United States include the following:

1. *Students who were in an elementary maintenance or a two-way bilingual program.* Depending on length of time in the elementary program these students may or may not have sufficient English-language academic proficiency for regular social studies instruction in English. Either way they would benefit from opportunities to continue to develop their first-language skills through social studies instruction that incorporates L_1. Although we are focusing our discussion here on language-minority students, it is important to note that students from English-speaking homes who have been in a two-way enrichment bilingual program would also benefit from the same opportunities to continue to learn social studies in a bilingual environment.

2. *Students who were in an elementary early-exit bilingual program.* They may not yet have reached nativelike proficiency in academic English, and they may also have a weak social studies background because of their very brief exposure to L_1 content-area instruction. They are likely to be unprepared for traditional, grade-level middle school social studies classes in which instruction is not modified to meet their needs.

3. *Students who have been in an ESL as opposed to a bilingual program in the elementary school.* Again, these students will often not yet have had the 5 to 10 years needed to develop academic English skills and would therefore benefit from social studies instruction adapted to their linguistic needs. Compounding the need for adapted instruction is the fact that without significant L_1 support during the elementary years, they will very likely be behind their English-proficient peers in social studies knowledge and skills.

school social studies classes for language-minority students reveals a complex array of organizational offerings. To begin to understand the range of programs that may be offered, we first need to look at the range of language-minority students we find in secondary social studies classes. They represent quite an array of backgrounds (Faltis & Arias, 1993).

We could add further to the complexity of the range of needs by going into the issue of sociocultural differences between immigrants and indigenous language minority students who are coming into the secondary level from U.S. elementary schools. Or we could also consider the amount of time that language minority students have spent with native-English speakers versus the amount of time spent isolated from them in special ESL or bilingual classes, which could also affect their preparedness for grade-level social studies classes. Or we could also consider the broad range of literacy levels that language-minority learners bring with them to social studies classes.

We add even more diversity to the mix when we turn to immigrant students who first enter U.S. schools at the middle school or secondary level:

1. *Students who have had a solid educational background in their country of origin.* These students will have a common underlying language proficiency in L_1 that will help them in acquiring academic English, and they will have an understanding of general social studies concepts such as forms of government and geographic regions of the world. However, they will have fairly limited background knowledge about U.S. history and geography. They would benefit from L_1 instruction in social studies while they are learning English, so that they have a better chance to begin to catch up with the district's curriculum in social studies.
2. *Students who have had little or no formal schooling in their country of origin.* These students have the most specialized needs. They will ideally need intensive and integrated opportunities to develop literacy in their native language at the same time that they begin to build their social studies knowledge base in L_1 and begin to acquire English.

Classroom settings for social studies at the middle school and secondary levels depend on such factors as the number and size of language groups represented in the school, the mix of immigrant versus indigenous language minorities, the educational background of the students, the availability of trained bilingual and ESL teachers and instructional assistants, community attitudes toward the use of L_1 in the schools, and the history of past bilingual or ESL programs (Lucas, 1993). Based on the work of Faltis & Arias (1993), Hornberger & Micheau (1993), King, Fagan, Bratt, & Baer (1987), Short (1994b), and Valdez Pierce (1987), we can identify six general types of social studies classes for language-minority students (this listing does not include submersion social studies, in which the English language learner receives no special services); see page 297.

All of the above types of classes can fit into the traditional high school structure. In this familiar format social studies classes for language minority students are simply scheduled in as special courses within the structure of a daily series of 45- or 55-minute class periods. However, this often may not be the best arrangement for language minority students, especially for beginning ELLs. Lucas (1993) notes that in her study of model secondary programs for language-minority students, *none* of the exemplary programs used this traditional, highly segmented structure. Instead, language minority students might attend a school-within-a-school or an entirely separate school for a half-day or the whole day. These types of programs are often called newcomer programs or high-intensity language training (HILT) programs, and have already been mentioned in the context of elementary settings. Such programs can have either a half-day or whole-day schedule, and social studies is an integral part of the curriculum. They are often targeted especially for students who enter school in the United States with few or no literacy skills in their native

Guidelines for Teaching

GENERAL TYPES OF SOCIAL STUDIES CLASSES

1. *Grade-level social studies classes with an add-on support system for English language learners.* In these classes the grade-level teacher does not significantly alter instruction, but bilingual or ESL teachers or instructional assistants come into the class to assist or tutor English language learners.

2. *Content ESL classes.* Specially designed for English-language learners, the primary purpose of such classes is to develop English language proficiency, but teachers use social studies content as a medium for instruction. A content ESL class may be devoted entirely to social studies, or it may also include science, math, or health as part of the curriculum. Such classes provide a meaningful context for language acquisition and simultaneously help to prepare students for grade-level instruction in social studies by building vocabulary, concepts, and learning strategies. Content ESL classes are generally taught by an ESL teacher who does not necessarily have specialized training in social studies education. The classes may be taught with input or collaboration from social studies teachers. In some cases the content ESL class is directly paired with a grade-level social studies class. ELLs attend the grade-level social studies class, but then they also attend a content ESL class in which the ESL teacher uses the vocabulary and concepts currently being studied in the grade-level class. This pairing of classes is referred to as the adjunct model.

3. *Sheltered social studies classes.* In content ESL the primary purpose is English-language development, but in sheltered classes the primary purpose is to provide social studies content similar to that of a grade-level classroom. However, the instructional approach in sheltered social studies classes is tailored to the linguistic needs of English-language learners. Sheltered social studies classes use specially adapted social studies materials and methods to make instruction comprehensible. The primary training of sheltered instruction teachers is generally social studies, but ideally they also have had training in ESL techniques. These classes may also be taught in collaboration with an ESL specialist.

4. *Language-sensitive mixed social studies classes.* In this setting, English-language learners are in heterogeneous classes with students who are proficient in English. Teachers in these classes have been trained to modify their language use and instructional style so that English-language learners may participate as fully as possible. Ideally, ESL teachers and social studies teachers work closely together to plan and carry out instruction in such mixed classes.

5. *Social studies classes taught primarily or entirely in a language other than English.* These classes might be part of a maintenance or a two-way bilingual program that carries over from the elementary level. They might also be offered for non-English-speaking newcomers at the secondary level as part of an effort to prepare them for high school graduation. For example, U.S. history is a standard requirement for high school graduation. Recent immigrants who are literate in their L_1 can take this class in L_1 and thus be able to successfully master the content of the course. This social studies knowledge base then transfers to English as English proficiency develops.

6. *Bilingual social studies classes that combine L_1 instruction with sheltered social studies instruction in English.* Teachers in these classes use a mixture of both English and the students' native languages depending on the context. For example, a concept might be introduced in the native language and then follow-up activities would be conducted in English.

language. In these supportive settings, students learn basic literacy in L_1 and survival skills and begin to develop English-language skills with intensive academic content in L_1. Social studies is often one of the main contexts for L_1 learning, as it dovetails with school and community survival skills and helps students begin to make sense out of their new social and geographic environment.

Beyond the school-within-a-school approach, there are the highly promising cases in which the entire middle school or secondary school has been restructured in ways that will benefit the quality of social studies instruction. Because middle schools are transitional institutions between elementary and high school instruction, they tend to exhibit more innovativeness than high schools in the design of social studies programs that can come closer to the NCSS ideals. Such instances of school reform offer highly creative opportunities for teaching social studies within a flexible, interdisciplinary framework. With this flexibility, for example, language arts and social studies instruction may be integrated into one block of time. Berman, Minicucci, McLaughlin, Nelson, and Woodworth (1996) describe an exemplary California middle school with a high proportion of language minority students in which such powerful social studies learning is occurring. To establish a greater sense of community in smaller groups, the school is divided into houses. The year-long theme for one of the houses in the 1993–1994 school year was "I Have a Dream," based on Martin Luther King's speech. As part of the theme, ELLs in sheltered core classes—classes that combined language arts and social studies— interviewed immigrants in their community and wrote essays in which they reflected on their interviewees' dreams for their new lives in the United States.

While in theory there are many promising practices for middle school and secondary social studies education in linguistically diverse contexts, in reality there are still many, many English-language learners who are not receiving the quality of social studies instruction that they need. Looking at secondary education in general, Faltis and Arias (1993) note, for example, that limited course offerings for ELLs in social studies and other key subjects often make it difficult for them to complete graduation requirements. Minicucci and Olsen (1992) found in their survey of 27 California secondary schools that almost half had few or no content-area courses designed to meet the needs of ELLs. Lucas concluded in her survey of secondary education for language minorities that overall the assessment was "gloomy." Many schools lacked bilingual and ESL-trained personnel, they did not have appropriate materials, they did not have a cohesive program, and consequently for most of the school day ELLs struggled to understand academic instruction, with few opportunities for "cognitively sophisticated thought and communication" (Lucas, 1993, p. 114). The needs are great not only for beginning and intermediate ELLs, but also for language-minority students who have been exited from bilingual or ESL programs. Many of these students are still not entirely prepared for instruction that does not take into account their continuing needs for the development of academic language proficiency in social studies contexts. We can conclude that without greater attention to this problem, we will be failing to provide a growing number of middle school and secondary language-minority students with the social studies knowledge and appreciation that they need to be active, responsible citizens.

Methods for Social Studies Instruction

We have just ended our discussion of classroom settings on a rather pessimistic note. However, turning to the question of how do you carry out day-to-day instruction in the social studies classroom, we can find cause for optimism. There are many exciting strategies that, in a supportive setting, can produce social studies teaching that is powerful, uses critical thinking, and is infused with a multicultural and global perspective. To guide our exploration of the possibilities, we will first consider the particular instructional challenges of social studies for language minority learners.

Challenges of Social Studies Instruction

Synthesizing from the work of Chamot and O'Malley (1994), King, Fagan, Bratt, and Baer (1987), and Short (1993, 1994a, 1994b) a number of factors can be identified that make social studies more context-reduced, cognitively challenging, and culturally alien than most other subject areas for language minority students.

1. *Limited background knowledge.* Immigrants may not have received any extensive social studies education in their home country. These students may be very unfamiliar with such underlying social studies concepts as a chronology of events, distances, and cultural variations. They may have little knowledge of map reading or of the history or geography of their home country—knowledge that would help them transfer concepts to their new setting. Even if immigrants have social studies instruction that can carry over, much of the content will have been very different and students will almost certainly not have the same schemata for U.S. history and government that U.S.-educated children have. Even children who have received a number of years of education in the United States (for example, a seventh-grader who had entered the United States in the third grade speaking no English) may have significant gaps because of lack of understanding of elementary school social studies content presented in English without L_1 language support (Chamot & O'Malley, 1994; King, Fagan, Bratt, & Baer, 1987).
2. *Limited points of view in many social studies materials.* As discussed earlier, some progress has been made in the addition of multicultural and global content, but materials still tend to lack significant infusion of multiple points of view into the main text. For example, textbooks usually tell the story of the American Revolution from the point of view of the rebels; the perspectives of the loyalists, the Native Americans, or the slaves are often omitted (Short, 1994b). The Eurocentric view found in many social studies materials adds to the difficulty that ELLs may have in relating to social studies content.

3. *Unfamiliarity with the formats and the instructional styles used in U.S. social studies classes.* Students may need to learn about the format of U.S. textbooks and may also be unfamiliar with procedures for report writing, oral presentations, classroom discussions, and so on (King, Fagan, Bratt, & Baer, 1987). For written assignments, students may not, for example, have had any prior experience with forming paragraphs, comparing and contrasting, or writing about cause and effect (Short, 1994a).

4. *High vocabulary density in social studies materials.* Social studies texts almost universally highlight key vocabulary as it is introduced, but for ELLs the number of unfamiliar terms and concepts usually goes far beyond what the text highlights. Furthermore, much of the vocabulary in social studies materials can be rather difficult to explain in a concrete manner. In just one short paragraph in a social studies book, for example, the ELL may come across the following terms that represent important concepts: *federalism, division, government, national, citizen, officials, derive, constitution, subjects,* and *supreme* (Chamot & O'Malley, 1994).

5. *A complex variety of genre and sentence structures in social studies materials.* Social studies texts generally use an expository style of writing with which ESL students are often unfamiliar, especially since ESL classes frequently focus heavily on narrative styles of writing. Also, the sentence structures in social studies materials are often very complicated, with embedded clauses and complicated verb structures such as "supposed to have spoken" and "need no longer fear." Referents can also be unclear for ELLs. For example, a sentence may begin with "It," "it" referring to something in the previous sentence or paragraph (Chamot & O'Malley, 1994). A number of studies of social studies books have found that, even for students proficient in English, texts often are very incoherent, have confusing visual organization, and do not use illustrations and headings appropriately (Short, 1994b). Such books, which can cause the reader to not see the forest for all of the trees, have been referred to aptly as "inconsiderate texts" (Armbruster & Gudbrandsen, 1986).

6. *Heavy reliance on advanced literacy skills, with limited opportunities for hands-on activities.* As traditionally taught, social studies assumes a high degree of literacy. ELLs often have not yet developed enough academic language proficiency to be able to carry out typical reading and writing assignments in English without effective instructional support. The issue becomes even more challenging for students who are not fully literate in their L_1 and therefore do not have a broad array of skills to transfer to the L_2 instructional context. In addition, as alluded to above in the context of vocabulary, social studies contains many concepts that are not always easy to demonstrate in a hands-on way. Compared to math and science, there are limits to the amount of manipulatives and real objects that can be used (Short, 1994a).

As we go through the remainder of this chapter, we will be looking at ways in which to effectively address these challenges. In this section we will first consider use of L_1 and L_2, and then we will look at examples of specific instructional strategies. In the final section of the chapter, we will explore the rich possibilities of theme-based, integrated social studies instruction for meeting the needs of language-minority learners.

Use of L_1 and L_2

Given the challenges of social studies for ELLs, the effective use of L_1 and L_2 is critical, and the key language use issues laid out in Chapter Four apply directly to social studies instruction. ELLs will best be served by social studies instruction that includes the use of L_1 until academic language proficiency is achieved in the second language. As we have just noted, social studies involves many abstract concepts and instruction is often carried out in an environment with limited context clues. When children are involved in such cognitively demanding learning, they "must be allowed to access their entire scope of linguistic resources in order to achieve full potential" (Milk, 1993, p. 102).

A social studies class may be taught entirely in L_1, or a bilingual approach may be used. To use both English and the L_1, an alternate approach or a concurrent approach can be taken. In the alternate approach, the language of instruction is clearly defined by alternating languages by subject area or theme, by time of day, by day of the week, or by week. Bilingual teacher educators have adopted the alternate approach as the preferred model. Research has shown that clear separation of the two languages leads to higher academic achievement in the long term (Christian, 1994; Crawford, 1999; Cummins & Swain, 1986; Lindholm, 1990; Milk, 1986).

The concurrent approach (Jacobson, 1981) allows for the use of both languages during social studies instructional time. However, this approach can be misused if not implemented carefully. In the concurrent approach, the teacher's language choice should not be random; instead, choices should be based among other things on a scaffolding concept in which teachers use the language and the knowledge students already have as a platform for increased language proficiency and conceptual growth. The principal mistake that bilingual teachers make with the concurrent approach is the extensive use of a pattern of quick translation from one language to the other. Besides becoming rather boring, it can also hinder conceptual understanding of content (Milk, 1993, p. 102). The distinction between cognitively rich concurrent use and concurrent-as-translation is rather difficult to perceive without classroom observation of the two patterns. However, it is also a very important distinction, and bilingual social studies teachers will want to make sure that they have opportunities to observe and practice the nontranslation approach in actual classrooms. Consider the following hypothetical example of translation without concept development in a class of ELLs:

TEACHER: Who can tell me what a constitution is?
STUDENT: Es una constitución. (It's a constitution.)
TEACHER: Good, that's right. Now let's look on page 51 . . .

In this example, the teacher might think that he was doing the right thing by checking for understanding before he went on with his point. However, by accepting a simple one-word translation rather than seeking a conceptual explanation, he would be failing to confirm or expand his students' understanding of the *concept* of a constitution. In a classroom where conceptual understanding rather than brief translations are emphasized the teacher would have prompted students toward a more elaborate explanation of the concept of a written document that describes the basic design of a particular form of government. It is easy to get into the translation habit, because on the surface it does have the effect of moving the lesson along quickly. However, in the long run, as Faltis (1996) argues, both content-area knowledge and language development suffer. The nontranslation approach not only results in a more cohesive, in-depth understanding of concepts, but also in a more language-rich environment in which complex, thought-provoking utterances are more frequent and inert one-word answers are less frequent. In a concurrent classroom in which teachers and students are weaned away from the translation habit, it is also possible to "push" the students to communicate in one language or the other for longer periods of time, which results in better development of both languages (Faltis, 1996). The effective use of the concurrent approach closely parallels Tharp & Gallimore's (1991) concept of "instructional conversations" (p. i). An instructional conversation is "a dialogue between teacher and learners in which the teacher listens carefully to grasp the students' communicative intent, and tailors the dialogue to meet the emerging understanding of the learners." Such conversations are used to work with children in the "zone of proximal development," and in bilingual social studies classrooms such concurrent instructional conversations serve to work within both the linguistic and content-area zones of proximal development.

Leaving bilingual settings, we turn now to language use within the ESL social studies context. Theoretically, the issue of language use in ESL social studies contexts is simply one of using proven content area second language acquisition techniques for the target language, English. In reality, however, the lines between bilingual and ESL programs are often blurred. There are so-called bilingual programs that use very little L_1, and there are ESL programs that make as much use of L_1 as they can given their circumstances. Lucas and Katz's (1994) survey of Special Alternative Instructional Programs (SAIPs) contains many examples of the use of L_1 in ESL contexts. Lucas and Katz studied nine exemplary SAIPs and found a "pervasive" variety of uses of students' L_1. At one site, for example, the teacher used Spanish to clarify a point with one student while the class was doing individual work. In this same setting, a Vietnamese student wrote in Vietnamese about three things learned in class the previous day. Students who were more proficient in English tutored less proficient English speakers in their L_1, or they explained instructions in L_1. These SAIPs also employed bilingual instructional assistants and made use of bilingual reference materials. A variety of the sites even offered some social studies courses in L_1—"History of Cambodia" in Khmer and "History of

Spanish-Speaking People" in Spanish, for example. Lucas and Katz (1994) concluded that "the use of the native language is so compelling that it emerges even when policies and assumptions mitigate against it" (p. 558). These SAIPs, which included social studies instruction, were successful because they focused less on the issue of which language to use per se and more on academic development and instructional dynamics that fostered meaningful interaction.

Instructional Strategies

We will look in more detail at examples of strategies that illustrate 7 of the below 12 principles. The principles that we will focus on are making connections with students' lives, using student knowledge about home countries, activating background knowledge, providing hands-on and performance-based activities, promoting critical thinking, paying attention to social studies language issues, and using graphic organizers. This is not to imply that the other five principles are less important. These principles (offering many different avenues for communication, using cooperative learning, modeling of

Guidelines for Teaching

SUCCESSFUL SOCIAL STUDIES INSTRUCTIONAL STRATEGIES

A good way to begin our survey of strategies is by referring to Short's list of guiding principles for successful social studies instruction. These principles integrate language development and cultural diversity into the process of social studies instruction. The list is based on a number of years of classroom research on social studies education for language-minority students. As we look at these strategies, we can see that they touch in a variety of ways on the NCSS characteristics of meaningful, integrative, value-based, challenging, and active social studies instruction.

1. Offer opportunities to communicate about social studies—in oral, written, physical, or pictorial forms.

2. Make connections between the content being taught and students' real-life experiences.

3. Use the students as resources for information about their native countries.

4. Activate students' background knowledge.

5. Provide hands-on and performance-based activities.

6. Promote critical thinking and study skills development.

7. Pay attention to language issues and employ strategies that will help students learn the language of social studies.

8. Use graphic organizers to help students represent information and identify relationships.

9. Incorporate cooperative learning activities and seek peer tutors among classmates.

10. Be process oriented and provide modeling for students to make transitions to academic tasks.

11. Open discussion to different perspectives of history.

12. Adjust instruction for the different learning styles of the students. (Short, 1993, p. 11)

assignments and learning processes, using multiple perspectives, and adjusting instruction to learning styles) are most likely already very familiar to readers because they are common to many second-language learning contexts and to good pedagogy in general. As we proceed to go through our focus strategies, please remember that the strategies we are not highlighting often cut across all of the others. For example, teachers may be using multiple perspectives as they activate students' background knowledge. Or they may be using modeling; cooperative learning; accommodation to learning styles; and a mixture of oral, written, and pictorial communication modes as they employ graphic organizers in their social studies classes.

Connections with Students' Lives, Home Countries, and Background Knowledge   In connecting with students' personal lives, home countries, and background knowledge, we can recognize a common theme in this book: the acknowledgement of students as highly important resources for their own learning. These connections are also closely related to the concept of identifying the learner's current schemata and expanding upon them. These schemata represent "networks of connected ideas" (Slavin, 1988b, p. 155). King et al. (1987, pp. 94–99) provide us with several examples of these kinds of connections that build schemata for social studies concepts. For instance, in a lesson on the movement of U.S. settlers into the western regions of North America, the teacher can compare and contrast this migration process with the patterns of settlement of recent immigrants to the United States. In preparing to study the Civil War, students can first develop the general concept that "differences can eventually lead to conflicts." The discussion could start with students' own problems with being different, and then expand to other situations in the United States or their home countries that illustrate social, political, and economic differences among groups of people. From here, students will be better prepared to understand some of the conflicts that led up to the Civil War. An example from Short (1997) demonstrates the development of a schema for understanding the concept of social classes. In one of the lessons from a unit on global conflicts that she and her colleagues developed (Short, Montone, Frekot, & Elfin, 1996) students learn about social classes within the Inca Empire. To activate their background knowledge, the teacher first guides the students in filling in a pyramid structure that illustrates the social hierarchy of their own school. With this background understanding in mind, the students are then able to better understand the concept of social classes as it applies to a pyramid depicting Incan social structure.

Social studies will offer numerous situations in which the students' own experiences can be used as a bridge to new knowledge and understanding. However, there also may be some social studies topics or concepts for which the student really has limited background knowledge. In such cases, the teacher may be able to begin to construct the schema in class by having students role play a situation. Duis (1996) gives an example in which the teacher gives students basic information about social and economic conditions after the Civil War and then the students have to develop a plan that addresses the questions "What are the most pressing problems?" and "What can the government do?" After going through the process of working on their own plans, the students have a schema—a network of ideas—that will help them understand their study of the actual reconstruction process after the Civil War.

Hands-On and Performance-Based Activities   While it may be true that social studies does not lend itself as much as math and science to actual materials that students can hold in their hands, the possibilities for concrete experiences and performance-based activities are actually quite extensive and exciting. Students can illustrate time-line murals, design dioramas and models, and create objects to place in a time capsule depicting a particular historical period. They can handle a variety of information sources beyond their textbooks. For example, they can use a clipping from the school newsletter about the upcoming student council elections before they go on to study about elections in their textbook.

Another example of the kind of material that can bring life to a social studies topic is the National Public Radio audiotape "Class of 2000: The Prejudice Puzzle" (Bartis & Bowman, 1994). This is a recording of interviews with young people about their experiences with prejudice and how they have dealt with it. Students can also use magazine and newspaper articles. Literature, diaries, speeches, posters, paintings, cartoons, and music from various historical periods and cultures also provide more concrete contexts for social studies. Visits to museums and other types of field trips enable students to have additional concrete experiences in material-rich environments.

Maps and globes are also important materials for language minority students—the more the better, and the more varied the better, such as local maps and world maps, physical maps and political maps, facsimiles of ancient maps, and the latest technologically advanced satellite maps. In one of the global education high schools mentioned at the beginning of this chapter, a world map was on every desk in virtually every classroom in the school (Fuss Kirkwood, 1990a, 1991b). The first gift that ESL and bilingual teachers doing social studies may want to give to their students is a map of the city or area in which they live. This map can be treated as a resource to be used throughout the year for a wide variety of activities involving such areas as language development, geography, history, and the environment. Many types of maps can be used to teach about multiple perspectives. A topographical map of the students' state shows a very different perspective than a road map. More important to global understanding is the availability of a variety of world maps. For example, maps that place North America in the center and cut Asia in half reflect the perspective of the map makers. The relative size of continents on varying maps is also very revealing. For example, Europe appears much larger on the traditional Mercator Projection map than it does on the more accurate Peters Projection map.

Performance-based activities also lend a sense of reality to social studies classes. One possibility is for students to role-play historical events or governmental processes. They may also conduct mock trials. For example, in *Seeing the Whole through Social Studies,* Lindquist (1995) describes how the students in her elementary class put Herschel the Sea Lion on trial for murdering Sam Steelhead. The trial grew out of a local controversy over what to do about sea lions who were decimating the salmon population as the fish entered a lock system in the Seattle area. In addition to providing a wealth of ideas for hands-on and performance-based social studies activities, the author—an elementary teacher—used her experiences in her own classes to show how social studies topics can become unifying themes for a variety of curricular areas throughout the entire school year. In the case of the mock trial, for example, students learned about the trial system and the Marine Mammal Protection Act (social studies), but they also learned about the life cycle of the salmon and the natural predator–prey relationship (science). Language arts—reading and writing and listening and speaking—were included throughout the entire unit.

As we will be seeing later in the chapter, students may also actively "do" social studies by designing communities, conducting interviews, developing life histories, taking on community service projects, and so on. Community members can also contribute to the richness of meaningful and active social studies classes. They can, for example, be used as guest speakers, classroom volunteers who share some type of expertise, colleagues in community service, subjects for interviews and data collection, or as an audience with whom students can interact as they make social studies presentations.

Electronic media and videos, while not precisely hands-on and performance-based activities, are another extremely important component of social studies programs that are designed to be comprehensible to language-minority students through the use of multiple modalities. A growing number of different kinds of electronic media resources and websites are available for social studies. Few if any have been designed specifically for bilingual or ESL students, but many can be used successfully. (One of the authors of this chapter still remembers how her ESL students loved to play one of the early and classic interactive computer games, "Oregon Trail.") There are interactive simulations of social phenomena, such as building cities, and there are electronic databases, multimedia programs, laser disks, and electronic networks that enable direct and immediate connections with people in many different parts of the country and the world.

Videos and films can provide the learner with a powerful sense of "being there," and they also provide ELLs with visual referents for spoken and written information. They are excellent instruments through which students can see other societies and themselves. Students can become involved in videotaping events or subjects, and the videotapes can be shown in class for instructional purposes. In this way the learner and teacher become not only knowledge consumers but also knowledge producers.

Guidelines for Teaching

THE USE OF VIDEOS OR DVDS IN THE SOCIAL STUDIES CLASSROOM

These are some things to consider when using videos:

1. *Does the video or DVD facilitate not only observation but also participation?* For example, the teacher can use prevideo or DVD questions to make the viewing more active or offer a class follow-up activity. Two different videos or DVDs can be compared and contrasted, or a video or DVD can be compared with a written source on the same subject. Students can take notes on certain types of information that they will be looking for during the video or DVD, or they may keep a journal on a series of videos or DVDs that they will be seeing.

2. *What is the language load of the video or DVD?* How much verbiage surrounds the videotape or DVD and how much commentary is really necessary? Would it be better to show the videotape or DVD without the running comments and let the viewers bring their experiences to the visual imagery? When you do this and ask the children what they saw, you may be surprised at the range of responses you get. After the material has been discussed, you may want to show the video or DVD again with sound. Now the question is: What did you hear?

3. *What perspective does the video or DVD portray?* When dealing with social studies content, it is very possible that the video or DVD will intentionally or unintentionally reflect the biases of the people who produced it. In some cases this may make the video or DVD inappropriate to use, but in other cases the class can analyze whose point of view is seen in the video or DVD and whose point of view is left out.

Critical Thinking and Study Skills Development

It is very important to prepare language minority students for the type of cognitively demanding academic work that they will be sure to encounter as they progress through high school and into higher education—critical thinking and study skills development are key components in this process. An example of a curricular package for ESL students that explicitly promotes critical thinking is *Making Peace: A Reading/Writing/Thinking Text on Global Community* (Brooks & Fox, 1994). This is a collection of readings and language development activities that engage ESL students in critical thinking and writing on highly relevant multicultural and global issues. As we proceed through the remainder of this section on instructional strategies and the next section on theme-based social studies units, we will see that the issue of critical thinking emerges repeatedly as an integral aspect of many different social studies activities for language-minority students.

Directed Reading Thinking Activity (DRTA) is an example of a specific classroom strategy that teachers can use in a wide range of contexts to help language-minority students develop critical thinking skills and deal with abstract content in social studies courses. With DRTA, students use higher-order thinking skills as they process a text in the following manner: (1) students brainstorm what they already know about the topic; (2) they predict what might be in the reading selection; (3) they read the text, confirming their predictions or making corrections and integrating the new information into their original knowledge base; and (4) they discuss what they learned from the text through follow-up questions and checks for comprehension (King et al., 1987).

Turning now to study skills, "Survey, Questions, Read, Recite, Record, Review" (SQ4R) is an example of a study skills routine that students can learn to use for outlining information from a text (King, Fagan, Bratt, & Baer, 1987). The point of the activity is not the outline per se, but the active use of the outline process to promote critical comprehension of key ideas. In the first step, "surveying," students skim the reading assignment to get an overall view of the topic headings, pictures, maps and graphs, and key vocabulary. Then they formulate questions about the selection based on the headings and subheadings in the chapter. On a sheet of paper that has been divided vertically in half, they write down their questions on the lefthand side. (For example, if one of the subheadings was "Spain's Empire Grows," a student might write on his paper, "How did Spain's empire grow?") Then the students read with a purpose in mind, that of answering their questions. They orally answer their question to themselves and then record them on the right-hand side of their outline form. The final step is a review of the material they have outlined. This process can be valuable in providing students with the skills needed to work independently on social studies assignments and research projects.

Paying Attention to Social Studies Language Issues

In the process of learning social studies content students develop a broad array of language skills, and in the process of learning new language skills they better prepare themselves for further understanding of social studies. Going back again to one of our introductory vignettes for an example, the students who wrote diamante poems based on their study of Incan social classes were developing vocabulary and writing skills in a new genre at the same time that they were developing the concept of social classes. In a previous section in this chapter we have already discussed the language issue of use of L_1 or L_2 for social studies. Here we focus more on issues of language development when students are learning social studies through their second language, as would happen in a content ESL class or a sheltered social studies class.

Of course, one of the most important language issues in such social studies classes is vocabulary development, and teachers need to use a very broad range of strategies to help students acquire new vocabulary in meaningful ways. Often visual representations can be used: Photographs of people demonstrating or picketing will help to convey the meaning of the word protest, for example. Sometimes vocabulary can be acted out physically. Another strategy is to use examples from the students' own experiences. For example, their familiarity with their school's student council can serve as a bridge to the meaning of *representative*. Semantic webs, which we will describe further in the section on graphic organizers, can help students associate the meaning of new words with related words that they already know (Short, 1994b).

Beyond the individual word level, social studies contexts offer many opportunities for students to develop sentence structures and skills with more extensive discourse patterns. For example, we can see this process happening at a beginning ELL level in which students use information about explorers to develop English sentence patterns for making comparisons. Students might have cards with a simplified summary of one explorer on each card. Then they make comparisons using a variety of modeled sentence patterns: "Columbus was a Spanish explorer, and so was Balboa," or "Columbus was a Spanish explorer and Balboa was too," or "Both Columbus and Balboa were Spanish explorers" (King, Fagan, Bratt, & Baer, 1987, p. 94). Another example involves learning how to paraphrase. Students listen to statements read to them and identify whether the statement was made by King George or Thomas Jefferson. Along with their choice, they have to give a reason for their answer. In the process of stating their reason, they are actually practicing paraphrasing (King, Fagan, Bratt, & Baer, 1987, pp. 112, 113).

Language experience is a very effective way to blend oral language development, literacy development, and social studies learning. Originally developed as a method for beginning reading instruction, the language experience approach starts with a concrete experience that students share. During or after the activity, the students and teacher generate vocabulary and sentences about the experience. These words, sentences, or both are recorded on large flash cards, sentence strips, or charts. The written materials are then used for follow-up literacy activities. When combined with social studies content they can also be used for follow-up social studies activities. For example, to develop vocabulary and concepts related to the electoral process, students carry out an election in the classroom. Step by step the teacher writes down in simplified language what is happening, introducing key vocabulary words such as nominate, campaign, and so on. With this language base students are then ready to apply the new concepts and vocabulary to the more abstract study of governmental electoral processes. Another type of concrete experience that lends itself to the language experience approach is roleplaying. For example, to develop the concept of decision making through compromise, students could role-play various interest groups arguing for or against a law. As they act out the process, the teacher would write down key sentences and vocabulary. The language and concepts that emerged from the role-playing would then serve, for instance, as a platform for the study of compromises made during the Constitutional Convention (King, Fagan, Bratt, & Baer, 1987).

One of the challenges of social studies that we have already noted is the range of writing styles and organizational structures in social studies activities. Language-sensitive teachers can help their students to develop proficiency with these formats. A good example of such a strategy is provided by a fifth-grade unit on explorers carried out in a mixed classroom of English proficient students and ELLs. As the unit progressed the teacher led the students through guided practice in five different writing styles. Students began with the style most familiar to them, narrative writing, and then moved on to descriptive writing, persuasive writing, and finally the least familiar genre, expository writing. This process was connected to social studies by having the students role play various explorers who needed to record their experiences in order to make reports to their rulers. In the first writing assignment the "explorers" told the story of their trip. In the second assignment they focused on a description of the new places they had seen. In the third they wrote to persuade others to join them or to persuade sponsors to provide more funding. In the final assignment they wrote reflective reports of the significance of their experiences. The teacher used modeling, thinking out loud, and joint text construction to prepare the students to complete their own writing assignments (Reppen, 1994/1995). This process again demonstrates the interconnectedness of language development and social studies understanding. The social studies information and concepts served as a natural context for the writing assignments, and the writing assignments helped the students to have a deeper understanding of various facets of the European age of exploration.

Just as students encounter a variety of writing genres, they also encounter a wide variety of discourse structures in social studies readings. Coelho (1982) has identified a variety of linguistic features of social studies discourse that can be explicitly taught to ELLs to improve their comprehension of social studies information. By developing an awareness of certain types of linguistic signals, ELLs can learn to recognize chronological markers and organizational structures such as cause–effect and compare–contrast. For example, ELLs can learn that the phrase "as a result" signals a cause-effect relationship. "In addition" and "furthermore" indicate enumeration—that a series of things are being listed (Short, 1997). Short (1994b) has identified six types of structures that are found in social studies texts: sequential (chronological), cause–effect, problem–solution, description, enumeration, and comparison–contrast. If teachers are aware of these structures in the materials they are using with their students, they will be better prepared to help students learn for themselves how to make sense out of social studies content. Because one of the ultimate goals of a social studies program for language-minority students is to enable them to participate fully in academically challenging social studies courses taught entirely in English, the development of their familiarity with these more advanced aspects of social studies discourse is extremely important.

Guidelines for Teaching

THE USE OF GRAPHIC ORGANIZERS

Graphic organizers is an umbrella term for a variety of kinds of diagrams that learners can use to literally *see* relationships. The type of graphic organizer that learners use depends on the nature of the relationships being portrayed. Graphic organizers can be used to help in understanding a written text, to give focus to a group discussion, or to serve as a prewriting framework for a writing assignment. When used with a written text, they can be developed before, during, or after reading the selection. Used before reading, they help as advance guides. During the reading process they are a way to organize information. After completing the reading assignment, they can be used to summarize relationships. The following are some examples of graphic organizers and some of their possible uses:

- *Semantic webs and tree diagrams.* These are composed of central hubs with extending spokes or tree trunks with branches and subbranches. They can work to show relationships between main ideas and subordinate details.

- *Time lines.* Time lines can be used to summarize the chronological relationship of various events.

- *Flow charts.* Flow charts can serve to demonstrate cause-and-effect relationships.

- *Venn diagrams.* Venn diagrams are composed of intersecting circles. Each circle represents a distinct subject, with characteristics of the subject listed inside the circle. Characteristics within the intersecting areas are common to all of the subjects, while characteristics outside of the intersections are unique to each separate component. Learners can use Venn diagrams to show relationships of comparison and contrast.

- *Charts or tables.* With their rectangles of rows and columns, charts can show how a group of details relate to each other to form a category that is distinct from other categories on the chart. (King et al., 1987; Short, 1997)

As ELLs progress in their second-language proficiency within the context of social studies classes, it is important for teachers to remember that listening, speaking, reading, and writing do not always develop in this sequence for second-language learners. McKay and Wong (1996) for example, in their case study of four adolescent immigrant Chinese students, found their subjects to be "extremely complex social beings" (p. 603) who were each unique in the amount of relative effort that they invested in listening and speaking skills versus reading and writing skills. It is also important to remember that even though some students may not be able to effectively convey complex ideas in writing, this does not necessarily mean that they lack understanding of concepts. Alternative assessment approaches such as political cartoons, illustrations, or semantic webs can also indicate higher level cognitive understanding.

We will look at two of Short's (1997) examples of the use of graphic organizers in bilingual or ESL contexts. One example involves the use of charts. Students who are learning about social classes in the Inca Empire (mentioned previously in another example) divide into groups, and the teacher distributes reading selections so that each group has a different social class to read about. After their group work, in which group members help each other understand their texts, all the groups come together to share their information, which they organize into a chart that depicts the various categories of people.

Another example involves students who are studying the Revolutionary War. They use a Venn diagram to compare and contrast the lives of Paul Revere and another important messenger, Sybil Ludington. After preparing the diagram, students are ready to write an essay about the two historical figures. One sample essay included in Short's article is clearly organized into three paragraphs, and the essay shows the student's use of language cues for enumeration and comparing and contrasting. In the first paragraph the student enumerates similarities between the two characters. In the second paragraph the student discusses differences. Both paragraphs include the use of linguistic cues such as "furthermore," "in addition," "on the other hand," and "for example." The student concludes her essay with the following opinion about Revere and Ludington's accomplishments:

> *Now that I have talked about these people. I'm going to choose one of them and that is Sybil Ludington as a hero because she is a girl, she was 16 year old, she was a brave girl who wanted to help her nation and she does things that men does that is why I think she is a hero. I think these two people did great thing to help their nation. (Short, 1997)*

In her essay, this student is clearly developing both language proficiency and social studies concepts, and in the process she is using critical-thinking skills as she chooses one character as her hero and defends this choice. She is developing a firm foundation for more advanced writing assignments in future social studies classes.

Bringing the Strategies Together: CALLA as an Example   Of course, all of the above language-sensitive strategies work together, and a large variety may be used at any one time. In the essays about Revere and Ludington, for example, students were using a graphic organizer, but they were also using what they had learned about words to show enumeration or comparison. To consider how all of these individual instructional strategies can be brought together cohesively within a unit of instruction, we will use the example of the Cognitive Academic Language Learning Approach, or CALLA (Chamot & O'Malley, 1994). The reader can refer back to Chapters Four and Six for a general description of the principles of CALLA instruction. In a social studies CALLA unit, the following preparatory steps might be involved: (1) teachers assess the students' background knowledge on the subject of the unit; (2) they then identify objectives that are appropriate in relation to the students' current knowledge bases; (3) they plan academic language objectives that will dovetail with the social studies objectives and include listening, speaking, reading, and writing activities as well as higher-order thinking skills; and (4) finally, in coordination with the social studies and language development component, they integrate use of learning strategies. In a sample CALLA unit on European colonies in North America (Chamot &

O'Malley, 1994, pp. 270, 271), some of the social studies, language and learning strategy objectives (not a total listing) include these:

> *Social studies:* Learn about Spanish, English, French, and Dutch colonists in North America and their interaction with Native Americans; use map skills to locate colonies; use a time line to highlight major events happening at this time in North America and in other parts of the world.

> *Language:* Discuss prior knowledge; develop vocabulary related to colonization; write summaries of information; describe photographs of the living museum of colonial life at Plymouth; write and present a report on colonies in other parts of the world.

> *Learning strategies:* Elaborate prior knowledge, use selective attention (e.g., scanning a reading selection), take notes, summarize, and work cooperatively.

Theme-Based, Integrated Social Studies Units

To further bring a sense of cohesiveness to the many effective strategies for social studies instruction for language-minority children, we close the chapter with examples of theme-based social studies units that integrate language arts and other subjects. We will look at two middle school units with the themes of protest and cultural conflict. Then we will describe three additional theme-based units—two elementary and one secondary—that emphasize the "doing" of social studies. These units develop such themes as the influence of location on living patterns and changes in communities over time.

Middle School Units on Protest and Conflict

The first two themes are "Protest and the American Revolution" (Short, Mahrer, Elfin, Liten-Tejada, & Montone, 1994) and "Conflict in World Cultures" (Short, Montone, Frekot, & Elfin, 1996). Short and her colleagues have spent a number of years developing and field testing these two theme-based units for use with middle school language-minority students. The units can be used in a broad range of types of classes: bilingual classes, content-area ESLs, sheltered social studies classes, or language-sensitive classes with a mix of ELLs and proficient English speakers.

We have already used some of the activities in these units as examples throughout the chapter, as these materials make extensive use of the successful principles which we listed at the beginning of this section on instructional methods. In these units, teachers strive for depth of understanding rather than accumulation of large numbers of details, and the activities clearly reflect the NCSS features of powerful teaching and the use of critical thinking. They also clearly employ a multicultural and global perspective. Like the CALLA model, the lessons include three kinds of objectives: social studies objectives, language objectives, and (similar to CALLA's learning strategies) critical thinking and study skills.

The first unit, "Protest and the American Revolution," obviously takes as its theme the concept of protest, with the subthemes of symbolism and point of view. As they integrated a multicultural perspective into the unit, the authors found that they had to bridge many gaps in textbooks in order to help students see the American Revolution from the point of view of such groups as the loyalists, women, Native Americans, and African Americans. The authors chose protest as the main theme because it can be connected to students' lives through their experiences as adolescents and possibly through their families' experiences in their home countries. In addition to being linked through the theme of protest, the lessons are also integrated with writing instruction. The examples of comparative writing about Paul Revere and Sybil Ludington were from this unit. Another writing assignment is to take on the role of a colonist and compose letters to the editor protesting an event. Students use many diverse activities as they explore the theme of protest through their study of the American Revolution: flow charts, Venn diagrams, tree diagrams, the writing process, vocabulary preview activities, art, authentic texts such as political cartoons and protest songs from the period, role playing, interviews, library research, and more (Short, et al., 1994). As a culminating project for the unit, students use their understanding about this historical period to publish a colonial newspaper.

The second thematic unit is "Conflicts in World Cultures." As indicated by the title, the unifying theme is conflict, with a subtheme of cultural influences on perception. Students become multicultural informants during this unit, as they use their own experiences with conflict in this country and in their families' countries of origin to bring meaning to the theme. Students explore the theme by studying five different examples of conflict: the conquest of the Inca Empire, the Protestant Reformation, the opening of Japan to U.S. trade, the defense of Ethiopian independence, and a series of culminating lessons on historical and personal conflicts and resolutions. Through the interdisciplinary, theme-based approach, students learn about different types of conflicts—political, cultural, economic, territorial, and religious—and they learn about possible types of resolutions—violence, resistance, negotiation, concession, and withdrawal. The unit is also integrated in its use of a variety of writing genres. For example, the students write haiku about the contact between Perry and the Japanese, and they write diamante poems about the Inca. (We used two examples of these poems at the beginning of the chapter.) Short (1997) notes that the variety of writing genres energizes the students and allows them to reflect in a different way on historical information, finding their own way to express ideas. As with the protest unit, a broad array of activities engage the learners. For example, in addition to the use of creative writing, they use graphic organizers and other reading scaffolds, and they gain experience with both commercial textbooks and other types of materials. They also engage in discussion and debate, form and justify opinions, use persuasion, take on multiple perspectives, and practice negotiation skills. Throughout the unit they make artifacts to put into a time capsule: illustrations, crafts, maps, diaries, and essays, for example. As a culminating activity they open the time capsule, hopefully with family members and other guests present. They describe the contents, recall information, answer questions, and elaborate on their explanations when requested (Short et al., 1996).

"Doing" Social Studies: Three Examples

The next three theme-based units that we describe illustrate an emphasis on "*doing* social studies" (Freeman & Freeman, 1991, p. 66). By "*doing* social studies," we mean the process in which students do the types of activities that social scientists might engage in: writing histories, conducting interviews, analyzing data, or recommending and planning courses of action, for example. As such, these units use the social science approach, combined with the critical-thinking approach. We have already looked very briefly at examples of students doing social studies at the beginning of this chapter. There was the vignette of the class that published a magazine about Southeast Asian immigrants' lives and the vignette about the Puerto Rican oral history video. In both of these examples, the students who produced the magazine and those who made the oral history video were "doing" social science. We will now look more closely at the oral history model, and then conclude with examples of two units that explore community themes.

The Puerto Rican oral history example is from an article by Olmedo (1993), in which she describes the process of bilingual high school students doing social studies as they produce oral histories. First, the teacher identifies a particular social studies concept, which becomes the theme for the oral history unit. Just some examples of the many themes that might be explored are acculturation, migration, the impact of economic or technological changes on people's lives, or the causes and results of wars. Based on the theme, the teacher and students develop an interview guide with questions that address the theme. If not already prepared in the L_1 of the people to be interviewed, students also become involved in the process of translating the interview guide, which has the additional benefit of giving practical value to their biliteracy. Then students practice using the interview guide on each other and also practice using a tape recorder or video camera. The next step is to invite a guest to be interviewed by the whole class, which provides more practice with the interview process. This class interview also serves as a model for the process of transcribing the interview and preparing a summary. Then a group of students select a person to interview and assign various tasks to group members, depending on their particular language and literacy skills. Finally, the students conduct the interview, transcribe the data, and prepare a class presentation.

After the class presentations, students use the oral histories as a springboard from which to develop a broader understanding of the theme or themes they are studying. For example, they may compare the themes found in their oral histories with examples from social studies texts, or they may compare and contrast the oral history experiences with the experiences of characters in a historical novel or a biography. The material from the interviews can be connected to the distant past by a common theme. For example, in preparation for the study of the colonial period in North America, students could collect oral histories about the reasons that their families came to the United States. Olmedo (1993) notes that oral history projects help students understand history as stories, and to see that "they and their communities are players on the historical stage" (p. 7). In addition, they serve to strengthen many different language skills and they involve community members as resources.

Our next model is a unit for elementary students with the general theme of the influence of location on community living patterns—in simple terms, "where we live influences how we live." As described by Freeman and Freeman (1991), this unit applies the principles of whole-language instruction to social studies in a multilingual classroom, using first-hand experiences and authentic reading selections (magazine articles) rather than textbooks. In this unit, students do social studies as they make observations about environments and make plans for social action. Students first develop an awareness of some of the characteristics of their own community. Next, using a variety of photographs, students analyze the characteristics of distant communities that they have never experienced directly. As they analyze the pictures, they develop lists of characteristics of the physical location (e.g., "hot," "rainy," "many tall buildings"). They also draw conclusions about community needs for survival and comfortable living, and the advantages and disadvantages of each location. With a schema now developed for their theme, they are better prepared to move on to written materials. They work in groups to read articles about diverse communities from such magazines as *World* (a *National Geographic* publication for children), and they use charts to organize their information, making one column about characteristics and another column about what people do as a result of these characteristics. For example, one characteristic might be "tall buildings with flat roofs," and one of the things that people do is "plant rooftop gardens." The next step is for children to return to look again at their local community, using such activities as field trips and guest speakers. Given their community's characteristics, they discuss advantages and disadvantages of the location. Focusing then on the disadvantages, they make and carry out a plan of action for improvement of some aspect of the quality of life. For example, they might write a letter to the editor of the local paper about a concern or an idea, or they might attend a city council meeting. All through the group process, children are actively "doing" social studies: observing, comparing, contrasting, identifying problems, and proposing solutions. In the process they are learning to value each others' contributions and they are coming to "see themselves as useful, contributing members of society as a whole" (Freeman & Freeman, 1991, p. 66).

Remember the question, "*¿Dónde agarraron los ladrillos?*" ("Where did they get the bricks?"). Our final example of doing social studies brings us back to the very first vignette at the beginning of the chapter. As mentioned there, the student who answered the question about the bricks was a member of a sixth-grade bilingual classroom involved in an "Island Project." Students were in mixed groups with monolingual English, monolingual Spanish, and bilingual students in each group, and all group-generated texts (for examples, charts and public records) were done in Spanish and English. Over the course of 10 weeks, the students developed their imaginary island communities. Working from the point of view of social scientists, they had to consider such aspects as survival, economics, religion, government, families, education, recreation, science, tools, and technology. They made portraits of their communities during the first two weeks on the island, in the 2nd year of existence and in the 10th year. Then students worked in pairs as historians to write about the development and changes that occurred in their communities. Throughout the course of the project there were many different ways to communicate—orally, pictorially and with written text—so that "access to knowledge was not constrained by reading test levels." The student-generated written texts that were used were more comprehensible to beginning readers than commercial texts would have been, because they were "talked into being [by the students]" (Heras, 1993, p. 292). The project was extremely rich in first-hand experience in social science processes and in classroom interactions that required extensive reasoning skills. Thus the unit effectively combined the social studies as social science approach with the critical-thinking/ transformative approach. Noting the highly interactive environment during final presentations, with students asking many interesting questions of each other, Heras (1993) noted that in this context "students themselves are knowledgeable beings who can talk from evidence, challenge each other in socially and academically appropriate ways, and take up new positions" (p. 294). In other words, they are informed, effective citizens of a community; they are putting into practice the essential aim of social studies education.

As we have seen throughout this chapter, there are many promising examples of powerful social studies contexts for language-minority students that can bring great energy to the classroom. Such success stories are the result of the hard work of dedicated educators. They come about through a challenging process of alignment of social studies and language objectives; design, trial, and redesign of activity-rich learning environments; countless hours of materials preparation and adaptation; and collaboration between social studies and bilingual/ESL specialists (Short, 1997). There is so much to learn about the world, and in the process of doing social studies there will probably never be enough time and enough resources to explore all of the concepts that we want to explore or to meet all of the disparate curricular guidelines. However, as long as we work toward a social studies program that is active, engaged, integrated, value-laden and challenging; as long as we work toward the *doing* of social studies and the pervasive use of critical thinking; and as long as we infuse a multicultural and global perspective into our work we will be helping language-minority students establish a strong social framework. They have a lifetime ahead of them in which to build on their knowledge as they grow up, work, raise families, and participate as citizens of their community, their state, their nation, and their world.

Summary

As with other content areas, this chapter argues that an effective social studies curriculum is necessarily grounded in the lived experiences of our English-language learner students. Bilingual and ESL educators, however, must challenge and ready students to go beyond their own racial, linguistic, cultural, and social class comfort zones before they venture into the often turbulent and uncharted waters of U.S. society. Notwithstanding, however, the dangers and opportunities associated with such processes, the chapter suggests that it is only through entering into dialogical encounters with "the other" that humans can make sense of each other's world. In this way of thinking, humans do not have the option to leave each other alone because "Cultures only flourish in contact with others; they perish in isolation" (Fuentes, 1992, p. 346). Focusing on the various frameworks for powerful and meaningful teaching, this chapter argues, that when taught in a manner appropriate to language-minority students, social studies provides a fascinating context for students to develop their own sociocultural and linguistic identity, to reach out and learn about the world and their place in it, and to begin to exercise their role as citizens in a democracy and as citizens of the world.

Key Terms

Social studies p. 280

Multicultural education p. 288

Multiple acculturation p. 290

Global education p. 290

Directed reading thinking activity (DRTA) p. 307

Reflection Questions

1. How would you apply the five features of "powerful" social studies teaching and learning promoted by the National Council for the Social Studies (NCSS) in your social studies classroom? What curricular activities would you include? How does each feature reflect effective social studies teaching?

2. How are the NCSS thematic standards related to the various social science disciplines?

3. What do the authors mean by social studies "as critical thinking"? Why do they maintain that this approach is superior to the more traditional conceptions of social studies taught as citizenship transmission or social science? How can bilingual and ESL teachers take a more critical approach in social studies classrooms?

4. How is Merkle's poem, *From the Other Side,* related to schooling in the global village? How would you respond to the poet's questions: "What is behind this? What drove people to condemn and execute so many so ruthlessly?" What role can schools play in promoting peaceful conflict resolution? If so, where does one start?

5. How are social studies classes typically organized for English-language learners in middle or high school? In your opinion, what are the advantages and disadvantages of each of the six types of social studies classes listed in this chapter? Why might ESL and bilingual students benefit more from alternative formats (e.g., a school-within-a-school, newcomer or high-intensity language training program) rather than a social studies class that fits within a traditionally segmented middle or high school structure?

6. Why is social studies considered by many educators and researchers to be more "context-reduced, cognitively challenging, and alien" than most other subjects for English-language learners? What are the implications of this for social studies instruction for these students?

7. What are some effective social studies instructional strategies that teachers can use with English-language learners? How would you use these strategies in your own classroom?

8. Why is a global education perspective ideally suited for the social studies classroom? Why is global education sometimes considered to be among the most controversial approaches to the teaching of social studies? In your opinion, are there ways in which bilingual and ESL teachers can mitigate some of this controversy?

Resources

Appleby, J., Hunt, L., & Jacob, M. *Telling the truth about history.* New York: W.W. Norton & Company, 1994.

• *Telling the Truth about History* is a histographical essay that confronts the uncertainty about values and truth seeking. It addresses the controversies about objective knowledge, cultural diversity, and the political imperatives of a democratic education. Its central argument is that skepticism and relativism about truth, not only in science but also in history and politics, have grown out of the insistent democratization of Western society. The authors challenge the idea of a single narrative of national history, and allude to the increasing emphasis on the diversity of ethnic, racial, and gender human experience.

Banks, J. A. *Teaching strategies for ethnic studies*. Boston: Allyn and Bacon, 1997.
- This book is designed to help teachers conceptualize, design and implement a democratic, thoughtful, and just curriculum that honors and reflects the experiences, hopes, and dreams of all Americans. It describes the knowledge, concepts, strategies, and resources that teachers need to implement a democratic curriculum by transforming the mainstream curriculum and incorporating content and concepts about diverse racial, ethnic, and cultural groups.

Brown, S. C., & Kysilka, M. L. *Applying multicultural and global concepts in the classroom*. Boston: Allyn and Bacon, 2002.
- *Applying Multicultural and Global Concepts in the Classroom* "offers advice to teachers on how to provide students with the conceptual tools to recognize how they can become empowered actors in a multicultural world. Arguing that the process has to begin with the teacher, they invite their readers to examine and challenge their own cultural preconceptions before delving into specific advice on classroom applications in relations to the students, school environment, curriculum, instruction, and assessment. Finally, they discuss how to make the material relevant to the students acting in the wider community."

Cortés, C. E. *The children are watching: How the media teach about diversity*. New York: Teachers College Press, 2000.
- *The Children Are Watching* is part of the *Multicultural Education Series* edited by James A. Banks. "The more I read and think about the relationship between the mass media and school education, particularly where diversity is concerned, the more I recognize the topic's tortuous complexities, puzzling inconsistencies, tantalizing paradoxes, and constant surprises," writes the author (p. xvii). Cortés analyzes the entertainment and news media and grapples with issues such as the way in which the media frame diversity and transmit values concerning identity, contribute to stereotypes, and influence thinking about topics like race, ethnicity, gender, religion, and sexual orientation.

Lee, E., Menkart, D., & Okazawa-Rey, M. *Beyond heroes and holidays: A practical guide to K–12 antiracist, multicultural education and staff development*. Washington, DC: Network of Educators on the Americas, 1998.
- *Beyond Heroes and Holidays* is an interdisciplinary guide for teachers, administrators, students, and parents. It offers lessons and readings developed by teachers that show how to analyze the roots of racism; investigate the impact of racism on all our lives, our families, and our communities; examine the relationship between racism and other forms of oppression such as sexism, classism, and heterosexism; and learn to work to dismantle racism in our schools, communities, and the wider society.

Loewen, J. W. *Lies my teacher told me: Everything your American history textbook got wrong*. New York: Touchstone, 1995.
- *Lies My Teacher Told Me* is a thought-provoking book that surveys a series of twelve leading high school American history texts and concludes that not one does a decent job of making history interesting or memorable because they omit almost all the ambiguity, passion, conflict, and drama from our past due to an

interesting combination of blind patriotism, mindless optimism, sheer misinformation, and outright lies.

Menzel, P. *Material world: A global family portrait.* San Francisco: Sierra Club Books, 1994.

- Through photographs and statistics, *Material World* captures both the common humanity of the peoples inhabiting our Earth and the great differences in material goods and circumstances that make rich and poor societies. This colorful and illustrative book artfully depicts a global family portrait.

Miller-Lachman, L. *Our family, our friends, our world: An annotated guide to significant multicultural books for children and teenagers.* New Providence, NJ: R.R. Bowker, 1992.

- *Our Family, Our Friends, Our World* is a reference guide on multicultural fiction and non-fiction literature for children. As children begin to socialize and encounter friends of diverse racial, ethnic, linguistic, and social backgrounds, it is important to afford them with literary experiences that foster a sense of solidarity with "the others"—our common humanity. The book contains fiction and nonfiction works that provide fair and accurate accounts of diverse heritages and experiences that will enhance the opportunity for our children to live and learn together.

Olsen, L. *Made in America: Immigrant students in our public schools.* New York: The New Press, 1997.

- *Made in America* is a compelling account of our contemporary version of the Americanization of immigrants—a complex process that requires immigrant students to give up their national identities and mother tongue to be accepted in an academic and social world that then, ironically, denies them full participation.

Assessment

by Lorraine Valdez Pierce

Kate Smith is concerned about one of her students. Eduardo speaks English well enough, but he is enrolled in the ESOL program due to his weak reading and writing skills. As a 7th grader, Eduardo has already taken a number of standardized tests, and he has yet to score at the norm. In fact, he usually scores around the 25th percentile. The school system requires that students pass the state standardized tests in order to graduate from high school. Both Kate and her student worry about how they are going to accomplish this. Eduardo makes good grades in ESOL and math, but he is not as strong in social studies and science. Kate is not sure how she will know when Eduardo will be ready to take the standardized tests. Based on his grades alone, he might be ready now, but Kate knows that grades don't tell the whole story. She even uses multiple-choice and fill-in-the-blank formats to help prepare Eduardo for the standardized tests. She just doesn't know what else she can do to show her hardworking student that he is making progress and to help him pass the standardized tests.

Introduction

This chapter addresses a number of issues in the assessment of English language learners. First, we begin with the political context for assessment, including trends in statewide testing and recent changes in federal legislation on education. We also review guidelines for appropriate test use with language minority students and principles for using tests with this population. Second, we examine basic issues in assessment, including assessment purpose, validity and threats to validity (types of bias), and reliability. Third, we introduce readers to the various types of assessments used in education today, from norm-referenced to performance-based assessments. We also look at assessment procedures used in the identification and placement of English language learners and school accountability systems. We provide an overview of trends in classroom-based assessment and offer five operating principles for the assessment of English language learners in classroom settings. This chapter focuses on how to increase the validity of assessments by linking assessment to instruction and gives examples of how to do this in oral language, reading, writing, and the content areas. Finally, we make recommendations for teachers who want to begin to make changes in their assessment practices and call for long-term professional development in assessment.

Context For Assessment

Over the last decade, assessment has been the hot-button topic in education. Everywhere we look in education today, we are met by legislators, school board members, business leaders, and parents demanding accountability for learning. Typically, these demands are made in light of local, state, or national standards in the content areas, and most recently, in the field of

English as a second language (TESOL Standards, 1997). While many teachers would like to think that what goes on in the classroom is far removed from politics, nothing could be further from the truth. This is especially true of classroom assessment practices. Most teachers already in the classroom live with the daily pressure of helping their ESOL/bilingual students pass statewide, standards-based, and local tests to demonstrate mastery of basic skills in reading, writing, social studies, and mathematics. In addition, professional education organizations such as the American Association for the Advancement of Science (AAAS), the National Council of Teachers of English (NCTE), the National Council of Teachers of Mathematics (NCTM), and the National Council of Teachers of Social Studies (NCTSS) have all set standards for what students need to know and be able to do at various grade levels in a number of subject-specific areas such as reading, writing, and content area conceptual development. Proposals for classroom-level testing have been made at all levels of government. Since public school systems are funded with taxpayer dollars, politicians at all three levels of government (local, state and national) are eager to show voters that their tax dollars are being well spent. In this section, we look at the political context for assessment at national, state, and local levels of government.

National Level

At the national level, in December 2001, the No Child Left Behind Act of 2001 was signed into federal law by President George Bush. This law requires annual testing of all students in Grades 3–8. The stated purpose of this testing is to ensure that students are caught at learning points that can be redirected or remediated toward success. Proponents of the testing initiative agree that it is better to catch students before they fail so that they don't fall between the cracks and ultimately drop out of school. Reasonable citizens might tend to agree with the stated motive behind the annual testing. However, the fallacy of this argument is that annual testing may provide a partial diagnosis of student learning at best, and at worst, it provides no assurances for providing students with the type of instruction and materials they need to succeed in school. Calling for annual national testing to improve student achievement might be comparable to requiring a doctor to take the temperature of each patient to ensure that he/she overcome the flu. One measure of health cannot cure anyone of a disease any more than a single test score or battery of test scores can increase student learning.

The Bush 2001 administration is not the first to propose national testing. In 1997, after repeated efforts, the Clinton administration put forth recommendations for voluntary national testing of students in Grades 4 and 8. This was part of President Clinton's Goals 2000 educational plan. Federal legislation has encouraged or required testing in the Educate America Act of 1994 (Goals 2000) and in Title I of the Elementary and Secondary Education Act of 1965. Prior to that, in 1991, President George Bush, Sr., proposed national testing as part of America 2000, a national school reform plan (Rothman, 1995). However, such proposals for national testing have met with resistance in Congress, most recently regarding the issue of how to provide funding to states to pay for testing programs. Nevertheless, federal legislation continues to promote the use of standardized tests and large-scale testing for program evaluation purposes.

State Level

At the state level, almost all states now have a mandated state testing program in place similar to that proposed at the national level. All states use tests to determine how well students are doing in school, and 49 states have set academic standards. Almost half the states (24) already require, or by 2008 will require, that students pass a standardized test in order to obtain a high school diploma. More than half the states (27) hold schools accountable for results by rating performance of all schools (*Education Week,* January 2001). Yet, only seven states use some type of performance assessment (such as a writing sample) at the state level, and only two states require use of portfolios (Vermont & Kentucky). State legislatures and/or Boards of Education have put into place predominantly traditional, multiple-choice tests in the content areas, some administered every year and others required in specific grades in elementary and secondary schools. Not surprisingly, then, teachers feel daily pressure to cover the content of these tests, often at the cost of more meaningful and substantive learning material.

Requiring language minority students and English language learners to pass a standardized test poses problematic issues. One problem with requiring students to pass a single state test or series of tests in order to graduate from high school, not considering grades or scores on other tests (such as SATs or ACTs), is that a single measure on one type of test cannot accurately reflect student learning or ensure that students have mastered all the standards set for high school. A series of studies conducted by McNeil and her colleagues at Rice University in Texas found that standardized tests in that state actually shut teachers and students out of the education equation, undermined educational quality, and promoted discrimination against minority students by watering down the curriculum (McNeil, 2000).

Another problem with requiring English language learners to attain a minimum score on a standardized test is that every standardized test administered in English in U.S. public schools is ultimately a test of the English language. If students are not proficient in the language, they won't do well on the test, not necessarily because they don't know the subject matter of the test, but because they don't know enough English to read the test. To avoid the misuse of norm-referenced standardized test results, students can be assessed in English reading and writing to determine if they are ready to take standardized tests. Since these tests allow comparisons between language minority students and native English speakers across the country, language minority students need to have attained a level of literacy that allows them to show their understanding on a standardized test in English, including following oral and written test directions, reading text passages, and using vocabulary appropriate to the subject matter of the test (Collier & Thomas, 1998). Thomas and Collier suggest that students with no proficiency in English who are enrolled in language support programs will take from two to four years to reach readiness to take norm-referenced tests. More specifically, their research has shown that students in ESL programs without access to native language instruction and who eventually move on to grade-level classes can reach the 50th NCE (normal curve equivalent) on standardized tests in English after seven to ten years of all-English schooling. Students in high quality bilingual programs took less time to reach this benchmark, approximately four to seven years (Collier & Thomas, 1998). However, we must remember that scoring at the 50th NCE is only a starting point and should not be considered an optimal level of attainment for English language learners. Ultimately, as Collier and Thomas point out, the goal of schooling is to eliminate the achievement gap between English language learners and native speakers of English at the same grade level.

Other recommendations for using standardized tests have been proposed by the Committee on Appropriate Test Use of the National Research Council. This committee recommends that high-stakes decisions such as graduation from high school be made with *multiple* measures rather than relying on a single test score (Heubert & Hauser, 1999). Multiple measures ensure reliability of the information; they are similar to looking at still snapshots of a person or thing from different angles or at different points in time. Multiple measures provide a fuller picture of a student's academic strengths and weaknesses than any single measure can show.

Does potential misuse of statewide standardized testing mean English language learners should be excluded from the process? The answer to this question depends on the level of English language proficiency attained by each student being tested. Statewide testing for accountability, when conducted in accordance with the guidelines provided in this section, can help improve the educational status of English language learners. Test scores that are used improperly can serve as an incentive to action and dialogue by concerned parents and educators (Heubert & Hauser, 1999).

Local Level

In addition to national and state mandates for testing, school systems find themselves scrambling to meet local standards-based assessments, as well. Whereas many schools ask teachers to meet each student's learning needs by "differentiating" instruction and placing them in special programs such as ESL and special education, not much special consideration is given at the assessment level. ESL and bilingual students are typically required to take state and local tests at some point in their school careers. Some school systems

Guidelines for Teaching

APPROPRIATE TEST USE FOR LANGUAGE MINORITY STUDENTS

NATIONAL RESEARCH COUNCIL

Specific recommendations by the National Research Council (NRC) can provide guidance on appropriate test use for language minority students, as well as for majority students. In particular, the NRC proposes three criteria and four basic principles of appropriate test use (Heubert and Hauser, 1999). The three criteria for determining whether test use is appropriate are:

1. *Measurement validity.* Does the test accurately measure a student's knowledge in the content area being tested?

2. *Attribution of cause.* Does a student's performance on a test reflect knowledge and skill based on appropriate instruction or is it a result of language proficiency, learning disabilities, or ineffective instructional approaches and programs?

3. *Effectiveness of the treatment.* Do test scores lead to placement in programs that help improve learning?
   These criteria are all critical when using tests with English language learners and language minority students.

The four basic principles of appropriate test use recommended by the National Research Council include the following:

1. Validity is based on *how* a test is used because tests are not inherently valid without regard to how the results are used.

2. Tests are not perfect, nor are they an exact measure of student learning. Therefore, no single test score can be considered a clear measure of a student's knowledge.

3. Educational decisions for high-stakes purposes (e.g., graduation from high school, grade promotion, program placement) should not be made solely on the basis of a single test score.

4. Test scores cannot justify a bad decision. When test scores are used to retain students in grade without providing special instructional support services that meet each learner's needs, even tests based on the highest standards will not produce increases in student learning.

give students a 1–3 year waiver or exclusionary period while in special-language programs. Other states and school systems allow for accommodations, including giving test directions in the native language and allowing the use of bilingual dictionaries. These accommodations vary from state to state, although not much research exists documenting their effectiveness.

A pernicious local policy that has the potential for doing more harm than good is the exclusion of ESL students' scores from the total school averages. School administrators often exclude (called *disaggregating*) the test scores of ESOL/bilingual students so that the total school averages at each grade level on various subtests will not be reduced by factoring in the low scores of those students. While school principals may look upon this policy as one that fairly represents their school's achievement, the truth is that it actually presents a distorted picture of reality. If a segment of the school population is excluded from the test score history, then who is the testing benefiting? This type of exclusionary policy, if it does not provide for alternative assessments to be given to the ESL/bilingual students in place of the state tests, can have the negative effect of limiting accountability for the progress of these students.

Growing Backlash

As many parents across the country have begun to understand that standardized tests are being used as de facto curricula to the exclusion of other types of learning (such as problem solving, social skills, art, music, and drama), there has been a growing backlash against the state testing movement. This backlash has taken aim at state legislatures and Boards of Education that propose using the tests as gatekeepers for a high school diploma (Kohn, 1999; McNeil, 2000; Ohanian, 1999). Examples can be found in states such as Massachusetts and Virginia. Parents in Massachusetts have asked their children to boycott classes on test days. In Virginia, parents have formed a coalition called Parents Across Virginia United to Reform the Standards of Learning (PAVURSOL). These parents speak out against the uses of state-mandated, standardized tests at state board meetings, public hearings, and community meetings across the state. As more and more majority parents speak out against these types of tests, state legislatures will begin to listen and modify their tests or testing policies. Already in Virginia, the State Board of Education has listened and allowed for alternatives to the state's Standards of Learning Tests (although the alternatives seem to be aimed at high-achieving children). Most recently, the state lowered passing scores on the social studies test in response to a public outcry over the content of the test.

Basic Assessment Concepts

To be able to use tests appropriately with English language learners, we need to first understand some basic concepts in assessment. In this section, we will examine assessment purpose and its role in helping determine the validity of an assessment, define validity and reliability as these terms are used in assessment, describe types of bias in assessment, and discuss the role of standards, both developmental and absolute, in determining student progress.

Assessment Purpose

Assessment is the process of gathering data on student achievement for the purpose of making educational decisions. These decisions may reflect a variety of purposes.

Guidelines for Teaching

The five most common purposes for conducting educational assessment with ESL/bilingual students include: (1) identification and placement in ESL, bilingual, special education, or regular classrooms; (2) determining readiness to exit or leave a special program; (3) monitoring student progress in special and regular classrooms; (4) accountability for meeting state and local standards; and (5) program evaluation to determine the effectiveness of a specific instructional program. Each of these will be described in the following sections of this chapter.

It is important to know one's purpose in assessment in order to determine the best type of test or measure to use. For example, in monitoring student progress in classrooms, both process and product data is needed. Teachers need to collect information not only on the processes of learning (e.g., use of reading or writing strategies) but also on the products, such as completed work samples or projects. By collecting both types of information, teachers are in a better position to recommend particular instructional approaches or activities to help students improve. If, on the other hand, school administrators are interested in determining whether students have met state or local standards, they will primarily focus on the products or outcomes of student performance.

Validity

Assessment purpose, in addition to guiding the selection of the most appropriate measure to use, also determines the level of validity that needs to be established for the assessment tools. The higher the stakes of the assessment purpose, the more important it is to verify the validity of the assessment tools and process. The **validity** of an assessment measure or tool indicates the extent to which it is an adequate measure of the curriculum and objectives it represents. For example, a test claiming to be a test of reading that consists of fifty vocabulary items outside of any reading context is probably not a valid test of reading ability since this ability itself was not measured. Several types of validity have been described in testing handbooks, but the most important types for classroom teachers to understand are *content validity* and *consequential validity*. **Content validity** is attained when there is a close match between the content of the assessment and that of the curriculum and instruction. When students are assessed on the material that they have been studying in the classroom, the assessment measure can be said to have content validity. **Consequential validity** refers to the way the assessment results are used to improve teaching and learning. When test or assessment results are used to redirect teaching and aid learning, the measure can be said to have consequential validity. In cases where state and local tests are used without giving teachers access to test results or information on how to support student learning through instructional activities, these tests can be said to lack consequential validity.

Validity of an assessment measure can be significantly threatened by the presence of systematic **bias.** Bias reduces the validity of an assessment. Types of bias in assessment are: cultural bias, attitudinal bias, assessment bias, and test or norming bias.

Cultural bias refers to an item or process that requires knowledge of a particular culture's values and shared experiences but is not intended for measuring this knowledge. For example, if a test of reading requires knowledge of a particular holiday in American culture that a language minority student or immigrant child is unfamiliar with, the test of reading becomes a test of cultural knowledge. In this case, cultural bias has changed the test from a test of reading to a test of culture.

Tests of language, such as commercially available English language proficiency tests, are inherently biased toward the culture of the native English-speaking population by whom they were developed (American, Australian, British, or Canadian). This is because all language tests have inherent cultural qualities. Language tests reflect the experiences, beliefs, and artifacts of the particular culture they represent. Is it possible to construct a culture-free test? No, according to Hamayan and Damico (1991), because representing culture on language tests is unavoidable. To limit the effects of cultural bias on language tests, assessors can use more than one measure of language and use tasks that are as natural and culturally neutral as possible (especially in assessment of oral language and reading).

Attitudinal bias refers to the assessor's attitude toward a language, dialect, or "accent" such as having a negative attitude toward students who speak English with a Spanish accent but having a positive attitude toward speakers of French or German (Hamayan & Damico, 1991). Having a bias toward one dialect or another can negatively affect assessment results, as when a teacher has lower expectations for students speaking the dialect or forms a permanent impression of students that clouds professional judgment of their work.

Assessment bias occurs when assessors do not take into consideration the potential effects on test scores of culturally different children being assessed. Cultural differences that may influence student responses or types of responses include: child-rearing practices, previous school setting or lack of schooling, previous life experiences in a significantly different environment, the value or nonvalue of competition in each student's culture, cultural mores, and the sociocultural status of the student's ethnic group within the larger society (Hamayan & Damico, 1991). All too often, ESL and bilingual students will not share or exhibit these values. Teachers and assessors need to become familiar with the second language acquisition process as well as the student's home culture in order to make appropriate interpretations of test scores.

Test or **norming bias** refers to the use of standardized tests that have not been shown to have conceptual, linguistic, and metric equivalence for cultural or racial populations not represented in the normative data (Suzuki,

Guidelines for Teaching

For example, a typical school system in the United States values the following elements for students taking a test:

- grade-level appropriate English language proficiency, including shared cultural meanings between students and assessors,
- analytical thinking skills,
- acceptance of the value of competition with other students,
- experience in taking timed, standardized tests,
- and knowledge of the way schools and classrooms work. (Garcia & Pearson, 1994; Hamayan & Damico, 1991)

Ponterotto, & Meller, 2001). This means that if students from particular language minority groups have not been part of the norming data, the results of the standardized test are not valid (accurate) for making decisions about these students (Garcia & Pearson, 1994). Even when tests claim to have included the test scores of language minority students, the ratio is so small as to make their inclusion meaningless (Hamayan & Damico, 1991). State tests that are criterion-referenced are typically also norm-referenced, with passing or cut scores set arbitrarily or based on scores of the native English-speaking population of the state. Assessors and teachers need to be aware of test bias on statewide tests, especially those that are required for high school graduation. Alternative means of assessment can be used for ESL and bilingual students who cannot get past the language demands of the standardized tests.

Another type of bias is that which is introduced when psychological tests have been translated from the original English into the native language of the students. Translated tests cannot be assumed to be valid or reliable because even though words can be translated, the measurement will not be equivalent in the order of difficulty of the items. Many cultural concepts cannot be translated. In addition, using interpreters for testing students in English lacks a strong research base (Valdes & Figueroa, 1994).

One way to limit bias in language and content area assessments used with ESL/bilingual students is to conduct dual-language testing. Testing is conducted in English *and* the student's native language to determine native-language literacy levels and knowledge of content area matter. Clearly specified scoring criteria can also help reduce the presence of bias in scoring student work by helping teachers focus on matching student performance to the established criteria rather than on comparing students to each other.

Reliability

Reliability of an assessment measure refers to the degree of consistency of the assessment in producing the same result with the same student in different testing settings or at different points in time or when being evaluated by different teachers or raters. As with validity, the higher the stakes for the assessment results, the more essential it is for a high level of reliability to be established in the assessment process and measures. For decisions concerning program placement or high school graduation, the level of reliability should be high. High levels of reliability can be established through the use of objective tests, multiple measures, multiple raters, and clearly specified scoring criteria. States typically use multiple raters to score student writing samples that are produced to show progress toward meeting state standards. Using multiple raters establishes **inter-rater reliability.**

Classroom teachers making weekly assessment decisions can also establish reliability of their assessments by using multiple and varied measures. Clearly specified scoring criteria in the form of checklists or scoring rubrics can also help ensure that teachers are evaluating each student's work using the same standards, not having higher expectations for some students than for others.

In some cases, however, it is appropriate to set different standards for individual students, especially in the case of students with learning or emotional disabilities or where classrooms display a wide variety of English language proficiency and cognitive ability. The notion of using standards appropriate to each student's current level of ability is called using **developmental** or **relative standards.** Developmental standards are appropriate for making decisions about individual student progress.

Teachers can also set standards that all students are expected to meet called **absolute standards.** An example of an absolute standard in oral language assessment might be:

> *Students will ask for and give directions for getting from one place to another with few errors in vocabulary, grammar, or pronunciation.*

Absolute standards are appropriate for making decisions about groups or for comparing individual progress to that of the group. Teachers of language-learning students can develop standards for individual students that vary with each individual's strengths and weaknesses. Rather than expecting *all* students to meet the same performance standard, teachers can set different standards for each student. For example, in a mixed-ability level ESL classroom, beginners would be expected to progress at a rate of learning and to master language features different from those to be mastered by a high intermediate or advanced language learner. Similarly, a student might attain high standards in oral language and not reach the performance levels in writing set for native English-speaking peers.

Types of Assessments

In the world of assessment, a wide variety of measurement tools has been developed for an even broader array of assessment purposes. The three most common types of assessments used in language proficiency and achievement testing are (1) norm-referenced, (2) criterion-referenced, and (3) performance-based assessments. These will each be described below.

Norm-referenced testing provides "a broad indication of relative standing" (Cohen, 1994). It gives an *overall, general estimate* of ability in content areas. Norm-referenced tests are used to see how well a student has learned specific concepts and skills when compared to other students in a large norming group. For example, a student who scores at the 75th percentile in reading has exceeded the reading score of 75 percent of the students in the comparison group. Norms can be established at national, state, and local levels. It is important to check test administration manuals to determine the groups that the test was normed on. In most cases, students in bilingual/ESL programs will not be part of a norming group for norm-referenced tests designed for use with mainstream students. For tests in a student's native language, such as Spanish, it is important that the dialect of the test be the same as that of the students. For example, a student who speaks the Spanish of the southwestern United States will most likely not be familiar with the vocabulary or some of the syntax of the Spanish spoken in Spain or Puerto Rico. All languages have a variety of dialects, and not all students will speak or read the standard dialect.

Norm-referenced tests are typically in a multiple-choice format where students mark their answers on answer sheets by filling in the bubbles or small circular spaces with Number 2 pencils. However, they can also consist of constructed-response items, where students complete a statement or respond to a prompt. Multiple-choice tests are used because they are objective (only one answer is correct) and reliable. One problem posed by norm-referenced tests is that they often lack content validity when they do not reflect the instructional activities of the classroom. Another concern is that teachers need to know how well English language learners can use functional and academic language in real contexts, and this cannot be directly determined through pencil and paper, fill-in-the-bubble tests. Since norm-referenced, standardized tests are administered only once or twice a year in most school systems, teachers are left to their own devices to collect information on student progress with regard to curricular goals during the rest of the year. Examples of norm-referenced rests are the Stanford-9, Terra Nova, and the Iowa Test of Basic Skills (ITBS) used in grades K–12 and the Test of English as a Foreign Language (TOEFL) and the Scholastic Aptitude Test (SAT).

Norm-referenced, standardized tests are useful for several purposes: to compare individual performance to that of the norming group, to identify relative areas of strength and weakness in learning, to monitor annual growth in skills such as reading and mathematics, and to evaluate program and school effectiveness. This type of test is not appropriate for monitoring the progress of students in language support programs such as ESL and bilingual education because these students do not yet have the English language skills to demonstrate their knowledge on these tests. However, they are useful for tracking the academic progress of these students once they are out of language programs and in mainstream classes.

Criterion-referenced assessments describe a student's performance according to established criteria (McTighe & Ferrara, 1998). Standards and performance criteria are used to determine the extent to which an individual has met local or state standardxss and instructional objectives. Criterion-referenced assessment lets students know exactly what they have to know and be able to do. When students know what and how they are to demonstrate their learning, they can learn how to become more responsible for their own learning (Cohen, 1994).

Criterion-referenced assessments may be multiple choice or may not look like tests at all. These assessment formats may be constructed-response items, where students construct a response, create a product, or perform a demonstration (McTighe & Ferrara, 1998). Constructed-response items also include portfolios and self-assessment logs. These formats allow for a broad range of responses rather than a single correct response, and because of this they require professional judgment in assessment.

Challenges in developing criterion-referenced assessments include: (1) determining which objectives are worth assessing; (2) learning how to construct items or tasks for those objectives; (3) learning how to administer or format the items and determining the number of items to use; and (4) deciding what constitutes attainment of an objective by individuals as well as the entire class (Cohen, 1994; McTighe & Ferrara, 1998; Wiggins, 1998).

Some problems with criterion-referenced tests, especially when used in statewide testing, are (1) the pressure put on teachers to "teach to the test"; (2) assessment of predominantly lower-order thinking skills; (3) arbitrarily set cut-scores; and (4) the difficulty of using enough items that represent mastery of a single objective in order to obtain an acceptable level of reliability (Collier & Thomas, 1998).

The main difference between norm-referenced and criterion-referenced tests lies in the manner that they are used. Norm-referenced tests are used to compare the mastery of broad objectives by groups and individuals to that of a norming group of learners. With criterion-referenced assessment, on the other hand, the learner's performance is judged based on his/her mastery of specific skills and objectives.

In addition to norm-referenced and criterion-referenced tests, **performance-based assessments** can be used to assess language proficiency and academic achievement. Performance-based assessments have come of age in the 1990s and appear to be here to stay. For example, in university teacher preparation programs across the country, for the first time, professors are being asked to use performance-based assessments to document outcomes for their graduates. Progress reports submitting course syllabi are no longer enough (National Council for Accreditation of Teacher Education, 2002).

Performance-based assessments require students "to actively accomplish complex and significant tasks, while bringing to bear prior knowledge, recent learning, and relevant skills to solve realistic or authentic problems" (Herman, Aschbacher, & Winters, 1992, page 2). These types of assessments require students to perform their competence and to apply knowledge and skills rather than simply recall and regurgitate facts (McTighe & Ferrara, 1998).

Performance-based assessments have been developed as a response to the perceived limitations of traditional standardized tests. Educators working primarily with general education students have questioned whether standardized tests represent significant learning outcomes.

Innovative aspects of performance-based assessments include making assessment criteria explicit and formal and assessing learning processes as well as products. Performance-based assessments "offer appealing ways to assess complex thinking and problem-solving skills, and, because they are grounded in realistic problems, are potentially more motivating and reinforcing for students" (Herman, Aschbacher, & Winters, 1992, page 9).

Teachers of English language learners can use performance-based assessments to gauge student progress toward meeting specific instructional goals and objectives. Performance-based assessments can be used to assess language proficiency and content skills through oral reports, presentations, demonstrations, essays, and portfolios. Performance-based assessments can have any number of formats, including oral interviews and essays and can include both processes (multiple drafts of a writing sample) and products (projects or essays). In assigning grades to student work, teachers can use evaluative scales called **scoring rubrics** that clearly delineate to students the standards and criteria by which their work will be assessed. Examples of evaluative scales used in performance-based assessment include scoring rubrics or rating scales, teacher observation checklists, anecdotal records, and self-assessment checklists. A sample scoring rubric for oral language appears in Figure 8.1.

Performance-based assessments become **authentic assessments** when they are based on classroom instruction and reflect tasks similar to those called for in the real world (Wiggins, 1998). Key elements of authentic assessment are clear performance criteria; higher-order thinking skills; meaningful, challenging tasks; integration of language skills; assessment of both process and product; and information on the depth (rather than breadth) of a student's knowledge over a wide array of skills. Another key element is self-assessment or the direct involvement of students in monitoring their own performance and setting learning goals for future work (Wiggins, 1998).

Among the challenges in using performance-based assessments are: (1) setting clear and fair criteria; (2) designing the tasks; (3) making professional judgments about student work; and (4) making the time to collaborate on the design of these assessments through professional development. Performance-based assessments do not typically produce one single, correct answer but promote a wide range of responses. Therefore, evaluation of student performances and products must be based on teacher judgment. This judgment is based on the criteria that have been specified for each task (McTighe & Ferrara, 1998). Professional development time for developing performance-based tasks and assessments competes with time needed for helping teachers assist students in meeting state standards on norm-referenced or criterion-referenced tests. Since the norm-referenced and criterion-referenced tests are the primary tools used in statewide assessment, very little time, if any, is available for teachers interested in developing performance-based assessments.

Student Name_____

Date_____

In-class Oral Report *
Scoring Rubric

Rating	Observed Performance
4	Presents a well-organized report. Conveys accurate information on the topic. Speaks loudly and clearly. Uses a variety of precise vocabulary. Designs visual aids that enhance meaning. Makes grammar or syntax errors that do not interfere with meaning. Responds accurately to questions.
3	Presents a report that is partially organized but may lose focus. Conveys accurate information on the topic. Speaks with some hesitation. Uses generic or repetitive vocabulary. Designs visual aids that support meaning. Makes grammar or syntax errors that interfere with meaning. May respond to questions with some inconsistencies.
2	Presents a report that lacks clear organization. Conveys inaccurate information on the topic. Speaks with some hesitation or long pauses. Uses generic or repetitive vocabulary. Designs visual aids that do not support meaning. Makes grammar or syntax errors that interfere with meaning. Responds to questions with some inconsistencies.
1	Presents a report that lacks organization. Conveys inaccurate information on the topic. Reads from notes or does not speak loudly enough. Uses limited or high frequency vocabulary. Does not use visual aids. Makes grammar or syntax errors that interfere with meaning. Responds to questions with many inconsistencies.

*Designed for Middle School Students of Intermediate English Language Proficiency

Figure 8.1

Over the past decade, with more importance being given to standardized, multiple-choice tests, educators have found it difficult to move away from the multiple-choice single-answer format. They want to prepare their students for the tests, so shouldn't they test this way in class? The answer is yes and no. Yes, teachers can provide students with test-taking skills that will help them show what they know on the standardized tests. No, curriculum shouldn't be narrowed to the lower-order thinking skills measured by single-answer, multiple-choice tests. This type of test may be useful for assessing basic skills, but it cannot possibly show the range of higher-order thinking skills and social interaction skills required in today's world, nor is the information generated by them useful for planning instruction to meet each student's learning needs. A good rule of thumb would be to use criterion-referenced and performance-based assessments to monitor learning in the classroom and to use norm-referenced tests, once students acquire basic proficiency in English, to compare their performance to that of students in general education classes at the same school as well as to a national norming group (Collier & Thomas, 1998).

In the following sections, we will be concerned with the two types of testing that are most frequently used with bilingual and ESL students: English language proficiency testing and achievement testing. Both of these types of assessment are administered at the program or schoolwide level, with ESL/bilingual specialists and teachers administering both types. School-based assessment will be described below as assessment of language for the purpose of placing students in language-support programs, such as ESL and bilingual education. Classroom-based assessment will be discussed from the teacher's perspective, including some tips for how to move forward with criterion-referenced and performance-based assessments that are linked to instruction.

School-Based Assessment

At the school or district level, English language learning students are assessed for a variety of reasons related to program placement and evaluation, including placement in language-based programs that meet their needs, moving out of those programs into the regular classroom, meeting state and local standards, and making progress in state and federally funded programs, such as Title I, Title VII (replaced in December 2001 by Title III), and special education programs. Each of these purposes will be described below.

Identification and Placement

The purpose of assessment for program placement is to identify those students who need special language services such as ESL or bilingual education. Federal law requires that students who cannot function in the regular, all-English classroom receive language instruction that helps them acquire English as rapidly as possible. However, the law does not prescribe the type of program in which the student should be enrolled. Three purposes of assessment in identification and placement of English language learners include: (1) the screening/identification of students needing special language-based services; (2) program placement to determine the language ability and content knowledge of students in order to place them at one of the various levels of an ESL or bilingual education program; and (3) reclassification or program exit to determine when a student no longer needs the language-based program and is ready to move out of it and into the regular classroom.

To identify those students who need special language services, we need to first have a definition of the characteristics required for eligibility for these services. While federal law specifies the needs of the limited English proficient student, each state must operationalize the definition with the ways and means to identify these students. Not surprisingly, there is tremendous variation across states as to who qualifies for English language services. This is problematic, because it means that not all students are identified using similar criteria. Only about one-third of the states require or recommend assessment procedures for identification of English language learners. Most of the states do not have procedures in place that can prevent inaccurate identification of students. In fact, not all states even have an operational definition for students who are limited English proficient (LEP) (O'Malley & Pierce, 1994). Without appropriate identification procedures, students cannot gain access to instructional programs that meet their learning needs. Furthermore, without accurate use of effective assessment tools or the resulting data, students may be inappropriately referred to special education or reading programs that are not designed to meet their language acquisition needs (see Chapter 9 on Special Education).

Those states that do require or recommend assessment procedures for identification and placement use a combination of assessment approaches, including a Home Language Survey to determine the language spoken in the home or most frequently used by the student, and assessment of oral language, reading, and/or writing. While the Home Language Survey can be used to identify the language minority background students, it alone cannot be used to identify those who need language-based services. States use a combination of commercially available language proficiency tests, criterion-referenced tests, achievement tests, grades, interviews, and teacher observations and referrals to assess students' language proficiency. Few states use classroom-based or performance-based assessments for identification and placement purposes.

Assessment of language proficiency in the native language is recommended to determine whether students have literacy skills. If they do, they can be assumed to have a reading/writing foundation upon which to base English language literacy instruction. Placement in ESL or bilingual programs will be most accurate when based upon multiple measures, as will program exit decisions.

Program exit assessment has as its purpose the determination of whether a student has gained the language skills and content area competencies needed to benefit from instruction in regular, grade-level classrooms. As with assessment for program placement, multiple measures should be used for determining student readiness to exit a language support program. These measures may include: language proficiency tests, grades, interviews, teacher recommendations, and standardized tests. In addition, monitoring ELL students with the use of content area achievement tests or statewide tests after reclassification/exit can help identify areas needing growth and support.

Achievement Testing/Accountability Systems

In addition to identification and placement assessment, schools administer achievement tests and statewide tests (including high school graduation tests) to ensure that students in the general population attain expected educational goals or standards. English language learners need to be included in these accountability systems. When test scores are available for these students, we have a clearer picture of their academic needs in the content areas. Caution should be used in interpreting test results, however. Since the focus of accountability testing is on groups rather than individuals, using test results to make high-stakes decisions about individual ESL/bilingual students cannot be justified. In fact, Valdes and Figueroa (1994) make one of the strongest statements on this position:

> *Standardized tests should not be used in any aspect of a decision-making process with bilingual populations. There is no way of minimizing the potential harm to this population resulting from seemingly "objective" and "scientific" psychometric tests. All such testing should be discontinued.* (p. 203).

When students are not eligible to take the statewide tests, then alternate measures such as criterion-referenced or performance-based assessments can be used to monitor their progress in the language-based or regular classroom.

Program Evaluation

When ELL students participate in specially funded programs, government agencies require that those programs be evaluated to determine their effectiveness in helping students learn. To determine the effects of federal, state, or local instructional programs, objective measures such as standardized tests are typically used to determine student progress.

These tests may be norm-referenced or criterion-referenced. Performance-based assessments such as writing samples can also be used for program evaluation. For program evaluation purposes, assessment measures are used to document student products or learning outcomes rather than learning processes.

Classroom-Based Assessment

Traditional and Student-Centered Teaching

Little has changed in classroom-based testing for at least the past fifty years (Bertrand, 1994). Traditional testing assumes that knowledge of facts is the priority assessment goal, and that these facts can be broken down into fragmented components. This approach has been questioned over the past decade, however, because it does not provide information on students' functional use of higher-order thinking skills (Bertrand, 1994; Glasser, 1990; Herman et.al, 1992). Another assumption of traditional testing formats is that using professional judgment is unreliable, and teachers cannot be trusted to use their own judgment in evaluating student work. A corollary assumption is that the only good test is an objective test (one correct answer only).

In this century, two movements have emerged in schools that have a direct impact on the way teachers assess students' work. First, teachers' rights and obligations to judge and evaluate students' work has become less important than scores obtained on objective tests. Second, standardized tests have become tremendously important in making judgments about individual students, schools, programs, teachers, principals, and school superintendents. Both of these movements have come under scrutiny and attack in this decade (Bertrand, 1994; Herman et. al., 1992).

To understand the battle between traditional testing proponents and supporters of more innovative approaches to assessment, we need to first examine what goes on in traditional and student-centered classrooms (Bertrand, 1994). Most teachers fall along a continuum ranging from traditional to student-centered teaching. Teachers on the "traditional" end of the continuum spend most of their time trying to "cover the curriculum" and follow a set of objectives in a minimal period of time, with little regard for meeting individual student needs and interests. These teachers also spend time correcting students' work and behavior, with the sole purpose of covering the instructional objectives and increasing test scores. Traditional teachers tend to spend little time on cooperative learning activities with students. Traditional teachers also use tests as periodic checks, typically at the end of a learning unit or grading period. Giving the tests takes up valuable time, as does grading the tests. As standardized tests increase in importance, we will continue to see more of this kind of teaching.

Teachers tend to assess the way they were assessed. This is because most teachers do not have access to practical assessment information in their teacher preparation programs. So, for example, for student essays, demonstrations, oral reports, and projects, teachers assign grades, usually based on the traditional 100-point scale that was used to assess their own school work, with 90 and above being an A, 80–89 being a B, and so on. However, most teachers do not have a systematic way to quantify or evaluate classroom-based activities and projects using constructed-response and performance-based assessments based on specific standards and criteria.

Teachers who lean more toward student-centered teaching tend to focus on student needs and interests as well as on learning processes rather than just the products of learning, such as test scores. Student-centered teachers assess student learning much of the time while also conducting instructional activities. These teachers have established collaborative classrooms where groups of students work together to meet learning objectives and standards. Using observation and criterion-based assessment, the student-centered teacher gathers assessment data while students are engaged in learning activities to determine their learning progress and identify learning needs. With increasing importance being placed on the role of standardized tests, teachers who aim to meet the learning needs of individual students are finding themselves in a time crunch to prepare students both to pass the standardized tests and also make progress toward individual learning goals. What to do?

Not surprisingly, many general education teachers and teachers of English language learners have responded to the need for students to pass standardized tests as a call to teach to the test using traditional formats, covering as much of the required curriculum as they can. These types of tests are seen to be in direct conflict with performance-based assessments. Therefore, emphasis on the use of performance-based assessments that focus on building on students' strengths continues to decrease in many classrooms. Does it have to be this way? Or can teachers meet students' learning needs *and* help prepare them to pass the standardized tests? We can respond in the affirmative if we understand that basic skills can be taught and assessed in meaningful contexts that promote the acquisition of problem-solving and higher-order thinking skills, as well. For example, teachers can collaborate with colleagues to prepare a matrix of state and local standards, define learning outcomes, and outline instructional activities that will engage the learner in applying knowledge and skills while also providing feedback on those skills, including basic skills to be assessed on the standardized tests.

Another way teachers can help prepare English language learners for standardized tests is to provide practice in test-taking skills. Practice tests are now available for many standardized tests, and teachers can use these to teach test-taking skills such as following oral and written directions, making inferences, and working within set time limits.

In the following section, we provide five fundamental assumptions and five operating principles for using fair and accurate classroom-based assessment procedures with English language learners. We will also provide some guidelines for getting started with classroom-based assessment that is objective, fair, and useful for providing feedback to students for learning and to the teacher for redirecting instruction.

 Guidelines for Teaching

FIVE FUNDAMENTAL ASSUMPTIONS

Classroom-based assessment of English language learners can be guided by five fundamental assumptions:

- it must be based on what we know about how language learners learn, in particular how they acquire reading and writing processes;
- it is integral to instruction, informs teaching, and improves learning;
- it uses multiple sources of information on a regular and systematic basis;
- it is culturally and developmentally appropriate; and
- it provides valid, reliable, and fair measures of learning. (Harp, 1994; O'Malley & Pierce, 1996; McTighe & Ferrara, 1998)

Classroom-based assessmnent of English language learners must begin with what we know about the second language acquisition process, including how students acquire skills in reading, writing, and the content areas. For example, if we know that writing is a process of revising multiple drafts of work after getting feedback on them, why do we test this construct differently (product only) from what the research suggests? Acquiring literacy skills in a second language means tapping prior knowledge, actively using reading and writing strategies, knowing something about text structure or how texts are organized, relating the topic to students' interests, and having students work collaboratively on reading-related activities. Do our classroom assessment tools capture student learning on any or all of these processes?

To inform teaching and improve learning, classroom assessment must be conducted on a regular, systematic basis, not just at the end of a unit of study. Effective teachers use assessment to collect baseline data or information on students' background knowledge and experiences prior to launching into a new unit of study. Teachers assess students weekly or biweekly to keep tabs on how they are progressing with regard to learning objectives. Teachers who are not able to judge student progress must resort to teaching without feedback, in a void, with no basis for judging the effectiveness of their teaching or follow a scripted curriculum or specific teaching method.

Classroom assessment also calls for collecting data from multiple sources in order to make a reliable judgment about student progress. The sources should also be varied in format, using a combination of assessments ranging from multiple-choice and fill-in-the blank tests to performance assessments such as written essays, oral reports, self-assessments, reading logs, and portfolios. The use of multiple sources is especially important when working with English language learners and special needs learners because it provides individual snapshots of student learning under a variety of conditions and skill requirements.

Classroom-based assessment must be culturally and developmentally appropriate to yield valid results. Culturally appropriate assessment begins with instruction. First, the language of the assessment should be the same as that of the instruction. So, for example, a student learning to read in Spanish would also be assessed in Spanish reading. In addition, students from traditional cultural backgrounds may not value competition with peers, and students from these cultures (including Latino students) may not respond to calls for individual achievement but instead may be more motivated to work as a team to help members attain a learning goal. Teachers can encourage group work while also showing students that individual competition in school is a highly-valued American principle. Developmentally appropriate assessment refers to using materials and tasks that have been designed for the age interest levels, and language proficiency of the student. For example, in the state of Virginia, much controversy has revolved around 3rd grade standards in social studies calling for knowledge of Egyptian kings and queens and forms of government. Many educators believe this topic is not developmentally appropriate for 3rd graders. A much more appropriate topic might be "My

Community," where students learn about people and places in the community in which they live.

A final assumption about classroom-based assessment is that it has *content* and *consequential validity*. Students are assessed on the instructional principles and activities presented in class (content validity), and assessment results are used to improve teaching and learning (consequential validity). Fairness is achieved when teachers assess students on the material and formats that have been presented in class. Assessments are unfair when teachers ask students to do something for assessment that has not been part of instruction, such as asking students to apply synthesis or evaluation skills when only knowledge and comprehension skills have been practiced in class. Assessment is also unfair when teachers show bias in their scoring or grading toward students whom they know to be "A" students or "F" students, based on previous performance. This phenomenon has been referred to as the "halo" and "pitchfork" effect by McTighe and Ferrara (1998). To avoid these effects, teachers can use blind scoring of student work. This entails covering up each student's name and assigning an individual number from 1–25 (or the total number of students in the class). When scoring student work, the student's identity is unknown, thereby reducing the potential for bias. Another approach to eliminating bias in the evaluation of student work is to use criterion-referenced assessment. Using a rating scale or checklist based on the presence or absence of specific criteria, teachers can guide their scoring against the criteria rather than against pre-conceived notions of students' abilities.

Five Operating Principles

In addition to the five fundamental assumptions discussed above, classroom-based assessment must also be based on five operating principles. These include: setting clear criteria for performance, scaffolding instruction and assessment for English language learners, using models or benchmarks, involving the learner in the assessment process, and assigning grades in an objective manner.

Setting Clear Criteria   A basic operating principle of authentic, classroom-based assessment is the specification of clear performance criteria that are shared with the students (Herman et al., 1992; McTighe & Ferrara, 1998). Many teachers *know* what they are looking for in student work and may think the *students know,* but in most cases, English language learners need help in understanding the teacher's expectations for performance in class. Some teachers propose assessment criteria and discuss these with the class. Other teachers ask students to generate criteria for evaluation of their work. To help make the criteria visible to the students, teachers can show examples of student work at various levels of achievement. In addition, teachers can document student progress and provide feedback on learning by assigning a score or grade using criteria listed on a checklist, rating scale, scoring rubric, or through oral and written feedback. See Figure 8.2 for an example of a rating scale for reading strategies.

Student Name_____

Date_____

Reading Strategies[*]
Rating Scale

Reading Strategies	Unassisted	With Assistance	Not Yet
1. Relates reading to prior knowledge			
2. Uses headings and pictures to make predictions			
3. Rereads sentences			
4. Identifies main idea			
5. Summarizes main idea			
6. Outlines main idea and supporting details			
7. Guesses meaning of words from context			
8. Analyzes ideas			
*Designed for High School Students of Advanced English Proficiency			

Figure 8.2

Scaffolding   In addition to setting clear criteria, teachers can reduce the language demand of any instructional or assessment task through the use of **scaffolding** (Chamot & O'Malley, 1994). Scaffolding refers to providing contextual supports for meaning through the use of simplified language, teacher modeling, visuals and graphics, cooperative learning, and hands-on experiences. Rather than water down the curriculum, teachers can provide access to higher-order thinking skills through scaffolded instruction and assessment. Scaffolding approaches are especially useful for content-based instruction or subject matter texts that have not been written with the English language learner in mind. By reducing the language demand of these content-based materials, teachers will be more likely to see students' strengths in the content areas.

Three types of scaffolding are: simplifying the language, asking for completion rather than generation, and using of visuals. Simplifying the language means using shorter sentences and paragraphs, giving less wordy directions, using the present tense, and avoiding idiomatic expressions. Asking for completion, not generation, can be acheived when teachers ask students to complete a task by selecting answers from a list or filling out a partially completed outline or paragraph. Using visuals includes presenting information and asking students to respond through the use of graphic organizers, tables and charts, graphs, and outlines. All of these scaffolding approaches can be used to assess what students can do with what they know without limiting assessment to evaluation of basic skills. As with the scaffolding used in buildings under construction, assessement scaffolding is temporary and can be removed when English language learners have the language skills to tackle assessments without it.

Using Benchmarks   Another way to help students succeed in the classroom is to use **benchmarks.** Benchmarks, also called *anchors* or *exemplars,* are models or examples of excellent work. If we want students to write a well-structured paragraph, then we need to show them many examples of these. Then we go through each one to show why it is a model paragraph, how it contains a topic sentence, sentences providing supporting details, and a concluding sentence that does not introduce a new topic. It would be helpful to put examples of excellent work on the bulletin board for students to see what an "A" or a "Level 4" paper looks like.

Involving the Learner in Assessment   Another operating principle of student-centered classrooms and authentic assessment is getting the learner involved in the assessment process. We can do this by asking for students' input in the generation of criteria for assessment of their work, teaching them to provide feedback to a peer, and showing them how to evaluate their own work. To make any of these approaches work, the teacher will have to feel comfortable in a collaborative classroom, where cooperative learning activities are regularly used for language and concept development. In addition, the teacher will need to be able to share his/her grading authority with the students. That is, the teacher must be open enough to student feedback that he/she is willing to elicit criteria and even change the criteria for evaluation if the students make reasonable requests to that effect. Teachers can also teach students the process and language of constructive feedback to peers. Guiding questions or partially completed peer interview sheets can help model the language of feedback so that it is positive rather than negative and destructive. Peers can provide feedback on writing using a writing checklist, for example. Once students have practiced the peer feedback process of applying criteria to a peer's work, they will be ready for self-assessment or applying criteria to their own work.

Grading   The final operating principle for fair classroom-based assessment of English language learners involves teacher grading practices. Grading can be a controversial topic, especially because it is idiosyncratic and varies from teacher to teacher. Subjectivity and unreliability of teacher grades were reasons why standardized tests were invented: Teachers couldn't be trusted to all grade the same way. Therefore, it would seem that major challenges of the student grading process are attaining objectivity, validity, reliability, and fairness. These challenges are compounded when we consider grading the English language learning student. How do we account for English language proficiency? And what about grading on the curve?

Teachers can make grades less subjective and more reliable by tying grades to criterion-referenced assessments and to the progress made by each individual student toward learning goals. Grades can be based on criteria specified on assessment tools such as checklists, scoring rubrics, and rating scales. These tools must be developmentally appropriate and match the level of language proficiency of the learner. In addition, grades can be assigned not only for student completion of work but for the quality of the work based on criteria. Finally, grades accompanied by constructive feedback can guide learners in setting learning goals for the next assignment (Wiggins, 1998). By linking grades to criteria for performance, teachers can ensure that they assign grades in a fair and reliable manner.

Grading on the curve, or using norm-referenced assessment to set arbitrary parameters for grades, is not a recommended practice for either English language learners or general education students. For example, a teacher who determines that he will only assign three As and three Fs in his class and that everyone else will fall in between, has set arbitrary limits for assigning grades that will not necessarily be fair or accurate. Statistical formulas for establishing norms on standardized tests do not apply to classroom grading practices and should not be used to assign grades to English language learners

Linking Assessment to Instruction

In the preceding section, we provided guidelines for achieving valid, fair, and reliable classroom-based assessments of English language learners. In this section, we give examples of how to ensure the validity of classroom-based assessments by linking assessment to instructional activities. This sounds like common sense, but let's take a look at an example of what happens when this principle is ignored.

Mary is a 3rd grade ESL teacher. She plans interactive, meaningful activities for her students such as Reader's Theater, literature discussion groups, and writers' workshop. Yet, when it comes to assessment, Mary relies on traditional multiple-choice and fill-in-the-blank tests that she makes herself or takes from textbook end-of-unit tests. She assesses writing by assigning a grade of A, B, and so on to writing samples depending on whether or not her young writers completed the five steps of the writing process (planning, drafting, editing, revising, publishing). When asked about using other forms of assessment, Mary rolls her eyes and says, "I don't need it. It takes time away from instruction, and besides, I already know how each student is doing. It's inside my head." Mary's version of assessment *does* take time away from instruction, but that is because Mary takes a traditional approach to assessment even though she provides student-centered instructional activities. Unusual? Not really. Without information or professional development on how to base assessment on instruction, most teachers are left without any sort of guidance for assessing student work. Here we provide some ideas for linking assessment to instructional activities that teachers conduct on a routine basis. By coordinating assessment with instructional activities, teachers can increase the content validity of their assessments and save time.

Oral Language

To begin planning for assessment of oral language, teachers need to first consider instructional activities they can conduct on a weekly basis for developing oral language. These same activities can often be used for gathering assessment data. That is, teachers can collect information on how students are using oral language simultaneously to the instructional activities in which the students are engaged. We need to begin to look at each instructional activity as an opportunity for assessment. We also need to plan for assessment just as we plan our lessons and activities. How will we collect data that shows that students are making growth in oral language? What criteria will we use? Will we conduct individual, pair, or group activities? Will we use a checklist, scoring rubric, or anecdotal records to document student learning? How often will we collect assessments on oral language? Weekly? Monthly? Quarterly? It is most useful to make a plan, collect potential assessment tools, set a preliminary time line for using them, draft or revise assessment tools to use, then try them out. Only by trying out our assessment tools can we judge their effectiveness. A tool is effective if it is valid, fair, and reliable. The students will tell us what they think of the assessment task and tools, and if we listen to their feedback, we can use the information to improve each assessment tool.

Oral language can be assessed most directly by conducting one-on-one interviews or story retelling sessions, pair discussions, and small group interviews, role-plays, or demonstrations, among other activities. Teachers can also use picture stories or wordless cartoon sequences for students to narrate. When planning for assessment, we need to set criteria for performance that reflect our instructional objectives. Will we be assessing language functions or how students use language (such as describing, requesting information, comparing)? What aspects of language structure or grammar will be assessed? What about vocabulary and pronunciation? How important will these domains be? Will they receive equal weight of importance as communicative effect? Or is communicative effectiveness more important than complete and total mastery of grammar? Is assessing delivery skills such as making eye contact with the audience something that has been taught and modeled in class?

Once the instructional activity and performance criteria have been identified, teachers can begin to draft an assessment tool such as a checklist or rating scale for assessing student's use of oral language. It is usually best to review sample assessment tools that can be adapted and modified rather than to attempt starting from scratch. The latter is likely to be more time-consuming and frustrating than the former and may not produce the desired result. For an example of a scoring rubric to be used for oral reports, see Figure 8.1.

Reading/Writing

As with the assessment of oral language, assessment of reading and writing must begin with instructional activities that require students to use these skills. For English language learners, it is especially important that literacy instruction be based on second language research as well as on what we know about what works for teaching reading and writing to native speakers of English. In second language reading, for example, we now know that prior knowledge about the reading topic is the number one predictor of reading comprehension in the target language. This makes sense, but how often do we stop to tap the prior knowledge of our students on the reading topic? And how often do we assess students' use of prior knowledge in making sense of what they read?

Research conducted with native speakers of English for over two decades suggests that readers need plenty of time to read during class, direct instruction in reading strategies, opportunities for collaboration on reading-related activities, and discussions of personal responses to readings (Fielding & Pearson, 1994). These findings do not contradict research on second language reading. It makes sense, then, to include research-based elements in instructional activities and to conduct assessments of reading to determine how well students are making use of prior knowledge and reading strategies, how they are making sense of what they read through personal interpretations of the readings, and how they are able to communicate this understanding in reading logs or literature discussion circles. Teachers may want to use reading strategies checklists or rating scales, story or text retelling maps, cloze tests (where words are omitted systematically to promote use of language structure and context clues), or reading logs, among other tools, to assess reading comprehension of English language learners. See Figure 8.2 for an example of a reading strategies rating scale.

From the research on teaching writing, we have learned that prior knowledge about the topic and how to plan for writing are essential to the success of the writer (Hillocks, 1987). Additionally, writers need to know how to organize their writing and how to synthesize knowledge into a written text. The research suggests that it is important to assess writing for more than just aspects of vocabulary and grammar. Writing assessment needs to provide feedback to the learner and the teacher on how the writer is working through the processes of writing, from brainstorming a topic and its details to editing a final draft and providing peer feedback on writing to others. Activities for teaching writing may include writing paragraphs, summaries, and essays; keeping dialogue journals and learning logs; and any number of writing tasks in the content areas. See Figure 8.3 for an example of a teacher checklist for paragraph writing.

Student Name: _____

Date:_____

Writing—Edited Paragraphs*
Teacher Review Checklist

Purpose & Organization

_____1. Clear topic sentence

_____2. Supporting details

_____3. Examples

_____4. Transitions link sentences

_____5. Concluding sentence

Grammar/Mechanics

_____6. Sentences begin with CAPITAL letter

_____7. Sentences/questions end with period/question mark

_____8. Paragraph indented

_____9. Few grammar errors

_____10. Spelling errors do not interfere with meaning

*Designed for Elementary Students of Intermediate English Proficiency

---

Figure 8.2

Once teachers determine what aspects of reading and writing they are going to assess, they can identify assessment tools to adapt or modify for this purpose and determine how often they will assess literacy skills. As with reading and oral language, to be assessed fairly and validly, writing must be assessed using some specified criteria that has been shared with students prior to the writing assignment. Students need to know the basis on which their writing will be assessed so that they can prepare for it. Analytic scoring rubrics assigning a separate score for each domain, such as organization, sentence structure, grammar, and mechanics can be used by the teacher to diagnose students' strengths and weaknesses in writing. Students can use a writing checklist to monitor their ability to follow steps of the writing process. In addition, teachers can use benchmark writing samples as models that show students what good writers do. Students will need to be given time and guidance to engage in self-assessment of their work. By assessing their own writing, English language learners can gain confidence in understanding the criteria by which their work will be evaluated.

Teachers may want to guide students in keeping reading/writing assessment portfolios. Assessment portfolios are not mere collections of student work. Collections of student work are called *work folders*. Assessment portfolios, on the other hand, require the input of each student in selecting the portfolio entries and in writing a justification for each entry. These explanations of each entry in a portfolio provide a self-assessment for the learner, guiding her in setting short- and long-term learning goals. In addition, assessment portfolios provide performance criteria for judging the merit of each student's portfolio based on academic standards and instructional objectives.

Content Areas

In addition to assessing oral language, reading, and writing skills, teachers of English language learners need to familiarize themselves with assessment approaches in the content areas. English language learners need to be monitored for growth in both language proficiency and content knowledge. Recent research suggests that language-based programs, to promote academic achievement, must go beyond the teaching of language skills such as pronunciation, vocabulary, and grammar. School programs need to teach and assess students' ability to process content area knowledge and skills (Chamot & O'Malley, 1994; Thomas & Collier, 1997).

Cummins' (1982, 1983) theoretical distinction between two types of language proficiency, communicative and academic language proficiency, serves as an important impetus for teaching and assessing both basic communicative and academic language skills of English language learners. Communicative language proficiency is highly contextualized and places minimal cognitive demands on thinking in a second language, while academic language provides fewer contextual clues for meaning and is more cognitively demanding. Since academic language proficiency takes longer to acquire than communicative language proficiency, it is imperative that teachers provide access to content concepts as well as to language skills development. Cummins' research, supported by that of Collier and Thomas (1997), provides direct support for teaching language through the content areas for English language learners in grades K–12.

The delivery of content-based language instruction for school-age English language learners raises a number of assessment-related questions. In particular, many of these students will be enrolled, at one time or another, in regular content area classrooms with native speakers of English. How can English language learners be assessed for both language proficiency and content area knowledge? Should language learners be assessed differently from native speakers? Should they be held to different standards? The answers to these questions depend on the instruction that is being provided to the English language learners. If these students are in regular classrooms, the assumption is that they can profit from instruction in English only or with language-based services outside of the regular classroom. These students should be assessed in English and held to the same standards as their proficient English-speaking peers. If English language learners have weak vocabulary or literacy skills, teachers can use developmental standards to determine student progress. It is in the students' best interests for ESL/bilingual and regular classroom teachers to collaborate on the instruction and assessment of their students. If students are enrolled in a bilingual or native language program, they should be assessed in the language of instruction.

When developing assessments in the content areas, teachers need to consider two kinds of knowledge: **declarative knowledge** and **procedural knowledge** (Gagne, Yekovich, & Yekovich, 1993; O'Malley & Pierce, 1996). Declarative knowledge can be defined as knowledge that can be declared or stated, such as historical, mathematical, or scientific facts. Procedural knowledge reflects what students can do with what they know. Declarative knowledge can be easily assessed through the use of graphic organizers, constructed-response formats, and matching, multiple-choice, and essay tests. Procedural knowledge, on the other hand, may require the use of checklists, rating scales, and scoring rubrics that detail the types of processes learners must demonstrate. In science, mathematics, and social studies, students can be asked to demonstrate what they know by following specific processes such as problem solving or experimental investigations, writing reports and summaries, and making oral presentations. It is important that teachers assess thinking skills and the processes by which students solve problems.

To aid students in showing what they know on content area assessments, teachers can add scaffolding to assessment tasks and tools. Teachers can provide scaffolding by using simplified language, visuals, demonstrations, graphic organizers, and cooperative learning activities to communicate the content of the lesson in mathematics, social studies, or science to the language learners. By using these instructional supports to reduce the linguistic demand, teachers are in a better position to find out what students know and can do in the content areas. It is especially important to determine each student's prior knowledge and level of study in the content areas so that teachers can plan instruction that builds on students' strengths and helps fill learning gaps.

Scaffolding assessments in the content areas can be as simple as tapping prior knowledge through brainstorming and allowing a pictorial response to a task or as complicated as designing a partially completed outline of a book chapter for students to fill in. Teachers need to provide the type of scaffolding needed by language learners at various levels of language proficiency. For example, beginners in reading and writing will need much more simplified language than high intermediates, and high intermediates will be able to handle longer written texts than beginners. Although we have little research data on scaffolding assessments with English language learners, research on the second language acquisition process would indicate that using manipulatives, physical demonstrations, graphics and visuals, and providing choices in tasks and responses can help provide access to meaningful input in content-based language classrooms as well as in regular classrooms. For intermediates, scaffolding can be provided through the use of graphic organizers such as tables, charts, and outlines, word banks for content-specific vocabulary, and manipulatives and games for presenting challenging conceptual knowledge. Evaluating student performance on scaffolded activities and tasks can give students the self-confidence that keeps them motivated to learn and teachers the information they need for diagnosing students' strengths and needs with regard to content area objectives.

As with assessment of language skills, teachers need to let students know the specific criteria by which their performance in the content areas will be assessed. These assessments need to be criterion-referenced and based on state and local standards for native speakers of English. Teachers need to aim for those standards so that English language learners do not fall behind in learning content knowledge that they will be held accountable for on annual standardized tests. Criteria for performance can be shared with students and discussed in class for clarity and fairness. Teachers can give students copies of the criteria in the form of scoring rubrics, rating scales, or self-assessment checklists.

An example from an ESL/social studies classroom shows how teachers can set criteria in content area assessments. In this classroom, students are being held responsible for knowing the names of various European explorers to the Americas, the dates of exploration, and each explorer's accomplishments. The teacher asks students to prepare a poster and make an oral presentation on a single explorer. Student performance is judged on accuracy of the content, clarity of the language used for the presentation, and presentation of the poster. Students receive subscores for each category of performance. Assigning subscores, one for language use and another for content knowledge, is called **differentiated scoring.** When teachers assign subscores for language, content knowledge, and artwork using clearly specified criteria, they are conveying useful feedback to language learners on their strengths and weaknesses, and this helps the learners set learning goals and become independent learners.

Need For Long-Term Professional Development

In a two-year study of the impact of teaching on student learning, The National Commission on Teaching and America's Future discovered that student achievement can be directly affected by the professional preparation obtained by teachers and that many teachers are not getting the preparation they need to help their students succeed in school (Report of the National Commission on Teaching and America's Future, 1996). In this chapter, we have presented a number of assessment issues pertaining to English language learners. However, this brief overview will not be sufficient for teachers to actually begin using valid and reliable assessments in their classrooms.

The National Commission proposed the need to "reinvent teacher preparation and professional development." Among the recommendations are mentoring programs for beginning teachers and high-quality, long-term professional development opportunities. This is not how most schools work, throwing in beginning teachers to sink or swim and providing a parade of one-shot workshops from external consultants that teachers must attend each year for professional credit points. The irony pointed out by this report is that while we may hold instruction for students to high standards, such as through problem solving, inquiry learning, collaborative learning, and learning by doing, we seldom hold professional development for teachers to the same high standards. This observation needs to be taken quite seriously, especially when we see teachers being told what to teach and in what time frame to teach it, as if they were mindless automatons hired to do someone else's bidding, with no professional judgment of their own. Recommendations for professional development include the need for:

> ". . . more useful forms of professional development, including support for teachers' in-school study groups, peer coaching, and other problem-solving efforts as well as teacher-to-teacher networks, teacher academies, and school university partnerships." (Report of the National Commission on Teaching & America's Future, p. 120).

Staff in-service days can be consolidated and used at the end of the year, allowing teachers to spend at least ten days planning and working together on "how to use curriculum and assessments" that are related to helping students attain learning standards. We now have research indicating that the type of professional development suggested by the National Commission produces favorable results for student learning. In particular, school–university partnerships have great potential for helping teachers increase the effectiveness of their assessment practices.

An example of a decade-long school–university partnership in assessment reform can be found in Northern Virginia, between George Mason University and two local school systems, Fairfax County Public Schools and Prince William County Public Schools. One system is large and the other is small, but both have instructional leaders in the form of ESOL Program Coordinators who have requested assistance with helping teachers use new forms of assessment for program placement. The ultimate goal has been to help change the way ESOL teachers teach and assess students in their own classrooms.

Both Virginia school systems are feeling the pressure of preparing ESOL students to meet stringent state standards (primarily declarative knowledge) in the content areas. ESOL students must also prepare a written essay on state tests. In a few years, students will have to pass all state tests to qualify for a high school diploma. Teachers need to know when ESOL students are ready to go out of the ESOL program and into regular classrooms, thus making them eligible to take statewide standardized tests. Students in language-support programs are currently excluded from taking state tests for three years, under a number of specific conditions. It was in this context that the university consultant approached each school system to invite them to collaborate in a school–university partnership aimed at aligning teacher assessment approaches with instructional practices in student-centered classrooms.

Since 1992, both school systems have worked with the George Mason University consultant (this writer) to improve assessment for the identification and placement of ESOL students in the ESOL program. Through this school–university partnership, small teams of elementary and secondary teachers come together, typically for at least five days during the school year and five more during the summer, to plan and develop assessment tools and procedures for program placement and classroom instruction. The number of teachers from each school system can range from 5 to 20 each year. At the end of the summer and after all their work has been completed, teachers present their work and assessment tools to all teachers in the school system for training and feedback. All teachers are invited to try out the tools during the year and provide feedback for improving them in the following year. This is a

Guidelines for Teaching

GETTING STARTED

We would like to provide a few tips for initiating improvements in your approach to instruction and assessment so that both you and your students can benefit from clear expectations for learning. Suggestions for getting started include: (1) start with your own classroom, (2) start small, (3) form or join a teacher support group, and (4) plan for the long term. First, start with your own classroom. Examine routine instructional activities to see how you can turn them, with a little planning, into assessment opportunities for data gathering. Second, start small. Tackle one language skill or content area first. Try out one assessment tool or format at a time. Reflect on your effectiveness and revise your tools. The revision of assessment tools and processes should be recurring and can take several years to perfect. Third, form or join a teacher support group in your school or school system. Joining a support group can give you the impetus you need for moving forward with your resolutions to make changes in assessment and instruction. Finally, plan on a long-term strategy for improving your assessment approaches with English language learners, because it can take up to five years for an innovation to become a routine.

recursive process that has been going on for the past decade, with all parties continuing to reap benefits from the process. If you have the opportunity to participate in a school–university partnership or a teacher academy, you will most likely get the support you need for making improvements to the assessment of ESOL students in your school system.

Summary

In this chapter, we have described the national context for assessment and how it got that way, and how standardized testing at the state and national levels has become a controversial topic among students, teachers, and parents. We also presented some key issues in assessment and described various types of assessments used with English language learners. We differentiated between assessment purposes for school-based assessment and classroom-based assessment. We described traditional and student-centered classrooms and the potential of each to move toward valid, fair, and reliable assessment of language learners. We also provided guidelines for linking assessment to instruction in order to increase the validity of classroom-based assessments. In addition, we discussed the need for teachers to demand and obtain professional development on assessment, not only for the benefit of their students, but also for improving their own teaching. Finally, we provided some tips for teachers who want to get started with making improvements to their assessment practices. We hope this chapter has been useful as an introduction to the topic of the assessment of English language learners and that you will explore more in depth many of these topics through university coursework, workshops sponsored by professional educational organizations, and professional readings in teacher journals and reference books.

Key Terms

Validity p. 329

Content validity p. 329

Consequential validity p. 329

Bias p. 329

Cultural bias p. 330

Attitudinal bias p. 330

Assessment bias p. 330

Test bias p. 331

Norming bias p. 331

Reliability p. 331

Reflection Questions

1. Find out whether ESL/bilingual students are included in state-mandated testing in your school system and whether their test scores are included in school averages. What alternative assessments would you recommend for including these students in your statewide testing programs?
2. Examine a language proficiency test or achievement test for evidence of bias. What types of bias do you find?
3. Why are criterion-referenced tests more useful than norm-referenced tests for judging the academic progress of students in ESL/bilingual programs?
4. Conduct a self-assessment of your teaching style. Do you tend to be more traditional or student-centered? What steps can you take to ensure the content and consequential validity of your assessments?
5. What scaffolding approaches do you use for assessment of language learners? How might you improve these?
6. What steps will you take to learn more about developing valid and reliable assessments for English language learners?

Resources

Heubert, J. P., & Hauser, R. M., eds. *High stakes: Testing for tracking, promotion, and graduation.* Washington, DC: National Academy Press, 1999.
   • This book examines how tests are used to make critical decisions for students in American schools. The following issues are discussed: political and legal back-

grounds of testing, misuses of tests, special populations (including English language learners), and recommendations for appropriate test use.

McNeil, L. M. *Contradictions of school reform: Educational costs of standardized testing*. New York, NY: Routledge, 2000.
- The author and her colleagues have actually collected research data on the impact of statewide testing on classroom teaching and learning. The book shatters the myth that standardization helps raise academic standards and improve learning. In particular, the authors found that standardized tests have a negative impact on poor and minority students.

McTighe, J., & Ferrara, S. *Assessing learning in the classroom*. Washington, DC: National Education Association, 1998.
- This book provides an introduction to classroom-based assessment, describing selected- and constructed-response formats and performance-based assessment. It includes guidelines for using various types of scoring instruments such as rubrics and rating scales.

O'Malley, J. M., & Pierce, L. V. *Authentic assessment for English language learners: Practical approaches for teachers*. White Plains, NY: Pearson Education, 1996.
- The authors provide research-based practical guidelines for how to design and use performance-based assessments with language minority and English language learners. The book contains chapters on assessment of oral language, reading, writing, and content areas and portfolio development, and contains numerous sample rubrics, rating scales, and other assessment tools for teacher use.

Wiggins, G. *Educative assessment: Designing assessments to inform and improve student performance*. San Francisco, CA: Jossey-Bass, 1998.
- The author focuses on using assessment as feedback for improving student learning and presents design standards for ensuring that performance-based assessments provide that feedback. The book contains a number of examples and templates for designing scoring tools.

CHAPTER 9

Bilingual Special Education

by Theresa A. Ochoa

Rethinking Identification and Referrals of English-language Learners for Special Education Services
Do We Really Want All CLD Students Out of Special Education?
How Do ELLs With Disabilities Benefit Orom Special Education?

Andrés

Andrés is a 6-year old boy at Orange Elementary School. He is, generally speaking, much like his first-grade peers. His classmates like him and he has a best friend. He sits with other children to eat in the cafeteria and dashes out to the playground after rushing through his lunch. However, although Ms. Toles, his teacher, describes him as a happy first grader, she is concerned about his academic progress. Unlike his peers, Andrés presents sustained and marked academic difficulties. He writes, according to his teacher, only the first letter of his name while the other children write their complete names independently. He can count to three but has difficulty with number correspondence. Coloring and writing are also difficult for him. He has trouble coloring within object lines and his strokes are noticeably more rudimentary compared to other children's work. His writing composition is also markedly different from that of his peers. Ms. Toles is concerned that Andrés is not making expected progress given the academic support provided to him throughout the year. She notes that he is falling behind all other students in her class. She is worried that his self-esteem may begin to diminish given his academic difficulties. A review of Andrés' school records indicates that he receives one-on-one tutoring for a half hour each day from a special education reading specialist who speaks Spanish. Their work together is an extension of their learning tutorial done last year, but Andrés still seems unable to recall the names and sounds of letters, which makes reading impossible for him at this point.

Mrs. González, Andrés' mother, is also concerned about his academic progress. Like Ms. Toles, Mrs. González notices that Andrés does not know the alphabet despite the time she spends at home reading to Andrés in Spanish and going over the alphabet. When she helps him complete his homework, she also notes his difficulties with numbers. Communication between Ms. Toles and Mrs. González is limited due to language barriers. Mrs. González speaks only Spanish while Ms. Toles speaks only English. Translators are necessary when they have to convey important information to each other about Andrés. A conversation with Ms. González through a translator about helping Andrés with homework revealed that his family shares an apartment with two other families totaling 11 individuals. Mrs. González said that she completed 6th grade in Mexico while her husband, whose family could afford to keep him in school, stayed in school two years longer than she did. She stated that Mr. González is involved with Andrés's schooling and wants him to have more opportunities to go to school than he had as a child. Mr. González is the one who mostly helps Andrés with math at the table, but his mother says that they have to do it while having dinner and watching television because that is the only time available. Sometimes, the older kids who live in the house also help Andrés with homework or translate the home-work directions written in English. Overall, Andrés's parents are certain that Ms. Toles cares about Andrés and is doing her best to help him at school. However, they are worried that his academic troubles are persisting and he is not learning.

What are the concerns expressed about Andrés by his teacher and parents?

Is it certain limited English proficiency accounts for Andrés' academic diffi-culties?

Is it possible that Andrés might have a legitimate disability?

Introduction

Both bilingual education and special education are interventions aimed at improving educational services to students whose needs have not been met by traditional methods of providing universal public education. Yet each has been criticized not only by those who want to preserve existing models of for-mal education and those who have negative attitudes towards the special populations they are designed to serve, but also by those who are advocates for reform of traditional education practices and those who advocate for these distinctive populations. Furthermore, those who are the strongest sup-porters of bilingual education have been among the most vocal critics of spe-cial education. If this is so, how has this come about, and how can we define a field called bilingual special education that meets the concerns of supporters and reformers of universal public education, and even more specifically, the criticisms of advocates for educational justice for linguistic minorities?

The authors defined bilingual education in Chapter One as an approach to teaching culturally and linguistically diverse (CLD) students English, encompassing a variety of program models each promoting different goals (e.g., one program model may endorse the simultaneous development of the student's first language and English, while another may merely incorporate the student's first language to facilitate a quick transition to English). **Special education** is defined as instruction and related services specifically designed and provided to meet the unusual needs of exceptional students (Hallahan & Kauffman, 2000). **Bilingual special education** refers to the use of the home language along with English in an individually designed program of instruc-tion provided to a student with exceptional educational needs for the purpose of maximizing his or her learning potential (Baca & Valenzuela, 1998; Carrasquillo, 1990; Tymitz, 1983).

How is it that there can be such strong negative feelings about such serv-ices? Advocates for minority racial, cultural, and linguistic groups have histor-ically attacked special education for inappropriately, and disproportionately, labeling, segregating, stigmatizing, and poorly educating their children. Amidst attacks against special education, advocates for persons with disabili-ties sought to remedy the lack of appropriate public education and related services for their children. Extensive litigation, legislation, and research beginning in the 1960s, building on the model of the earlier initiated civil rights movement, particularly efforts to end racial discrimination in schools, ultimately resulted in the accumulation of considerable research, court decisions, and laws to support the validity of many of these juxtaposed claims.

Among the most dramatic research findings was the disproportionately high rate of identification and placement of ethnic-minority students in special education. For example, Mercer's seminal work in California found that Mexican-American students were tested using standardized IQ tests in English and were inappropriately overrepresented in programs for the mentally retarded. Similar studies in other states, and for other minority groups clearly justified the criticisms against special education, including those within the field itself (e.g., Dunn, 1968), and led in 1975 to a major federal law called the Education for All Handicapped Children Act (PL 94–142), which required extensive changes in referral, testing, and placement for special education services. The most relevant of these changes for bilingual special education is the requirement to use nonbiased assessments with language-minority students when determining special education eligibility.

Thus, close to three decades later, and considering the efforts to resolve the problem, one should expect the misplacement of culturally and diverse students to be corrected. Are linguistic minority students still misidentified and misplaced in special education? Are they still likely to be segregated from their English-speaking counterparts? Are they likely to be getting appropriate educational services?

This chapter is written to empower conscientious and devoted educators who continue to strive to meet the needs of linguistically diverse and exceptional students in their classrooms. In particular, it targets general and bilingual education teachers working with children with exceptionalities and English-language limitations. The chapter begins with a brief presentation of the history of special education services and its intersection with bilingual education. It continues with a description of what bilingual special education could be like and describes bilingual education programs across the United States developed to provide bilingual special education services to exceptional children. Statistics on the disproportional representation of English-language learners (ELLs) in programs of exceptionality are presented, and include the underidentification of students with disabilities for special education services. The last section, and perhaps most important, is a description of the prereferral, assessment, and placement processes that are all important in the education of students with disabilities.

How Many Culturally and Linguistically Diverse (CLD) Students Also Have Disabilities?

Undoubtedly, most educators reading this chapter are personally acquainted with the challenge of educating the growing number of students from CLD backgrounds in public schools across the United States. Baca and Valenzuela (1998) suggest that there are an estimated 10 million school-age language-minority students across the United States for whom English is not their first language, with heavier concentrations of these students in the Southwest and Northwest and with half of all speakers of languages other than English residing in California, Texas, and New York. Of the estimated 10 million CLD students, a large number of them have disabilities that require specialized services (Carrasquillo, 1990, p. 13). Under the assumption that disabilities are distributed among language minority students the same way they are in the normal population of students, Baca and Valenzuela (1998) note that using the language-minority population figure of 9,985,000 from the 1990 census in combination with the estimated disability rates of 12 percent provided by the U.S. Office of Special Education, 1,198,200 children ages 5–17 have disabilities and are linguistically diverse.

Given the stigma still associated with special education, however, and the fact that some CLD students continue to be misplaced in special education—not because of disabilities but because of English-language limitations—educators are justified in being hesitant to identify these students for special education. It is important for all general educators to exercise caution and exhaust the resources available to them before making a referral for special education assessment. Richard Hungerford's words (in Hallahan & Kauffman, 2000) are useful as we all grapple with the highly complex and controversial task of addressing the needs of CLD students with disabilities while avoiding the mistakes we have made in the past.

Only the brave dare look upon the gray –
Upon the things which cannot be easily explained,
Upon the things which often engender mistakes,
Upon the things whose cause cannot be understood,
Upon the things we must accept and live with.
And therefore only the brave dare look upon difference
Without flinching.

Increases in the number of students from diverse language backgrounds and the advancement of the **full inclusion** movement, which promotes the practice that students with disabilities be reintegrated in general education classrooms and taught alongside their peers without disabilities, will result in larger numbers of English-language learners with disabilities coming into contact with general education teachers.

Foundations for Bilingual Special Education

Legislation

Legislation specific to bilingual special education does not exist. Linguistically diverse students with disabilities are, however, protected by both bilingual and special education legislation. As discussed in Chapter

Two, in 1968 Congress passed the Bilingual Education Act (PL 90–247) that provided opportunities for school districts to obtain competitive funding to develop and implement programs to appropriately address the needs of culturally and linguistically diverse students (Baca & Valenzuela, 1998). Tymitz (1983) suggests that bilingual education came about as a direct response to the needs of general educators who mistakenly viewed students with English-language limitations as having mental retardation.

Several special policy mandates give individuals with disabilities the right to a public education and protect them against exclusion from public schools. Section 504 of the 1973 Rehabilitation Act stipulates that a child must be furnished with an individualized education program (IEP) appropriate for his or her needs and entitles the individual to a due process hearing if educational appropriateness is in doubt (Baca & Valenzuela, 1998). The 1974 Educational Amendments Act (PL 93–380) was the first time special education legislation included a provision for students with English language limitations by mandating nondiscriminatory testing. However, the 1975 Education for All Handicapped Children Act (PL 94–142), renamed in 1990 as the Individuals with Disabilities Education Act (IDEA), is the most comprehensive and significant legislation on behalf of individuals with disabilities. As noted by Baca (1998) the IDEA legislation is the foundation for bilingual special education because it mandates nondiscriminatory testing and an individualized and appropriate program of instruction for each student through an IEP in the least restrictive environment (LRE).

Litigation

Litigation has played a major role in advancing the services available to students with English-language limitations and disabilities (Baca, 1998). The *Pennsylvania Association of Retarded Children* v. *Commonwealth of Pennsylvania* and *Mills* v. *the Board of Education of the District of Columbia* established that no student can be excluded from or denied a public education based on disability. Prior to this, many students with disabilities were forced to stay at home without any formal education. *Lau* v. *Nichols* is without question the landmark case in the field of bilingual education. On behalf of 1,800 Chinese students, the U.S. Supreme Court unanimously ruled that students with English-language limitations were entitled to a "meaningful education" which could include a bilingual education or English as a second-language instruction. Chapter Two provides additional discussion on the impact of the *Lau* v. *Nichols* decision on bilingual education programs for students with English-language needs.

Three cases relate directly to the improper placement of English-language learners in special education programs: *Arreola* v. *Board of Education, Diana* v. *State Board of Education,* and *Covarrubias* v. *San Diego Unified School District.* Collectively, these cases "challenged the validity of using IQ tests to measure the mental ability of linguistically and culturally diverse students"

(Baca, 1998). *Arreola* provided parents the right to a due process hearing before their children are placed in classes for students with mental retardation. The *Diana* case ordered that children be tested in their primary language, mandated the use of nonverbal tests, and the collection and use of extensive supporting data when assessing students for special education evaluation. Nonetheless, while the problem of overrepresentation of linguistic-minority children has been at least partially addressed and resolved through nonbiased testing, a new problem of *underrepresentation* has developed (Baca, 1998).

The *Jose P.* v. *Amback* (1979) decision found that students with disabilities were being denied an appropriate public education because they were not being referred or evaluated in a timely fashion nor placed in special education programs. The *Dyrcia S. et al.* v. *Board of Education of the City of New York et al.* (1979) found that Puerto Rican and other Hispanic children with disabilities and English-language limitations were being denied a public education because they were not being assessed or placed in bilingual special education programs (Baca, 1998 p. 94). The decision required the following:

1. Identification of children needing special education services with the inclusion of an outreach office with adequate bilingual resources.
2. Appropriate evaluation through the establishment of school-based support teams to evaluate children in their own environment with a bilingual nondiscriminatory evaluation process.
3. Appropriate programs in the least restrictive environment, including a comprehensive continuum of services with the provision of appropriate bilingual programs at each level of the continuum for children with limited English proficiency.
4. Due process and parental student rights, including a Spanish version of a parent's rights booklet, that explains all of the due process rights of children and parents. Also included is the hiring of neighborhood workers to facilitate parental involvement in the evaluation and development of the individualized educational program.

English-Language Learners in Special Education

Disproportional representation of students from minority ethnic and linguistic backgrounds in special education programs continues to be problematic in U.S. public schools. Over the course of nearly thirty years, since it was noted that too many students from ethnic minority backgrounds were in special education, the term disproportion has to some extent become synonymous with overrepresentation. However, this is clearly not the case. Disproportionality, or disproportional representation, refers to the difference in actual occurrence rates among a given population compared to the expected occurrence rates given their representation in the general population. Certainly, documenting the overrepresentation of CLD students in special education programs and their underrepresentation in programs for the gifted and talented have been the focus of both research and attacks against special education. However, albeit to a lesser extent, underidentification and placement in special education disability categories have also been noted as problematic. This section provides a brief reaffirmation that overrepresentation of CLD students continues to be of major concern and stresses that underreferral and placement of CLD students with disabilities denies those students of the services guaranteed to them under special education law.

Overrepresentation in Special Education and Underrepresentation in Gifted and Talented Programs

Certainly, problems in the appropriate placement and education of culturally and linguistically diverse students existed prior to Dunn's seminal article in 1968 arguing that special education was unjustified for many and alleging that far too many students from minority groups were misplaced in special education programs. Research conducted by Mercer (1973) and Bryen (1974) noted that the placement of students in special education classes was discriminatory and educationally unsound because the tests used to evaluate students' intelligence were biased. Bryen (1974) concluded that placement of CLD students in special education programs was due to their limited English proficiency. Based on early findings and allegations that CLD students were misplaced in special education, efforts to ameliorate the problem have focused, in large measure, on developing culturally sensitive and language appropriate tests and reducing the number of CLD students in special education.

Today, as in the past, assertions persist that students from ethnic and linguistically diverse backgrounds are misplaced in special education (e.g., Artiles & Trent, 1994; Hallahan & Kauffman, 2000; Jitendra & Rohena-Diaz, 1996; Ortiz, 1994; Robertson & Kushner, 1994; Schiff-Myers, Djukic, McGovern-Lawler, & Perez 1993). While CLD students are overrepresented in special education categories of disability, few of them are in programs for the gifted and talented. According to Rodriguez (1992) "...educators have completely ignored the gifted child within the Mexican American population" (p. 27). Rodriguez (1992) suggests that IQ tests are limited in their ability to identify minority students and identify only one out of three gifted minority students.

Underidentification and Referral of Culturally and Linguistically Diverse Students for Special Education Evaluation

Underidentification and referral of ELLs for special education services is not a new phenomenon (Omark & Erickson, 1983; Pacheco, 1983; Tymitz, 1983). In fact, an increasing number of special education scholars have noted that underreferral of CLD students with disabilities is a concern (Baca & Valenzuela, 1998; Carrasquillo, 1990; Hallahan & Kauffman, 2000; Robertson, Kushner,

Starks, & Drescher, 1994). As noted previously, an estimated 1,198,200 children ages 5–17 are both linguistically diverse and have disabilities (Baca & Valenzuela, 1998). Despite needs for specialized services, however, bilingual students experiencing academic problems are underreferred and placed in special education programs (Artiles & Trent, 1994; Baca & Valenzuela, 1998; Benavides, 1988; Carrera, 1988; Grossman, 1998; Horner, Maddux, & Green, 1986; National Commission on Migrant Education, 1992; Ortiz, 1994; Robertson & Kushner, 1994). Clearly, a significant number of CLD students have real disabilities that require special education services.

Historically, advocates of language-minority students have been severely critical of special education principally because many students with English-language limitations were misplaced in special education classes not because of disabilities, but because of their limitations in the English language. Although some criticism against special education has to some extent abated (Arreaga-Mayer, Carta, & Tapia , 1994), attacks on special education as an effective and appropriate pedagogy abound (Baca & Valenzuela, 1998, Starks, Bransford, & Baca, 1998, Tymitz, 1983). For many critics, special education is racially biased, instructionally ineffective, and psychologically and socially damaging to students. In the least favorable description, special education is a dumping ground where, ill-intended, general educators send students from low status minority backgrounds they cannot or will not teach. Bryen (1974), for example, indicated that special education is a covert extension of ethnic discrimination and a way to exclude ethnically and linguistically diverse students from the mainstream student population. Similarly, McCarty and Carrera (1988) and Cummins (1985) declare that special education is a place where students from ethnic and linguistic minorities are "deported" and segregated from their peers without disabilities. A less critical description of bilingual special education suggests that it is no different from bilingual education. Cummins (1989), for example, begins his theoretical conceptualization of bilingual special education with a statement indicating that he makes "no a priori distinction between bilingual education or bilingual special education" (p. 11).

Notwithstanding criticism, bilingual special education is concerned with addressing the academic and behavioral needs of CLD students by responding to weaknesses within the student and modifying the student's environment to ensure that it nurtures existing strengths within the student and is respectful of the student's culture and language (Carrasquillo, 1990). Hallahan and Kauffman (2000) believe that bilingual special education must extend beyond the scope of multicultural education by ensuring that "ethnicity is not mistaken for educational exceptionality" (p. 98). Hence, the goal of bilingual special education is to provide an individualized program of instruction for a student with disabilities in the least restrictive environment that focuses on the cognitive development of the child in the child's first language at the same time it promotes the acquisition of English (Carrasquillo, 1990).

Understanding the Prereferral, Evaluation, and Placement Processes

There are classrooms across America where the majority of students are culturally and linguistically different from their teachers and where general educators are expected to teach students with behavioral and cognitive challenges for which they are unprepared to teach. Bilingual educators and special educators should commend them for their efforts to embrace the diversity within their classrooms and their staunch efforts to teach all students as best they can. Moreover, in cases where general educators hesitate to refer a CLD student, that hesitation is likely due to caution rather than neglect, given the stigma still associated with special education and the fact that some culturally and linguistically diverse students are misplaced in special education classes on the basis of their English-language needs. However, having emphasized the importance of exercising caution and exhausting available resources before making a referral for special education evaluation, it is equally important that educators understand that there are students with English-language limitations who also have legitimate and real disabilities. There are discrete steps to be taken in the process of determining eligibility for special education placement.

Prereferral Process

On the surface, it appears that CLD students are capriciously and impulsively identified, referred, and placed in special education programs. Brown, Gable, Hendrickson, and Algozzine (1991) report that 5 percent of the school-age population is referred annually for special education services; 92 percent of this number is tested for disabilities, and 73 percent of those tested is generally found to meet the eligibility criteria for special education placement. **Prereferral interventions** are educational and behavioral strategies recommended to general educators by a prereferral team for teaching students who are having behavioral or learning difficulties in the general education classroom before referring them for special education evaluation. While the individuals who make up the prereferral team vary, they typically include general and special educators. The goal of prereferral interventions is two-pronged: to reduce the number of special education referrals and to promote general education teachers assuming responsibility for teaching students experiencing academic and/or behavioral problems rather than transferring that responsibility to special educators. In other words, prereferral interventions intend to empower general educators to work with students through collaborative problem solving within a nonhierarchical group of colleagues (Del'Homme, Kasari, Forness, & Bagley, 1996; Flugum & Reschly, 1994; Graden, 1989; Nelson, Taylor, Dodd, & Reavis, 1991). Prereferral interventions modify the general education curriculum prior to referring a student for evaluation and possible placement in special education (Brown, Gable, Hendrickson, & Algozzine, 1991; Fuchs, Fuchs, Bahr, Fernstrom, & Stecker, 1990). Graden

Guidelines for Teaching

PREREFERRAL CHECKLIST

Obtain and review all the school's records of the child in question. Look for information that could help you understand the student's academic and behavioral problems. In particular review the records to determine if the student:

- Has had a psychological evaluation.

- Qualified for special services in the past.

- Has ever been included in other programs (e.g., programs for disadvantaged children or speech and language therapy).

- Has scored far below average on standardized tests.

- Has been retained in a grade level.

- Indicates good progress in some areas and poor progress in others.

- Has any physical or medical problems.

- Is taking medication.

In addition, to viewing records, you should also:

- Talk to other educators who have worked with the student to determine if they share similar concerns and have found successful ways of responding to the student.

- Talk with the student's family and make a home visit if possible to assess and understand the student's home environment.

As you are implementing preferral interventions:

- Document the strategies used in the general education classroom.

- Note those that have been successful and unsuccessful.

Applied to ethnic and linguistic-minority groups, a prereferral intervention could prevent an erroneous referral and subsequent placement in a special education program when information about second-language acquisition and learning characteristics of a student with disabilities is considered.

(1989) describes the process as "collaborative consultation" between special and general education. Research suggests that prereferral screening reduces bias and idiosyncratic opinions about students (Benavides, 1988). The prereferral checklist above provides guidelines that all educators are encouraged to implement while working with a CLD student experiencing academic and/or behavioral difficulties.

Identification and Referral for Special Education Evaluation

A **referral for special education** evaluation is a written statement, submitted by any number of individuals (e.g., school personnel, parents, or the student), to the school's multidisciplinary team of educational professionals requesting an evaluation to determine if a student meets the criteria for a federally recognized special education category such as a learning disability, mental retardation, or an emotional or behavioral disorder. A referral for special education is the culmination of informal concerns about the progress of a specific child in a general education classroom. For students with mild disabilities the general education teacher is typically the one to identify and refer a student for special education evaluation. Referral occurs only after all resources available to the teacher are exhausted and recommendations provided from the child study team are implemented to attend to the needs of students experiencing academic and/or behavioral difficulties in the general education classroom. In essence, the referral to special education is a statement by the teacher documenting the interventions he or she has implemented to help the child succeed in the classroom but acknowledging that she or he has not met nor improved the outcomes for a specific student in his or her classroom. Figures 9.1, 9.2, and 9.3 are examples of a referral form used in one school district. According to special education law and best practice, parents should be notified in their primary language when their child is being referred for special education evaluation. Spanish and Chinese translations of the English special education referral form are provided and can be adapted for use to notify parents. See Figures 9.2 and 9.3.

Special Education Placement

Not all referrals result in special education placements. As noted previously, 27 percent of all students referred for special education evaluation does not meet the criteria for special services. Discussion of the special education assessment process is beyond the scope of this chapter. However, in general, assessment is the process of collecting information about students for the purpose of making educational decisions (Hallahan & Kauffman, 2000). Best assessment practice includes formal testing using standardized and nonstandardized measures, interviews, and observations. Alternative educational assessments for CLD students include curriculum-based assessments. According to Rueda (1997), and Rueda and Garcia (1997) curriculum-based assessments focus on the educational tasks the student is expected to do rather than on how he or she performs on limited, and often biased, standardized tests. Additionally, good assessments take into account not only student characteristics but also the instructional environment to determine its relationship to the student's academic and/or behavioral problems. In the best possible scenario, special education assessment (a) identifies the student's strengths and weaknesses (b) determines which federally recognized disability best captures the student's disability or disabilities, and (c), informs about the educational program needed to maximize the students learning potential. Formal special education categories recognized by the federal government are provided in Guidelines for Teaching on page 375. They include the prevalence rates for each category of exceptionality.

Figure 9.1   *Referral Form—Special and Related Services*

Referral Form—Special Education and Related Services

_____ School District

☐ Initial Referral   ☐ Reevaluation

Name of child (last, first, middle)	Date of birth	Grade	School

Name of parent or legal guardian	Address (street, city, state, zip code)

Telephone (area/number)	Person making referral/title	Date parent notified of intent to refer

Method of notifying parent of intent to refer	Is an interpreter needed?
☐ Conference ☐ Phone Call ☐ Written	☐ Yes ☐ No

Parent's or adult student's primary language or other primary mode of communication if other than English (specify): _____

Child's primary language or other primary language mode of communication if other than English (specify): _____

Date (month/day/year) of receipt of referral by school district/Local Education Agency

(LEA) _____ (Note: this date begins the 90-day time line.)

State the reason for referral. Why do you believe this child has a disability (impairment and a need for special education)—such as academic or nonacademic performance and medical information; any special programs, services, interventions used to address this student's needs and the results of those interventions.

Figure 9.2   *Referral Form—Special and Related Services (Spanish)*

Forma de Referencia para Servicios de Educación Especial y Servicios Relacionados

_____ Distrito Escolar

☐ Referencia Inicial   ☐ Reevaluación

Nombre del Estudiante (apellido, nombre)	Fecha de nacimiento	Grado	Escuela
Nombre del padre/madre o guardián legal	Domicilio (calle, ciudad, estado, zona postal)		

Teléfono (área/número)	La persona que dio la referencia	Fecha en la cual se mandó aviso del intento de dar referencia al estudiante

Método del aviso a los padres del intento de referir	Se necesita un interprete?
☐ Conferencia ☐ Teléfono ☐ Escrito	☐ Sí ☐ No

Cuál es la lengua maternal de los padres o del estudiante sí es adulto? O cuál es la forma principal de communicación si no es inglés (especifique): _____

Cuál es la lengua materna del estudiante o la forma principal de communicación si no es inglés (especifique): _____

Fecha (mes, día, año) en la cual el distrito escolar o Agencia de Educación Local recibió notificación de la referencia para servicios especiales _____ (Nota: A partir de esta fecha se empiezan a contar los 90 dias de la evaluación)

Explique la razón por la cual se refirió al estudiante. Por qué piensa que el estudiante tiene una inhabilidad (tal cual requira educación especial) – como rendimiento académico o no académico e información médica; cualquier programa especial, servicios o intervenciones usadas para remediar las necesidades del estudiante y los resultados de las intervenciones.

Figure 9.3   *Referral Form —Special and Related Services (Chinese)*

特殊教育及相關服務轉介申請單

學生所屬學區_____

☐ 新個案   ☐ 復審個案

學生姓名		出生日期	年級	學校
父母或監護人		住址		
電話		轉介人姓名職稱	支會父母或監護人日期	

經由下列途徑支會父母或監護人   經由翻譯支會父母或監護人？

☐ 面談   ☐ 電話通知   ☐ 書面通知   ☐ 是   ☐ 否

父母或已成年學生母語非英語或需經由特殊溝通管道 (請詳細說明):

未成年學生母語非英語或需經由特殊溝通管道 (請詳細說明):

收件日期_____ (學區及地方教育單位收受轉介申請表日期。
此日期即特殊教育法規 "九十日期限" 之首日。)

請説明提出轉介原因. 請依據學生的學術記錄及非學術表現，健康情況，特殊需要
及以往參與類似課程活動之記錄説明學生需要特殊教育或特殊服務之理由。

Guidelines for Teaching

FEDERAL SPECIAL EDUCATION CATEGORIES BY PREVALENCE RATES AND EDUCATIONAL NEEDS

Federal Category	Prevalence in Total School-Age Population (percent)	Category as Percent of All Students with Disabilities	Primary Special Education Needs
Specific learning disability	3.90	49.9	Improving basic academic skills and social skills
Speech or language impairment	1.73	22.2	Reducing speech problems; Improving language skills and academic skills
Mental retardation	0.96	12.3	Improving functional skills, social skills, and academic skills
Serious emotional disturbance	0.69	8.9	Improving social skills, social relationships, and academic skills
Multiple disabilities	0.17	2.2	Improving academic skills, mobility skills, and functional skills
Hearing impairment	0.11	1.3	Improving language skills and academic skills
Other health impairments	0.10	1.3	Improving physical skills and functional skills
Orthopedic impairments	0.09	1.1	Improving physical skills and academic skills
Visual impairment	0.04	0.5	Developing reading skills and improving academic skills
Deaf/Blindness	Less than 0.01	Less than 0.1	Improving mobility and developing communication
Autism	Less than 0.01	Less than 0.1	Improving social skills and developing communication
Traumatic brain injury	Less than 0.01	Less than 0.1	Improving physical skills and academic skills
Gifted and talented	3-5	—	Faster pacing in curriculum, broadening curriculum, and maintaining positive social relationships

Table adapted from James E. Ysseldyke, & Bob Algozinne, Special Education: A practical approach for teachers (Third edition), Boston, Toronto: Houghton Mifflin Company, 1995.

Guidelines for Teaching

CATEGORIES OF EXCEPTIONALITY IN ENGLISH, SPANISH, AND CHINESE

Exceptionality /English	Excepcionalidad / Spanish	特殊教育類別/ Chinese
1. Language and speech disorders	1. Impedimentos del habla y de la lengua	1. 語言障礙
2. Specific learning disability	2. Discapacidades específicas de aprendizaje	2. 學習障礙
3. Mental retardation	3. Retardación mental	3. 智能障礙
4. Emotional and behavioral disorders	4. Trastornos emocionales y del comportamiento	4. 情緒及行為異常（性格異常）
5. Visual impairments	5. Impedimentos visuals	5. 視覺障礙
6. Hearing impairments	6. Impedimentos auditivos	6. 聽覺障礙
7. Other health impairment	7. Otros impedimentos de salud	7. 其他健康障礙（指身體病弱）
8. Physical disabilities	8. Impedimentos físicos	8. 肢體傷殘
9. Autism	9. Autismo	9. 自閉症
10. Multiple handicaps	10. Multiples discapacidades	10. 多重障礙
11. Gifted and talented	11. Estudiantes superdotados	11. 資賦優異

Each category consists of an operational definition and criteria which students have to meet in order to be assigned to it. Hallahan and Kauffman's textbook *Exceptional Learners: Introduction to Special Education* (8th Edition) is the recommended source for obtaining a detailed description of the definition of and criteria for each federally recognized special education category. In keeping with the need to communicate the disability with parents who do not speak English, the Guidelines for Teaching above provide the list of federal categories of exceptionalities (to the right, are their Spanish and Korean equivalents).

Rethinking Identification and Referrals of English-Language Learners for Special Education Services

Clearly, distinguishing between academic difficulties caused by cognitive disabilities from those related to second-language limitations is a formidable task. When students with limited English proficiency skills do poorly in school, it is often difficult to identify the cause. Are the problems these students experience related to limited English language proficiency or are they related to a handicapping condition?

Do We Really Want All CLD Students out of Special Education?

Does the need to decrease the number of students misidentified and placed in programs of special education exceed the need to identify and serve linguistically diverse students with legitimate handicaps? Some educators view the reduction in the numbers of students in programs for students with disabilities as an improvement because they think that fewer ELLs are being misplaced in special education programs. However, a large number of students with disabilities are left to linger without special education services in general education classrooms (Grossman, 1998, NCAS, 1992) because they do not speak English.

How Do ELLs with Disabilities Benefit from Special Education?

Some English-language learners require special education because they have disabilities. While placement in special education is not justified for a student without a disability, leaving a student with a legitimate disability in general education is not only inappropriate—it is a violation of the Individuals with Disability Education Act (IDEA). As bilingual education grew and as administrators attempted to compensate for the high numbers of minority children enrolled in special education, bilingual education teachers began to notice an increased placement of children with handicaps in their classrooms. Thus not only were minority children often mistakenly labeled as handicapped and in need of special services, other students with disabilities were not correctly identified as eligible to receive the necessary services to help them attain their educational potential (Erickson & Walker, 1983). Ovando and Collier suggest that in some cases, bilingual education programs serve as an alternative placement for minority students with disabilities (in Baca & Valenzuela, 1998). In other cases, students' special needs are ignored and specialized services are inappropriately withheld from them (Hallahan & Kauffman, 2000). Robertson and Kushner (1994) suggest that perhaps efforts to reduce the number of culturally and linguistically diverse students in special education ironically have been all too successful and have discouraged educators from referring students to special education when academic difficulties are considered to be bilingual, not cognitive in nature. In other words, they suggest that referral is postponed until the student learns English. Clearly, the postponement denies students with disabilities access to the "meaningful education" provision stipulated in IDEA. Baca and Valenzuela (1998, p. 17) point out that while overidentification and placement remain a concern there are some students, with legitimate and real disabilities, who remain unidentified for special education services. Grossman (1998), writing on ways to end discrimination in special education, notes that some students with English-language limitations are underrepresented in special education and concludes that for these students, they "still do not yet get their fair share of the American educational pie" (p. 3). Put yet another way, he equates underrepresentation of English-language learners with disabilities to denial of fair educational treatment.

Consistent with Grossman (1998), Baca and Valenzuela (1998) and Robertson and Kushner (1994) stress that those students with disabilities kept in general education classrooms are deprived of the special education services they are entitled to and which their disabilities require. The 1992 Final Report of the National Commission on Migrant Education stressed that language-minority students are more likely to be underrepresented in mild disability categories (e.g., learning disabilities, mild mental retardation) because they are easily masked by limited English skills. Maldonado-Colon (1983) suggests that educators are unable to distinguish when learning problems are the result of disabilities or whether speech and language behaviors are characteristics of students who learn English as a second language. Thus, there is a demand to develop assessment instruments and procedures to ensure that English-language learners are neither misdiagnosed nor overlooked for special education services (National Commission on Migrant Education, 1992). What are the consequences for students with English-language limitations and suspected disabilities when they are not referred for special education evaluation?

While educators need to continue to focus on reducing the number of students inappropriately placed in special education programs, they also need to guard against withholding the provision of special education services for students with disabilities who need them. If, in addition to being limited in English proficiency, students are also handicapped, they are very unlikely to receive any sort of instruction or assistance in their own language. A study conducted by Advocates of Children in New York found that only 16 percent of bilingual evaluations for special education qualification were carried out within the period required by law (Carrera, 1988). A Burmese mother in New York City public schools described her frustrations trying to get services for her daughter and indicated that "There was a gap of three months (March to May) when the Committee on the Handicapped did not get in touch with me. When I called them, I was informed that I should try and locate an individual or agency to do the evaluation "for my daughter Tu Tu." An education advocate representing the Burmese family to help them gain appropriate educational services for their daughter continued the story and stated, "I believe that if we had not intervened, Tu Tu would still be at home . . . she has a lot of catching up to do."

Summary

While some CLD students continue to be misplaced in special education programs, close to 2 million language-minority students with legitimate disabilities are not receiving the special education services they need to reach their learning potential. It appears that educators are hesitant to identify and refer English-language learners for special education evaluation because of uncertainties about the extent to which learning problems are related to cognitive disabilities and not to English-language limitations. An increasing number of special educators, however, point out that decisions to withhold identification and referral to special education for such students is detrimental and denies them the opportunity to benefit from school. The chapter made note that referring a student for special education evaluation does not always result in special education placement and encouraged teachers to refer CLD students who are experiencing sustained academic and/or behavioral problems in their classrooms for special education evaluation in order to maximize the learning potential of all students who are from different cultures and linguistic backgrounds.

Key Terms

Special education p. 360

Bilingual special education p. 360

Full inclusion p. 362

Prereferral interventions p. 367

Referral for special education p. 368

Reflection Questions

1. Why is referring culturally and linguistically diverse students to special education controversial?
2. Why is it difficult to differentiate the nature of the academic difficulties experienced by CLD students? Are the academic problems experienced by CLD students related to limited language proficiency? Or are they related to a handicapping condition?
3. What are the consequences for students with English-language limitations and suspected disabilities when they are not referred for special education evaluation?
4. What is the relationship between legislation and litigation in bilingual special education?
5. How do English-language learners with disabilities benefit from bilingual special education?

Resources

Baca, L. M., & Cervantes, H. T. *The bilingual special education interface.* Upper Saddle River, New Jersey: Prentice Hall, 1998.

*   This book is a resource for educators of English-language learners with disabilities. Baca and Cervantes emphasize the overlap between bilingual and special education. The sequence of the topics and organization of content is written to familiarize education professionals with the major and varied needs of students who do not speak English in order to improve delivery of education.

Hallahan, D. P., & Kauffman, J. M. *Exceptional learners: Introduction to special education.* (8th edition) . Needham Heights, MA: Allyn & Bacon, 2000.

*   Written for both special and general education educators, this book provides an introduction to special education. The first three chapters provide a historical background and current trends with particular attention to the full inclusion movement and issues related to multicultural and bilingual aspects of special education. Subsequent chapters (4–12) introduce specific categories of exceptionality (e.g., mental retardation, learning disabilities, emotional and behavioral disorders, attention deficit hyperactivity disorders, hearing and visual impairments) and myths, facts, and issues related to each are discussed.

Figueroa, R., Ruiz, N. T., & Díaz-Guerrero, R., eds. *The bilingual special education dictionary: A resource for special educators.*

*   This book is a practical resource for school personnel to communicate with Spanish-speaking parents. Where necessary, authors supplement technical special education terminology with communicable explanations for use with parents and pupils. The goal of the dictionary is to provide accurate information to educators and parents of all socioeconomic and educational backgrounds.

Endnote

Theresa A. Ochoa, the author of this chapter, is a Special Education Assistant Professor of Emotional and Behavioral Disorders in the School of Education at Indiana University. As a former behavior specialist, she has research interests in cognitive behavior interventions for students with emotional and behavioral needs. Her current research agenda includes the systematic evaluation of the effectiveness of problem-based learning CD-ROM technology in the preparation of teachers for students from Hispanic backgrounds, those with limited English proficiency, and those with behavior problems.

School and Community

Pathways to Partnerships
Legislation for Parent Participation
Issues in the Development of Partnerships
Family Literacy Programs and Other School–Community Partnerships
Case Studies of Change from the Inside Out

To give people help, while denying them a significant part in the action, contributes nothing to the development of the individual. In the deepest sense it is not giving but taking—taking their dignity. Denial of the opportunity for participation is the denial of human dignity and democracy. It will not work. (p. 123)

> *Saul Alinsky (1971), an outspoken community organizer whose ideas spawned a variety of grassroots organizations dedicated to solving local problems.*

With the spirit of Alinsky's quote in mind, in this chapter we explore the many ways in which partnerships between the school and its surrounding community can provide a firm foundation for effective bilingual and ESL programs. By linking the life of the school with that of its corresponding mainstream and ethnic communities, parents and other community members can achieve a strong sense of ownership in the education of their children.

Strong parent involvement is one factor that research has shown time and time again to have positive effects on academic achievement and school attitudes. Greenwald, Hedges, and Laine (1996) provide a general summary of the remarkably consistent results of this type of research. Given this reality, it is rather surprising that efforts to involve the community in the life of the school are so often given a backseat to other seemingly more pressing pedagogical concerns. Focusing specifically on language-minority populations, Goldenberg (1993) concludes that for these groups as well, the research shows that the promotion of strong home-school partnerships enables all children, from preschool through high school, to be more successful.

When educators make decisions about what languages to use in instruction, usually more is at stake than supposedly rational, research-based pedagogical and language development issues. Spolsky (1977) suggested that the underlying motivation for the establishment of a bilingual program is usually not a purely linguistic one. Rather, social, economic, political, psychological, or cultural factors trigger the desire for something other than monolingual instruction. It follows that when a particular language education program is not locally initiated, community reaction to it will not be based solely on linguistic factors, but more likely on socioeconomic, political, psychological, and cultural factors.

Lamenting the tendency of educational planners to focus on rather specific pedagogical issues, Kjolseth (1972) once stated that "most programs are patchwork affairs, each searching for some distinctive gimmick and focusing its rhetoric and design toward the individual pupil in isolation from his family, peers, neighborhood, and community" (pp. 109–10). This statement was written 30 years ago, and we would like to think that bilingual programs today have grown beyond "patchwork affairs" with "distinctive gimmicks." However, in many instances today educators still tend to focus too much on narrow pedagogical concerns, overlooking the important influence of our students' community context.

Illustrative of this phenomenon of neglect of community context is Valdés's (1996) experience studying 10 immigrant families in the Texas borderlands. She was participating in a three-year research project on the role of oral language in literacy development among young children. However, as she came to know the children, their families, and their schools, she concluded that there were other crucial aspects of the children's lives that she was not exploring that might have much more to do with the youngsters' success or failure in school. She noticed that the children's development of language skills frequently was unrelated to the teachers' perceptions about the children's general abilities. Instead these perceptions were influenced by the teachers' views about recent immigrant families, views that were significantly lacking in a realistic understanding of everyday life in the local community.

In this chapter we will refer often to the local community as a geographic and sociocultural entity surrounding a particular school, but we will also be referring to "the **bilingual community**." The term *bilingual community* means to us more than just the parents, guardians, and extended families of language-minority children attending a specific school. We extend the concept of bilingual community to include a complex coalition of families, bilingual/ESL educators, university researchers, neighbors, community organizations, and businesses that are connected in some way to the local schools. We take this broader view of the community because it is through the activation of a broad array of community resources, and through the cooperation of many different professional educators and laypersons, that we can develop the best programs for language-minority students.

In his book *Improving Schools from Within,* Roland Barth reflects on his years as a teacher, a principal, and a university faculty member. He proposes that it is through the establishment of positive relationships among teachers, students, and parents at the local level that school reform can best be achieved. The relationships that he envisions foster a "community of learners" and a "community of leaders." This vision of such communities reflects the kind of real-life, locally sensitive learning environment that is so important for any culturally and linguistically diverse setting. Barth defines his "community of learners" as "a place where students and adults alike are engaged as active learners in matters of special importance to them and where everyone is thereby encouraging everyone else's learning." He defines a "community of leaders" as a place where "students, teachers, parents and administrators share opportunities and responsibilities for making decisions that affect all the occupants of the schoolhouse" (Barth, 1990, p. 9). Barth gives as one example of a community of learners the case of an all-English-speaking elementary school that would in the following year be receiving for the first time a large number of Cambodian students. Learning about Cambodia became the school's curriculum for the spring preceding the new students' arrival, with integration through virtually all of the subject areas. Everyone—parents, custodians, lunch workers, secretaries, and administrators—was involved in learning about who these students were, where they were from, and why they would be coming to the local school. The sense of community was real, the learning had a clear purpose, and in the fall the community felt that it was prepared to welcome the newcomers into the life of the school (Barth, 1990, p. 44).

In this chapter, we will look at ways in which we can move toward the establishment of a community of learners and a community of leaders within the bilingual or ESL context. Throughout the chapter we will survey a variety of approaches to school and community relationships. However, to initially give the reader a flavor for the many different ways in which parents and schools can work together to raise their children, we will begin with highlights from two well-established districtwide plans for community partnerships—one in McAllen, Texas, and the other in Arlington County, Virginia. After looking at these programs, the chapter is then divided into three sections: (1) the historical context of language-minority communities; (2) developing a portrait of the community; and (3) pathways to community partnerships.

Examples of Community Programs

Community Programs in McAllen, Texas

Located on the Mexican border, the school district in McAllen serves a population that is approximately 87 percent Hispanic, with a large number of migrant families. As described by Rioux and Berla (1993, pp. 296–98), the McAllen Parent Involvement Program, staffed by bilingual parent coordinators and bilingual paraprofessional community aides, included a large array of projects:

- An adopt-a-school program, through which local businesses, churches, or other organizations provided financial or volunteer assistance or both to their school.

- Parent/student community evening study centers, where students could receive assistance at the centers with school assignments, and parents simultaneously attended classes in such areas as ESL, parenting skills, basic literacy, and computer-assisted instruction.

- Parent education programs that provided courses on child development.

- An orientation program for fifth-graders and their parents that prepared the families to make a smooth transition to enrollment in junior high school.

- A "Keys for a Better Life" course that helped parents build strong families through the keys of faith, enthusiasm, self-confidence, imagination, communication, determination, and love.

- A dropout prevention program that provided parents with information on ways to ensure that their children completed high school.

- Programs that provided families with home educational activities, such as materials to help children prepare for statewide competency tests.

- A radio talk show, *"Discusiones Escolares,"* in which the community could discuss school-related topics.

- Parent involvement in school governance through participation in such organizations as PTAs, Chapter I Parent Advisory Councils, and membership on school-based management committees.

In addition to these programs, Goldenberg (1993, p. 236) described how parents in the McAllen district could sign a contract in which they agreed to do the following: ensure that their children did their homework; talk with their children about what they learned each day; instill a sense of discipline; and provide at least three TV-free hours per week devoted to educational activities.

Community Programs in Arlington County, Virginia

The schools in Arlington County serve a number of different language-minority groups, and their parent involvement programs have been designed to serve a highly diverse population. According to Violand-Sánchez, Sutton, and Ware (1991) the district plan for community partnerships at the time of their writing included:

- Multilingual intake centers for new language-minority families, in which translation services were provided as parents went through the process of enrolling their children.

- Orientation for new parents in a variety of languages, with handbooks also translated into target languages.

- Interpreters for back-to-school nights and parent-teacher conferences.

- Multilingual family learning materials that parents and their children could use at home to reinforce school activities.

- Native-language parent groups that provided a means for disseminating information to parents. These groups also gave parents a sense of community and opportunities for involvement in school decision-making processes.

- Efforts to recruit language-minority parents to participate in the district's citizen advisory councils.

- District support of staff involvement in family outreach activities.

- Organization of an annual multicultural conference, in which the community's diversity was celebrated.

- Development of a long-range plan to promote the continued involvement of language-minority parents.

From looking just at these two districts, we can see that there are many different ways in which schools and communities can work together for the education of language-minority children. And there are many different roles that community members can assume: volunteer, paid employee, teacher at home, audience, decision maker, and adult learner (Delgado-Gaitán, 1990). To these roles we would add that of curricular resource person. However, as we go through this chapter we will also see that the creation of a community of learners and a community of leaders is not a simple question of the implementation of a list of "good ideas" that educators come up with at planning meetings. A variety of powerful linguistic, cultural, economic, and sociopolitical forces influence the outcomes of efforts to create a community of learners. There will be disagreements. For example, what seems like a valid and effective program to one educational practitioner may seem like a hegemonic intrusion into the integrity of the home to another observer. We will discuss such dilemmas in the final section of the chapter, "Pathways to Partnerships," but in order to establish a context we will first consider the historical context of language-minority communities in the United States.

The Historical Context of Language-Minority Communities

We will examine the history of language-minority communities from several perspectives. First, we discuss changes in attitudes toward minority communities in the United States over the past 200 years, using Havighurst's stages of pluralism. Then we will focus in on the 1970s and 1980s—important years in the establishment of contemporary bilingual and ESL programs. We will examine court cases during this time that have significantly affected language-minority communities, and then we will describe three cases of community-initiated bilingual programs during the 1970s.

Stages of Pluralism in the United States

Many educators and leaders in the United States have traditionally pinned high hopes on the schools to serve as efficacious instruments of national unity and democratic pluralism (Cremin, 1976; Dewey, 1916; Handlin, 1951; Kaestle, 1983; Tyack, 1974). Yet the process of unification has always tugged at the national fabric as ideals have had to confront reality. To keep the nation from falling apart, early political leaders designed and tried to implement a national agenda that would be capable of adjusting to the complex sociocultural and linguistic diversity that characterized the embryonic nation. As Hechinger (1978) argues:

> The facts of history are quite clear; they cannot be rewritten or revised. Those facts show clearly that the founding fathers viewed the United States as a country with a unified history, with unified traditions, and with a common language. For proof you need only to read Benjamin Franklin and his virtual phobia of foreign-language enclaves. The history of nation building is clear in any view of the American past. The concept of the melting pot was very much part of the American tradition, and it was accepted virtually by all. The reason why the melting pot is in disrepute today, and rightly so, is not because the concept was not a good one but because it was used dishonestly. Some people were excluded from the unified country. The melting pot's main failure was that it did not include all persons from all groups at all times. (p. 130)

What the early leaders in fact had in mind by a "country with a unified history, with unified traditions, and with a common language" was a United States ruled by institutions of English origin and by the English language. Therefore, early in the nation's history, the stage was set for tensions associated with the cultures and languages of non-English-speaking groups—both American Indian communities and new immigrant groups arriving in the United States in large numbers.

The educational sociologist Havighurst (1978) illustrates the sociocultural drama Hechinger described in the following chronology of 200 years of U.S. history. In looking at the status of ethnic communities in the United States, he identified four overlapping stages: defensive pluralism, the melting pot phase, laissez-faire pluralism, and constructive pluralism. During the 1800s, the general period of defensive pluralism, large numbers of immigrants formed ethnic enclaves in which they struggled to keep ethnic loyalties alive while still participating in the larger civic society. Toward the end of the century, however, the concept of the melting pot challenged the desirability of such defensive pluralism. The idea was that through the schools, the workplace, and public life in general, the great diversity of immigrants would meld into citizens who would share the same cultural patterns as the prototypical "American." However, as noted earlier in Hechinger's quote, the concept was not honest in the process of selecting *who* should be melted. (Spring [1997], in his historical analysis of the educational experiences of American Indians and Puerto Ricans, referred to schooling practices for these groups during this period as a process of "deculturalization" or an explicit attempt to strip away the native culture and replace it with the dominant culture.)

With a relative decrease in immigration after World War I and other social changes, the ideology of the melting pot gradually began to be less vigorously promoted. Social scientists began to affirm that it was acceptable for ethnic groups to socialize and enculturate their children in such a way that their own beliefs and values were nurtured while they concurrently participated in the civic, economic, and educational life of the larger society.

However, the pluralism was laissez-faire in the sense that the government did not involve itself in issues of ethnic rights or equal opportunity. Such government involvement gradually emerged through the effects of the civil rights movement, and Havighurst identified the phase of constructive pluralism as beginning in the 1970s. Unlike laissez-faire pluralism, this is a phase in which the heterogeneous texture of American society has been actively promoted. For example, as a result of constructive pluralism, one now finds multicultural education, bilingual education, and ethnic studies in the public schools and teacher preparation institutions.

Despite the sociopolitical changes that Havighurst identified, a lingering legacy of the melting pot concept has remained throughout the 20th century. Although highly explicit Americanization programs have disappeared, schools up to the present day have to varying degrees conveyed the implicit message of the desirability of assimilation. Havighurst published his chronology in 1978, and it would be interesting to know how he would characterize the current state of pluralism in the United States, given the fact that the 1990s have brought a variety of powerful and potentially destructive challenges to the stance of constructive pluralism. There is, for example, the English Only movement, whose xenophobic and potentially racist ramifications we discussed in Chapter Two. Another significant example, only one of a variety that we could cite, is California's Proposition 187, which was passed in 1994. Called the "Save Our State" initiative, Proposition 187 stated that "the people of California declare their intention to provide for cooperation between their agencies of state and local government with their federal government and to establish a system of required notification by and between such agencies to prevent illegal aliens in the United States from receiving benefits or public services in the state of California" (Suárez-Orozco, 1995, p. 17). The potential effect of such a proposition on school-community relations was tremendous, as the initiative required that school personnel report students whom they "reasonably suspected" to be undocumented. Not surprisingly, the day after the proposition passed, a coalition of immigrants' rights groups filed a lawsuit in federal court, and within one week there was a temporary restraining order against enforcement. Also, school boards in Los Angeles, San Francisco, and Sacramento filed suit in state court and got an order blocking the ban on public school for illegal immigrants. One teacher organized a drive for educators to sign a pledge refusing to enforce Proposition 187. Reflecting the pressure under which these educators made their voices heard, Governor Wilson warned the public that school and health care personnel who refused to enforce the initiative "ought to be fired" (Simpson, 1995, p. 17). Initiatives such as Proposition 187, coupled with immigration policies and procedures, have worked to create climates of fear and harassment in many language-minority communities, and such climates negatively effect the conditions under which schooling for language-minority students occurs.

Unfortunately, while backlash movements such as the one that resulted in Proposition 187 focus national attention on issues that strongly affect language-minority communities throughout the United States, they do not do very much to solve the local social and economic problems that result from changes in the world economic order. As Suárez-Orozco argues, California's immigration "problem" of the 1990s is only a symptom of a worldwide crisis because it reflects the contemporary economic realities of multinational corporations—realities such as the need for cheap foreign workers in the wealthy industrial countries and the policy of privatization of Third World economies. For example, economic changes related to the North American Free Trade Agreement (NAFTA) are estimated to potentially drive as many as 2 to 3 million small-scale farmers in Mexico off of their land. It should not be any great surprise that many of these individuals would try desperately to earn a living in the United States. Thus, as the United States continues to struggle with its commitment to constructive pluralism, such phenomena as Proposition 187 and the English Only movement can be seen as a type of catharsis—they discharge anger over such issues as economic recession, crowded schools, and demographic changes, but they fail to solve the problem of how to build healthy, pluralistic communities in changing economic and political times (Suárez-Orozco, 1995, p. 18).

Many of the challenges to such pluralistic concepts as immigrants' rights and affirmative action stem from the nation's chronic fear that cultural diversity will lead to political disintegration and to changes in the traditional positions of power and status held disproportionately by European-American males. However, despite all of the conflict in the 1990s over the alleged "tribalization" of the United States, some historians argue that late 20th-century immigrants are actually assimilating faster today than they have in the past, for example, by learning English faster and by having a higher rate of marriages outside of ethnic groups (Jost, 1995, p. 114). It is unfortunate that this historical perspective is often lost amidst all the rhetoric in which critics argue that because of such policies as bilingual education and affirmative action, there are supposedly less incentives for immigrants to incorporate themselves into American society.

Court Cases as Reflections of Community Activism

As seen in Havighurst's four stages—defensive pluralism, the melting pot, laissez-faire pluralism, and constructive pluralism—the theme of ethnic diversity and how to deal with it starts early in American history and remains unresolved today. Even when free public schooling began to be made available to all children after the middle of the 19th century, such groups as African Americans and American Indians were excluded from participating in policy decisions affecting the schooling of their children (Tyack, 1981). These decisions in turn resulted in highly inequitable education practices. With such endemic inequity ultimately came challenges through the legal system. A variety of court cases from the 1970s to the present have involved ethnic communities and the issues of education, language, culture, and racial isolation. During this time, historically stigmatized ethnic communities have used the court system as an instrument of social reform with varying degrees of success. In Chapter Two we surveyed the role of a series of major court cases in determining bilingual education policies for language-minority students. We return now to look at these and other court cases again from the perspective of the role of language-minority communities in the development of bilingual education. All of these cases involve community efforts to redress injustices that affect the lives of minority children. First we will look at a court case from Alaska that clearly effected the general quality of community life, and then we will turn to *Lau* v. *Nichols* and subsequent court cases that focus specifically on bilingual education.

In *Tobeluk* v. *Lind* (1976) parents from bush communities of Alaska brought a civil class-action suit against the state on behalf of their children, arguing that it was discriminatory for these students to be required by law to leave their homes to attend school. At the time, it was necessary for rural students to leave their small, remote villages to attend distant boarding high schools. The practice brought with it great costs: significant disruption to family life, the erosion of a sense of community, and the loss of native languages and knowledge. In the settlement the governor of Alaska signed a consent decree stating that it was the right of every child to attend school in his or her local community, and that educational facilities had to be provided for local villages. This was a major victory for the integrity and development of language-minority communities in rural Alaska, as well as for the establishment of native-language maintenance and revitalization programs in the schools.

In the pivotal case of *Lau* v. *Nichols* (1974) members of the Chinese-American community in San Francisco organized on behalf of their children, whom they felt were not receiving an equitable education in the San Francisco school system. *Lau* v. *Nichols* remains today as the most significant victory for parents who want their children to receive comprehensible instruction while adapting to American linguistic, academic, and cultural norms. However, *Lau* v. *Nichols* and the ensuing Equal Educational Opportunities Act (see Chapter Two) did not specify how school districts' efforts to meet the needs of ELLs should be measured, and therefore the decision set the stage for a variety of future court cases in which community members sought better educational opportunities for their children (Jiménez, 1992).

In both *Ríos* v. *Read* (1977) and *Cintrón* v. *Brentwood Union Free School District Board of Education* (1978) community activists challenged the quality of already implemented bilingual education programs, pitting community expectations against school policy (Teitelbaum & Hiller, 1978). In both cases, the community won the decisions, with the courts determining that the mere existence of programs for ELLs was not in and of itself sufficient. The districts' programs had to meet certain standards of quality in order to be in compliance with families' civil rights.

In *Plyler* v. *Doe* (1981) community advocates for the rights of the children of illegal immigrants won a Supreme Court ruling that declared unconstitutional a Texas statute that had denied access to public schools to undocumented immigrants. As Justice Brennan wrote, the Texas law was clearly unconstitutional because it "imposes a lifetime hardship on a discrete class of children not accountable for their disabling status" (*Plyler* v. *Doe*, 1981, 219–20).

Castañeda v. *Pickard* (1981) was a class action lawsuit of the Mexican-American community against the Raymondville, Texas, school district. Quality was an issue here again as advocates for the community argued that the district did not have an adequate bilingual program to overcome language barriers. As discussed in Chapter Two, the most significant result of this case was actually the three-part test devised by the court to determine whether or not a district met the Equal Educational Opportunities Act (EEOA) requirement of "appropriate action." With *Castañeda* there was now a yardstick with which to measure the quality of bilingual programs.

In *Keyes* v. *School District No. 1* (1983) a group of parents and educators in Denver argued that the rights of English-language learners were being violated because of the district's weak bilingual and ESL programs. Influenced by the three-part test that emerged from the *Castañeda* decision, the court here ruled that the district had failed to meet standards of quality. The case was also significant because the district had argued that it had been acting in "good faith" in its efforts to provide programs for English-language learners, and therefore, it was not guilty of violation of the students' civil rights. However, the court ruled that good intentions were not sufficient; results rather than intent should be the basis for determination of discrimination.

Communities, however, have not always won their cases. In *Teresa P.* v. *Berkeley Unified School District* (1989) the "intent" pendulum swung back in the other direction. In this case, the court accepted that the Berkeley school district had made good faith efforts to implement a program for language-minority students, and therefore could not be found in violation of the law because of shortcomings in its program. In other words, the fact that bilingual and ESL services might not be adequate was considered acceptable if it was not the *intent* of the district to discriminate.

The sometimes conflicting conclusions found in court cases involving bilingual education reveal unresolved issues in the interplay between language-minority communities and the schools that serve them. As Jiménez (1992) stated in her review of court cases affecting the use of bilingual instruction, "the ideological debate over whether and to what extent other languages should be used in instruction for children not yet proficient in English will likely be with us for years to come" (p. 25). Still, it is through such legal evolution that community members and educators who are strong advocates for language-minority children can continue to work together as a community of leaders in the struggle to provide the best education possible for their children.

Despite periodic setbacks, the predisposition to use the legal system will continue to shape school policy slowly as communities of leaders push for quality language-minority education. While some observers of the American experience sense that the country may be experiencing "compassion fatigue"—exhaustion from all the civil rights and human welfare campaigns of the 1950s, 60s, and 70s—ethnic groups have gained a momentum for potential power far greater than that available to them in the past. As Gamboa (1980, p. 236) pointed out, the initial development of language-minority programs received its greatest impetus from the courts rather than from research. Today, we have much more research to back up the value of quality bilingual and ESL programs, but issues affecting the experience of language-minority students will continue to be played out in the courts as bilingual communities continue to organize to advocate for their children.

Community-Initiated Bilingual Programs in the 1970s

As important as court cases have been in the establishment of language-minority education programs, community organization for negotiation with school districts outside the courtroom has been another approach used successfully by communities throughout the country. We briefly discuss the history of three such cases here, all of them casting bilingual education programs within the larger context of the communities from which they grew. All of these cases, which developed in the 1970s, reflect the effort to establish a climate of constructive pluralism. At the time, many communities throughout the United States were struggling to simply establish the *right* to develop bilingual programs, and they were working with educators who by and large had very little training in bilingual and ESL concepts.

Guskin (1981) studied the implementation of bilingual education programs in Milwaukee, Wisconsin. These programs grew out of the civil rights movement of the 60s, becoming not only a means of instruction for English-language learners, but also a symbol of recognition and respect for the Hispanic-American community. Because Hispanic Americans in Milwaukee had little political power at the time, the community's strategy was a mixture of confrontation and cooperation. Crucial to the success of their movement were (1) a cadre of parent advocates who had been trained by community organizers; (2) a mainstream non-Hispanic administrator who was knowledgeable about bilingual education and served as a broker between the community and the school district; and (3) a few supportive school board members. However, once the programs were begun the battle was not over. Court-ordered school desegregation plans threatened to disperse Hispanic-American students throughout the city in such a way that bilingual classrooms could not be organized. It was, according to Guskin, through community activism that the court agreed to consider the impact of desegregation on bilingual schools and to save them from being dismantled.

Activism for bilingual education brings with it challenges and mixed success for communities. However, it is also a source of community development, as seen in the following two instances, one involving bilingual education development in Wilmington, Delaware, and the second the evolution of bilingual education in Washington, D.C. Waserstein (1975) documented the development of bilingual education through community efforts in Wilmington, Delaware, and found that as an important spin-off the process served as a natural training ground for leadership within the ethnic community. The movement was started through the efforts of the bilingual community in the broadest sense—a mixture of minority and majority group laypersons and professionals. This core of interested people developed parent support through extensive personal contact and through already-established institutions such as the church, school, and local community center. Community meetings served as a forum for the development of community organization strategies and leadership skills. In this case, the community chose to negotiate with the school district rather than sue. At the beginning of the negotiations, school district negotiators perceived community members as outsiders, but toward the end they were seen as the local experts on bilingual education, and their opinions carried considerable weight in deciding district bilingual policies. As a result of their efforts, the community not only achieved the implementation of bilingual programs but also gained valuable skills for organizing themselves over future local issues.

One of the authors of this book (Collier, 1980), in her study of the development of bilingual education over nine years in Washington, D.C., found a similar pattern of community involvement. Here, too, efforts to implement bilingual programs began with the community in the large sense of the word—community leaders, priests, and local bureaucrats. As the movement evolved, however, it facilitated the establishment of a grassroots Hispanic-American community identity, and it made the local community more visible as a political reality in the schools and the larger urban community. As the bilingual program developed, community members became more politically active and more experienced in the strategies of bringing about change. The schools themselves enhanced the development of civic participation and leadership skills through the following initiatives: the use of school-community coordinators; the hiring of bilingual teachers and aides who lived in and participated actively in the community; and parent participation in community advisory councils and in Saturday workshops on language development and math. Collier found that bilingual school administrators played an important role in raising community consciousness, so that the community itself took on new characteristics in the process of working with school staff for the improvement of educational opportunities for their children.

Whether we look at community activism through the courts or community organizing efforts in the 1970s to establish bilingual programs, we see that community activism has always played an important role behind the headlines in bilingual education. Even though the big scenes in language-minority education rights generally get played out in state capitals and in Washington, countless local leaders have paved the way for a better education for their community's children. And behind those community leaders are many other parents with issues and concerns, talents and ideas. Local communities constitute a tremendous resource for educators, and in order to appreciate this resource it is necessary to know the community well—which brings us to our next topic, the development of community portraits.

Developing a Portrait of the Community

A wealth of linguistic, cultural, and socioeconomic detail can be found in every community—detail that *should* affect the planning and definitely *will* affect the outcome of language-minority schooling efforts. Based on the analysis of a variety of studies of bilingual education programs, Jacobson (1979) suggested that the success of the effort "depends to a large extent upon the social, cultural, and attitudinal conditions prevailing in the immediate neighborhood of the school hosting such a program" (p. 483). And yet there is often a notable lack of knowledge about these important details of community life when programs are being planned, implemented, or evaluated. Guzmán (1978), for example, concluded in his study of a bilingual program in Oregon that unexamined community attitudes negatively affected the outcome of the project. There was a value conflict in the community between supporters of pluralism and supporters of assimilation, and because planners did not directly address the issue in the design and implementation stages, it became a hidden factor in the ineffectiveness of the resulting program.

While reading this section on community portraits, it is important to keep in mind that we will be concluding the chapter with a discussion of pathways toward strong partnerships between families and schools. Although this section and the final one are separate for organizational reasons, the ability to build a strong partnership is intimately connected with the picture that educators have of the local community. Without an understanding of the community, school-initiated parent involvement programs may have unintended results. For example, taking a hard look at the possible problems with programs for parents in lower-income language-minority communities, Valdés (1996) stated, "parent involvement is an attempt to find small solutions to what are extremely complex problems. I am concerned that this 'new' movement—because it is not based on sound knowledge about the characteristics of the families with which it is concerned—will fail to take into account the impact of such programs on the families themselves" (p. 31). A parent involvement program may indeed be perceived as a David battling against the Goliath of an inequitable society that reproduces itself through the schools. However, parent programs become more powerful to the extent that they are firmly rooted in a sound knowledge of the communities in which they operate.

The goal of development of a community portrait is somewhat challenging. Bilingual and ESL programs just do not come equipped with full-time sociolinguists and ethnographers. Yet the accumulation of cultural, socioeconomic, and linguistic detail is the basis for a realistic understanding of the community, and without this realistic understanding, pedagogical innovations and parent partnerships may not thrive. While research literature on the patterns of similar communities can provide some orientation, administrators and teachers who want to develop a sound local knowledge base will have to rely largely on themselves and their ties with community members for the acquisition of a detailed community perspective. However, acquiring this perspective is not something that a single school employee has to do alone over a short period of time. It is a continual process that teachers, administrators, university researchers, instructional assistants, interns, student teachers, and community members establish together over a long period of time. Doing community research in this context seldom means a formal research agenda with complicated data-gathering techniques. A lot of information and understanding can be gained over time through experience and interaction with the community, provided one is prepared to notice the relevant details and to build them into a sense of the structure of community life. It means finding frequent opportunities to interact with community members and organizations, being very observant about aspects of community life as we encounter them, listening to and learning from students as they share aspects of their lives, reflecting on the meaning of our observations and remembering that our perceptions are colored by our own experiences, and sharing and comparing our observations with other members of the school community. Perhaps most importantly, it also means incorporating the community knowledge into the curriculum, into the ways in which teaching and learning take place, and into the way we interact with families.

To provide a framework for the numerous themes educators can consider when developing a profile of a particular community, we will first look at an example of one teacher's initial description of the community in which she taught. We will then organize our discussion of community portraits around the topics of (1) characteristics of ethnicity in the community; (2) the socioeconomic structure of the community; (3) language use in the community; (4) the use of funds of knowledge and community-based research; and (5) ethnographies as resources.

Community Observations: One Teacher's Perspective

An extremely important goal in the development of bilingual and ESL education is to train increased numbers of language-minority individuals to become credentialed teachers. However, the fact remains that all too often the teachers who work in language-minority programs are outsiders to the community in which they teach, often in several different ways—culturally, socioeconomically, and geographically. However, such teachers can make themselves more fully members of the school's community of learners and community of leaders by making efforts to get to know the local community on its own terms. Combined with the effort must be an ability to reflect on how their own sociocultural backgrounds affect their perceptions of the community. The following thoughts by one of the authors of this chapter, who was an outsider to the community in which she worked as a novice teacher in the 1970s, portray her ongoing development as she took the first steps in coming to know her community.

In this portrait, she happened to touch briefly on each of the community themes that we will be exploring: characteristics of ethnicity, socioeconomic structure, language use, funds of knowledge, and community-based research.

The Teacher's View and the Child's-Eye View

The area served by my school is the most economically depressed of the city. Less than a third of the adults have completed high school. The average annual family income is well below the national median, and nearly a third of the students receives Aid for Dependent Children. Nearly all of the students receive free or reduced-price breakfasts and lunches at school. According to the California Assessment Program Background Factor Summary, normed for all schools in California, the area's socioeconomic indicator is at the 1st percentile, the parent education index is at the 4th percentile, and the number of children on Aid for Dependent Children is at the 78th percentile.

The community lacks full development of many basic urban services. Until recently there were several unpaved streets, and most alleys are still unpaved. There are few health services available in the immediate community. There are only a few small neighborhood stores, and bus stops are as much as half a mile away from many of the homes. Many of the small homes are well maintained and have pleasing gardens, but much of the housing is substandard, consisting of tiny one- to three-room rental units.

The community is at least 80 percent Hispanic and about 10 percent black. That, of course, adds up to at least 90 percent minority residents. It would be very safe to say that the dominant language in the community is Spanish. Many of the business establishments are named after places in Mexico; there is a Spanish-language theater; and billboards commonly appear in Spanish.

There is a strong network of family and church relationships. Most children have grandparents, aunts, uncles, cousins, or godparents who live close by. Many families frequently make return trips to visit family in rural Mexico. The local Catholic church serves many families and operates a K–6 parochial school in which many upwardly mobile families enroll their children. The Catholic Youth Organization also maintains a community center across the street from the school. This center provides many youth and senior citizen activities. Much social interaction occurs within the homes, in front of the homes, on the sidewalks, and in the streets.

Seen from the inside, however, the community is not homogeneous. There are devout Catholic Hispanics and devout Protestant Hispanics. There are Hispanics who get along well with blacks and those who have strong racial prejudices. There are rural Mexicans who still wear the kinds of hats and boots that they wore on the ranches in Mexico, and many residents slaughter goats, pigs, and chickens in their backyards. But there are also Chicanos who buy their children's clothes at Sears, take vacations in campers, and barely speak Spanish. There are parents who take their children to the library and there are parents who can't sign their own name. There are teenagers who keep the neighborhood walls decorated with graffiti, use drugs, and vandalize the school. And there are teenagers who belong to religious organizations or attend college.

Most parents in the community place great importance on the role of schooling for their children. They want them to do well. What they don't realize is the extent to which schools such as the one in their community have traditionally failed to keep students competitive with the national norms. Neither do most parents realize that schools such as theirs are often singled out by policymakers as problems that can be given assorted labels and attacked with money for special remedial programs. For example, of the 1,200 students at school this year, 91 percent are Hispanic and 5 percent are black, making it a minority, segregated school. This qualifies it for special court-ordered funding that is supposed to alleviate the adverse effects of racial isolation. Also, first-graders score each year at the first percentile in the California Assessment Program's test of entry-level skills. This, along with the economic status of the community, entitles the school to federal Title I funding.

Despite the gap between the aspirations of parents for their children and the highly politicized and institutionalized intricacies of the public school system, bilingual education has enabled parents to become more closely involved in the elementary schooling process. Because the language barrier has been removed, they can talk to most of the teachers, participate in meetings, understand programs, and help children with their homework. Most of the educational aides at the school are members of the community. The Hispanic-dominated PTA and the school decision-making committees have provided opportunities for Hispanic community leaders to emerge and to develop their leadership skills. Most parents are supportive of bilingual education, in varying degrees, although the program is not the result of a grass-roots community movement. Some parents favor a maintenance bilingual program, and some favor a transitional bilingual program. A few are against bilingual education altogether. And many aren't quite sure what is happening but want to trust the school and out of respect sign just about anything they're asked to sign.

The "standard" English and "standard" Spanish that we use at school are imports from outside the community, and we the teachers are imports too. Nearly all the teachers, myself included, come into the barrio to teach and then retreat to our own enclaves by 4:30 every afternoon. Despite extensive use of Spanish and recognition of Mexican and Chicano cultural traditions, we still comprise an alien and often puzzling institution. The teachers at school vary in their degree of support for bilingual education, especially with respect to maintenance of the home language. Some teachers seem to be holding their noses as they warily implement the bare requirements, and this message must get through to the students. By second grade many LEP students have already figured out that English speakers seem to have more status among peers and more verbal interactions with teachers. By sixth grade former Spanish-dominant students frequently claim to know little or no Spanish. And in some instances former Spanish speakers really have lost their Spanish fluency.

In the eyes of the outside world, the community where I work seems to have developed into one large, negative stereotype. I remember the principal telling me about an incident involving a large mural at the school entrance that some local teen-age boys were painting under the auspices of a local artist. Most of the boys involved wore the clothing of the cholo [which can be associated with gang membership]. The principal was proud of the mural project and wanted the area newspaper to cover it. However, he told me he was repeatedly unsuccessful in getting *a reporter out until he finally called and hinted that the mural had something to do with gangs. That got the story printed.*

Despite the many negative traits of the community from an outsider's point of view, from the child's point of view it is home, and the neighborhood houses, stores, playgrounds, gardens, parks, vacant lots, railroad tracks, repair shops, junkyards, and industries carry many emotional connotations. Although teachers may think in terms of the undesirable nature of the community, the children have found a great deal of joy and warmth there. Without romanticizing poverty, it is important to remember that an outsider's perception of the community is different from the insider's. This struck me clearly one day when a group of first-graders in my class had completed a writing assignment. We were studying the local community as a social studies unit and had just returned from a long neighborhood walk. After some group discussion I modeled a mixture of sentences, both positive and negative, based on my comments and theirs. Biased by my own awareness of the less-than-optimal socioeconomic and environmental realities of the community, I expected a lot of sentences reflecting negative traits from the students. To my surprise, every child came up with a product that began along the lines of "(name of community) is pretty." I had also been surprised, when we first began the community unit, to see how quickly the students learned to read and spell the rather long name of the community. Another incident that made me think about the community from the child's-eye view was the following conversation between a group of first-graders and myself:

> *Arturo: Teacher! Teacher! They cut a boy all up, on his face, last night. From here to here (pointing).*
> *Angela: They were cholos.*
> *Nakia: Cholos are bad.*
> *Me: Well, some cholos do some bad things. But some do good things too.*
> *Alejo: Teacher, some cholos live in my house. They're good.*

Being "sensitive" to the community involves more than celebrating holidays read about in a book or trying an ethnic recipe. It involves beginning to see the community the way the parents and children do—as an ethnographer would.

We cannot discuss each issue extensively in this chapter, but we will look more closely at the first question regarding immigrant versus indigenous minority status. In looking at this issue, we also will be touching indirectly on a number of the other questions listed above. While in many if not most cases, both immigrants and families that have been here for several generations live within the same neighborhood, it is useful to consider their characteristics separately in order to better know the types of issues that may be encountered.

Immigrant Communities

Ethnic communities composed primarily of foreign-born parents represent a diverse configuration of backgrounds, talents, needs, and aspirations. The United States is a nation of immigrants who have uprooted their families and left homes, friends, relatives, customs, food, and language. To make such a

Guidelines for Teaching

CHARACTERISTICS OF ETHNICITY IN THE COMMUNITY

Looking at the community "as an ethnographer would" we find a variety of factors that contribute to the characteristics of local ethnicity. The following questions give an idea of the types of issues that may be considered in coming to understand the ethnic composition of a community:

- How is ethnicity reflected in the immigrant or in the indigenous status of community members?

- What is the ethnic and mainstream mix within the neighborhood?

- What are the characteristics of the relationships between the various groups?

- How isolated from or integrated with the mainstream community are the language-minority communities?

- To what degree does the community represent a stable or a mobile population?

- What are the reasons for the stability or mobility of community members?

- What is happening to community members in terms of maintenance of ethnicity and acculturation or assimilation?

- How have minority status, acculturation, or both, affected the relationships between younger and older generations?

dramatic move, family decision makers must have reflected carefully on the pros and cons of the geographic shift and concluded that the overall benefits outweighed any social, cultural, or emotional advantage of staying home. There are very strong economic, political, professional, ideological, religious, or educational forces that push immigrants from their home country and pull them toward another nation.

Some immigrants, despite numerous hardships, may feel a strong sense of optimism in their lives. Many immigrants, after all, perceive the United States as a place in which resourcefulness, intelligence, and perseverance are rewarded. But equally important to remember is the fact that along with the original voluntary immigrants may be involuntary ones—children, spouses, relatives, or other dependents who joined the migration without a strong say in the matter and who as a result may have mixed feelings about the move. Besides the matter of initial choice, there are other important factors that fundamentally affect the way immigrants feel about the host country, such as age, marital status, economic condition, educational experience, occupation, language barriers, health, size of family, extent of personal ties in the new country, and the political and economic situation of the home country. Immigrants' feelings also may be strongly affected by the way in which they feel they are perceived by mainstream United States citizens. All too often, immigrants correctly discern that they are not entirely welcome by people whose own ancestors arrived here several generations before.

For immigrant families with children, the school becomes one of the first and most important places where the adjustment process begins. The outcome of this acculturation process through the schools is closely linked to the age and previous schooling experience of the child, as well as to the attitudes and philosophy of the parents. Generally, we can say that younger children may experience less difficulty learning everyday social English and may make a smoother cultural transition. But perhaps they will not do as well academically as older siblings if these siblings have had extensive formal schooling in the home country. A significant correlation seems to exist between the academic performance in the United States and the age and literacy skills of the learner before immigrating. (See Chapter Four, for research related to this topic.) Adolescent immigrants experience other problems, however. This is not surprising given that even under the best of circumstances teenagers often face challenging developmental stress.

Immigrant parents vary a great deal in how they wish to have their children acculturate to American society. Some parents, wanting to allow their children time to come to grips with the variety of new experiences, or concerned that their children will lose very important traditional values, are not in a hurry to push their children to become Americanized. Others, on the other hand, may want to encourage their children to quickly adopt American cultural patterns—for example, by dressing the part of middle class Americans and anglicizing their children's names. Some parents feel nostalgic about their ancestral lands, while others wish to forget their past. Some parents are accepting of religious changes or marriage outside the ethnic boundaries, while others feel quite strongly about keeping their ethnic identity at least partially insulated from the dominant culture lifestyles. Some families wish to construct a division between their private ethnic lives and their public lives. For example, they may wish the school to focus on a monolingual, monocultural English curriculum while they take care of the native language and culture at home or in private weekend or after-school classes.

In addition to the mode and speed of cultural transmission found in ethnic communities, we have to consider the broad range of perceptions that ethnic parents may have of the school itself as an institution. We may start by noting that what foreign-born parents expect from the American experience for them and for their children is affected by the nature of their educational and socioeconomic experiences in their ancestral countries. In most cases, therefore, their notions about the American school experience may be highly speculative. They generally do not have first-hand experience with schooling in the United States, and they may have somewhat inaccurate perceptions from the information their children bring home. Their awareness of how schools function in the United States is often limited, and they may have insufficient knowledge about the social, cultural, and academic skills it takes to succeed in the new education system.

A variety of attitudes toward school may limit the extent to which parents feel at ease playing active roles. Some community members may feel very grateful to have come to the United States, and therefore may feel that it is

Guidelines for Teaching

FOUR STAGES OF ADJUSTMENT EXPERIENCED BY NEWCOMER PARENTS

In their work with immigrant families, Violand-Sánchez, Sutton, and Ware (1991, p. 5) have identified four stages of adjustment that newcomer parents may experience. Summarizing from their work, the four stages are these:

1. *Arrival survival.* During this stage, the parents' time for participation in school affairs may be limited as they establish a new household, find their way around the community, and seek employment. However, the interest level will be very high for such basic information as enrollment procedures, school schedules, and lunch routines. Provision of information in the native language is particularly important at this time.

2. *Culture shock.* This is an emotionally stressful time during which families may find their energies drained from having to cope day after day with the new sociocultural environment. During this stage they may be disillusioned with American ways. Support groups are helpful at this point, along with personal contacts from school personnel. It is important to keep lines of communication open during this difficult period, while limiting school demands on the parents' time.

3. *Coping.* Coming out of culture shock, families feel more confident that they can deal with the new system and establish a role for themselves within it. As they are now more familiar with the new cultural system, it is a good time to encourage more participation in school activities, making sure that the tasks or responsibilities are clearly defined so that the parents feel comfortable in their role. Families at this stage can also be enlisted to help other families in the previous two stages who need assistance in adjustment.

4. *Acculturation.* At this stage, if the school has been successful in establishing a sense of community, parents feel comfortable in their setting. In addition to basic participation in school activities, they should be provided with opportunities for leadership and also for more extensive mentoring of other parents.

not appropriate for them to complain or to critique American educational institutions. To some immigrants these institutions may seem superior to what they had in their native countries. On the other hand, many parents may find United States schools to be too lax or undemanding compared to the schools in their home country. Because community involvement in educational decision making is not significant in many other countries, some parents may believe that the right thing is to place all the responsibility for educating their children on school personnel. Such parents might not consider it appropriate to go beyond seeing that their children's homework is completed, requiring that their children behave well in school, or attending an open house. Foreign-born parents are profoundly interested in the education of their children, but because of experiences rooted in the past they may tend to be tentative about taking too much ownership of the formal schooling process. This may mean that their children are sometimes left on their own to make sense out of American schools. Without a strong partnership between schools and parents, older students may have to make choices regarding graduation and vocational or academic programs independently—choices that will have an impact on career opportunities later in life.

Indigenous Minority Communities   *"Ni chicha ni limonada"* is a popular saying in Latin America that roughly translates to English as "neither fish nor fowl." In a vivid way such a saying captures the cultural dilemma surrounding many indigenous minorities in this country such as American Indians, Puerto Ricans, and other language minorities who have been here for more than one or two generations. As individuals in these groups define and redefine their identities, the choices that they make between sociocultural alternatives can sometimes offer many unresolved propositions.

There is a troubling tendency in the United States for European Americans to perceive indigenous minorities as being non-American, even if they have been here for generations. It is not uncommon, for example, for a European American to mentally place all Mexican Americans as "belonging" somewhere south of the Rio Grande. Ronald Takaki, a historian who is Japanese American, tells of a situation he has repeatedly encountered in various forms. In this particular instance, Takaki was in Virginia, in a taxi driven by a middle-aged European American:

> "How long have you been in this country?" he [the taxi driver] asked. "All my life," I replied, wincing. "I was born in the United States." With a strong southern drawl, he remarked: "I was wondering because your English is excellent!" Then, as I had many times before, I explained: "My grandfather came here from Japan in the 1880s. My family has been here, in America, for over a hundred years." He glanced at me in the mirror. Somehow I did not look "American" to him. (Takaki, 1993, p. 1)

At the same time that indigenous minorities often feel unaccepted as fullfledged citizens of the United States, their status in their ancestral country can often be problematic. Mexican Americans frequently tell of being ostracized by native Mexicans, particularly when their Spanish is faulty by Mexican standards. The somewhat derogatory term *pocho*—what a Mexican sometimes calls a Mexican American—reflects the potentially ethnocentric view of Mexican nationals toward Mexican Americans. It is sometimes difficult for them to view Mexican-American culture as a long-term, rational adaptation to a specific linguistic and cultural context in the United States. This *"ni chicha ni limonada"* experience is not unique to Hispanic Americans. It is also reflected, for example, in the statement of a Japanese American regarding her trips to Japan: "I feel American when I'm in Japan, but when I'm in the United States I feel Japanese."

It is difficult to make generalizations about indigenous communities, as their experiences vary greatly depending on racial or ethnic background, region, and urban or rural status. A tiny bush community of Inuit living on the northern coast of Alaska—people who have never been "from" anywhere else in recorded history—have little in common with urban Puerto Ricans on the East Coast who have been in this country for two or three generations. However, one generalization that can be made is that the majority of indigenous language-minority communities in the United States have experienced over the years various kinds of discrimination and tend to reflect a pattern of socioeconomic inequality.

On the surface the differences between indigenous minority communities and mainstream communities may in some cases be easy to overlook. Indigenous minority communities are composed of English speakers who have been educated in the United States and who are generally very familiar with popular culture. However, despite the superficial homogeneity, indigenous minority groups over generations tend to maintain cultural differences, such as the type of English used, the ways family members interact with each other, learning styles, and patterns of family structure. In looking at the conquered or colonized status of many indigenous minorities, the anthropologist John Ogbu (1992) argues that such groups tend to maintain such differences over time as a natural response in defense of their identity as they are subjected to unequal treatment by the dominant society.

While immigrant students often arrive at school with "a clean slate," so to speak, indigenous minorities often arrive with an all-too-familiar history of past generations' experiences in the classroom. They frequently come to the classroom surrounded by negative stereotypes about the support that their community will offer to the learning process. To begin, educators often see the language of their community as a strike against them. School personnel who are often very sympathetic to the language needs of non-English-speaking immigrants sometimes have a less than enlightened attitude toward the language patterns indigenous minorities bring to school. Rather than seeing the language resources that such children have, they see defects—the nonstandard version of English the children speak is not accepted as a naturally evolved expression of the uniqueness of the community. In addition, teachers may see the fact that the children may speak a limited or "incorrect" version of their ancestral language, or that they may mix English with the other language, as a defect. In terms of behavior patterns, teachers are readily prepared to expect that immigrant children may differ significantly from dominant culture children, but teachers who have not had appropriate training and who do not have an unprejudiced familiarity with the local community often assume "normalcy" patterns for indigenous minorities that are in reality based on the teachers' own culture and experiences. When supposedly "American" indigenous language minorities do not conform to these "normalcy" patterns, an adversarial relationship develops between the teacher and the student (Delpit, 1995).

Another aspect of the indigenous community that is often cast in negative stereotypes is their attitude toward schooling. Because of the past inequalities in schooling, indigenous minorities as a group have tended to have high dropout rates and lower test scores. This becomes a cycle as teachers come to expect less from students from these groups. Educators often assume that the community puts little value on education. When parents or community members question school practices, some administrators or teachers may see this as confrontational militancy rather than as a reflection of a deep caring for the well-being of their children. One of the writers of this book once asked a high school principal to comment on his school's relations with ethnic groups in the community. The administrator pointed out first that a good principal is skillful in selecting community members to work with him and for him—persons who can help put out the frequent fires in school and community relations. Then he went on to point out that his main problems had been with indigenous minority parents who were frequently a thorn in his side. According to him, these parents tended to be more assertive, single-issue-oriented, and ill-informed than immigrant parents. He described recent immigrant parents, on the other hand, as cooperative and easy to work with. This anecdote points out the critical issue of stereotyped perceptions. Intentionally or not, school personnel may tend to treat indigenous parents less positively than immigrant parents.

In the case of immigrant families, community members and school personnel often quickly erect bridges between the culture of the school and the immigrant community because of the urgent need for bilingual individuals to facilitate communication with non-English-speaking parents. Beyond simple removal of the language barrier, a positive side effect may be that these translators also serve as cultural brokers between the school and the home. In the case of indigenous minority families, translators are generally not needed, and consequently the school may lack cultural brokers who can work well with the community. One important solution to this problem is to increase the number of indigenous minority students who become educators; another aspect is to provide training for all educators, regardless of their backgrounds, that will enable them to approach the indigenous minority community as a resource rather than as a source of impediments to learning.

The Socioeconomic Structure of the Community

Socioeconomic characteristics of a community reflect such issues as wealth distribution, education, employment, and social mobility. Through a consideration of socioeconomic issues, educators become more aware of another important dimension of community life. As we have stated in Chapter One, language-minority families—despite the stereotype of low-income levels—come from a very broad range of backgrounds. Among both immigrant and indigenous groups there are middle-income as well as lower-income families.

We will look at two examples of socioeconomic factors in the community that can affect the outcome of bilingual programs. First, we will look at the case of a Spanish/Quiche bilingual program in Ecuador, in which groups of differing SES had very different views of the region's bilingual program. Then we will consider Guthrie's **ethnography** (1985) of a Chinese-American community in California.

Guidelines for Teaching

**SOCIOECONOMIC ISSUES TO ADDRESS IN THE
DEVELOPMENT OF A COMMUNITY PORTRAIT**

- How is wealth distributed in the community?

- How is the local economy tied in to the national and international economy?

- Which community groups or members tend to have higher social status than others?

- Who are the leaders in the community and how are they perceived by other community members?

- To what extent is upward socioeconomic mobility a part of the community's definition of success?

- What are the perceived socioeconomic rewards for literacy and school achievement?

- What are the socioeconomic costs and benefits of membership in a particular ethnic group?

In the case of the Otavalo Indians of highland Ecuador (Carpenter, 1983) the Ecuadorian government had implemented Spanish/Quichua bilingual programs with the stated goal of facilitating the sociocultural and economic integration of the Quichua-speaking minorities. However, planners based the program design on the erroneous assumption of homogeneity among the Otavalo Indians. In reality, there were two rather distinct socioeconomic classes among the Otavaleños, and their reactions to the bilingual program were quite different. This in turn affected the potential for success of the programs. Otavaleños derived their livelihood largely from subsistence agriculture and traditional weaving, for which there was a substantial tourist market. The weaving was sold principally in a famous regional artisan market that was held every Saturday. The more wealthy (relatively speaking) Otavaleños who marketed the Otavalo crafts were generally urban Protestants who were already bilingual in Spanish and Quichua and who alternated between traditional and modern dress depending on the situation. The poorer Otavalo Indians were generally rural, Catholic subsistence farmers and were more likely to be monolingual Quichua speakers who tended to wear traditional clothing. Carpenter reported that the wealthy, urban Otavalo Indians, concerned over their childrens' loss of Quichua, warmly accepted bilingual education as a means of maintaining their ethnic identity. The maintenance of this identity was crucial to their economic success as Otavalo Indians in the artisan market. On the other hand, the rural Otavaleños saw the transitional bilingual program—in which reading was first introduced in Quichua—as an attempt to keep them from attaining fluency in Spanish and thus to bar them from socioeconomic advancement. As one rural, antibilingual-education Quichua informant put it, "almost nothing is written in Quichua, so why on earth would anyone want to learn to read and write that language? Anything to be read is in Spanish, and anything worth writing about will also be in that language" (Carpenter, 1983, p. 104). Carpenter (1983) concluded that for a bilingual education program to be successful, program designers could not assume homogeneity within any particular ethnic group and must be prepared to "incorporate the concerns of the target population in their design" (p. 106).

In Guthrie's ethnography of public bilingual education in a Chinese-American community in California, she also found SES to be a factor in attitudes toward the program, but in different ways than was the case in Carpenter's study. In her study, the lower-income residents, who were generally the more recent immigrants, tended to be the most supportive of the use of Chinese in the public schools. Preoccupied as they were with day-to-day survival, they often did not have the resources to enroll their children in private Chinese-language classes or to provide such instruction at home. Furthermore, they saw a pragmatic need for Chinese-language skills if their children were to survive within the local ethnic economy. Middle-class and upper-class parents, on the other hand, saw beyond the local ethnic economy and appeared to be primarily concerned with their children's advancement within the dominant socioeconomic structure. They saw an emphasis on English and math as the means to that goal; and therefore tended to be less supportive of the public school's bilingual program (Guthrie, 1985, pp. 224–25).

Language Use in the Community

To more fully understand the significance of the languages that teachers and children use in school, it is important to understand language use in the community. By language use we mean, essentially, who uses which language, with whom, and for what purposes. As Aguirre (1980) pointed out, it is perhaps ironic that "much implementation of bilingual education programs has occurred without comprehensive sociolinguistic analyses of the target student populations, and their respective school-community environments" (p. 47). For example, if educators are cognizant of the varieties of languages that community members use, as well as the level of proficiency in the various codes, they are better able to select linguistically appropriate materials or to anticipate language difficulties that may come up because of the materials that are available. Information on community language use may also be of value in the evaluation of programs. For example, as Cohen (1983) points out, if one of the goals of a program is native language maintenance, then long-term research on patterns of language use in the community can help to determine if that goal is being met. At a much deeper level, knowledge of language use in the community is also extremely important as a resource for curriculum and instruction. Virtually all learning in school is mediated through language, and therefore, as we saw in Chapter Five when we examined ethnographic studies of language usage patterns, the ways in which children and adults use language can have an effect on the quality of the experience. By

Guidelines for Teaching

LANGUAGE USE IN THE COMMUNITY

Among the types of questions that we can ask about language use in the community are these:

- Who speaks which languages, and when are the various languages spoken?

- Which languages do individuals read and write in the community? If they read and write in more than one language, which languages are used for which kinds of literacy events?

- What is the level of proficiency of community members in the various languages, including literacy levels?

- What language variation is present within each language? For example, is a particular dialect of the language or a nonstandard version of the language used?

- To what extent do community members use code-switching, and what are the patterns of its use?

- What prestige or stigma is attached to the various types of language present in the community?

- What value do community members place on speaking, reading, and writing the various languages present in the community?

- How is language use changing or remaining the same within the community?

accepting community language patterns in the classroom, teachers are capitalizing on the skills that children and their parents bring to the learning environment. If we look more specifically at patterns of literacy in the community, an awareness of which languages people use for various reading and writing activities and for what purposes they use literacy in their daily lives is crucial to the cultural appropriateness of formal literacy instruction in school, especially at the beginning levels of reading and writing.

To get a feeling for language-use issues, we will look briefly at the concept of **diglossia** and changes in language use. Then we will look at the role of language goals in the school and community in effecting the outcome of bilingual programs.

Diglossia, a term coined by Ferguson (1959), refers to a situation in which two languages or varieties of languages are both used within the same community but in separate circumstances or contexts. The pattern of language use found among the Mississippi Band of the Choctaw Indians in the 1970s provides one example of a pattern of diglossia. Young people could use Choctaw well in informal conversations with family and friends, but for more formal uses they changed to English, because they did not have the skills they needed in Choctaw to carry on more extended formal discourse.

As we will see later in the chapter, the development of the Choctaw community's awareness of this pattern of diglossia resulted in the establishment of a bilingual program (York, 1979).

Fishman's sociolinguistic study (1980) of private ethnic language schools in New York suggested a relationship between the nature of diglossia in the community and the success of schools in producing **biliteracy.** In the French, Hebrew, Chinese, Armenian, and Greek communities he studied in New York, literacy in each language had a separate function in the community. There was a *reason* for learning to read and write in each language, and children were immersed in two "cultures of reading." Based on his research, Fishman suggested that language educators' concern over specific methods of literacy instruction for bilingual children may not be as crucial to promoting biliteracy as a consideration of the uses of reading and writing in the immediate and wider communities.

As community circumstances change, patterns of diglossia also change. Thus, the next language-use question that we consider is "How is language use changing or remaining the same in the community?" Over a period of time a community may maintain the use of a particular language in predictable contexts, or the community may experience a shift in language use such that one language is replaced by another language. For example, Portes and Schauffler (1996) found evidence in their survey of second-generation youth in Miami (which included Cuban, Haitian, and Nicaraguan youth as well as other groups) of a surprisingly rapid degree of language shift. Nearly 100 percent of the young people in the study reported speaking English well or very well, and 80 percent of the entire sample reported preferring to use English to their native language. The authors described the situation as a context of "overwhelming language assimilation" (Portes & Schauffler, 1996, p. 22).

Looking at a different region, however, Jaramillo (1995) found a different pattern of "reverse diglossia" in progress within the Spanish-speaking community of the Tucson area. In the Tucson of the 1940s, Mexican Americans tended to exhibit a diglossic language-use pattern of Spanish for intimate and familiar relations and English for more impersonal and formal relations, even when all speakers were fluent in Spanish (Barker, 1975). Today, however, Jaramillo found that "the previously differentiated functional allocation of Spanish for private domains and English for public domains has given way to what appears to be a far more open use of Spanish for public life" (Jaramillo, 1995, p. 81).

Many different factors affect language maintenance or language shift in the community. For example, some factors that may contribute to language maintenance are a large, homogeneous group of speakers; frequent returns to the country of origin; reinforcement through the frequent arrival of new immigrants, and the existence of a variety of modes of language use in the community (reading and writing as well as listening and speaking). Among the factors that may contribute to language loss are low social status of speakers of the language and the lack of necessity for the language in social advancement (Cohen, 1975; Gaarder, 1971; Weinreich, 1953).

In the specific case of Tucson's "reverse diglossia," Jaramillo identified a variety of macrosociolinguistic factors that could continue to contribute to the growth of Spanish as a public language: proximity to Mexico; a continual influx of new speakers of the language; the size and geographic density of the Spanish-speaking population in the community's *barrios;* the general socioeconomic subordination and distance of the Spanish-speaking population from dominant society; the presence of ethnolinguistic pride as well as a small but visible Spanish-speaking elite; the market value of the language for employment (especially due to the international trade effects of NAFTA); and the presence of newspapers, radio, television, and religious services in Spanish.

Traditionally, schools have tended to replicate the patterns of social status, and thus language status, of the larger society. Therefore, we need to look more specifically at the potential influence of school language policies in language maintenance or language shift. For example, the decades of emphasis on English in Bureau of Indian Affairs schools certainly had a tremendously negative effect on the fate of many American Indian languages. On the other hand, when language shift has occurred or begins to occur in a particular community, the schools can also become involved in efforts to revitalize or maintain the language that is losing ground. As Holm and Holm (1995) note, reflecting on American Indian language revitalization movements, "Certainly schools alone cannot 'save' a language. But conversely, we know of no successful efforts to reverse language shift in the twentieth century that have ignored the school" (p. 165).

In considering the role of schools in language maintenance or shift, it is important to identify the language goals of community members and compare those to the school program's language goals. Regarding the value that community members place on the various languages present in their particular setting, Aguirre (1980) reported on a situation in a rural Colorado community in which the language goals of the teachers and parents were not congruent. Community members generally preferred their children to use Spanish among friends and family, but the teachers (although predominantly Mexican American) tended to prefer the use of English in the home. Thus, while the parents indicated a preference for a language maintenance bilingual program, the teachers indicated a preference for a transitional model. Aguirre attributed the conflicts that arose between the school and community regarding the program to these consistently differing attitudes, and he concluded that the lack of match had damaged the effectiveness of the community's bilingual program.

Funds of Knowledge and Community-Based Research

As we said when we began this section on community profiles, schools don't come equipped with full-time ethnographers and sociolinguists. However, there are many ways in which bilingual and ESL educators can begin to identify and use community resources. We will look more closely now at how school personnel, in cooperation with community members and outsiders such as university researchers, can improve their knowledge of the community by using funds of knowledge and community-based research.

Community knowledge is a valuable commodity in the classroom because the child does not arrive at school as a *tabula rasa*. In fact, by the time children enroll in school they have had myriad and complex experiences—for example, learning to read a few things on their own; using a variety of mathematical concepts in everyday situations; learning to understand the cultural and social demands placed on them; adopting some values and bypassing others; and developing the ability to communicate their needs, interests, and ideas. Such learners come to school already equipped with a wide array of skills that enable them to negotiate life successfully within their community.

The child exists within the context of the community, and this community therefore is a vast resource for the development of the child. In fact, Moll (1992), like other researchers we have cited in this chapter, has suggested that too much research time and energy is spent on such pedagogical issues as how to measure language dominance, when to transfer from L_1 reading to English reading, and so on. He feels that this research emphasis reflects a dominant culture bias toward bilingual and ESL education as remedial education that will "fix" language "problems." In focusing on this type of classroom-oriented research, bilingual educators are missing the more important issue of using research to discover how communities can enhance instruction.

All too often, unfortunately, the public sees communities in which language-minority children reside as barriers to learning. For example, English-dominant Americans often negatively stereotype communities with many recent immigrants as "ghettos" that impede the incorporation of the newcomers into American society. However, the historian Ueda (cited in Jost, 1995, p. 114) argues that ethnic neighborhoods in reality assist immigrants in the acculturation and socialization process. The mix of newcomers with immigrants who already have had some experience living in the United States, coupled with relatively easy access to bilingual individuals who can translate as needed, gives the newcomers a base from which to establish survival networks and to make sense out of all of the new cultural and social patterns. Rather than seeing such communities as "problems," they can be perceived as providers of resources that the local schools can also capitalize on to establish a community of learners.

Another cost of educators' ignorance of the community, according to Moll, is a distortion in our knowledge about children's cognitive abilities. Moll feels that by being largely unaware of the kinds of activities, responsibilities, and interactions that the child has in the community, teachers are consequently unaware of what the children are actually able to do intellectually in the everyday context of their neighborhood and family. Not knowing about these skills, teachers don't take advantage of them in the classroom, resulting in a watered-down curriculum.

Moll and González and their colleagues have developed the funds of knowledge perspective as a means of enabling educators to capitalize on the resources communities can provide for learning (González, 1995; González et al., 1995; Moll, 1992; Moll et al., 1992; Moll & González, 1997). Discussing the guiding principle of his funds of knowledge perspective, Moll states that "the students' community represents a resource of enormous importance for educational change and improvement. We have focused our [funds of knowledge] research on the sociocultural dynamics of the children's households, especially on how these households function as part of a wider, changing economy, and how they obtain and distribute resources of all types through the creation of strategic social ties or networks." He goes on to say that "the essential function of the social networks is that they share or exchange what we have termed *funds of knowledge:* the essential cultural practices and bodies of knowledge and information that households use to survive, to get ahead, or to thrive" (Moll, 1992, p. 21).

Schools are often on the lookout for individuals in the community who have special artistic talents—musicians, artists, weavers, artisans, photographers, writers, dancers, storytellers, and so on. However, there are so many other—often more everyday—talents and skills that we overlook. For example, in a sample of 30 working-class Latino families in Tucson, Moll found such household funds of knowledge as ranching, farming, hunting, mining, building codes, appraising, renting, selling, budgets, child care, cooking, carpentry, roofing, masonry, vehicle repair, first aid, midwifery, herbal knowledge, catechism, and Bible studies.

The funds of knowledge approach combines the fields of anthropology, psychology, linguistics, and education, but Moll's ethnographic surveys are user-friendly to general educators. With adequate training in issues of cultural sensitivity, teachers are very capable of collecting a wealth of data on community knowledge and skills and personal and work histories. They can accomplish this through home visits and a variety of community activities. However, the data gathering is not data gathering for its own sake. It has to be paired in the classroom with active learning: the community funds of knowledge provide real-life contexts for classroom activities in which literacy and numeracy are tools for real communication and thinking. The effect of funds of knowledge on instruction is seen in Moll's account of one sixth-grade unit on construction, which was based on community funds of knowledge. (In Chapter Six, we very briefly referred to this unit as an example of activation of community knowledge for integrated math instruction.) Over 20 parents and other community members visited the class to share their knowledge and skills, and the unit culminated with the students' construction of a model community, which incorporated students' written and oral reports about the design and building process. The teacher involved in the project had never before engaged in this type of teaching, and her teaching style changed dramatically as the unit progressed. Through real-life locally relevant activities she tapped into the students' real communicative and problem-solving skills, bringing her classroom alive linguistically and intellectually (Moll, 1992).

Various groups of teachers and researchers in several different settings in the Southwest have used the funds of knowledge approach, and the community knowledge that the teachers gain becomes a part of their developing language-rich, intellectually challenging learning environments for their students. Recently Mercado has been developing a funds of knowledge approach in East Harlem (Mercado & Moll, 1997). The results of this work suggest that funds of knowledge, as an approach, to improved educational opportunities, can work in large inner-city neighborhoods as well as in the smaller cities and towns where it was originally developed. Predating the expansion of the funds of knowledge approach, but clearly reflecting the potential of a similar framework, is the literacy work of Taylor and Dorsey-Gaines (1988) with African-American inner-city children. Looking beyond the stereotype of functional illiteracy in such low-income communities, the researchers used ethnographic approaches to learn firsthand how community members in reality used literacy. They then applied this knowledge to ways in which to approach literacy instruction in the schools that would build on the community uses of literacy, and thus make sense to young children.

The work of Pease-Alvarez and Vásquez (1994) provides another example of community-based research. Looking at language socialization, for example, they found that many of the language resources that children bring to school may be wasted in a classroom in which the predominant format is teacher-asks-a-question/student-responds/teacher-evaluates. Doing research on language socialization in a predominantly Hispanic community, they found some community language-use patterns that were unique to the bilingual community, and some that were the same as those of mainstream middle-class parents. Among the unique traits was the style of the family histories and storytelling from Mexico. Also unique to the bilingual children was the process of young children learning through real-life experience how to be translators for parents—a process that makes language socialization a mutual endeavor between parents and children and that requires some degree of metalinguistic awareness. One of the patterns that Mexican-American families tended to share with European-American families was parents' perception of themselves as active participants in the child's language development (for example, by "talking" with a two-month-old baby). Another similarity was helping a small child recount an event that happened at preschool (for example, by asking for clarification and making requests for elaboration). Like the funds of knowledge researchers, Pease-Alvarez and Vásquez feel that community-based research should be an integral part of educators' ongoing design of their students' learning environment. Again, without having an elaborate research design, they believe that much can be accomplished by school personnel with home visits and other community contacts. Once rapport has been established with parents, teachers might explore such topics as information sources in the community (for example, how do people find out about community events), areas of parental expertise, family histories, language use practices, children's everyday life at home, parents' theories about how children learn, and parents' views on schooling (Pease-Alvarez & Vásquez, 1995, pp. 96, 97).

Community-based research and use of community funds of knowledge in the design of curriculum and instruction are promising means toward the end of a community of learners. However, they do require an adequate level of cultural sensitivity on the part of practitioners. For example, teachers involved with funds of knowledge projects participate in study groups in which they explore theoretical issues of culture and community as well as methodological techniques for household visits. However, even with training in cross-cultural communication, blunders can occur when the outsider, the educator, attempts to gain knowledge from community members. This may be particularly true in communities in which the schools have a long history of failure to meet the needs of language-minority children. Due to possible differences in education, language use, and social class, misunderstandings can occur even when the educator and the community member are of the same ethnic background. Many families might well be apprehensive or offended when a person who they do not yet know well (and who they possibly see as an authority figure) begins to ask questions about such topics as family recreational activities, circumstances of arrival in the United States, and ideas about how to help their children learn. Thus, enthusiasm for community-based research must be tempered with a realistic appraisal of the cross-cultural skills of its practitioners and the degree of preliminary rapport that will need to be established. Notice that we say "preliminary" rapport, because once trust has been established, community-based research and funds of knowledge certainly hold the promise of close and extremely beneficial ties between the school and the community.

The following reflections by an elementary teacher at a predominantly Mexican-American school in Tucson, Arizona, portray the way that use of funds of knowledge can improve learning environments for language-minority children. The teacher first commented that she used to feel that parents were "more disruptive than an asset" and that they were "an added problem that would occasionally make dittos for me."

⊠ *Now I've realized that they're far more valuable. I've had parents teach and interact with the students and assist in the classroom activities. Parents have taught classes in a variety of subjects, from making tortillas to the multiple uses of cacti. They have told stories to the class and shared their family histories. It's fascinating listening to students explain to adults how they discovered an answer to a problem, and them having the adult respond with how he or she approached it. Everyone is welcome in our classroom, but no one is allowed to just sit and observe. (Fahr in Heckman, 1996, pp. 163, 164)*

Ethnographies as Resources

While educators must build their community portraits at the local level, published ethnographies can serve as valuable models of the kinds of insights that can be gained from community portraits. They can also provide us with lessons from their particular contexts that may be applicable to our local situations.

We now refer to four such ethnographic accounts. Each book is written from a very different perspective and for different purposes, but they all serve to remind us powerfully of the importance of community understanding in developing a realistic view of the relationship between the home and the school.

A School Divided (Guthrie, 1985) is an ethnography of bilingual education in a Chinese-American community in California. We have already referred to this work recently in our discussion of socioeconomic status as part of the portrait of a community. Guthrie portrays the Chinese-American community in depth, and she also describes the local school's bilingual programs. Using these ethnographic accounts, she analyzes the interaction between the school and the community. She identifies positive outcomes of the bilingual program, but she also identifies significant areas of conflict, both within the school and between the school and the community. These conflicts have important implications for our understanding of the effect of top-down versus bottom-up approaches to public programs of bilingual education. In the case of *A School Divided*, the top-down history of the bilingual program had, in Guthrie's opinion, a deleterious effect on the bilingual program.

Of Borders and Dreams (Carger, 1996) is a chronicle of the education of a learning disabled Mexican-American boy in Chicago, from the age of 10 through his decision to drop out of high school. In telling the story of this child's struggles at both Catholic and public schools, the author also draws a clear picture of the tenuous relations between the child's remarkably dedicated parents and the schools.

We refer to Delgado-Gaitán's research several times throughout this chapter because of her work in understanding the texture of local families' lives and its relationship to school learning. Her book, *Literacy for Empowerment* (1990), is an ethnographic study of approximately 20 Hispanic families in California. She began her research with the idea of looking for ways in which family practices affected children's literacy development. Her objective was to learn through observation and interviews about the ways in which Spanish-speaking parents helped their children learn to read and write. She was also studying how these parents socialized with each other as they adapted to the United States education system. The book provides insights into such specific topics as home literacy-related activities. But the study took an unexpected turn when Delgado-Gaitán became involved via her research in a process through which parents began to organize together to assume more active leadership roles as advocates for their children. This process resulted in the formation of COPLA, the parent group discussed in the last section of this chapter.

Valdés' ethnography, *Con Respeto: Bridging the Distances between Culturally Diverse Families and Schools* (1996), is a controversial and thought-provoking look at the lives of immigrant mothers from Mexico who are trying very hard to raise good children in their new environment in Texas. Although Valdés acknowledges the good intentions of educators in trying to provide opportunities for parent involvement to these kinds of families, she concludes that such efforts almost inherently tend to become cultural deficit programs because they are based on middle-class notions of involvement and success. She feels that efforts to bring school learning activities into the home may actually undermine the important types of socialization that such parents normally and effectively engage in.

Valdés has been criticized for her work because at times she seems to be arguing that parent involvement programs may be futile. However, she emphasizes that she is not advocating that all efforts to promote parent involvement be abandoned. Rather, she is asking that we be very realistic in assessing our objectives and in identifying our underlying philosophies. She argues for an awareness of how some types of parent education programs may adversely affect the already-established home environment. For example, she found *consejos,* the advice of adults to the younger generation, to be a valuable parenting method in the Mexican-American homes she studied, and she suggested that the replacement of *consejos* with educator-designed home activities could be detrimental to the quality of family life. She also argued for a greater acceptance of a diversity of definitions of success, because such underlying definitions affect the nature of parent involvement programs. For example, not all language-minority families may define success as upward socioeconomic mobility if this comes at the cost of loss of cultural identity and family ties. As we turn to the next section, "Pathways to Partnerships," we will see that the types of concerns Valdés voices do indeed have to be addressed as educators and parents work together to improve education for language-minority children.

Pathways to Partnerships

In an effort to improve student achievement, educators in the 1980s and 1990s have increasingly talked about the importance of "parent involvement." Because the term is used so much in practice and in the literature, we have referred to *involvement* often throughout this chapter. However, the word is somewhat dangerous because it can imply a one-way relationship in which the school exists as a separate entity to which parents come to engage in activities that school personnel define and design. In interviews conducted with bilingual and ESL staff in a Massachusetts community, Ringawa (1980) found that many teachers perceived the primary functions of parent involvement to be improving such things as school attendance, discipline, and parent attitudes toward the teachers and school. To see these as principal reasons for parent involvement reflects a one-sided attitude in which teachers see parents and their children as objects that need to be changed to fit the school, rather than as individuals with interests, aspirations, expectations, resources, and skills that can contribute to the improvement of the school. As Ringawa put it, teachers seemed to be willing to work with parents within the confines of the school— on the teachers' terms—but they were somewhat reluctant to go out into the community and to see the home–school partnership from that perspective.

Empowerment is another term that educators use frequently when talking about parent participation in school affairs. The idea has been adapted from the Brazilian educator Paulo Freire's *conscientizaçao* work with adult literacy programs. Through this conscientization process, Freire (1973) found that learners gained literacy through dialogues in which they became aware of the inequalities in their society as they were manifested at the local level. Valdés (1996), whose ethnography we referred to in the previous section, argues that while many well-intentioned individuals describe their parent programs as avenues toward empowerment, the accuracy of the term may be somewhat questionable. Such programs do provide valuable information on such topics as how schools function, how parents can advocate for their children, and what legal resources are available to them. However, they do not generally develop an awareness of issues such as racism, social inequality, and economic exploitation. Neither do they tend to address the fact that low achievement in school is an extremely complex result of many powerful social factors over which parents do not have very much control. Valdés suggests that those who strive toward empowerment programs are idealistic believers in the myth that schools have the power "to right all social wrongs" (p. 195). She would argue that powerful macro forces of socioeconomic inequality make it impossible for schools to be fully equitable. From this point of view one does have to accept the fact that affluence matters. As long as the nation's wealthiest districts are spending as much as $18,000 per student per year while the poorest ones are spending $4,000, the playing field will not be level despite any amount of parent empowerment (Kozol, 1997).

Despite Valdés' pessimism, or realism (depending on how you view it), there is also the important fact that a broad range of educators and parents have repeatedly found much value in their efforts to strengthen home–school ties. We believe that despite the power of sociopolitical macro forces, teachers as advocates for and members of the bilingual community, as we have defined it broadly, do have the potential to work with parents to make improvements in schooling experiences. However, to avoid the one-way implications of the term *involvement* and the debatable meaning of *empowerment*, we have chosen to cast our discussion of program development in terms of *partnerships*. The term *partnership* does not make any potentially inflated claims about empowerment, but it does suggest a two-way relationship of cooperation toward a common goal.

In the best of all possible worlds, there should be an equitable partnership between the schools and the community. In reality, however, there is an imbalance of power between the school and the language-minority community. This imbalance is built partially on the power that institutions of public education wield as part of the sociopolitical system, and partially on the division between the professional educators' jargon-coded pedagogical knowledge and the community layperson's pedagogical knowledge. Therefore, they are almost always bound to be tensions even as well-intentioned educators and community members work toward a community of learners and leaders.

As such, when we talk about "pathways" to partnerships, we imply that there are various approaches depending on the context, and that the establishment of a community of learners and leaders is an ongoing process.

As transmitters of consensual values, schools traditionally tend to homogenize students cognitively and socioculturally. They transmit cultural objectives appropriate to the functioning of a large, anonymous, technological society. This process happens through school socialization and enculturation—a process by which children learn to respond to the demands placed on them by American society. Meanwhile, socialization and enculturation go on intensively in the home, and with quite a head start. At the interface between the home and the school in ethnically diverse settings, the ongoing perceptions that educators and families have about each other are often wired to conflicting socioeconomic, linguistic, and cultural frameworks. Therefore, educators and parents cannot always assume a common basis of understanding. Such perceptions, moreover, are often reflections of issues that contain shades of gray rather than black and white. To complicate matters, ethnic children—as culture makers—often have their own notions, apart from those of the school or parents, of what is and is not important in their lives (Handlin, 1951).

To explore pathways toward a common basis of understanding at the same time that we acknowledge the shades of gray, we will look at four areas: (1) the role of legislated parent participation; (2) issues to be addressed as partnerships develop; (3) programs and case studies that reflect in varying ways the ethos of communities of learners and communities of leaders; and (4) resources for the development of community-school partnerships.

Legislation for Parent Participation

Although court cases such as *Lau* v. *Nichols* have been pivotal in the establishment of bilingual and ESL programs throughout the nation, one of the costs of court-mandated services for language-minority students has been the lack of grassroots community involvement in the establishment of many such programs. The unfortunate result is that a deficit framework for such programs has possibly been established from the start: "Help" is brought in from the outside to provide remedial services.

On the other hand, legislative mandates and court mandates do not preclude community involvement. Guidelines for formal community involvement are generally built into federal and state legislation for language-minority education. Going back to the years of the Johnson administration, the Elementary and Secondary Education Act of 1965 (ESEA) was designed with the specific goal of redressing social and economic inequality through improved educational opportunities. The concept of structured requirements for parent involvement began through such ESEA programs as Title I and Head Start, and some of the parent programs that we will be describing later have been funded through Title I. The Bilingual Education Act of 1968, an offspring of ESEA, also included provisions for parent involvement in the planning, implementation, and evaluation of Title VII programs. Six years later, the Bilingual Education Act of 1974 mandated such provisions for parent participation. The role of parent and community participation continued to expand in the 1994 Bilingual Education Act. For example, the act acknowledged that "parent and community participation in bilingual education programs contributes to program effectiveness" (P.L. 103–382, Section 7102, cited in Crawford, 1999), and included a stipulation that applications for grants must have been "developed in consultation with an advisory council, the majority of whose members are parents and other representatives of the children and youth to be served in such programs" (P.L. 103–382, Section 7116, cited in Crawford, 1999, p. 277). Among the categories of programs that could be funded by the 1994 act were those that implemented "family education programs and parent outreach and training activities designed to assist parents become active participants in the education of their children" (P.L. 103–382, Section 7112, cited in Crawford, 1999, p. 273). State bilingual education programs today also generally specify mechanisms for community involvement in programs implemented at the local level. As a result, bilingual programs throughout the nation generally include some type of parent advisory council. In some cases, such councils can serve as training grounds and springboards for greater parent participation in the politics of education. Some parents who work on advisory councils have become well known in the larger community's educational circle, and in some cases have become members of local school boards.

More often than not, however, parent advisory councils seem to have fallen short of their goals. For example, research findings for Title VII in 1981 indicated that "with few exceptions, Community Advisory Committees were not deeply involved in governance" (as reflected in decisions regarding program content, project budget, and project personnel), and that "most did not advise or otherwise contribute to decisions" (System Development Corporation, 1981). The researchers also found that the rare instances in which parents were involved in policy formulation were a reflection of the ideology of the project director, who clearly wanted an articulate, strong, and caring cadre of parents who would participate in meaningful ways. In most other cases parents played perfunctory roles such as signing forms or being supportive on social occasions when it was symbolically important to be seen with the bilingual/ESL project director and staff. The fact is that school personnel generally want parents to buttress the school's norms, exhibit a positive attitude toward the school, trust its teachers, help children with their homework, ensure that their children attend school regularly and punctually, instill a drive for academic achievement in their children, participate in school social functions, and attend parent conferences—but not be overly interested in school policy matters. Educators may well feel very satisfied if most parents come to school sparingly but faithfully on the appropriate symbolic occasions.

However, there are cases in which advisory councils do take on stronger roles. Shannon and Latimer's ethnographic account of parental empowerment through a Bilingual Parent Advisory Council (BPAC) demonstrates the importance of the presence of a strong advocate for parental empowerment within the school's staff. In this case a teacher who worked to organize the BPAC took on the role of advocate. She worked very hard to establish a climate in which parents and teachers could come to know each other better and in which parents felt confident to state their needs, opinions, and suggestions. These meetings had become an important forum in which parents knew that they had a role to play and in which they could be heard. Thus, when a new principal who was considered to be possibly racist or at least culturally insensitive by many parents of language-minority students arrived at the school, the BPAC took on a change agent role to challenge the principal's policies (Shannon & Latimer, 1996).

Issues in the Development of Partnerships

The establishment of mutual partnerships between parents and schools can be a complex undertaking even when there is a strong match between the culture of the school and the culture of the community. Thus, it can potentially become even more complex within the context of the language-minority community. Consequently, we often hear educators talk about "barriers" to parent participation. However, we have intentionally chosen not to use the term *barriers* as we talk about the development of partnerships, because it brings to our mind a negative, conflictive "us versus them" mentality. In reality, of course, *barriers* can be an apt term for describing a situation in which there are chronic, unresolved conflicts between the school and the community, but we want to focus on the kinds of partnerships that we believe can develop under the right circumstances. Even within these two-way partnerships there will be conflicts, but they do not have to lead to the erection of barriers. Therefore, rather than organizing our discussion around a list of so-called barriers, we look at a series of questions that establish a less conflictive perspective.

As we go through these questions, two things are important to keep in mind: (1) the ability to adequately address these questions requires that school personnel maintain an ongoing portrait of their community; and (2) we are all seeing these questions through our personal sociocultural lenses or through the sociocultural lenses of our institution, the school system. There are, unfortunately, numerous ways in which well-intentioned educators can sabotage the construction of a partnership by unwittingly applying the assumptions of a majority institution to minority contexts. As we discuss the upcoming questions, we will see a variety of examples of how institutional bias can have a negative impact on home–school relationships. Celebration of diversity is a mantra within school walls today, and yet we are not always so willing to perceive and accept diversity when it comes to relationships with students' families.

As we look more closely now at the development of partnerships between families and schools, we will organize the questions into five general areas: language, survival and family structure, educational background and values, knowledge about education and beliefs about learning, power and status, and resources for the development of programs.

Language   How does language affect communication between the home and the school?

It seems rather obvious to state that communication with parents should be in a language they can understand, but in reality this is sometimes overlooked. Constantino, Cui, and Faltis (1995) describe a school in southern California that provided parent communications in Spanish, but the same support structure was not available in Chinese. After talking with Chinese families to understand better their perspective on the low level of Chinese parent involvement, school personnel took two actions. They began to translate forms, newsletters, signs, and other communications into Chinese, and teachers began to take in-service classes on Chinese language and culture. Subsequent to these interventions, more Chinese parents began to attend school functions, and Chinese parents took on a greater role as advocates for their children in school.

What are community members' attitudes toward the use of the home language in school?

Just because parents speak a language other than English does not automatically mean that they are in favor of bilingual education. For example, Watahomigie (1995) tells how many families reacted negatively when Hualapai/English bilingual education was begun in Peach Springs, Arizona, in the 1970s: "Parents and grandparents were upset because they had been brainwashed for over 100 years that the native language and culture were to be forgotten" (p. 190). Today Peach Springs has a high-technology, integrated bilingual program through the high school level and the school has very strong community support, but this was achieved through a conscious effort of local advocates to win over the skeptics.

Parents and other interested community members need a variety of opportunities to learn about bilingual education and second-language acquisition. One first step might be an assessment of parents' entry-level knowledge and opinions regarding bilingual education. To get such information would require an "informal, natural environment in which honest comments would emerge" (Cohen, 1983, p. 147). According to Cohen, if parents are to make a real difference in the planning, operation, and evaluation of their child's bilingual program, they need information that will enable them to do more than just endorse bilingual education as an abstraction. A survey of parents of bilingual program students in East Austin, for example, found that the majority were unfamiliar with the objectives of bilingual education (Santelices, 1981). Despite plans on paper to inform the community about bilingual education, it is unrealistic to assume that the community will automatically absorb such information without face-to-face interaction and closer ties between the school and the community, which would provide opportunities for first-hand observation and discussion through social networks that are meaningful to the parents.

How can educators bridge the gap between educators' jargon and everyday language?

A teacher and a parent may be speaking the same language, or may be supposedly communicating with each other via a translator, but if the teacher is using terms that are unfamiliar to the listener, it is obviously difficult for meaningful communication to occur. Written communication can also be translated into the home language and still be virtually incomprehensible. For example, a typical elementary report card assumes much previous knowledge about U.S. educational practices—knowledge that many newcomers to this country will not have.

In her ethnographic study of Puerto Rican families in the special education system, Harry (1992) found that miscommunication was a very important factor in the loss of trust between parents and the system. Terms such as *borderline range, decoding,* and *spatial memory tasks* can be translated into the home language and still be meaningless unless one has had some training in education. While Harry found such miscommunication rampant in the district in which she conducted her ethnographic research, she did find a "pocket of excellence" at one school. Along with other innovations, personnel at this school had made very deliberate efforts to build rapport and problem-solving capacities between school personnel and parents by making sure that terms were understood. School personnel explicitly taught key education terminology to the families, and for other less salient terms the family liaison worker insisted that special education staff and teachers use plain English. This plain English could then be translated into plain Spanish when needed. This helped tremendously to turn meetings into dialogues in which parents and teachers could learn from each other about their childrens' achievements and needs.

Survival and Family Structure   *How will the struggles of day-to-day survival affect the nature of the home–school partnership?*

As they work to feed, clothe, and house their families—often in a new and unfamiliar setting—some parents will simply not have enough time and energy to devote to extensive participation in school activities. Language-minority parents who work long hours at extremely low wages for economic survival, often at more than one job, will have little time for additional school responsibilities, especially during school hours.

When social services are extremely segmented and transportation services are inadequate, families can also face many daily challenges in their efforts to secure needed housing, health care, social services, and adult education opportunities—challenges that also compete with time for school-related activities. Valdés found in the immigrant community that she studied that "surviving, using what was available in the system, and learning how to work within it required energy, hard work, and information. Some families were lucky and had excellent networks of experienced relatives ready to help them. Others did not. Even with help, however, the everyday lives of the adults and children in the study were not easy" (Valdés 1996, p. 114). Later in the chapter when we look at programs, we will see that some schools have addressed this issue by working together with the community for better coordination of social services.

These day-to-day survival challenges do not mean that a partnership cannot be established, but they do mean that the supposed quality of the family's school involvement cannot be judged by standards based on a middle-class lifestyle. In reality, though, the expectations that are built into many parent involvement plans are indeed based on such assumptions of relative socio-economic stability.

How will differences in family structure affect the relationship?
A teacher who is looking at the world through cultural lenses that define the nuclear family as the norm may misjudge a family that does not fit this pattern. One of the authors still recalls the exasperation in an elementary teacher's voice as she complained to a colleague that her Filipino students' families were so "clannish." But does "clan" necessarily have to carry a negative connotation? Various extended family patterns that are characteristic of a variety of language-minority groups generally have an important role in providing networks for survival as parents negotiate the American socioeconomic system. However, because of institutional or personal biases, teachers may attribute negative characteristics to such families, rather than capitalizing on the positive role that extended family members can have in raising children. For example, Robledo Montecel (1993) noted that for many Puerto Rican families, extended family members can be seen as legitimate representatives for the parents in school activities, and the acceptance of their role will improve the partnership between the home and the school.

Educational Background and Attitudes toward the Value of Schooling *To what degree do school expectations match the educational background of parents?*
The more that school personnel know about the educational background of their students' families, the more they will be able to anticipate the issues that they need to address, or the information and training that they may want develop with parents in order to make the current generation's educational experience meaningful to the parents. School–parent interfaces generally assume a basic degree of literacy on the part of the parents, along with a general understanding of how American school systems work. For example, understanding a report card or a letter to the parents about an upcoming

career day requires both reading skills and some background knowledge of school subjects, teaching methods, and behavioral expectations. Therefore, when language-minority parents have not had opportunities for extensive schooling, it becomes very difficult for them to negotiate their child's school system. Teachers who learn something about the education system in the country of origin of immigrant parents will be better prepared to know what will make sense and what will not make sense to parents as their children go through the American system.

Besides basic literacy, there may be attitudes associated with lack of schooling that can affect the home–school relationship. Delgado-Gaitán (1990) found in a community study of Hispanic-American parents that some—generally those with more education—had an active stance in their childrens' learning: They believed that their children could learn and took action when that was not happening. However, other parents felt powerless because of their own limited schooling experiences. These parents tended to blame their children's learning difficulties on their own low level of schooling, and they also tended to blame their children for lack of motivation. They had less faith than more educated parents did in their children's abilities to learn and in their abilities as parents to contribute to that learning. The children of the powerless parents in Delgado-Gaitán's study were more likely to be in the lower reading groups, thus creating a situation of "perpetuated inequity" (1990, pp. 138, 139). Unless educators and other parents find ways to help less educated parents step into the community of learners, such inequities can indeed be perpetuated.

The case of negative educational experiences is another example of the influence of parents' educational backgrounds. Many indigenous minorities have had very unpleasant experiences in their own schooling, often resulting in failure to complete high school. Illiteracy or a history of school failure can work in two ways for parents. It can make them have little trust in their own abilities to support their childrens' education, and it can make them mistrustful of the school in which their children are enrolled.

What assumptions do educators have about the attitudes of parents toward schooling?

It is a common refrain among teachers and administrators in general that they really want parents to be involved, but that the parents just do not care. The refrain is even more common among educators working in lower-income, ethnically diverse communities. However, ethnic parents, in turn, could argue that schools do a very effective job of making them feel unwanted. They often don't want to be involved where they sense or see that they are being treated as nonequals. The adage of parents' "lack of interest" may in reality be a reflection of educators' "lack of interest" in empowered parent participation. In other words, if community members sense that their participation really does not matter to the administration, they may feel that an active stance is not worth their time and effort.

Despite myths that marginalized social groups do not value education, individual members of ethnic communities generally do perceive formal schooling to be an important instrument for upward mobility (Carger, 1996). There is a stereotype that many minority parents are more apathetic than their nonminority counterparts. However, research indicates that low parent participation has more to do with low education levels and low income than with minority or ethnic group membership. In other words, controlling for education and income, Juan and Juana Fulano are no more likely than John or Jane Doe to have low involvement in their children's education (Goldenberg, 1993).

Lareau and Benson (1984), in a comparative study of two schools, explored the myth of parent apathy, and Lareau (1989) expanded on the theme in a subsequent book. They were studying the phenomenon from the point of view of socioeconomic class rather than ethnicity, but their study has important implications for language-minority education. They found that the middle-class school they studied had established a much stronger partnership with the parents than had the working-class school. The difference, however, was not related to the amount of parental interest in the education of their children. It was related to sociocultural differences in family life and the ways in which the schools responded to these differences. Social network patterns and child socialization networks were some of the principal sociocultural factors that produced the different home–school relationships. Among families in the lower-class school, for example, kinship played a more important role in social networks than contact with fellow parents through the school network. The middle-class families, on the other hand, being more socially and geographically mobile, tended to be more isolated from their relatives, and consequently depended more on other parents in their neighborhood rather than on relatives for their social relationships. Through these frequent school-related contacts with neighborhood peers, middle-class parents had much more information about what actually happened in the classroom. They also had more information about funding, school policy, and staffing procedures. The lower-class children were more likely to be involved in informal, often family-related activities, while the middle-class children were more likely to be involved in such formal activities as Brownies, organized athletics, or piano lessons. These formal activities, in turn, strengthened the middle-class parental social network and won the approval of teachers, who judged the activities to be educational and enriching. Even though parents at both schools had a comparable level of interest in their children's education, the ultimate result of the social network patterns was that teachers tended to develop higher expectations for the middle-class children because it *appeared* to them that the middle-class parents were more interested. Lareau and Benson concluded that teachers should be prepared to take some initiative in fostering a climate of mutual interdependence, and they must be willing to explore a variety of partnership alternatives based on varied sociocultural patterns.

In the case of language-minority families, although their care may not be *perceived* by the school, parents generally *do* wonder: How well are my children doing in school? Are they being prepared for jobs or college? Are the teachers properly equipped to do their job? Is the curriculum prolearner? What is the bilingual or ESL program doing for my child? Are my children safe in school? Do teachers and administrators care? Because of the middle-class biases which have historically been built in to our educational system, however, it takes willingness, creativity, and a strong community knowledge base in order for school personnel to hear and to accept the questions which language-minority parents ask.

Knowledge and Beliefs About Education *How much knowledge do parents have about school culture and the role of parents in schools in the United States?*

Just about any school system that immigrant parents are coming from will have been significantly different than the system in which their children are now enrolled. Therefore, families will benefit greatly from frequent opportunities to ask questions and to learn how the new system works. Without this knowledge, they may be unable to be strong advocates and supporters for their children as they find their way through the system. Delgado-Gaitán found that a broad range of Hispanic parents that she studied, both those who felt somewhat empowered and those who felt powerless, expressed much confusion over exactly what the school expected of them and indicated that they felt frustrated about how to help their children (Delgado-Gaitán, 1990, p. 109). In a case study of three Mexican-origin families in California, the same researcher (Delgado-Gaitán, 1987) found that the parents were very effective in teaching their children to work cooperatively, to respect adults, and to do well in school by obeying teachers. However, beyond having them "learn English" and "stay in school" the parents had very little knowledge about how to guide their children through the system. The parents, for example, needed opportunities to learn about available career and higher education paths, so that they could provide clearer direction for their children. When we survey actual programs at the end of this chapter, we will see that several of these programs have addressed such issues through various types of opportunities for parents to learn about American school systems.

How much do parents know about the specific methods being used in their child's classroom, and how comfortable would they be reinforcing these methods at home?

Language-minority parents on the whole are less likely than majority parents to be familiar with the types of learning activities that teachers expect their children to do in the classroom and at home. Consequently, opportunities for home learning can be lost because of discrepancies between the approaches of parents and teachers. Goldenberg tells of two cases: In one case a literate Mexican mother was teaching her first-grade daughter the letters of the alphabet at home, thinking that she was helping her to learn to read. The daughter's teacher told the mother that this was not the way that she taught reading in her classroom, but she didn't provide the mother with alternative activities. As a result, the mother stopped working with her child. In the second case, a Salvadoran mother was helping her child with reading at home based on the methods that she was familiar with from her country. The father, who had some familiarity with United States schools, asked her to stop because *"los métodos de la maestra son distintos"* (the teacher's methods are different) (Goldenberg, 1993, p. 232). In both cases, Goldenberg reports, the children ended the year below grade level in reading, and he suggested that this might not have been so if there had been better communication between the home and the school.

Beliefs about how children learn can also have an effect on the nature of the partnerships between the home and school. For example, the degree of congruence between the *type* of homework assigned and parents' *beliefs* about learning may affect children's learning outcomes. In a study involving two language-minority kindergarten groups, one group was using a basal text and phonics-oriented worksheets; the other group was using a whole-language approach. This latter group of children had simple storybooks to read at school and then to read again at home with their parents. Comparing the two groups, the class using storybooks did better overall than the readiness and phonics class in development of reading skills. However, looking at individual children, the extent to which parents actually used the storybooks at home was unrelated to the literacy development of the children in the whole-language group. In other words, children whose parents used the storybooks were no further along in reading than children whose parents hadn't used the assigned storybooks. However, use of the phonics worksheets at home was strongly related to higher literacy development for children in the phonics group. The Hispanic-American parents in both groups tended to equate learning to read with decoding, which they believed was learned through repetitious drills. Therefore, according to Goldenberg, the storybook parents were unlikely to see the point of the whole-language approach of "pretend" reading and talking about the meaning of the texts. As Goldenberg concluded, "There was a congruence between the [phonics] worksheets and parents' beliefs about learning to read; this congruency led, we believe, to their more effective use in the home" (Goldenberg, 1993, p. 244).

What differences exist between parents and teachers in the perception of the home-school relationship?

Parents' perceptions of their role in their children's education may differ from school ideas about the role of parents. Perceptions may differ in many ways. For example, some parents may believe in a separation between home life and school life, entrusting the education of their children to the teachers and not feeling that it is their role to challenge the authority of the school. However, the absence of challenges to the school's authority cannot necessarily be equated with trust in the school. In Harry's previously mentioned ethnographic study of 12 Puerto Rican families with learning disabled children, the researcher concluded that while parents generally showed *deference* to school authorities, they did not necessarily *trust* them: "Inadequate provision of information regarding the meaning of various events, as well as the school district's reliance upon formalized, written communication, led to mistrust and withdrawal on the part of parents. A habitual deference to authority, however, tended to disguise parents' real opinions" (Harry, 1992, p. 471). The parents in this study were reluctant to openly challenge school personnel, despite the obvious blunders that school personnel sometimes made. (For example, in two instances children were promoted to the next grade "by accident" and then had to be sent back to their previous grade after they had been in their new classroom for several days.) Such experiences often resulted in withdrawal and resignation (Harry, 1992, p. 486).

Power and Status   *How will the inherent inequality of the educator/layperson relationship affect the quality of the partnership?*
Except in the case of community members who have degrees in education, educators have a repertoire of educational concepts and a specialized lexicon that are alien to community members, especially those coming from a very different educational system. Coupled with specialized training, educators often convey the feeling that they alone know what is best for the students. To add to the feeling of inequality, when educators and parents are interacting, educators are acting as part of a fairly large and powerful institution—the school district—while parents are acting in most cases as a single family. The inequality is a given—it exists whether we like it or not—but unless we address it constructively, it can certainly impede the establishment of a partnership. Because of this inequality, many language-minority parents are very uncertain of their role within the school, and they may have a fear of being judged negatively by school personnel because of their lack of education or their limited familiarity with the dominant cultural system. It is natural for people to feel ill at ease in unfamiliar territory, and schools often feel extremely unfamiliar to language-minority parents.

Do programs for parents convey a message of cultural deficiency?
You may be groaning and thinking, "Oh, no, I can't believe the authors are bringing this up again! Cultural deficit frameworks are a thing of the past. We are much more enlightened today." However, we believe that cultural deficiency is an issue that will not go away entirely because it is a product of power and status disparity. A parent education program can easily come to represent a cultural deficit framework as educators work to promote certain parent behaviors. Specific kinds of parent behavior have been shown to have an effect on academic achievement, and consequently it might seem desirable to change more parents' behavior to fit that pattern. For example, among the home environment factors that Martínez (1981) found would predict higher

achievement of students in bilingual education programs in northern New Mexico were verbal interaction, time spent reading with the child, and parental aspirations for their children. According to Delgado-Gaitán (1993), "family practices have been shown to be more important than parent education, race, marital status, or family size in affecting children's reading success" (p. 141).

Such findings suggest the desirability of intervention in parenting practices. However, there can be a tension between educators' desires to provide parents with what they consider to be the best possible tools for helping their children succeed and the danger that such efforts will in reality be designs to remedy supposed family deficiencies. Schools that convey to students and parents an attitude of sociocultural devaluation are also schools that are most likely failing to tap and develop the experiences, skills, and abilities of their community members. As valuable as parent education programs may be in many contexts, there is also a danger of their misuse. Cultural and social differences have a track record of being misconstrued as deficiencies, and it is very easy to put the burden on the parent to change to fit the school. In a well-intentioned attempt to strengthen the role of the parent as a partner, the degree of mutuality—inherent to the concept of partnership—instead may be diminished. Therefore, forays into parent education will most likely have positive effects on the partnership only if they are conceived and developed as mutual parent–professional dialogues.

As an example of such mutual dialogue, Flores and Hendricks (1984) reported on a series of discussions for Hispanic-American parents in Fairbanks, Alaska, on child development and the role of the parent in academic development. As rapport grew, the sessions became opportunities to share mutual concerns, worries, successes, or problems. In many areas the parents concurred with the "professional" advice presented in a series of filmstrips. However, one professional prescription with which the parents tended to disagree was that young children should be encouraged to establish social relationships apart from their family's own network. In the workshop environment the parents felt free to disagree, and the objective of the discussion coordinators—who were bilingual teachers—was not necessarily to change anybody's mind. However, as a result both the teachers and the parents became aware of and more sensitive to this cultural difference.

Delgado-Gaitán provides another example of a parent-training program that did not operate out of a deficit framework. She examined a bilingual preschool parent training program, asking herself whether the bilingual teacher was promoting a deficit theory by teaching parents ways to interact with their preschoolers. She concluded that in this case, the parents were not getting a message of deficiency for three reasons: (1) the teacher used the family's natural home activities, enabling parents to become more aware of the educational potential in these activities; (2) the program included a parent advisory committee that was involved in actual decision-making activities; and (3) the students' culture was incorporated into the daily school curriculum. This made the experience a two-way street, in which the home life was incorporated into the school, and the school perspective was incorporated into home life (Delgado-Gaitán, 1990, p. 163).

To what degree are language-minority community members a part of the school in instructional and administrative positions?

One way in which status inequality between the school and the community can begin to be lessened is through active efforts to employ community members in the school. As we will be seeing shortly when we survey some types of programs, positive school–community relationships can evolve from the presence of cultural brokers who work on a personal level to build natural bridges between the school and the community. It cannot be said enough that we all have our own socioculturally based worldview, and no matter how much an outsider may have studied about and interacted with members of a different cultural group, she or he will almost never have the same perspective that a community member has. Reflecting on the development of the Hualapai bilingual/bicultural program in Peach Springs, Arizona, Watahomigie (1995) reported that one of the factors in the success of the program had been the effort to "grow our own" Hualapai teaching staff. As the number of Haulapai certified teachers gradually increased over the years, the school truly became the *community's* school. With a community school that looked to parents and grandparents for support and knowledge, dramatic improvements occurred in the number of Peach Springs students who went on to graduate from high school (100 percent in some years) and the number of graduates who went on to some form of postsecondary education (pp. 190, 191).

However, membership in a particular ethnic group does not automatically mean that one will have a better understanding of the reality and needs of other members of that group. Given differences in the amount of education, socioeconomic background, place of birth, personal philosophy, and the like, as much variation often occurs within broad language-minority groups as between such groups. Valdés, for example, found in her study of young immigrant children in a predominantly Mexican-American community that "both Anglos and Hispanics varied in their response to the same children. We found sensitive teachers in both ethnic groups who believed these children could succeed. But we also found very mainstream-oriented teachers in both groups who had little patience with [the perceived shortcomings] of newly arrived Mexican children and their families" (Valdés, 1996, p. 148).

Family Literacy Programs and Other School–Community Partnerships

A broad range of programs throughout the United States with the goal of ultimately improving student learning reflects a variety of pathways toward partnerships. As we look at some of these programs, we can see how they address many of the issues we discussed in our preceding series of focusing questions.

We will first examine family literacy programs, and then we will conclude by looking at other programs that may include family literacy components but also have other objectives. We will describe these programs in the present tense, but the reader needs to remember that such programs depend on a variety of funding sources, as well as on the support of school and community personnel. As funds come and go, and as administrators, teachers, and community members come and go, the programs we describe here may no longer be in existence or may have been modified.

Family Literacy Programs

Family literacy projects expand the scope of literacy beyond the classroom doors and reach out into the community to provide parents, as well as children, with learning opportunities. The general components of family literacy projects are adult education, use of intergenerational educational activities, and classes on parenting or parent support groups. While the development of literacy habits, parenting skills, and the use of classroom-type activities at home may seem like laudable objectives, family literacy programs, not surprisingly, have been criticized as new manifestations of cultural deficit theories. For example, such programs may ignore literacy in the home language. They may not recognize the many types of informal but valuable learning experiences that occur within the natural home context, or they may ignore parents' vast knowledge about their own children. Building on their work with immigrant families and using Auerbach's (1989) sociocontextual approach to family literacy, Lee and Patel (1994) make several suggestions for family literacy programs in which families participate as individuals with resources rather than as defective parents who need remediation. Lee and Patel recommend the establishment of respect for the families' identities by using lessons that are culturally relevant; visiting families in their homes to build an understanding of their strengths; a focus on language learning as it occurs in the natural environment (for example through family games, mealtimes, bedtimes, recreation, and worship); helping parents to find culturally comfortable ways to advocate for their children; providing appropriate training for educators in empowering styles of adult education; and use of an integrated approach in which community agencies collaborate with schools and parents.

Project FLAME (Family Literacy: Aprendiendo, Mejorando, Educando) is a family literacy program from the Center for Literacy at the University of Illinois at Chicago. FLAME helps limited-English-speaking Hispanic parents develop their own literacy in order to increase the academic achievement of their children. Designed as a resource model rather than a deficit model, FLAME addresses the parents' personal goals. It also values the home language and encourages shared literacy experiences within the home social network. The program has two prongs: Parents as Teachers and Parents as Learners. In the Parents as Teachers component, parents attend meetings conducted in Spanish in which they learn ways to model literacy at home and how to employ parent-child interactions that build literacy. The Parents as Learners component consists of ESL lessons that are designed to complement the goals of the Parents as Teachers sessions. The program has achieved success as measured by children's increased scores on standardized tests and less need for special services. Just as important, it has resulted in increased parent participation in school governance and has served as a springboard from which parents can aspire to further education or improved job opportunities (Mulhern, Rodríguez-Brown, & Shanahan, 1994).

The Lao Family English Literacy Project in St. Paul, Minnesota, includes extended family members in the home–school connection. Serving immigrant Hmong and Vietnamese families, the project focuses on cultural preservation, achievement of economic self-sufficiency, and academic achievement for children. The services include ESL classes for extended family members, a preschool and child care, development of native language literacy, and "parent-child time." The ESL classes focus on survival skills, parent involvement in school activities, homework assistance, and child development. The family literacy staff is from the local community and is bilingual and bicultural (McCollum & Russo, 1993).

Another program in St. Paul is the Family English School, which is sponsored by the Lao Family Community. The program is for Hmong and Latino parents and their preschoolers, and it is staffed by bilingual teachers, ESL teachers, early childhood teachers, and bilingual community volunteers who range from high school age to senior citizens. The program introduces parents and children to the U.S. school setting, but just as importantly, it establishes a context in which parents can voice their opinions and capitalize on their important role as their child's first teacher. School personnel work with parents and community agencies to develop a culturally relevant curriculum. For example, using the families' experiences, the school produced a story about a Hmong child's life in Laos, and they also made a video entitled "Learning Happens Everywhere" that illustrates in the local community's context the role of parents as teachers (Patel & Kaplan, 1994).

In the Hmong Literacy Project in Fresno, California, parents work to preserve their past as well as to ensure a better future for their children. Beyond developing literacy in Hmong and English, this parent-designed program strives to record oral histories, develop skills that will enable parents to help their children academically, and strengthen intergenerational ties. Through the literacy component of this program, parents have produced a community newsletter. They also learn math skills and computer literacy, which enables them to better help their children with schoolwork. Through this program parents have developed their literacy and increased their ability to understand communications sent home by teachers The program has also resulted in greater involvement at school, as measured by attendance at school events and parent-teacher conferences (Kang, Kuehn, & Herrell, 1996).

The Families Together Project at Hawthorne School in San Francisco is an example of a program that coordinates its work with other community agencies. The program is open to the community at large rather than just to parents of children at the school. In addition to native-language literacy, ESL and parenting classes, the program offers translation services, legal services, and assistance with other social services. The results of a needs assessment survey determine class topics, and activities can range from learning how to fill out government forms to learning about American folk songs and board games. Through the family stories project, participants tell their life stories, which are then published in Spanish and English so that they can be used in future classes. Rioux and Berla (1993) note that as a result of the workshops in which parents learn about their rights and responsibilities within the school, parents are more confident in visiting the school and have become more involved in school activities.

Our final family literacy program is that of Seward Park High School in New York City. The program organizers begin with a questionnaire, available in Chinese, Spanish, and English, through which they identify topics of interest to the parents. They then develop these topics into themes for the classes. Parents participate in ESL classes and also take a class called "Parent, Child, and School." The curriculum develops from everyday life situations and school-related situations, and it includes such relevant topics as family health and HIV/AIDS prevention. Parents also receive strong support and encouragement to attend school meetings and to speak with teachers and administrators about concerns regarding their children (Patel & Kaplan, 1994).

School-Community Partnerships   We now look at a variety of other community programs that, although they may include a family literacy component, illustrate additional aspects of school-community partnerships.

At Eugene Field Elementary School in Albuquerque, New Mexico, the nerve center for home–school relations is the Parent Room. Parents and teachers together have opportunities to learn from each other as they explore such issues as the role of parents and the role of teachers in child development; clarifications of parents' goals for their children; the use of a problem-solving approach to child rearing and instruction; and parents' and teachers' respect for each other as equals who both contribute resources and who work together. With day care provided, parents can observe classes to help them learn about classroom teaching methods, attend workshops, check out materials from the family center, receive training to become substitute classroom aides, maintain communication with teachers, and participate in school governance. In addition to the activities centered around the Parent Room at the school, home visits are also an important aspect of the program (Navarette, 1996).

Hollibrook Elementary School in Houston, Texas, is located in a neighborhood characterized by poverty, violence, and gang activity. Like Eugene Field Elementary School, Hollibrook has a Parent Center where parents can hold meetings, work on projects, participate in ESL classes, and socialize. In addition, the school has bilingual social workers who work with neighborhood apartment building managers, police, and community agencies to develop an awareness of the whole child and to coordinate services. Teachers also do outreach at the apartment buildings where many of the students live. To further increase the bond between teachers and families, students stay with the same teacher for several years. Teacher volunteers and city parks employees offer an after-school program in which community members can work with tutors and can participate in recreational activities (Berman, Minicucci, McLaughlin, Nelson, & Woodworth, 1995).

The *Instituto Familiar* at Carr Middle School in southern California puts into action Moll's "funds of knowledge" approach. In the initial process of establishing the institute, parents on the school's advisory board surveyed families to identify their interests and concerns. Then, parents worked together to choose topics for workshops and to organize the workshops to meet the needs of working parents' schedules. As a result of the institute's activities, parents have come to feel more comfortable in the school and more confident about their place and voice in the education of their children. They also have developed a better understanding of the role of education in shaping their childrens' futures, and through their activities in the institute they have found a way to close "the cultural and linguistic gap that commonly exists, especially as adolescents become increasingly absorbed into the cultural norms and expectations of the dominant society" (Zúñiga & Westernoff, 1996, p. 216).

The Trinity-Arlington Teacher-Parent Training for School Success Program in Virginia provides services in Spanish, Vietnamese, Khmer, and Lao. The program has three components: teacher training in parent involvement techniques, parent training in tutoring strategies for home use, and curriculum development. Project participants developed the Vocationally Oriented Bilingual Curriculum that parents and students can use at home to learn together about procedures and resources for career planning. For example, it includes a lesson about the role of the school counselor. Parents and children discuss the lesson together and then make a list of three reasons why they might need to see a guidance counselor. Besides providing very practical information for students and their families, the program has resulted in discussions with siblings and extended family members as well as parents. Another reported result is that parents' contacts with the school have increased as they became more knowledgeable about how the school system functions (Simich-Dudgeon, 1993).

Turning now to a program for indigenous language minorities, *Ciulistet* is a teacher study group for educators in southwestern Alaska. (*Ciulistet* means "leaders" in the Yup'ik language.) At the time of this writing, the group had been operating for 15 years with the participation of community elders, teachers, administrators, and university consultants. The meetings are conducted in Yup'ik, and the goal is to find ways to connect traditional holistic knowledge with school knowledge. For example, "the elders' storytelling through dance, storyknifing, and drumming are intimately related to Western forms of literacy, and elders' environmental knowledge is directly related to Western science and mathematics" (Lipka & Ilutsik, 1995, p. 201). Through *Ciulistet,* participants develop ways to make these connections in the classroom. Along with community-based curriculum development, *Ciulistet* participants hold community meetings throughout southwestern Alaska to open up a dialogue with the many parents who feel that the use of Yup'ik in the classroom only "gets in the way" of English. Through their work, they want the next generation of Yup'ik children to be able to see "that their language holds wisdom, and that their stories teach values, science, and literacy" (Lipka & Ilutsik, 1995, p. 201).

The final approach to school–community partnerships that we consider here is that of the community organization at Ochoa Elementary School in Tucson, Arizona. As part of a comprehensive and intensive process of teacher-designed reform at the school in this lower-income, predominantly Mexican-American neighborhood, teachers radically altered their views of parent participation. They realized that they had traditionally been operating out of a deficit perspective. Influenced by the funds of knowledge approach, they instead began to identify and use many of the resources that parents and other family members could bring to the learning process. At the same time, the teachers recognized that the community's poverty did bring with it serious conditions that impacted the learning environment and that could not realistically be ignored—for example, a preponderance of low-paying jobs, substandard housing, and inadequate health care access. As part of their reform efforts they hired a staff member to work on community organization. A group of parents and other neighborhood residents formed a community coalition that later expanded to collaborate with other community organizing agencies. In conjunction with the funds of knowledge approach to curriculum and instruction, the community organizing activities significantly changed the relationships among teachers, parents, and students. For example, they would all work together to investigate community issues. In the process of these investigations, students might be learning content area by taking on such roles as historians, mathematicians, and scientists. The principal investigator of the project described the new relationships among parents, students, and teachers: "as they seek and find solutions to local problems, they together advocate for changes in their community structures" (Heckman, 1996, p. 154). Of all of the programs that we have described here, this one perhaps comes closest to parent involvement that is empowering.

Case Studies of Change from the Inside Out

To conclude this chapter we look at three examples of community activism in which change comes predominantly "from the inside out," to use the phrase of the authors of one of the cases we will discuss (Begay, Dick, Estell, Estell, McCarty, & Sells, 1995). In these cases, we are not looking at program features as we have done so far. We are looking at the processes through which community members have become highly active. First we will look at the development of the Choctaw bilingual program in Mississippi, and then we will consider the history of the Rough Rock program in Arizona. Finally we will look at the development of an Hispanic parent organization in a community in central California.

The Mississippi Choctaw Bilingual Program   The community participates in three important roles in the Mississippi Choctaw bilingual program: making decisions, providing resources, and developing parents' skills. As we described earlier in the chapter, the program grew out of the community's awareness of a need to develop their children's bilingual skills. As described by York (1979), the situation involved children who could use Choctaw informally with family and friends but were unable to carry on discourse in Choctaw in formal situations such as public meetings. Survey results indicated that most parents favored using both Choctaw and English in the school, and the community applied for and received a Title VII grant so that 12 Choctaw teachers could be certified; consequently, children's Choctaw as well as English skills could be developed in school. Parents participated in decision making for the program through the advisory board and in the development of instructional materials. As resource persons, community members demonstrated crafts, music, and dance; told stories; and organized special events and activities. As learners, the parents participated in a variety of activities. For example, they enrolled in literacy programs and learned the school orthography for Choctaw. They learned about the school curriculum and had opportunities to clarify conflicting values and goals. Some community members participated in a writers' workshop so that they could create Choctaw literature based on their experiences (York, 1979).

The Choctaw bilingual program no longer receives Title VII support, and program design has changed over the years. However, with tribal funding and monies from the Indian Students Equalization Program, the Choctaw schools continue to thrive today and to be an integral part of the Choctaw community. The Mississippi Band of the Choctaw Indians now locally operates six schools that were once administered through the Bureau of Indian Affairs. Parents conduct their activities out of the school system's central office, and this physical location reflects their status within the organization. Twenty percent of the parents volunteer in classrooms on a daily basis, and parents participate actively in every type of committee work—for example, textbook adoption, grant money allocations, and modification of programs to meet student needs (Dr. Ada Belton, Dr. Patricia Kwachka, and Ms. Mandy Hemphill, personal communication, February 11, 1997).

The Rough Rock English-Navajo Language Arts Program   In 1966 Rough Rock became known as the first American Indian school to be governed by a locally elected Navajo school board. Since then the community has been a leader and innovator in Navajo education. The Rough Rock English-Navajo Language Arts Program (RRENLAP) was initiated in the 1980s in an effort to strengthen what had previously been a very unstructured bilingual education program at the K through third-grade level. As the program has developed over the past 10 years, teachers, administrators, and university consultants have perceived a process of evolution from the inside out as they have changed "the relations of indigenous educators to the larger school power structure" (Begay et al., 1995, p. 121). The RRENLAP program has come to involve "community educators teaching according to community norms, utilizing local cultural and linguistic knowledge" (p. 122). This has not happened in complete isolation, however. Local educators have benefited enormously from collaboration with outsiders with whom they have built long-term mutual relationships. (RRENLAP was established in close collaboration with KEEP researchers from Hawaii. See Chapter Five for a discussion of the KEEP concept of culturally compatible classrooms.) However, RRENLAP participants conclude that "those best equipped to mediate between an educational system of exogenous origin and the local language and culture, are local educators themselves" (p. 137). Looking at their experience with RRENLAP, Begay et al. state that in order for successful community schools to develop, three factors must be present: a school culture that values and rewards local knowledge, a stable staff that is committed to program goals and has opportunities for staff development, and democratic power relations so that teachers can have control over their own pedagogy.

El Comité de Padres Latinos (COPLA)   Our third illustration is an ethnographic account of the development of a parent advocacy group among Hispanic parents in Carpintería, California. Parents organized COPLA–Comité de Padres Latinos–as a way to provide support for one another in their interactions with the school. The organization has helped many Hispanic parents develop from isolation to activism. With the assistance of several advocates within the school system, COPLA has worked to establish time for teachers to interact more with parents, to help parents learn about the school system and about their rights and responsibilities, and to give parents an active role in decision making. Through COPLA, parents who have the social and cultural capital to be more active have trained less active parents in community and school leadership. COPLA has also fostered valuable dialogue between school personnel and parents. For example, in a discussion about teenagers' academic motivation, "the parents began to understand more fully the extent of teachers' workloads and pressures and the teachers and principal gained a new appreciation of the contributions and responsiveness of parents" (Delgado-Gaitán, 1993, p. 153).

The emergence of COPLA as an important community organization did not happen easily, however. The first step was development of an awareness among parents of their rights and of their need to learn more about how the school system worked. The school district's migrant education director, a bilingual preschool teacher, and an outside researcher—Delgado-Gaitán—played an advocacy role in helping to develop this awareness. With awareness, parents began to mobilize. At a meeting in which the researcher presented data about parent participation, one parent said, "some of us have more knowl-edge about this topic and we need to organize into a group to help other fam-ilies who do not have as much experience. That way we can help each other" (Delgado-Gaitán, 1990, p. 145). The immediate response of other parents was not enthusiastic, but a core of interested parents did form a leadership group that began to meet. They learned as they went along about how to con-duct a meeting, how to listen to divergent points of view, and how to share responsibilities for getting things done. Despite many organizational chal-lenges, they ultimately obtained formal district recognition, access to funds for parent training, and the part-time services of a district employee to help with organizational details. None of this came about easily, however. Twice, for example, the parents had to meet outside because through an oversight they had been locked out of their meeting room despite having made prior arrangements to use it.

Reflecting on the value of COPLA's work, one parent said, "I felt very iso-lated before, and now in this group these meetings have been very good for me." Another parent said, "One loses one's shyness. We can visit the schools more confidently" (Delgado-Gaitán, 1990, p. 156). Delgado-Gaitán identifies some of the results of COPLA's development as less social isolation among parents, a greater parental sense of expertise in child rearing, opportunities to work collectively with school personnel, improved communication between the home and the school, improved programs and services for Latino chil-dren, and academic gains for Latino children (Delgado-Gaitán, 1993, p. 153).

Summary

Throughout this chapter we have referred to many different examples of approaches to school–community partnerships. It would be unrealistic to claim that any of the many programs we have surveyed are unmitigated success stories. A closer look at any of the examples, depending on the lenses of the viewer, could probably reveal flaws or short-comings. What one observer sees as true community empowerment, another could see as school imperialism clothed in the fashionable rhetoric of empowerment. Looking underneath the labels, however, you will find extremely dedicated parents, teachers, and other community advocates who make things happen and who are committed to establishing partnerships that will improve education for language-minority children. Such efforts require thoughtful planning, a sincerely open and supportive administra-tion, informed and energetic staff, and collaborative parents and students. They also require the willingness of all concerned to work hard, experience joys and sorrow, and accept times of conflict along with partial answers to complex questions.

Language-minority families and communities want the best for their children, and they pin great hopes on the school to enable their children to succeed, however that may be defined. Families may not always have the time, energy, self-confidence, or institutional understanding to demonstrate that concern in ways that the school has traditionally recognized, but language-minority parents, as any parents, do want the quality of the schools to measure up to their aspirations for their children. School matters to these parents, and they do notice when learning is not occurring; when their schools resemble maximum security prisons rather than gardens of the mind; when their children sit in overcrowded classrooms; when teachers lose the sense that their work can really make a difference in the lives of their students; when they as parents don't feel welcome in the schools; when they and their children are treated as sociocultural pariahs and problems rather than as full community members; when their children's education lacks enrichment on the grounds that such children need remedial work in reading, writing, and mathematics; when their children are told that to get a good education they will have to be driven across town to areas in which affluent families live; or when their schools pay lip service to linguistic and cultural issues but in reality practice benign neglect.

For partnerships to develop, the communication of expectations between parents and educators cannot be a one-way street. Educators, parents, and students all impact and change each other in predictable and unpredictable ways. If we want to have engaging and supporting working relationships with each other, we have to be in tune with each other's sometimes strident, sometimes soft, sometimes calm, sometimes anxious (and sometimes silent) voices. Language-minority parents, like all parents, will participate in varying ways in mutual efforts that value their contributions, yield solid academic results, and encourage positive interpersonal and intercultural relationships—efforts that aspire toward a community of learners and a community of leaders.

Key Terms

Bilingual community p. 382   Diglossia p. 406

Ethnography p. 403   Biliteracy p. 407

Reflection Questions

1. How do the authors define the term *bilingual community*? Why do they argue for a broader conception of this term, rather than a more traditional definition that includes only the parents, guardians, and extended families of language-minority children attending a specific school?

2. Why do the authors argue that educators should develop a community portrait of the area served by their particular school? How would you write such a portrait? What characteristics would you include in your community portrait?

3. What are community *funds of knowledge*? How can educators incorporate a funds of knowledge perspective into the curriculum and instruction of their bilingual or ESL classrooms?

4. According to the authors, what makes a home–school–community partnership effective? What questions should educators ask themselves as they develop such a partnership?

Resources

As with virtually all aspects of education, there are no all-purpose formulas for the establishment of mutual home-school partnerships. We can, however, learn from effective school and community partnerships as reflected in the following resources.

Hepworth Berger, E. *Parents as partners in education: Families and schools working together,* 5th edition. Upper Saddle River, NJ: Merrill, 2000.

- *Parents as Partners in Education* analyzes strategies for helping regular and special educators, community workers, and other professionals effectively involve parents in their children's education. The author examines past and current research, special concerns and challenges of working with minority and culturally diverse families, school and home-based programs, conducting parent conferences, involving parents of children with disabilities, among other topics. The book covers the essential aspects of parent participation and society's impact on education and addresses recent research on child and brain development, family resource centers, and the focus on involving parents from the beginning of the educational process.

McGee Banks, C. Families and teachers working together for school improvement. In J. A. Banks & C. A. McGee Banks, eds., *Multicultural education: Issues and perspectives,* 4th edition. John Wiley & Sons, Inc, 2001, pp. 402–20.

- "Families and Teachers Working Together for School Improvement" addresses the importance of parent–community involvement for improving student learning and for providing the rationale, motivation, and social action necessary for educational reform. McGee Banks elaborates on various "steps" to establish effective parent-community involvement.

Mulhern, M., Rodríguez-Brown, F. V., & Shanahan, T. *Family literacy for language-minority families: Issues for program implementation.* http://www.ncbe.gwu.edu/ncbepubs/pigs/pig17.htm

- *Family Literacy for Language-minority Families* is a publication of the National Clearinghouse for Bilingual Education (NCBE). Using Project FLAME as a model, the authors briefly address the following questions: What are the first steps in establishing a literacy program? Where and when should classes take place? How should the curriculum be designed? What languages should be used for instruction? How do ESL classes fit within the literacy framework? How should instructional materials be selected? How can programs best be staffed? How can parent participation be sustained? How should the program be evaluated? The booklet includes a model lesson plan for parent education on how to share books with children in ways that will build literacy.

Violand-Sánchez, E., Sutton, C. P., & Ware, H. W. *Fostering home–school cooperation: Involving language-minority families as partners in education,* 1991. http://www.ncbe.gwu.edu/ncbepubs/pigs/pig6.htm

- *Fostering Home-School Cooperation* is also a publication from the National Clearinghouse for Bilingual Education. Using Arlington County, Virginia, as an example, the authors describe a district-wide model for involvement. The model includes such components as an intake center, parent education projects, native-language resource materials for parents, leadership training for parents, staff networking and development opportunities, and long-range planning for minority achievement. Focusing in more closely, the authors then describe the components of the school-community partnership at one elementary school within the district.

Afterword

This new edition of *Bilingual and ESL Classrooms* continues the tradition of its previous editions with its comprehensive treatment of a growing and highly complex set of educational challenges for schools in the United States. It brings together in one volume the issues of critical importance in understanding development and learning. It does so by relating to constructing optimal conditions and environments (schools, classrooms, lessons) that educators can use to enhance educational success in a large population of students that arrive at our schools speaking a language other than English. Never lost in this treatment is that these students do not arrive like blank slates, instead, they bring with them linguistic, cultural, and educational assets that can be leveraged in achieving educational success.

In this context of challenges, schools and the educational professionals who inhabit them often spend their time classifying and separating/segregating students as if these students were invisible, and would become visible only after being classified as limited English proficient, poor (free lunch/Title I), low performing, immigrant, etc., etc. These educational circumstances generate a remarkably new and expanded set of challenges for teachers who choose to serve these school populations. A recent e-mail from an urban high school teacher says it best:

> Hi . . .
> Here's the report from the Western Front. Please pass it around.
> What I initially perceived to be innovative use of year-round scheduling seems to be more mechanization run amok. Although they apparently were able to split the kids into three separate tracks with different vacations with little or no problem, the track system has virtually NO academic benefit, at least the way it operates here. There are about 600 9th- and 10th-graders per track and about 200 11th- and 12th-graders per track. Look at the dropout rate (near 50 percent if not more). And the school just received a 3 year accreditation rather than a 7 year so things are pretty bad.
> In short, this school and school district are nightmares.

Reading and writing levels are grotesque. I have only four students who are operating above grade level. That's out of 150 on the rolls.

Teacher support is nil. I still don't have a stapler or even file folders for portfolio writing assessment. The trash is emptied maybe once a week. The floors are filthier than some bars I've been in, and the bathrooms and stairwells stink. There is one computer lab for Math, four or five computers in the library and that's about it. The textbooks left for me to use were 1980 copyright 10th-grade lit books, and there were only enough for a classroom set. And, of course, all except one of the short stories was about teenage white (male) characters, and these kids Just Don't Relate to that. Plus, despite this being a major ESL school, no supplementary resources "enrichment" materials exist that I can find that contain black or brown or multinational short stories or poems.

I have 21 students with perfect attendance and no discipline problems. Half of them turn in work that is perhaps 4th- or 5th-grade level; the others don't turn in anything at all. I asked other teachers what to do about grades. Well, if they make it every day, pass them with a D even if they don't do anything.

I asked the Union Steward if all the schools in the district were as screwed up as this one. He said that he has taught only here but that he hears it is the same way, but the sad thing is that it doesn't have to be that way. Indeed. The English teachers here are cold, intelligent, and superb. But they all tell me to forget everything I know and just do the best you can with what tools you have and forget how it could be. The faculty has rich experience, but I have never seen so many good ideas from attendance to technology disappear into such a black hole.

These kids are sweet. What lives they have led. Its too bad this system here just processes them through. *(García, 2001, pp. 21–24)*

This edition confronts theses realities and challenges. Its treatment of the most recent theories regarding language and learning combined with the historical-to-present analysis of schooling of culturally and linguistically diverse students in this country are unique. They challenge the reader to go beyond the usual educational practice routines that often are utilized to prepare teachers for this student population. In the nomenclature of recent formulations within the school reform movement, this text serves as a "coach" for an already committed audience that needs to move from where they are to where they should be, particularly in those schools and circumstances that are challenged by a diverse cultural and linguistic student body.

Eugene E. García, Ph.D.
Arizona State University

Glossary

Absolute standards Setting standards that all students must meet, regardless of language proficiency level or ability.

Academic language The "complex network of language cognitive skills and knowledge required across all content areas for eventual successful academic performance at secondary and university levels of instruction" (Collier & Thomas, 1989, p. 27). Like the term *social language, academic language* was initially popularized by Cummins as "cognitive academic language proficiency" or "context-reduced, decontextualized" language. It represents a dimension of language proficiency that extends into increasingly cognitively demanding uses of language, with fewer contextual clues to meaning.

Accelerated learning A comprehensive approach to school change developed in 1986 at Stanford University that aims at creating school success for all students. By redesigning and integrating complex curricular, instructional, and organizational practices, accelerated learning strategies seek to narrow the achievement gap between mainstream and culturally and linguistically diverse students. The program assumes that remedial approaches fail to close these gaps because they don't build on the students' strengths and they don't tap into the resources of teachers, parents, and the community.

Acculturation A process whereby an individual or group incorporates one or more cultural traits of another group, resulting in a blend of cultural patterns. Cultural change and accommodation through acculturation does not necessarily mean loss of the original cultural identity.

Active learning An instructional approach to teaching and learning that understands education as a dynamic process. AL strategies engage students in activities involving the application of content area in "real-life" situations. AL classrooms foster a learning environment where students develop their own knowledge structures through dialogue, reading and writing, and reflecting and acting upon engaging material.

Alternative assessment Any type of assessment for finding out what students know or can do that is not a traditional multiple-choice or standardized test.

Assessment bias Bias that occurs when the cultural background of diverse students is not considered.

Assimilation A process in which an individual or group completely takes on the traits of another culture, leaving behind the ancestral culture.

Attitudinal bias Bias resulting from differences in attitudes toward a particular language or dialect.

Authentic assessment Assessments that are linked both to the instruction delivered in the classroom and to real-world activities.

Authorization/reauthorization This is the process by which Congress amends an existing law in an effort to change or improve it.

Benchmarks Models or examples of student work used to demonstrate various levels on a scoring rubric.

Bias Threatens the validity of an assessment by factors irrelevant to what the test intends to measure, such as by favoring one group (cultural, racial, language, or gender) over another, or ignoring variations in the language proficiency or cultural background of students being assessed, especially when compared to a norming group.

Biculturalism The capacity to negotiate effectively within two different cultural systems. Being bicultural does not necessarily mean, however, giving equal time to both cultures in terms of behavior.

Bilingual community Traditionally *bilingual community* has been defined in terms of parents, guardians, and extended families of minority children attending a specific school. The authors, however, have extended the concept to encompass bilingual educators, university researchers, neighbors, community organizations, and businesses that are connected in some way to the local schools. The authors argue that it is through the cooperation of many different community resources, including professional educators and laypersons that the best programs for language-minority children can be developed.

Bilingual Education Act Formerly Title VII of the Elementary and Secondary Education Act (ESEA) signed by President Lyndon B. Johnson on January 2, 1968. Through this Act, the federal government made its first attempt at addressing the educational needs of language-minority students. (See James Crawford's *Bilingual Education: History, Politics, Theory and Practice*, 1999, for a detailed explanation of its genesis and further developments.)

Bilingual special education Refers to the use of the home language along with English in an individually designed program of instruction provided to a student with disabilities for the purpose of maximizing his or her learning potential.

Biliteracy At its most basic level, biliteracy refers to a person's ability to read and write in two languages. The concept, however, has taken on a sociopolitical dimension, especially as reflected in the work of the Brazilian educator Paulo Freire, who links literacy with issues of social justice and empowerment.

Common underlying proficiency/interdependence of languages The theory, supported by research, that academic skills, literacy development, concept formation, subject knowledge, and learning strategies all transfer from the first to the second language as the vocabulary and communicative patterns are developed in L_2 to express that academic knowledge.

Consequential validity Validity obtained when assessment results are used to improve both learning and teaching by responding to student needs criterion-referenced tests. Tests scored on mastery of specified criteria or content.

Content validity Validity resulting from a match between assessment purpose and classroom instruction.

Cooperative learning An instructional strategy that facilitates a social and linguistically interactive classroom environment. Cooperative learning structures draw from the individual knowledge and talents of learners to facilitate team building, communication building, content mastery, and other interactive skills. Because interaction is a major feature of cooperative learning, language-minority students tend to benefit from increased contact and richer linguistic experiences.

Critical pedagogy An ambitious and wide-ranging ideological project usually situated within educational contexts and linked to the work of Brazilian educator Paulo Freire. Critical pedagogy represents a montage of ideas and approaches questioning how knowledge is individually constructed and legitimized institutionally. Critical pedagogy offers individuals a lens to examine how human beings—regardless of their status in life—construct knowledge and their lived experiences.

Critical thinking A process that stresses an attitude of suspended judgment, incorporates logical inquiry and problem solving, and leads to an evaluative decision or action. Students that exhibit sound critical thinking skills distinguish between fact and opinion;

ask questions; make detailed observations; uncover assumptions; and make assertions based on sound logic and solid evidence. Critical thinking is an intellectually disciplined process of actively and skillfully conceptualizing, applying, analyzing, synthesizing, and/or evaluating information gathered from, or generated by, observation, experience, reflection, reasoning, or communication, as a guide to belief and action.

Cultural bias Bias in favor of the cultural majority group and against minority groups.

Cultural relativism An important social science concept that involves "Tolerance based on skepticism of universal, objective standards of value as well as the idea of progress" (Bidney, 1968).

Culture A deep, multilayered, somewhat cohesive interplay of language, values, beliefs, and behaviors that pervades every aspect of every person's life, and that is continually undergoing modifications. Culture is *not* an isolated aspect of life that can be used mechanistically to explain phenomena in a multicultural classroom or that can be learned as a series of facts.

Declarative knowledge Knowledge of facts (names, dates, characteristics) typical of that measured on standardized tests.

Developmental or maintenance bilingual education An additive or enrichment model designed to preserve and enhance students' primary language skills while they are acquiring English. In general, students participating in this program come from language-minority backgrounds, although some may already be fluent in English. There is less emphasis on exiting students into an all-English classroom and more emphasis on academic development in the home language. In the United States, this model is relatively uncommon.

Developmental standards Standards based on each student's individual growth in language and content skills.

Differentiated scoring Assigning separate scores for language and content on content area work samples.

Diglossia A term coined by Ferguson (1959). It refers to a relatively stable arrangement of two languages existing together in a society, namely primary dialects of the language (which may include a standard or regional standard) coexisting with a divergent and often grammatically more complex variety that serves as the vehicle of a respected body of written literature. *Diglossia* is used to describe a situation where two languages or language varieties are used within the same community, but within separate circumstances or contexts.

Directed reading thinking activity (DRTA) DRTA is a classroom strategy that teachers can use in a wide range of contexts to help language-minority students develop critical thinking skills and deal with abstract content in social studies courses. It involves brainstorming, predicting, reading and confirming, or making corrections about predictions.

Elementary and Secondary Education Act First authorized by Congress in 1965, the ESEA is the federal government's largest omnibus education legislation. This legislation provides public funding for numerous educational programs, including programs serving English-language learners.

English as a second language (ESL) A system of instruction that enables students who are not proficient in English (English-language learners) to acquire both interpersonal communication skills and academic proficiency in spoken and written English. ESL is an essential component of all bilingual education programs in the United States.

English-language learner (ELL) A term favored over 'Limited English Proficiency,' for it conveys that the student is in the process of learning English, without having the connotation that the student is in some way defective until full English proficiency is attained. Like the term *LEP*, however, the *ELL* designation is still somewhat problematic in that it focuses on the need to learn English without acknowledging the value of the child's proficiency in L_1. The term is superficially less offensive, but it is also less precise. It conveys single-minded focus on learning English that tends to restrict discussion about student's pedagogical needs.

Equal Educational Opportunities Act of 1974 Originally passed by Congress as an anti-busing statute, the EEOA also prohibits states from denying equal educational opportunity to individuals on the basis of race, color, sex, or national origin. This legislation requires school districts to "take appropriate action to overcome language barriers that impede equal participation by its students in instructional programs."

ESL content (or sheltered) classes An instructional approach used to make academic instruction in English understandable to language-minority students. Its aim is to help such students develop academic competence while also developing English proficiency. Students in these classes are "sheltered" in that they do not compete academically with native English speakers since the class includes only nonmajority language students. In the regular classroom, English fluency is assumed. In contrast, in the sheltered English classroom, teachers use physical activities, visual aids, and the environment to teach important new words for concept development in mathematics, science, history, home economics, and other subjects.

Ethnocentrism The belief in the superiority of one's own ethnic group.

Ethnomathematics Refers to the study of mathematics that takes into consideration the culture in which mathematics arises. Mathematics is usually associated with the study of "universals." It is important to be aware, however, that often something we think of as universal is merely universal to those who share our cultural and historical perspectives. According to Power and Frankenstein (1997), ethnomathematics refers to the "mathematical ideas of peoples, manifested in written or nonwritten, oral or nonoral forms, many of which have been either ignored or otherwise distorted by conventional histories of mathematics."

Ethnoscience Kessler and Quinn (1987) define ethnoscience as comprised of "theories and procedures for learning about the physical world that have evolved informally within cultures to explain and predict natural phenomena."

Full inclusion Refers to an educational movement promoting the idea that students with disabilities be reintegrated in general education classrooms and taught alongside their peers without disabilities. The term is the most current trend among its predecessors mainstreaming and inclusion.

Global education *Global education* is an educational approach that involves learning about the problems and issues that cut across national boundaries, and about the interconnectedness of systems—ecological, racial, cultural, economic, political, and technological. Global educators exhibit open-mindedness and the ability to find the threats that interconnect the myriad range of human affairs and their subsequent effects. The world, as a global community, is interdependent. The task of the global educator and students is to forge a dialogue through which cause–effect interconnections are uncovered, analyzed, and understood.

Immersion An approach originally developed in Canada to help English-speaking children achieve proficiency in the French language. Bilingualism in two high status languages was the intended outcome, with children becoming bilingual and bicultural without a loss of academic achievement.

Indigenous or heritage languages A term used to designate non-English languages spoken in the United States that are not spoken by the dominant culture. (See Krashen, Tse, & McQuillan, 1998, p. 3; see also http://www.cal.org/heritage/.)

Interrater reliability Level of agreement reached between raters scoring the same work sample or student performance.

Lau plans Negotiated "consent agreements" between OCR and school districts found to be out-of-compliance with federal civil rights statutes.

Lau regulations Formal and federally mandated regulations for implementing bilingual and ESL programs (proposed by the Carter Administration in 1980 and later withdrawn by the Reagan Administration in 1981).

Lau remedies Guidelines developed after the *Lau v. Nichols* decision about the implementation of bilingual and ESL programs (concerning, for example, identification of students' language dominance, appropriate placement into programs, curriculum design, assessment, and analysis of achievement data).

Learning strategies Techniques, strategies, and activities that students use across subject areas to understand and retain information, to solve problems, and to "learn *how* to learn."

Limited English Proficient (LEP) A controversial term used to describe children with limited English language skills due to their mother tongue background. The term has recently been criticized for its negative connotations. It has been argued that it defines children in terms of what they "lack" rather than what they already possess, namely valuable skills in a language other than English. The term is favored over "limited English speaking" (LES), for it encompasses proficiencies in reading, writing, and listening (for a more detailed explanation, see James Crawford, 1999, p. 17).

Marked languages and cultures The concept refers to the status assigned to particular languages, cultures, and social groups within a pluralistic society.

Mathematics standards As defined by the National Council of Teachers of Mathematics, math standards are "descriptions of what mathematics instruction should enable students to know and do—statements of what is valued for school mathematics education."

Melting pot Our best-known assimilationist metaphor that implies dissolving individuals into a boiling mixture, whether in the foundry or the kitchen, to be poured into molds of mass production. Although originally intended to equalize the sociocultural and racial playing field in the United States, the melting pot metaphor has been criticized for being discriminatory in practice.

Multicultural education Multicultural education is an idea or concept, an educational reform movement, and a process that forms the basis for teaching and learning based on democratic values and beliefs. It seeks to affirm cultural pluralism within culturally diverse soci-

eties and an interdependent world. It incorporates the ideas of democratic challenges and opportunities for school achievement regardless of race, ethnic background, gender, or socioeconomic status.

Multiple acculturation A term that suggests that the U.S. common culture is a product of the intersection of diverse cultural, racial, and ethnic elements within U.S. society.

Multiple modalities Refers to teaching strategies that allow teachers to frame much of their teaching in such a way that students are able to develop cognitive skills in the subject areas as they receive instruction in L_2. Through the use of multiple modalities in the mathematics classroom (i.e., manipulatives, demonstrations, experiments), math educators can involve their students not only in the discovery of new knowledge, but also in the practice of newly acquired L_2.

National Association for Bilingual Education (NABE) A nonprofit professional development and advocacy professional membership association working to ensure educational excellence and equity for language-minority Americans. NABE is the only national organization exclusively concerned with the education of language-minority students in American schools. It promotes educational excellence and equity through bilingual education. (for detailed information log on to http://www.nabe.org).

National Defense Education Act of 1958 The Soviet Union's successful launching in late 1957 of Sputnik, the world's first satellite, spurred Congress to pass the NDEA, legislation that provided federal expenditures for science, engineering, technology, and the study of foreign languages.

Norming bias Bias resulting from establishing test norms with one cultural or linguistic group and using the test with a different group.

Norm-referenced test Determines how a student's test score compares to the scores of other students who took the test.

Passive learning A traditional approach to teaching based on the "banking model" of education. Within the passive learning model, students are expected to learn new information through absorption and by rote repetition of facts without an attempt to interact with the material, especially in terms of problem solving, critical thinking, and applications to new situations.

Prereferral interventions These are educational and behavioral strategies recommended to general educators by a prereferral team for teaching difficult to teach students in the general education classrooms before referring them for special education evaluation. While the individuals who make up the prereferral team vary, they typically include general and special educators.

Procedural knowledge Knowledge of processes, how to do something with reliability. The degree of consistency with which an assessment provides information about a student.

Referral for special education This is a written statement, submitted by any number of individuals (e.g., school personnel, parents, or the student), to the school's multidisciplinary team of educational professionals requesting an evaluation to determine if a student meets the criteria for a federally recognized special education category such as a learning disability, mental retardation, emotional or behavioral disorder.

Scaffolding Reducing the linguistic demand of instructional and assessment materials so that students can show what they know.

Semilingualism A controversial and mostly discredited idea that some language-minority children do not know any language at all, or speak their native and target languages with only limited ability.

Silent period A natural stage of beginning L_2 acquisition observed in some young second-language learners, in which these learners mostly listen to the new language without producing it.

Social language First conceptualized by Jim Cummins as "basic interpersonal communicative skills" (BICS) or "context-embedded, conversational" or "contextualized" language, this is a dimension of language proficiency in which meaning is negotiated through a wide range of contextual clues. Given access to L_2 speakers and social settings that encourage natural interaction, L_2 speakers may acquire social language in two or three years.

Social studies Social studies is the integrated study of the social sciences and humanities to promote civic competence. Within the school program, social studies provides coordinated, systematic study drawing upon such disciplines as anthropology, archeology, economics, geography, history, law, philosophy, political science, psychology, religion, and sociology. It also draws appropriate content from the humanities, mathematics, and the natural sciences. The primary purpose of social studies is to help young people develop the ability to make informed and reasoned decisions for the public good as citizens of a culturally diverse, democratic society in an interdependent world. (See National Council for the Social Studies, 1993.)

Special education Instruction and related services specifically designed and provided to meet the unusual needs of exceptional students.

Stereotype "A conventional, formulaic, and over simplified conception, opinion, or image." (From *The American Heritage Dictionary of the English Language*.)

Structured English immersion A model typically promoted by English Only supporters, in which subject matter instruction is provided in English, along with direction in English grammar. This approach also allows for some instruction in the students' first language for clarification or explanation. Ideally, sheltered/structured English immersion teachers have specialized training in instructional strategies designed to meet the linguistic and cultural needs of English-language learners.

Submersion Although included with definitions of various curriculum models, it is *not* actually a program model because it is not in compliance with federal legal standards (review the discussion on the Supreme Court's 1974 decision in *Lau* v. *Nichols*). Also known as "sink or swim," submersion is an approach to the education of English-language learners characterized by no special assistance of any kind. Language-minority students who are developing proficiency in English are placed in the same classes with language-majority students and all receive instruction in English only. Teachers and students are expected to use English, not the home language. In the United States, this kind of education is *illegal*.

Teachers of English to Speakers of Other Languages (TESOL) An international and professional education association. Its mission is to develop the expertise of its members and others involved in teaching English to speakers of other languages to help them foster effective communication in diverse settings while respecting individuals' language rights. In English-speaking countries, ESL teachers work with immigrants and refugees at all levels of the education system—in primary, secondary, and higher education. According to the TESOL organization, ESL should be part of a larger bilingual program that also involves instruction in the student's L_1 (for detailed information log on to http://www.tesol.org).

Test bias Exists when equally able groups perform differently on the same test.

Threshold Hypothesis The theory that academic and cognitive difficulties will occur for L_2 learners if a certain academic and literacy *threshold* in their L_1 is not first achieved.

Title VI of the Civil Rights Act of 1964 This title serves as the basis for much civil rights litigation on behalf of language-minority students, and bans discrimination on the basis of "race, color or national origin" in any "program or activity receiving federal financial assistance."

Transitional bilingual education A compensatory or remedial model designed to prepare linguistic minority students to enter mainstream (all English) classes. A portion of the overall instruction is in the child's first language. After a period of time, generally two or three years, students are "transitioned" into the mainstream curriculum. TBE is the most common bilingual education model in the United States.

Two-way, dual-language, or bilingual immersion education An additive or enrichment model that is designed to achieve bilingualism in both the minority and majority language. In general, it serves two linguistically diverse population groups: speakers of the minority language and speakers of the majority language. It is designed to cultivate the native language skills of both groups. These programs provide content area instruction and language development in both languages. In order to achieve the full benefits of two-way bilingual education, students from the two language backgrounds are in each class, and they are integrated for most or all of their content instruction.

U.S. Office for Civil Rights (OCR) This is an agency of the U.S. Department of Education that monitors school district delivery of services to language-minority students in order to determine whether those districts are in compliance with the requirements of Title VI of the Civil Rights Act, the Equal Educational Opportunity Act, and other civil rights statutes.

Validity The degree to which a test measures what it is intended to measure or the accuracy of the interpretation of test scores.

References

Ada, A. F. (1980). Creative reading: A new approach to teaching ethnic minority students to read. *Aids in Bilingual Communication Report, 1*(2), 1–8.

Ada, A. F. (1988). The Pájaro Valley experience: Working with Spanish-speaking parents to develop children's reading and writing skills in the home through the use of children's literature. In T. Skutnabb-Kangas & J. Cummins (Eds.), *Minority education: From shame to struggle* (pp. 223–38). Clevedon, England: Multilingual Matters.

Ada, A. F. (1991). Creative reading: A relevant methodology for language minority children. In C. E. Walsh (Ed.), *Literacy as praxis: Culture, language, and pedagogy* (pp. 89–102). Norwood, NJ: Ablex.

Adams, D. W. (1988). Fundamental considerations: The deep meaning of Native American schooling, 1880–1900. *Harvard Educational Review, 58*, 1–28.

Adams, J. (1780). A letter to the president of Congress. Rpt. in Charles Francis Adams (Ed.), *Works* (vol. 7, pp. 249–51). Boston: Little, Brown, 1852.

Adamson, H. D. (1993). *Academic competence: Theory and classroom practice: Preparing ESL students for content courses.* New York: Longman.

Adkins, K., Fleming, K., & Saxena, D. (1995). Three teachers' views on critical pedagogy: An educational Woodstock. In J. Frederickson (Ed.), *Reclaiming our voices: Bilingual education, critical pedagogy and praxis* (pp. 197–209). Los Angeles: California Association for Bilingual Education.

Adler, P. S. (1972). Beyond cultural identity: Reflections on cultural and multicultural man. In L. Samovar & R. Porter (Eds.), *Intercultural communication: A reader* (pp. 362–80). Belmont, CA: Wadsworth.

Affeldt, J. T. (1996). Legal/legislative policy. In *Revisiting the Lau decision: 20 years after* (pp. 43–48). Oakland, CA: ARC Associates.

Aguirre, A., Jr. (1980). The sociolinguistic survey in bilingual education: A case study of a bilingual community. In R. V. Padilla (Ed.), *Ethnoperspectives in bilingual education research, Vol. 2: Theory in bilingual education* (pp. 47–61). Ypsilanti, MI: Eastern Michigan University.

Ahmad, K., Corbett, G., Rogers, M., & Sussex, R. (1985). *Computers, language learning and language teaching.* Cambridge: Cambridge University Press.

Airasian, P. (1997). *Classroom assessment* (2nd ed.). New York: McGraw-Hill.

Alatis, J. E. (1993). Building an association: TESOL's first quarter century. In S. Silberstein (Ed.), *State of the art TESOL essays: Celebrating 25 years of the discipline* (pp. 382–414). Alexandria, VA: Teachers of English to Speakers of Other Languages.

Alcoze, T. (1993). Multiculturalism in mathematics, science and technology: *Readings & activities.* Reading, MA: Addison-Wesley.

Aldridge, B. G. (Ed.). (1995). *A high school framework for National Science Education Standards (Vol. III): Scope, sequence, and coordination of secondary school science.* Arlington, VA: National Science Teachers Association.

Alinsky, S. D. (1971). *Rules for radicals.* New York: Random House.

Allan, M. (1985). *Teaching English with video.* New York: Longman.

Allwright, D., & Bailey, K. M. (1991). *Focus on the language classroom: An introduction to classroom research for language teachers.* Cambridge: Cambridge University Press.

American Association for the Advancement of Science. (1993). *Benchmarks for science literacy: Project 2961.* Oxford: Oxford University Press.

Anderson, C. C. (1990). Global education and the community. In K. A. Tye (Ed.), *Global education: From thought to action* (pp. 125–41). Alexandria, VA: Association for Supervision and Curriculum Development.

Andersson, T., & Boyer, M. (Eds.). (1970). *Bilingual schooling in the United States* (1st ed., Vols. 1–2). Washington, DC: Government Printing Office.

Apple, M. W. (1992). Do standards go far enough? Power, policy, and practice in mathematics education. *Journal for Research in Mathematics Education, 23*(5), 412–31.

Apple, M. W., & Beane, J. A. (Eds.). (1995). *Democratic schools.* Alexandria, VA: Association for Supervision and Curriculum Development.

Applebome, P. (1996, January 7). Is experience the best teacher? Debating almost everything about how to train new educators. *New York Times,* p. 4A22.

Appleton, N. (1983). *Cultural pluralism in education: Theoretical foundations.* New York: Longman.

Areola v. Santa Anna Board of Education (1968). No. 160-577, Orange County, California.

Arias, M. B. (1986). The context of education for Hispanic students: An overview. *American Journal of Education, 95*(1), 26–57.

Arias, M. B., & Casanova, U. (1993). *Bilingual education: Politics, practice, and research.* Chicago: University of Chicago Press.

Armas, G. C. (2001). *Census data shows more immigrants in U.S.* 2001 Nando Media/2001 AP Online.

Armbruster, B., & Gudbrandsen, B. (1986). Reading comprehension instruction in social studies programs. *Reading Research Quarterly, 21,* 36–48.

Armstrong, T. (1994). *Multiple intelligences in the classroom.* Alexandria, VA: Association for Supervision and Curriculum Development.

Arnberg, L. (1987). *Raising children bilingually: The pre-school years.* Clevedon, England: Multilingual Matters.

Aronson, E., Blaney, N., Stephan, C., Sikes, J., & Snapp, M. (1978). *The Jigsaw classroom.* Newbury Park, CA: Sage.

Arreaga-Mayer, C., Carta, J. J., & Tapia, Y. (1994). Ecobehavioral assessment: A new methodology for evaluating instruction for exceptional culturally and linguistically diverse students. In S.B. Garcia (Ed.), *Addressing cultural and linguistic diversity in special education: Issues and trends* (pp. 10–29). Reston, Virginia, The Council for Exceptional Children.

Artiles, A. J., & Trent, S. C. (1994). Overrepresentation of minority students in special education: A continuing debate. *The Journal of Special Education, 27*(4), 410–37.

Arvizu v. Waco Independent School District, 373 F. Supp. 1264 (W.D. Tex. 1973), *aff'd in part, rev'd in part, and remanded,* 495 F.2d 499 (5th Cir. 1974).

Ascher, M. (1991). *Ethnomathematics: A multicultural view of mathematical ideas.* Pacific Grove, CA: Brooks/Cole.

Asher, J. (1982). *Learning another language through actions: The complete teacher's guide book* (2nd ed.). Los Gatos, CA: Sky Oaks Productions.

Ashton-Warner, S. (1963). *Teacher.* New York: Simon & Schuster.

Aspira of New York v. Board of Education of the City of New York, 72 Civ. 4002 (S.D.N.Y., consent decree, August 29, 1974), 394 F. Supp. 1161 (S.D.N.Y. 1975), 423 F. Supp. 647 (S.D.N.Y. 1976).

Associated Press. (1987, Feb. 14). Survey: Most think English is official U.S. language.

Au, K. H. (1993). *Literacy instruction in multicultural settings*. Fort Worth, TX: Harcourt Brace Jovanovich.

Au, K. H., & Jordan, C. (1981). Teaching reading to Hawaiian children: Finding a culturally appropriate solution. In H. T. Trueba, G. P. Guthrie, & K. H. Au (Eds.), *Culture and the bilingual classroom: Studies in classroom ethnography* (pp. 139–52). New York: Newbury House.

Auerbach, E. R. (1989). Toward a social-contextual approach to family literacy. *Harvard Educational Review, 59*, 165–81.

August, D., & Hakuta, K. (Eds.). (1998). *Educating language-minority children*. Washington, DC: National Academy Press.

August, D., Hakuta, K., Olguin, F., & Pompa, D. (1995). *LEP students and Title I: A guidebook for educators*. Washington, DC: National Clearinghouse for Bilingual Education.

August, D., Hakuta, K., & Pompa, D. (1994). *For all students: Limited English proficient students and Goals 2000*. Washington, DC: National Clearinghouse for Bilingual Education.

August, D., & McArthur, E. (1996). *Proceedings of the Conference on Inclusion Guidelines and Accommodations for Limited English Proficient Students in the National Assessment of Educational Progress*. Washington, DC: National Center for Education Statistics and Office of Educational Research and Improvement, U.S. Department of Education.

Baca, L. M., & Cervantes, H. T. (1989). *The bilingual special education interface* (2nd ed.). Columbus, OH: Merrill.

Baca, L. M., & de Valenzuela, J. S. (1994). *Reconstructing the bilingual special education interface*. Washington, DC: National Clearinghouse for Bilingual Education.

Baca, L. & de Valenzuela, J. S. (1998). Background and rationale for bilingual special education. In L. M. Baca & H. T. Cervantes (Eds.), *The bilingual special education interface* (pp. 2–25). Upper Saddle River, New Jersey: Prentice Hall.

Bachman, L. F., & Palmer, A. S. (1996). *Language testing in practice: Designing and developing useful language tests*. Oxford: Oxford University Press.

Baker, C. (1988). *Key issues in bilingualism and bilingual education*. Clevedon, England: Multilingual Matters.

Baker, C. (1996). *Foundations of bilingual education and bilingualism* (2nd ed.). Clevedon, England: Multilingual Matters.

Bancroft, W. J. (1978). The Lozanov method and its American adaptations. *Modern Language Journal, 62*, 167–75.

Banks, J. A. (1988). Ethnicity, class, cognitive and motivational styles: Research and teaching implications. *Journal of Negro Education, 57*,(4), 452–66.

Banks, J. A. (1991a). Introduction. *Curriculum guidelines for multicultural education: NCSS Position Statement & Guidelines*. Washington, DC: National Council for the Social Studies.

Banks, J. A. (1991b). Multicultural education: Its effects on students' ethnic and gender role attitudes. In J. P. Shaver (Ed.), *Handbook of research on social studies teaching and learning* (pp. 459–69). New York: Macmillan.

Banks, J. A. (1991c). *Teaching strategies for ethnic studies* (5th ed.). Boston: Allyn & Bacon.

Banks, J. A. (1993). Multicultural education: Development, dimensions, and challenges. *Phi Delta Kappan, 75*(1), 22–35.

Banks, J. A. (1995). Multicultural education: Historical development, dimensions, and practice. In J. A. Banks & C. A. M. Banks (Eds.), *Handbook of research on multicultural education* (pp. 4–5). New York: Macmillan.

Banks, J. A., & McGee Banks, C. A. (2001). *Multicultural education: Issues and perspectives* (4th ed.). New York: John Wiley & Sons.

Barba, R. H. (1995). *Science in the multicultural classroom: A guide to teaching and learning*. Boston: Allyn and Bacon.

Barker, G. C. (1975). Social functions of language in a Mexican-American community. In E. Hernández-Chávez, A. D. Cohen, & A. F. Beltramo (Eds.), *El lenguaje de los chicanos* (pp. 183–201). Arlington, VA: Center for Applied Linguistics.

Barr, R. D., Barth, J. L., & Shermis, S. S. (1977). Defining the social studies. *National Council of Social Studies Bulletin*, no. 51.

Barreras, R. (1992). Ideas a literature can grow on: Key insights for enriching and expanding children's literature about the Mexican American experience. In V. Harris (Ed.), *Teaching multicultural literature in Grades K-8* (pp. 203–42). Norwood, MA: Christopher-Gordon.

Barringer, F. (1991, March 11). Census shows profound change in racial makeup of the nation. *New York Times*, p. A1.

Barth, F. (1967). On the study of social change. *American Anthropologist, 69,* 661–69.

Barth, R. S. (1990). *Improving schools from within: Teachers, parents, and principals can make the difference.* San Francisco: Jossey-Bass.

Bartis, P., & Bowman, P. (1994). *A teacher's guide to folklife resources for K–12 classrooms.* Washington, DC: American Folklife Center & Library of Congress.

Becijos, L. (1997). *SDAIE Strategies for teachers of English learners.* Bonita, CA: Torch Publications.

Becker, H. J. (1990). *How computers are used in United States schools: Basic data from the 1989 I.E.A. computers in education survey.* Baltimore, MD: Johns Hopkins University, Center for Social Organization of Schools.

Bedell, F. (1992). Educational needs of minorities with disabilities and reactions. In T. J. Wright & P. Leung (Eds.), *The unique needs of minorities with disabilities: Setting an agenda for the future.* Conference proceedings (Jackson, Mississippi, May 6–7, 1992).

Beebe, C., & Evans, J. (1981). Clarifying the Federal role in education. In R. Miller (Ed.), *Federal role in education* (pp. 39–48). Washington, DC: Institute for Educational Leadership.

Begay, S., Dick, G. S., Estell, D. W., Estell, J., McCarty, T. L., & Sells, A. (1995). Change from the inside out: A story of transformation in a Navajo community school. *Bilingual Research Journal, 19*(1), 121–39.

Bem, D. (1970). *Beliefs, attitudes, and human affairs.* Belmont, CA: Brook/Cole Publishing.

Benavides, A. (1988). High risk predictors and prereferral screening for language minority students. In A. A. Ortiz & B. A. Ramirez (Eds.), *Schools and the culturally diverse exceptional student: Promising practices and future directions.* (pp. 19–31). Boston: The Council for Exceptional Children.

Bennett, C. I. (1995a). *Comprehensive multicultural education: Theory and practice* (3rd ed.). Boston: Allyn and Bacon.

Bennett, C. I. (1995b). Research on racial issues in American higher education. In J. A. Banks & C. A. M. Banks (Eds.), *Handbook of research on multicultural education* (pp. 663–82). New York: Macmillan.

Bennett, J. A., & Berry, J. W. (1991). Cree literacy in the syllabic script. In D. R. Olson & N. Torrance (Eds.), *Literacy and orality* (pp. 90–104). Cambridge: Cambridge University Press.

Bennett, W. J. (1984). To reclaim a legacy: Report on humanities in education. *The Chronicle of Higher Education, 29*(14), 16–21.

Bennett, W. J. (1985, September 26). Speech to the Association for a Better New York. Rpt. in J. Crawford (Ed.) (1992), *Language loyalties: A source book on the Official English controversy* (pp. 358–63). Chicago: University of Chicago Press.

Bensusan, G., & Carlisle, C. (1978). *Raíces y ritmos: Our heritage of Latin American music.* Flagstaff, AZ: Northern Arizona University.

Berelson, B., & Steiner, G. A. (1964). *Human behavior: An inventory of scientific findings.* New York: Harcourt, Brace & World.

Berger, P. (1967). *The sacred canopy.* New York: Doubleday.

Berko Gleason, J. (1993). *The development of language* (3rd ed.). New York: Macmillan.

Berliner, D. C., & Biddle, B. J. (1995). *The manufactured crisis: Myths, fraud, and the attack on America's public schools.* Reading, MA: Addison-Wesley.

Berman, P., Minicucci, C., McLaughlin, B., Nelson, B., & Woodworth, K. (1995). *School reform and student diversity: Case studies of exemplary practices for LEP students.* Santa Cruz, CA: National Center for Research on Cultural Diversity and Second Language Learning.

Bertrand, J. E. (1994). Student assessment and evaluation. In B. Harp (Ed.) *Assessment and evaluation for student centered learning* (2nd ed.). Norwood, MA: Christopher-Gordon Publishers.

Beyer, L. E. & Apple, M. W. (1988). *The curriculum: Problems, politics, and possibilities.* Albany: State University of New York Press.

Bialystok, E. (Ed.). (1991). *Language processing in bilingual children.* Cambridge: Cambridge University Press.

Bialystok, E., & Hakuta, K. (1994). *In other words: The science and psychology of second-language acquisition.* New York: BasicBooks.

Bidney, D. (1968). Cultural relativism. In D. L. Sills (Ed.), *International Encyclopedia of the Social Sciences* (Vol. 3, pp. 543–47). New York: Macmillan.

Bikales, G. (1987, March 12). Presentation to Georgetown University Round Table on Languages and Linguistics, Washington, DC.

Bingham, S., & Bingham, J. (1979). *Navajo farming.* Chinle, AZ: Rock Point Community School.

Birdwhistell, R. (1970). *Kinesics and context: Essays on body motion communication.* Philadelphia: University of Pennsylvania.

Blair, R. W. (Ed.). (1982). *Innovative approaches to language teaching.* New York: Newbury House.

Bloom, A. (1987). *The closing of the American mind.* New York: Simon & Schuster.

Bloom, B. S. (Ed.). (1956). *Taxonomy of educational objectives: The classification of educational goals, Handbook I: Cognitive domain.* New York: Longman.

Bloomfield, L. (1933). *Language.* New York: Holt.

Blumer, H. (1969). *Symbolic interactionism.* Englewood, NJ: Prentice Hall.

Borba, M. C. (1990). Ethnomathematics and education. *For the Learning of Mathematics, 10*(1), 39–43.

Bosma, B. (1992). *Fairy tales, fables, legends, and myths: Using folk literature in your classroom* (2nd ed.). New York: Teachers College Press.

Bourdieu, P., & Passeron, J. C. (1977). *Reproduction in education, society and culture.* Newbury Park, CA: Sage.

Bowen, J. D., Madsen, H., & Hilferty, A. (1985). *TESOL techniques and procedures.* New York: Newbury House.

Bowles, S., & Gintis, H. (1976). *Schooling in capitalist America.* New York: Basic Books.

Bradley v. Milliken, 402 F. Supp. 1096 (E.D. Mich. 1975).

Bretzer, J. (1992). Language, power, and identity in multiethnic Miami. In J. Crawford (Ed.), *Language loyalties: A source book on the official English controversy* (pp. 209–16). Chicago: The University of Chicago Press.

Brinton, D. M., Snow, M. A., & Wesche, M. B. (1989). *Content-based second language instruction.* New York: Newbury House.

Brooks, E., & Fox, L. (1994). *Making Peace: A Reading/Writing/Thinking Text on Global Community.* New York: St. Martin's Press.

Brooks, J. G., & Brooks, M. G. (1993). *In search of understanding: The case for constructivist classrooms.* Alexandria, VA: Association for Supervision and Curriculum Development.

Brophy, J. (1992). Probing the subtleties of subject-matter teaching. *Educational Leadership, 49*(7), 4–8.

Broudy, S. (1977). Educational unity in a pluralistic society: An abstract. *Viewpoints, 53*(6), 1–3.

Brown, H. D. (1994a). *Principles of language learning and teaching* (3rd ed.). Englewood Cliffs, NJ: Prentice Hall Regents.

Brown, H. D. (1994b). *Teaching by principles: An interactive approach to language pedagogy.* Upper Saddle River, NJ: Prentice Hall Regents.

Brown, K. (1993). Balancing the tools of technology with our own humanity: The use of technology in building partnerships and communities. In J. V. Tinajero & A. F. Ada (Eds.), *The power of two languages: Literacy and biliteracy for Spanish-speaking students* (pp. 178–98). New York: Macmillan/McGraw-Hill.

Brown, K., & Cuéllar, J. C. (1995). Global learning networks as a catalyst for change: Confronting prejudice between "minority" groups. *NABE News, 18*(6), 9, 12–14.

Burt, M. K., Dulay, H. C., & Hernández-Chávez, E. (1975). *Bilingual Syntax Measure.* New York: Harcourt Brace Jovanovich.

Bryen, D. N. (1974). Special education and the linguistically different child. *Exceptional Children, 40*(8), 589–99.

Calderón, M. (1994). Cooperative learning for bilingual settings. In R. Rodríguez, N. J. Ramos, & J. A. Ruiz-Escalante (Eds.), *Compendium of readings in bilingual education: Issues and practices* (pp. 95–110). San Antonio, TX: Texas Association for Bilingual Education.

Calderón, M. (1996). *Educational change for language and discourse development of teachers and students in two-way bilingual programs.* Paper presented at the annual meeting of the American Educational Research Association, New York City.

Calderón, M., & Carreón, A. (1994). Educators and students use cooperative learning to become biliterate and bilingual. *Cooperative Learning, 14*(3), 6–9.

Calderón, M., Tinajero, J., & Hertz-Lazarowitz, R. (1992). Adopting cooperative integrated reading and composition to meet the needs of bilingual students. *The Journal of Educational Issues of Language Minority Students, 10,* 79–106.

California Achievement Tests (5th ed.). (1992). Monterey, CA: CTB McGraw-Hill.

California Department of Education. (1981). *Schooling and language minority students: A theoretical framework.* Los Angeles: Evaluation, Dissemination, and Assessment Center, California State University, Los Angeles.

California Department of Education. (1984). *Studies on immersion education: A collection for United States educators.* Sacramento, CA: Author.

California Department of Education. (1986). *Beyond language: Social and cultural factors in schooling language minority students.* Los Angeles: Evaluation, Dissemination, and Assessment Center, California State University, Los Angeles.

California Department of Education. (1991). Los Angeles Unified achieves excellence with bilingual approach. *Bilingual Education Office Outreach, 2*(2), 12–13, 15.

Campos, S. J., & Keatinge, H. R. (1988). The Carpintería language minority student experience: From theory, to practice, to success. In T. Skutnabb-Kangas & J. Cummins (Eds.), *Minority education: From shame to struggle* (pp. 299–307). Clevedon, England: Multilingual Matters.

Cancian, F. (1968). Varieties of functional analysis. In D. Sills (Ed.), *International Encyclopedia of the Social Sciences* (Vol. 6, pp. 29–43). New York: Macmillan.

Cantieni, G., & Tremblay, R. (1979). The use of concrete mathematical situations in learning a second language: A dual learning concept. In H. T. Trueba & C. Barnett-Mizrahi (Eds.), *Bilingual multicultural education and the professional* (pp. 246–55). New York: Newbury House.

Cantoni, G. (Ed.). (1996). *Stabilizing indigenous languages.* Flagstaff, AZ: Center for Excellence in Education, Northern Arizona University.

Cantoni-Harvey, G. (1987). *Content-area language instruction: Approaches and strategies.* Reading, MA: Addison-Wesley.

Cantoni-Harvey, G. (1992). Facilitating the reading process. In P. A. Richard-Amato & M. A. Snow (Eds.), *The multicultural classroom: Readings for content-area teachers* (pp. 175–97). New York: Longman.

Caplan, N., Choy, M. H., & Whitmore, J. K. (1992). Indochinese refugee families and academic achievement. *Scientific American, 266*(2), 36–42.

Carger, C. L. (1996). *Of borders and dreams: A Mexican-American experience of urban education.* New York: Teachers College Press.

Carlson, P. E., & Stephens, T. M. (1986). Cultural bias and identification of behaviorally disordered children. *Behavioral Disorders,* May 1986, 191–99.

Carmody, D. (1989, September 12). Minority students gain on college entrance tests. *New York Times,* p. A16.

Carpenter, L. K. (1983). Social stratification and implications for bilingual education: An Ecuadorian example. In A. W. Miracle, Jr. (Ed.), *Bilingualism: Social issues and policy implications* (pp. 96–106). Athens, GA: University of Georgia Press.

Carrasco, R. L. (1981a). Expanded awareness of student performance: A case study in applied ethnographic monitoring in a bilingual classroom. In H. T. Trueba, G. P. Guthrie, and K. H. Au (Eds.), *Culture and the bilingual classroom* (pp. 153–77). New York: Newbury House.

Carrasco, R. L. (1981b). Review of Chicano sociolinguistics: A brief introduction by F. Peñalosa. *Harvard Educational Review, 51,* 191–193.

Carrasquillo, A. L. (1990). Bilingual special education: The important connection. In A. L. Carrasquillo & R. E. Baecher (Eds.), *Teaching the bilingual special education student* (pp. 4–24). Norwood, New Jersey: Ablex Publishing Corporation.

Carrasquillo, A. L., & Baecher, R. E. (Eds.). (1990). *Teaching the bilingual special education student.* Norwood, NJ: Ablex.

Carrasquillo, A. L., & Hedley, C. (Eds.). (1993). *Whole language and the bilingual learner.* Norwood, NJ: Ablex.

Carrell, P. L. (1981). Culture-specific schemata in L_2 comprehension. In R. Orem & J. Haskell (Eds.), *Selected papers from the ninth Illinois*

TESOL/BE annual convention (pp. 123–32). Chicago: Illinois Teachers of English to Speakers of Other Languages/Bilingual Education.

Carrell, P. L., & Eisterhold, J. C. (1983). Schema theory and ESL reading pedagogy. *TESOL Quarterly, 17*, 553–73.

Carrera, J. W. (1989). *Immigrant students: Their legal right of access to public schools.* Boston: National Coalition of Advocates for Students.

Carrillo Hocker, B. (1993). Folk art in the classroom. In B. J. Merino, H. T. Trueba, & F. A. Samaniego (Eds.), *Language and culture in learning: Teaching Spanish to native speakers of Spanish* (pp. 153–59). Bristol, PA: Falmer Press.

Carroll, J. B. (1961). Fundamental considerations in testing for English proficiency of foreign students. In *Testing the English proficiency of foreign students.* Washington, DC: Center for Applied Linguistics.

Carson, J. G., & Leki, I. (Eds.). (1993). *Reading in the composition classroom: Second language perspectives.* Boston, MA: Heinle & Heinle.

Carter, D. J., & Wilson, R. (1994). *Minorities in higher education: Twelfth annual status report.* Washington, DC: American Council on Education.

Castañeda v. Pickard, 648 F.2d 989 (5th Cir. 1981).

Castro Feinberg, R. (1990). Bilingual education in the United States: A summary of *Lau* compliance requirements. *Language, Culture and Curriculum, 3*(2), 141–52.

Cazden, C. B. (1988). *Classroom discourse: The language of teaching and learning.* Portsmouth, NH: Heinemann.

Cazden, C. B. (1992). *Whole language plus: Essays on literacy in the United States and New Zealand.* New York: Teachers College Press.

Cazden, C. B., John, V. P., & Hymes, P. (Eds.). (1972). *Functions of language in the classroom.* New York: Teachers College Press.

Cazden, C. B., & Leggett, E. L. (1981). Culturally responsive education: Recommendations for achieving Lau Remedies II. In H. T. Trueba, G. P. Guthrie, K. H. Au (Eds.), *Culture and the bilingual classroom* (pp. 69–86). New York: Newbury House.

Cazden, C. B., & Snow, C. E. (1990). Preface to C. B. Cazden and C. E. Snow (Eds.) *English*

Plus: Issues in Bilingual Education. (The Annals of the American Academy of Political and Social Science, Vol. 508). London: Sage.

Celce-Murcía, M. (Ed.). (1991). *Teaching English as a second or foreign language* (2nd ed.). Boston: Heinle & Heinle.

Center for Applied Linguistics. (1990). *Communicative math and science teaching.* (Videotape). Washington, DC: Author.

Chambers, J., & Parrish, T. (1992). *Meeting the challenge of diversity: An evaluation of programs for pupils with limited proficiency in English: Vol. 4. Cost of programs and services for LEP students.* Berkeley, CA: BW Associates.

Chamot, A. U., Dale, M., O'Malley, J. M., & Spanos, G. A. (1992). Learning and problem solving strategies of ESL students. *Bilingual Research Journal, 16*(3–4), 1–34.

Chamot, A. U., & O'Malley, J. M. (1986). *A Cognitive Academic Language Learning Approach: An ESL content-based curriculum.* Washington, DC: National Clearinghouse for Bilingual Education.

Chamot, A. U., & O'Malley, J. M. (1987). The Cognitive Academic Language Learning Approach: A bridge to the mainstream. *TESOL Quarterly, 21*, 227–49.

Chamot, A. U. & O'Malley, J. M. (1988). *Language development through content: Mathematics Book A.* Reading, MA: Addison-Wesley.

Chamot, A. U., & O'Malley, J. M. (1994). *The CALLA handbook: Implementing the Cognitive Academic Language Learning Approach.* Reading, MA: Addison-Wesley.

Chapman, L., & Chapman, J. (1993, September). Interview. *ASCD Curriculum Update,* p. 7.

Chastain, K. (1988). *Developing second-language skills: Theory and practice* (3rd ed.). San Diego: Harcourt Brace Jovanovich.

Chaudron, C. (1988). *Second language classrooms: Research on teaching and learning.* Cambridge: Cambridge University Press.

Chiang, R. A. (1994). Recognizing strengths and needs of all bilingual learners: A bilingual/multicultural perspective. *NABE News, 17*(4), 11, 22–23.

Chomsky, N. (1957). *Syntactic structures.* The Hague: Mouton.

Chomsky, N. (1965). *Aspects of the theory of syntax.* Cambridge, MA: MIT Press.

Christian, D. (1994). *Two-way bilingual education: Students learning through two languages.* Washington, DC: Center for Applied Linguistics.

Christian, D., & Whitcher, A. (1995). *Directory of two-way bilingual programs in the United States* (Rev ed.). Washington, DC: Center for Applied Linguistics.

Christison, M. A., & Bassano, S. (1992) *Earth and physical science: Content and learning strategies.* Reading, MA: Addison-Wesley.

Chu, H. S. (1981). *Testing instruments for reading skills: English and Korean (Grades 1–3).* Fairfax, VA: Center for Bilingual/Multicultural/ESL Education, George Mason University.

Cintrón v. Brentwood Union Free School District Board of Education, 455 F. Supp. 57 (E.D.N.Y. 1978).

Clair, N. (1994). Informed choices: Articulating assumptions behind programs for language minority students. *ERIC Clearinghouse on Languages and Linguistics News Bulletin, 18*(1), 1, 5–8.

Clark, M., Kaufman, S., & Pierce, R. C. (1976). Explorations of acculturation: Toward a model of ethnic identity. *Human Organization, 35,* 231–38.

Clark, R. M. (1983). *Family life and school achievement: Why poor black children succeed or fail.* Chicago: University of Chicago Press.

Cloud, N., Genesee, F., & Hamayan, E. (2000). *Dual language education: A handbook for enriched education.* Boston, MA: Heinle & Heinle.

Cocking, R. R., & Chipman, S. (1983). *Conceptual issues related to mathematics achievement of language minority children.* Washington, DC: National Institute of Education.

Cocking, R. R., & Mestre, J. P. (Eds.) (1988). *Linguistic and cultural influences on learning mathematics.* Hillsdale, NJ: Lawrence Erlbaum.

Coelho, E. (1982). Language across the curriculum. *TESL Talk, 13,* 56–70.

Coelho, E. (1992). Jigsaw: Integrating language and content. In C. Kessler (Ed.), *Cooperative language learning* (pp. 129–52). Englewood Cliffs, NJ: Prentice Hall Regents.

Coelho, E. (1994). Social integration of immigrant and refugee children. In F. Genesee (Ed.), *Educating second language children: The whole child, the whole curriculum, the whole community* (pp. 301–27). Cambridge: Cambridge University Press.

Cohen, A. D. (1975). Assessing language maintenance in Spanish speaking communities in the southwest. In E. Hernández-Chávez, A. D. Cohen, & A. F. Beltramo (Eds.), *El lenguaje de los chicanos* (pp. 202–15). Washington, DC: Center for Applied Linguistics.

Cohen, A. D. (1976). The case for partial or total immersion education. In A. Simoes, Jr. (Ed.), *The bilingual child* (pp. 65–89). New York: Academic Press.

Cohen, A. D. (1980). *Describing bilingual education classrooms: The role of the teacher in evaluation.* Washington, DC: National Clearinghouse for Bilingual Education.

Cohen, A. D. (1983). Researching bilingualism in the classroom. In A. W. Miracle. Jr.(Ed.), *Bilingualism: Social issues and policy implications* (pp. 133–48). Athens, GA: University of Georgia Press.

Cohen, A. D. (1994). *Assessing language ability in the classroom* (2nd ed.). Boston, MA: Heinle & Heinle.

Education Week. January 11, 2001. Quality counts 2001. A better balance: Standards, tests, and the tools to succeed. Vol. XX, No. 17.

Cohen, K. J. (1993, July 24). Roth hits bilingual education. *Milwaukee Sentinel.*

Cole, M. (1992). Context, modularity, and the cultural constitution of development. In L. T. Winegar & J. Valsiner (Eds.), *Children's development within social context* (Vol. 2, pp. 5–32). Hillsdale, NJ: Lawrence Erlbaum.

Cole, M., & Scribner, S. (1974). *Culture and thought: A psychological introduction.* New York: Wiley.

Coleman, J., Campbell, J. E., Hobson, C., McPartland, J., Mood, A., & York, R. (1966). *Equality of educational opportunity.* Washington, DC: U.S. Government Printing Office.

Collier, V. P. (1980). A sociological case study of bilingual education and its effects on the schools and the community (Doctoral dissertation, University of Southern California).

Dissertation Abstracts International, 41, 2481A.

Collier, V. P. (1981). A sociological case study of bilingual education and its effects on the schools and the community. In *Outstanding dissertations in bilingual education: Recognized by the National Advisory Council on Bilingual Education.* Washington, DC: National Clearinghouse for Bilingual Education. (Doctoral dissertation available from University of Southern California, 304 pp.)

Collier, V. P. (1985). University models for ESL and bilingual teacher training. In *Issues in English language development* (pp. 81–90). Washington, DC: National Clearinghouse for Bilingual Education.

Collier, V. P. (1986). Cross-cultural policy issues in minority and majority parent involvement. In *Issues of parent involvement and literacy* (pp. 73–78). Washington, DC: National Clearinghouse for Bilingual Education.

Collier, V. P. (1987). Age and rate of acquisition of second language for academic purposes. *TESOL Quarterly, 21,* 617–41.

Collier, V. P. (1988). *The effect of age on acquisition of a second language for school.* Washington, DC: National Clearinghouse for Bilingual Education.

Collier, V. P. (1989a). *Academic achievement, attitudes, and occupations among graduates of two-way bilingual classes.* Paper presented at the annual meeting of the American Educational Research Association, San Francisco, CA.

Collier, V. P. (1989b). Education: Bilingualism. In *1989 Americana Annual/Encyclopedia Year Book.* Danbury, CT: Grolier.

Collier, V. P. (1989c). How long? A synthesis of research on academic achievement in second language. *TESOL Quarterly, 23,* 509–31.

Collier, V. P. (1991). *Language minority students and higher education: Access, programs, and policies.* Trenton, NJ: New Jersey Department of Higher Education.

Collier, V. P. (1992a). The Canadian bilingual immersion debate: A synthesis of research findings. *Studies in Second Language Acquisition, 14,* 87–97.

Collier, V. P. (1992b). Reforming teacher education. In *Proceedings of the Second National Research Symposium on Limited-English-Proficient Student Issues: Focus on evaluation and measurement* (Vol. 2, pp. 417–21). Washington, DC: Office of Bilingual Education and Minority Language Affairs, U.S. Department of Education.

Collier, V. P. (1992c). A synthesis of studies examining long-term language minority student data on academic achievement. *Bilingual Research Journal, 16*(1–2), 187–212.

Collier, V. P. (1993). Review of Ofelia García (Ed.), *Bilingual education: Focusschrift in honor of Joshua A. Fishman* (Vol. 1). *Language in Society. 22,* 316–22.

Collier, V. P. (1995a). *Acquiring a second language for school.* Washington, DC: National Clearinghouse for Bilingual Education.

Collier, V. P. (1995b). *Promoting academic success for ESL students: Understanding second language acquisition for school.* Elizabeth, NJ: New Jersey Teachers of English to Speakers of Other Languages–Bilingual Educators.

Collier, V. P. (1995c). Second language acquisition for school: Academic, cognitive, sociocultural, and linguistic processes. In J. E. Alatis et al. (Eds.), *Georgetown University Round Table on Languages and Linguistics 1995* (pp. 311–27). Washington, DC: Georgetown University Press.

Collier, V. P., & Thomas, W. P. (1988, April). *Acquisition of cognitive-academic second language proficiency: A six-year study.* Paper presented at the annual meeting of the American Educational Research Association, New Orleans, LA.

Collier, V. P., & Thomas, W. P. (1989). How quickly can immigrants become proficient in school English? *Journal of Educational Issues of Language Minority Students, 5,* 26–38.

Collier, V. P., & Thomas, W. P. (1998). Assessment & Evaluation. In C. J. Ovando, & V. P. Collier (Eds.), *Bilingual and ESL Classrooms: Teaching in Multicultural Contexts* (pp. 240–68). Boston: McGraw-Hill.

Collins, A., Brown, J. S., & Newman, S. E. (1989). Cognitive apprenticeship: Teaching the craft of reading, writing, and mathematics. In L. B.

Resnick (Ed.), *Knowing, learning, and instruction: Essays in honor of Robert Glaser.* (pp. 453–94). Hillsdale, NJ: Lawrence Erlbaum.

Condon, J. C., & Yousef, F. S. (1975). *An introduction to intercultural communication.* Indianapolis: Bobbs-Merrill.

Connor, U., & Kaplan, R. B. (Eds.). (1987). *Writing across languages: Analysis of L₂ text.* Reading, MA: Addison-Wesley.

Constantino, R., Cui, L., & Faltis, C. (1995). Chinese parental involvement: Reaching new levels. *Equity & Excellence in Education* 28(2), 46–50.

Cook, B., & Urzua, C. (1993). *The literacy club: A cross-age tutoring/paired reading project.* Washington, DC: National Clearinghouse for Bilingual Education.

Cortés, C. E. (1986). The education of language minority students: A contextual interaction model. In *Beyond language: Social and cultural factors in schooling language minority students* (pp. 3–33). Sacramento, CA: California Department of Education.

Cortés, C. E. (1993). Power, passivity and pluralism: Mass media in the development of Latino culture and identity. *Latino Studies Journal, 4,* 1–22.

Covarrubias v. San Diego Unified School District (1971). No. 70394–T (SD Calif.).

Crandall, J. (Ed.). (1987). *ESL through content-area instruction: Mathematics, science, social studies.* Englewood Cliffs, NJ: Prentice Hall Regents.

Crandall, J. A. (1993). Content-centered learning in the United States. *Annual Review of Applied Linguistics, 13,* 111–26.

Crandall, J. A., Dale, T. C., Rhodes, N., & Spanos, G. (1989). *English skills for algebra.* Englewood Cliffs, NJ: Prentice Hall Regents.

Crawford, J. (1992a). *Hold your tongue: Bilingualism and the politics of "English Only."* Reading, MA: Addison-Wesley.

Crawford, J. (1992b). What's behind official English? In J. Crawford (Ed.), *Language loyalties: A source book on the Official English controversy* (pp. 171–77). Chicago: University of Chicago Press.

Crawford, J. (1997). *Best evidence: Research foundations of the Bilingual Education Act.* Washington, DC: National Clearinghouse for Bilingual Education.

Crawford, J. (1999). *Bilingual education: History, politics, theory, and practice* (4th ed.). Los Angeles, CA: Bilingual Educational Services.

Crawford, J. (2000). *At war with diversity: U.S. language policy in an age of anxiety.* Clevedon, England: Multilingual Matters.

Cremin, L. A. (1976). *Public education.* New York: Basic Books.

Cross, P. (1976). *Accent on learning.* San Francisco: Jossey Bass.

Crump, T. (1992). *The anthropology of numbers.* Cambridge: Cambridge University Press.

Cummins, J. (1976). The influence of bilingualism on cognitive growth: A synthesis of research findings and explanatory hypotheses. *Working papers on Bilingualism, 9,* 1–43.

Cummins, J. (1977). Cognitive factors associated with the attainment of intermediate levels of bilingual skills. *Modern Language Journal, 61,* 3–12.

Cummins, J. (1979a). Cognitive/academic language proficiency, linguistic interdependence, the optimal age question, and some other matters. *Working papers on Bilingualism, 19,* 197–205.

Cummins, J. (1979b). Linguistic interdependence and the educational development of bilingual children. *Review of Educational Research, 49,* 222–51.

Cummins, J. (1981a). *Bilingualism and minority-language children.* Toronto: Ontario Institute for Studies in Education Press.

Cummins, J. (1981b). The role of primary language development in promoting educational success for language minority students. In *Schooling and language minority students* (pp. 3–49). Sacramento, CA: California Department of Education.

Cummins, J. (1982). *Tests, achievement, and bilingual students.* Wheaton, MD: National Clearinghouse for Bilingual Education.

Cummins, J. (1983). Conceptual and linguistic foundations of language assessment. In S. S. Seidner (Ed.), *Issues of language assessment: Language assessment and curriculum planning.* Wheaton, MD: National Clearinghouse for Bilingual Education.

Cummins, J. (1984a). *Bilingualism and special education: Issues in assessment and pedagogy.* Clevedon, England: Multilingual Matters.

Cummins, J. (1984b). Wanted: A theoretical framework for relating language proficiency to academic achievement among bilingual students. In C. Rivera (Ed.), *Language proficiency and academic achievement* (pp. 2–19). Clevedon, England: Multilingual Matters.

Cummins, J. (1986a). Empowering minority students: A framework for intervention. *Harvard Educational Review, 56,* 18–36.

Cummins, J. (1986b). Language proficiency and academic achievement. In J. Cummins & M. Swain, *Bilingualism in education* (pp. 138–61). New York: Longman.

Cummins, J. (1989a). *Empowering minority students.* Los Angeles: California Association for Bilingual Education.

Cummins, J. (1989b). Language and affect: Bilingual students at home and at school. *Language Arts, 66,* 29–43.

Cummins, J. (1989c). The sanitized curriculum: Educational disempowerment in a nation at risk. In D. M. Johnson & D. H. Roen (Eds.), *Richness in writing: Empowering ESL students* (pp. 19–38). New York: Longman.

Cummins, J. (1989d). A theoretical framework for bilingual special education. *Exceptional Children, 56(3),* 111–19.

Cummins, J. (1991). Interdependence of first- and second-language proficiency in bilingual children. In E. Bialystok (Ed.), *Language processing in bilingual children* (pp. 70–89). Cambridge: Cambridge University Press.

Cummins, J. (1992). Bilingual education and English immersion: The Ramírez report in theoretical perspective. *Bilingual Research Journal, 16(1–2),* 91–104.

Cummins, J. (1993). Keynote address. In C. Minicucci & L. Olsen (Eds.), *Educating students from immigrant families: Meeting the challenge in secondary schools* (pp. 8–9). Santa Cruz, CA: National Center for Research on Cultural Diversity and Second Language Learning.

Cummins, J. (1995). Power and pedagogy in the education of culturally-diverse students. In J. Frederickson (Ed.), *Reclaiming our voices: Bilingual education, critical pedagogy and praxis* (pp. 139–62). Los Angeles: California Association for Bilingual Education.

Cummins, J. (1996a). Foreword. In S. Nieto, *Affirming diversity. The sociocultural context of multicultural education* (pp. xv–xvii). New York: Longman.

Cummins, J. (1996b). *Negotiating identities: Education for empowerment in a diverse society.* Los Angeles: California Association for Bilingual Education.

Cummins, J. (2000). Beyond adversarial discourse: Searching for common ground in the education of bilingual students. In C. J. Ovando & P. McLaren (Eds.), *The politics of multiculturalism and bilingual education: Students and teachers caught in the cross fire* (pp. 127–47). Boston: McGraw-Hill.

Cummins, J., & Sayers, D. (1990). Education 2001: Learning networks and educational reform. In C. J. Faltis & R. A. DeVillar (Eds.), *Language minority students and computers* (pp. 1–29). Binghamton, NY: Haworth Press.

Cummins, J., & Sayers, D. (1995). *Brave new schools: Challenging cultural illiteracy through global learning networks.* New York: St. Martin's Press.

Cummins, J., & Swain, M. (1986). *Bilingualism in education.* New York: Longman.

Curran, C. A. (1976). *Counseling-learning in second languages.* Apple River, IL: Apple River Press.

Dalton, S., & Sison, J. (1995). *Enacting instructional conversation with Spanish-speaking students in middle school mathematics.* Santa Cruz, CA: National Center for Research on Cultural Diversity and Second Language Learning.

Danoff, M. N., Coles, G. J., McLaughlin, D. H., & Reynolds, D. J. (1977–78). *Evaluation of the Impact of ESEA Title VII Spanish/English Bilingual Education Programs,* 3 vols. Palo Alto, CA: American Institutes for Research.

Dasen, P. (Ed.). (1977). *Piagetian psychology: Cross-cultural contributions.* New York: Gardner Press.

Davison, D. M., & Pearce, D. L. (1992). The influence of writing activities on the mathematics learning of American Indian students. *The*

Journal of Educational Issues of Language Minority Students, 10, 147–157.

De Avila, E. A., Duncan, S. E., & Navarrete, C. (1987). *Finding out/Descubrimiento.* Northvale, NJ: Santillana.

De George, G. P. (1988). *Assessment and placement of language minority students: Procedures for mainstreaming.* Washington, DC: National Clearinghouse for Bilingual Education.

Del'Homme, M., Kasari, C., Forness, S. R., & Bagley, R. (1996). Prereferral intervention and students at-risk for emotional or behavioral disorders. *Education and Treatment of Children, 19*(3), 272–85.

De Luca, F. P. (1976). Research in science education. *News, Notes, and Quotes: Newsletter of Phi Delta Kappan, 20*(6), 3.

de Villiers, J. G., & de Villiers, P. A. (1978). *Language acquisition.* Cambridge, MA: Harvard University Press.

Del Vecchio, A., Guerrero, M., Gustke, C., Martínez, P., Navarrete, C., Nelson, C., & Wilde, J. (1994). *Whole-school bilingual education programs: Approaches for sound assessment.* Washington, DC: National Clearinghouse for Bilingual Education.

Delgado-Gaitán, C. (1987). Parent perceptions of school: Supportive environments for children. In H. T. Trueba (Ed.), *Success or failure? Learning and the language minority student* (pp. 131–55). New York: Newbury House.

Delgado-Gaitán, C. (1990). *Literacy for empowerment: The role of parents in children's education.* Bristol, PA: Falmer Press.

Delgado-Gaitán, C. (1991). Linkages between home and school: A process of change for involving parents. *American Educational Journal, 100*(1), 20–46.

Delgado-Gaitán, C. (1993). Research and policy reconceptualizing family-school relationships. In P. Phelan & L. Davidson (Eds.), *Renegotiating cultural diversity in American schools* (pp. 139–57). New York: Teachers College Press.

Delgado-Gaitán, C. (1994). Socializing young children in Mexican-American families: An intergenerational perspective. In P. M. Greenfield

& R. R. Cocking (Eds.), *Cross-cultural roots of minority child development* (pp. 55–86). Hillsdale, NJ: Lawrence Erlbaum.

Delgado-Gaitán, C., & Trueba, H. (1991). *Crossing cultural borders: Education for immigrant families in America.* Bristol, PA: Falmer Press.

Delpit, L. (1995). *Other people's children: Cultural conflict in the classroom.* New York: The New Press.

Dentzer, E., & Wheelock, A. (1990). *Locked in/locked out: Tracking and placement practices in Boston Public Schools.* Boston: Massachusetts Advocacy Center.

DeVillar, R. A., & Faltis, C. J. (1991). *Computers and cultural diversity: Restructuring for school success.* Albany, NY: State University of New York Press.

Dewey, J. (1916). *Democracy and education.* New York: Macmillan.

Diana v. *California State Board of Education, No. C-70-37 R.F.P. (N.D. Cal., February 3, 1970).*

Díaz, R. M. (1983). Thought and two languages: The impact of bilingualism on cognitive development. In E. W. Gordon (Ed.), *Review of Research in Education,* Vol. 10 (pp. 23–54). Washington, DC: American Educational Research Association.

Díaz, R. M., & Klingler, C. (1991). Towards an explanatory model of the interaction between bilingualism and cognitive development. In E. Bialystok (Ed.), *Language processing in bilingual children* (pp. 167–92). Cambridge: Cambridge University Press.

Díaz, S., Moll, L. C., & Mehan, H. (1986). Sociocultural resources in instruction: A context-specific approach. In *Beyond language: Social and cultural factors in schooling language minority students* (pp. 187–230). Sacramento, CA: California Department of Education.

Diebold, A. R. (1961). Incipient bilingualism. *Language, 37,* 97–112.

Diebold, A. R. (1968). The consequences of early bilingualism on cognitive development and personality formation. In E. Norbeck, D. Price-Williams, & W. McCord (Eds.), *The study of personality* (pp. 218–45). New York: Holt, Rinehart & Winston.

Diller, K. C. (1978). *The language teaching controversy.* New York: Newbury House.

Dinnerstein, L., Nichols, R., & Reimers, D. M. (1979). *Natives and strangers: Ethnic groups and the building of America*. Oxford: Oxford University Press.

Dobbs, J. P. B. (1992). Music as multicultural education. In P. A. Richard-Amato & M. A. Snow (Eds.), *The multicultural classroom: Readings for content-area teachers* (pp. 364–69). New York: Longman.

Dolson, D. P. (1985). The effects of Spanish home language use on the scholastic performance of Hispanic pupils. *Journal of Multilingual Multicultural Development, 6*, 135–55.

Dolson, D. P., & Lindholm, K. J. (1995). World class education for children in California: A comparison of the two-way bilingual immersion and European school models. In T. Skutnabb-Kangas (Ed.), *Multilingualism for all*. Lisse, The Netherlands: Swets & Zeitlinger.

Dolson, D. P., & Mayer, J. (1992). Longitudinal study of three program models for language-minority students: A critical examination of reported findings. *Bilingual Research Journal, 16*(1–2), 105–57.

Donegan, C. (1996). Debate over bilingualism. *The Congressional Quarterly Researcher, 6*(3), 49–72.

D'Souza, D. (1991). *Illiberal education*. New York: Free Press.

Duis, M. (1996). Using schema theory to teach American history. *Social Education, 60*(3), 144–46.

Dulay, H., & Burt, M. (1980). The relative proficiency of limited English proficient students. In J. E. Alatis (Ed.), *Georgetown University Round Table on Languages and Linguistics 1980* (pp. 181–200). Washington, DC: Georgetown University Press.

Dulay, H., Burt, M., & Krashen, S. (1982). *Language two*. Oxford: Oxford University Press.

Duncan, J. (1987). *Technology assisted teaching techniques*. Brattleboro, VT: Pro Lingua Associates.

Duncan, S. E., & De Avila, E. A. (1979). Bilingualism and cognition: Some recent findings. *NABE Journal, 4*(1), 15–20.

Duncan, S. E., & De Avila, E. A. (1990). *Language Assessment Scales-Oral*. Monterey, CA: CTB McGraw-Hill.

Duncan, S. E., & De Avila, E. A. (1994). *Language Assessment Scales-Reading/Writing*. Monterey, CA: CTB McGraw-Hill.

Dunkel, P. (Ed.). (1991). *Computer-assisted language learning and testing*. New York: Newbury House.

Dunn, L. M. (1968). Special education for the mildly retarded: Is much of it justifiable? *Exceptional Children, 23*, 5–21.

Duran, R. P. (1989). Assessment and instruction of at-risk Hispanic students. *Exceptional Children, 56*(2), 154–58.

Dyrcia S. et al. v. Board of Education of the City of New York et al. 557 F. Supp. 1230 (EDNY, 1983).

Echevarria, J., & Graves, A. (1998). *Sheltered content instruction: Teaching English-language learners with diverse abilities*. Boston, MA: Allyn and Bacon.

Edelsky, C. (1986). *Writing in a bilingual program: Había una vez*. Norwood, NJ: Ablex.

Edelsky, C. (1990). *With literacy and justice for all: Rethinking the social in language and education*. London: The Falmer Press.

Edelsky, C. (1996). *With literacy and justice for all: Rethinking the social in language and education*. (2nd ed.). Bristol, PA: Taylor & Francis.

Edelsky, C., Altwerger, B., & Flores, B. (1991). *Whole language: What's the difference?* Portsmouth, NH: Heinemann.

Edelsky, C., Hudelson, S., Flores, B., Barkin, F., Altweger, B., & Jilbert, K. (1983). Semilingualism and language deficit. *Applied Linguistics, 4*, 1–22.

Education Week. January 11, 2001. Quality Counts 2001. A better balance: Standards, tests, and the tools to succeed. Vol. XX, No. 17.

Elam, S. M., Rose, L. C., & Gallup, A. M. (1993, October). The 25th annual Phi Delta Kappa/Gallup Poll of the public's attitudes toward the public schools. *Phi Delta Kappan*, 137–52.

Ellis, R. (1985). *Understanding second language acquisition*. Oxford: Oxford University Press.

Ellis, R. (1990). *Instructed second language acquisition*. Oxford: Blackwell.

Ellis, R. (1994). *The study of second-language acquisition*. Oxford: Oxford University Press.

Ember, C. R., & Ember, M. (1988). *Cultural anthropology* (5th ed.). Englewood Cliffs, NJ: Prentice Hall.

English for the Children. 1997. The 1998 California "English for the Children" initiative. Online document: http://www.onenation.org/facts.html.

English Language in Public Schools. 1998. Initiative statute (Proposition 227). Online document: http://Primary98.ss.ca.gov/VoterGuide/Propositions/227.htm.

English Plus Information Clearinghouse. (1992). In J. Crawford (Ed.), *Language loyalties: A source book on the Official English controversy* (pp. 151–53). Chicago: University of Chicago Press.

Enright, D. S., & McCloskey, M. L. (1988). *Integrating English: Developing English language and literacy in the multilingual classroom*. Reading, MA: Addison-Wesley.

Epstein, N. (1977). *Language, ethnicity, and the schools: Policy alternatives for bilingual-bicultural education*. Washington, DC: Institute for Educational Leadership, George Washington University.

Erickson, F. (1981). Some approaches to inquiry in school-community ethnography. In H. T. Trueba, G. P. Guthrie, & K. H. Au (Eds.), *Culture and the bilingual classroom* (pp. 17–35). New York: Newbury House.

Erickson, F. (1987). Transformation and school success: The politics and culture of educational achievement. *Anthropology and Education Quarterly, 18*(4), 335–56.

Erickson, F. (1996). Ethnographic microanalysis. In S. L. McKay & N. H. Hornberger (Eds.), *Sociolinguistics and language teaching* (pp. 283–306). Cambridge: Cambridge University Press.

Erickson, F. (1997). Culture in society and in educational practice. In J. A. Banks & C. A. M. Banks (Eds.), *Multicultural education: Issues and perspectives* (pp. 32–60). Boston: Allyn and Bacon.

Erickson, J. G., & Omark, D. R. (Eds.). (1981). *Communication assessment of the bilingual bicultural child: Issues and guidelines*. Baltimore: University Park Press.

Erickson, J. G., & Walker, C. L. (1983). Bilingual exceptional children: What are the issues. In D. R. Omark & J. G. Erickson (Eds.), *The bilingual exceptional child* (pp. 3–22). San Diego, CA: College Hill Press.

Escamilla, K., Andrade, A. M., Basurto, A., & Ruiz, O. A. (1996). *Instrumento de observación de los logros de la lecto-escritura inicial*. Portsmouth, NH: Heinemann.

Evans v. Buchanan, 416 F. Supp. 328 (D. Del. 1976).

Falgout, S. (1992). Hierarchy vs. democracy: Two strategies for the management of knowledge in Pohnpei. *Anthropology & Education Quarterly, 23*(1), 30–43.

Faltis, C. J. (1996). Learning to teach content bilingually in a middle school bilingual classroom. *Bilingual Research Journal, 20*(1), 29–44.

Faltis, C. J. (2001). *Joinfostering: Teaching and Learning in Multilingual Classrooms* (3rd ed.). Upper Saddle River, NJ: Merrill.

Faltis, C. J., & Arias, M. B. (1993). Speakers of languages other than English in the secondary school: Accomplishments and struggles. *Peabody Journal of Education, 69*(1), 6–29.

Faltis, C. J., & DeVillar, R. A. (Eds.). (1990). *Language minority students and computers*. Binghamton, NY: Haworth Press.

Faltis, C. J., & DeVillar, R. A. (1993). Effective computer uses for teaching Spanish to bilingual native speakers: A socioacademic perspective. In B. J. Merino, H. T. Trueba, & F. A. Samaniego (Eds.), *Language and culture in learning: Teaching Spanish to native speakers of Spanish* (pp. 160–70). Bristol, PA: Falmer Press.

Faltis, C. J., & Hudelson, S. (1998). *Bilingual education in elementary and secondary school communities: Toward understanding and caring*. Boston: Allyn & Bacon.

Farr, R., & Tone, B. (1994). *Portfolio and performance assessment: Helping students evaluate their progress as readers and writers*. Fort Worth, TX: Harcourt Brace.

Fathman, A. K., & Quinn, M. E. (1989). *Science for language learners*. Englewood Cliffs, NJ: Prentice Hall Regents.

Fathman, A. K., Quinn, M. E., & Kessler, C. (1992). *Teaching science to English learners,*

Grades 4–8. Washington, DC: National Clearinghouse for Bilingual Education.

Ferguson, C. A. (1959). Diglossia. *Word, 15,* 325–340.

Ferguson, C. A., & Heath, S. B. (Eds.). (1981). *Language in the USA.* Cambridge: Cambridge University Press.

Fern, V., Anstrom, K. & Silcox, B. (1995). *Active learning and the limited English proficient student.* Washington, DC: National Clearinghouse for Bilingual Education.

Fielding, L. G., & Pearson, P. D. (1994). Reading comprehension: What works. *Educational Leadership, 51 (5),* 62–68.

Figueroa, R. A. (1980). Intersection of special education and bilingual education. In J. Alatis (Ed.), *Georgetown University Round Table on Languages and Linguistics 1980* (pp. 147–61). Washington, DC: Georgetown University Presss.

Figueroa, R. A. (1991). Bilingualism and psychometrics. *Diagnostique, 17,* 70–85.

Figueroa, R. A. (1989). Psychological testing of linguistic-minority students: Knowledge gaps and regulations. *Exceptional Children, 56(2),* 145–52.

Figueroa, R. A. (1995). When minority concerns become majority imperatives: A California case study. *Educational Record, 76(2-3),* 72–78.

Figueroa, R. A., Fradd, S. H., & Correa, V. I. (1982). Bilingual special education and this special issue. *Exceptional Children, 56(2),* 174–78.

Figueroa, R. A., Sandoval, J., & Merino, B. (1984). School psychology and limited-English-proficient (LEP) children: New competencies. *Journal of School Psychology, 22,* 131–43.

Figueroa, R. A., & Sassenrath, J. M. (1989). A Longitudinal study of the predictive validity of the system of multicultural pluralistic assessment (SOMPA*). Psychology in the Schools, 26,* 5–19.

Finn, C., Ravitch, D., & Fancher, R. (1984). *Against mediocrity: The humanities in America's high schools.* New York: Holmes and Meier.

First, J. M., & Carrera, J. W. (1988). *New voices: Immigrant students in U.S. public schools.* An NCAS research and policy report. Boston: National Coalition of Advocates for Sudents.

Fishman, J. A. (1966). The implications of bilingualism for language teaching and language learning. In A. Valdman (Ed.), *Trends in language teaching.* New York: McGraw-Hill.

Fishman, J. A. (1976). *Bilingual education: An international sociological perspective.* New York: Newbury House.

Fishman, J. A. (1980). Ethnocultural dimensions in the acquisition and retention of biliteracy. *Basic Writing, 3(1),* 48–61.

Fishman, J. A. (1992). The displaced anxieties of Anglo-Americans. In J. Crawford (Ed.), *Language loyalties: A source book on the Official English controversy* (pp. 165–70). Chicago: University of Chicago Press.

Fishman, J. A., & Keller, G. D. (Eds.). (1982). Bilingual education for Hispanic students in the United States. New York: Teachers College Press.

Flanders, N. A. (1970). *Analyzing teacher behavior.* Reading, MA: Addison-Wesley.

Fleischman, H. L., Arterburn, S., & Wiens, E. M. (1995). *State certification requirements for teachers of limited-English-proficient students.* Arlington, VA: Development Associates.

Flores, J. L. B. (Ed.). (1996). *Children of la frontera: Binational efforts to serve Mexican migrant and immigrant students.* Charleston, WV: Clearinghouse on Rural Education and Small Schools.

Flores, P., & Hendricks, S. (1984, February). *Raising children whose linguistic and cultural background is different from the common school setting.* Paper presented at the Alaska Bilingual Multicultural Education Conference, Anchorage.

Fordham, S., & Ogbu, J. U. (1986). Black students' school success: Coping with the "burden of 'acting white.' " *Urban Review, 18(3),* 176–206.

Forman, E. A., Minick, N., & Stone, C. A. (Eds.). (1993). *Contexts for learning: Sociocultural dynamics in children's development.* Oxford: Oxford University Press.

Fradd, S. H., & Correa, V. I. (1989). Hispanic students at risk: Do we abdicate or advocate? *Exceptional Children, 56(2),* 105–10.

Frederickson, J. (Ed.). (1995). *Reclaiming our voices: Bilingual education, critical pedagogy and praxis.* Los Angeles: California Association for Bilingual Education.

Freeman, D. E., & Freeman, Y. S. (1991). "Doing" social studies: Whole language lessons to promote social action. *Social Education, 55*(1), 29–32, 66.

Freeman, D. E., & Freeman, Y. S. (1994). *Between worlds: Access to second language acquisition.* Portsmouth, NH: Heinemann.

Freeman, Y. S., & Freeman, D. E. (1992). *Whole language for second language learners.* Portsmouth, NH: Heinemann.

Freire, P. (1970). *Pedagogy of the oppressed.* New York: Continuum.

Freire, P. (1973). *Education for critical consciousness.* New York: Continuum.

Freire, P. (1978). *Pedagogy-in-process.* New York: Continuum.

Freire, P. (1981). The people speak their word: Learning to read and write in São Tomé and Principe. *Harvard Educational Review, 51,* 27–30.

Freire, P. (1985). *The politics of education: Culture, power and liberation.* New York: Bergin & Garvey.

Freire, P., & Macedo, D. (1987). *Literacy: Reading the word and the world.* S. Hadley, MA: Bergin & Garvey.

Fuchs, D., Fuchs, L. S., Bahr, M. W., Fernstrom, P., & Stecker, P. M. (1990). Prereferral intervention: A prescriptive approach. *Exceptional Children, 56*(6), 493–513.

Fuentes, C. (1992). *The buried mirror: Reflections on Spain and the new world.* Boston: Houghton Mifflin.

Fuss Kirkwood, T. (1990a). Global education as a change agent. In K. A. Tye (Ed.), *Global education: From thought to action* (pp. 142–56). Alexandria, VA: Association for Supervision and Curriculum Development.

Fuss Kirkwood, T. (1990b). Miami High School. In K. A. Tye (Ed.), *Global education: School-based strategies* (pp. 109–16). Orange, CA: Interdependence Press.

Gaarder, A. B. (1971, November). *Language maintenance or language shift: The prospect for Spanish in the United States.* Paper presented at the Child Language Conference, Chicago.

Gaer, S., & Ferenz, K. (1993). Telecommunications and interactive writing projects. *CAELL Journal, 4*(2), 2–5

Gagne, E.D., Yekovich, C. W., & Yekovich, F. R. (1993). *The cognitive psychology of school learning* (2nd ed.). New York: Harper Collins.

Gallas, K. (1994). *The languages of learning: How children talk, write, dance, draw, and sing their understanding of the world.* New York: Teachers College Press.

Gallimore, R., Boggs, J. W., & Jordan, C. (1974). *Culture, behavior, and education: A study of Hawaiian-Americans.* Newbury Park, CA: Sage.

Gamboa, R. (1980). Cultures, communities, courts, and educational change. In R. V. Padilla (Ed.), *Ethnoperspectives in bilingual education research, Vol. 2: Theory in bilingual education* (pp. 234–49). Ypsilanti, MI: Eastern Michigan University.

Gamoran, A. (1990). How tracking affects achievement: Research and recommendations. *National Center on Effective Secondary Schools Newsletter, 5*(1), 2–6.

Garbarino, J. (1992). Cited in Goleman, D. (1992, December 6). Conversation/James Garbarino: Attending to the children of all the world's war zones. *New York Times,* Section 4, p. E7.

García, E. E. (1991). *Education of linguistically and culturally diverse students: Effective instructional practices.* Santa Cruz, CA: National Center for Research on Cultural Diversity and Second Language Learning.

García, E. E. (1993). Language, culture, and education. In L. Darling-Hammond (Ed.), *Review of research in education* (Vol. 19, pp. 51–98). Washington, DC: American Educational Research Association.

García, E. E. (1994). *Understanding and meeting the challenge of student cultural diversity.* Boston: Houghton Mifflin.

García, E. E. (2001). *Hispanic education in the United States: Raíces y alas.* Lanham: Rowman & Littlefield Publishers, Inc.

Garcia, G. E., & Pearson, P. D. (1994). Assessment and diversity. *Review of Research in Education, 20,* 337–91.

García, G. N. (1994). *Bilingual education: A look to the year 2000.* Washington, DC: National Clearinghouse for Bilingual Education.

García, J. (1993). The changing image of ethnic groups in textbooks. *Phi Delta Kappan, 75*(1), 29–35.

García, S. B., & Ortiz, A. A. (1988). *Preventing inappropriate referrals of language minority students to special education.* Washington, DC: National Clearinghouse for Bilingual Education.

Gardner, H. (1983). *Frames of mind: The theory of multiple intelligences.* New York: Basic.

Gardner, H. (1993). *Multiple intelligences: The theory in practice.* New York: Basic.

Gass, S., & Madden, C. (Eds.). (1985). *Input in second language acquisition.* New York: Newbury House.

Gattegno, C. (1976). *The common sense of teaching foreign languages.* New York: Educational Solutions.

Gay, J., & Cole, M. (1967). *The new mathematics and an old culture.* New York: Holt, Rinehart & Winston.

Gee, J. P. (1990). *Social linguistics and literacies: Ideologies in discourse.* Bristol, PA: Falmer Press.

Geertz, C. (1973). *The interpretation of cultures.* New York: Basic Books.

Geisinger, K. F. (1992). Testing LEP students for minimum competency and high school graduation. In *Proceedings of the Second National Research Symposium on Limited English Proficient Student Issues: Focus on evaluation and measurement,* Vol. 2 (pp. 33–67). Washington, DC: Office of Bilingual Education and Minority Languages Affairs, U.S. Department of Education.

Genesee, F. (1987). *Learning through two languages.* New York: Newbury House.

Genesee, F. (Ed.). (1994). *Educating second language children: The whole child, the whole curriculum, the whole community.* Cambridge: Cambridge University Press.

Genishi, C. (1993). Assessing young children's language and literacy: Tests and their alternatives. In B. Spodek & O. N. Saracho (Eds.), *Language and literacy in early childhood education* (pp. 60–81). New York: Teachers College Press.

Gibran, K. (1951). *The prophet.* New York: Knopf.

Gibson, C. J., & Lennon, E. (1999, February). Historical census statistics on the foreign-born population of the United States: 1850–1990. Retrieved October 13, 2001 http://www.census.gov/population/www/documentation/twps0029/twps0029.html.

Gidich, D. (1990). Northeast magnet school. In K. A. Tye (Ed.), *Global education: School-based strategies* (pp. 67–73). Orange, CA: Interdependence Press.

Ginsburg, H. (1978). Poor children, African mathematics, and the problem of schooling. *Educational Research Quarterly, 2*(4), 26–44.

Ginsburg, H. (1981). Social class and racial influences on early mathematical thinking. *SRCD Monographs #193, 46*(6).

Ginsburg, H. (1986). The myth of the deprived child: New thoughts on poor children. In U. Neisser (Ed.), *The school achievement of minority children: New perspectives* (pp. 169–89). Hillsdale, NJ: Lawrence Erlbaum.

Giroux, H. A. (1988). *Teachers as intellectuals: Toward a critical pedagogy of learning.* New York: Bergin & Garvey.

Giroux, H. A. (1992). *Border crossings: Cultural workers and the politics of education.* New York: Routledge.

Giroux, H. A. (1993). *Living dangerously: Multiculturalism and the politics of difference.* New York: Peter Lang.

Giroux, H. A., & Simon, R. I. (Eds.). (1989). *Popular culture, schooling and everyday life.* New York: Bergin & Garvey.

Glasser, W. (1990). The quality school. *Phi Delta Kappan, 71*(6), 425–35.

Glassie, H. (1992). *First thoughts.* Lecture given at a conference on folklore and history-making in the classroom, Indiana University, Bloomington.

Glazer, N. (1981). Ethnicity and education: Some hard questions. *Phi Delta Kappan, 62,* 386–89.

Glazer, N. (1984). *The public interest on education.* Cambridge, MA: ABT Books.

Glazer, N. (1985). *Clamor at the gates: The new American immigration.* San Francisco, ICS Press.

Glendale Unified School District (1990). *Sheltered instruction: Bringing subjects to life for language minority students.* Glendale, CA: Author.

Glock, C. Y., Wutnow, R., Piliavin, J. A., & Spencer, M. (1975). *Adolescent prejudice.* New York: Harper & Row.

Golden, T. (1993, February 18). Mexico pulls out of fund that has roiled trade issue. *The New York Times,* p. C1.

Goldenberg, C. (1991). *Instructional conversations and their classroom application.* Santa Cruz, CA: National Center for Research on Cultural Diversity and Second Language Learning.

Goldenberg, C. (1993). The home-school connection in bilingual education. In M. B. Arias & U. Casanova (Eds.), *Bilingual education: Politics, practice, and research* (pp. 225–50). Chicago: University of Chicago Press.

Gómez v. Illinois State Board of Education, 811 F.2d 1030 (7th Cir. 1987).

González, J. M. (1975). Coming of age in bilingual/bicultural education: A historical perspective. *Inequality in education, 19,* 5–17.

González, J. M. (1994). Bilingual education: A review of policy and ideologies. In R. Rodríguez, N. J. Ramos, & J. A. Ruiz-Escalante (Eds.), *Compendium of readings in bilingual education: Issues and practices* (pp. 3–13). San Antonio, TX: Texas Association for Bilingual Education.

González, N. (1995). Educational innovation: Learning from households. *Practicing Anthropology 17(3),* 2–32.

González, N., Moll, L. C., Floyd-Tenery, M., Rivera, A., Rendón, P., Gonzales, R., & Amanti, C. (1995). Funds of knowledge for teaching in Latino households. *Urban Education 29(4),* 443–70.

González, V., Brusca-Vega, R., & Yawkey, T. (1997). *Assessment and instruction of culturally and linguistically diverse students with or at-risk of learning problems.* Needham Heights, MA: Allyn & Bacon.

González-Edfelt, N. (1993). An introduction to computer-assisted Spanish language learning. In B. J. Merino, H. T. Trueba, & F. A. Samaniego (Eds.), *Language and culture in learning: Teaching Spanish to native speakers of Spanish* (pp. 171–99). Bristol, PA: Falmer Press.

Goodlad, J. (1984). *A place called school: Prospects for the future.* New York: McGraw-Hill.

Goodluck, H. (1991). *Language acquisition.* Oxford: Blackwell.

Goodman, K. (1986). *What's whole in whole language?* Portsmouth, NH: Heinemann.

Goodman, K. S., Bird, L. B., & Goodman, Y. M. (1991). *The whole language catalog.* Santa Rosa, CA: American School Publishers.

Goodman, K. S., Bird, L. B., & Goodman, Y. M. (1992). *The whole language catalog supplement on authentic assessment.* New York: SRA Macmillan/McGraw-Hill.

Goodman, K. S., Goodman, Y. M., & Flores, B. (1979). *Reading in the bilingual classroom: Literacy and biliteracy.* Washington, DC: National Clearinghouse for Bilingual Education.

Goodman, Y. M. (Ed.). (1990). *How children construct literacy.* Newark, DE: International Reading Association.

Goodman, Y. M., & Wilde, S. (Eds.). (1992). *Literacy events in a community of young writers.* New York: Teachers College Press.

Goodwin, A. A., Hamrick, J., & Stewart, T. C. (1993). Instructional delivery via electronic mail. *TESOL Journal, 3(1),* 24–27.

Goodwin, M. H. (1990). *He-said-she-said: Talk as social organization among Black children.* Bloomington: Indiana University Press.

Goodz, N. (1994). Interactions between parents and children in bilingual families. In F. Genesee (Ed.), *Educating second language children: The whole child, the whole curriculum, the whole community* (pp. 61–81). Cambridge: Cambridge University Press.

Goor, M. B., & Schwenn, J. O. (1993). Accommodating diversity and disability with cooperative learning. *Intervention in School and Clinic, 29(1),* 6–16.

Gottlieb, J., & Alter, M. (1994). *An analysis of referrals, placement, and progress of children with disabilities who attend New York City public schools. Final report.* Unpublished final report submitted to New York State Education Department, Office of Children with Handicapping Conditions. New York: New York University, School of Education.

Gottlieb, J., & Alter, M. (1994). Special education in urban America: It's not justifiable for many. *Journal of Special Education, 27(4),* 453–65.

Gottlieb, J., & Gottlieb, B. W. (1991). Parent and teacher referrals for a psychoeducational evaluation. *Journal of Special Education, 25(2),* 155–67.

Gottlieb, J., & Weinberg, S. (1999). Comparison of students referred and not referred for special education. *Elementary School Journal, 99(3),* 187–99.

Graden, J. L. (1989). Redefining "prereferral" intervention as intervention assistance: Collaboration between general and special education. *Exceptional Children, 56(3),* 227–31.

Graff, G. (1992). *Beyond the culture wars: How teaching the conflicts can revitalize American education.* New York: Norton.

Grallert, M. (1991). Working from the inside out: A practical approach to expression. *Harvard Educational Review, 61,* 260–69.

Grant, C. A., & Gómez, M. L. (1996). *Making schooling multicultural: Campus and classroom.* Englewood Cliffs, NJ: Prentice Hall Regents.

Grant, C. A., & Sleeter, C. E. (1989). *Turning on learning: Five approaches for multicultural teaching plans for race, class, gender, and disability.* Columbus, OH: Merrill.

Gray, P. (1991, July 8). Whose America? *Time,* pp. 12–17.

Gray, T., Convery, S., & Fox, K. (1981). *Bilingual education series, No. 9: The current status of bilingual education legislation: An update.* Washington, DC: Center for Applied Linguistics.

Greene, M. (1993). *Dialogue and plurality: Education in a public space.* Lecture presented at the Annual Education Conference, Indiana University, Bloomington.

Greenwald, R., Hedges, L. V., & Laine, R. D. (1996). The effect of school resources on student achievement. *Review of Educational Research, 66(3),* 361–96.

Grosjean, F. (1982). *Life with two languages: An introduction to bilingualism.* Cambridge, MA: Harvard University Press.

Gregory, D. A., Starnes, W. T., & Blaylock, A. W. (1988). Finding and nurturing potential giftedness among black and Hispanic students. In A. A. Ortiz & B. A. Ramirez (Eds.), *Schools and the culturally diverse exceptional student:*

Promising practices and future directions. (pp. 76–85). Boston: The Council for Exceptional Children.

Grossman, H. (1984). *Educating Hispanic students: Cultural implications for instruction, classroom management, counseling, and assessment.* Springfield, IL: Charles C. Thomas.

Grossman, H. (1995). *Special education in a diverse society.* Boston: Allyn & Bacon.

Grossman, H. (1998). *Ending discrimination in special education.* Springfield, Illinois: Charles C. Thomas Publisher, LTD.

Gumperz, J. J. (1996). On teaching language in its sociocultural context. In D. I. Slobin, J. Gerhardt, A. Kyratzis, and J. Guo (Eds.), *Social interaction, social context, and language: Essays in honor of Susan Ervin-Tripp* (pp. 469–80). Mahwah, NJ: Lawrence Erlbaum Associates.

Guskin, J. T. (1981, April). *Bilingual education community study: Implementing bilingual education in an urban midwestern context.* Paper presented at the American Educational Research Association, Los Angeles.

Guthrie, G. P. (1985). *A school divided: An ethnography of bilingual education in a Chinese community.* Hillsdale, NJ: Lawrence Erlbaum.

Guthrie, L. F., & Hall, W. S. (1983). Continuity/discontinuity in the function and use of language. In E. W. Gordon (Ed.), *Review of Research in Education* (Vol. 10, pp. 55–77). Washington, DC: American Educational Research Association.

Guzmán, J. (1978). Community conflict: A case study of the implementation of a bilingual education program (Doctoral Dissertation, Oregon State University). *Dissertation Abstracts International, 39,* 1465A.

Hakuta, K. (1986). *Mirror of language: The debate on bilingualism.* New York: Basic Books.

Hakuta, K. (1987). The second-language learner in the context of the study of language acquisition. In P. Homel, M. Palij, & D. Aaronson (Eds.), *Childhood bilingualism: Aspects of linguistic, cognitive, and social development* (pp. 31–55). Hillsdale, NJ: Lawrence Erlbaum.

Hakuta, K. (1990). Language and cognition in bilingual children. In A. M. Padilla, H. H. Fairchild, & C. M. Valadez (Eds.), *Bilingual education: Issues and strategies* (pp. 47–59). Newbury Park, CA: Sage.

Hakuta, K., Butler, Y., & Witt, D. (2000). *How long does it take English learners to attain proficiency?* University of California Linguistic Minority Research Institute. Policy Report 2000–2001. Los Angeles: LMRI.

Hakuta, K., & Díaz, R. M. (1985). The relationship between degree of bilingualism and cognitive ability: A critical discussion and some new longitudinal data. In K. E. Nelson (Ed.), *Children's language,* Vol. 5 (pp. 319–44). Hillsdale, NJ: Lawrence Erlbaum.

Hall, E. T. (1959). *The silent language.* New York: Doubleday.

Hall, E. T. (1976). *Beyond culture.* New York: Anchor Press.

Hallahan, D. P., & Kauffman, J. M. (2000). *Exceptional learners: Introduction to special education, 8th ed.* Needham Heights, MA: Allyn & Bacon.

Halliday, M. A. K., & Strevens, P. (1964). *The linguistic sciences and language teaching.* London: Longmans, Green.

Hamayan, E. V. (1993). Current trends in ESL curriculum. In *English as a second language curriculum resource handbook: A practical guide for K–12 ESL programs* (pp. 16–34). Millwood, NY: Kraus International.

Hamayan, E. V., & Damico, J. S. (1991). Limiting bias in the assessment of bilingual students. Austin, TX: Pro-Ed.

Hamers, J. F., & Blanc, M. H. A. (1989). *Bilinguality and bilingualism.* Cambridge: Cambridge University Press.

Hamp-Lyons, L. (Ed.). (1991). *Assessing second language writing in academic contexts.* Norwood, NJ: Ablex.

Handlin, O. (1951). *The uprooted: The epic story of the great migration that made the American people.* Boston: Little, Brown.

Hanushek, E. (1972). *Education and race: An analysis of the educational production process.* Lexington, MA: D.C. Heath.

Harding, E., & Riley, P. (1986). *The bilingual family: A handbook for parents.* Cambridge: Cambridge University Press.

Hardisty, D., & Windeatt, S. (1989). *CALL.* Oxford: Oxford University Press.

Harley, B. (1986). *Age in second language acquisition.* Clevedon, England: Multilingual Matters.

Harley, B., Allen, P., Cummins, J., & Swain, M. (Eds.). (1990). *The development of second language proficiency.* Cambridge: Cambridge University Press.

Harmin, M. (1994). *Inspiring active learning: A handbook for teachers.* Alexandria, VA: Association for Supervision and Curriculum Development.

Harp, B. (Ed.). (1994). Assessment and evaluation for student centered learning (2nd ed.). Norwood, MA: Christopher-Gordon Publishers.

Harris, H. (1994). "Soft" and "hard" domain theory for bicultural education in indigenous groups. *Peabody Journal of Education, 69*(2), 140–53.

Harris, V. (Ed.). (1992). *Teaching multicultural literature in Grades K–8.* Norwood, MA: Christopher-Gordon.

Harris, V. (1993). Children's trade books: A guide to resources. In *English as a second language curriculum resource handbook: A practical guide for K–12 ESL programs* (pp. 155–67). Millwood, NY: Kraus International.

Harry, B. (1992). An ethnographic study of cross-cultural communication with Puerto Rican-American families in the special education system. *American Educational Research Journal, 29,* 471–94.

Harste, J., Burke, C., & Woodward, V. A. (1981). *Children, their language and world: Initial encounters with print.* Bloomington, IN: Language Education Department.

Hatano, G. (1982). Learning to add and subtract: A Japanese perspective. In T. P. Carpenter, J. M. Moser, & T. A. Romberg (Eds.), *Addition and subtraction: A cognitive perspective* (pp. 211–23). Hillsdale, NJ: Lawrence Erlbaum.

Hatch, E. (1978). *Second language acquisition.* New York: Newbury House.

Hatch, E. (1983). *Psycholinguistics: A second language perspective.* New York: Newbury House.

Haugen, E. (1969). *The Norwegian language in America: A study in bilingual behavior* (2nd ed.). Bloomington, IN: Indiana University Press.

Havighurst, R. J. (1978). Structural aspects of education and cultural pluralism. *Educational Research Quarterly, 2*(4), 5–19.

Hayakawa, S. I. (1982). Testimony on the "Bilingual Education Improvement Act." In U.S. Senate Committee on Labor and Human Resources, Subcommittee on Education, Arts and Humanities, *Hearings on S. 2002,* 97th Cong., 2d Sess. (pp. 14–28). Washington, DC: U.S. Government Printing Office.

Hayden, D., & Cuevas, G. (1990). *Pre-Algebra Lexicon.* Washington, D.C.: Center for Applied Linguistics.

Heald-Taylor, G. (1989). *Whole language strategies for ESL students.* San Diego, CA: Dormac.

Heath, S. B. (1976). A national language academy? Debate in the new nation. *International Journal of the Sociology of Language, 11,* 9–43.

Heath, S. B. (1983). *Ways with words: Language, life, and work in communities and classrooms.* Cambridge: Cambridge University Press.

Heath, S. B. (1986). Sociocultural contexts of language development. In *Beyond language: Social and cultural factors in schooling language minority students* (pp. 143–86). Sacramento, CA: California Department of Education.

Heath, S. B., & Mangiola, L. (1991). *Children of promise: Literate activity in linguistically and culturally diverse classrooms.* Washington, DC: National Education Association.

Hechinger, F. M. (1978). Political issues in education: Reflections and directions. In W. I. Israel (Ed.), *Political issues in education* (pp. 127–35). Washington, DC: Council of Chief State School Officers.

Heckman, P. E. (1996). *The courage to change: Stories from successful school reform.* Thousand Oaks, CA: Corwin Press.

Henderson, R. W., & Landesman, E. M. (1992). *Mathematics and middle school students of Mexican descent: The effects of thematically integrated instruction.* Santa Cruz, CA: National Center for Research of Cultural Diversity and Second Language Learning.

Heras, A. I. (1993). The construction of understanding in a sixth-grade bilingual classroom. *Linguistics and Education, 5*(3 & 4), 275–99.

Herman, J. L., Aschbacher, P. R., & Winters, L. (1992). *A practical guide to alternative assessment.* Alexandria, VA: Association for Supervision and Curriculum Development.

Hernández-Chávez, E. (1977). Meaningful bilingual-bicultural education: A fairytale. *NABE Journal, 1*(3), 49–54.

Hernández-Chávez, E. (1984). The inadequacy of English immersion education as an educational approach for language minority students in the United States. In *Studies on immersion education: A collection for United States educators* (pp. 144–83). Sacramento, CA: California Department of Education.

Hernández-Chávez, E., Cohen, A. D., & Beltramo, A. F. (Eds.). (1975). *El lenguaje de los chicanos.* Washington, DC: Center for Applied Linguistics.

Herrnstein, R. J., & Murray, C. (1994). *The bell curve: Intelligence and class structure in American life.* New York: The Free Press.

Hertz-Lazarowitz, R., & Calderón, M. (1994). Facilitating teachers' power through collaboration: Implementing cooperative learning in elementary schools. In S. Sharan (Ed.), *Handbook of cooperative learning methods* (pp. 300–17). New York: Praeger.

Heubert, J. P., & Hauser, R. M. (Eds.). (1999). High stakes: Testing for tracking, promotion, and graduation. Washington, D.C.: National Academy Press.

Hewett, K. A. (In press). Our culture: Your good intentions. *Primary Voices, 4*(3). National Council of Teachers of English.

Hidalgo, N. M., Siu, S. F., Bright, J. A., Swap, S. M., & Epstein, J. L. (1995). Research on families, schools, and communities: A multicultural perspective. In J. A. Banks & C. A. M. Banks (Eds.), *Handbook of research on multicultural education* (pp. 498–524). New York: Macmillan.

Hiebert, E. H. (Ed.). (1991). *Literacy for a diverse society: Perspectives, practices, and policies.* New York: Teachers College Press.

Higham, J. (1992). Crusade for Americanization. In J. Crawford (Ed.), *Language loyalties: A source book on the Official English controversy* (pp. 72–84). Chicago: University of Chicago Press.

Hill, J. E. (1972). *The educational sciences.* Bloomfield Hills, MI: Oakland Community College Press.

Hilliard, A. G. (1980). Cultural diversity and special education. *Exceptional Children, 46,* 584–88.

Hillocks, G. (1987). Synthesis of research on teaching writing. *Educational Leadership* 4(8), 71–82.

Kohn, A. (2000). *The case against standardized testing: Raising the scores, ruining the schools.* Portsmouth, N.H.: Heinemann.

Hirsch, Jr., E. D. (1991). *The dictionary of cultural literacy.* Boston: Houghton Mifflin.

Hirsch, Jr., E. D. (1987). *Cultural literacy: What every American needs to know.* Boston: Houghton Mifflin.

Holm, A., & Holm. W. (1995). Navajo language education: Retrospect and prospects. *Bilingual Research Journal, 19*(1), 141–67.

Holt, D. D. (Ed.). (1993). *Cooperative learning: A response to linguistic and cultural diversity.* McHenry, IL: Delta Systems.

Homel, P., Palij, M. & Aaronson, D. (Eds.). (1987). *Childhood bilingualism: Aspects of linguistic, cognitive, and social development.* Hillsdale, NJ: Lawrence Erlbaum.

Hooker, C. P. (1978). Issues in school desegregation litigation. In C. P. Hooker (Ed.), *The courts and education* (Part I, pp. 84–115). Chicago: University of Chicago Press.

Hopfenberg, W. S., & H. M. Levin & Associates. (1993). *The accelerated schools resource guide.* San Francisco: Jossey-Bass.

Hornberger, N. H., & Micheau, C. (1993). "Getting far enough to like it": Biliteracy in the middle school. *Peabody Journal of Education, 69*(1), 30–52.

Horne, G. (Ed.). (1988). *Thinking and rethinking U.S. history.* New York: Council on Interracial Books for Children.

Horner, C. M., Maddux, C. D., & Green, C. (1986). Minority students and special education: Is overrepresentation possible? *NASSP Bulletin,* Oct. 1986, 89–93.

Horton, J., & Calderón, J. (1992). Language struggle in a changing California community. In J. Crawford (Ed.), *Language loyalties: A source book on the official English controversy* (pp. 186–94). Chicago: The University of Chicago Press.

Huddy, L., & Sears, D. O. (1990). Qualified public support for bilingual education: Some policy implications. *Annals of the American Association for Political and Social Science, 508,* 119–34. Hudelson, S. (1989). *Write on: Children writing in ESL.* Englewood Cliffs, NJ: Prentice Hall Regents.

Hudelson, S. (1989). *Write on: Children writing in ESL.* Englewood Cliffs, NJ: Prentice Hall Regents.

Hudelson, S. (1991). Contexts for literacy development for ESL children. In C. E. Walsh (Ed.), *Literacy as praxis: Culture, language, and pedagogy* (pp. 103–14). Norwood, NJ: Ablex.

Hudelson, S. (1994). Literacy development of second language children. In F. Genesee (Ed.), *Educating second language children: The whole child, the whole curriculum, the whole community* (pp. 129–58). Cambridge: Cambridge University Press.

Hunt, N. (1993). A review of advanced technologies for L2 learning. *TESOL Journal, 3*(1), 8–9.

Hutchings, J. (1984). Producing videotapes for teaching English. *ERIC/CLL News Bulletin, 7*(2), 1, 6–7.

Hymes, D. (1979). Ethnographic monitoring. In E. J. Brière (Ed.). *Language development in a bilingual setting* (pp. 73–88). Los Angeles: National Evaluation, Dissemination, and Assessment Center, California State University, Los Angeles.

Igoa, C. (1995). *The inner world of the immigrant child.* New York: St. Martin's.

Indiana Daily Student (1993, January 26). Editorial, p. 13.

International Reading Association and National Council of Teachers of English. (1994). *Standards for the assessment of reading and writing.* Newark, DE: Authors.

Iowa Tests of Basic Skills. (1993). Chicago: Riverside Publishing.

Irvine, J. J., & York, D. E. (1995). Learning styles and culturally diverse students: A literature review. In J. A. Banks & C. A. M. Banks (Eds.), *Handbook of research on multicultural education* (pp. 484–97). New York: Macmillan.

Jackson, G., & Cosca, C. (1974). The inequality of educational opportunity in the Southwest: An observational study of ethnically mixed classrooms. *American Educational Research Journal, 10,* 219–29.

Jackson, P. W. (1968). *Life in classrooms.* New York: Holt, Rinehart & Winston.

Jacob, E. (1999). *Cooperative learning in context.* Albany, NY: State University of New York Press.

Jacob, E., & Jordan, C. (Eds.). (1993). *Minority education: Anthropological perspectives.* Norwood, NJ: Ablex.

Jacob, E., Rottenberg, L., Patrick, S., & Wheeler, E. (1996). Cooperative learning: Context and opportunities for acquiring academic English. *TESOL Quarterly, 30,* 253–80.

Jacobson, R. (1979). Can bilingual teaching techniques reflect bilingual community behaviors? In R. V. Padilla (Ed.), *Ethnoperspectives in bilingual education research, Vol. 1: Bilingual education and public policy in the United States* (pp. 483–97). Ypsilanti, MI: Eastern Michigan University.

Jacobson, R. (1981). The implementation of a bilingual instruction model: The new concurrent approach. In R. V. Padilla (Ed.), *Ethnoperspectives in bilingual education research, Vol. 3: Bilingual Education Technology* (pp. 14–29). Ypsilanti, MI: Eastern Michigan University.

Jacobson, R., & Faltis, C. (Eds.). (1990). *Language distribution issues in bilingual schooling.* Clevedon, England: Multilingual Matters.

Jaramillo, J. A. (1995). The passive legitimization of Spanish. A macrosociolinguistic study of a quasiborder: Tucson, Arizona. *International Journal of the Sociology of Language 114,* 67–91.

Jencks, C., Smith, M., Acland, H., Bane, M. J., Cohen, D., Gintis, H., Heyns, B., & Michelson, S. (1972). *Inequality: A reassessment of the effect of family and schooling in America.* New York: Basic Books.

Jensen, A. (1969). How much can we boost IQ and scholastic achievement? *Harvard Educational Review, 39,* 1–123.

Jiménez, M. (1992). The educational rights of language-minority children. In J. Crawford (Ed.), *Language loyalties: A source book on the official English controversy* (pp. 243–51). Chicago: University of Chicago Press.

Jitendra, A. K., & Rohena-Diaz, E. (1996). Language assessment of students who are lin-guistically diverse: Why a discrete approach is not the answer. *School Psychology Review, 25(1),* 40–56.

Johnson, D. M., & Roen, D. H. (Eds.). (1989). *Richness in writing: Empowering ESL students.* New York: Longman.

Johnson, D. W., Johnson, R. T., & Holubec, E. J. (1986). *Circles of learning* (revised ed.). Edina, MN: Interaction.

Johnson, D. W., Johnson, R. T., & Smith, K. A. (1991). *Active learning: Cooperation in the college classroom.* Edina, MN: Interaction.

Johnson, P. (1981). Effects on reading comprehension of language complexity and cultural background of a text. *TESOL Quarterly, 15,* 169–81.

Johnson, P. (1982). Effects on reading comprehension of building background knowledge. *TESOL Quarterly, 16,* 503–16.

Johnston, J., & Johnston, M. (1990). *Content points A, B & C: Science, mathematics and social studies activities.* Reading, MA: Addison-Wesley.

Jones, R. L. (Ed.). (1988). *Psychoeducational assessment of minority group children: A casebook.* Berkeley, CA: Cobb & Henry.

Jordan, C. (1977, November). *A multidisciplinary approach to research in education: The Kamehameha Early Education Program* (Technical Report No. 81). Symposium delivered at the American Anthropological Association, Houston.

Jordan, C. (1984). Cultural compatibility and the education of Hawaiian children: Implications for mainland educators. *Educational Research Quarterly, 8(4),* 59–71.

Jose P. v. Amback, 557 F. Supp. 1230 (EDNY, 1983).

Jost, K. (1995, February 3). Cracking down on immigration. *Congressional Quarterly 5(5), Researcher,* pp. 99–115.

Kaestle, C. F. (1983). *Pillars of the republic: Common schools and American society, 1780–1860.* New York: Hill and Wang.

Kagan, S. (1986). Cooperative learning and socio-cultural factors in schooling. In *Beyond language: Social and cultural factors in schooling language minority students* (pp. 231–98). Sacramento, CA: California Department of Education.

Kagan, S. (1992). *Cooperative learning.* San Juan Capistrano, CA: Kagan Cooperative Learning.

Kagan, S. (1993). The structural approach to cooperative learning. In D. D. Holt (Ed.), *Cooperative learning: A response to linguistic and cultural diversity* (pp. 9–17). McHenry, IL: Delta Systems.

Kagan, S., & McGroarty, M. (1993). Principles of cooperative learning for language and content gains. In D. D. Holt (Ed.), *Cooperative learning: A response to linguistic and cultural diversity* (pp. 47–66). McHenry, IL: Delta Systems.

Kane, M. B. (1970). *Minorities in textbooks: A study of their treatment in social studies texts.* Chicago: Quadrangle Books.

Kang, H. W., Kuehn, P., & Herrell, A. (1996). The Hmong literacy project: Parents working to preserve the past and ensure the future. *The Journal of Educational Issues of Language Minority Students, 16,* 17–32.

Kaplan, R. B. (1988). Contrastive rhetoric and second language learning: Notes toward a theory of contrastive rhetoric. In A. C. Purves (Ed.), *Writing across languages and cultures: Issues in contrastive rhetoric* (pp. 275–304). Newbury Park, CA: Sage.

Kessler, C. (with M. E. Quinn). (1986). Bilingual children's cognition and language in science learning. In J. J. Gallagher & G. Dawson (Eds.), *Science education and cultural environments in the Americas* (pp. 32–39). Washington, DC: National Science Teachers Association.

Kessler, C. (Ed.). (1992). *Cooperative language learning: A teacher's resource book.* Englewood Cliffs, NJ: Prentice Hall Regents.

Kessler, C., & Quinn, M. E. (1980). Positive effects of bilingualism on science problem-solving abilities. In J. Alatis (Ed.), *Georgetown University Round Table on Languages and Linguistics 1980* (pp. 295–308). Washington, DC: Georgetown University Press.

Kessler, C., & Quinn, M. E. (1987). ESL and science learning. In J. Crandall (Ed.), *ESL through content-area instruction* (pp. 55–87). Englewood Cliffs, NJ: Prentice Hall Regents.

Kessler, C., Quinn, M. E., & Fathman, A. K. (1992). Science and cooperative learning for LEP students. In C. Kessler (Ed.), *Cooperative language learning* (pp. 65–83). Englewood Cliffs, NJ: Prentice Hall Regents.

Keyes v. School District No. 1, 576 F. Supp. 1503, 1516–18 (D. Colorado 1983).

Khodabakhshi, S. C., & Lagos, D. C. (1993). Reading aloud: Children's literature in college ESL classes. *The Journal of the Imagination in Language Learning, 1,* 52–55. Jersey City, NJ: Jersey City State College.

Kim, Y. Y. (1988). *Communication and cross-cultural adaptation.* Clevedon, England: Multilingual Matters.

King, M., Fagan, B., Bratt, T., & Baer, R. (1987). ESL and social studies instruction. In J. Crandall (Ed.), *ESL through content-area instruction: Mathematics, science, social studies* (pp. 89–120). Englewood Cliffs, NJ: Prentice Hall Regents.

Kjolseth, R. (1972). Bilingual education programs in the United States: For assimilation or pluralism? In B. Spolsky (Ed.), *The language education of minority children* (pp. 94–121). New York: Newbury House.

Kleinfeld, J. S. (1979). *Eskimo school on the Andreafsky: A study of effective bicultural education.* New York: Praeger.

Kloss, H. (1977). *The American bilingual tradition.* New York: Newbury House.

Kohn, A. (1999). *The schools our children deserve: Moving beyond traditional classrooms and "tougher standards."* Boston: Houghton Mifflin Company.

Kohonen, V. (1992). Experiential language learning: Second language learning as cooperative learner education. In D. Nunan (Ed.), *Collaborative language learning and teaching* (pp. 14–39). Cambridge: Cambridge University Press.

Kolker, A., & Alvarez, L. (Producers & Directors). (1991). *The Japanese Version.* (Videotape). New York: The Center for New American Media.

Kozol, J. (1992). *Savage inequalities.* New York: Harper Perennial.

Kozol, J. (1997, February). Saving public education. *The Nation, 264*(6), 16–18.

Krashen, S. D. (1977). Some issues relating to the Monitor Model. In H. Brown, C. Yorio & R. Crymes (Eds.), *On TESOL '77* (pp. 144–58).

Alexandria, VA: Teachers of English to Speakers of Other Languages.

Krashen, S. D. (1981). *Second language acquisition and second language learning.* Oxford: Pergamon.

Krashen, S. D. (1982). *Principles and practices in second language acquisition.* Oxford: Pergamon.

Krashen, S. D. (1985). *The input hypothesis: Issues and implications.* New York: Longman.

Krashen, S. D., & Biber, D. (1988). *On course: Bilingual education's success in California.* Los Angeles: California Association for Bilingual Education.

Krashen, S. D., Scarcella, R. C., & Long, M. H. (Eds.). (1982). *Child-adult differences in second language acquisition.* New York: Newbury House.

Krashen, S. D., & Terrell, T. D. (1983). *The Natural Approach: Language acquisition in the classroom.* Oxford: Pergamon.

Krashen, D., Tse, L., & McQuillan, J. (Eds.). (1998). *Heritage language development.* Culver City, California: Language Education Associates.

Krauss, M. (1994). Extending inquiry beyond the classroom: Electronic conversations with ESL students. *CAELL Journal, 5*(1), 2–11.

Krauss, M. (1996). Status of Native American language endangerment. In G. Cantoni (Ed.), *Stabilizing indigenous languages* (pp. 16–21). Flagstaff, AZ: Northern Arizona University.

Kroeber, A. L., & Kluckhohn, C. (1963). *Culture: A critical review of concepts and definitions.* New York: Vintage Books.

LaCelle-Peterson, M. W., & Rivera, C. (1994). Is it real for all kids? A framework for equitable assessment policies for English language learners. *Harvard Educational Review, 64,* 55–75.

Lado, R. (1961). *Language testing.* London: Longmans, Green.

Ladson-Billings, G. (1994). *The dreamkeepers: Successful teachers of African American children.* San Francisco: Jossey-Bass.

Lambert, W. E. (1975). Culture and language as factors in learning and education. In A. Wolfgang (Ed.), *Education of immigrant students.* Toronto: Ontario Institute for Studies in Education.

Lambert, W. E. (1984). An overview of issues in immersion education. In *Studies on immersion education: A collection for United States educators* (pp. 8–30). Sacramento, CA: California Department of Education.

Lambert, W. E., & Klineberg, O. (1967). *Children's views of foreign peoples.* New York: Appleton-Century-Crofts.

Lamy, S. L. (1990). Global education: A conflict of images. In K. A. Tye (Ed.), *Global Education: From thought to action* (pp. 49–63). Alexandria, VA: Association for Supervision and Curriculum Development.

Lancy, D. F. (1983). *Cross-cultural studies in cognition and mathematics.* New York: Academic Press.

Langdon, H. W. (1989). Language disorder or difference? Assessing the language skills of Hispanic students. *Exceptional Children, 56(2),* 160–67.

Lareau, A. (2000). *Home advantage: Social class and parental intervention in elementary education* (2nd ed.). Lanham, Md.: Rowman & Littlefield.

Lareau, A., & Benson, C. (1984). The economics of home/school relationships: A cautionary note. *Phi Delta Kappan, 65,* 401–404.

Larsen-Freeman, D. (1985). Overview of theories of language learning and acquisition. In *Issues in English language development* (pp. 7–13). Washington, DC: National Clearinghouse for Bilingual Education.

Larsen-Freeman, D. (1986). *Techniques and principles in language teaching.* Oxford: Oxford University Press.

Larsen-Freeman, D., & Long, M. H. (1991). *An introduction to second language acquisition research.* New York: Longman.

Larson, C. L., & Ovando, C. J. (2001). *The color of bureaucracy: The politics of equity in multicultural school communities.* Belmont, CA: Wadsworth.

Lau v. Nichols, 414 U.S. 563 (1974).

LeCompte, M. D. (1981). The procrustean bed: Public schools, management systems, and minority students. In H. T. Trueba, G. P. Guthrie, & K. H. Au (Eds.), *Culture and the bilingual classroom* (pp. 178–95). New York: Newbury House.

Lee, V. W., & Patel, N. (1994). Making literacy work for immigrant families. *New Voices, 4*(1), 1–2.

Legarreta, D. (1979). The effects of program models on language acquisition by Spanish-speaking children. *TESOL Quarterly, 13,* 521–34.

Legarreta, D. (1981). Effective use of the primary language in the classroom. In *Schooling and language minority students* (pp. 83–116). Sacramento, CA: California Department of Education.

Leibowitz, A. H. (1969). English literacy: Legal sanction for discrimination. *Notre Dame Lawyer, 45,* 7–67.

Leibowitz, A. H. (1971). *Educational policy and political acceptance: The imposition of English as the language of instruction in American schools.* Washington, DC: Center for Applied Linguistics.

Leibowitz, A. H. (1980). *The Bilingual Education Act: A legislative analysis.* Washington, DC: National Clearinghouse for Bilingual Education.

Leinhardt, G. (1992). What research on learning tells us about teaching. *Educational Leadership, 49*(7), 20–25.

Leithwood, K. A. (1992). The move toward transformational leadership. *Educational Leadership, 49*(5), 8–12.

Lemlech, J. K. (1984). *Curriculum and instructional methods for the elementary school.* New York: Macmillan.

Lesh, R., Lamon, S. J., Behr, M., & Lester, F. (1992). Future directions for mathematics assessment. In R. Lesh & S. J. Lamon (Eds.), *Assessment of authentic performance in school mathematics* (pp. 379–425). Washington, DC: American Association for the Advancement of Science.

Lessow-Hurley, J. (1996). *The foundations of dual language instruction.* New York: Longman.

Levin, H. M. (1987). Accelerated schools for disadvantaged students. *Educational Leadership, 44*(6), 19–21.

Levin, H. M. (1988). Accelerating elementary education for disadvantaged students. In Council of Chief State School Officers, *School success for students at risk* (pp. 209–26). Orlando, FL: Harcourt Brace Jovanovich.

Levin, H. M., & Hopfenberg, W. (1991). Don't remediate: Accelerate! *Principal, 70*(3), 11–13.

Levine, D. U., & Havighurst, R. J. (1992). *Society and education* (8th ed.). Boston: Allyn and Bacon.

Levine, L. (1988). *Highbrow/lowbrow: The emergence of cultural hierarchy in America.* Cambridge, MA: Harvard University Press.

Lindholm, K. J. (1990). Bilingual immersion education: Criteria for program development. In A. M. Padilla, H. H. Fairchild, & C. M. Valadez (Eds.), *Bilingual education: Issues and strategies* (pp. 91–105). Newbury Park, CA: Sage.

Lindholm, K. J. (1991). Theoretical assumptions and empirical evidence for academic achievement in two languages. *Hispanic Journal of Behavioral Sciences, 13,* 3–17.

Lindholm, K. J., & Aclan, Z. (1991). Bilingual proficiency as a bridge to academic achievement: Results from bilingual/immersion programs. *Journal of Education, 173,* 99–113.

Lindholm, K. J., & Molina, R. (in press). Learning in dual language education classrooms in the U.S.: Implementation and evaluation outcomes. In *Proceedings of the 3rd European Conference on Immersion Programmes.*

Lindholm-Leary, K. (2001). Dual language education. Clevedon, England: Multilingual Matters.

Lindholm, K. J., & Molina, R. (2000). Two-way bilingual education: The power of two languages in promoting educational success. In J. V. Tinajero & R. A. DeVillar (eds.), *The power of two languages 2000: Effective dual-language use across the curriculum.* New York: McGraw Hill, pp. 163–74 .

Lindholm, K. J., & Molina, R. (1998). Learning in dual language education classrooms in the U.S.: Implementation and evaluation outcomes. In J. Arnau & J. M. Artigal (Eds.), *Immersion programmes: a European perspective.* Barcelona, Spain: Universitat de Barcelona.

Lindquist, T. (1995). *Seeing the whole through social studies.* Portsmouth, NH: Heinemann.

Linse, C. T. (1993). Assessing student needs. In *English as a second language curriculum resource handbook: A practical guide for K–12 ESL programs* (pp. 35–48). Millwood, NY: Kraus International.

Lipka, J., & Ilutsik, E. (1995). Negotiated change: Yup'ik perspectives on indigenous schooling. *Bilingual Research Journal, 19*(1), 197–207.

Lockwood, A. T., & Secada, W. G. (1999). *Transforming education for Hispanic youth: Exemplary practices, programs, and schools.* New York: Teachers College Press.

Lollock, L. (2001, January). The foreign-born population of the United States: March 2000. Current population reports (P20-534). Retrieved October 13, 2001, from http://www.census.gov/prod/2000pubs/p20-534.pdf.

Lomawaima, K. T. (1995). Educating Native Americans. In J. A. Banks, & C. A. M. Banks (Eds.), *Handbook of research on multicultural education* (pp. 331–47). New York: Macmillan.

Lonergan, J. (1984). *Video in language teaching.* Cambridge: Cambridge University Press.

Long, M. H. (1990). Maturational constraints on language development. *Studies in Second Language Acquisition, 12,* 251–85.

Long, M. H., & Richards, J. C. (Eds.). (1987). *Methodology in TESOL: A book of readings.* New York: Newbury House.

Longstreet, W. S. (1978). *Aspects of ethnicity: Understanding differences in pluralistic classrooms.* New York: Teachers College Press.

Lott, S. W., Hawkins, M. S. G., & McMillan, N. (Eds.). (1993). *Global perspectives on teaching literature: Shared visions and distinctive visions.* Urbana, IL: National Council of Teachers of English.

Lovett, C. J. (1980). Bilingual education: What role for mathematics teaching? *Arithmetic Teacher, 27*(8), 14–17.

Lowe, P., Jr., & Stansfield, C. W. (Eds.). (1988). *Second language proficiency assessment.* Englewood Cliffs, NJ: Prentice Hall Regents.

Lozanov, G. (1978). *Suggestology and outlines of Suggestopedy.* New York: Gordon and Breach.

Lozanov, G., & Gateva, E. (1988). *The foreign language teacher's Suggestopedic manual.* New York: Gordon and Breach.

Lucas, T. (1993). Secondary schooling for students becoming bilingual. In M. B. Arias & U. Casanova (Eds.), *Bilingual education: Politics, practice, research* (pp. 113–43). Chicago: University of Chicago Press.

Lucas, T., Henze, R., & Donato, R. (1990). Promoting the success of Latino language-minority students: An exploratory study of six high schools. *Harvard Educational Review, 60,* 315–40.

Lucas, T., & Katz, A. (1994). Reframing the debate: The roles of native languages in English-only programs for language minority students. *TESOL Quarterly, 28,* 537–61.

Lutz, S. (1994). *Multiculturalism: An easy target.* Unpublished paper, Department of Curriculum and Instruction, Indiana University, Bloomington.

Lyons, J. J. (1990). The past and future directions of federal bilingual-education policy. In C. B. Cazden & C. E. Snow (Eds.), *The Annals of the American Academy of Political and Social Science,* Vol. 508 (pp. 66–80). Newbury Park, CA: Sage.

Lyons, J. J. (1992). *Legal responsibilities of education agencies serving national origin language minority students* (2nd ed.). Washington, DC: Mid-Atlantic Equity Center.

Macbeth, D. R. (1974). The extent to which pupils manipulate materials, and attainment of process skills in elementary school science. *Journal of Research in Science Teaching, 77,* 45–52.

Mace-Matluck, B. J. (1982). *Literacy instruction in bilingual settings: A synthesis of current research.* Los Alamitos, CA: National Center for Bilingual Research.

Macías, J. (1991). Informal education, sociocultural expression, and symbolic meaning in popular immigration music text. *Explorations in Ethnic Studies, 14*(2), 15–32.

Macías, R. F. (1994). California adopts Proposition 187: Voters pass measures prohibiting education, welfare and medical services to undocumented immigrants; challenge to constitutionality yields temporary relief. *NABE News, 18*(3), 1, 24–25.

Mackey, W. F. (1962). The description of bilingualism. *Canada Journal of Linguistics, 7,* 51–85.

Mackey, W. F., & Andersson, T. (Eds.). (1977). *Bilingualism in early childhood.* New York: Newbury House.

MacMillan, D. L., Gresham, F. M., Lopez, M. F., & Bocian, K. M. (1996). Comparison of students nominated for prereferral interventions by ethnicity and gender. *The Journal of Special Education, 30*(2), 133–51.

Macnamara, J. (1967). The bilingual's performance: A psychological overview. *Journal of Social Issues, 23,* 58–77.

MacSwan, J. (2000). The threshold hypothesis, semilingualism, and other contributions to a deficit view of linguistic minorities. *Hispanic Journal of Behavioral Sciences, 22(1),* 3–45.

MacSwan, J., & Rolstad, K. (In press). Linguistic diversity, schooling, and social class: Rethinking our conception of language proficiency in language minority education. In C. B. Paulston and G. R. Tucker (Eds.), *Essential Readings in Sociolinguistics,* Oxford: Blackwell.

Marker, G. (1994). Speculating about the future of change in social studies: Seeking answers to some basic questions. In M. R. Nelson (Ed.), *The future of the social studies* (pp. 81–88). Boulder, CO: Social Science Education Consortium.

Martin-Jones, M., & Romaine, S. (1986). Semilingualism: A half-baked theory of communicative competence. *Applied Linguistics* 7, 26–38.

Martínez, P. E. (1981, May). Home environment and academic achievement: There is a correlation. Paper presented at the National Association for Bilingual Education, Boston.

Marzano, R. J. (1992). *A different kind of classroom: Teaching with dimensions of learning.* Alexandria, VA: Association for Supervision and Curriculum Development.

Matthews-DeNatale, G. (1993). *Building bridges between school and community.* Columbia, SC: University of Southern Carolina, McKissick Museum.

Maxwell, M. A. (1983). Off-air and commercial video recordings in ESL classes. *ERIC/CLL News Bulletin, 7(1),* 1, 7.

McCarty, J., & Carrera, J. W. (1988). New voices: Immigrant students in U.S. public schools. In *An NCAS research and policy report* (pp. 40–55). Boston, MA.

McCarty, T. L., Wallace, S., Lynch, R. H., & Benally, A. (1991). Classroom inquiry and Navajo learning styles: A call for reassessment. *Anthropology and Education Quarterly, 22,* 42–59.

McCollum, H., & Russo, A. W. W. (1993). *Model strategies in bilingual education: Family literacy and parent involvement.* Washington, DC: U.S. Department of Education.

McCormick, E. (2000, September 3). Asians will soon be biggest S.F. group. *The San Francisco Examiner* A1, A12.

McFee, J., & Degge, R. (1977). *Art, culture, and environment: A catalyst for teaching.* Belmont, CA: Wadsworth.

McGroarty, M. (1989). The benefits of cooperative learning arrangements in second language instruction. *NABE Journal, 13(2),* 127–43.

McKay, S. L., & Hornberger, N. H. (Eds.). (1996). *Sociolinguistics and language teaching.* Cambridge: Cambridge University Press.

McKay, S. L., & Wong, S. C. (Eds.). (1988). *Language diversity: Problem or resource?* Boston, MA: Heinle & Heinle.

McKay, S. L., & Wong, S. C. (1996). Multiple discourses, multiple identities: Investment and agency in second-language learning among Chinese adolescent immigrant students. *Harvard Educational Review, 66,* 577–608.

McKeon, D. (1992). Introduction. In *TESOL resource packet* (p. 1). Alexandria, VA: Teachers of English to Speakers of Other Languages.

McKeon, D. (1994). When meeting "common" standards is uncommonly difficult. *Educational Leadership, 51(8),* 45–49.

McKeon, D., & Malarz, L. (1991). *School-based management: What bilingual and ESL program directors should know.* Washington, DC: National Clearinghouse for Bilingual Education.

McKnight, A., & Antinuez, B. (1999). *State survey of legislative requirements for educating limited English proficient students.* Washington, DC: National Clearinghouse for Bilingual Education (NCBE). http://www.ncbe.gwu.edu/askncbe/faqs/09certifi.htm.

McLaren, P. (1989). *Life in schools: An introduction to critical pedagogy in the foundations of education.* New York: Longman.

McLaughlin, B. (1984). *Second language acquisition in childhood: Vol. 1. Preschool children* (2nd ed.). Hillsdale, NJ: Lawrence Erlbaum.

McLaughlin, B. (1985). *Second language acquisition in childhood: Vol. 2. School-age children* (2nd ed.). Hillsdale, NJ: Lawrence Erlbaum.

McLaughlin, B. (1987). *Theories of second-language learning.* London: Arnold.

McLaughlin, B. (1992). *Myths and misconceptions about second language learning: What every teacher needs to unlearn.* Santa Cruz, CA: National Center for Research on Cultural Diversity and Second Language Learning.

McLeod, B. (1996). *School reform and student diversity: Exemplary schooling for language minority students.* Washington, DC: National Clearinghouse for Bilingual Education.

McNeil, L. M. (2000). *Contradictions of school reform: Educational costs of standardized testing.* New York, NY: Routledge.

McTighe, J., & Ferrara, S. (1998). *Assessing learning in the classroom.* Washington, DC: National Education Association.

Mead, M. (1963). Socialization and enculturation. *Current Anthropology, 4,* 184–88.

Mead, M. (1978). *Culture and commitment* (Rev ed.). New York: Anchor Press.

Mehan, H. (1989). *Understanding inequality in schools: The contribution of interpretive studies.* Paper presented at the meeting of the American Sociological Association.

Mehan, H. (1991). *Sociological foundations supporting the study of cultural diversity.* Santa Cruz, CA: National Center for Research on Cultural Diversity and Second Language Learning.

Mercado, C., & Moll, L. C. (1997). The study of funds of knowledge: Collaborative research in Latino homes. *Centro, 9*(9), 26–42.

Mercer, J. (1973). *Labeling the mentally retarded.* Berkeley: University of California Press.

Merino, B. J., Trueba, H. T., & Samaniego, F. A. (Eds.). (1993). *Language and culture in learning: Teaching Spanish to native speakers of Spanish.* Bristol, PA: Falmer Press.

Met, M. (1994). Teaching content through a second language. In F. Genesee (Ed.), *Educating second language children: The whole child, the whole curriculum, the whole community* (pp. 159–82). Cambridge: Cambridge University Press.

Mettler. S. (1983). Exercising language options: Speech into writing. *TESOL Newsletter, 17*(5), 1, 3–4.

Meyer, M. M., & Feinberg, S. E. (Eds.). (1992). *Assessing evaluation studies: The case of bilingual education strategies* (pp. 111–12). Washington, DC: National Academy Press.

Michaels, S. (1981). "Sharing time": Children's narrative styles and differential access to literacy. *Language in Society, 10,* 423–42.

Middleton, S. (1992). Equity, equality, and biculturalism in the restructuring of New Zealand schools: A life-history approach. *Harvard Educational Review, 62,* 301–22.

Mielke, A., & Flores, C. (1994). Bilingual technology equalizes opportunities in elementary classrooms. In L. M. Malavé & J. A. Parla (Eds.), *Annual Conference Journal: NABE '92–'93* (pp. 81–92). Washington, DC: National Association for Bilingual Education.

Milk, R. (1986). The issue of language separation in bilingual methodology. In E. García & B. Flores (Eds.), *Language and literacy research in bilingual education* (pp. 67–86). Tempe, AZ: Center for Bilingual Education, Arizona State University.

Milk, R. D. (1993). Bilingual education and English as a second language: The elementary school. In M. B. Arias & U. Casanova (Eds.), *Bilingual education: Politics, practice, research* (pp. 88–112). Chicago: University of Chicago Press.

Minami, M., & Ovando, C. J. (In press). Language issues in multicultural contexts. In J. A. Banks & C. A. M. Banks (Eds.), *Handbook of research on multicultural education* (2nd Ed.) New York: Longman.

Minicucci, C., & Olsen, L. (1992). *Programs for secondary limited English proficient students: A California study.* Washington, DC: National Clearinghouse for Bilingual Education.

Minicucci, C., & Olsen, L. (Eds.). (1993). *Educating students from immigrant families: Meeting the challenge in secondary schools.* Santa Cruz, CA: National Center for Research on Cultural Diversity and Second Language Learning.

Mirel, J., & Angus, D. (1994). High standards for all: The struggle for equality in the American high school curriculum, 1890–1990. *American Educator, 18*(2), p. 4–9, 40–42.

Mohan, B. A. (1986). *Language and content.* Reading, MA: Addison-Wesley.

Mohatt, G., & Erickson, F. (1981). Cultural differences in teaching styles in an Odawa school: A sociolinguistic approach. In H. T. Trueba, G. P. Guthrie, & K. H. Au (Eds.),

Culture and the bilingual classroom (pp. 105–19). New York: Newbury House.

Moll, L. C. (1981). The microethnographic study of bilingual schooling. In R. V. Padilla (Ed.), *Ethnoperspectives in bilingual education research, Vol. 3: Bilingual education technology* (pp. 430–46). Ypsilanti, Ml: Eastern Michigan University.

Moll, L. C. (1988a). Educating Latino students. *Language Arts, 64,* 315–24.

Moll, L. C. (1988b). Some key issues in teaching Latino students. *Language Arts, 65*(5), 465–72.

Moll, L. C. (1989). *Vygotsky and education.* Cambridge: Cambridge University Press.

Moll, L. C. (1992). Bilingual classroom studies and community analysis: Some recent trends. *Educational Researcher, 21*(2), 20–24.

Moll, L. C., Amanti, C., Neff, D., & González, N. (1992). Funds of knowledge for teaching: Using a qualitative approach to connect homes and classrooms. *Theory into Practice, 31*(2), 132–41.

Moll, L. C., & Díaz, S. (1993). Change as the goal of educational research. In E. Jacob & C. Jordan (Eds.), *Minority education: Anthropological perspectives* (pp. 67–79). Norwood, NJ: Ablex.

Moll, L. C., & González, N. (1997). Teachers as social scientists: Learning about culture from household research. In P. M. Hall (Ed.), *Race, ethnicity and multiculturalism,* Vol. 1 (pp. 89–114). New York: Garland.

Moll, L. C., Vélez-Ibáñez, C., Greenberg, J., & Rivera, C. (1990). *Community knowledge and classroom practice: Combining resources for literacy instruction.* Arlington, VA: Development Associates.

Monroe, R. (1993). *Writing and thinking with computers: A practical and progressive approach.* Urbana, IL: National Council of Teachers of English.

Moran, C., & Hakuta, K. (1995). Bilingual education: Broadening research perspectives. In J. A. Banks & C. A. M. Banks (Eds.), *Handbook of research on multicultural education* (pp. 445–62). New York: Macmillan.

Morgan v. Kerrigan, 401 F. Supp. 216 (D. Mass. 1975), *aff'd,* 523 F.2d 917 (1st Cir. 1976).

Morine-Dershimer, G. (1983). Instructional strategy and the "creation" of classroom status. *American Educational Research Journal, 20,* 645–62.

Morris, C. C. (1997). *A study of labeling narratives for self and cultural voice.* Doctoral dissertation, George Mason University, Fairfax, VA.

Moses, R.P. (2001). *Radical equations: Math literacy and civil rights.* Boston: Beacon Press.

Mulhern, M., Rodriguez-Brown, F. V., & Shanahan, T. (1994). *Family literacy for language minority families: Issues for program implementation.* Washington, DC: National Clearinghouse for Bilingual Education.

Mullis, I. V. S., Dossey, J. A., Owen, E. H., & Phillips, G. W. (1993). *Executive summary of the NAEP 1992 mathematics report card for the nation and the states.* Washington, DC: Office of Educational Research and Improvement.

NAEP trends show turnaround in students' achievement. (1994, August 18). *Education Daily,* pp. 1–3, 5–6.

National Advisory Council for Bilingual Education. (1978–79). *The fourth annual report.* Rosslyn, VA: InterAmerica Research Associates.

National Association for Bilingual Education. (1992). *Professional standards for the preparation of bilingual/multicultural teachers.* Washington, DC: Author.

National Center for Education Statistics. (1993). *Language characteristics and schooling in the United States, a challenging picture: 1979 and 1989.* Washington, DC: U.S. Government Printing Office.

National Coalition of Advocates for Students. (1988). *New voices: Immigrant students in U.S. public schools.* Boston: Author.

National Coalition of Advocates for Students. (1991). *The good common school: Making the vision work for all children.* Boston, MA: Author.

National Council for Accreditation of Teacher Education. (2002). *Professional Standards for the Accreditation of Schools, Colleges, and Departments of Education.* NCATE: Washington, DC. 2002.

National Council for the Social Studies. (1993). A vision of powerful teaching and learning in the social studies: Building social understanding and civic efficacy. *Social Education, 57*(5), 213–23.

National Council for the Social Studies. (1997). *A sampler of curriculum standards for social studies: Expectations of excellence.* Excerpted from the original by Walter C. Parker and John Jarolimek. Upper Saddle River, NJ: Prentice-Hall.

National Council of Teachers of Mathematics. (1989). *Curriculum and evaluation standards for school mathematics.* Reston, VA: Author.

National Council of Teachers of Mathematics. (1991). *Professional standards for teaching mathematics.* Reston, VA: Author.

National Council of Teachers of Mathematics (NCTM). (2000). *Principles and Standards for School Mathematics.* Reston, VA: Author.

National Council for Accreditation of Teacher Education. (2002). *Professional Standards for the Accreditation of Schools, Colleges, and Departments of Education.* NCATE: Washington, DC. 2002.

National Science Foundation. (1980). *Science education data book.* Washington, DC: Author.

National Science Teachers Association. (1993). *Science for all cultures: A collection of articles from NSTA's journals.* Arlington, VA: Author.

National Science Teachers Association. (1995). *A high school framework for national science education standards: Scope, sequence, and coordination of secondary school science* (Vol.III). Arlington, VA: Author.

Navarette, Y. (1996). Family involvement in a bilingual school. *The Journal of Educational Issues of Language Minority Students, 16,* 77–84.

Nelson, J. R., Smith, D. J., Taylor, L., Dodd, J. M., & Reavis, K. (1991). Prereferral intervention: A review of the research. *Education and Treatment of Children, 14*(3), 243–53.

Neu, J., & Scarcella, R. (1991). Word processing in the ESL writing classroom: A survey of student attitudes. In P. Dunkel (Ed.), *Computer-assisted language learning and testing: Research issues and practice* (pp. 169–87). New York: Newbury House.

Neuman, D. (1994). Technology and equity. *NABE News, 18*(1), 17–18, 32.

Neuman, S. B., & Koskinen, P. S. (1990). *Using captioned television to improve the reading proficiency of language minority students.* Falls Church, VA: National Captioning Institute.

Nieto, S. (1992). We have stories to tell: A case study of Puerto Ricans in children's books. In V. Harris (Ed.), *Teaching multicultural literature in Grades K–8* (pp. 171–202). Norwood, MA: Christopher-Gordon.

Nieto, S. (1994). Lessons from students on creating a chance to dream. *Harvard Educational Review, 64,* 392–426.

Nieto, S. (2000). *Affirming diversity: The sociopolitical context of multicultural education* (3rd ed.). New York: Longman.

Noden, H. R., & Vacca, R. T. (1994). *Whole language in middle and secondary classrooms.* New York: HarperCollins.

Norris, W. E. (1977). TESOL Guidelines for the Preparation of ESOL Teachers with comments. In J. F. Fanselow & R. L. Light (Eds.), *Bilingual, ESOL and foreign language teacher preparation: Models, practices, issues* (pp. 26–35). Alexandria, VA: Teachers of English to Speakers of Other Languages.

Northcutt Gonzales, L. (1994). *Sheltered instruction handbook.* San Marcos, CA: AM Graphics & Printing.

Nunan, D. (Ed.). (1992). *Collaborative language learning and teaching.* Cambridge: Cambridge University Press.

Nunes, T., Schliemann, A. D., & Carraher, D. W. (1993). *Street mathematics and school mathematics.* Cambridge: Cambridge University Press.

Oakes, J. (1985). *Keeping track: How schools structure inequality.* New Haven: Yale University Press.

Oakes, J. (1990). *Multiplying inequalities: The effects of race, social class, and tracking on opportunities to learn math and science.* Santa Monica, CA: The RAND Corporation.

Oakes, J. (1992). Can tracking research inform practice? Technical, normative, and political considerations. *Educational Researcher, 21*(4), 12–21.

Oakes, J., Wells, A. S., Yonezawa, S., & Ray, K. (1997). Equity lessons from detracking schools. In A. Hargreaves (Ed.), *Rethinking educational change with heart and mind* (pp. 43–72). Alexandria, VA: Association for Supervision and Curriculum Development.

Odlin, T. (1989). *Language transfer: Cross-linguistic influence in language learning.* Cambridge: Cambridge University Press.

Ogbu, J. U. (1974). *The next generation: An ethnography of education in an urban neighborhood.* New York: Academic Press.

Ogbu, J. U. (1978). *Minority education and caste: The American system in cross-cultural perspective.* New York: Academic Press.

Ogbu, J. U. (1986). The consequences of the American caste system. In U. Neisser (Ed.), *The School achievement of minority children: New perspectives* (pp. 19–56). Hillsdale, NJ: Lawrence Erlbaum.

Ogbu, J. U. (1987). Opportunity structure, cultural boundaries, and literacy. In J. Langer (Ed.), *Language, literacy, and culture: Issues of society and schooling.* Norwood, NJ: Ablex.

Ogbu, J. U. (1992). Understanding cultural diversity and learning. *Educational Researcher, 21*(8), 5–14, 24.

Ogbu, J. U. (1993). Variability in minority school performance: A problem in search of an explanation. In E. Jacob & C. Jordan (Eds.), *Minority education: Anthropological perspectives* (pp. 83–111). Norwood, NJ: Ablex.

Ohanian, S. (1999). *One size fits few: The folly of educational standards.* Portsmouth, NH: Heinemann.

Oller, J. W., Jr. (1979). *Language tests at school.* New York: Longman.

Oller, J. W., Jr. (1992). Language testing research: Lessons applied to LEP students and programs. In *Proceedings of the Second National Research Symposium on Limited English Proficient Student Issues: Focus on Evaluation and Measurement,* Vol. 1 (pp. 43–123). Washington, DC: Office of Bilingual Education and Minority Languages Affairs, U.S. Department of Education.

Oller, J. W., Jr. (1993). *Methods that work: Ideas for literacy and language teachers* (2nd ed.). Boston: Heinle & Heinle.

Olmedo, I. M. (1993). Junior historians: Doing oral history with ESL and bilingual students. *TESOL Journal, 2*(4), 7–10.

Olsen, L. (with M. T. Chen). (1988). *Crossing the schoolhouse border: Immigrant students and the California public schools.* San Francisco, CA: California Tomorrow.

Olsen, L. (1997). *Made in America: Immigrant students in our public schools.* New York: The New Press.

Olson, D. R. (1977). From utterance to text: The bias of language in speech and writing. *Harvard Educational Review, 47,* 257–81.

Omaggio Hadley, A. (1993). *Teaching language in context* (2nd ed.). Boston: Heinle & Heinle.

O'Malley, J. M., & Chamot, A. U. (1990). *Learning strategies in second language acquisition.* Cambridge: Cambridge University Press.

O'Malley, J. M., & Valdez Pierce, L. (1994). State assessment policies, practices, and language minority students. *Educational Assessment, 2*(3), 213–55.

O'Malley, J. M., & Valdez Pierce, L. (1996). *Authentic assessment for English language learners: Practical approaches for teachers.* White Plains, NY: Addison Wesley Longman.

Omark, D., & Erickson, J. G. (1983). *The bilingual exceptional child.* San Diego, CA: College-Hill Press.

O'Neil, J. (1993). Using technology to support 'authentic' learning. *ASCD Update, 35*(8), 1, 4–5.

Ortiz, A. A. (1992). Assessing appropriate and inappropriate referral systems for LEP special education students. In *Proceedings of the Second National Research Symposium on Limited English Proficient Student Issues: Focus on evaluation and measurement,* Vol. 1 (pp. 315–42). Washington, DC: Office of Bilingual Education and Minority Languages Affairs, U.S. Department of Education.

Ortiz, A. A. (1994). Editor's corner. *The Bilingual Special Education Perspective, 14*(1), 2.

Ortíz, A. A., & García, S. B. (1988). A Prereferral process for preventing inappropriate referrals of Hispanic students to special education. In A.A. Ortiz & B.A. Ramírez (Eds.), *Schools and the culturally diverse exceptional student: Promising practices and future directions.* (pp. 6–18). Boston: The Council for Exceptional Children.

Ortíz, A. A., & García, S. B. (1995). Serving Hispanic students with learning disabilities: Recommended policies and practices. *Urban Education, 29*(4), 471–81.

Ortíz, A. A., & Maldonado-Colón, E. (1986). Recognizing learning disabilities in bilingual children: How to lessen inappropriate referrals of language minority students to special education. *Journal of Reading, Writing, and Learning Disabilities International, 2(1),* 43–56.

Ortíz, A. A., Wilkinson, C. Y., Robertson-Courtney, P., & Bergman, A. (1990). *AIM for the BESt: Assessment and intervention model for bilingual exceptional students.* Arlington, VA: Development Associates.

Ortiz, A. A., & Yates, J. R. (1983). Incidence of exceptionality among Hispanics: Implications for manpower planning. *NABE Journal, 7(3),* 41–53.

Ortiz, A. A., & Yates, J. R. (1988). Characteristics of learning disabled, mentally retarded, and speech-language handicapped Hispanic students at initial evaluation and reevaluation. In A. A. Ortiz & B. A. Ramirez (Eds.), *Schools and the culturally diverse exceptional student: Promising practices and future directions* (pp. 51–62). Boston: The Council for Exceptional Children.

Ovando, C. J. (1978a). Female and male Latino college aspirations: Implications for pluralistic education. *Educational Research Quarterly,* 2(4), 106–22.

Ovando, C. J. (1978b). Political issues in bilingual/bicultural education. In W. I. Israel (Ed.), *Political issues in education* (pp. 101–15). Washington, DC: The Council of Chief State School Officers.

Ovando, C. J. (Ed.). (1984). Culture, language and education in Alaska, Canada, Hawaii, Guam, Puerto Rico, Australia and New Zealand: Implications for U.S. mainland educators. [Special issue]. *Educational Research Quarterly, 8(4),* 1–121.

Ovando, C. J. (1990). Politics and pedagogy: The case of bilingual education. *Harvard Educational Review, 60,* 341–56.

Ovando, C. J. (1992). Teaching science to American Indian students. In J. Reyhner (Ed.), *Teaching American Indian students* (pp. 223–40). Norman: University of Oklahoma Press.

Ovando, C. J. (1993). Language diversity and education. In J. A. Banks & C. A. Banks (Eds.), *Multicultural education: Issues and perspectives* (2nd ed.), (pp. 215–35). Boston: Allyn and Bacon.

Ovando, C. J. (1994). Change in school and community attitudes in an Athapaskan village. *Peabody Journal of Education, 69(2),* 43–59.

Ovando, C. J. (1997). Language diversity and education. In J. A. Banks & C. A. M. Banks, (Eds.), *Multicultural education: Issues and perspectives* (3rd ed.), (pp. 272–96). Boston: Allyn and Bacon.

Ovando, C. J. (1999). *Bilingual education in the United States: Historical development and current issues.* Paper presented at the annual meeting of the American Educational Research Association, Montreal, Canada.

Ovando, C. J. (2000). The case of the Asian "model minority." *Rice Paper.* Indiana University: Asian Culture Center.

Ovando, C. J., & Gourd, K. (1996). Knowledge construction, language maintenance, revitalization, and empowerment. In J. A. Banks (Ed.), *Multicultural education, Transformative knowledge and action: Historical and contemporary perspectives* (pp. 297–322). New York: Teachers College Press.

Ovando, C. J., & McCarty, L. P. (1992). *Multiculturalism in U.S. society and education: Why an irritant and a paradox?* Paper presented at the Seventh Triennial Conference of the World Council for Curriculum and Instruction, Cairo, Egypt.

Ovando, C. J., & McLaren, P. (Eds.). (2000). *The politics of multiculturalism and bilingual education: Students and teachers caught in the cross fire.* Boston: McGraw-Hill.

Ovando, C. J., & Pérez, R. (2000). The politics of bilingual immersion programs. In C. J. Ovando, & P. McLaren (Eds.), *The politics of multiculturalism and bilingual education: Students and teachers caught in the cross fire* (pp. 148–65).Boston: McGraw-Hill.

Oxford, R. L. (1990). *Language learning strategies: What every teacher should know.* New York: Newbury House.

Pacheco, R. (1983). Bilingual mentally retarded children: Language confusion or real deficits? In D. R. Omark & J. G. Erickson (Eds.), *The bilingual exceptional child* (pp. 233–53). San Diego, California, College-Hill Press.

Padilla, A. M., Fairchild, H. H., & Valadez, C. M. (Eds.). (1990). *Bilingual education: Issues and strategies.* Newbury Park, CA: Sage.

Pally, M. (1994). Lingua franca: Film and video in second language acquisition. *NABE News, 18*(3), 11–13, 17, 34.

Panfil, K. (1995). Learning from one another: A collaborative study of a two-way bilingual program by insiders with multiple perspectives. *Dissertation Abstracts International, 56–10A,* 3859. (University Microfilms No. AAI96-06004)

Parker, W., & Jarolimek, J. (1997). Social studies in elementary education. Upper Saddle River, NJ: Merrill.

Patel, N., & Kaplan, J. (1994). Literacy programs for immigrant families. *New Voices, 4*(1), 4–6.

Paulston, C. B. (1976). *Teaching English to speakers of other languages in the United States, 1975: A dipstick paper.* Alexandria, VA: Teachers of English to Speakers of Other Languages.

Paulston, C. B. (1992). *Sociolinguistic perspectives on bilingual education.* Clevedon, England: Multilingual Matters.

Peal, E., & Lambert, W. E. (1962). The relation of bilingualism to intelligence. *Psychological Monographs: General and Applied, 76,* 1–23.

Pease-Alvarez, C., & Vásquez, O. (1994). Language minority socialization in ethnic minority communities. In F. Genesee (Ed.), *Educating second language minority children: The whole child, the whole curriculum, the whole community* (pp. 82–102). Cambridge: Cambridge University Press.

Peña, A. A. (1976a). Bilingual education: The what, the why and the how? *NABE Journal, l*(1), 27–33.

Peña, A. A. (1976b). Letter from the president. *NABE Journal, 1*(1), 9–10.

Peñalosa, F. (1980). Chicano bilingualism and the world system. In R. V. Padilla (Ed.), *Ethnoperspectives in bilingual education research, Vol. 2: Theory in bilingual education* (pp. 3–17). Ypsilanti, MI: Eastern Michigan University.

Penfield, J. (1987). *The media: Catalysts for communicative language learning.* Reading, MA: Addison-Wesley.

Peng, S. S., Owings, J. A., & Fetters, W. B. (1984). *School experiences and performance of Asian American high school students.* Washington, DC: National Center for Education Statistics, U.S. Department of Education.

Pennsylvania Association of Retarded Children v. Commonwealth of Pennsylvania (PARC), 334 F. Supp. 1257 (E.D. PA, 1971).

Peregoy, S. F., & Boyle, O. F. (1997). *Reading, writing, and learning in ESL.* (2nd ed.). White Plains, NY: Longman.

Pérez, B., & Torres-Guzmán, M. E. (1996). *Learning in two worlds: An integrated Spanish/English biliteracy approach* (2nd ed.). New York: Longman.

Pérez-Bustillo, C. (1992). What happens when English Only comes to town? A case study of Lowell, Massachusetts. In J. Crawford (Ed.), *Language loyalties: A source book on the Official English controversy* (pp. 194–201). Chicago: University of Chicago Press.

Perlmann, J. (1990). Historical legacies: 1840–1920. In C. B. Cazden & C. E. Snow (Eds.), *The Annals of the American Academy of Political and Social Science: Vol. 508. English Plus: Issues in bilingual education* (pp. 27–37). Newbury Park, CA: Sage.

Perspectives on inequality. (1973). *Harvard Educational Review,* Reprint Series No. 8.

Peters, J.Y. (1979). *Neurologically and perceptually impaired bilingual students: Their identification and evaluation.* Unpublished EdD dissertation, Rutgers University, The State University of New Jersey, New Brunswick.

Peyton, J. K. (Ed.). (1990). *Students and teachers writing together: Perspectives on journal writing.* Alexandria, VA: Teachers of English to Speakers of Other Languages.

Peyton, J. K., & Mackinson-Smyth, J. (1989). Writing and talking about writing: Computer networking with elementary students. In D. M. Johnson & D. H. Roen (Eds.), *Richness in writing: Empowering ESL students* (pp. 100–19). New York: Longman.

Peyton, J. K., & Reed, L. (1990). *Dialogue journal writing with nonnative English speakers: A handbook for teachers.* Alexandria, VA: Teachers of English to Speakers of Other Languages.

Philips, S. U. (1983). *The invisible culture: Communication in classroom and community on the Warm Springs Indian Reservation.* New York: Longman.

Phinney, M. (1991). Computer-assisted writing and writing apprehension in ESL students. In

P. Dunkel (Ed.), *Computer-assisted language learning and testing* (pp. 189–204). New York: Newbury House.

Piaget, J. (1929). *The child's conception of the world*. London: Routledge & Kegan Paul.

Piaget, J. (1954). *The construction of reality in the child*. New York: Basic Books.

Piaget, J. (1966). *The origins of intelligence in children*. New York: International Universities Press. (Original work published 1954).

Piestrup, A. M. (1973). *Black dialect interferences and accommodations of reading instruction in first grade*. Washington, DC: National Institute of Mental Health. (ERIC Document Reproduction Services No. 119113.)

Pitsch, M. (1994). O.C.R. stepping up civil-rights enforcement. *Education Week, 14*(10), 15, 20.

Plyler v. Doe, 457 U.S. 202, 102 S.Ct. 2382 (1982).

Polgar, S. (1960). Biculturation of Mesquakie teenage boys. *American Anthropologist, 62*, 217–35.

Porter, A. (1989). A curriculum out of balance: The case of elementary school mathematics. *Educational Researcher, 18*(5), 9–15.

Portes, A., & Schauffler, R. (1996). Language and the second generation: Bilingualism yesterday and today. In A. Portes (Ed.), *The new second generation* (pp. 8–29). New York: Russell Sage Foundation.

Pottinger, J. S. (1970, May 25). *Memorandum to school districts with more than five percent national origin-minority group children regarding identification of discrimination and denial of services on the basis of national origin*. Washington, DC: Office for Civil Rights, Department of Health, Education and Welfare.

Powell, A. B., & Frankenstein, M. (Eds.). (1997). *Ethnomathematics: Challenging eurocentrism in mathematics education*. Albany, NY: State University of New York Press.

President's Commission for a National Agenda for the Eighties. (1980). *A national agenda for the eighties*. Washington, DC: U.S. Government Printing Office.

Pulchalska, E., & Semadeni, Z. (1987). Children's reaction to verbal arithmetic problems with missing, surplus or contradictory data. *For the Learning of Mathematics, 7*(3), 9–16.

Purves, A. C. (Ed.). (1988). *Writing across languages and cultures: Issues in contrastive rhetoric*. Newbury Park, CA: Sage.

Ramírez, J. D. (1992). Executive summary. *Bilingual Research Journal, 16*(1–2), 1–62.

Ramírez, J. D., Yuen, S. D., Ramey, D. R., & Pasta, D. J. (1991). *Final report: Longitudinal study of structured English immersion strategy, early-exit and late-exit transitional bilingual education programs for language-minority children* (Vols. I and II). San Mateo, CA: Aguirre International.

Ramírez. M., & Castañeda, A. (1974). *Cultural democracy, bicognitive development, and education*. New York: Academic Press.

Randall, N. (1996). The World Wide Web: Interface on the Internet. In *Discover the World Wide Web* (2nd ed.), (pp. 1–8). Indianapolis, IN: Sams.net.

Ravitch, D. (1985). *The schools we deserve: Reflections on the educational crises of our time*. New York: Basic Books.

Ravitch, D. (1990, Summer). Multiculturalism: E pluribus plures. *The American Scholar, 337–54.

Ravitch, D., & Asante, M. K. (1991, Spring). Multiculturalism: An exchange. *The American Scholar, 267–76.

Reppen, R. (1994/1995). A genre-based approach to content writing instruction. *TESOL Journal, 4*(2), 32–35.

Reyhner, J. (Ed.). (1986). *Teaching the Indian child: A bilingual/multicultural approach*. Billings, MT: Eastern Montana College.

Reyhner, J. (1996). Rationale and needs for stabilizing indigenous languages. In G. Cantoni (Ed.), *Stabilizing indigenous languages* (pp. 3–15). Flagstaff, AZ: Northern Arizona University.

Report of the National Commission on Teaching & America's Future. (1996). *What matters most: Teaching for America's future*. New York, NY: The National Commission on Teaching & America's Future.

Reschly, D. J. (1984). Beyond IQ test bias: The National Academy Panel's analysis of minority EMR overrepresentation. *Educational Researcher, 15–19.

Reschly, D. J. (1991). Bias in cognitive assessment: Implications for future litigation and professional practices. *Diagnostique, 17(1), 86–90.

Reynolds, A. G. (1991). The cognitive consequences of bilingualism. In A. G. Reynolds (Ed.), *Bilingualism, multiculturalism, and second language learning* (pp. 145–82). Hillsdale, NJ: Lawrence Erlbaum.

Rich, A. C. (1986). *Blood, bread, and poetry: Selected prose, 1979–1985.* New York: Norton.

Richard-Amato, P. A. (1996). *Making it happen: Interaction in the second language classroom* (2nd ed.). New York: Longman.

Richard-Amato, P. A., & Snow, M. A. (Eds.). (1992). *The multicultural classroom: Readings for content-area teachers.* New York: Longman.

Richards, J. C., & Rodgers, T. S. (1986). *Approaches and methods in language teaching.* Cambridge: Cambridge University Press.

Rigg, P., & Enright, D. S. (Eds.). (1986). *Children and ESL: Integrating perspectives.* Alexandria, VA: Teachers of English to Speakers of Other Languages.

Ringawa, M. (1980). Cultural pedagogy: The effects of teacher attitudes and needs in selected bilingual bicultural education environments. In R. V. Padilla (Ed.), *Ethnoperspectives in bilingual education research, Vol. 2: Theories in bilingual education* (pp. 347–71). Ypsilanti, MI: Eastern Michigan University.

Ríos v. Read, 73 F.R.D. 589 (E.D.N.Y. 1977), 480 F. Supp. 14 (E.D.N.Y. 1978).

Rioux, J. W., & Berla, N. (1993). *Innovations in parent and family involvement.* Princeton Junction, NJ: Eye on Education.

Rivera, C. (Ed.). (1983). *An ethnographic/sociolinguistic approach to language proficiency assessment.* Clevedon, England: Multilingual Matters.

Rivera, C. (Ed.). (1984). *Communicative competence approaches to language proficiency assessment: Research and application.* Clevedon, England: Multilingual Matters.

Rivera, C. (1990). *IARP project, purposes, and approaches.* (Final Performance Report, Innovative Approaches Research Project.) Arlington, VA: Development Associates.

Rivera, C., & Vincent, C. (In press). High school graduation testing: Policies and practices in the assessment of English Language Learners. *Educational Assessment.*

Rivera, C., & Zehler, A. (1990). *Collaboration in teaching and learning: Findings from the Innovative Approaches Research Project.* Arlington, VA: Development Associates.

Robert, S., & Lichter, L. S. (1988). Does TV shape ethnic images? *Media & Values, 43,* 5–7.

Roberts, L. (1988). *Power on! New tools for teaching and learning.* Washington, DC: U.S. Government Printing Office.

Roberts, N., Blakeslee, G., Brown, M., & Lenk, C. (1990). *Integrating telecommunications into education.* Englewood Cliffs, NJ: Prentice Hall.

Robertson, P., Kushner, M. I., Starks, J., & Drescher, C. (1994). An update of participation rates of culturally and linguistically diverse students in special education: The need for a research and policy agenda. *The Bilingual Special Education Perspective, 14*(1), 1,3–9.

Robledo Montecel, M. (1993). *Hispanic families as valued partners: An educator's guide.* San Antonio, TX: Intercultural Development Research Association.

Rodríguez, A. M. (1980). Empirically defining competencies for effective bilingual teachers: A preliminary study. In R. V. Padilla (Ed.), *Ethnoperspectives in bilingual education research, Vol. 2: Theory in bilingual education* (pp. 372–87). Ypsilanti, MI: Eastern Michigan University.

Rodríguez, R. F. (1982). *The Mexican American child in special education.* ERIC Clearinghouse on Rural Education and Small Schools. Washington, D.C.: National Institute of Education.

Romo, H. (1999). *Reaching out: Best practices for educating Mexican-origin children and youth.* Charleston, WV: Clearinghouse on Rural Education and Small Schools.

Rosebery, A. S., Warren, B., & Conant, F. R. (1992). *Appropriating scientific discourse: Findings from language minority classrooms.* Santa Cruz, CA: National Center for Research on Cultural Diversity and Second Language Learning.

Rosier, P., & Holm, W. (1980). *The Rock Point experience: A longitudinal study of a Navajo school program.* Washington, DC: Center for Applied Linguistics.

Rothman, R. (1991). Schools stress speeding up, not slowing down. *Education Week, 11*(9), 1, 14–15.

Rothman, R. (1995). *Measuring up: Standards, assessment, and school reform*. San Francisco, CA: Jossey-Bass.

Rueda, R. (1989). Defining mild disabilities with language-minority students. *Exceptional Children, 56(2)*, 121–28.

Rueda, R., & García, E. (1994). *Teachers' beliefs about reading assessment with Latino language minority students*. Santa Cruz, CA: National Center for Research on Cultural Diversity and Second Language Learning.

Rutherford, F. J., & Ahlgren, A. (1990). *Science for all Americans*. Oxford: Oxford University Press.

Salavert, R. (1991). Integrating computerized speech and whole language in the early elementary school. In C. E. Walsh (Ed.), *Literacy as praxis: Culture, language, and pedagogy* (pp. 115–29). Norwood, NJ: Ablex.

Samuda, R. J. (1975). *Psychological testing of American minorities: Issues and consequences*. New York: Dodd, Mead & Co.

Samuda, R. J. (1983). Classifying and programming ethnic minority immigrants in the public schools. In R. J. Samuda & S. L. Woods (Eds.), *Perspectives in immigrant and minority education*. (pp. 175–85). Lanham, MD: University Press of America.

Samway, K. D. (1992). *Writers' workshop and children acquiring English as a non-native language*. Washington, DC: National Clearinghouse for Bilingual Education.

Samway, K. D., & McKeon, D. (1999). *Myths and realities: Best practices for language minority students*. Portsmouth, NH: Heinemann.

Sánchez, R. (1996, March 17). California schools sound out change: Renewed emphasis on phonics could reverberate nationwide. *Washington Post*, pp. A1, A20.

Santelices, A. C. (1981, May). *Actitudes de los padres hacia la educación bilingüe en una comunidad chicana*. Paper presented at the National Association for Bilingual Education, Boston.

Santos, S. L. (1992). Mathematics instruction in bilingual education. In R. V. Padilla & A. H. Benavides (Eds.), *Critical perspectives on bilingual education research* (pp. 242–56). Tempe: AZ: Bilingual Press/Editorial Bilingüe.

Saravia-Shore, M. (1979). An ethnographic evaluation/research model for bilingual programs. In R. V. Padilla (Ed.), *Ethnoperspectives in bilingual education research, Vol. 1: Bilingual education and public policy in the United States* (pp. 328–48). Ypsilanti, Ml: Eastern Michigan University.

Saravia-Shore, M., & Arvizu, S. F. (Eds.). (1991). *Cross-cultural literacy: Ethnographies of communication in multiethnic classrooms*. New York: Garland.

Sasser, L. (1992). Teaching literature to language minority students. In P. A. Richard-Amato & M. A. Snow (Eds.), *The multicultural classroom: Readings for content-area teachers* (pp. 300–15). New York: Longman.

SAT score seesaw; math up, verbal down. (1994, August 25). *Education Daily*, p. 1.

Saunders, G. (1988). *Bilingual children: From birth to teens*. Clevedon, England: Multilingual Matters.

Saville-Troike, M. (1978). *A guide to culture in the classroom*. Washington, DC: National Clearinghouse for Bilingual Education.

Saville-Troike, M. (1980). Cross-cultural communication in the classroom. In J. Alatis (Ed.), *Georgetown University Round Table on Languages and Linguistics 1980* (pp. 348–55). Washington, DC: Georgetown University Press.

Saville-Troike, M. (1984). What *really* matters in second language learning for academic achievement? *TESOL Quarterly, 18*, 199–219.

Saville-Troike, M. (1991). *Teaching and testing for academic achievement: The role of language development*. Washington, DC: National Clearinghouse for Bilingual Education.

Saville-Troike, M., & Kleifgen, J. A. (1986). Scripts for school: Cross-cultural communication in elementary classrooms. *Text, 6(2)*, 207–21.

Saxe, G. B. (1983). *Linking language with mathematics achievement: Problems and prospects*. Washington, DC: National Institute of Education.

Saxe, G. B., & Posner, J. (1983). The development of numerical cognition: Cross-cultural perspectives. In H. P. Ginsburg (Ed.), *The development of mathematical thinking* (pp. 291–317). New York: Academic Press.

Sayers, D. (1993a). Distance team teaching and computer learning networks. *TESOL Journal, 3*(1), 19–23.

Sayers, D. (1993b). Helping students find their voice in nonfiction writing: Team teaching partnerships between distant classes. In J. V. Tinajero & A. F. Ada (Eds.), *The power of two languages: Literacy and biliteracy for Spanish-speaking students* (pp. 164–77). New York: Macmillan/McGraw-Hill.

Sayers, D. (1996). Technology and language minority students: Annotated listing of Internet resources for bilingual/ESL education: "People connection" tools. *NABE News, 19*(4), 21–22, 27–29.

Scarcella, R. C. (1990). *Teaching language minority students in the multicultural classroom.* Englewood Cliffs, NJ: Prentice Hall Regents.

Scarcella, R. C., & Oxford, R. L. (1992). *The tapestry of language learning: The individual in the communicative classroom.* Boston: Heinle & Heinle.

Schafer, L. (1982). Native cultural contexts and formal education. In R. Barnhardt (Ed.), *Cross-cultural issues in Alaskan education, Vol. 2* (pp. 93–105). Fairbanks, AK: University of Alaska.

Schiff-Myers, N. B., Djukic, J., McGovern-Lawler, J., & Perez, D. (1993). Assessment considerations in the evaluation of second-language learners: A case study. *Exceptional Children, 60(3),* 237–48.

Schindler, D. E., & Davison, D. M. (1985). Language, culture, and the mathematics learning of American Indian learners. *Journal of American Indian Education, 24*(3), 27–34.

Schlesinger, A. M., Jr. (1992). *The disuniting of America: Reflections on a multicultural society.* New York: W.W. Norton.

Schnaiberg, L. (1994a). California Board reinstates $4.9 million for bilingual education in Oakland. *Education Week, 13*(26), 6.

Schnaiberg, L. (1994b). L.E.P. students' access to services elevated to policy priority at O.C.R. *Education Week, 13*(30), 17.

Schnaiberg, L. (1995). Judge rejects Proposition 187 bans on California Services. *Education Week, 15*(13), 13.

Schnaiberg, L. (1996). Pressure builds to nix school ban for illegal immigrants. *Education Week, 15*(39), 25.

Schoenfeld, A. H. (2002). Making mathematics work for all children: Issues of standards, testing, and equity. *Educational Researcher, 31*(1), pp. 13–25.

Schorr, B. (1983, November 30). Grade-school project helps Hispanic pupils learn quickly. *The Wall Street Journal,* p. 1.

Schuman, J. M. (1992). Multicultural art projects. In P. A. Richard-Amato & M. A. Snow (Eds.), *The multicultural classroom: Readings for content-area teachers* (pp. 349–55). New York: Longman.

Schumann, J. (1978). The acculturation model for second language acquisition. In R. Gingras (Ed.), *Second language acquisition and foreign language teaching* (pp. 27–50). Washington, DC: Center for Applied Linguistics.

Schumann, J. (1980). Affective factors and the problem of age in second language acquisition. In K. Croft (Ed.), *Readings in ESL* (2nd ed.). Cambridge, MA: Winthrop.

Scott, J. (Ed.). (1993). *Science and language links: Classroom implications.* Portsmouth, NH: Heinemann.

Scovel, T. (1988). *A time to speak: A psycholinguistic inquiry into the critical period for human speech.* New York: Newbury House.

Scribner, S., & Cole, M. (1978). Literacy without schooling: Testing for intellectual effects. *Harvard Educational Review, 48,* 448–61.

Scribner, S., & Cole, M. (1981). *The psychology of literacy.* Cambridge, MA: Harvard University Press.

Secada, W. G. (1990). Research, politics, and bilingual education. In C. B. Cazden & C. E. Snow (Eds.), *The Annals of the American Academy of Political and Social Science,* Vol. 508 (pp. 81–106). Newbury Park, CA: Sage.

Secada, W. G. (1991). Degree of bilingualism and arithmetic problem solving in Hispanic first graders. *Elementary School Journal, 92*(2), 213–31.

Secada, W. G. (1992a). Evaluating mathematics education of LEP students in a time of educational change. In *Proceedings of the Second National Research Symposium on Limited*

English Proficient Student Issues: Focus on evaluation and measurement, Vol. 2 (pp. 209–56). Washington, DC: Office of Bilingual Education and Minority Languages Affairs, U.S. Department of Education.

Secada, W. G. (1992b). Race, ethnicity, social class, language, and achievement in mathematics. In D. A. Grouws (Ed.), *Handbook of research on mathematics teaching and learning* (pp. 623–60). New York: Macmillan.

Secada, W. G., & Carey, D. A. (1990). *Teaching mathematics with understanding to limited English proficient students.* New York: ERIC Clearinghouse on Urban Education.

Secada, W. G., & De La Cruz, Y. (1996). Teaching mathematics for understanding to bilingual students. In J. L. Flores (Ed.), *Children of la frontera* (pp. 285–308). Charleston, WV: ERIC Clearinghouse on Rural Education and Small Schools.

Serna v. *Portales Municipal Schools,* 351 F. Supp. 1279 (D.N.M. 1972), *aff'd,* 499 F.2d 1147 (10th Cir. 1974).

Seymour-Smith, C. (1986). *Dictionary of anthropology.* Boston, MA: G.K. Hall.

Shanker, A. (1974, November 3). Bilingual education: Not why but how. *New York Times,* p. E11.

Shannon, S. M., & Latimer, S. L. (1996). Latino parent involvement in schools: A story of struggle and resistance. *The Journal of Educational Issues of Language Minority Students, 16,* 301–19.

Sharan, S., & Sharan, Y. (1976). *Small-group teaching.* Englewood Cliffs, NJ: Educational Technology Publications.

Sharpe, M. N. (1997). *Disproportionate representation of minorities in special education: A focus group study of parent perspectives. Final report phase II: Minority parents.* St. Paul: Minnesota State Dept. of Children, Families and Learning, St. Paul. Office of Special Education.

Sharpe, M. N. (1997). *Disproportionate representation of minorities in special education: A focus group study of professional educator perspectives. Final report phase I: Professional groups.* St. Paul: Minnesota State Dept. of Children, Families and Learning, St. Paul. Office of Special Education.

Shepard, L. (1991a). Negative policies for dealing with diversity: When does assessment and diagnosis turn into sorting and segregation? In E. H. Hiebert (Ed.), *Literacy for a diverse society: Perspectives, practices, and policies* (pp. 279–98). New York: Teachers College Press.

Shepard, L. (1991b). Will national tests improve student learning? *Phi Delta Kappan, 73,* 232–38.

Shor, I., & Freire, P. (1987). *A pedagogy for liberation: Dialogues on transforming education.* New York: Bergin & Garvey.

Short, D. J. (1991). *How to integrate language and content instruction: A training manual* (2nd ed.). Washington, DC: Center for Applied Linguistics.

Short, D. J. (1993). *Integrating language and culture in middle school American history classes.* Washington, DC: Center for Applied Linguistics.

Short, D. J. (1994a). The challenge of social studies for limited English proficient students. *Social Education, 58*(1), 36–38.

Short, D. J. (1994b). Expanding middle school horizons: Integrating language, culture, and social studies. *TESOL Quarterly 28,* 581–608.

Short, D. J. (1997). Reading, 'riting and . . . social studies: Research in integrated language and content secondary classrooms. In D. Brinton & M. A. Snow, *The content-based classroom: Perspectives on integrating language and content* (pp. 213–32). Reading, MA: Addison-Wesley Longman.

Short, D. J., Mahrer, C. A., Elfin, A. M., Liten-Tejada, R. A., & Montone, C. L. (1994). *Protest and the American Revolution: An integrated language, social studies and culture unit for middle school American history.* Washington, DC: Center for Applied Linguistics.

Short, D. J., Montone, C., Frekot, S., & Elfin, A. M. (1996). *Conflicts in world cultures: An integrated language, social studies and culture unit for middle school world studies.* Washington, DC: Center for Applied Linguistics.

Siegel, F. (1991, February 18). The cult of multiculturalism. *The New Republic,* pp. 34–39.

Silcox, B. (1997). *A summary of the survey of states' limited-English-proficient students and available educational programs and services, 1994–1995.* Washington, DC: National Clearinghouse for Bilingual Education.

Sills, D. L. (Ed.). (1968). *International Encyclopedia of the Social Sciences* (Vol. 1). New York: Macmillan.

Simeone, W. E. (1982). *A history of Alaskan Athapaskans.* Anchorage, AK: Alaskan Historical Society.

Simich-Dudgeon, C. (1993). Increasing student achievement through teacher knowledge about parent involvement. In N. F. Chavkin (Ed.), *Families and schools in a pluralistic society* (pp. 189–203). Albany, NY: State University of New York Press.

Simpson, M. D. (February, 1995). Immigrant backlash puts kids at risk. *NEA Today,* p. 17.

Singleton, D., & Z. Lengyel (Eds.). (1995). *The age factor in second language acquisition.* Clevedon, England: Multilingual Matters.

Sirotnik, K. (1983). What you see is what you get—consistency, persistency, and mediocrity in classrooms. *Harvard Educational Review, 53,* 16–31.

Skutnabb-Kangas, T. (1981). *Bilingualism or not: The education of minorities.* Clevedon, England: Multilingual Matters.

Skutnabb-Kangas, T., & Cummins, J. (Eds.). (1988). *Minority education: From shame to struggle.* Clevedon, England: Multilingual Matters.

Slate, C. (1993). On reversing Navajo language shift. *Journal of Navajo Education, 10*(3), 30–35.

Slavin, R. E. (1988a). Cooperative learning and student achievement. In R. E. Slavin (Ed.), *School and classroom organization* (pp. 129–56). Hillsdale, NJ: Erlbaum.

Slavin, R. E. (1988b). *Educational psychology: Theory and practice.* Englewood Cliffs, NJ: Prentice Hall.

Slavin, R. E. (Ed.). (1988c). *School and classroom organization.* Hillsdale, NJ: Lawrence Erlbaum.

Slavin, R. E. (1989). Research on cooperative learning: An international perspective. *Scandinavian Journal of Educational Research, 33,* 231–43.

Slavin, R. E. (1990). *Cooperative learning: Theory, research, and practice.* Englewood Cliffs, NJ: Prentice Hall.

Slavin, R. E., Sharan, S., Kagan, S., Hertz-Lazarowitz, R., Webb, C., & Schmuck, R. (Eds.). (1985). *Learning to cooperate, cooperating to learn.* New York: Plenum.

Sleeter, C. E., & Grant, C. A. (1994). *Making choices for multicultural education: Five approaches to race, class, and gender* (2nd ed.). New York: Merrill.

Smallwood, B. A. (1991). *The literature connection: A read-aloud guide for multicultural classrooms.* Reading, MA: Addison-Wesley.

Smallwood, B. A. (1992). *Input or interaction: Which strategies contribute to second language acquisition in elementary literature-based classrooms?* Unpublished manuscript, Center for Bilingual-Multicultural/ESL Education, George Mason University, Fairfax, VA.

Smith, G. P. (1993, September). Interview. *ASCD Curriculum Update,* p. 7.

Snell, N. (1996). Using the Internet for education. In *Discover the World Wide Web* (2nd ed.). (pp. 93–98). Indianapolis, IN: Sams.net.

Snow, C. E. (1983). Literacy and language: Relationships during the preschool years. *Harvard Educational Review, 53,* 165–89.

Snow, C. E. (1990). Rationales for native language instruction: Evidence from research. In A. M. Padilla, H. H. Fairchild, & C. M. Valadez (Eds.), *Bilingual education: Issues and strategies.* (pp. 60–74). Newbury Park, CA: Sage.

Snow, C. E., & Ferguson, C. A. (Eds.). (1977). *Talking to children: Language input and acquisition.* Cambridge: Cambridge University Press.

Snow, M. A., Met, M., & Genesee, F. (1989). A conceptual framework for the integration of language and content in second/foreign language instruction. *TESOL Quarterly, 23,* 201–17.

Social Science Research Council. (1954). Acculturation: An exploratory formulation. *American Anthropologist, 56,* 973–1102.

Solís, A. (1989). Use of the Natural Approach Teaching Model: Application of second language acquisition research by teachers of limited-English-proficient students. *Dissertation Abstracts International, 51–01A,* 0071. (University Microfilms No. AAG90–15621).

Sosa, A. S. (1996). Twenty years after *Lau:* In pursuit of equity, not just a language response program. In *Revisiting the Lau decision: 20 years after* (pp. 34–42). Oakland, CA: ARC Associates.

Soska, M. (1994). *An introduction to educational technology.* Washington, DC: National Clearinghouse for Bilingual Education.

Sowell, T. (1990). *Preferential policies: An international perspective.* New York: Morrow.

Sowell, T. (1993). *Inside American education.* New York: Free Press.

Spangenberg-Urbschat, K., & Pritchard, R. (Eds.). (1994). *Kids come in all languages: Reading instruction for ESL students.* Newark, DE: International Reading Association.

Spanish Assessment of Basic Education (2nd ed.). (1991). Monterey, CA: CTB McGraw-Hill.

Spanos, G., & Smith, J. J. (1990). *Closed captioned television for adult LEP literacy learners.* Washington, DC: National Clearinghouse on Literacy Education. (ERIC Document Reproduction Service No. ED 321 623).

Spener, D. (1988). Transitional bilingual education and the socialization of immigrants. *Harvard Educational Review, 58,* 133–53.

Spindler, G., & Spindler, L. (1990). *The American cultural dialogue and its transmission.* Bristol, PA: Falmer Press.

Spiridakis, J. N. (1981). Diagnosing the learning styles of bilingual students and prescribing appropriate instruction. In R. V. Padilla (Ed.), *Ethnoperspectives in bilingual education research, Vol. 3: Bilingual education technology* (pp. 307–20). Ypsilanti, Ml: Eastern Michigan University.

Spolsky, B. (1977). The establishment of language education policy in multilingual societies. In B. Spolsky & R. L. Cooper (Eds.), *Frontiers of bilingual education* (pp. 1–21). New York: Newbury House.

Spolsky, B. (1978). Language and bicultural education. *Educational Research Quarterly, 2*(4), 20–25.

Spring, J. (1997). *The American school 1642–1996* (4th ed.). New York: McGraw-Hill.

Stanford Working Group. (1993). *Federal education programs for limited-English-proficient students: A blueprint for the second generation.* Palo Alto, CA: Stanford University.

Starks, J., Bransford, J., & Baca, L. (1998). Issues in policy development and implementation. In L. M. Baca & H. T. Cervantes (Eds.), *The bilingual special education interface* (pp. 372–410). Upper Saddle River, New Jersey: Prentice Hall.

Stempleski, S., & Tomalin, B. (1990). *Video in action: Recipes for using video in language teaching.* New York: Prentice Hall International.

Stern, H. H. (Ed.). (1963). *Foreign languages in primary education: The teaching of foreign or second languages to younger children.* Hamburg: International Studies in Education, UNESCO Institute for Education.

Stevenson, H. (1994). Moving away from stereotypes and preconceptions: Students and their education in East Asia and the United States. In P. M. Greenfield & R. R. Cocking (Eds.), *Cross-cultural roots of minority child development* (pp. 315–22). Hillsdale, NJ: Lawrence Erlbaum.

Stevick, E. W. (1976). *Memory, meaning and method.* New York: Newbury House.

Stevick, E. W. (1980). *Teaching language: A way and ways.* New York: Newbury House.

Stewart, D. W. (1993). *Immigration and education: The crisis and the opportunities.* New York: Macmillan.

Stewart, W. A. (1987). Coping or groping? Psycholinguistic problems in the acquisition of receptive and productive competence across dialects. In P. Homel, M. Palij, & D. Aaronson (Eds.), *Childhood bilingualism: Aspects of linguistic, cognitive, and social development* (pp. 281–98). Hillsdale, NJ: Lawrence Erlbaum.

Stiggins, R. J. (1992). *In teachers' hands: Investigating the practices of classroom assessment.* Albany, NY: State University of New York Press.

Strickland, D. S., & Morrow, L. M. (Eds.). (1989). *Emerging literacy: Young children learn to read and write.* Newark, DE: International Reading Association.

Suárez M. (1973). El hoyo. In L. O. Salina & L. Faderman (Eds.), *From the barrio. A Chicano anthology* (pp. 101–2). San Francisco: Canfield Press.

Suárez-Orozco, C., & Suárez-Orozco, M. M. (1995). *Transformations: Immigration, family life, and achievement among Latino adolescents.* Stanford, CA: Stanford University Press.

Suárez-Orozco, M. M. (1987). Towards a psy-chosocial understanding of Hispanic adapta-tion to American schooling. In H. T. Trueba (Ed.), *Success or failure? Learning and the language minority student* (pp. 156–68). New York: Newbury House.

Suárez-Orozco, M. M. (1989a). *Central American refugees and U.S. high schools: A psychoso-cial study of motivation and achievement.* Stanford, CA: Stanford University Press.

Suárez-Orozco, M. M. (1989b). Psychosocial aspects of achievement motivation among recent Hispanic immigrants. In H. T. Trueba & G. L. Spindler (Eds.), *What do anthropolo-gists have to say about dropouts?* (pp. 99–116). Bristol, PA: The Falmer Press.

Suárez-Orozco, M. M. (1993). "Becoming some-body": Central American immigrants in U.S. inner-city schools. In E. Jacob & C. Jordan (Eds.), *Minority education: Anthropological perspectives* (pp. 129–43). Norwood, NJ: Ablex.

Suárez-Orozco, M. M. (1995). The need for strangers: Proposition 187 and the immigra-tion malaise. *Multicultural Review, 4*(2), 17–23, 56–58.

Sue, S., & Padilla, A. (1986). Ethnic minority issues in the United States: Challenges for the educa-tional system. In *Beyond language: Social & cultural factors in schooling language minority students* (pp. 35–72). Sacramento, CA: California Department of Education.

Sullivan, N. (1993). Teaching writing on a com-puter network. *TESOL Journal, 3*(1), 34–35.

Susser, B. (1993). ESL/EFL process writing with computers. *CAELL Journal, 4*(2), 16–22.

Sutherland, J., & Black, P. (1993). Finding com-mon ground: International e-mail penpals. *CAELL Journal, 4*(2), 6–15.

Suzuki, L. A., Ponterotto, J. G., & Meller, P. J. (Eds.). (2001). *Handbook of multicultural assessment* (2nd ed.). San Francisco: Jossey-Bass.

Swain, M. (1981). Time and timing in bilingual education. *Language Learning, 31,* 1–15.

Swain, M. (1985). Communicative competence: Some roles of comprehensible input and com-prehensible output in its development. In S. Gass & C. Madden (Eds.), *Input in second language acquisition* (pp. 235–53). New York: Newbury House.

Swain, M., & Lapkin, S. (1981). *Bilingual educa-tion in Ontario: A decade of research.* Toronto: Ontario Institute for Studies in Education.

Swain, M., Lapkin, S., Rowen, N., & Hart, D. (1990). The role of mother tongue literacy in third language learning. *Language, Culture and Curriculum, 3,* 65–81.

System Development Corporation. (1981). *Preliminary report in the study of parental involvement in four federal education pro-grams.* Santa Monica, CA: Author.

Takaki, R. (1993). *A different mirror: A history of multicultural America.* Boston: Little, Brown.

Tashakkori, A., & Ochoa, S. H. (Eds.). (1999). *Education of Hispanics in the United States: Politics, policies and outcomes.* New York: AMS Press.

Taylor, D., & Dorsey-Gaines, C. (1988). *Growing up literate: Learning from inner-city families.* Portsmouth, NH: Heinemann.

Teachers of English to Speakers of Other Languages. (1976). *Position paper on the role of English as a second language in bilingual education.* Alexandria, VA: Author.

Teachers of English to Speakers of Other Languages. (1992a). *TESOL resource packet: Is your school helping its language minority students meet the national educational goals?* Alexandria, VA: Author.

Teachers of English to Speakers of Other Languages. (1992b). TESOL statement on the education of K–12 language minority stu-dents in the United States (1992). In *TESOL resource packet: Is your school helping its language minority students meet the national education goals?* Alexandria, VA: Author.

Teachers of English to Speakers of Other Languages. (1993). *Bilingual basics: The offi-cial publication of the bilingual interest sec-tion, TESOL.* Alexandria, VA: Author.

Teachers of English to Speakers of Other Languages. (1997). *ESL Standards for Pre-K-12 Students.* Alexandria, VA: Author.

Teitelbaum, H., & Hiller, R. J. (1977a). Bilingual education: The legal mandate. *Harvard Educational Review, 47,* 138–70.

Teitelbaum, H., & Hiller, R. J. (1977b). The legal perspective. In *Bilingual education: Current perspectives, Vol. 3: Law* (pp. 1–64). Washington, DC: Center for Applied Linguistics.

Teitelbaum, H., & Hiller, R. J. (1978). Trends in bilingual education and the law. In H. LaFontaine, B. Persky, & L. Golubchick (Eds.), *Bilingual education* (pp. 43–47). Wayne, NJ: Avery Publishing.

Teresa, P. et al. v. *Berkeley Unified School District et al.* (1989). U.S. District Court Case for the Northern District of California, Case No. C–87–2396–DLJ.

TerraNova. (1996). Monterey, CA: CTB McGraw-Hill.

Terrazas, B. (1995). Struggling for power and voice: A high school experience. In J. Frederickson (Ed.), *Reclaiming our voices: Bilingual education, critical pedagogy and praxis* (pp. 279–309). Los Angeles: California Association for Bilingual Education.

Terrell, T. D. (1981). The Natural Approach in bilingual education. In *Schooling and language minority students* (pp. 117–46). Sacramento, CA: California Department of Education.

Tharp, R. G. (1994). Intergroup differences among Native Americans in socialization and child cognition. In P. T. Greenfield & R. R. Cocking (Eds.), *Cross-cultural roots of minority child development* (pp. 315–22). Hillsdale, NJ: Lawrence Erlbaum.

Tharp, R. G., & Gallimore, R. (1988). *Rousing minds to life: Teaching, learning, and schooling in social context*. Cambridge: Cambridge University Press.

Tharp, R. G., & Gallimore, R. (1991). *The instructional conversation: Teaching and learning in social activity*. Santa Cruz, CA: National Center for Research on Cultural Diversity and Second Language Learning.

Tharp, R. G., Jordan, C., Speidel, G. E., Au, K. H., Klein, T. W., Calkins, R. P., Sloat, K. C. M., & Gallimore, R. (1984). Product and process in applied developmental research: Education and the children of a minority. In M. E. Lamb & L. Brown, (Eds.), *Advances in developmental psychology* (Vol. 3) (pp. 91–144). Hillsdale, NJ: Lawrence Erlbaum.

Thomas, L. (1975). *The lives of a cell*. New York: Viking Press.

Thomas, W. P. (1992). An analysis of the research methodology of the Ramírez study. *Bilingual Research Journal, 16*(1–2), 213–245.

Thomas, W. P. (1994). *The Cognitive Academic Language Learning Approach project for mathematics*. Fairfax, VA: Center for Bilingual/Multicultural/ESL Education, George Mason University.

Thomas, W. P., & Collier, V. P. (1997). *School effectiveness for language minority students*. Washington, DC: National Clearinghouse for Bilingual Education.

Thomas, W. P., Collier, V. P., & Abbott, M. (1993). Academic achievement through Japanese, Spanish, or French: The first two years of partial immersion. *Modern Language Journal, 77*, 170–79.

Thonis, E. (1981). Reading instruction for language minority students. In *Schooling and language minority students* (pp. 147–81). Sacramento, CA: California Department of Education.

Thornburg, D. G., & Karp, K. S. (1992). Lessons learned: (Mathematics + science + higher-order thinking) × second-language learning = ? *The Journal of Educational Issues of Language Minority Students, 10*, 159–84.

Thorndike, R. M. (1997). *Measurement and evaluation in psychology and education* (6th ed.). Upper Saddle River, NJ: Prentice-Hall.

Thornton, S. J. (1994). The social studies near century's end: Reconsidering patterns of curriculum and instruction. In L. Darling-Hammond (Ed.), *Review of Research in Education*, Vol. 20 (pp. 223–54). Washington, DC: American Educational Research Association.

Tiedt, P. L., & Tiedt, I. M. (1990). *Multicultural teaching: A handbook of activities, information, and resources* (3rd ed.). Boston: Allyn & Bacon.

Tikunoff, W. J. (1985). *Applying significant bilingual instructional features in the classroom*. Washington, DC: National Clearinghouse for Bilingual Education.

Tikunoff, W. J., Ward, B. A., von Broekhuizen, D., Romero, M., Castañeda, L. V., Lucas, T., & Katz, A. (1991). *Final report: A descriptive study of significant features of exemplary special alternative instructional programs*. Los Alamitos, CA: Southwest Regional Educational Laboratory.

Timm, L. A. (1993). Bilingual code-switching: An overview of research. In B. J. Merino, H. T. Trueba & F. A. Samaniego (Eds.), *Language and culture in learning: Teaching Spanish to native speakers of Spanish* (pp. 94–112). Bristol, PA: Falmer Press.

Tinajero, J. V., & Ada, A. F. (Eds.). (1993). *The power of two languages: Literacy and biliteracy for Spanish-speaking students*. New York: Macmillan/McGraw-Hill.

Tinajero, J. V., Calderón, M. E., & Hertz-Lazarowitz, R. (1993). Cooperative learning strategies: Bilingual classroom applications. In J. V. Tinajero & A. F. Ada (Eds.), *The power of two languages: Literacy and biliteracy for Spanish-speaking students* (pp. 241–53). New York: Macmillan/McGraw-Hill.

Tinajero, J. V., & Huerta-Macías, A. (1993). Enhancing the skills of emergent writers acquiring English. In J. V. Tinajero & A. F. Ada (Eds.), *The power of two languages: Literacy and biliteracy for Spanish-speaking students* (pp. 254–63). New York: Macmillan/McGraw-Hill.

Tirrell, P. B. (1981, December). *Innovative teaching in anthropology: New approaches for new students*. Paper presented at the American Anthropological Association, Los Angeles.

Tobeluk v. Lind, No. 72–2450 (3rd Judicial District, Anchorage; Superior Court, Alaska, 1976).

Torres-Guzmán, M. E. (1993). Critical pedagogy and Bilingual/Bicultural Education Special Interest Group update. *NABE News, 17*(3), 14–15, 36.

Troike, R. D. (1982). Zeno's paradox and language assessment. In S. S. Seidner (Ed.), *Issues of language assessment, Vol. 1: Foundations and research* (pp. 3–5). Evanston, IL: Illinois State Board of Education.

Trueba, H. T. (1979). The Mexican-American family: The use of life history materials. In H. T. Trueba & C. Barnett-Mizrahi (Eds.), *Bilingual multicultural education and the professional* (pp. 149–56). New York: Newbury House.

Trueba, H. T. (Ed.). (1987). *Success or failure? Learning & the language minority student*. New York: Newbury House.

Trueba, H. T. (1991). The role of culture in bilingual instruction: Linking linguistic and cognitive development to cultural knowledge. In Ofelia García (Ed.), *Bilingual education* (pp. 43–55). Amsterdam: John Benjamins.

Trueba, H. T., Guthrie, G. P., & Au, K. H. (Eds.). (1981). *Culture and the bilingual classroom: Studies in classroom ethnography*. New York: Newbury House.

Trueba, H. T., Jacobs, L., & Kirton, E. (1990). *Cultural conflict and adaptation: The case of Hmong children in American society*. Bristol, PA: Falmer Press.

Trueba, H. T., Spindler, G., & Spindler, L. (Eds.). (1989). *What do anthropologists have to say about dropouts?* Bristol, PA: Falmer Press.

Trujillo, A., & Zachman, J. M. (1981). Toward the practice of culturally relevant teaching. In R. V. Padilla (Ed.), *Ethnoperspectives in bilingual education research, Vol. 3: Bilingual education technology* (pp. 30–48). Ypsilanti, Ml: Eastern Michigan University.

Tsang, S. L. (1982). Asian American education. In H. E. Mitzel, J. H. Best, & W. Rabinowitz (Eds), *Encyclopedia of educational research* (Vol. 1, pp. 171–73). New York: Free Press.

Tucker, G. R. (1980). *Implications for U.S. bilingual education: Evidence from Canadian research*. Washington, DC: National Clearinghouse for Bilingual Education.

Tyack, D. B. (1974). *The one best system: A history of American urban education*. Cambridge, MA: Harvard University Press.

Tyack, D. B. (1981). Governance and goals: Historical perspectives on public education. In D. Davies (Ed.), *Communities and their schools* (pp. 11–31). New York: McGraw-Hill.

Tye, K. A. (Ed.). (1990a). *Global education: From thought to action*. Alexandria, VA: Association for Supervision and Curriculum Development.

Tye, K. A. (Ed.). (1990b). *Global education: School-based strategies*. Orange, CA: Interdependence Press.

Tymitz, B. L. (1983). Bilingual special education: A challenge to evaluation practices. In D. R. Omark & J. G. Erickson (Eds.), *The bilingual exceptional child* (pp. 359–77). San Diego, CA: College Hill Press.

Ulanoff, S., & Pucci, S. (1993, April). *Is concurrent-translation or preview-review more effective in promoting second language vocabulary acquisition?* Paper presented at the annual meeting of the American Educational Research Association, Atlanta, GA.

Ulibarri, S. R. (1972). The word made flesh: Spanish in the classroom. In L. Valdez & S. Steiner (Eds.), *Aztlán: An anthology of Mexican American literature* (p. 295). New York: Alfred Z. Knopf House.

United Nations Educational, Scientific and Cultural Organization. (1953). *The use of vernacular languages in education*. Monographs on Fundamental Education VIII. Paris: Author.

United States Census Bureau, (2000). *Statistical abstract of the United States 2000*. Washington, DC: Author.

United States Census Bureau, (2001). Current population survey, March 2000. Washington, DC: Ethnic and Hispanic Statistics Branch, Population Division. Retrieved October 13, 2001, from http://www.census.gov/population/socdemo/foreign/p20-534/tab0306.pdf.

United States Commission on Civil Rights. (1975). *A better chance to learn: Bilingual/bicultural education*. Washington, DC: U.S. Government Printing Office.

United States Congress. (1968, January 2). *Congressional Record* (Section 702 of Public Law 90–247, Bilingual Education Act). Washington, DC: Author.

United States Congress. (1990). *United States Code Congressional and Administrative News: 101st Congress—Second Session 1990*, Volume 8. St. Paul, MN: West Publishing.

United States v. *State of Texas*, 342 F. Supp. 24 (E.D. Tex. 1971), aff'd, 466 F.2d 518 (5th Cir. 1972).

United States v. State of Texas, 506 F. Supp. 405 (E.D. Tex. 1981), rev'd, 680 F.2d 356 (5th Cir. 1982).

U.S. Census Bureau, (1992). Selected social characteristics: 1990. CPH-L-80, Table 1.

U.S. Department of Commerce: Economics and statistics administration, Bureau of the Census. (1992). *Current population reports. Population projections of the United States by age, sex, race, and Hispanic origin: 1992 to 2050* (Report No P25–1092). Washington, DC: Author.

U.S. Department of Education. (1991). *America 2000: An education strategy*. Washington, DC: Author.

U.S. Department of Education. (1995). *Forming new partnerships for educating all students to high standards*. Washington, DC: National Clearinghouse for Bilingual Education.

U.S. English. (1990, May 21). The door to opportunity. *Roll Call*.

U.S. General Accounting Office, (1987). *Bilingual education: A new look at the research evidence*. GAO/PEMD–87–12BR. Washington, DC: U.S. Government Printing Office.

U.S. Office for Civil Rights. (1975). *Remedies available for eliminating past educational practices ruled unlawful under* Lau *v.* Nichols. Washington, DC: U.S. Department of Health, Education, and Welfare.

Valdés, G. (1978). *Code switching and the classroom teacher*. Washington, DC: Center for Applied Linguistics.

Valdés, G. (1980). Is code-switching interference, integration, or neither? In E. L Blansitt, Jr. & R. V. Teschner (Eds.), *A Festschrift for Jacob Ornstein: Studies in general linguistics and sociolinguistics* (pp. 314–25). New York: Newbury House.

Valdés, G. (1981). Pedagogical implications of teaching Spanish to the Spanish-speaking in the United States. In G. Valdés, A. G. Lozano, & R. García-Moya (Eds.), *Teaching Spanish to the Hispanic bilingual: Issues, aims, and methods* (pp. 3–20). New York: Teachers College Press.

Valdés, G. (1996). *Con respeto: Bridging the distance between culturally diverse families and schools: An ethnographic portrait*. New York: Teachers College Press.

Valdés, G. (2001). *Learning and not learning English: Latino students in American schools*. New York: Teachers College Press.

Valdés, G., & Figueroa, R. A. (1994). *Bilingualism and Testing: A special case of bias*. Norwood, NJ: Ablex.

Valdés, G., Lozano, A. G., & García-Moya, R. (Eds.). (1981). *Teaching Spanish to the Hispanic bilingual: Issues, aims, and methods*. New York: Teachers College Press.

Valdez Pierce, L. (Ed.). (1987). *Language and content-area instruction for secondary LEP students with limited formal schooling: Language arts and social studies*. Washington, DC: National Clearinghouse for Bilingual Education.

Valdez Pierce, L. (1988). *Facilitating transition to the mainstream: Sheltered English vocabulary development*. Washington, DC: National Clearinghouse for Bilingual Education.

Valdez Pierce, L. (1991). *Effective schools for language minority students*. Washington, DC: Mid-Atlantic Equity Center.

Valdez Pierce, L., & O'Malley, J. M. (1992). *Performance and portfolio assessment for language minority students*. Washington, DC: National Clearinghouse for Bilingual Education.

Valencia, S. W., Hiebert, E. H., & Afflerbach, P. P. (Eds.). (1994). *Authentic reading assessment: Practices and possibilities*. Newark, DE: International Reading Association.

Vanderplank, R. (1993). A very verbal medium: Language learning through closed captions. *TESOL Journal, 3*(1), 10–14.

Vargas, A. (1988). *Literacy in the Hispanic community*. Washington, DC: National Council of La Raza.

Vélez-Ibáñez, C. G. (1993). U.S. Mexicans in the borderlands: Being poor without the underclass. In J. Moore & R. Pinderhughes (Eds.), *In the barrios: Latinos and the underclass debate* (pp. 195–220). New York: Russell Sage Foundation.

Vélez-Ibáñez, C. G., & Greenberg, J. B. (1992). Formation and transformation of funds of knowledge among U.S.-Mexican households. *Anthropology & Education Quarterly, 23*(4), 313–35.

Veltman, C. (1988). *The future of the Spanish language in the United States*. Washington, DC: Hispanic Policy Development Project.

Viadero, D. (1994). Get smart: A Yale psychologist says that understanding the different kinds of intelligence can help both students and teachers excel. *Education Week, 14*(13), 33–34.

Violand-Sánchez, E., Sutton, C. P., & Ware, H. W. (1991). *Fostering home-school cooperation: Involving language minority families as partners in education*. Washington, DC: National Clearinghouse for Bilingual Education.

Vogt, L. A., Jordan, C., & Tharp, R. G. (1993). Explaining school failure, producing school success: Two cases. In E. Jacob & C. Jordan (Eds.), *Minority education: Anthropological perspectives* (pp. 53–65). Norwood, NJ: Ablex.

Vonnegut, K. (1974). Afterword. In M. Thomas (Ed.), *Free to be you and me* (p. 139). New York: McGraw-Hill.

Vygotsky, L. S. (1962). *Thought and language*. Cambridge, MA: Harvard University Press.

Vygotsky, L. S. (1978). *Mind and society*. Cambridge. MA: Harvard University Press.

Waggoner, D. (1991). *The Numbers News: Ethnic and Linguistic Minorities in the United States, 1*, 1–2.

Walberg, H. (1986). What works in a nation still at risk. *Educational Leadership, 44*(1), 7–11.

Walker, S. (1996). *Prevalence of disabling conditions among diverse racial/ethnic groups in the United States*. Washington, D.C.: Howard University, Center for Disability and Socioeconomic Policy Studies.

Walsh, C. E. (Ed.). (1991a). *Literacy as praxis: Culture, language, and pedagogy*. Norwood, NJ: Ablex.

Walsh, C. E. (1991b). *Pedagogy and the struggle for voice: Issues of language, power, and schooling for Puerto Ricans*. New York: Bergin & Garvey.

Walsh, C. E. (1995). Critical reflections for teachers: Bilingual education and critical pedagogy. In J. Frederickson (Ed.), *Reclaiming our voices: Bilingual education, critical pedagogy and praxis* (pp. 79–98). Los Angeles: California Association for Bilingual Education.

Walsh, C. E. (Ed.). (1996). *Education reform and social change: Multicultural voices, struggles, and visions*. Hillsdale, NJ: Lawrence Erlbaum.

Warren, B., & Rosebery, A. S. (1992). Science education as a sense-making practice: Implications for assessment. In *Proceedings of the Second National Research Symposium on Limited English Proficient Student Issues: Focus on evaluation and measurement*, Vol. 2 (pp. 273–304). Washington, DC: Office of Bilingual Education and Minority Languages Affairs, U.S. Department of Education.

Warren, B., & Rosebery, A. S. (1995). *"This question is just too, too easy!" Perspectives from the classroom on accountability in science*. Santa Cruz, CA: National Center for Research on Cultural Diversity and Second Language Learning.

Warren, B., Rosebery, A. S., & Conant, F. (1990). *Cheche konnen: Collaborative scientific inquiry in language minority classrooms.* Arlington, VA: Development Associates.

Waserstein. A. (1975). Organizing for bilingual education: One community's experience. *Inequality in Education, 19,* 23–30.

Watahomigie, L. (1995). The power of American Indian parents and communities. *Bilingual Research Journal, 19*(1), 189–94.

Wax, M. L. (1993). "How culture misdirects multiculturalism." *Anthropology & Education Quarterly, 24*(2), 99–115.

Weinreich, U. (1953). *Languages in contact: Findings and problems.* New York: Linguistic Circle of New York.

Weinstein-Shr, G. (1992). *Family and intergenerational literacy in multilingual families.* Washington, DC: National Clearinghouse on Literacy Education.

Wells, G. (1985). *Language development in the pre-school years.* Cambridge: Cambridge University Press.

Wells, G., & Chang-Wells, G. L. (1992). *Constructing knowledge together: Classrooms as centers of inquiry and literacy.* Portsmouth, NH: Heinemann.

Wenden, A., & Rubin, J. (Eds.). (1987). *Learner strategies in language learning.* Englewood Cliffs, NJ: Prentice Hall Regents.

Wheelock, A. (1992). *Crossing the tracks: How "untracking" can save America's schools.* New York: The New Press.

Whorf, B. J. (1956). *Language, thought, and reality.* Cambridge, MA: Massachusetts Institute of Technology Press.

Wiggins, G. P. (1993). *Assessing student performance: Exploring the purpose and limits of testing.* San Francisco: Jossey-Bass.

Wiggins, G. P. (1997). *Assessment for excellence: Designing assessment to inform and improve student performance.* San Francisco: Jossey-Bass.

Wiggins, G. (1998). *Educative assessment: Designing assessments to inform and improve student performance.* San Francisco: Jossey-Bass.

Wiley, T. G. (1996). *Literacy and language diversity in the United States.* Washington, DC: Center for Applied Linguistics and Delta Systems.

Wilkinson, C., & Ortiz, A. A. (1986). Reevaluation of learning disabled Hispanic students: Changes over three years. *Bilingual Special Education Newsletter, 5*(1), 3–6.

Williams, J. D., & Snipper, G. C. (1990). *Literacy and bilingualism.* New York: Longman.

Willis, J. W., Stephens, E. C., & Matthew, K. I. (1996). *Technology, reading, and language arts.* Boston: Allyn and Bacon.

Willis, S. (1993). Whole language in the '90s. *Association for Supervision and Curriculum Development Update, 35*(9), 1, 5–6, 8.

Willis, S. (1995, Fall). Whole language: Finding the surest way to literacy. *ASCD Curriculum Update,* pp. 1–8.

Wilson, A. H. (1994). Teaching toward a global future and the future of global teaching. In M. R. Nelson (Ed.), *The future of the social studies* (pp. 53–59). Boulder, CO: Social Science Education Consortium.

Wolf, D., Bixby, J., Glenn, J., & Gardner, H. (1991). To use their minds well: Investigating new forms of student assessment. In G. Grant (Ed.), *Review of Research in Education,* Vol. 17 (pp. 31–74). Washington, DC: American Educational Research Association.

Wolfram, W., & Christian, D. (1989). *Dialects and education: Issues and answers.* Englewood Cliffs, NJ: Prentice Hall Regents.

Wong Fillmore, L. (1985). Second language learning in children: A proposed model. In *Issues in English language development* (pp. 33–42). Washington, DC: National Clearinghouse for Bilingual Education.

Wong Fillmore, L. (1989). Teachability and second language acquisition. In R. Schiefelbusch & M. Rice (Eds.), *The teachability of language* (pp. 311–32). Baltimore, MD: Paul Brookes.

Wong Fillmore, L. (1991a). Second language learning in children: A model of language learning in social context. In E. Bialystok (Ed.), *Language processing in bilingual children* (pp. 49–69). Cambridge: Cambridge University Press.

Wong Fillmore, L. (1991b). When learning a second language means losing the first. *Early Childhood Research Quarterly, 6,* 323–46.

Wong Fillmore, L., & Valadez, C. (1986). Teaching bilingual learners. In M. C. Wittrock (Ed.),

Handbook of research on teaching (3rd ed.). (pp. 648–85). New York: Macmillan.

Worthen, B. R., Sanders, J. R., & Fitzpatrick, J. L. (1997). *Program evaluation: Alternative approaches and practical guidelines* (2nd ed.). New York: Longman.

Worthen, B. R., White, K. R., Fan, X., & Sudweeks, R. R. (1999). *Measurement and assessment in schools* (2nd ed.). New York: Longman

Wraga, W. G., & Hlebowitsh, P. S. (1991). STS education and the curriculum field. *School, science and mathematics, 81*(7), 575–80.

Yager, R. E. (1990). STS: Thinking over the years. *The Science Teacher, 57*(3), 52–55.

York, K. H. (1979). Parent/community involvement in the Mississippi Choctaw bilingual education program. In *Working with the bilingual community* (pp. 29–36). Washington, DC: National Clearinghouse for Bilingual Education.

Y. S. v. School District of Philadelphia. (1988). C.A. 85-6924 (E.D. PA 1986).

Yates. J. R. (1988). Demography as it affects special education. In A. A. Ortiz & B. A. Ramirez (Eds.), *Schools and the culturally diverse exceptional student: Promising practices and future directions.* (pp. 1–5). Boston: The Council for Exceptional Children.

Ysseldyke, J. E., Algozzine, B., & Richey, L. (1982). Judgment under uncertainty: How many children are handicapped? *Exceptional Children, 48*(6), 531–34.

Zapata, J. A. (1996). 104th Congress and minority-language communities. *NABE News, 20*(2), 3.

Zaslavsky, C. (1996). *The multicultural math classroom: Bringing in the world.* Portsmouth, NH: Heinemann.

Zavala, J., & Mims, J. (1983). Identification of learning disabled bilingual Hispanic students. *Learning Disability Quarterly, 6,* 479–88.

Zehler, A. M., Hopstock, P. J., Fleischman, H. L., & Greniuk, C. (1994). *An examination of assessment of limited English proficient students.* Arlington, VA: Development Associates.

Zentella, A. C. (1981). *Ta' bien,* you could answer me *en cualguier idioma:* Puerto Rican code switching in bilingual classrooms. In R. Durán (Ed.), *Latino language and communicative behavior* (pp. 109–31). Norwood, NJ: Ablex.

Zúñiga C., & Westernoff, F. (1996). Parents as resources in schools: A community-of-learners perspective. *The Journal of Educational Issues of Language Minority Students, 16,* 207–23.

Author Index

Subject Index

Italic type indicates page reference to a text box or table.

AAAS. *See* American Association for the Advancement of Science
Academic language
  acquisition of, 128–129, 130–132
  cognition and, 144–145
  content ESL and, 249, 348
  multimodal teaching and, 253
  social studies instruction and, 301
Accelerated learning, 92, 99–100
Accountability, in education, 339
Acculturation, 193, 197–198, 399
  multiple, 290
Achievement, in mathematics and science, 236–240
Achievement tests. *See* Standardized testing
Active learning, 89–92
Advocates of Children, 376
Alternate language approach, 247
America 2000, 324–325
American Association for the Advancement of Science (AAAS), 240, 271, 324
American Federation of Teachers, 44
Ancestral languages. *See* Heritage languages
Anchors, 345
Anthropology, and culture, 188–192
  characteristics of, *189*
  context, 190–191
  interrelated components, 191–192
  learned patterns, 189–190
Arreola v. Board of Education, 363
Art, 104–106
Arvizu v. Waco (1973), 66
Aspira v. Board of Education of the City of New York (1974), 66
Assessment, 323–355
  bias in, 330–331
  classroom-based, 339–343

criterion-referenced, 334, 343
  and instruction linkage, 346–350
  norm-referenced, 333
  of oral language, 347–348
  performance-based, 334–335
  political context for, 323–328
  program exit assessment, 338
  purpose of, 328–329
  of reading and writing, 348–350
  reliability, 331–332
  school-based, 337–339
  validity, 329–331
Assessment bias, 330
Assimilation, 193, 198, 387
At-risk students, 99–100
Attitudinal bias, in assessment, 330
Audiolingual method, 147–148
Authentic assessments, 335

Benchmarks, 345
Biculturalism, and cultural identity, 195–197
Bilingual classrooms, 164–170
  defining proficiency for, 165–166
  dialect diversity in, 166–169
  language distribution in, 169–170
Bilingual communities, definition of, 382
Bilingual education. *See also* Bilingual education programs; Bilingual special education
  in early twentieth century, 52–53
  monolingual students and, 25–26
  in 1960s, 55
  in nineteenth century, 51–52
Bilingual Education Act (1968), 5, 26, 38, 43, 56, 68, 363, 416–417
Bilingual Education Act (1974), 417
Bilingual Education Act (1994), 49, 417
Bilingual education programs
  basic characteristics of, 6

community-initiated programs, 391–392
  content ESL or sheltered instruction, 74–75
  developmental bilingual instruction, 49, 59, 78–79
  early-exit, 49, 76–78, 165
  enrichment or remediation, 72–73
  ESL pullout, 73–74
  immersion, 79–80
  late-exit, 49, 78–79
  maintenance, 78–79
  math and science in, 247–249
  newcomer programs, 75
  recommendations on role of, 7
  in social studies, 301–302
  special alternative instruction, 49
  structured immersion, 49, 76
  transitional bilingual education, 49, 76–78, 165
  two-way, 26, 62, 80
  use of primary language in, 72
  varied goals of, 5–6
Bilingual Parent Advisory Council (BPAC), 419
Bilingual special education, 359–377
  definition of, 360
  identification and placement issues, 361, 362, 363–366, 374–376
  identification and placement processes, 367–373
  legislation on, 362–363
  litigation on, 363–364
Bilingualism
  and abilities, 233n1
  definitions of, *165*
  math and science and, 264
  as norm, 135–136
  subtractive, 136

505